THE MARINE OFFICER'S GUIDE

8TH EDITION

THE MARINE OFFICER'S GUIDE

8TH EDITION

COLONEL CHRISTIAN HALIDAY,
UNITED STATES MARINE CORPS (RET.)

FOREWORD BY GENERAL ALFRED M. GRAY JR.,
UNITED STATES MARINE CORPS (RET.)

NAVAL INSTITUTE PRESS
Annapolis, Maryland

Naval Institute Press
291 Wood Road
Annapolis, MD 21402

Library of Congress Cataloging-in-Publication Data
Title: The Marine officer's guide / Colonel Christian N. Haliday, U.S. Marine Corps (Ret.).
Description: Eighth edition. | Annapolis, Md. : Naval Institute Press, [2017] | Includes index.
Identifiers: LCCN 2017038139 | ISBN 9781612518268 (hbk.)
Subjects: LCSH: United States. Marine Corps—Officers' handbooks.
Classification: LCC VE153.E85 2017 | DDC 359.9/60973—dc23
LC record available at https://lccn.loc.gov/2017038139

♾ Print editions meet the requirements of ANSI/NISO z39.48-1992 (Permanence of Paper).
Printed in the United States of America.

25 24 23 22 21 20 19 18 17 9 8 7 6 5 4 3 2 1
First printing

Photographs, unless otherwise indicated, are Department of Defense, U.S. Marine Corps, or U.S. Navy official photographs. Diagrams, where not original, have been reproduced from various official publications.

To all Marine officers

Into whose keeping
The Corps is year by year entrusted.

Once a Marine, always a Marine.

CONTENTS

PART II
AN OFFICER OF MARINES

PART III
PERSONAL, FAMILY, AND SOCIAL MATTERS

ILLUSTRATIONS

FIGURES

TABLES

PHOTOS

FOREWORD

We make Marines. We win our nation's battles.
We develop quality citizens.

—The Marine Corps' simple promises
to the nation and its Marines

Congratulations! Your interest and investment in *The Marine Officer's Guide* represents a determined first step to become an effective Marine officer and join the storied profession of arms. By absorbing its contents, you are sure to begin your contribution to fulfilling two of the Marine Corps' promises: "making Marines" and "developing quality citizens." The *Guide* will help shape you as a Marine and, in turn, help you lead, train, educate, mentor, and develop Marines during your career. And it includes some universal advice and guidance that will contribute more generally to your personal growth and development as a citizen of our great nation.

The Marine Officer's Guide did not exist when I gained my commission in 1952, but I acquired a copy not long after the original edition's publication in 1956. I immediately found the *Guide* useful. It reinforced some of the lessons that I had learned in "the school of hard knocks" and delivered early insights on the Marine Corps and the profession of arms that might otherwise have taken years to accumulate.

A central theme in the *Guide* is the notion of the Marine officer as leader. The Marine Corps' style of warfare, *maneuver warfare,* requires intelligent, informed leaders with a bias for bold action. Marine Corps Doctrinal Publication 1, *Warfighting*, defines maneuver warfare: "Maneuver warfare is a warfighting philosophy that seeks to shatter the enemy's cohesion through a variety of rapid, focused, and unexpected actions, which create a turbulent and rapidly deteriorating situation with which the enemy cannot cope."

In addition to obvious traits, such as courage and endurance, that the profession of arms requires, the Marine Corps' warfighting philosophy demands of its officers the temperament to cope with uncertainty; a flexibility and independence of mind; and initiative, boldness, and moral courage. These desirable traits must be tempered by self-discipline, good judgment, and loyalty to both seniors and juniors. And maneuver warfare requires leaders to think at an echelon above their own—understanding *commander's intent*—and take bold action consistent with the requirements of the bigger picture. Several of the *Guide*'s chapters contain concise information and broad lessons, as well as practical anecdotes, insights, and advice, that will help you to latch onto and embrace many of these tenets of maneuver warfare.

Marine Corps warfighting philosophy also relies on continuous and progressive professional military education throughout a career. As you embark on this first stage of your professional military career and education, which is, practically speaking, your apprenticeship, make *The Marine Officer's Guide* a close companion. Read it, study it, take it to heart!

Finally, in recommending this *Guide* to you, I am reminded of something I have thought and said often over the years: "Take all the help you can get. There are no crowded battlefields."

Semper Fidelis! Thank you for your commitment to Corps and country, and welcome aboard!

—GENERAL ALFRED M. GRAY JR.

UNITED STATES MARINE CORPS (RET.)

PREFACE
TO THE 8TH EDITION

Having just passed the sixtieth anniversary of its debut, *The Marine Officer's Guide* has no doubt helped legions of young officers and officer candidates take their places in this brotherhood we know as the United States Marine Corps. I suspect that over the years it helped many enthusiastic young officers rapidly develop the knowledge, skills, and abilities to become fine leaders of Marines, while hopefully avoiding some of the common pitfalls of inexperience; I know the fifth edition provided me a head start. In a period of rapid and incessant change in global affairs, power politics, and the profession of arms, the *Guide* is a reassuring constant that offers its reader the wherewithal to launch a promising Marine Corps career.

Why read a guide book in an age of automation and computers? It is worth recalling the insight of Daniel J. Boorstin, American historian and twelfth Librarian of Congress, on books in the information era: "A wonderful thing about a book, in contrast to a computer screen, is that you can take it to bed with you." While I am not necessarily advocating the *Guide* as bedtime reading, in book form it retains many attributes. It is more portable and durable than a computer. Unlike the screen of a smart phone, it is gentle on your eyesight and comes without a low-battery indicator. And perhaps most importantly, the *Guide* offers a single, curated collection of information and wisdom on the Corps, which would require countless searches and careful vetting by an aspiring

Marine officer who seeks the same information online. It thus seems a useful supplement to even the most modern sources of information on the Corps.

This eighth edition of *The Marine Officer's Guide* continues in the tradition of its predecessors. As Colonel Robert D. Heinl Jr., one of its originators, noted, the *Guide* aims "to assist new officers to learn the ropes as quickly as they can, to digest for all readers the continuing changes which have beset the Defense Establishment, and to help the entire officer corps keep professionally up to date." I have completely reviewed and, where required, revised this edition. It retains a similar general outline of twenty-two chapters and several appendices as in previous editions, although I have reorganized the work into three parts. After the largely intact introductory chapter, Part I addresses the Marine Corps as a military service, an institution, and, yes, in some degree, a bureaucracy. This part touches upon the Corps' storied history; places the service in the nation's defense and naval establishments, the treatments of which are completely updated; describes its mission, organization, and infrastructure; and reveals inter alia its culture, the sum total of its beliefs and ways of thinking, working, and behaving. Part II turns to topics related to becoming and being an effective officer of Marines. Most important here are discussions of leadership and the profession of arms, but the updated and expanded chapters on such mundane but essential topics as unit and individual administration, pay and allowances, and military justice are also worth the effort. Part III provides useful information on personal, family, and social matters. In sum, this new edition is current and applicable to today's Corps.

I am grateful to General Al Gray for agreeing to offer the foreword to this edition. General Gray is a Marine icon whom I have admired over many years, although I did not come to know him personally until after I retired. I value his thoughtful, helpful suggestions and envy his apparently boundless energy as he continues to find ways to contribute to the Corps' advancement.

I thank Ken Estes, who prepared the previous three editions of *The Marine Officer's Guide.* I have profited greatly from our long association and friendship, which began more than three decades ago after I became a midshipman at Duke University where he was the Marine Officer Instructor. To say he influenced me is an understatement. I believe he takes no small degree of pride in "stealing" me from the Navy in that he helped me change course as I entered my junior year and opted for a pathway into the Marine Corps. Ken has been a superb sounding board, mentor, supporter, and friend over these many years. He provided me invaluable advice through my own career. And he arranged for me to take the helm of this work, which I am finding a challenging and rewarding experience. I am in his debt.

I also thank the many officers and Marines with whom I served over almost three decades and with whom I continue to interact since leaving active service. Fellow Marines—both seniors and juniors—shaped my understanding of and stoked my love for the Corps. They contributed to my successes in the Marine Corps and to my accumulation of knowledge, expertise, and experience that enables me to complete this project. They have my gratitude.

And I am, of course, profoundly grateful to my wife, Anne, and our family, who supported me in this endeavor. Their encouragement, which kept me going, and indulgence, when I was perhaps not quite myself during the past year, contributed greatly to this revision of the *Guide.*

Finally, I express my appreciation to the Naval Institute Press and its acquisition, editorial, and production staffs, who assisted and supported me during this edition's preparation over more than a year. Tom Cutler guided me expertly through the revision process. Jim Dolbow and Lisa Yambrick added their editorial skills and provided valuable feedback to improve the original manuscript. And I know that countless others worked behind the scenes to bring this project to fruition. Altogether, they were unsurpassed in their guidance, expertise, support, and, above all, patience as I researched and revised this new version of the *Guide.*

I welcome insights, comments, suggestions, and corrections from all readers, but particularly those who are part of this work's primary audience: prospective and new Marine officers. Does this *Guide* help you become a Marine officer and make a good start in your career? Does it answer your questions? Is it accurate and complete? What would make it better or more useful? Please send your suggestions to the Editor, *The Marine Officer's Guide,* Naval Institute Press, 291 Wood Road, Annapolis, MD, 21402-5034. With your help, this volume will continue to improve and prepare future leaders to rapidly make their own contributions to the Corps.

Semper Fidelis, Marines!

—CHRISTIAN N. HALIDAY

INTRODUCTION
TO THE 1ST EDITION

Preparation of this book was a project which began during my tenure as Commandant of the Marine Corps, and it was one to which I lent sympathetic attention. Now that I see the results, I am well satisfied that I helped to the extent that I did.

It is high time that the Marine Corps had a work of this kind.

Within the memory not of a few senior officers on the verge of retirement, but of the bulk of our most experienced field officers, the Corps has expanded immensely and has pursued its traditional role of national force in readiness on a vastly larger scale.

Thus, the Marine Corps is—or could be—in a time of transition. At such times it is all too easy to forget, depart from, or discard the well-tested ways which have brought us where we are. Fortunately, those ways are still with us, and such a book as *The Marine Officer's Guide* must be of the greatest value in keeping them with us.

As I write this to readers of *The Marine Officer's Guide*, I am reminded of what must be one of the earliest surviving "fitness reports" on a young Marine officer, submitted by Captain Daniel Carmick, USMC, in April 1799: "Lt Amory is very ignorant of Military duty, as he acknowledges, but he is a smart Gentleman and far preferable to the others." For the young officer of today who (like Lt Amory) is not ashamed to admit the limits of his own experience, and is intelligent enough to profit by the experience of others, *The Marine Officer's Guide* should prove indispensable.

—GENERAL L. C. SHEPHERD JR.
UNITED STATES MARINE CORPS (RET.)

1

THE U.S. MARINE CORPS

First to fight.
Retreat, hell! We just got here.
Gone to fight the Indians—will be back when the war is over.
Uncommon valor was a common virtue.
The Marines have landed, and the situation is well in hand.

Phrases like these say more about the United States Marine Corps than all the handbooks ever written. As you read this guide, therefore, remember that there is far more to the Marine Corps than can ever be expressed in any manual. If you are fortunate enough to become a Marine, you will soon realize what the Corps is and what it represents.

101. What Is a Marine Corps?

Beyond the statutes and official definitions, what is a marine corps?

To many observers, it is a military anomaly—a marine is a "soldier and sailor, too." But any cursory reading of military history tells us that navies from their inception had a fundamental need for expert troops to guard ships and stations, as well as to extend the force of naval power ashore.

Every world power has an army. Most powers have navies and air forces. Few throughout history have had marine corps, but more such corps, based on the examples of their eminent usefulness, have been formed since World War II. Some fifty nations now field marine corps or naval infantry units in their orders of battle: Argentina, Bolivia, Brazil, Cameroon, Chile, China, Colombia, Cuba, Dominican Republic, Ecuador, France, Greece, Guatemala, Guinea, Honduras, India, Indonesia, Italy, Republic of Korea, Kuwait, Malawi, Maldives, Mauritania, Mexico, Morocco, Netherlands, Pakistan, Paraguay, Peru, Philippines, Poland, Portugal, Romania, Russia, Saint Lucia, Saudi Arabia, Spain, Sudan, Sweden, Taiwan, Thailand, Tonga, Turkey, Ukraine, United Kingdom, Uruguay, Venezuela, Vietnam, and Yemen. Several other countries have naval commando or coastal defense organizations that perform missions similar to those of marines.

Nowhere but in the United States, however, has any marine corps attained the status of our own. This status was not foreseen when the Continental Congress, on 10 November 1775, formed two battalions of Marines. The Corps has gained its unique position through long evolution.

Much of the anomalous quality of the U.S. Marine Corps stems from the fact that the Corps possesses many individual attributes of its brother services. As a result, you can usually discern something suggestive of the other services in the Marine Corps, and this is only natural in a Corps that has spent most of its time spearheading, supporting, or serving alongside the Army, Navy, and Air Force. But you can also see much more that belongs only to the Marine Corps.

Certainly, the Marine Corps attitude is peculiar to the Corps.

Fully as important as its attitude, however, is the fundamental mission of the Corps. This primary mission—readiness—combined with the Marine state of mind makes the Corps what it is today: a national force in readiness, prepared in fact and required by law to "perform such other duties as the President may direct"—which implies, "ready for anything."

Most Americans, including some who know few specifics about the Corps, recognize Marines as the national force in readiness. Such tried and true phrases as "Call out the Marines!" or "The situation is well in hand," or "Tell it to the Marines" have entered the American lexicon and voice the country's attitude. The existence of this nationwide feeling makes the Marine Corps a national institution.

As a Marine, therefore, you represent a national institution whose standing and reputation are in your hands.

102. What the U.S. Marine Corps Stands For

The U.S. Marine Corps exists for one purpose—to fight. Whether the Marine Corps is engaged in shipboard combat, landing operations, or a land campaign, the fundamental reason for its establishment remains unchanged.

The qualities that the Marine Corps stands for might seem old-fashioned. Nevertheless, these attributes have shaped the Corps since 1775, from Princeton to Belleau Wood, from Trenton to Chosin Reservoir to Khe Sanh, and from Granada to Fallujah. Here are some things that the Corps stands for.

Quality and Competence. Simply stated, a Marine must be first-rate. In the Marine Corps, your best is just the acceptable minimum. It is expected, as a matter of course, that the technical performance of a single Marine or a whole Marine outfit, whether on parade or in the attack, will be outstanding.

Discipline. Of all the principles of the Marine Corps, its insistence on discipline is the most unvarying and most uncompromising.

Valor. Displaying great courage in the face of danger or adversity is another Marine Corps hallmark. After the seizure of Iwo Jima, Fleet Admiral Chester W. Nimitz epitomized the performance of the Marines who took the island. "Uncommon valor," wrote the admiral, "was a common virtue." Three hundred Medals of Honor have been awarded to U.S. Marines. Valor is the Marines' stock in trade. "Retreat, hell! We just got here" was originally uttered in 1918 by a company commander of U.S. Marines.

Esprit de Corps. A Marine is intensely proud of the Corps, loyal to his or her comrades, and jealous for the good name of the Corps. This spirit is nowhere better expressed than in a letter, written in 1800, from William Ward Burrows, second commandant of the Marine Corps, to a junior Marine officer who had been insulted by an officer in the Navy:

> Camp at Washing., Sept 22, 1800
> Lt. Henry Caldwell,
> Sir—
>
> When I answer'd your letter, I did not Know what Injuries you had received on board the *Trumbull.* . . . Yesterday the Secretary told me, that he understood one of the Lieutenants of the Navy had struck you. I lament that the Capt. of yr ship cannot Keep Order on board of her. . . . As to yourself I can only say, that a Blow ought never to be

forgiven, and without you wipe away this Insult offer'd to the Marine Corps, you cannot expect to join our Officers.

I have permitted you to leave the Ship . . . that you may be on an equal Footing with the Captain, or any one who dare insult you, or the Corps. I have wrote to Capt. Carmick, who is at Boston to call on you & be your Friend. He is a Man of Spirit, and will take care of you, but don't let me see you 'till you have wip'd away this Disgrace. It is my Duty to support my Officers and I will do it with my Life, but they must deserve it.

On board the *Ganges*, about 12 mos. ago, Lt. Gale was struck by an Officer of the Navy, the Capt. took no notice of the Business, and Gale got no satisfaction on the Cruise: The moment he arrived he call'd the Lieut. out, and shot him; afterwards Politeness was restor'd.

. . .

Yr obdt Svt,
W. W. Burrows
LtCol Comdt, MC

Pride. Every Marine is intensely proud of Corps and country and does his or her utmost to build and uphold the Corps.

Loyalty and Faithfulness. Semper Fidelis ("Always Faithful") is the motto of the Corps. In addition, every honorable discharge certificate from the Marine Corps bears the phrase *Fideli certa merces* ("A sure reward to the faithful"). Marines understand that these are not idle words. Absolute loyalty to the Corps, as well as devotion to duty, is required of every Marine. The percentage of Marines missing in action or taken prisoner by the enemy is minute. A good Marine places the interests of the Marine Corps at the top of his or her list.

The Individual. The Marine Corps cherishes the individuality of its members and, although sternly consecrated to discipline, has cheerfully sheltered a legion of nonconformist, flamboyant individuals and irradiant personalities. It is a perennial prediction that colorful characters are about to vanish from the Corps. They never have and never will. No Marine need fear that the mass will ever absorb the individual.

The Volunteer. Despite occasional acceptance of draftees in times of peak demand, as in World War II and the Vietnam War, the Marine Corps is "a volunteer outfit." The Corps relies on those who want to be Marines. There is no substitute. In the old phrase, "One volunteer is worth ten pressed men."

The Infantry. The Corps is unique in that no matter what military specialty Marines acquire, be it combat, combat support, or combat service support specialty, ground or aviation, they are all trained initially as riflemen. All officers, in addition, must be morally and professionally prepared to function as infantry officers.

Relations between Officers and Enlisted Marines. A commandant of the Marine Corps once wrote: "The relation between officers and enlisted men should in no sense be that of superior and inferior nor that of master and servant, but rather that of teacher and scholar [i.e., student]. In fact, it should partake of the nature of the relation between father and son, to the extent that officers, especially commanding officers, are responsible for the physical, mental, and moral welfare, as well as the discipline and military training, of the young men under their command." These words now stand as an enduring testimony to the comradeship among all Marines, whether officer or enlisted.

Traditions. Saint Paul's injunction, "Hold the traditions which ye have been taught," could be a Marine motto. Respect for the traditions of the Corps is deeply felt. Every Marine adheres to the traditions that have shaped the Corps.

Professionalism. U.S. Marines are professionals who stand ready to fight any enemy, anytime, anywhere, as designated by the president and Congress, and to do so coolly and capably. They are not trained to hate, nor are they whipped up emotionally for battle or for any other duty the Corps is called on to perform. Patriotism and professionalism are their only two "isms."

Readiness. The Corps is perhaps most needed when the nation is demobilized and at peace. Marines are prepared mentally and physically for immediate employment, as individuals and in trained units. A former secretary of state once remarked that, as a crisis loomed, his first question to his staff was, "Where are the Marines and the carriers?"

Above all, the public has maintained a consistent view of the Corps; that view is taken for granted, but all Marines could use it as a daily measure of effectiveness. It contains no sophisticated concept of national defense or the exercise of sea power but rather reflects the public appreciation of decades of consistent Marine Corps performance. It goes like this: First, that wherever there is a crisis demanding U.S. military action, there will be Marines ready and able to go there in an instant. Second, once on the scene, those Marines will perform in a highly effective manner and restore the situation in our favor, without exception. Finally, the public believes that the Corps is a good thing to have around and consists of sound, energetic young men and women upon whom the national trust can be bestowed.

103. A Commandant Writes to His Officers

Years ago, Major General John A. Lejeune, thirteenth commandant of the Marine Corps, opened his heart to his officers in a collective letter.

> TO THE OFFICERS OF THE MARINE CORPS:
>
> I feel that I would like to talk to each of you personally. This, of course, it is impossible for me to do. Consequently, I am going to do the next best thing, by writing letters from time to time which will go to all the officers. In these letters, I will endeavor to embody briefly some of the thoughts which have come into my mind concerning our beloved Corps.
>
> In the first place, I want each of you to feel that the Commandant of the Corps is your friend and that he earnestly desires that you should realize this. At the same time, it is his duty to the Government and to the Marine Corps to exact a high standard of conduct, a strict performance of duty, and a rigid compliance with orders on the part of all the officers.
>
> You are the permanent part of the Marine Corps, and the efficiency, the good name, and the esprit of the Corps are in your hands. You can make or mar it.
>
> You should never forget the power of example. The young men serving as enlisted men take their cue from you. If you conduct yourselves at all times as officers and gentlemen should conduct themselves, the moral tone of the whole Corps will be raised, its reputation, which is most precious to all of us, will be enhanced, and the esteem and affection in which the Corps is held by the American people will be increased.
>
> Be kindly and just in your dealings with your men. Never play favorites. Make them feel that justice tempered with mercy may always be counted on. This does not mean a slackening of discipline.

Obedience to orders and regulations must always be insisted on, and good conduct on the part of the men exacted. Especially should this be done with reference to the civilian inhabitants of foreign countries in which Marines are serving.

The prestige of the Marine Corps depends greatly on the appearance of its officers and men. Officers should adhere closely to the Uniform Regulations, and be exceedingly careful to be neatly and tidily dressed, and to carry themselves in a military manner. They should observe the appearance of men while on liberty, and should endeavor to instill into their minds the importance of neatness, smartness, and soldierly bearing.

1-1. General John A. Lejeune

A compliance with the minutiae of military courtesy is a mark of well-disciplined troops. The exchange of military salutes between officers and men should not be overlooked. Its omission indicates a poor state of discipline. Similarly, officers should be equally careful to salute each other. Courtesy, too, demands more than an exchange of official salutes between officers. On all occasions when officers are gathered together, juniors should show their esteem and respect for their seniors by taking the initiative in speaking to and shaking hands with their seniors. Particularly should this be done in the case of commanding officers. The older officers appreciate greatly attention and friendliness on the part of younger officers.

We are all members of the same great family, and we should invariably show courtesy and consideration, not only to other officers, but to members of their personal families as well. Do not fail to call on your commanding officers within a week after you join a post. On social occasions the formality with which all of us conduct ourselves should be relaxed, and a spirit of friendliness and good will should prevail.

In conclusion, I wish to impress on all of you that the destiny of our Corps depends on each of you. Our forces, brigades, regiments, battalions, companies, and other detachments are what you make them. An inefficient organization is the product of inefficient officers, and all discreditable occurrences are usually due to the failure of officers to perform their duties properly. Harmonious cooperation and teamwork, together with an intelligent and energetic performance of duty, are essential to success, and these attributes can be attained only by cultivating in your character the qualities of loyalty, unselfishness, devotion to duty, and the highest sense of honor.

Let each one of us resolve to show in himself a good example of virtue, honor, patriotism, and subordination, and to do all in his power, not only to maintain, but to increase the prestige, the efficiency, and the esprit of the grand old Corps to which we belong.

With my best wishes for your success and happiness, I am, as always,

Your sincere friend,
John A. Lejeune,
Major General Commandant

General Lejeune's timeless and persuasive words make it evident that the Corps' reputation, its virtue, and indeed its future lie in the hands of its Marines—and particularly its officers. Read on to gain a deeper understanding of our Corps of Marines and what it takes to be an officer of Marines.

Letter to All Hands—We are going back into the brawl.

—Major General James N. Mattis
Iraq, March 2004

PART I

A CORPS OF MARINES

2

THE STORY OF THE MARINE CORPS

The Marine Corps dates from 10 November 1775. On that day, the Continental Congress authorized formation of two battalions of Marines. Samuel Nicholas of Philadelphia was commissioned captain on 28 November 1775 and was charged with raising the Marines authorized by Congress to form part of the naval service. Nicholas remained senior officer in the Continental Marines for the duration of the American Revolution and is properly considered our first commandant.

201. Marines in the Revolution

The initial Marine recruiting rendezvous opened at Tun Tavern in Philadelphia, and by early 1776, the organization had progressed to the extent that the Continental Marines were ready for their first expedition. The objective was New Providence Island (Nassau) in the Bahamas, where a British fort and large supplies of munitions were known to be. With Captain Nicholas in command, 234 Marines sailed from Philadelphia in Continental warships. On 3 March 1776, Captain Nicholas led his men ashore, took the fort, and captured the powder and arms for Washington's army.

For the first time in U.S. history, the Marines had landed, and the situation was well in hand.

During the succeeding years, Nicholas, now a major, commanded a battalion of Marines that fought in the Middle Atlantic campaigns of 1776 and

1777, at Trenton, Morristown, Assunpink, and Fort Mifflin. At sea (notably under John Paul Jones), shipboard Marines played traditional parts as prize crews, sharpshooters, and landing forces (such as in the Penobscot Bay expedition in 1779).

202. Early Years, 1783–1811

After the end of the Revolution in 1783, both the Continental Navy and the Marines waned into temporary obscurity. Although individual Marines continued to be enlisted to serve in the few U.S. armed vessels of the period (such as revenue cutters), no Corps organization again existed until 1 July 1798, when Congress reconstituted the Marine Corps as a military service. Major William Ward Burrows, another Philadelphian with Revolutionary War experience, was appointed major commandant of the Corps.

During the decade that followed, the Naval War with France (1798–1800) and the campaign against the Barbary corsairs (1801–5) provided employment for the Corps. Other noteworthy events were the organization of the Marine Band in 1798, the movement of Marine Corps Headquarters to Washington in 1800, and the retirement of Burrows as commandant in 1804.

The third commandant, Lieutenant Colonel Franklin Wharton, found approximately 65 percent of his small Corps on duty in the Mediterranean. Here, in 1805, First Lieutenant Presley Neville O'Bannon led a mixed force, including Marines, six hundred miles across the Libyan desert to attack the fortress at Derna. O'Bannon's handful of Marines was the first U.S. force to hoist the Stars and Stripes over territory in the Old World. The Mameluke sword, carried by Marine officers to this day, symbolizes O'Bannon's feat.

While events in the Mediterranean held the spotlight, Marines, together with Army and Navy forces, were active in Georgia, East Florida, and the lower Mississippi, where, in 1804, a 106-man detachment was established at New Orleans.

203. The War of 1812

During the first two years of the War of 1812, the main American achievements were at sea or on the Great Lakes. Marines fought in the great frigate duels of the war, as well as at the Battle of Lake Erie.

The outstanding record among seagoing Marines, however, was set by Captain John M. Gamble, captain of Marines in USS *Essex*, the raider that virtually destroyed England's Pacific whaling trade. In April 1813, Gamble, with a crew of fourteen Marines and seamen, was placed in command of a prize, the recommissioned USS *Greenwich*. Late in 1813, Gamble and his tiny force joined Captain David Porter in the Marquesas Islands and established a base where they could rest and refit over the winter. In the spring, Porter sailed for the coast of South America and left Gamble with twenty-two volunteers and six prisoners of war to man the base, should it be needed after a battle with the British. In May, a mutiny broke out aboard the *Seringapatam*, and Gamble was put in a small boat with four others. They made it back to another ship that had been left in the Marquesas. When the natives attacked the small party, Gamble, who had been wounded in the foot during the mutiny, hopped from cannon to cannon to fire them and beat off the attack. Gamble somehow got the ship under way with no charts and a crew of eight scarcely able to sail. He and his men made the Hawaiian Islands, only to be captured in 1814 by a British man-of-war. For all these exploits, he was awarded a richly deserved brevet as lieutenant colonel.

2-1. Sharpshooting Marine riflemen dominate the action between USS *Wasp* and HMS *Reindeer* in 1814.

In mid-1813, British forces under Admiral George Cockburn and Major General Robert Ross began a campaign of raids against the Middle Atlantic seaboard. A year later, in August 1814, a column of British soldiers, sailors, and Marines advanced on Washington, D.C. On 24 August, after the government had fled to Frederick, Maryland, an irresolute force of American soldiers and militia under Army Brigadier General William H. Winder attempted to halt the much smaller British column at Bladensburg, just east of Washington. Reinforcing Winder's 6,000 soldiers were 114 Marines from the barracks at "Eighth and Eye" and a contingent of seamen gunners with five guns, the whole force being under Commodore Joshua Barney of the United States Navy.

Winder's soldiers broke and ran at the first volley from the British, who advanced unconcernedly until they hit a piece of high ground occupied by the Marines and seamen, who were standing firm. Marine volleys and Navy gunnery forced the British (seven times stronger) to halt, to deploy, and finally, three times in succession, to charge—at a cost of 249 casualties. After having suffered more than 20 percent casualties and being forced rearward by a double envelopment, the Marines and sailors withdrew in good order, with at least a moral victory to their credit.

The British, having put Washington to the torch, were now determined to seize New Orleans.

Although a peace treaty was even then being signed in Europe, the British expedition forced its way up the Mississippi. On 28 December 1814, the first enemy attack spent itself against an American line led by General Andrew Jackson, with Marines (under Major Daniel Carmick) holding the center. Less than two weeks later, on 8 January, the British tried again. Despite a courageous assault by the redcoats, Jackson's main battle position stood unbroken. As the British commander, Sir Robert Pakenham, fell mortally wounded, the attack ebbed, New Orleans was saved, and the Marines shared in the glory when Congress recognized "the valor and good conduct of Major Daniel Carmick and Marines under his command."

204. Archibald Henderson Takes Over

The most important event in the history of the Marine Corps following the War of 1812 took place on 17 October 1820, when the adjutant and inspector, Archibald Henderson, succeeded Lieutenant Colonel Anthony Gale and became fifth commandant. Gale's term as commandant had been cut short by a poorly timed dispute with Secretary of the Navy Smith Thompson, followed by a court-martial.

During the thirty-nine years and ten presidential administrations that followed, Henderson dominated the Corps and gave it the high military character it holds to this day. Had it not been for Henderson's firmness, reinforced by a sympathetic Congress, the Corps might well have been abolished as a result of President Andrew Jackson's attempt in 1829 (with connivance from certain influential naval officers) to transfer the Marines into the Army. After the smoke of controversy had drifted clear, Congress in 1834 placed the Corps directly under the Secretary of the Navy—and increased its strength to boot. This was the first instance of congressional redress and rescue for the Marine Corps—something that has recurred repeatedly since then.

2-2. Commandant Archibald Henderson held the position for thirty-nine years and shaped the character of the Corps in the nineteenth century.

205. Actions against the Creeks and Seminoles, 1836–42

From 1836 through 1842, the Army, Navy, and Marine Corps collaborated to transfer the Creek and Seminole Indians of Georgia and Florida to new reservations. Commandant Henderson spent part of this time in the field at the head of a mixed brigade of Army troops and a Marine regiment (the first organization of that size in the history of the Corps). At the Battle of Hatchee Lustee, Florida, in 1837, Colonel Henderson won one of the few decisively successful victories of the campaign and was thereupon brevetted brigadier general—the first general officer in the Corps. Despite this success, as well as others against the Creeks, the Seminoles continued an obstinate resistance, and, in 1842, the war ended—with most of the Seminoles still in Florida.

206. To the Halls of the Montezumas

The war with Mexico included three distinct campaigns: Zachary Taylor's against Monterrey; Winfield Scott's against Mexico City; and that against California and the west coast of Mexico. Marines took part in two of these, and were, in

2-3. Marines took part in the campaigns against the Creek and Seminole Indians, including service in the Navy's "Mosquito Fleet" of river patrol boats.

fact, the first U.S. forces to set foot on the soil of Mexico proper (at Burrita on 18 May 1846).

A battalion of Marines formed part of General Scott's column that advanced from Veracruz toward Mexico City. The key to the capital was Chapultepec Castle, set on a crag commanding the swamp causeways into the city. In the assault on Chapultepec, the Marines were divided into storming parties to head the attack up the south approach.

Under a hail of fire, the Marines moved out. Major Levi Twiggs, the battalion commander, fell early in the attack, while Captain George H. Terrett, a company commander, pressed home a separate assault toward the city. After a night in the outskirts of Mexico City, the Marines marched into town, in the van of their division—the first U.S. troops to enter—and occupied the palace of the Montezumas on 14 September 1847. A new phrase had been added to the annals of the Corps, and the exploit was eventually forever memorialized in the first line of the Marine's Hymn.

In the Pacific, Marines joined naval landing parties taking possession of Monterey, Yerba Buena (San Francisco), Los Angeles, and San Diego, while First Lieutenant Archibald Gillespie acted both as confidential agent of President James Polk in the Bear State diplomatic intrigues and subsequently as a bold combat leader.

With California uneasily at rest by 1847, Marines of the Navy's Pacific Squadron secured the Mexican west coast ports of Mazatlán, Guaymas, Mulejé, and San José del Cabo. Mazatlán was garrisoned by Marines until June 1848, when peace was concluded.

207. Between the Wars

The decade following the peace with Mexico was hardly one of peace for the Marine Corps, despite its postwar reduction to approximately twelve hundred officers and men.

The opening of Japan in 1853–54 provided a historic setting for the landing of almost one-sixth of the Corps (six officers and two hundred Marines, commanded by Major Jacob Zeilin, Mexican War hero and future commandant). In the best traditions of the Corps, Major Zeilin's Marines were the first Americans to set foot on Japanese soil.

Hardly as peaceful were the landings at Shanghai (1854) and Canton (1856). In each, the conflicts represented trials of strength between Chinese and the Americans bent on "opening" China. At Canton's "Barrier Forts," 176 Chinese cannon were taken and five thousand Chinese put to flight.

A hemisphere away, in Nicaragua, Panama, Paraguay, and Uruguay, Marines were scarcely less active. With discovery of gold in California, the Panamanian isthmus assumed great importance in 1855, when a rickety U.S. railroad was finally completed across it. Soon Panama became a hotbed of disorder, which necessitated several landings by Marines, ultimately including a brigade-sized force in 1885. In Uruguay and Paraguay, the story was the same—unsettled times, immature governments—and Marines protected American interests.

And at home, in Washington itself, Marines were called out in 1859 to stand off the "Plug-Uglies," a gang of Baltimore mobsters that carried a loaded brass cannon for emphasis. While Marines and rioters faced each other across a downtown square, an old man, armed only with a gold-headed cane, stepped forward and placed his body across the muzzle of the mobsters' cannon. It was Brevet Brigadier General Archibald Henderson, fifth commandant of the Marine Corps, now seventy-four years old. While the thugs milled about the steadfast old man, a squad of his Marines rushed the cannon, ending the confrontation.

208. The Civil War

For the Marine Corps, the opening shots of the Civil War sounded almost two years before Fort Sumter. On 17 October 1859, shortly after John Harris had succeeded Henderson as colonel commandant, eighty-eight Marines were dispatched by the president to Harpers Ferry, Virginia, to recapture the U.S. Arsenal, which had been seized by the insurrectionist John Brown. Upon arrival, the Marine forces reported to Colonel Robert E. Lee, the senior U.S. Army officer present. When John Brown refused to surrender, the Marines, led by First Lieutenant Israel Green, smashed their way under fire into Brown's stronghold, wounded the old abolitionist, and quelled the insurrection.

After 1861, the Marine Corps—like the regular Army—was never large enough to fill the demands upon it. A Marine battalion fought in the first Battle of Bull Run (Manassas), and other Marine forces served ashore in the Mississippi Valley and in the defenses of Washington. All along the Confederate seaboard, from Hatteras Inlet to Hilton Head and Fort Pickens, shipboard Marines, sometimes in provisional battalions, executed successful landings, which put teeth into the Union blockade. Only at Fort Fisher did Marines share with the Navy a bloody defeat.

By and large, the reputation of the Corps did not gain during the Civil War. Its strength was kept small at only 4,161 officers and men. And, as a Corps, Marines were not called on to perform either the readiness or amphibious tasks peculiar to the organization. As early as 1864 (and again in 1867), attempts were made to disband the Marine Corps and merge it with the Army. Both times, however, Congress stepped into the breach, and the Corps was saved.

209. Post–Civil War Era

Although the period from 1865 to 1898 has sometimes been spoken of as one of marking time by the Marine Corps, this scarcely holds up. During that time, U.S. Marines landed to protect American lives and property in Egypt, Colombia, Mexico, China, Cuba, the Arctic, Formosa, Uruguay, Argentina, Chile, Haiti, Alaska, Nicaragua, Japan, Samoa, and Panama.

In addition to these and many minor landings, a combined Marine-Navy Asiatic Fleet landing force was sent in to the west coast of Korea in 1871, where, after storming an elaborate system of Korean forts along the Han River, it captured 481 guns and 50 Korean battle standards. In this fighting, two Marines tore down the Korean flag over the enemy citadel under intense fire and consequently were awarded Medals of Honor, the first of many to be awarded for action on the soil of the Hermit Kingdom.

Three able commandants (Jacob Zeilin, Charles G. McCawley, and Charles Heywood) did much to spark the Corps out of the Civil War doldrums, and despite its small strength (still below three thousand), the Marine Corps was in excellent shape when the United States declared war with Spain in 1898.

210. War with Spain

On the night of 15 February 1898, USS *Maine* (ACR-1) suddenly exploded and sunk in Havana Harbor. Twenty-eight Marines were among the 266 casualties. The gallantry of Private William Anthony, the captain's orderly, in rescuing Captain Charles D. Sigsbee despite great personal danger made Anthony the first U.S. hero of the impending war.

2-4. Private Hugh Purvis received one of several Medals of Honor awarded to Marines who stormed the Han River forts of Korea in 1871.

On 1 May 1898, less than a week after the declaration of war, Commodore George Dewey destroyed the Spanish squadron in Manila Bay. Two days later, Dewey landed his Marine detachments to secure Cavite Navy Yard and settled down for a three-month wait until the Army could get troops to the Philippines.

Just as Marines were first to land in the Philippines, so also were they the first U.S. forces to land and fight in Cuba. On 10 June 1898, an Atlantic Fleet battalion of Marines, commanded by Lieutenant Colonel R W. Huntington, landed under cover of ships' guns at Guantánamo Bay, Cuba, and seized an advanced base for the fleet. Four days later, at Cuzco Well, Huntington routed the remaining Spanish forces, destroyed their water supply, and completed the victory. The hero of the day was Sergeant John H. Quick, who was awarded the Medal of Honor for semaphoring while under U.S. and Spanish shellfire for an emergency lift of the naval bombardment.

Huntington's battalion was not the conventional ship's landing party of the nineteenth century but rather a self-contained Marine expeditionary force, which included infantry, artillery, and a headquarters complement of specialist and service troops. The battalion formed part of the fleet—a miniature fleet marine force whose primary mission was landing on hostile shores to secure an advanced base, as well as a precursor to the modern Marine air-ground task force.

2-5. Lieutenant Colonel R. W. Huntington (center) led the Floating Battalion of the Navy's Caribbean flotilla to quick success in Cuba in 1898.

211. "Our Flag's Unfurl'd to Every Breeze"

Between 1899 and 1916, the Marine Corps participated in eight major expeditions or campaigns: the Philippine Insurrection, the Boxer Uprising, Panama, the Cuban Pacifications, Veracruz, Haiti, Santo Domingo, and Nicaragua.

At least as important, and possibly more so, Marine Corps developments of this period laid the foundation of American amphibious warfare techniques and ensured the future survival and growth of the Corps.

Long oppressed by Spain, the Philippines in 1899 sought to make a clean break with colonialism and launched the Philippine Insurrection—or rather transferred its insurrection from the Spanish to the Americans. This three-year campaign included the first modern Marine brigade ever organized, as well as three exploits for which the Corps will be remembered: Major Littleton W. T. Waller's march across Samar, the storming of Sojoton Cliffs in Samar (where Captains David Porter and Hiram Bearss distinguished themselves in action, resulting in the award of Medals of Honor for both), and the pacification of the Subic Bay area on Luzon.

2-6. Between expeditions, the Marine Corps stood guard over stations and on ships of the U.S. Navy. This detachment guarded the Naval Station, Pensacola, Florida, at the turn of the twentieth century.

As 1900 dawned, China was undergoing one of its periods of antiforeignism—the Boxer Rebellion. In Tientsin and Peking, foreign missions were besieged by bloodthirsty Chinese mobs. In Peking, together with other foreign garrisons, U.S. and British Marines linked arms, as so often in the past, this time to defend the beleaguered Legation Quarter throughout the summer of 1900. In the international relief column dispatched to save Tientsin and Peking was a U.S. Marine force commanded by Major Waller and later by Major W. P. Biddle. By midsummer, Tientsin was relieved, and the legations were relieved on 14 August.

At almost the same time, conditions in Panama began to threaten free transit of the isthmus. In 1903, on orders from President Theodore Roosevelt, a U.S. Marine brigade—led by Major General G. F. Elliott, the commandant—landed at Colón to protect U.S. rights during Panama's revolt against Colombia. Marines remained in the Canal Zone until the situation became fully routine in 1911, when the Army took over.

First in 1906 and again in 1912, Marine brigades were sent to Cuba to restore order under the so-called Platt Amendment, by which the United States had the right to intervene in that newly liberated country. Twenty-four towns were occupied in 1906 and twenty-six in 1912; considerable fighting took place in eastern Cuba before peace was finally attained.

In 1901, the Marine Corps began special training and organization for the seizure and defense of advanced bases. Succeeding years saw increased use of battalions and regiments based in Navy transports as a means of projecting naval power across the shoreline. In 1910, at New London, Connecticut, General Elliott, the tenth commandant, established the Marine Corps Advanced Base School. For the first time in U.S. history, a school had been created to focus the thinking of an entire service on the unsolved problems of amphibious warfare and to develop expeditionary readiness in the Corps.

Hand in hand with establishment of the Advanced Base School was the organization of the Advanced Base Force, a Marine brigade containing all the necessary combined arms, maintained in readiness for immediate expeditionary service with the fleet. The Advanced Base Force was the prototype of the Fleet Marine Force (FMF).

When President Woodrow Wilson was obliged to protect American rights, property, and citizens in Mexico in 1914, Marines from the Advanced Base Force were the first to land, at Veracruz. Army forces followed. Veracruz provided the first field test of the Advanced Base Force, a test passed with flying colors.

Early in 1915, Haiti was wracked by revolution. Ships' detachments landed, but Haiti's troubles called for reinforcement by units of the Advanced Base Force. The pacification of Haiti proved to be long and arduous. Bandits were firmly established in the north, where the rugged country gave them every advantage. Under the dynamic leadership of now-Colonel Waller and Major Smedley Butler, Marines finally brought the bandits to battle in their stronghold at Fort Rivière. During the storming of the fort, Butler displayed gallantry that led to his second Medal of Honor, having been awarded his first for actions at Veracruz. The resulting victory brought peace to northern Haiti. The Marines rebuilt civil government, and, for the time being, Haiti breathed easily.

On 7 May 1916, Marine forces were dispatched to restore order in the Dominican Republic and again dramatized the ability of the Corps to take effective action on short notice. More than two thousand Marines landed in Santo Domingo, where, until 18 September 1924, a protracted campaign was waged to suppress banditry and enable a Dominican civil government to regain control of the country.

2-7. After the war with Spain, U.S. Marines remained in the Philippines on guard duty. The contingent swelled to brigade size to assist in suppressing the insurrection.

By the end of 1916, the Corps had ended a major era of growth. It had become, in fact if not in law, a national force in readiness. In addition, the seeds of Marine amphibious development had been sown, and the leadership of the Corps had been hardened in continual combat and expeditionary experience, which was destined to pay off for years to come.

212. Marines "Over There"

Although Marines served faithfully around the globe during World War I, and although Marine commitments in Haiti, Santo Domingo, Cuba, and Nicaragua remained little changed, the preeminent Marine story of World War I is that of the 4th Marine Brigade in France.

The 4th Brigade was the largest unit of Marines ever assembled. Composed of the 5th and 6th Regiments and the 6th Machine Gun Battalion, it totaled some 9,444 officers and men. Of the brigade's succession of notable actions (Belleau Wood, Soissons, Saint Mihiel, Blanc Mont Ridge, the Argonne), Belleau Wood was the most significant because it was the greatest battle, up to that

2-8. The 4th Marine Brigade arrived in France, among the "First to Fight," and joined the Army 2nd Infantry Division in 1918.

time, in the history of the Corps. The casualties of the 4th Marine Brigade in assaulting the well-organized German center of resistance in Belleau Wood were unmatched until the hardest-fought beach assaults of World War II. After Belleau Wood, German intelligence evaluated the Marine brigade as "storm troops"—the highest rating on the enemy scale of fighting men.

By 11 November 1918, the 4th Marine Brigade and Marine aviation units in France had sustained more casualties in eight months of almost-continuous combat than had the entire Corps during the preceding 143 years. The grim total was 11,366.

213. Marine Aviation

Founded in 1914 as part of the Advanced Base Force, Marine Corps aviation was still in the experimental stages when World War I began. During the war, Marine aviation units flew in combat over France and supported the fleet from an advanced base in the Azores. The spark plug of aviation's participation in the war was Major A. A. Cunningham, the Corps' first pilot. Starting from a strength of 7 officer pilots and 43 enlisted men in 1917, Marine aviation mustered 282 officers and 2,180 enlisted men by war's end. In the best traditions of the Corps, the 1st Aeronautical Company, destined for the Azores, was the first completely equipped American aviation unit to leave the United States for service overseas.

214. "Beyond the Seas"

While the 4th Brigade was gaining immortal victories, the Advanced Base Force remained hard at work in Haiti, Santo Domingo, and Cuba. One regiment, the 8th Marines (later reinforced by the 9th Marines) was held in east Texas to protect the Mexican oil fields should the Germans try (as intelligence indicated they intended to do) to disrupt that source of the Navy's oil supply.

The 5th Marine Brigade was sent to France, but the Army refused it permission to enter combat. Instead, the Marines were parceled out in noncombatant duties, mainly provost marshal and military police, in the Army communications zone.

215. Expeditions between World Wars

In addition to continuing commitments in the Caribbean, the year 1919 found the Corps performing occupation duty along the Rhine.

2-9. Marines in World War I faced a well-trained and modern opponent for the first time on a major scale.

Marines were also occupying eastern Cuba, which was ultimately pacified in 1922. Two years later, in 1924, six hard-fought campaign years in Santo Domingo came to an end, and Marines were finally withdrawn.

Between 1918 and 1920, Haiti was at a boil, with banditry again in full cry. Following suppression of bandit forces in 1922, Brigadier General John H. Russell, an expert in Haitian affairs, was appointed U.S. High Commissioner to Haiti to administer the American protectorate over the troubled republic. It was not until 1934 that the 1st Marine Brigade hauled down its Colors in Port-au-Prince and boarded ship for home.

The year 1927 was marked by trouble in both hemispheres—in Nicaragua and China. Naturally, Marines were soon involved.

As early as 1912, Marines had landed in Nicaragua to preserve order but were withdrawn in 1925. No sooner were they out of the country, however, when the worst civil war in the history of Nicaragua erupted, and Marines (spearheaded by the ships' detachments) were again dispatched in 1927 at the mutual request of the leaders of both warring factions. Marine occupation continued after an uneasy peace and consisted of disarming dissidents, conspicuous among whom was Augusto Sandino, a self-styled "patriot" guerrilla supported from Mexico and neighboring Honduras. A native *Guardia Nacional*, much like the *Gendarmerie d'Haiti* (also Marine-trained), was organized under the Marines to facilitate the hard job of policing a population that included thousands of demobilized revolutionary soldiers.

Marine aviation not only played a leading role in supporting ground operations in Nicaragua but also pioneered tactical and logistic air support on a scale hitherto unknown. The technique of dive-bombing (invented by Marine aviators in Haiti in 1919) was greatly refined. Practically all the isolated patrols and outposts in the heavy jungles of northern Nicaragua were maintained by air supply. To evacuate Marine wounded, First Lieutenant C. F. Schilt made ten landings and takeoffs from a village street in Quilali in a fabric-covered scout plane under murderous fire. Lieutenant Schilt was awarded the Medal of Honor.

When the Marines left Nicaragua in 1933, they turned over to the Nicaraguan government a well-organized *Guardia*, a military academy, a system of communications, and a first-rate public health service, plus many less obvious improvements.

As in Nicaragua, Marine embassy guards had been stationed in China for many years before 1927. There, too, civil disturbances of increasing violence reached a peak in 1927, and additional forces—the 4th Marines to Shanghai and a brigade to North China—were hurried in. Mainly because of these precautions, the threatening situation eased, and the brigade was withdrawn. The remaining units in Shanghai and Peking, and ultimately Tientsin as well, faced crisis after crisis with Chinese warlords and the Japanese until World War II closed the ledger.

216. Guarding the U.S. Mail

In 1921, after a series of violent mail robberies, President Warren G. Harding directed the Marine Corps to guard the "United States mails." Within a matter of hours, Marine armed guards were riding mail cars and trucks, with orders to shoot to kill. Not a single successful mail robbery took place against a Marine guard, and in less than a year the Marines were withdrawn. Five years later, when mail robberies again broke out, Marines were called in a second time; this time as well, the robberies ended at once.

2-10. Major General John A. Lejeune (left) and Brigadier General Wendell C. Neville returned from France in 1919 to lead the Corps into its amphibious era as the thirteenth and fourteenth commandants.

217. Amphibious Pioneering

In the early 1920s, it became clear to Marines that a war with Japan would entail amphibious seizure of a chain of advanced bases across the Pacific, the world's greatest ocean. In 1921, the year after Marine Corps Schools opened at Quantico, the course of a war with Japan was forecast by Lieutenant Colonel Earl Ellis, who subsequently died while on an intelligence mission in the Japanese Palaus in 1923.

To Major General John A. Lejeune, thirteenth commandant, the prospect of amphibious war was a bleak one. The British failure at Gallipoli had convinced orthodox military thinkers that an amphibious operation could not succeed against strong opposition. Despite the forbidding nature of the problem, General Lejeune set the Marine Corps to solving it.

Quantico was well equipped to undertake the task and became the focal point of American fleet-centered amphibious development. Marine Corps Schools attacked the problem and, by 1934, produced the first comprehensive U.S. manual of amphibious doctrine—*Tentative Landing Operations Manual*. This historic document was adopted intact by the U.S. Navy in 1938, under the title Fleet Training Publication-167, *Landing Operations Doctrine, U.S. Navy*. In 1941, when the U.S. Army issued its first amphibious publication, Quantico's book was again borrowed verbatim, even down to the illustrations, and appeared this time as War Department Field Manual 31-5. The tenets of

2-11. These primitive tactical exercises carried out by U.S. Marines between the wars forged the vital doctrine that ensured the defeat of Japan in World War II.

Tentative Landing Operations Manual still constitute much of the basis for publications that compose today's amphibious "bible."

To deal with matériel aspects of amphibious problems, the Marine Corps Equipment Board was established in 1933. Most notable among the board's pre–World War II achievements was the amphibian tractor, or LVT (landing vehicle, tracked), which joined the FMF in 1940.

During these pioneering years, the Advanced Base Force was redesignated in 1921 as the East Coast Expeditionary Force, and in 1933 as the Fleet Marine Force, after Major General John H. Russell, later the sixteenth commandant, had persuaded the Secretary of the Navy that Marine expeditionary troops should form an integral part of the U.S. Fleet. The Fleet Marine Force not only constituted a force in readiness but also performed an invaluable role in testing the doctrines and matériel evolved by Marine Corps Schools and the Equipment Board, respectively. From 1935 on, annual fleet landing exercises

2-12. Marine aviation came of age in the 1930s. It would prove an essential ingredient to success in the coming war.

enabled the fledgling FMF to find its footing as well as to keep the thinkers at Quantico progressing along sound lines.

Because of its pioneering efforts during the 1920s and 1930s, the Marine Corps—ground and aviation—was ready for amphibious war, and ready also to train others to wage it, when the opening salvos of World War II rocked the world. Before the war had run its course, seven U.S. Army divisions (including the first three Army divisions ever to receive amphibious training) were trained in landing operations by the Marine Corps, and the doctrines of Quantico girdled the globe.

2-13. Two architects of amphibious victory: Commandant Thomas Holcomb (left) and future Pacific amphibious corps commander H. M. Smith (right) at Quantico in late 1940.

218. Occupation of Iceland

In 1941, under the seventeenth Marine Corps commandant, Major General Thomas Holcomb, the Fleet Marine Force was called on to demonstrate its capabilities.

Iceland, garrisoned by British forces, was critical in the Battle of the Atlantic. President Franklin D. Roosevelt, who well knew Iceland's strategic importance, agreed with British Prime Minister Winston Churchill that the island should be more adequately secured, and that U.S. forces should be employed to deny Iceland to Germany. After the Army found itself unable to provide ready forces for the Iceland mission, the president turned to the Marine Corps. Less than one week later, on 22 June 1941, the 1st Provisional Marine Brigade had been organized and had embarked and sailed. On 7 July, more than four thousand Marines debarked at Reykjavik. Once again first on the spot, the Corps had proved itself the national force in readiness.

219. "Uncommon Valor"

When the United States entered World War II in 1941, the Marine Corps totaled some 70,425 men and was organized into two Marine divisions, two aircraft wings, and seven defense battalions (advanced base artillery units). By 1944, the Corps included six divisions, four wings, and corps and force troops to support the two amphibious corps, which were the FMF's highest formations. The Corps' top strength was 471,905.

Despite differences in terrain and character of operations, both the South Pacific and Central Pacific campaigns of World War II displayed two of the Marine Corps' unique attributes: the South Pacific highlighted *readiness,* and the Central Pacific, *amphibious assault virtuosity.*

The Guadalcanal campaign (1942) not only typified the South Pacific, but, more important, it dramatized to the American public the function of the Fleet Marine Force.

In 1942 (on the heels of valiant Marine defensive fighting at Wake Island, Midway, and Corregidor), it became clear that a U.S. advance base had to be established in the southern Solomons. Guadalcanal, where the Japanese were already building an airstrip, was the logical target. Despite high-level prophecies of disaster and recommendations that the assault be delayed until the following year—the earliest that Army troops could be trained to participate—the 1st Marine Division was given the job of retaking Guadalcanal and adjacent Tulagi. On 7 August 1942, the Marines landed.

It was the first U.S. offensive of World War II; the long road back had begun. Margins were never slimmer during the Pacific War than on Guadalcanal. But by late November 1942, when Army troops began to arrive in strength, battered Henderson Field was firmly secured by U.S. Marine ground and air, and, in the inner councils of Japan, it was already acknowledged that the turning point of the war had been reached.

The lesson of the Guadalcanal campaign was that without a *ready* Marine Corps, the operation could never have taken place. Undertaken as a purely naval campaign by fleet units and Marines, Guadalcanal demonstrated the dependence of sea power on fleet expeditionary forces, as well as the degree to which the Marine Corps had placed itself in readiness for just such an occasion.

2-14. Success on Tarawa, as in other battles, rested on the fighting abilities of the individual Marine.

If Guadalcanal and subsequent operations in the South Pacific—New Georgia, Bougainville, Choiseul (all in 1943), and New Britain (in 1944)—proved that the Corps was ready for war, the campaign across the Central Pacific displayed the Marine Corps' virtuosity in amphibious assault.

The succession of Central Pacific battles—Tarawa (1943), the Marshalls, Saipan, Guam, Tinian, Peleliu (all 1944), and Iwo Jima and Okinawa (both 1945)—was by hard necessity mostly a series of frontal assaults from the sea against positions fortified with every refinement that Japanese ingenuity and pains could produce. To reduce such strongholds, the amphibious assault came of age.

On Iwo Jima, toward the end, as on Tarawa at the beginning, the fighting ability of the individual Marine came into sharp focus. Each battle was one of frontal assault and close combat against fortified positions. Tarawa was the first combat test of the Marine Corps doctrines for amphibious assault, and Tarawa demonstrated that those doctrines worked. Two years later, at Iwo Jima—the largest all-Marine battle in history—Marines reaped the benefit of their Tarawa experience (and experience from many other hard-fought assaults) in the form of a tested, combat-proven assault technique. Without Tarawa, Iwo would not

2-15. In many respects, the Great Pacific War, 1941–45, truly cemented the Marine Corps as an armed service of the United States.

have been possible. Without the U.S. Marine Corps (and without the years of study, experimentation, and development at Quantico), neither Tarawa nor Iwo (or the battles between) could have succeeded, let alone taken place.

But the record of the Corps in World War II was not only the great record of its seaborne assaults. Beginning on 7 December 1941 at Wake, Marine aviation was also in the war. At Midway, Guadalcanal, Bougainville, and the northern Solomons, in the Marshalls, at Peleliu, Iwo Jima, and Okinawa, Marine fliers again helped to forge the concept of the air-ground team. And just as World War II brought to fruition the long-studied amphibious assault doctrines of the Corps, so also World War II witnessed the introduction of Marine close air support. In the reconquest of the Philippines, four Marine aircraft groups working with Marine air-liaison parties on the ground reached a high point in Marine tactical air support (even though this support was for Army comrades).

By the end of the war, the Fleet Marine Force, with aviation and ground units, was poised for the invasion of Japan—an invasion rendered unnecessary after Japan's surrender on 2 September 1945. The Corps had grown from 19,354 in 1939 to nearly 500,000 in 1945. The victories in World War II cost the Corps 86,940 casualties. In the eyes of the American public, the Marine Corps was second to none and seemed destined for a long and useful career. Fleet Admiral Chester W. Nimitz's ringing endorsement of Marine fighting on Iwo Jima might very well be applied to the entire Marine Corps during World War II: "Uncommon valor was a common virtue."

220. The Postwar Marine Corps

Although the Corps enjoyed high public prestige at the end of World War II and seemed here to stay, the years 1946–49 were devoted to a searching examination into the mission of (and behind closed doors in high quarters, even the need for) the Marine Corps. These doubts were inspired, as two commandants testified before Congress, by the Army General Staff, whose long-term objective (since before World War I) had been the restriction of the development of the Marine Corps or, some asserted, its reduction to a minor security and ceremonial unit. The question was firmly—and, Marines hoped, finally—resolved by the National Security Act of 1947 (discussed in the next chapters), which gave the Corps firm missions and reaffirmed its status as the service uniquely charged with primary amphibious development responsibility for landing force tactics, technique, and doctrine. Subsequently, the Douglas-Mansfield Act, enacted in 1952, afforded the commandant coequal status with the Joint Chiefs of Staff in all matters concerning the Marines and legislated today's organization of the Corps.

While the roles, missions, and status of the Marine Corps were being debated in both executive and legislative branches of the government, the Corps maintained occupation forces in Japan and northern China and completed an orderly demobilization unmarred by indiscipline or untoward incident.

The postwar FMF comprised two major forces, Fleet Marine Force Pacific and Fleet Marine Force Atlantic, assigned respectively to the Pacific and the Atlantic fleets. Each force embodied a Marine division and an aircraft wing (both on reduced manning for budgetary reasons) with supporting logistic units.

221. The Korean War

Like the story of the Corps in World War II, the Marines' part in the Korean War is covered by the official histories. Therefore, this narrative confines itself only to high spots of a grueling three-year war, at the outset of which, to quote Hanson Baldwin of the *New York Times*, "The Marines were ready to fight; if they had not been, we might still be fighting in the Korean peninsula."

On 25 June 1950 (24 June in the United States and Europe), when the Russian- and Chinese-supported North Korean troops attacked South Korea, the Corps numbered approximately seventy-five thousand. The FMF was deployed in two shrunken divisions at Camps Pendleton and Lejeune. Aviation, which had narrowly missed transfer to the Air Force by Defense Secretary Louis Johnson, was even thinner: eighteen squadrons, divided into two wings at Cherry Point and El Toro, but thirty fighter squadrons in the Marine Corps Reserve. The chairman of the Joint Chiefs of Staff, General Omar Bradley, had predicted publicly, hardly eight months before, that the world would never again see a large-scale amphibious landing.

On 2 July, faced with mounting catastrophe, General Douglas MacArthur sent his first request to the Joint Chiefs of Staff for help from the Marines. In the days that followed, General MacArthur sent five more pleas, culminating in a request for a war-strength Marine division and a war-strength aircraft wing.

Less than two weeks later, the 1st Provisional Marine Brigade was crossing the Pacific as it headed for the Pusan perimeter, into which shaken U.S. Army

2-16. Colonel L. B. Puller (right), who distinguished himself during the Inchon landings, studies the terrain before advancing to another enemy objective beyond Inchon.

and Republic of Korea units were already streaming rearward. On 3 August, Marine F4Us from USS *Sicily* (CVE-118) scored first blood for the Corps in an air strike over Inchon; on 7 August, eight years after Guadalcanal, ground elements of the brigade were plugging holes in the Pusan perimeter, and, for the first time, helicopters were flown in support of ground close combat—by Marines.

In Tokyo, U.S. Marine and Navy planners were translating into reality General MacArthur's plan to relieve Pusan and retake Seoul by an amphibious stroke to be delivered at the Korean west coast port of Inchon. Because of extreme tidal fluctuation, 15 September was the only suitable D-day until mid-October.

Despite unprecedented haste in preparation and numerous calculated risks of enemy opposition, geography, and hydrography, the Inchon landing was almost anticlimactic in its success. As favorable reports poured in throughout D-day, General MacArthur signaled: "The Navy and Marines have never shone more brightly than this morning." Largely as a result of the amphibious capability and readiness of the Marine Corps, the United Nations forces were able to rout the North Korean army south of the 38th parallel, leaving it all but destroyed.

On 25 November 1950, after an eerie lull, Chinese troops hit the right wing of the Eighth U.S. Army, routed and dispersed at least one U.S. Army division, and launched an entire army group, eight divisions, against the 1st Marine Division.

The blow fell when the division's forward elements were west of Chosin Reservoir, at Yudam-Ni. It is enough to record that, in the face of "General Winter" and of every weapon, artifice, and attack in overwhelmingly superior strength, the division concentrated promptly; rescued and evacuated surviving remnants of adjacent, less ready Army formations; and commenced one of the great marches of American history, from Chosin Reservoir to the sea.

Following amphibious withdrawal and a short "breather," the 1st Division spearheaded the IX Corps spring offensive of 1951. At the same time, the 1st Marine Aircraft Wing continued to provide the preponderance of all close-support sorties nominally credited to the Fifth Air Force, under whose control the wing now operated.

In spring 1952, the 1st Division moved to the arena of its final battles in Korea: the line of the Imjin River, astride the Munsanni corridor to Seoul. Here, holding a frontage greater than that of any other division in Korea, the division kept Seoul safe, anchored the United Nations' left flank, and overlooked the Panmunjom truce site. From these positions, the Marines fought a series of bloody trench-warfare actions of a type and scale unheard of in the Corps since World War I.

Korea tested "the new Marine Corps" in readiness and fighting quality, and the Corps was found wanting in neither. Korea demonstrated to doubters, in high places and low, that amphibious operations were anything but dead. Korea proved, as had World War II before it, the high caliber and readiness of the Marine Corps Reserve. Marine Corps close air support distinguished itself as an unrivaled capability. Most of all, in a time of immense upheaval in military techniques, Korea underscored the fact that the military principles for which the Marine Corps stood remained as sound in 1953 as they had been in 1775.

222. At Mid–Twentieth Century

There had been no victory in Korea, so there was no demobilization. The Corps continued within the structure of three divisions and three wings that Congress had established in 1952, with one of each on the East and West coasts of the United States and the third in the Far East (Okinawa and mainland Japan). From these major forces, floating battalions were maintained on station with the U.S. fleets in the Mediterranean and the Far East and frequently in the West Indies as well. A thorough modernization of the war-tested amphibious doctrines of the Navy and Marine Corps, originally conceived in Quantico in the late 1940s, gave these forces assault helicopters and specially designed helicopter carriers as transports. Blending these sophisticated and original methods with the tried and true ones of seaborne assault by landing craft and amphibious tractors, or amtracs, the amphibious assault now had even greater shocking power and flexibility than before.

In the decade following Korea, it became clear that, despite the ever-present threat of nuclear war, the characteristic pattern of the Cold War was one of limited operations, of politico-military guerrilla warfare—in short, the type of small war in which the Marine Corps had become so thoroughly versed during the first 150 years of its existence. In the Far East, between 1955 and 1963,

2-17. Improved helicopters brought a new dimension to postwar Marine amphibious doctrine.

Marines landed in the Tachen Islands, Taiwan, Laos, Thailand, and South Vietnam in countermoves against Communist pressure. In the Mediterranean, not only did Marines land at Alexandria to help evacuate U.S. and foreign nationals during the Suez incident of 1956, but, on an appeal from the Lebanese government, Marines also secured Beirut against a Communist coup in July 1958. A Marine brigade, subsequently reinforced by Army troops, stood by for ten weeks until peaceful elections had been completed and a constitutional change of government had been duly carried out. In the Caribbean, the nation's October 1962 confrontation with Communism saw Cuba ringed with floating Marine landing forces, while other FMF units ensured that Guantánamo Bay remained safe and secure against Fidel Castro's aggression.

223. Explosion in Santo Domingo

On 24 April 1965, what had started as a military coup d'état escalated into an attempt by rebel factions to gain control of the Dominican Republic. In a five-day blood bath, the government of Santo Domingo ceased to exist. The American embassy and seven other foreign embassies came under fire or were violated by revolutionaries. In the late afternoon of 28 April, President Lyndon B. Johnson ordered the landing of the 3rd Battalion, 6th Marines, at Ciudad Santo Domingo, from USS *Boxer* (LPH-4) lying offshore. It had been thirty-nine years since U.S. Marines last landed in the Caribbean (at Bluefields, Nicaragua, in 1926).

Quickly augmented to brigade size, the landing force, despite sporadic resistance in some areas, established a demilitarized international zone protecting the American and other embassies. When, in due course, Army airborne units arrived, the Marines came under command of the Army. Marine forces were withdrawn once pacification of the city was complete.

224. War in Vietnam

Meanwhile, on the other side of the globe, the dragging war in Vietnam heated up. Marine helicopter units (flying half the total sorties and flight hours with 20 percent of the helicopter lift capability in the country) had been in Vietnam since 1962. So had Marine radio reconnaissance troops and a U.S. Marine advisory mission to train the Vietnamese marine corps.

2-18. Among the innovative technical developments pioneered by the Corps in the 1950s, the Ontos demonstrated the potential of mobile, lightweight antitank weapons for the landing force.

In accordance with long-standing contingency plans, elements of the 3rd Marine Division, supported by squadrons of the 1st Marine Aircraft Wing, deployed to a highly strategic enclave, centered around Da Nang and the existing air base complex, in the north of the Republic of Vietnam. This area had not been chosen by chance: it had a port, independent of Saigon and others, to the south; it had beaches; and it commanded defiles in the coastwise road and rail networks. Its main and enduring disadvantage was that it was adjacent to some of the most hard-core Vietcong regions in-country, both south and inland to the west.

On the heels of the 3rd Division followed the 1st Marine Division and Marine Aircraft Group 36, being split between Vietnam and Okinawa. By the end of the year, almost two-thirds of the combat units of the Marine Corps were thus committed to the Vietnam war.

Adjacent Marine coastal enclaves were established at Da Nang and Chulai, with the objective of not only protecting these important air bases but also pacifying a populous and productive region using the "oil-stain" tactics originated in this very region by France's master of colonial warfare, Marshal Lyautey.

Consolidated under Headquarters, III Marine Amphibious Force, the Marines soon came to grips with the Vietcong. Late 1965 was marked by sustained patrolling, ambushes, and intermittent battles to connect the Da Nang and Chulai enclaves. Not only did 1966 bring more of the same but also more troops. By the end of 1966, approximately sixty thousand Marines—more than one-sixth of all U.S. forces in Vietnam—were ashore and in the field. These units included troops from the newly reformed 5th Marine Division, not seen on the active list since World War II. In hard fighting throughout I Corps area and especially along the 17th parallel demilitarized zone separating North and South Vietnam, Marines repeatedly turned back stubborn North Vietnamese Army (NVA) units.

Yet even as successes in combat and pacification mounted for the U.S. forces and their allies, the war was being lost. The native Vietnamese government proved unsuited to gain and sustain the loyalty and obedience of its population. In the United States, another people grew weary and impatient of the war, amplified on a daily basis on television and the printed media to the extent that President Lyndon B. Johnson chose not to pursue re-election and Congress began to apply halters to the war effort.

2-19. Marine helicopter tactics played an important part in the Vietnam War.

In mid-1969, as the Vietnamese armed forces began to take on more of their own war, American troop withdrawals commenced. By October, the first-in 3rd Division and 1st Wing had been phased out. By this time, the Communists had reverted almost completely to the level of terrorism and guerrilla war. At the year's end, 90 percent of the population of the Marines' northern provinces was living in secure areas. Even so, the 1st Division still had ample work holding NVA forays at arm's length from the vital Da Nang area. More and more, however, the Army of the Republic of Vietnam was out front, while the Marines were in support.

One landmark Marine Corps achievement had been to forge the capable, high-spirited Vietnamese marine corps, whose splendid fighting during the all-out Communist offensive of 1972 did so much to hold the northern provinces. Yet in the end it was all in vain: abandoned by an America that cut off its weapons and supplies, Vietnam was destined to fall to Communist aggression, which outlasted its foes.

By that time, however (save for Marine landing forces that covered the final evacuation of American embassies in Phnom Penh and Saigon), the Marines' long war was over. In the words of General Robert E. Cushman, twenty-fifth commandant, in April 1972, "We are pulling our heads out of the jungle and redirecting our attention seaward, reemphasizing our partnership with the Navy and our shared concern in the maritime aspects of our national strategy. . . . With respect to our standards—we will maintain them: in appearance, discipline, personal proficiency, and unit performance. Without them, we would not be Marines."

225. History of the Women Marines

In August 1918, the first women ever to wear the Globe and Anchor enlisted in the U.S. Marine Corps. They totaled 305 in all and were immediately nicknamed "Marinettes," an obvious derivative of the Navy's contemporary "Yeomanettes." Although the duties and scope of action of a Marinette (whose top possible rating was sergeant) were much more limited than today, the spirit was similar.

The "new" women's component was organized on 13 February 1943, when Lieutenant General Thomas Holcomb, seventeenth commandant, authorized creation of the Marine Corps Women's Reserve. The first officers and enlisted women were trained beside Navy WAVES (Women Accepted for Volunteer

Emergency Service) in existing naval schools for women. By May 1943, 75 women had completed officer training in a special course at Mount Holyoke College in South Hadley, Massachusetts, and 722 had weathered recruit training. July 1943 saw establishment of the Women Reserve Schools at Camp Lejeune. Here at Lejeune were centralized recruit and officer candidate training, together with a number of specialist schools for the 18,000 enlisted women and 821 officers of the Women's Reserve, or "WR," as it was soon short-titled.

2-20. Violet van Wagner (center) and Florence Weidinger enlisted as the first women to serve in the United States Marine Corps. World War I jackets, a campaign hat, and a helmet were hastily borrowed from male Marines for the official swearing-in ceremony.

It was an emphatic tradition of the new branch of the Corps that there would be no trick nicknames for the group. As far as women Marines were—and are—concerned, any cute, coy, or punning sobriquet, official or otherwise, would merely demean the Marine Corps Emblem, which they proudly wore. Today, this tradition is stronger than ever, and since the late 1990s Marines who happen to be women are known simply as "Marines," or female Marines when a distinction is relevant.

Much of the initial tone and standard of the Marine Corps Women's Reserve was set in ordinary course by the parent Corps, but quite as much, if not more, was due to the ability and effort of the first director of the Women's Reserve, Colonel Ruth Cheney Streeter. Colonel Streeter made it her objective to integrate the women reservists into the framework of the Corps. It was her vision that lifted the World War II women from clerical specialization (the World War I role of the Marinettes) into more than two hundred separate occupational specialties and billets at every major Marine Corps post in the continental United States and ultimately overseas.

At the end of World War II, save for about one hundred women officers and enlisted women retained on duty at Marine Corps Headquarters under Major Julia E. Hamblet (later to become a director of women Marines), the Women's Reserve went home. In 1948, however, Congress passed the Women's Armed Services Integration Act, and a new chapter opened. Henceforth, each service would have a career cadre of regulars, in addition to the reservists.

To head the regulars (then called "WM" for women Marines), General Clifton B. Cates, nineteenth commandant, chose Colonel Katherine A. Towle, former assistant dean of women at the University of California and wartime successor of Colonel Streeter. On 12 June 1948, the Women's Reserve went out of existence, and on the succeeding 4 November, the women Marines came into being.

Members of the former Women's Reserve were reenlisted into the Marine Corps Reserve, and many became members of the Organized Reserve. Like the remainder of the Organized Reserve, the women found themselves mobilized only days after the onset of war in Korea, with thirteen Organized Reserve women's platoons responding to the call. During the years ahead, regular women Marines continued as an increasingly important part of the Corps, and during Vietnam (on a strength of some two thousand) filled many key billets, which released other Marines for field service. (A symbolic watershed for the WMs came in 1965 when, during the Dominican revolt, a staff sergeant on duty at the American embassy earned the first combat campaign medal ever awarded to a woman Marine.)

With the signing of the Paris Peace Accords on 27 January 1973, the war in Vietnam was declared officially ended. Not only a war, but also an era, was coming to an end.

The draft was replaced by the all-volunteer force policy, and societal roles for women were changing rapidly. Both these factors would soon be reflected in the increasing number and widening role of women in the military.

On 1 February 1973— almost thirty years to the day that the first director was sworn into office—Colonel Margaret A. Brewer became the seventh, and final, director of women Marines. The only director without World War II service, she had entered the Marine Corps during the Korean War, immediately following graduation from the University of Michigan at Ann Arbor in 1952.

In many ways, her service career paralleled that of the previous directors. She was commissioned during a war, at a time of acute personnel shortages, and faced the unexpected demands that wartime service entailed. Colonel Brewer served as director during a period of sweeping change. In the post-Vietnam years, the Marine Corps took positive steps, within the limits of its combat mission and organization, to integrate women more fully. Many of the actions that were to take place in coming years stemmed from recommendations made by a specially formed ad hoc committee on increased effectiveness and utilization of women in the Marine Corps. In November 1973, the committee's recommendations were approved by the commandant with the written comment, "Let's move out!" Among the most significant recommendations were the establishment of a pilot program to train women for duty with selected stateside elements of the Fleet Marine Forces; the assignment of women Marines to all occupational fields except the combat arms; and the elimination of the regulation that prohibited women from commanding units other than women's units.

In 1974, the commandant approved a change in policy permitting the assignment of women to specified rear-echelon elements of the Fleet Marine Forces, on the condition that women Marines not be deployed with assault units or units likely to become engaged in combat. The decision came at the conclusion of a successful six-month pilot program and carried the provision "that such assignment not adversely affect combat readiness." Three years later, out of a total of approximately 3,830 women Marines on active duty, 600 were serving in Fleet Marine Force assignments. Another major step was taken in the following year. The Marine Corps approved the assignment of women Marines to all occupational fields except the four designated as the combat arms (infantry, artillery, armor, and pilot and air crew).

Of necessity, some assignment restrictions did remain, including the preservation of a rotation base for male Marines; the need for adequate facilities for women; the availability of nondeployable billets for women; and the legal restrictions prohibiting the assignment of women Marines to combat ships and aircraft.

2-21. Within a year, proper uniforms were designed and issued to the Women's Reserve, in which more than three hundred served in 1918–19.

As women became more fully integrated in the Marine Corps, the decision was made to disestablish the Office of the Director of Women Marines following thirty-four years of existence, and its functions were transferred to other Marine Corps staff agencies. And today, the complete integration of women in the Marine Corps appears near, for in January 2014, Defense Secretary Leon Panetta ordered all specialties and positions throughout the Defense Department opened to women to take effect beginning in January 2016 unless a service formally requests and receives approval to exempt selected specialties.

226. The Cutting Edge of Sea Power

In the aftermath of Vietnam, the Corps trained for conventional contingencies involving the reinforcement of the North Atlantic Treaty Organization (NATO) and South Korea but also found its operating forces in the Sixth and Seventh Fleets involved in patrolling waters off the Middle East and West Asian hot spots. Middle East tensions brought Marines ashore again in Lebanon during 1983–84. This time, Marines in Beirut drew fire as they interposed themselves between warring factions as part of a four-nation peacekeeping force. On 23 October 1983, 241 U.S. service personnel, including 220 Marines, 18 sailors, and 3 soldiers, were killed by a terrorist truck bomb at a Marine compound in Beirut, Lebanon. Emerging undaunted from the rubble, the survivors and a relief battalion continued in their presence mission until withdrawn six months later.

Almost immediately after the Beirut disaster, other Marines played a successful role in the U.S. liberation of the Caribbean island of Grenada that commenced on 25 October 1983 and ousted the Cubans and radicals in control there. Marines exploited light resistance to dash across the island and relieve pressure on bogged-down Army paratroopers and rangers in a model ninety-six-hour intervention.

Expeditionary action short of war proved especially heavy and varied as Marine Corps units participated in the U.S. intervention in Panama on 20 December 1989 and evacuated foreign nationals and secured the U.S. embassy in Liberia during a civil war there on 6 August 1990. Finally, the greatest U.S. deployment since the Vietnam War found the majority of the Fleet Marine Force in and afloat off Saudi Arabia as part of the international expedition sent to protect Saudi Arabia and subdue the Iraqi forces in the 1990–91 Gulf War.

227. The Gulf War and Aftermath, 1990–2001

In the wake of the Iraqi seizure of Kuwait in August 1990, the president of the United States ordered the U.S. Central Command (USCENTCOM) to reinforce and defend Saudi Arabia and the other Persian Gulf states, in concert with a growing coalition determined to resist and ultimately expel the Iraqi forces. Among the first U.S. forces to arrive in Saudi Arabia for this purpose was the 7th Marine Expeditionary Brigade, which deployed to the key port and petroleum center of Al Jubayl, with its aviation based farther south on the Gulf of Bahrain. Offloading heavy equipment from its habitually linked Maritime Prepositioning Squadron 1, the brigade reported ready for operations on 25 August, a mere ten days after arrival in theater.

The brigade stood alone only for a few days, as the follow-on elements of the I Marine Expeditionary Force (I MEF) began to arrive. Eventually growing to a force of over ninety thousand Marines and attached Navy personnel, U.S. Marine Corps Forces Central Command, the Marine component command for USCENTCOM, included two reinforced divisions, an enlarged aircraft wing containing the majority of the Marine Corps aircraft inventory, and the bulk of two force service support groups. Over twenty thousand Marines and Navy personnel of the 4th and 5th Marine Expeditionary Brigades remained afloat while I MEF moved to the Kuwaiti-Saudi frontier.

This, the most rapid and complex strategic deployment in Marine Corps history, used all forms of transportation, including military and commercial aircraft, naval and merchant shipping, and the ferrying of hundreds of Marine Corps aircraft, from fighters to the ubiquitous observation planes, from bases in California, Arizona, North and South Carolina, Hawaii, and Japan. Thousands of reservists and retired Marines were mustered to reinforce or augment the forces, as well as to replace deployed units and personnel in their former garrisons. An infantry regiment, battalions, squadrons, and smaller units of the Marine Corps Reserve took their places in line with regular units in both combat and support echelons.

After long periods of training, marshaling, and waiting, the campaign began with the air offensive against the Iraqi forces on 16 January 1991. Marine aircraft from Saudi bases and the amphibious ships in the Persian Gulf mainly struck targets in Kuwait, with Marine fighter and electronic warfare cover being provided to the coalition forces at large. After air superiority had been established, the ground units began to assemble along the frontier and prepare for

2-22. Marines train annually in Arctic warfare conditions in support of their global contingency responsibilities.

their assault. The two reinforced Marine divisions stood south of the Kuwaiti border, free from the observation of the Iraqi defenders, who were being pounded mercilessly by the coalition air forces.

On 24 February, the 1st and 2nd Marine Divisions attacked into Kuwait. They forced their way through the Iraqi barriers and brushed aside the frontline resistance. Mounted in a variety of tanks, assault amphibious vehicles, light armored vehicles, and trucks, the attacking regiments destroyed or captured whole battalions of Iraqi troops and swept through the burning oil fields toward the capital, Kuwait City. Artillery barrages and repeated strikes by fighter-bombers and attack helicopters supported the advance of the regiments. After one hundred hours of combat, Marines dominated southern Kuwait, and the capital was mopped up by neighboring Arab coalition forces. The cease-fire came too soon for many elements of the Marine force to come into play. The Marines of the landing force, afloat in the Gulf, raided a few islands, landed a tactical reserve in the MEF rear, and provided aviation support to their comrades ashore.

Even faster than their initial deployment to the crisis area, the withdrawal of Marines from the theater proved breathtaking. Except for the service support Marines needed to remove the bulk of the accumulated supplies, the I Marine Expeditionary Force returned to its bases in barely six weeks' time. A total of twenty-four Marines were killed and ninety-two wounded in action. The sudden withdrawal of the forces left untouched and unscarred the semifeudal Arab principalities to which the coalition forces had rallied.

Marines in the same year found themselves on humanitarian support missions in Bangladesh, Somalia, and Kurdistan. They would return in strength to Mogadishu, Somalia, on 9 December 1992, as the leading edge of a great United Nations effort to end starvation and lawlessness there. Later, a Marine expeditionary unit (MEU) formed the U.S. ground cutting edge for the NATO-led intervention in Kosovo in 1998. Increased naval and Marine Corps presence in the Indian Ocean littorals also marked the decade.

228. 9/11 and Aftermath, 2001–14

The 9/11 terrorist attacks led to the deployment of U.S. forces to Afghanistan, the initial terrorist base, and then the widening of the prosecution of what came to be called the "Global War on Terror" into Yemen and Somalia and the invasion of Iraq in 2003. These measures produced crushing military defeats of the enemy in each case. However, they also led to long-term campaigns in Iraq and Afghanistan to occupy, pacify, and conduct security and stabilization operations to establish and support governments that would lead the nations into the peaceful international community.

The initial Marine Corps contribution for the campaign in Afghanistan, called Operation Enduring Freedom, began on 7 October 2002, consisting in the main of the deployment of two MEUs—15th MEU and 26th MEU—combined to form Naval Expeditionary Task Force 58 under then–Brigadier General James N. Mattis. This provisional Marine expeditionary brigade launched combat forces and supporting aviation hundreds of miles inland to envelop the southeast portion of the country around Kandahar. These actions, combined with the U.S.-assisted anti-government forces of Afghans in the north, caused the flight of the Taliban leaders and the terrorist bands they had sheltered. A U.S.-approved provisional government took office in December, and although Marine Corps forces departed Afghanistan in 2014 after thirteen years of security and stability operations, the ensuing pacification program continues to this day against a resurgent Taliban.

Such an unusual campaign, harkening back to Marine Corps anti-bandit operations of the early twentieth century, paled in comparison to the Corps' major contribution to the invasion and occupation of Iraq, called Operation Iraqi Freedom (OIF), beginning on 20 March 2003. The Marine Corps provided half of the initial U.S. assault forces and a third of the forces in the initial campaign. The I Marine Expeditionary Force employed the 1st Marine Division and a regimental task force of 2nd Division with a reinforced 3rd Marine Aircraft Wing and 1st Force Service Support Group to sweep into southeastern Iraq. Detaching British army and Royal Marine contingents and the 15th MEU to take Basra and the Faw Peninsula, I MEF continued onward, routing the Iraqi army in a fast-moving battle and pursuit between the Euphrates and Tigris Rivers, past Kut, and into Baghdad from the south. As the Iraqi government and military collapsed, the collective Marine Corps and Army forces secured Baghdad, while a mobile Marine Corps light armored task force swept northward to Tikrit and Kirkuk to prevent any consolidation by Iraqi remnant forces and to link up with U.S. and free Kurdish forces to complete the seizure of the country in a matter of five weeks. These operations remained unprecedented in scope and sweep for Corps forces and remain under study to date.

Marine Corps forces then undertook the occupation of south-central Iraq between Baghdad and Basra for another six months while the United Nations sorted out an international coalition to relieve U.S. forces. In the end, a continuing U.S. presence emerged as a requirement, and I MEF returned to Iraq in February 2004 after a brief absence. A continuous occupation of western Iraq by Marine Corps forces (I and II MEF in rotation) ensued.

Fielding I MEF for combat operations in OIF caused considerable reverberation in the Operating Forces and Supporting Establishment of the Marine Corps during 2002–03. The Corps mobilized some 22,000 reservists by 1 May 2003 and still retained over 10,500 on duty in mid-October. Up to ten thousand would remain on active duty after March 2004 for augmentation and reinforcement tasks by continued call-up and demobilization of reservists. Active duty end strength had also climbed because of the stop-loss and stop-move directives, reaching a peak of 179,630 in July 2003, but then subsiding to 177,756 at the end of September and returning to the authorized 175,000 by March

2004. As security and stability operations continued in Afghanistan and the insurgent conflict in Iraq deepened in intensity, however, authorized strength of the Corps began to grow again, peaking at 202,441 in 2010.

The commandant's key decision and planning guidance on 27 November 2003 settled the future of Marine Corps deployments to Iraq. U.S. Marine Corps Forces Central Command would be provided with a reduced MEF (forward) for operations in Iraq. In addition to the MEF command element, a reduced Marine division with nine maneuver battalions would meet the Joint Staff and Central Command requirement and would be accompanied by the doctrinal aircraft wing and force service support group, both tailored for the smaller ground combat element envisioned. A seven-month unit rotation policy figured as the keystone of the planning guidance. Although the Army and other services earmarked their deployments to Iraq for a thirteen-month cycle, the Corps maintained the customary deployment of six to seven months that had the best chance of preserving the continuing operations and sustaining the health of the Corps in its global commitments.

2-23. Marine rifle squads go into action from their amphibious assault vehicles in Iraq, 2005.

As over twenty thousand Marines and sailors of I MEF took up their new positions in Iraq during 2004, equipped as well as the hurried measures and changing military environment allowed, the age-old problem remained: Who is the enemy, where is he, and what are his intentions? The combat operations of the campaign beginning in 2004 were characterized by major urban battles in the cities of Fallujah and Ramadi, counterinsurgency operations—both rural and urban—all over al Anbar Province, and a continuing effort to rebuild, protect, and nourish the native society and economy of a former enemy nation.

The Second Battle of Fallujah deserves special mention, as many regard it as the peak of conflict for Marine Corps forces during the Iraq War. In November and December 2004, Marine Corps forces led the combined American, Iraqi, and British offensive—code-named Operation Phantom Fury and Operation Al-Fajr—against the stronghold of Iraqi insurgents in the city of Fallujah. This battle represented the second major operation in Fallujah; earlier, in April 2004, coalition forces fought the First Battle of Fallujah to capture or kill insurgent elements considered responsible for the gruesome murder of four civilian contractors that year.

After a period of time shaping the battlespace, coalition ground operations began during the night of 7 November 2004 as the Iraqi 36th Commando Battalion, supported by their U.S. Army Special Forces advisers and other U.S. Army and U.S. Marine Corps units, attacked from the west and south. The main assault commenced on 8 November as the 1st Marine Division attacked with two Marine regimental combat teams, Regimental Combat Team 1 (RCT-1) and Regimental Combat Team 7 (RCT-7), along the northern edge of the city. Two U.S. Army heavy battalion-sized units, the 2nd Battalion, 7th Cavalry Regiment and the 2nd Battalion, 2nd Infantry Regiment (Mechanized), joined RCT-1 and RCT-7 in the attack. The British Army's 1st Battalion, known as "The Black Watch," patrolled the main highways to Fallujah's east. While coalition forces achieved their principal objectives and most of the fighting subsided by 13 November, the operation continued until 23 December 2004, when coalition forces neutralized the last pockets of resistance in the city.

This second battle was the bloodiest of the entire Iraq War and the bloodiest battle involving U.S. military forces since the Vietnam War, and it is notable for being the first major engagement of the Iraq War fought solely against insurgents rather than the forces of Saddam Hussein's Ba'athist Iraqi government, which coalition forces had deposed in 2003. Based on figures collected from multiple sources, coalition forces suffered 107 killed and 613 wounded during Operation Phantom Fury/Operation Al-Fajr. Most estimates place the figure for insurgent casualties in the range of twelve hundred to two thousand killed, and the Red Cross estimates that the operation resulted in eight hundred non-combatant deaths. The Second Battle of Fallujah marked some of the heaviest urban combat for U.S. Marines since the 1968 Battle of Hué City during Vietnam.

After a relatively brief respite, insurgent activity in and around Fallujah resumed in 2005 and heightened in 2006. Tactics developed during this period of counterinsurgency operations—and applied on a wider scale in the surrounding areas, including Ramadi—led to what became known as the "Anbar Awakening," whereby Sunni tribes that had previously tolerated and even supported the insurgency against the Shiite-led Iraqi government were persuaded to partner with U.S. forces to eject the insurgency from their communities. After four years of bitter fighting, Fallujah was ultimately turned over to Iraqi forces and provincial authorities during the autumn of 2007. Three years later, Marine Corps forces completed their planned withdrawal from Iraq.

229. Birth of Marine Corps Special Operators

The intensification of global counterterrorism operations following 9/11 increased the demand for forces specifically organized, trained, and equipped for special operations and focused attention on U.S. Special Operations Command (USSOCOM), headquartered at MacDill Air Force Base in Tampa, Florida. Since USSOCOM formed in 1986, the prospect of a Marine Corps service component for USSOCOM has been a topic of recurring discussion and debate. Some held that the Marine Corps must have a presence in this important combatant command, while others believed that the creation of such a service component would sap the Marine Corps of critical organic capabilities. In October 2005, however, the secretary of defense effectively ended the debate, directing formation of a Marine Corps service component at USSOCOM.

U.S. Marine Corps Forces Special Operations Command (MARSOC) activated in phases beginning on 24 February 2006 at Camp Lejeune, North Carolina. MARSOC initially comprised a small headquarters staff and the Foreign Military Training Unit, which in short order became the Marine Special

Operations Advisor Group (MSOAG). MARSOC rapidly absorbed both 1st and 2nd Force Reconnaissance Companies from I and II MEF during the year following its activation, and these two units grew to form 1st and 2nd Marine Special Operations Battalions (MSOB). As MARSOC's capabilities expanded, the MSOAG was redesignated the Marine Special Operations Regiment during April 2009, with the 1st, 2nd, and 3rd MSOBs as subordinate units. To round out its capabilities and achieve a degree of self-sustainability, MARSOC eventually formed the Marine Special Operations Support Group (MSOSG), providing organic combat support and combat service support to MARSOC, and the Marine Special Operations School, responsible to screen, assess, select, and train Marine special operators, as well as to review, develop, and refine special operations doctrine for the Marine Corps.

Almost a decade after its initial activation, MARSOC incorporated the term "Raider" into the names of its subordinate operational units in June 2015. Thus, the Marine Special Operations Regiment became the Marine Raider Regiment; the MSOBs, Marine Raider Battalions; and the MSOSG, Marine Raider Support Group. "Raider" evokes the rich heritage of MARSOC's predecessors from World War II, the four Marine Raider battalions first activated in February 1942 that operated as special, amphibious light-infantry forces, waging irregular warfare across the Pacific and often operating behind enemy lines.

MARSOC units first deployed six months after initial activation in August 2006. Since then, MARSOC has continuously deployed Marine Special Operations Teams, conducting foreign internal defense, and Marine Special Operations Companies, conducting foreign internal defense, special reconnaissance, and direct action.

230. Ever Present, Ever Ready

Concurrent with and following operations in Afghanistan and Iraq, Marines remained engaged and active around the globe. In addition to conducting scheduled deployments to execute forward presence and theater engagement missions in support of combatant commanders, Marine Corps forces continued to respond to crises worldwide. After a catastrophic magnitude 7.0 earthquake shook Haiti in January 2010, the Marine Corps rapidly deployed both the 22nd and 24th MEUs to restore order, provide security, and distribute support. A year later in 2011, Marines returned to the shores of Tripoli in support of

Operation Odyssey Dawn in Libya. Positioned off the coast of Libya, Marines of the 26th MEU were among the first to enforce the no-fly zone, and the MEU also conducted a successful tactical recovery of aircraft and personnel (TRAP) mission using the MEU's MV-22 Ospreys, CH-53E Super Stallions, and KC-130J Hercules aircraft.

In the Western Pacific, Marines stationed in Okinawa responded with supplies and support to a magnitude 9.0 earthquake and resulting 124-foot tsunami that decimated parts of mainland Japan in 2011. With over forty-five thousand buildings in ruins and a snowstorm dropping temperatures to 15 degrees Fahrenheit, the 31st MEU joined forces with the Japan Self-Defense Forces to deliver vital water, heating fuel, and other supplies to displaced residents in difficult to reach areas.

In response to the 2012 attack on the U.S. consulate in Benghazi, Libya, the Marine Corps established Special Purpose Marine Air-Ground Task Force Crisis Response Africa (receiving the rather awkward acronym SPMAGTF-CR-AF) in 2013 as a self-sustaining Marine air-ground task force (MAGTF) designed for response to a range of potential crises in Africa. Commanded by a colonel and operating from Morón Air Base in Spain, the unit comprises a command element, company-sized ground combat element, robust aviation combat element (a reinforced Marine medium tiltrotor squadron providing, among other capabilities, extraordinary mobility), and compact logistics combat element. SPMAGTF-CR-AF participates in bilateral and multilateral training with regional partners, while remaining ready to execute missions such as embassy reinforcement, noncombatant evacuation operations, tactical recovery of aircraft and personnel, humanitarian assistance, and disaster relief. In January 2014, SPMAGTF-CR-AF executed an embassy reinforcement mission in response to a crisis in South Sudan, and later that year during October the unit deployed to Liberia to participate in Operation United Assistance, supporting a U.S. Agency for International Development–led effort to contain the outbreak of the Ebola virus in West Africa.

While Marines supported coalition operations in Libya, responded to natural disasters half a world away, and conducted theater engagement and crisis response operations across Africa, a new threat emerged in the Middle East from the remnants of al Qaeda in Iraq (AQI), which had faded into relative obscurity with the U.S. troop surge into Iraq during 2007; a new mission awaited the

Marines. Despite the surge, Iraq never achieved durable stability. Meanwhile, catalyzed by the Arab Spring, neighboring Syria descended into civil war. In this vacuum of effective governance, AQI resurfaced in 2011 and capitalized on growing instability in Iraq and Syria, carrying out successful attacks and bolstering its ranks over the next few years. Revealing its true ambitions in 2013, the terror group renamed itself the Islamic State of Iraq and Syria (ISIS), alternately known as the Islamic State of Iraq and the Levant and colloquially by its Arabic language acronym Daesh. ISIS became the object of serious global concern by 2014, having seized control of Fallujah and portions of Ramadi in 2013 and captured Mosul, Tikrit, and Raqqa, Syria, in 2014. From its "capital" in Raqqa, the group proclaimed a worldwide caliphate in June 2014 and referred to itself as simply the Islamic State. As the group's strength and ambitions grew, reports of atrocities spread, refugees multiplied, and the threat of global terror intensified. U.S and coalition forces undertook a campaign to contain and eventually defeat ISIS, beginning with air strikes against ISIS targets in Iraq during August 2014 and in Syria during September 2014. The Pentagon finally named the campaign against ISIS Operation Inherent Resolve in October 2014. By early 2015, the coalition included Australia, Bahrain, Belgium, Canada, Denmark, France, Jordan, the Netherlands, Saudi Arabia, the United Arab Emirates, the United Kingdom, and the United States.

MARSOC was active against ISIS and Marines assumed staff and advisory positions with the coalition, but perhaps the Marine Corps' most visible contribution to Operation Inherent Resolve was the creation and deployment of Special Purpose Marine Air-Ground Task Force Crisis Response Central Command (SPMAGTF-CR-CC) beginning in November 2014. Commanded by a colonel and operating from Al Asad Air Base, Iraq; Al Jaber Air Base, Kuwait; and Sheik Isa Air Base, Bahrain, as well as several undisclosed locations, the unit is essentially a land-based, reinforced Marine expeditionary unit numbering 2,300 personnel. SPMAGTF-CR-CC performs a bilateral training and advisory mission, while remaining ready to execute missions such as embassy reinforcement, noncombatant evacuation operations, tactical recovery of aircraft and personnel, humanitarian assistance, and disaster relief. From 2014 to 2017, the SPMAGTF's Marines spent countless hours training and advising units of the Iraqi 7th Division, its fixed-wing aircraft struck ISIS targets in Iraq and Syria, and its TRAP team spent months on strip alert, plus 145 hours loitering airborne in direct support of large coalition air strikes against ISIS.

As was the case with Iraq, stability proved elusive in Afghanistan in the face of a recalcitrant and reconstituted Taliban. In January 2017, the Marine Corps announced plans to deploy a task force to Afghanistan's unruly Helmand Province, with which Marines had grown intimately familiar during a particularly challenging period from 2009 to 2014. Security in this enduring Taliban stronghold deteriorated following the withdrawal of U.S. forces from Helmand in 2014, and the three-hundred-person task force joined Operation Resolute Support to advise and assist units of the Afghan National Army and National Police in their efforts to reverse Taliban gains in the region. Staffed predominantly by more experienced senior personnel, Task Force Southwest, as it is named, aims to enhance the Afghan units' abilities to develop and interpret intelligence, integrate their operations, and sustain their forces.

In addition to the combat, security, and stability operations in Afghanistan and Iraq encompassing 2001 to 2014, these most recent actions illustrate the continuity in the Marine Corps story. In every clime and place Marines have stood vigil ashore and afloat. Readiness, versatility, amphibious expertise, prowess in expeditionary operations, and ferocity in combat remain hallmarks of the Corps. As long as our nation remains a maritime nation with global interests and global responsibilities, Marines will form its cutting edge.

No-one can say that the Marines have ever failed to do their work in handsome fashion.

—Major General Johnson Hargood, USA

3

THE DEPARTMENT OF DEFENSE AND THE ORGANIZATION FOR NATIONAL SECURITY

Numerous organizations within the government play a role in U.S. national security. To set the stage for an explanation of the Marine Corps' role in national security, it is important first to provide an overview of the principal individuals, organizations, and agencies responsible for decisions, policies, and plans affecting national security and military operations. The Department of Defense (DOD), the largest department of the federal government, is obviously central to this discussion, but we begin with the president of the United States and the National Command Authorities.

THE PRESIDENT AND THE NATIONAL COMMAND AUTHORITIES

301. Executive Office of the President

Although the U.S. Constitution gives the sole power to declare war to Congress, the president bears ultimate responsibility to protect national security. To fulfill this responsibility, the president is the commander in chief of the armed forces as set forth in Article 2, Section 2 of the Constitution. The Cabinet and the Executive Office of the President provide the broad support that the president needs to govern effectively, and several individuals, agencies, and offices within the Executive Office of the President provide direct and indirect support to the president in the national security domain. Among the entities within the Executive Office of the President, the National Security Council (NSC) and the Office of Management and Budget (OMB) are particularly important to the armed forces. Beyond the Executive Office of the President, we must also consider a third, the Central Intelligence Agency, at this high level.

The term National Command Authorities (NCA) refers collectively to the president and the secretary of defense. The NCA signifies the constitutional authority to direct the armed forces in their execution of military action. The president, as commander in chief, is the ultimate authority. The secretary of defense carries out NCA decisions and directives by tasking the military departments, combatant commands, and separate defense agencies.

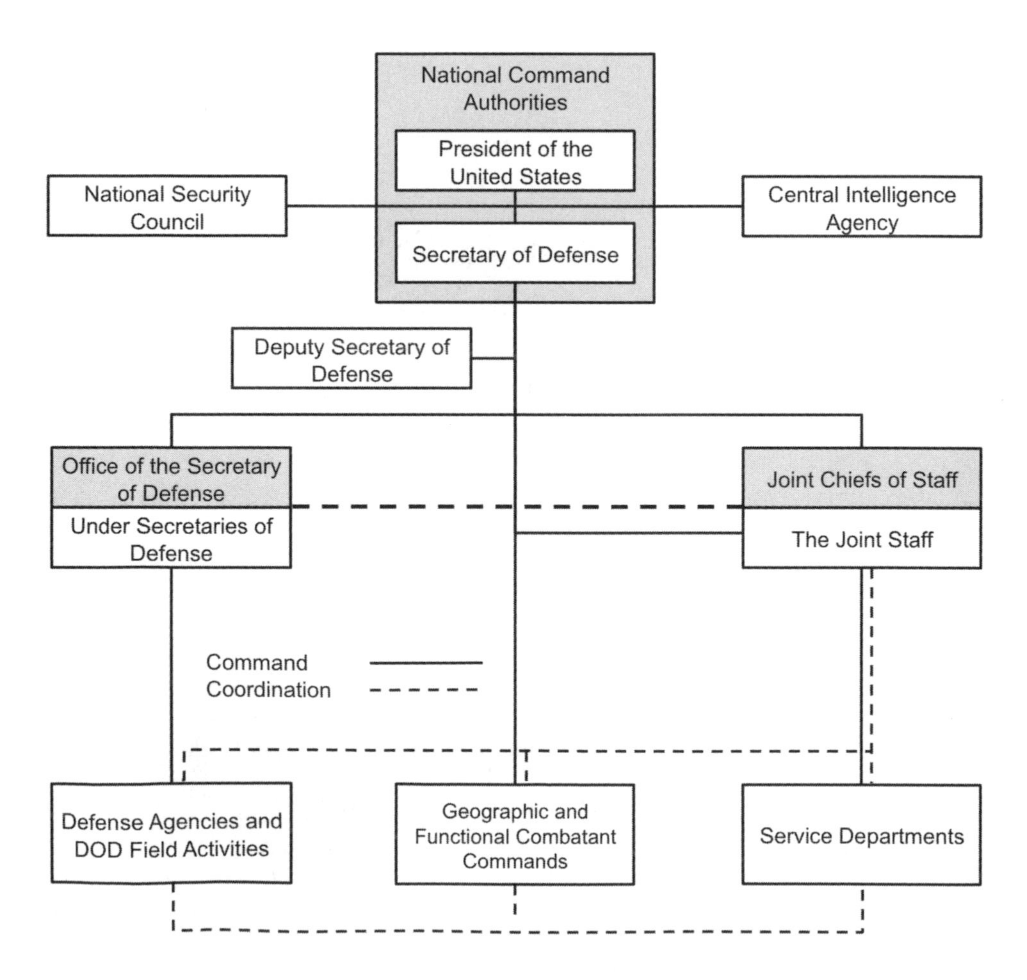

Figure 3-1. Organization for National Security (2016)

Figure 3-1 shows the flow of authority and direction through the organization for national security from the president as commander in chief to the secretary of defense and the three military departments, nine unified combatant commands, and multitude of separate defense agencies and field activities.

302. National Security Council

The NSC is the president's principal forum for considering national security and foreign policy matters with senior advisers and cabinet officials. Since its inception in 1947, the NSC's function has been to advise and assist the president on national security and foreign policies. It also serves as the president's principal arm for coordinating these policies among various government agencies.

The NSC has as statutory members the president, the vice president, the secretary of state, the secretary of defense, and the secretary of energy. The secretary of the treasury and the assistant to the president for national security affairs, commonly known as the national security adviser, are regular nonstatutory participants. Secretaries and under secretaries of other executive and military departments may serve as members of the council when appointed by the president and confirmed by the Senate. In addition, other government officials attend meetings as "standing request members" or on an ad hoc basis. The staff that supports the council is usually headed by a civilian executive secretary appointed by the president; it includes officers and civilian officials primarily from DOD and the Department of State and the five military services. The chairman of the Joint Chiefs of Staff is the statutory military adviser to the NSC, and the director of national intelligence is the intelligence adviser; subject to the direction of the president, they may attend and participate in NSC meetings. The chief of staff to the president, counsel to the president, and assistant to the president for economic policy are normally invited to attend any NSC meeting. The attorney general and the director of the Office of Management and Budget are invited to attend meetings pertaining to their responsibilities. The heads of other executive departments and agencies, as well as other senior officials, may attend meetings of the NSC when appropriate.

The NSC was established by the National Security Act of 1947 and amended by the National Security Act Amendments of 1949. Later in 1949, as part of the Reorganization Plan, the NSC was placed in the Executive Office of the President.

303. Office of Management and Budget

Established in 1970, the OMB has a number of functions: it helps the president prepare the government's budget, including the defense budget; it supervises administration of the budget; it improves government administrative management; it helps the president bring about more efficient and economical conduct of government service; it coordinates departmental advice on proposed legislation and makes recommendations as to presidential action on legislative enactments; it assists in consideration, clearance, and preparation of executive orders and proclamations; it improves, develops, and coordinates federal and other statistical services; and it informs the president of the progress of government work proposed, initiated, or completed.

Thus, the OMB is actually far more than its title or even its mechanical functions suggests. It functions, in fact, as a civilian general staff for the president. The power of the office—the ultimate power of the purse—and the continuity of its work give OMB considerable influence over DOD and the defense policies of the government.

304. Office of the Director of National Intelligence (ODNI) and the Intelligence Community

The ODNI is headed by the director of national intelligence (DNI), a position established in 2005. The DNI functions as the head of the somewhat diffuse Intelligence Community, overseeing and directing the implementation of the national intelligence program and acting as the principal adviser to the president, the NSC, and the Homeland Security Council for intelligence matters related to national security. The president appoints the DNI with the advice and consent of the Senate. The director is assisted by a Senate-confirmed principal deputy director of national intelligence, recommended by the DNI and appointed by the president, and by several deputy directors and mission managers who lead various directorates, centers, and offices. Collectively, these compose the ODNI, whose overarching goal is to integrate foreign, military, and domestic intelligence in defense of the nation and of U.S. interests abroad.

The U.S. Intelligence Community is a coalition of seventeen agencies and organizations, including the ODNI, that work both independently and collaboratively to gather and analyze the intelligence necessary to conduct foreign relations and national security activities. In addition to the ODNI, the following organizations compose the Intelligence Community:

- Air Force Intelligence
- Army Intelligence
- Central Intelligence Agency
- Coast Guard Intelligence
- Defense Intelligence Agency
- Department of Energy
- Department of Homeland Security
- Department of State
- Department of the Treasury
- Drug Enforcement Administration
- Federal Bureau of Investigation
- Marine Corps Intelligence
- National Geospatial-Intelligence Agency
- National Reconnaissance Office
- National Security Agency
- Office of Naval Intelligence.

As is clear from the list above, the members of the Intelligence Community represent a diverse range of intelligence interests based primarily on the missions and functions of their parent organizations and the particular intelligence needs of their "customers." Several members of the Intelligence Community merit further discussion here given their relatively important roles in military intelligence, complementing the intelligence arms of each of the military services.

The Central Intelligence Agency (CIA), established in 1947, is a civilian foreign intelligence agency responsible for providing national security intelligence to senior U.S. policymakers. The director of the CIA heads the agency and, since 2005, reports to the DNI. The director is nominated by the president with the advice and consent of the Senate. The director and deputy director can be either military officers or civilians; if officers, they retain their service grades and status, being carried as an extra number in grade, but are otherwise exempt from normal military responsibilities. The director manages the operations, personnel, and budget of the CIA. Beneath the Office of the Director are five major components: the Directorate of Operations, the Directorate of Analysis, the Directorate of Science and Technology, the Directorate of Support, and the Directorate of Digital Innovation. Additionally, there are several mission centers, each with a specific geographical or functional orientation. Together, these directorates and centers carry out the "intelligence cycle," the process of collecting, analyzing, and disseminating intelligence information to top U.S. government officials.

The agency provides the president and senior advisers with accurate, comprehensive, and timely foreign intelligence relating to national security. It also conducts counterintelligence activities, special activities, and other functions relating to foreign intelligence and national security as the president may direct.

To fulfill its mission, the CIA must collect, process, exploit, analyze, and disseminate foreign intelligence by employing a highly skilled, diverse workforce and state-of-the-art technical systems and devices; protect intelligence sources and methods; conduct research on, develop, and procure technical systems and devices; protect the security of its installations, activities, and people; and provide necessary administrative and logistical support, as well as services of common concern to the Intelligence Community. The CIA does not possess police, subpoena, or law enforcement powers, nor does it deal with internal security questions. In carrying out its functions, the CIA prepares "national intelligence estimates," analyses of strategic intelligence that serve as the basis for policy decisions.

The Defense Intelligence Agency (DIA) is a combat support agency within DOD. With more than 16,500 military and civilian employees worldwide, DIA is a major producer and manager of foreign military intelligence. It collects, analyzes, and disseminates military intelligence to warfighters, planners, and policymakers in DOD and the Intelligence Community, thus supporting military planning, military operations, and weapons systems acquisition. DIA is led by a director, typically a military officer, who serves as principal adviser to the secretary of defense and to the chairman of the Joint Chiefs of Staff on matters of military intelligence. The director also chairs the Military Intelligence Board, which coordinates activities of the Intelligence Community's military members.

The National Geospatial-Intelligence Agency (NGA) provides civilian and military officials and organizations of the United States with geospatial intelligence about human activity on earth derived from the analysis and exploitation of various forms of overhead imagery and geospatial information. NGA is a unique combination of intelligence agency and combat support agency. In fact, anyone who sails a U.S. ship, flies a U.S. aircraft, makes national policy decisions, fights wars, locates targets, responds to natural disasters, or even navigates with a cellphone relies on NGA.

The National Security Agency/Central Security Service (NSA/CSS) serves as the national cryptology organization. It coordinates, directs, and performs highly specialized activities to protect U.S. government information systems and produce foreign signals intelligence information. A high-technology organization, the NSA/CSS is on the frontier of communications and data processing. It is also one of the most important centers of foreign language analysis and research within the government.

305. Other Organizations

Several other organizations, under direct control of the Executive Office of the President, are connected with national security.

The Department of Energy (DOE) contributes to the nation's security and prosperity by addressing energy, environmental, and nuclear challenges. In particular, it administers programs in the areas of energy production and distribution, energy science and innovation, and nuclear safety and security. The principal connection between DOE and DOD is the Nuclear Weapons Council (NWC), which in 1986 succeeded the Military Liaison Committee that was established by the 1946 Atomic Energy Act to coordinate nuclear defense activities. The NWC is a joint DOD-DOE organization responsible for facilitating cooperation and coordination, reaching consensus, and establishing priorities between the two departments as they fulfill their dual-agency responsibilities for U.S. nuclear weapons stockpile management.

The National Aeronautics and Space Administration (NASA) deals with problems of flight in space and in the earth's atmosphere, develops and operates space vehicles, and leads the nation's exploration of space.

The Selective Service System provides nationwide standby machinery for the registration and induction—in other words, the draft—of individuals for military service.

The second largest of the federal government agencies (based on total workforce), the Department of Veterans Affairs (VA) administers all laws authorizing benefits for former members of the armed forces and their dependent beneficiaries, together with all government insurance and health programs open to members of the armed forces. (For benefits and services of the VA, see Chapter 21.)

The Department of Homeland Security (DHS) took form in the aftermath of the 11 September 2001 attack on the United States. The third largest of all departments, this extraordinary and debated entity comprises several agencies, offices, and directorates, including most notably the Management Directorate, National Protection and Programs Directorate, and Science and Technology Directorate. It also directs the field activities of numerous components and agencies, including, among others, the U.S. Coast Guard, U.S. Secret Service, U.S. Citizenship and Immigration Services, U.S. Customs and Border Protection, U.S. Immigration and Customs Enforcement, Federal Emergency Management Agency, and the Transportation Security Administration. DHS provides the unifying core for the vast national network of organizations and institutions involved in efforts to secure our nation, and the department executes five core missions: prevent terrorism and enhance security, secure and manage borders, enforce and administer immigration laws, safeguard and secure cyberspace, and ensure resilience to disasters.

DEPARTMENT OF DEFENSE

306. Overview

DOD is the largest agency in the federal government. The central functions of DOD are to provide for the military security of the United States and to support and advance the national policies and interests of the United States. It spends approximately one-sixth of the national budget in an ordinary fiscal year (2015), not counting inevitable "supplemental" bills. In the six and a half decades since its creation, the department has grown to number more than 1.4 million men and women on active duty, supported by approximately 718,000 civilian personnel. As such, the department is the nation's largest employer.

DOD includes the Office of the Secretary of Defense (OSD); the Joint Chiefs of Staff (JCS) and their supporting staff; the Departments of the Army, Navy, and Air Force, and the four military services (Army, Marine Corps, Navy, and Air Force) within those departments; the unified and specified commands; and such other agencies and field activities as the secretary of defense establishes to meet specific requirements (see Figure 3-2).

307. The National Security Act

The National Security Act of 1947, as amended, is an important piece of legislation of the United States, for it directed a major restructuring of U.S. military and intelligence organizations following World War II, and much of its impact endures today. The policy section of the act reads: "It is the intent of Congress to provide a comprehensive program for the future security of the United States; to provide for the establishment of integrated policies and procedures for the departments, agencies, and functions of the Government relating to the national security." In so doing, the act:

1. Provides three military departments, separately organized, for the operation and administration of the Army, the Navy (including naval aviation) and the Marine Corps, and the Air Force, with their assigned combatant and service components
2. Provides for coordination and direction of the three military departments and four services under a secretary of defense
3. Provides for strategic direction of the armed forces, for their operation under unified control, for establishment of unified and specified commands, and for the integration of the four services into an efficient team of land, naval, and air forces. The act does not establish a single chief of staff over the armed forces or an armed forces general staff.

The National Security Act unified the military establishment by giving the secretary of defense authority and virtual military control over the four services, although the secretary does not administer directly the departments of the Army, Navy, and Air Force. The secretary also has authority in procurement, supply, transportation, storage, health, and research and engineering. The secretary's greatest power lies in administration of the DOD military budgets.

The secretaries of Army, Navy, and Air Force no longer enjoy cabinet status, but each secretary has the right to make representations directly to the OMB or to Congress. However, he or she must first inform the secretary of defense of the intention to do so.

308. Office of the Secretary of Defense

Since its inception, the OSD has mushroomed from a handful of policymakers (in 1949 the secretary of defense had only three special assistants) to a major

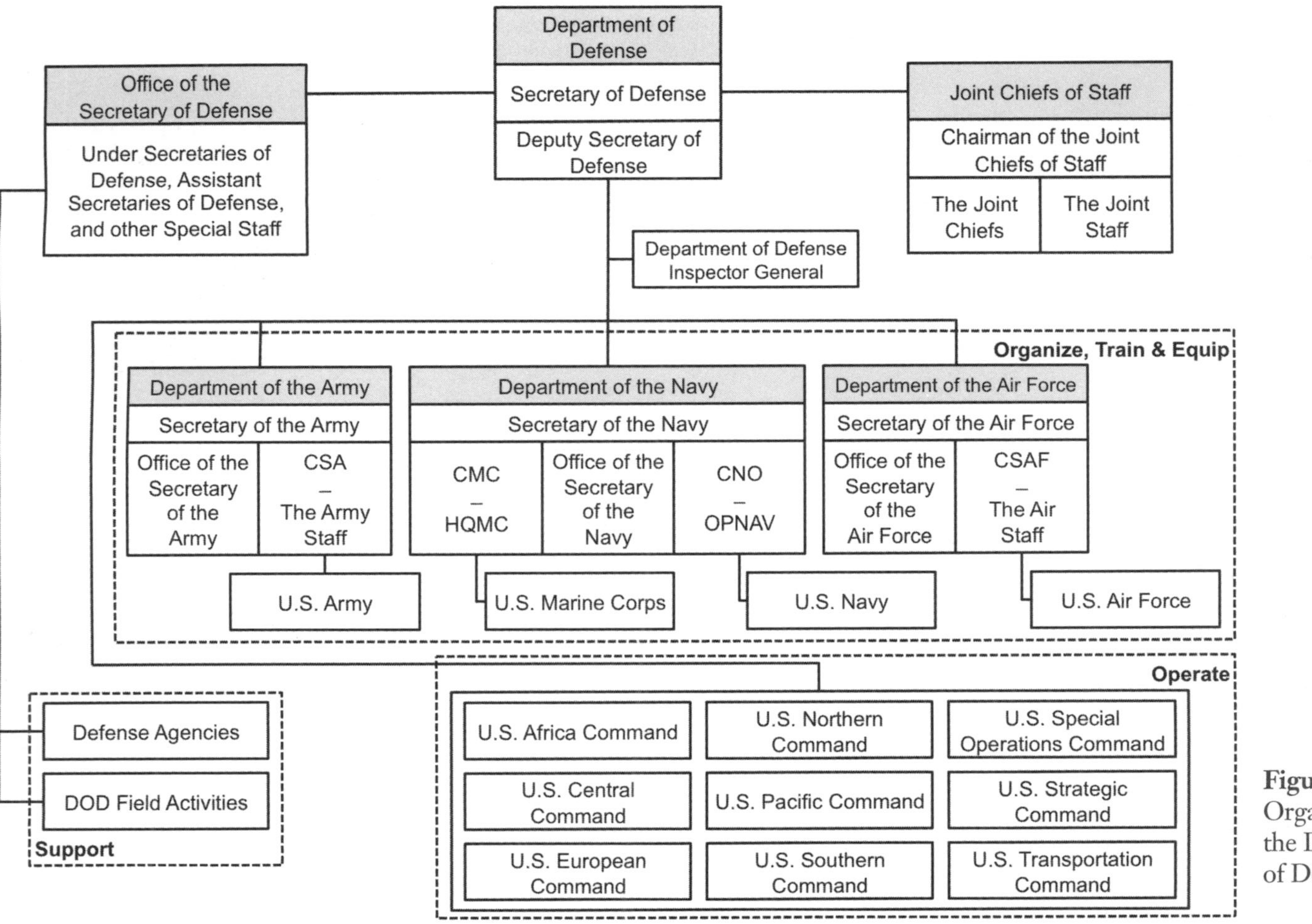

Figure 3-2. Organization of the Department of Defense (2016)

bureaucracy within the government. It serves as the principal staff element of the secretary of defense in the exercise of policy development, planning, resource management, and program evaluation responsibilities.

The secretary of defense, principal assistant to the president in all matters relating to DOD, is appointed from civil life by the president with the advice and consent of the Senate. Under the president, the secretary exercises authority, direction, and control over the Defense Department. The secretary is a member of the president's cabinet and the NSC.

The OSD (see Figure 3-3) includes the immediate offices of the secretary and deputy secretary of defense, under secretaries of defense, director of defense research and engineering, assistant secretaries of defense, general counsel, director of operational test and evaluation, assistants to the secretary of defense, director of administration and management, and such other agencies, offices, and positions as the secretary establishes to assist in carrying out assigned responsibilities. Several key positions within OSD merit further discussion.

Reporting directly to the secretary of defense, the deputy secretary of defense is delegated full power and authority to act for the secretary and is responsible for supervising and coordinating DOD activities.

The under secretary of defense for acquisition, technology, and logistics is the principal adviser and staff assistant to the secretary of defense in scientific, technical, and logistic matters. He or she exercises staff supervision over all research and engineering activities in DOD and wields extensive coordinating and directive authority over virtually all matériel programs of the defense establishment. However, the 2017 National Defense Authorization Act effectively split the duties of this under secretary, forming two new positions: an under secretary of defense for research and engineering, who will be the third ranking civilian leader in the department and whose duties will focus on technology innovation, and an under secretary of defense for acquisition and sustainment, who will remain the senior DOD acquisition official. The act provided for a delay in implementation of this change until February 2018.

The under secretary of defense (comptroller) serves as the principal adviser to the secretary of defense on all budgetary and financial matters, including the development and execution of the department's annual budget.

The under secretary of defense for intelligence is the principal intelligence adviser to the secretary of defense. He or she exercises staff supervision on behalf

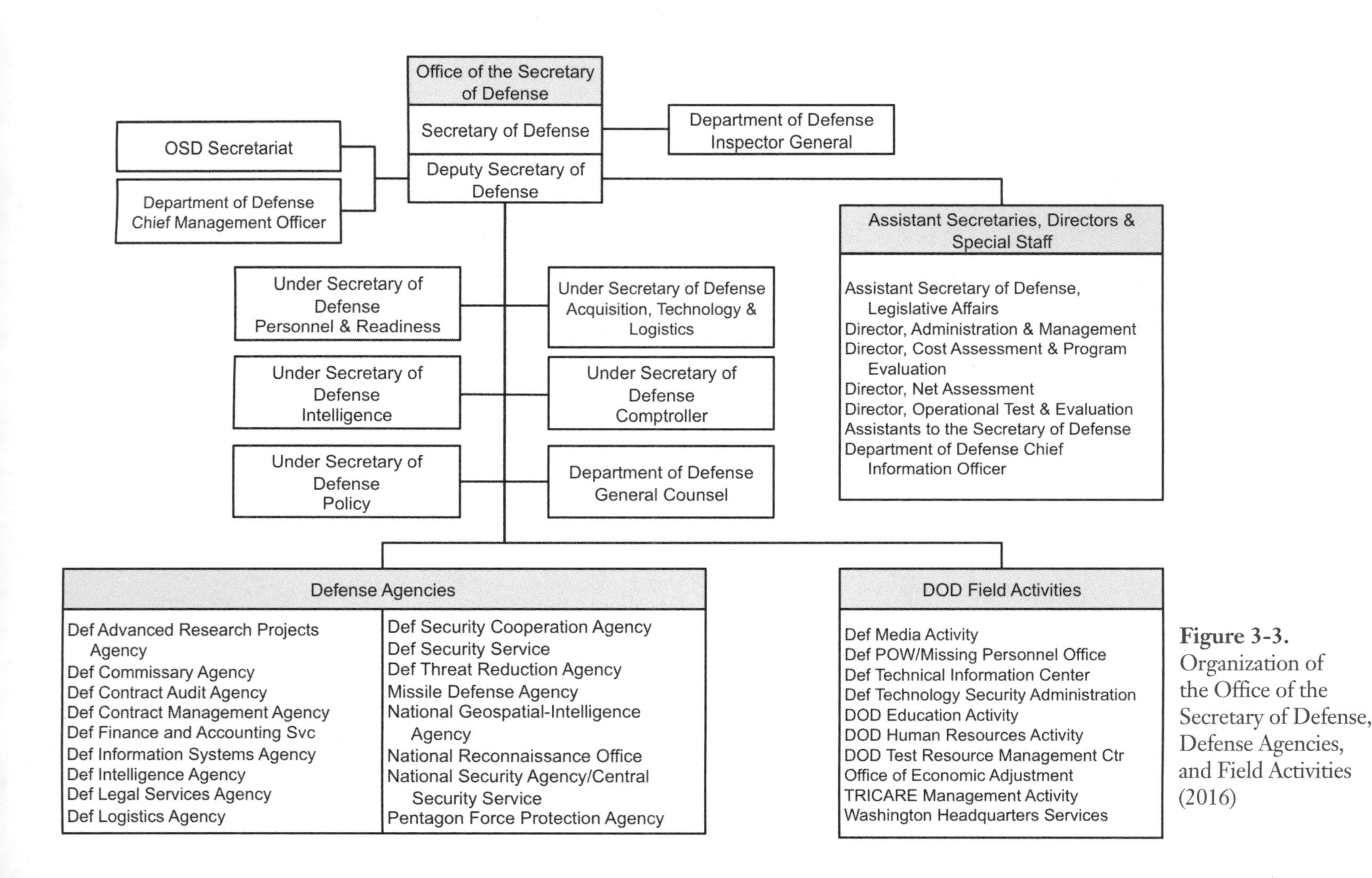

Figure 3-3. Organization of the Office of the Secretary of Defense, Defense Agencies, and Field Activities (2016)

of the secretary of defense over intelligence organizations within DOD, including NSA/CSS, DIA, NGA, and the National Reconnaissance Office.

The under secretary of defense for personnel and readiness is the principal staff assistant and adviser to the secretary of defense for total force management as it relates to readiness; National Guard and Reserve component affairs; health affairs; training; and personnel requirements and management, including equal opportunity, morale, welfare, recreation, and quality of life matters.

The under secretary of defense for policy is the principal adviser and staff assistant to the secretary of defense in matters of defense and security policy. These include the formulation of national strategy in line with resources and national security requirements, regional security arrangements, nuclear armaments regulation, and special measures for crises short of open warfare. He or she coordinates the formulation of strategic concepts into military force programs and security policies.

The assistant secretaries of defense, including the general counsel and certain special assistants, are responsible to the secretary for particular areas. In 2016, there were over a dozen of these areas, embracing such fields as health affairs, legislative affairs, program analysis, regional security affairs, manpower reserves and logistics, public affairs, and intelligence oversight.

The agencies, offices, and positions that compose the Office of the Secretary of Defense are not fixed across administrations or over time. Each secretary of defense may periodically rearrange responsibilities and functions according to existing requirements.

309. Joint Chiefs of Staff

To promote more personal control of the Army and Navy, to ensure direct access to the president for principal military advisers, and to improve coordination between the Army and Navy, President Franklin D. Roosevelt directed organization of the JCS in 1942. With the passage of the National Security Act in 1947, the JCS became a permanent part of the defense organization of the United States. The joint chiefs consist of a chairman, a vice chairman, the chief of staff of the Army, the commandant of the Marine Corps, the chief of naval operations, the chief of staff of the Air Force, and the chief of the National Guard Bureau.

Amended in 1949, the National Security Act authorized a chairman who would preside at JCS meetings and expedite the conduct of business. The president appoints the chairman from one of the four services with the advice and consent of the Senate. The chairman is the principal military adviser to the president, secretary of defense, and NSC; all JCS members, however, are by law military advisers, and they may respond to a request or voluntarily submit, through the chairman, advice or opinions to the president, secretary of defense, or NSC. The chairman, who takes precedence over all officers of the armed forces, serves as presiding officer for the JCS, provides the agenda for meetings, and manages the Joint Staff, through its director.

The executive authority of the JCS has evolved. During World War II, the joint chiefs acted as executive agents in dealing with theater and area commanders, but the National Security Act of 1947 regarded the JCS as planners and advisers, not as commanders of combatant forces. Despite this, the 1948 Key West Agreement permitted JCS members to serve as executive agents for unified commands, a responsibility that allowed the executive agent to originate direct communication with the combatant command. Congress abolished this authority in a 1953 amendment to the National Security Act. Today, the joint chiefs have no executive authority to command combatant forces. The issue of executive authority was clearly resolved by the Goldwater-Nichols Department of Defense Reorganization Act of 1986, which established that the chain of command to a combatant command shall run from the president through the secretary of defense to the combatant commander.

The joint chiefs do not operate on a voting basis. If, after discussing an issue, the joint chiefs agree unanimously, all chiefs and the chairman sign (or, as the process is called, "red-band") a paper giving their decision to the secretary of defense and the services. But after all views are presented, if disagreement remains, the joint chiefs come to what is known as a "split." It is the statutory duty of the chairman to inform the secretary of defense and the president of such disagreement.

As principal military advisers to the president, secretary of defense, and NSC, the joint chiefs prepare strategic plans and provide strategic direction of the military forces; prepare joint logistic plans and assign logistic responsibilities in accordance with such plans; formulate policies for joint training of the military forces and coordinate the education of members of the military forces;

review major matériel and personnel requirements of the military forces in accordance with strategic and logistic plans; and provide U.S. representation on the Military Staff Committee of the United Nations.

310. Organization of the Joint Chiefs of Staff

The supporting establishment of the JCS comprises the Joint Staff and a group of other agencies outside the Joint Staff that report directly to the JCS.

The Joint Staff assists the chairman of the Joint Chiefs of Staff (CJCS) in accomplishing the responsibilities for the unified strategic direction of the combatant forces, their operation under unified command, and their integration into an efficient team of land, naval, and air forces. The Joint Staff comprises approximately equal numbers of officers from the Army, Navy and Marine Corps together, and Air Force. In practice, the Marines make up about 20 percent of the number allocated to the Navy.

The director of the Joint Staff, an officer of three-star grade, attends meetings of the JCS and serves, in effect, as the expediter and coordinator of the JCS organization. The Joint Staff is divided into directorates: Manpower and Personnel (J-1), Intelligence (J-2), Operations (J-3), Logistics (J-4), Strategic Plans and Policy (J-5), Command, Control, Communications, and Computers/Cyber (J-6), Joint Force Development (J-7), and Force Structure, Resources, and Assessment (J-8). There are also various special assistants.

Other entities within the JCS organization, but not part of the Joint Staff, include the Joint Secretariat, the Directorate of Management, and various councils, boards, committees, and representatives.

311. Unified Combatant Commands

Organized directly under the secretary of defense, with orders transmitted by the CJCS, are the unified combatant commands, predominantly located outside the United States and covering the geographic and functional areas of greatest strategic importance. A unified command is a command with a broad continuing mission, under a single commander, composed of components of two or more services. The combatant commander's staff includes representatives from all services, and the command includes subordinate "service component commanders" who command all units from their respective services within the unified command.

There are nine unified combatant commands. Six are oriented geographically, broadly responsible for military operations within a designated geographical area:

U.S. Africa Command (USAFRICOM)
U.S. Central Command (USCENTCOM)
U.S. European Command (USEUCOM)
U.S. Northern Command (USNORTHCOM)
U.S. Pacific Command (USPACOM)
U.S. Southern Command (USSOUTHCOM).

The remaining three unified commands are oriented functionally, each responsible for global military operations within a specialized functional area:

U.S. Special Operations Command (USSOCOM)
U.S. Strategic Command (USSTRATCOM)
U.S. Transportation Command (USTRANSCOM).

312. Other DOD Agencies and Field Activities

In addition to the unified commands, a number of major agencies, field activities, and joint service schools come under the aegis of DOD or the Joint Chiefs of Staff. These entities are established by the secretary of defense to perform an administrative, supply, or service activity common to more than one military department. Certain of these agencies are of commanding size and stature and perform major functions for DOD that were once considered to be within the operating and administrative purview of the military departments. The list of defense agencies and field activities is extensive:

Defense Advanced Research Projects Agency
Defense Commissary Agency
Defense Contract Audit Agency
Defense Contract Management Agency
Defense Finance and Accounting Service
Defense Health Agency (formerly TRICARE Management Activity)
Defense Human Resources Activity
Defense Information Systems Agency

Defense Intelligence Agency
Defense Legal Services Agency
Defense Logistics Agency
Defense Media Activity
Defense POW/MIA Accounting Agency
Defense Security Cooperation Agency
Defense Security Service
Defense Technical Information Center
Defense Technology Security Administration
Defense Threat Reduction Agency
DOD Education Activity
Missile Defense Agency
National Geospatial-Intelligence Agency
National Reconnaissance Office
National Security Agency/Central Security Service
Office of Economic Adjustment
Pentagon Force Protection Agency
Test Resource Management Center
Washington Headquarters Services.

The Joint Service Schools include the National Defense University (National War College, Eisenhower School for National Security and Resource Strategy, and Joint Forces Staff College) and over a dozen specialty schools, including the Defense Acquisition University, National Intelligence University, and Uniformed Services University of the Health Sciences.

For detailed, up-to-date information on the organization and functioning of the Joint Chiefs of Staff, its supporting organization, and the unified and specified command structure, consult the current version of Joint Publication 1, *Doctrine for the Armed Forces of the United States.*

DEPARTMENT OF THE ARMY

313. Overview

The Department of the Army is one of the three military departments within DOD. It is the federal government agency within which the United States Army is organized, and it is led by the secretary of the Army who prescribes its regulations and directs its affairs, subject to the limits of the law and the directions of the secretary of defense and the president. The term "Department of the Army" normally refers to the secretariat and headquarters, located in the nation's capital, and all field headquarters, forces, reserve components, installations, activities, and functions under the control or supervision of the Department of the Army.

314. The United States Army

As provided in the National Security Act, the United States Army, within the Department of the Army, includes land combat and service forces, including certain organic water transport, aviation, space, and cyberspace forces. It is organized, trained, and equipped primarily for prompt and sustained combat incident to operations on land. It is responsible for the preparation of land forces necessary for the effective prosecution of war or military operations short of war and, in accordance with integrated joint mobilization plans, for the expansion of peacetime components of the Army to meet the needs of war.

315. Mission and Functions of the Army

The Army's stated mission is "to fight and win the nation's wars by providing prompt, sustained land dominance across the full range of military operations and spectrum of conflict in support of combatant commanders." The Army accomplishes this by executing Title 10 and Title 32 U.S. Code directives, to include organizing, training, and equipping forces for the conduct of prompt and sustained combat operations on land, and by performing additional tasks assigned by the president, secretary of defense, and combatant commanders.

In addition to the functions common to all military services, the Army is responsible, per Department of Defense Directive (DODD) 5100.01, *Functions of the Department of Defense and Its Major Components*, to organize, train, equip, and provide forces with expeditionary and campaign qualities—as well as develop the appropriate concepts, doctrine, tactics, techniques, and procedures—to perform the following specific functions:

1. Conduct prompt and sustained combined arms combat operations on land in all environments and types of terrain, including complex urban environments, in order to defeat enemy ground forces, and seize, occupy, and defend land areas

3-1. A fireball erupts from the muzzle of a U.S. Army M1 Abrams tank during gunnery training. (U.S. Army photo by MAJ Adam Weece)

2. Conduct air and missile defense to support joint campaigns and assist in achieving air superiority
3. Conduct airborne, air assault, and amphibious operations. The Army has primary responsibility for the development of airborne doctrine, tactics, techniques, and equipment.
4. Conduct civil affairs operations
5. Conduct riverine operations
6. Occupy territories abroad and provide for the initial establishment of a military government, pending transfer of this responsibility to other authority
7. Interdict enemy sea, space, air power, and communications through operations on or from the land
8. Provide logistics to joint operations and campaigns, including joint over-the-shore and intra-theater transport of time-sensitive, mission-critical personnel and matériel
9. Provide support for space operations to enhance joint campaigns, in coordination with the other military services, combatant commands, and other federal departments and agencies

10. Conduct authorized civil works programs, to include projects for improvement of navigation, flood control, beach erosion control, and other water resource developments in the United States, its territories, and its possessions, and conduct other civil activities prescribed by law
11. Provide intra-theater aeromedical evacuation
12. Conduct reconnaissance, surveillance, and target acquisition
13. Operate land lines of communication.

316. Structure of the Army

Command flows from the president, through the secretary of defense and the secretary of the Army, to Army units and installations throughout the world (see Figure 3-4). The Army comprises two distinct and equally important components: the active component and the reserve components, including both the Army National Guard and the Army Reserve.

The Army's active component, or Regular Army, contains the forces capable of performing the majority of the Army's functions in both peacetime and wartime. It is also the framework upon which the nation builds wartime armies.

The Army National Guard is one of the Army's two reserve components. In time of peace, the National Guard of any state can be called to active duty by the governor of that state to perform emergency duties. Units or individual members of the National Guard can be called to active duty by the federal government only during war or national emergency, or with their own consent in time of peace.

Like the National Guard, the Army Reserve units train in local armories and are subject to orders to active duty under similar conditions. Individual members are assigned to Army Reserve organizations in or near their hometowns. Historically, the Reserve was not subject to state control; however, this changed in 2004 with the establishment of dual status command authority, which was created primarily to cope with multistate disasters or national events requiring military support. A designated dual status commander, established based on an agreement between the president and a state governor, may now direct multicomponent Army forces based on orders of the president or the governor.

Regardless of component, Army structure includes both operational and institutional elements. The operational Army consists of numbered armies, corps, divisions, brigades, and battalions that conduct operations around the world. A field army comprises a headquarters and two or more corps, each in turn composed of two or more divisions. The division is the smallest unit that permanently contains a balanced proportion of the combined arms and services and that therefore is constituted to operate independently. Below division level, standing units are mainly composed of the separate arms or services of the Army. The company is the smallest administrative unit in the Army.

The institutional Army supports the operational Army just described. Institutional organizations provide the infrastructure necessary to raise, train, equip, deploy, and ensure the readiness of all Army forces. Within the institutional Army, the training base provides military skills and professional education to every soldier—as well as members of sister services and allied forces. It also allows the Army to expand rapidly in time of war. Complementing the training base, the industrial base provides equipment and logistics for the Army. Army installations provide the platforms required to deploy land forces promptly to support combatant commanders. Once those forces are deployed, the institutional Army provides the logistics needed to support them.

In addition to understanding the basic structure of the Army, it is useful to be familiar with how the Army organizes its personnel. To provide a framework for personnel management, the Army assigns its personnel to branches, grouping them in five categories: (1) Maneuver, Fires, and Effects, (2) Operational Support, (3) Force Sustainment, (4) Health Services, and (5) Special. Some of these are further divided into subcategories. Maneuver, Fires, and Effects branches are subcategorized as Maneuver, encompassing *Infantry*, *Armor*, and *Aviation*; Maneuver Support, encompassing *Corps of Engineers*, *Military Police Corps*, and *Chemical Corps*; Fires, encompassing *Field Artillery* and *Air Defense Artillery*; and Special Operations Forces, encompassing *Special Forces*, *Psychological Operations*, and *Civil Affairs Corps*. Operational Support branches include *Military Intelligence Corps* and *Signal Corps*. Force Sustainment branches are subcategorized as Integrated Logistics, encompassing *Transportation Corps*, *Ordnance Corps*, *Quartermaster Corps*, and *Logistics Corps*; and Soldier Support, encompassing *Adjutant General Corps* and *Finance Corps*. Health Services branches include *Medical Corps*, *Medical Service Corps*, *Medical Specialist Corps*, *Nurse Corps*, *Dental Corps*, and *Veterinary Corps*. Finally, Special branches include *Chaplain Corps* and *Judge Advocate General's Corps*.

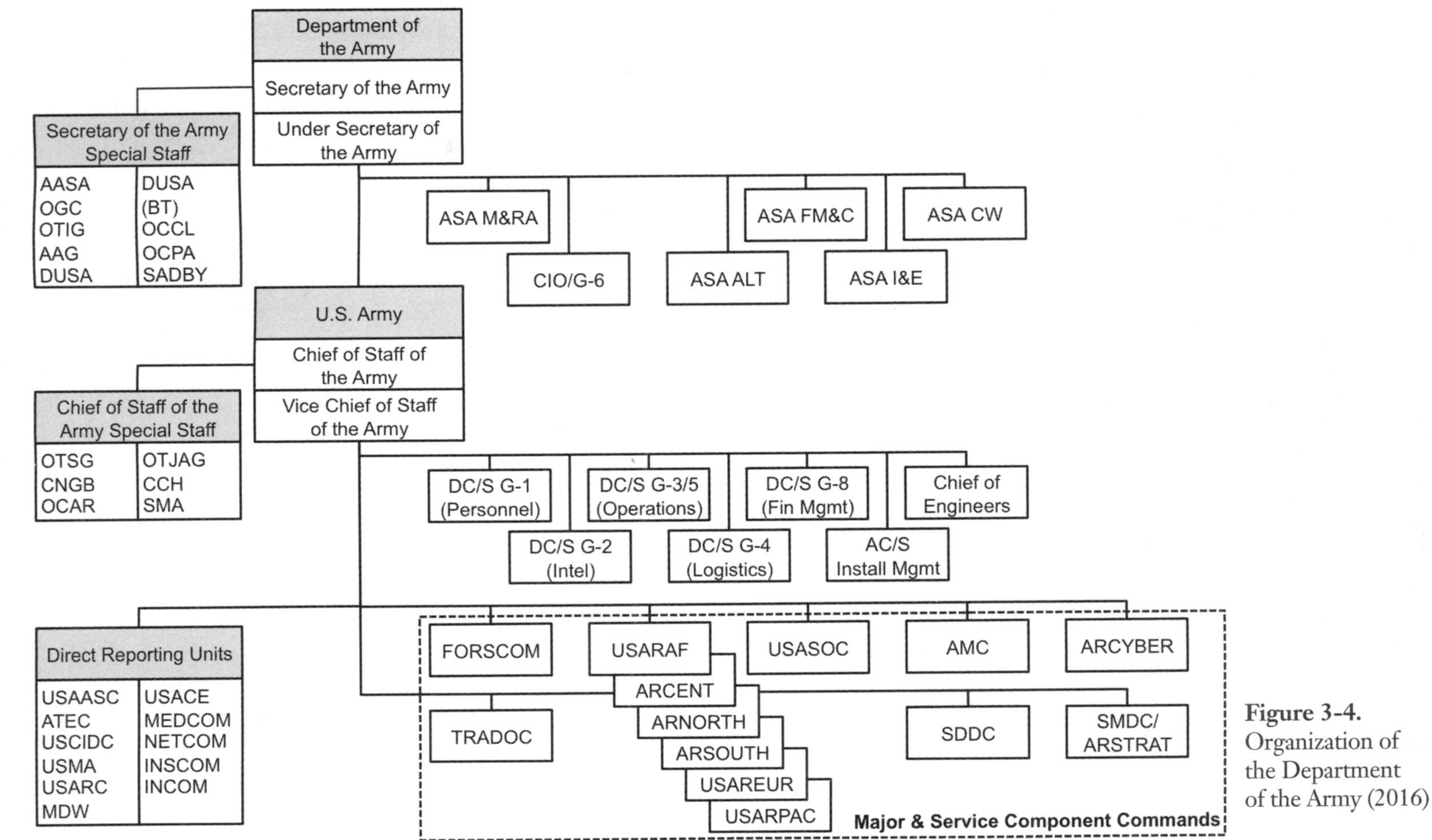

Figure 3-4. Organization of the Department of the Army (2016)

317. Major Army Commands and Activities

The Army is composed of the Army headquarters, Army commands, Army service component commands, and Army direct reporting units. Army commands include:

- U.S. Army Forces Command
- U.S. Army Training and Doctrine Command
- U.S. Army Materiel Command.

Army service component commands include:

- U.S. Army Africa
- U.S. Army Central
- U.S. Army North
- U.S. Army South
- U.S. Army Europe
- U.S. Army Pacific
- U.S. Army Special Operations Command
- Military Surface Deployment and Distribution Command, the Army service component command for USTRANSCOM
- U.S. Army Space and Missile Defense Command/Army Strategic Command
- U.S. Army Cyber Command.

Army direct reporting units include:

- U.S. Army Network Enterprise Technology Command/9th Signal Command (Army)
- U.S. Army Medical Command
- U.S. Army Intelligence and Security Command
- U.S. Army Criminal Investigation Command
- U.S. Army Corps of Engineers
- U.S. Army Military District of Washington
- U.S. Army Test and Evaluation Command
- U.S. Military Academy
- U.S. Army Reserve Command

- U.S. Army Acquisition Support Center
- U.S. Army Installation Management Command.

318. Education of Army Officer Candidates

Three education systems train candidates for commissions in the Army—the U.S. Military Academy, Officer Candidate School, and the Reserve Officers' Training Corps.

The United States Military Academy, West Point, New York, was established in 1802 to train young gentlemen as commissioned officers. "Duty, Honor, Country"—motto of the Corps of Cadets—has long served to set West Point's high standard. Colonel Archibald Henderson, fifth commandant of the Marine Corps, remarked in 1823: "It but rarely happens that a graduate from West Point is not a gentleman in his deportment, as well as a soldier in his education."

The Military Academy is commanded by a superintendent, an Army general officer. Marine officers now serve on West Point's academic staff. The four-year curriculum is typical of a four-year undergraduate program in the United States, though it also includes cultural subjects and military science. The cadet graduates with a B.S. degree and, if physically fit, is commissioned as a second lieutenant in the Army, the Marine Corps, or the Air Force.

Officer Candidate School is located at Fort Benning, Georgia. It is a two-phased training program designed to produce commissioned officers. Basic Officer Leader Course A lasts twelve weeks, and it is followed by Basic Officer Leader Course B (six to sixteen weeks), which is specific to the officer's branch assignment. Many candidates are chosen from enlisted men and women of the Regular Army, the Reserve, and the National Guard.

The Army Reserve Officers' Training Corps (ROTC) was born when President Woodrow Wilson signed the National Defense Act of 1916. Since its inception, Army ROTC has provided leadership and military training at schools and universities across the country and has commissioned more than a half million officers. ROTC has long been a major source of officers for the Army (and from time to time for the Marine Corps as well), and it is the largest commissioning source in the American military. Army ROTC has more than 270 host programs with more than eleven hundred partnership and affiliate schools across the country. It produces approximately 60 percent of the second lieutenants who join the Regular Army, the Reserve, and the National Guard.

DEPARTMENT OF THE AIR FORCE

319. Overview

Established in 1947 by the National Security Act, the Department of the Air Force is one of the three military departments within DOD. It is the federal government agency within which the United States Air Force is organized, and it is led by the secretary of the Air Force who prescribes its regulations and directs its affairs, subject to the limits of the law and the directions of the secretary of defense and the president. The term "Department of the Air Force" refers to the secretariat and headquarters, located in the nation's capital, and all field headquarters, forces, reserve components, installations, activities, and functions under the control or supervision of the Department of the Air Force.

320. The U.S. Air Force

As provided in the National Security Act, the United States Air Force, within the Department of the Air Force, includes aviation combat and service forces. It is organized, trained, and equipped primarily for prompt and sustained offensive and defensive air operations. The Air Force is responsible for the preparation of the air forces necessary for the effective prosecution of war and, in accordance with integrated joint mobilization plans, for the expansion of the peacetime components of the Air Force to meet the needs of war.

321. Mission and Functions of the Air Force

The Air Force's stated mission is "to fly, fight and win . . . in air, space and cyberspace." It organizes, trains, and equips forces to defend the United States against air attack, to gain and maintain general aerospace supremacy, to defeat enemy air forces, to control vital air areas, and to establish local air supremacy as required. The Air Force has the primary responsibility to develop doctrine and procedures (in coordination with the other services) for the defense of the United States against air attack; organize, train, and equip Air Force forces for strategic air warfare; organize and equip Air Force forces for joint amphibious and airborne operations, in coordination with the other services; furnish close combat and logistical air support to the Army; provide air transport for the armed forces, except as otherwise assigned; and to develop, in coordination with the other services, doctrine, procedures, and equipment for shore-based air defense, including the continental United States.

3-2. A U.S. Air Force KC-10 Extender refuels an F-22 Raptor. (U.S. Air Force photo by SSgt Andy M. Kin)

In addition to the functions common to all military services, the Air Force is responsible per DODD 5100.01 to develop concepts, doctrine, tactics, techniques, and procedures and to organize, train, equip, and provide forces to perform the following specific functions:

1. Conduct nuclear operations in support of strategic deterrence, to include providing and maintaining nuclear surety and capabilities
2. Conduct offensive and defensive operations, to include appropriate air and missile defense, to gain and maintain air superiority, and air supremacy as required, to enable the conduct of operations by U.S. and allied land, sea, air, space, and special operations forces
3. Conduct global precision attack, to include strategic attack, interdiction, close air support, and prompt global strike
4. Provide timely, global integrated intelligence, surveillance, and reconnaissance capability and capacity from forward-deployed locations and globally distributed centers to support world-wide operations
5. Conduct offensive and defensive operations to gain and maintain space superiority to enable the conduct of operations by U.S. and allied land, sea, air, space, and cyberspace forces. Conduct space operations to

enhance joint campaigns, in coordination with the other military services, combatant commands, and U.S. government departments and agencies.

6. Provide rapid global mobility to employ and sustain organic air and space forces and other military service and U.S. Special Operations Command forces, as directed, to include airlift forces for airborne operations, air logistical support, tanker forces for in-flight refueling, and assets for aeromedical evacuation
7. Provide agile combat support to enhance the air and space campaign and the deployment, employment, sustainment, and redeployment of air and space forces and other forces operating within the air and space domains, to include joint air and space bases, and for the armed forces other than which is organic to the individual military services and U.S. Special Operations Command in coordination with the other military services, combatant commands, and U.S. government departments and agencies
8. Conduct global personnel recovery operations including theater-wide combat and civil search and rescue, in coordination with the other military services, USSOCOM, and DOD components
9. Conduct global integrated command and control for air and space operations.

322. Structure of the Air Force

Command flows from the president, through the secretary of defense and the secretary of the Air Force, to Air Force units and installations throughout the world (see Figure 3-5). As with the Army, the Air Force is composed, in its entirety, of the Regular Air Force, Air National Guard, and Air Force Reserve.

The basic organizational structure of the Air Force includes the headquarters, major commands, direct reporting units, and field operating agencies. The Air Force headquarters consists of two major entities: the Secretariat (including the secretary of the Air Force and the secretary's principal staff) and the Air Staff.

Major commands (MAJCOMs) represent major subdivisions of the Air Force that are each assigned a major part of the Air Force mission. A MAJCOM is directly subordinate to the Air Force chief of staff, and it normally includes the word "command" its name. MAJCOM headquarters are management headquarters and thus have the full range of functional staff. MAJCOMs, in turn, may be further subdivided into numbered air forces, wings, groups, squadrons, and flights.

Numbered Air Force. This intermediate command echelon is designed to control and administer a grouping of combat wings. It is flexible in organization and can vary in size. Usually, a numbered air force has one of three missions—strategic, tactical, or defensive.

Wing. This is the smallest Air Force unit manned and equipped to operate independently in sustained action until replacement and resupply can take place.

Group. A flexible unit, a group is composed of two or more squadrons whose functions may be either tactical or administrative in nature.

Squadron. The basic unit in the organizational structure, a squadron is manned and equipped to best perform a specific military function, such as combat, maintenance, food service, or communications.

Flight. The lowest tactical echelon recognized in the Air Force structure, flights are not formally designated in the structure but are subdivisions of combat squadrons. They provide the basis for combat formations and are used for training.

Not all Air Force major commands follow this unit-oriented internal structure. Some, particularly those with an administrative or support focus, rely on alternate organizational structures. When this is the case, they are normally subdivided into centers, directorates and/or divisions, branches, and sections.

Direct reporting units, another subdivision of the Air Force, are—as the term implies—directly subordinate to the Air Force chief of staff. A direct reporting unit performs a mission that does not fit into any of the major commands; however, it has many of the same administrative and organizational responsibilities as a major command.

Field operating agencies are directly subordinate to a functional manager at the Air Force headquarters. A field operating agency (FOA) performs field activities beyond the scope of any of the major commands. The activities are specialized or associated with an Air Force–wide mission and do not include functions performed in management headquarters, unless specifically directed by a DOD authority. Air Force FOAs usually have the word "agency" as part of their designation.

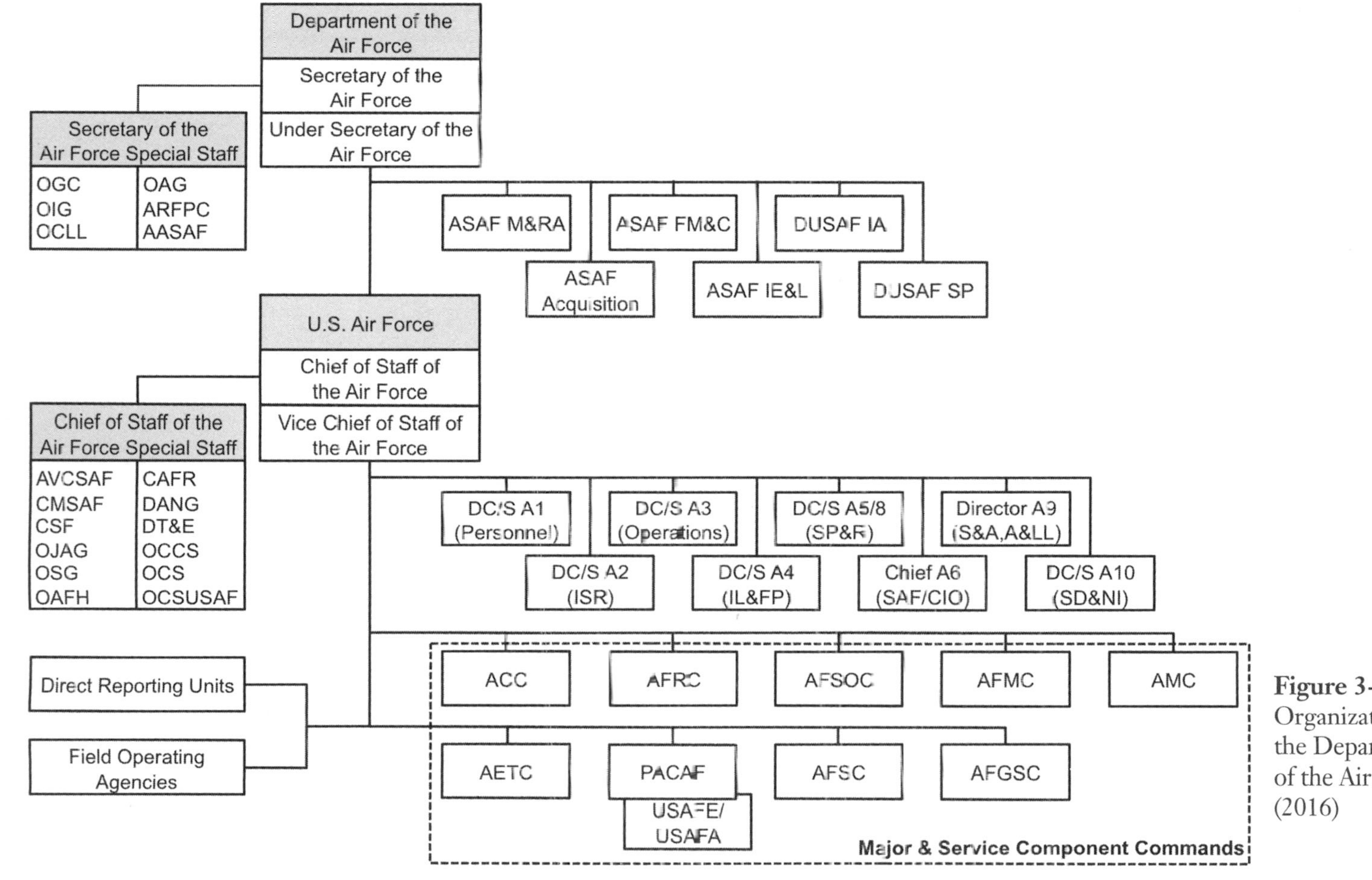

Figure 3-5. Organization of the Department of the Air Force (2016)

323. Major Air Force Commands and Activities

Subordinate to the headquarters, twelve major commands, six direct reporting units, and more than fifteen field operating agencies represent the field organization of the Air Force. The commands are organized on a functional basis in the United States and on an area basis overseas. Here are the twelve Air Force major commands:

- Air Combat Command provides Air Force component units for USSOUTHCOM, USNORTHCOM, and USSTRATCOM.
- Pacific Air Forces provides Air Force component units for USPACOM.
- U.S. Air Forces Central Command provides Air Force component units for USCENTCOM.
- U.S. Air Forces in Europe and Air Forces Africa provide Air Force component units for USEUCOM and USAFRICOM.
- Air Force Special Operations Command provides Air Force component units for USSOCOM.
- Air Education and Training Command recruits, trains, and educates airmen.
- Air Mobility Command provides global air mobility through airlift and aerial refueling for all the armed forces, including the Marine Corps, and serves as the Air Force component for USTRANSCOM.
- Air Force Global Strike Command develops and provides combat-ready forces for nuclear deterrence and global strike operations.
- Air Force Materiel Command conducts research, development, testing, and evaluation, and provides the acquisition management services and logistics support necessary to keep Air Force weapons systems ready for war.
- Air Force Reserve Command provides operational capability, strategic depth, and surge capacity as an integrated total force partner in every Air Force core mission.
- Air Force Space Command develops and operates military space and cyberspace technologies.
- Air National Guard maintains well-trained, well-equipped units available for prompt mobilization during war and provides assistance during national emergencies (such as natural disasters or civil disturbances).

Air Force direct reporting units include the following:

- Air Force District of Washington
- Air Force Network Integration Center
- Air Force Operational Test and Evaluation Center
- Air Reserve Personnel Center
- Arnold Air Force Base and Arnold Engineering Development Complex
- U.S. Air Force Academy.

The list of Air Force field operating agencies is extensive and covers wide-ranging functions, but the following are some of the more noteworthy:

- Air Force Agency for Modeling and Simulation
- Air Force Audit Agency
- Air Force Civil Engineer Center
- Air Force Flight Standards Agency
- Air Force Historical Research Agency
- Air Force Inspection Agency
- Air Force Intelligence, Surveillance, and Reconnaissance Agency
- Air Force Office of Special Investigations
- Air Force Personnel Center
- Air Force Petroleum Agency
- Air Force Public Affairs Agency
- Air Force Safety Center
- Air Force Security Forces Center
- Air Force Spectrum Management Office
- Air Force Weather Agency
- Global Cyberspace Integration Center.

324. Education of Air Force Officer Candidates

Candidates for Air Force commissions receive their training in a number of different institutions: the U.S. Air Force Academy, Officer Training School, Air Force ROTC, and Airman Education and Commissioning Program.

The U.S. Air Force Academy, located at Colorado Springs, Colorado, is one of the principal sources for regular Air Force officers. The curriculum includes both academic and military subjects and leads to a B.S. degree and a commission as a second lieutenant in the Air Force (or the Army, Marine Corps, or Navy).

The Officer Training School is located at Lackland Air Force Base, Texas. College graduates may apply for this three-month course. The curriculum includes administration, organization, supply, military law, world affairs, leadership, and human relations. Graduates are either assigned directly to duty or pursue additional training in an aircrew (pilot or navigator) or technical course. Graduates may apply for regular commissions.

The Air Force ROTC is similar in purpose and organization to the Army and Navy ROTC programs.

The Airman Education and Commissioning Program provides undergraduate education, followed by officer training and a commission, for selected career-minded airmen on active duty.

DEPARTMENT OF THE NAVY

325. Overview

The Department of the Navy is one of the three military departments within DOD. It is the federal government agency within which the United States Navy and United States Marine Corps are organized, and it is led by the Secretary of the Navy who prescribes the regulations for and directs the affairs of both the Navy and Marine Corps, subject to the limits of the law and the directions of the secretary of defense and the president. The term "Department of the Navy" encompasses the secretariat, Navy headquarters, and Marine Corps headquarters, all located in the nation's capital; the entire Operating Forces of the United States Navy and the United States Marine Corps, including naval aviation and the reserve components of such forces; all field activities, headquarters, forces, bases, installations, activities, and functions under the control or supervision of the Department of the Navy; and the United States Coast Guard *when operating as part of the Navy* pursuant to law.

The Department of the Navy occupies coequal status with the Department of the Army and Department of the Air Force in the organization for national security (see Figure 3-1) and in DOD. The organization of the Department of the Navy and the place of the U.S. Marine Corps in the naval establishment are described in greater detail in Chapters 4, 5, and 6.

3-3. *Wasp*-class amphibious assault ships are one means by which the U.S. Navy projects power across the seas. (U.S. Navy photo by MCS3 Eric Zeak)

COAST GUARD

326. Overview

The Coast Guard is a military service and a branch of the U.S. armed forces. It operates under the Department of Homeland Security during peacetime and under the Department of the Navy when directed by the president, or upon a declaration of war.

Coast Guard personnel receive the same pay and benefits as men and women in the other armed forces, and they are also subject to the Uniform Code of Military Justice. The service's rank and rating system is similar to the Navy's, with one major difference: there are fewer enlisted ratings. The Coast Guard is led by the commandant of the Coast Guard, a four-star admiral.

327. Role, Missions, and Status

The Coast Guard performs a wide range of functions in the United States and around the world. There are three broad mission areas: maritime safety, law enforcement, and military readiness. To carry out these missions, the service operates approximately 1,400 boats and more than 100 cutters larger than 65 feet; mans hundreds of facilities, mostly small units, throughout the United States and a few abroad; and operates the world's seventh largest naval air force with over 200 aircraft.

Coast Guardsmen are best known for their lifesaving mission, but search and rescue is only one of their duties. They maintain lighthouses, buoys, and other aids to navigation; operate electronic navigation stations; track icebergs and operate America's icebreakers; inspect vessels for safety violations; and enforce maritime environmental laws. Their law enforcement responsibility also includes enforcing fisheries laws and stopping drug smuggling. The service is the primary maritime law enforcement agency in the war against drugs and against maritime piracy and terrorism.

The Coast Guard has recently assumed an increased military emphasis. It is the lead agency in the Maritime Defense Zone, which is in charge of the defense of America's coast. In past wars, the Coast Guard has engaged in escort duties, antisubmarine warfare, cold-weather operations, riverine warfare, amphibious warfare, port and coastal security, and much more.

3-4. National security cutters are the centerpiece of the Coast Guard's fleet.

Today, the Coast Guard has more than 42,000 active duty servicemembers, of which approximately one-sixth are officers; more than 7,800 reservists; more than 8,700 civilian employees; and roughly 32,000 volunteer auxiliary members. The service has an academy at New London, Connecticut. Appointment is by competitive examination, which is open to civilians and enlisted men and women from any armed service between the ages of seventeen and twenty-two. Cadets have a choice of several different majors and graduate with a B.S. degree.

The service was created on 4 August 1790 by the secretary of the treasury, Alexander Hamilton, and was initially a simple system of cutters known as the Revenue Cutter Service. In 1915, the Revenue Cutter Service combined with the United States Lifesaving Service to form the United States Coast Guard. Its motto is *Semper Paratus* ("Always Ready").

The principal foundations of all states are good laws and good arms; and there cannot be good laws where there are not good arms.

—Niccolo Machiavelli, *The Prince*

4

THE DEPARTMENT OF THE NAVY

The facts that 71 percent of the globe is covered by water and that the U.S. seacoast exceeds twelve thousand miles in length have long caused the nation to appreciate the need for strong naval forces. The United States is a maritime power, and American security strategy must always be fundamentally maritime. In two world conflicts, superior sea power was vital to U.S. success. Without control of the seas, we could not have transported fighting men, equipment, and supplies to distant battles, nor could we ever project our fighting power from the seas onto the land.

Today, freedom of navigation and control of the seas are more important than ever. The oceans connect the nations of an increasingly interdependent world. The maritime domain—the world's oceans, seas, bays, estuaries, islands, coastal areas, and littorals, and the airspace above them—supports 90 percent of the world's trade, which is vital to global prosperity and, by extension, the prosperity of the United States. By maintaining control of the seas, we also remain capable of helping allied and friendly nations and confronting and defeating aggression far from our shores. More important, we ensure the use of the seas for the offensive operations that victory requires. For all these reasons, we must maintain the nation's maritime forces. The Navy Department's *A Cooperative Strategy for 21st Century Seapower* (2015) highlights the importance of naval forces: "Seapower has been and will continue to be the critical foundation of national power and prosperity and international prestige for the United States of America. . . . Naval forces operate forward to shape the security environment, signal U.S. resolve, protect U.S. interests, and promote global prosperity by defending freedom of navigation in the maritime commons."

In the service of these interests, the Department of the Navy (DON) aims to capitalize on the global reach, persistent presence, and operational flexibility of Navy and Marine Corps forces to accomplish six principal tasks. The DON postures the Navy-Marine Corps team to:

- limit regional conflict with forward deployed, decisive maritime power
- deter major power war
- win the nation's wars, as an integral part of the joint force
- contribute to homeland defense in depth
- foster and sustain cooperative relationships with more international partners
- prevent or contain local disruptions before they impact the global system.

Critical to accomplishing these tasks is the maintenance of a powerful fleet—ships, aircraft, and shore-based fleet activities, together with multi-purpose Marine Corps forces—capable of controlling the seas, projecting power ashore, and protecting friendly forces and civilian populations from attack.

4-1. The high mobility of naval forces, coupled with their staying power, makes them highly useful in forwarding national policy around the globe. That is the essence of the classical notion of sea power.

As you reflect on these key features of the nation's maritime strategy, remember the words of General Lemuel C. Shepherd, twentieth commandant: "Both the functions and the future of the Marine Corps are intimately linked with those of the U.S. Navy."

401. Mission of the Department of the Navy

The National Security Act, as amended, outlines in some detail the mission and responsibilities of the Department of the Navy as follows:

> Sec. 206 (a) The term "Department of the Navy" as used in this Act shall be construed to mean the Department of the Navy at the seat of government; the headquarters, United States Marine Corps; the entire operating forces of the United States Navy, including naval aviation, and of the United States Marine Corps, including the reserve components of such forces; all field activities, headquarters, forces, bases, installations, activities, and functions under the control or supervision of the Department of the Navy; and the United States Coast Guard when operating as a part of the Navy pursuant to law.
>
> (b) The Navy, within the Department of the Navy, includes, in general, naval combat and service forces and such aviation as may be organic therein. The Navy shall be organized, trained, and equipped primarily for prompt and sustained combat incident to operations at sea. It is responsible for the preparation of naval forces necessary for the effective prosecution of war except as otherwise assigned and is generally responsible for naval reconnaissance, antisubmarine warfare, and protection of shipping.
>
> All naval aviation shall be integrated with the naval service as part thereof within the Department of the Navy. Naval aviation consists of combat and service and training forces, and includes land-based naval aviation, air transport essential for naval operations, all air weapons and air techniques involved in the operations and activities of the Navy, and the entire remainder of the aeronautical organization of the Navy, together with the personnel necessary therefor.
>
> The Navy shall develop aircraft, weapons, tactics, technique, organization, and equipment of naval combat and service elements.

> Matters of joint concern as to these functions shall be coordinated between the Army, the Air Force, and the Navy.
>
> The Navy is responsible, in accordance with integrated joint mobilization plans, for the expansion of the peacetime components of the Navy to meet the needs of war.
>
> (c) The Marine Corps, within the Department of the Navy, shall be so organized as to include not less than three combat divisions and three air wings, and such other land combat, aviation, and other services as may be organic therein. The Marine Corps shall be organized, trained, and equipped to provide fleet marine forces of combined arms, together with supporting air components, for service with the fleet in the seizure or defense of advanced naval bases and for the conduct of such land operations as may be essential to the prosecution of a naval campaign. In addition, the Marine Corps shall provide detachments and organizations for service on armed vessels of the Navy, shall provide security detachments for the protecting of naval property at naval stations and bases, and shall perform such other duties as the President may direct. However, these additional duties may not detract from or interfere with the operations for which the Marine Corps is primarily organized.
>
> The Marine Corps shall develop, in coordination with the Army and the Air Force, those phases of amphibious operations that pertain to the tactics, technique, and equipment used by landing forces.

The Marine Corps is responsible, in accordance with integrated joint mobilization plans, for the expansion of peacetime components of the Marine Corps to meet the needs of war. As of FY 17, the authorized active duty end strength is 182,000 Marines. However, the U.S. Congress could adjust this level year by year given the security environment or fiscal constraints.

The functions of the Navy and Marine Corps were further defined in the 1948 Key West Agreement (see Figure 4-1). Although its primary purpose was to amplify the functions of the Army and Air Force, the agreement did assign collateral functions to the Navy and the Marine Corps and did spell out some basic functions in more detail. Nonetheless, the primary source for Marine Corps functions is the National Security Act, not the agreement.

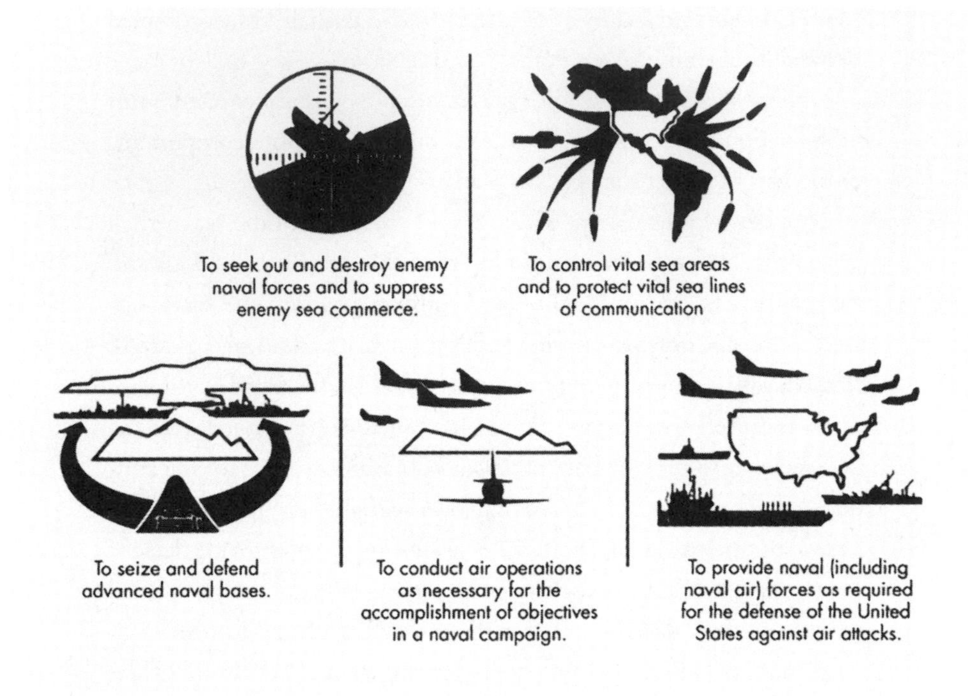

Figure 4-1. The Primary Functions of the Navy as Set Forth in "The Functions Paper"

402. The Executive Branch and the Department of the Navy

The DON, as one of the military departments within the Department of Defense, is organized under the president and the secretary of defense. Its organization and executive duties are covered later in this chapter.

403. The Legislative Branch and the Department of the Navy

Under our Constitution, Congress is given the authority "to provide and maintain a navy . . . and to make rules for the government of the land and naval forces." In the words of Supreme Court Chief Justice Charles Evans Hughes, "Congress provides; the President commands." Congress therefore enacts laws governing the size, scope, functions, and authority of the Navy and the Marine Corps. Congress also authorizes and provides funds for construction of ships and shore bases, procurement of weapons systems and equipment, and for conduct of all Navy and Marine Corps activities.

Members or committees of Congress, the DON, and other offices of the Department of Defense may originate legislation affecting the Navy and the Marine Corps. The Department of Defense then submits comments and recommendations on such military legislation. Officials of the department are frequently summoned to appear at hearings on proposed legislation and at congressional investigations.

404. The Judicial Branch and the Department of the Navy

The DON also interacts with the nation's judiciary. For example, it may sue or be sued. The department has a right to appear in its own defense or in defense of its officials or members of the services. It may enter briefs and may argue and appear before the courts, and it is bound by decisions of federal courts.

405. Organization

The Department of the Navy consists of three principal parts: the Navy secretariat, the United States Navy, and the United States Marine Corps. (see Figure 4-2)

The Navy secretariat supports the Secretary of the Navy in exercising the authority, under Title 10 (Armed Forces), U.S. Code, to conduct all the affairs of the DON. The secretariat includes the Secretary of the Navy, with his or her personal staff; the under Secretary of the Navy; the assistant secretaries of the Navy; and several additional chiefs, deputies, and directors who assist the Secretary of the Navy in the administration of the department.

The United States Navy is one of two uniformed services within the Department of the Navy, and it comprises the Navy headquarters, the Operating Forces, and the Shore Establishment. The Navy headquarters encompasses all the offices, boards, and agencies reporting to and performing duties for the chief of naval operations (CNO), and these are collectively referred to as the Office of the Chief of Naval Operations (OPNAV). The Operating Forces of the Navy include the several fleets, including the Fleet Marine Forces and other assigned Marine Corps forces; the service components assigned to the combatant commands; the naval reserve forces; several specialized commands, such as the Fleet Forces Command, Naval Special Warfare Command, Naval Network Warfare Command, Military Sealift Command, and Navy Installations Command; and such other Navy field activities and commands as are assigned by the Secretary of the Navy. The Shore Establishment consists of all activities of the Navy not assigned to the Operating Forces and not a part of OPNAV. These include various commands, centers, and groups that primarily provide administrative, matériel, technical, and training support to the Operating Forces.

The U.S. Marine Corps, the second of two uniformed services within the Department of the Navy, includes Headquarters, U.S. Marine Corps; the Operating Forces of the Marine Corps; the Marine Corps Supporting Establishment; and the Marine Corps Reserve (see Chapters 6, 7, and 8).

406. Secretary of the Navy

The Secretary of the Navy (SECNAV) heads the Department of the Navy and is responsible for the direction, control, and policies of the department, including its organization (except as otherwise prescribed in law), administration, operation, and efficiency. With regard to DON personnel, the SECNAV oversees recruiting, organizing, supplying, equipping, training, mobilizing, and demobilizing. The secretary also oversees the construction, outfitting, and repair of naval ships, equipment, and facilities. As far as practical, the secretary discharges these responsibilities through civilian executive assistants and other military and civilian assistants. The secretary, however, normally retains personal direction over activities relating to legislation and to Congress and maintains relationships with the secretary of defense, other principal government officials, and the public.

The secretary may communicate directly with any principal official of the DON, the Operating Forces, or the Shore Establishment.

The secretary is responsible for the formulation and implementation of policies and programs that are consistent with the national security policies and objectives established by the president and the secretary of defense.

The secretary recommends to the secretary of defense and the president appointments, removals, or reassignments of the legally constituted positions of the DON. In his or her own discretion, the SECNAV controls the selection and assignment of all other principal officials of the department.

407. Under Secretary of the Navy

The under Secretary of the Navy is the deputy and principal assistant to the Secretary of the Navy, and the under secretary acts with the SECNAV's authority in managing the Department of the Navy. He or she serves as the department's

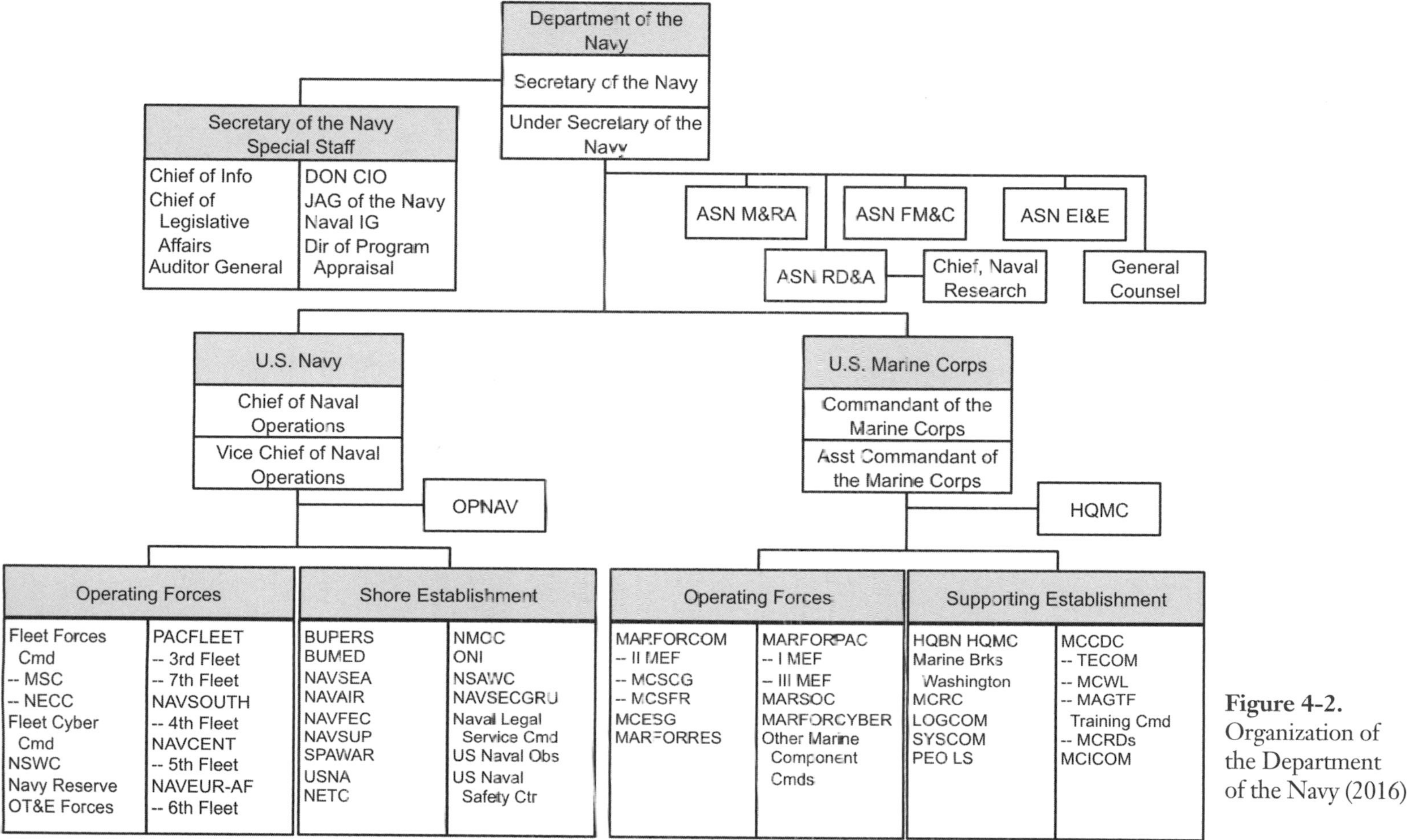

Figure 4-2. Organization of the Department of the Navy (2016)

chief operating officer and must promptly and fully inform the SECNAV regarding any matter or action taken involving or affecting the DON. Additionally, the under secretary oversees intelligence activities, intelligence-related activities, special access programs, DON critical infrastructure, and sensitive activities within the DON. The under secretary is supported by two assistants: a deputy under Secretary of the Navy (management) and a deputy under Secretary of the Navy (policy).

The deputy under Secretary of the Navy (management), or DUSN(M), serves as the principal deputy to the under Secretary of the Navy and is the senior adviser on business systems, information technology, information management, administrative services, innovation initiatives, and management processes. The DUSN(M) notably oversees the administration and management of the Navy secretariat.

The deputy under Secretary of the Navy (policy), or DUSN(P), serves as the principal civilian adviser to the secretary and under secretary on defense and foreign policy; sensitive activities, intelligence, and intelligence-related support activities; policy implications of emerging naval capabilities and concepts; military readiness; and special operations and irregular warfare.

408. Civilian Executive Assistants

The Office of the Secretary of the Navy also includes civilian executive assistants who are authorized and directed to act for the secretary and under secretary within SECNAV-assigned areas of responsibility, as well as to supervise all functions and activities internal to their offices and to any designated field activities. These principal civilian executives include the general counsel of the Navy, the assistant Secretary of the Navy (research, development, and acquisition), the assistant Secretary of the Navy (financial management and comptroller), the assistant Secretary of the Navy (energy, installations, and environment), and the assistant Secretary of the Navy (manpower and reserve affairs). They exercise top management, oversight, and coordination over the bureaus and offices of the Navy Department.

The assistant Secretary of the Navy (research, development, and acquisition), or ASN(RD&A), supervises all research, development, engineering, test, evaluation, and procurement efforts within the DON, naturally including the Marine Corps. The ASN(RD&A) is assisted in the execution of duties by two principal deputies, one military and one civilian. Among several agencies under this assistant secretary is the Office of Naval Research, with which the Marine Corps interacts regularly. In addition, the assistant secretary chairs the Research and Development Committee.

The assistant Secretary of the Navy (financial management and comptroller), or ASN(FM&C), is the SECNAV's principal financial adviser and is responsible for all matters relating to financial management and comptrollership within the DON, including budgeting, accounting, financing, progress and statistical reporting, and auditing. No other office or entity may be established or designated therein to perform these responsibilities.

The assistant Secretary of the Navy (energy, installations, and environment), or ASN(EI&E), supervises all matters relating to the acquisition and disposal of real property; construction and maintenance of installations; improvement of energy efficiency and security; protection, safety, and occupational health of the department's military and civilian personnel; environmental protection, planning, and restoration ashore and afloat; and conservation of natural and cultural resources.

The assistant Secretary of the Navy (manpower and reserve affairs), or ASN (M&RA), supervises all manpower and reserve matters, including the development of programs and policy related to military personnel (active, reserve, and retired), their family members, and the civilian workforce, including morale- and performance-related matters; the tracking of the contractor workforce; and the oversight of the DON's human resources systems. The various naval personnel boards and the Office of Naval Disability Evaluation function under the ASN(M&RA). Several of these boards affect Marines, including the Board for Correction of Naval Records, Naval Clemency and Parole Board, Navy Discharge Review Board, and Naval Physical Disability Review Board.

The general counsel (GC) of the Department of the Navy is the chief legal officer of the department and heads the Office of the General Counsel (OGC). The OGC furnishes legal services in the field of commercial law. The general counsel is responsible for legal aspects of procurement, contracts, property disposition, and renegotiation. The GC maintains a close working relationship with the Navy's judge advocate general and the staff judge advocate to the commandant of the Marine Corps on all matters of shared interest. The general counsel's legal opinions are the controlling legal opinions within the DON.

In the event of death, incapacitation, or resignation of the Secretary of the Navy, the order of succession as acting secretary is as follows: the under Secretary of the Navy; assistant secretaries, in the order prescribed by the secretary and approved by the secretary of defense, or, if no order is prescribed, then the order in which the respective assistant secretaries took office; the general counsel; the chief of naval operations; and the commandant of the Marine Corps.

Within the Office of the Secretary of the Navy, there are also several staff assistants who support the Secretary of the Navy in the leadership and direction of the DON. Within assigned areas of responsibility, they supervise all functions and activities internal to their offices and to assigned field activities, if any. Several of these staff assistants and their offices within the Navy secretariat merit special mention.

The chief of legislative affairs leads the Office of Legislative Affairs, advising and assisting the secretary and all other principal military and civilian officials of the DON in connection with legislative affairs and congressional relations. The chief of legislative affairs does not, however, conduct liaison with the appropriations committees of Congress; this authority is, by law, vested with the comptroller of the Navy.

The chief of information (CHINFO) leads the Office of Information, which performs public information and public relations functions for the Navy Department. The CHINFO also has collateral public relations responsibility to the chief of naval operations.

The chief of naval research (CNR) directs the Office of Naval Research and assigned shore activities. The CNR is the DON's science and technology executive, and a deputy assistant Secretary of the Navy–level official responsible for science and technology management, policy, and oversight for the SECNAV.

The judge advocate general leads the Office of the Judge Advocate General, which supports the secretary by providing legal and policy advice. Additionally, the office advises and assists the chief of naval operations in formulating and implementing policies and initiatives pertaining to the provision of legal services within the Navy.

Led by the DON's inspector general, the Office of the Inspector General conducts independent investigations and inspections on behalf of the SECNAV and formulates policies and procedures governing the conduct of the same at lower levels within the department.

The director of the DON Sexual Assault Prevention and Response Office serves as the SECNAV's direct source of subject matter expertise on sexual assault prevention and response, as well as primary adviser and representative for related matters throughout the DON.

The Office of Program Appraisal provides the secretary with an independent capability to appraise progress against approved programs, as well as to analyze proposed programs.

409. Naval Executives to the Secretary of the Navy

The *chief of naval operations* (CNO), an admiral, is the senior officer of the Department of the Navy and principal naval adviser to the president and to the Secretary of the Navy. The CNO commands the Navy and is responsible to the Secretary of the Navy for its operation. As Navy member of the Joint Chiefs of Staff, the CNO is responsible additionally to the president and secretary of defense for certain duties external to the Department of the Navy.

The chief of naval operations has nine principal responsibilities:

1. To command the Operating Forces of the Navy
2. To organize, train, prepare, and maintain the readiness of Navy forces for assignment to unified commands. This responsibility includes determination of training required by all members of the Navy and Navy Reserve for combat.
3. To plan and determine the matériel support needs of the Operating Forces of the Navy (less Fleet Marine Forces and other assigned Marine Corps forces)
4. To identify present and future needs, qualitative and quantitative, for regular and reserve personnel of the Navy; to make available to all hands education, training, and equal opportunities for promotion; to maintain the morale and motivation of the Navy and the prestige of a naval career
5. To provide for the health of members of the Navy and their dependents
6. To budget for the operating costs of the fleets and shore activities of the Operating Forces of the Navy (except as otherwise directed by the Secretary of the Navy) and to supervise the performance of the shore activities assigned to the Operating Forces of the Navy

7. To formulate Navy strategic plans and policies and to participate in the formulation of joint and combined strategic plans and policies
8. To supervise, except with respect to the Marine Corps, the military administration of the Department of the Navy in such matters as security, intelligence, discipline, communications, and customs and traditions
9. To serve as a member of the Joint Chiefs of Staff.

The *commandant of the Marine Corps* (CMC), a general and the senior officer in the Corps, commands the U.S. Marine Corps and is directly responsible to the Secretary of the Navy. The commandant has additional responsibility to the CNO for the forces of the Marine Corps assigned to the Operating Forces of the Navy and to the civilian executive assistants for matters related to them, as well as to the president and secretary of defense for certain duties external to the Department of the Navy.

The commandant's seven principal responsibilities are as follows:

1. To determine the needs of the Corps for equipment, weapons, matériel, supplies, facilities, maintenance, and supporting services, including deciding upon the characteristics of matériel to be procured and the training required to prepare Marines for combat
2. To develop, in coordination with the Army, Navy, and Air Force, the doctrine, tactics, techniques, procedures, and equipment employed by landing forces in amphibious operations
3. To plan for the future needs, qualitative and quantitative, of regular and reserve personnel of the Marine Corps. This includes ensuring a high degree of competence on the part of all hands through education, training, and equal opportunity and providing leadership to maintain the esprit of Marines and the prestige of a Marine Corps career.
4. To provide for the health of Marines (in coordination with the surgeon general of the Navy)
5. To budget for the Marine Corps (except as otherwise directed by the Secretary of the Navy) and supervise the performance of its Supporting Establishment
6. To formulate Marine Corps strategic plans and policies and also support development of joint and combined strategic plans and policies
7. To serve as a member of the Joint Chiefs of Staff.

The *commandant of the Coast Guard* is a naval executive to the Secretary of the Navy when the Coast Guard is attached to the Navy in time of war or emergency (see Chapter 3).

THE UNITED STATES NAVY

410. Overview

As provided in the National Security Act, the United States Navy, within the Department of the Navy, includes naval, land, air, space, and cyberspace forces, both combat and support, not otherwise assigned, to include those organic forces and capabilities necessary to operate and support the Navy and Marine Corps, the other military services, and joint forces. Together with the Marine Corps, the Navy constitutes the nation's principal maritime force. Providing global reach, persistent presence—through forward-stationed and rotationally based forces—and operational flexibility, the Navy helps to secure the nation from direct attack; ensures strategic access to vital areas and retains global freedom of action; strengthens existing and emerging alliances and partnerships; establishes favorable security conditions; deters aggression and violence; and, should deterrence fail, conducts the full range of military operations in support of U.S. national interests.

411. Mission and Functions of the Navy

The Navy's stated mission is "to maintain, train, and equip combat-ready naval forces capable of winning wars, deterring aggression, and maintaining freedom of the seas." The Navy accomplishes this by executing directives under Title 10, U.S. Code, to include organizing, training, and equipping forces for the conduct of prompt and sustained combat operations on, above, below, and in proximity to the sea, and by performing additional tasks assigned by the president, secretary of defense, and combatant commanders.

In addition to the functions common to all military services, the Navy is responsible per DODD 5100.01 to develop concepts, doctrine, tactics, techniques, and procedures and to organize, train, equip, and provide forces to perform the following specific functions:

1. Conduct offensive and defensive operations associated with the maritime domain, including achieving and maintaining sea control and covering subsurface, surface, land, air, space, and cyberspace operations

2. Project power through sea-based global strike, including nuclear and conventional capabilities; interdiction and interception capabilities; maritime and/or littoral fires, to include naval surface fires; and close-air support for ground forces
3. Conduct ballistic missile defense
4. Conduct oceanic, hydrographic, and river survey and reconstruction
5. Conduct riverine operations
6. Establish, maintain, and defend sea bases in support of naval, amphibious, land, air, or other joint operations as directed
7. Provide naval expeditionary logistics to enhance the deployment, sustainment, and redeployment of naval forces and other forces operating within the maritime domain, including joint sea bases, and provide sea transport for the armed forces other than that which is organic to the individual military services and U.S. Special Operations Command
8. Provide support for joint space operations to enhance naval operations, in coordination with the other military services, combatant commands, and U.S. government departments and agencies
9. Conduct nuclear operations in support of strategic deterrence, to include providing and maintaining nuclear surety and capabilities.

412. Structure of the Navy

Command flows from the president, through the secretary of defense and the Secretary of the Navy, to Navy units and installations throughout the world (see Figure 4-3). The Navy is composed of regular and reserve components. It does not include national guard forces, as are included components of the Army and Air Force.

The Navy's basic organization structure includes the Office of the Chief of Naval Operations, the Operating Forces, and the Shore Establishment.

OFFICE OF THE CHIEF OF NAVAL OPERATIONS

413. Chief of Naval Operations

As previously discussed, the CNO leads and directs the activities of the Navy. Assistants to the CNO include the vice chief of naval operations, the deputy chiefs of naval operations, the assistant chiefs of naval operations, and a number of other ranking officers. These officers and their staffs are collectively known as the Office of the Chief of Naval Operations. Within OPNAV, several individuals perform critical functions in support of the CNO.

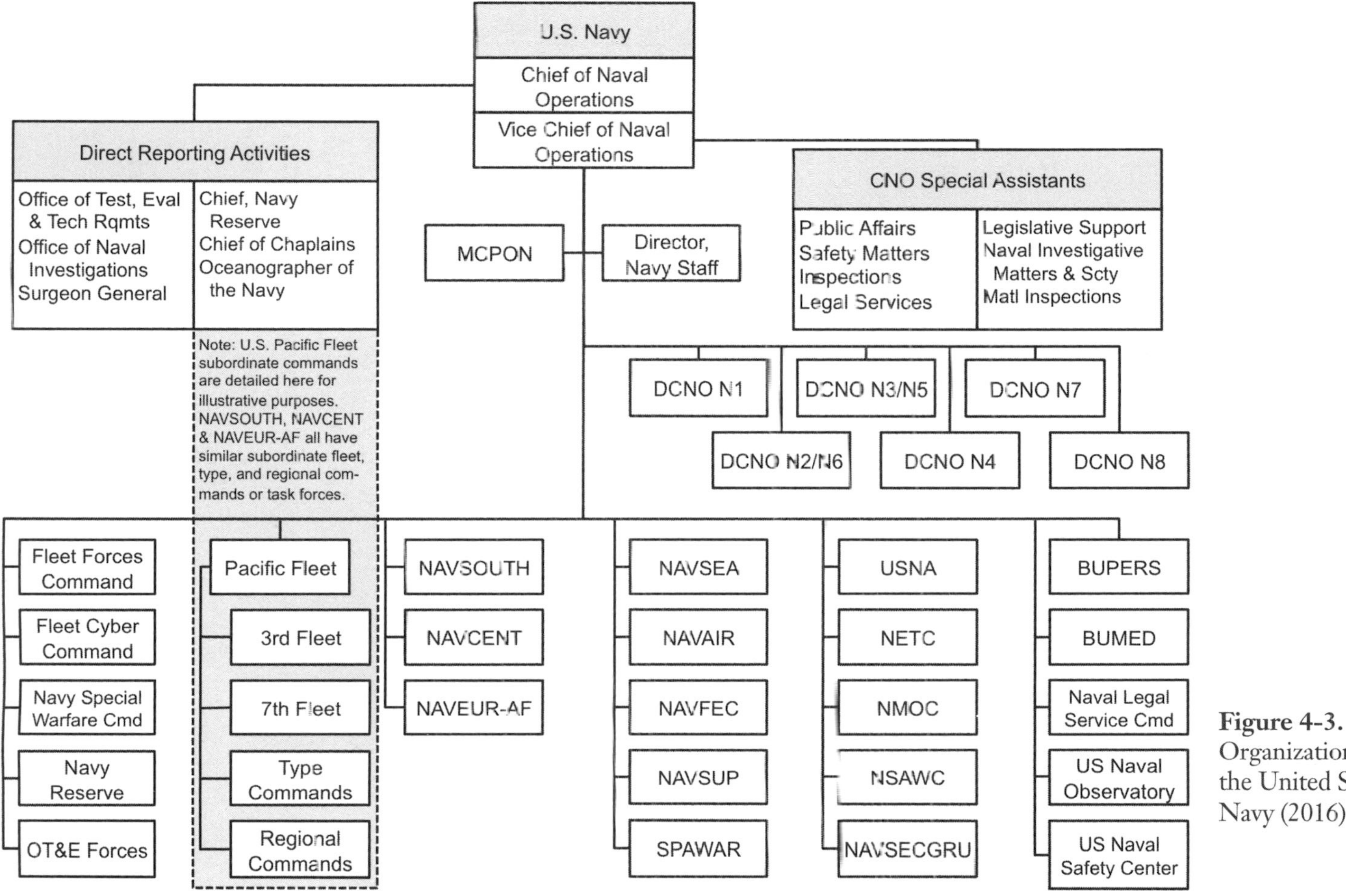

Figure 4-3. Organization of the United States Navy (2016)

414. Vice Chief of Naval Operations

The vice chief of naval operations (VCNO) acts for the CNO on all matters not specifically assigned solely to the CNO, performs the duties of the CNO during the CNO's absence, and is principal adviser to the CNO. Under the vice chief of naval operations are the special assistants for Public Affairs (N09C), Safety Matters (N09F), Inspections (N09G), Legal Services (N09J), Legislative Support (N09L), Naval Investigative Matters and Security (N09N), and Material Inspections and Surveys (N09P).

There is also a director of the Navy staff (DNS) who functions on behalf of the CNO and VCNO as the coordinator among the deputy chiefs of naval operations and the field activities reporting directly to the CNO. The latter include the Office of Test and Evaluation and Technology Requirements (N091), Surgeon General of the Navy (N093), Chief of Navy Reserve (N095), Oceanographer of the Navy (N096), and the Chief of Chaplains of the Navy (N097).

415. Deputy Chiefs of Naval Operations

Six deputy chiefs of naval operations (DCNOs) assist the CNO by performing the following functions.

The DCNO for Manpower, Personnel, Education, and Training (N1) is responsible for instituting personnel policies and coordinating basic training for the Navy and Navy Reserve. The same officer serves as chief of naval personnel.

The DCNO for Warfare Dominance (N2/N6) exercises staff responsibility for battlespace awareness (N2) and communications and network matters (N6) and serves as the Navy's top-level advocate for information management and information technology resources throughout the Navy and the joint environment. He or she also serves as the deputy chief information officer (CIO) for the Department of the Navy.

The DCNO for Operations, Plans, and Strategy (N3/N5) has cognizance over the monitoring of daily operations and readiness of the Navy, service planning for present and future military strategy, and working with the Joint Staff on the myriad of military policy matters that occupy the Washington scene.

The DCNO for Fleet Readiness and Logistics (N4) has cognizance over the logistic requirements of the Operating Forces of the Navy, including ships' matériel readiness, shore facilities programming, and inspection and survey of warships.

The DCNO for Integration of Capabilities and Resources (N8) plans the allocation of resources, providing a Navy-wide perspective and independent analysis. He or she assesses strategy, requirements, and resources during the budget formulation process. Key divisions include Programming (N80), Assessment (N81), Fiscal Management (N82), Joint Capabilities and Integration (N83), Innovation, Test and Evaluation, and Technology Requirements (N84), and Special Programs (N85).

The DCNO for Warfare Systems (N9) is responsible for the integration of manpower, training, sustainment, modernization, and procurement of the Navy's warfare systems. Key divisions include Program Integration (N91), Expeditionary Warfare (N95), Surface Warfare (N96), Undersea Warfare (N97), and Air Warfare (N98).

OPERATING FORCES OF THE NAVY

416. Overview

The Operating Forces, as the name implies, conduct naval operations around the world in support of the unified combatant commanders. The Navy's Operating Forces comprise the following major commands: U.S. Fleet Forces Command, U.S. Pacific Fleet, U.S. Naval Forces Central Command, U.S. Naval Forces Southern Command, U.S. Naval Forces Europe/U.S. Naval Forces Africa, U.S. Fleet Cyber Command, U.S. Navy Reserve, U.S. Naval Special Warfare Command, Naval Sea Systems Command, and Operational Test and Evaluation Force. Collectively, these commands encompass the six "numbered" fleets, seagoing forces, district forces, shore activities, and such other forces as may be assigned by the president or the Secretary of the Navy. The fleet commanders and commanders in the Operating Forces function under a dual chain of command. Administratively, they report to the CNO and provide, train, and equip naval forces. Operationally, they provide naval forces and report to the appropriate component commanders of the unified combatant commands.

Technically, the fleets in the Navy take on the role of force provider. They do not carry out military operations independently; rather, they train and maintain naval units that will subsequently be provided to the naval forces component of each unified combatant command. Practically speaking, however, the fleet commander is often also dual-hatted as the naval forces component commander.

All naval units within the major fleets are also organized into categories by type (for example, aviation, submarine, etc.), reporting administratively to an appropriate type commander. Aircraft carriers, aircraft squadrons, and air stations are under the administrative control of an appropriate commander, Naval Air Forces. Submarines come under a commander, Submarine Forces. Other ships and Navy units fall under a commander, Surface Forces. Marine forces, when assigned, report to their own type commander, a commanding general, Fleet Marine Forces. The purpose of this "type organization" is to prepare and provide forces for operations—not to conduct operations.

417. Major Components

United States Fleet Forces Command is a unique operational and administrative command. Its commander trains, certifies, and provides combat-ready Navy forces to unified combatant commanders; commands and controls subordinate Navy forces and shore activities during the planning and execution of assigned service functions in support of the CNO; provides operational planning and coordination support to the commanders of USNORTHCOM, North American Aerospace Defense Command's U.S. Element, and USSTRATCOM; and commands and controls subordinate forces during the planning and execution of joint missions as the Joint Forces Maritime Component Commander North.

U.S. Fleet Forces Command includes five type commands (Naval Surface Forces Atlantic, Naval Air Forces Atlantic, Submarine Force Atlantic, Navy Expeditionary Combat Command, and Navy Cyber Forces); Navy Warfare Development Command, whose mission is "to develop and integrate innovative solutions to complex naval warfare challenges to enhance current and future warfighting capabilities"; Military Sealift Command, which serves the U.S. Navy and the entire Department of Defense as an ocean carrier of equipment, fuel, ammunition, and other goods essential to the smooth function of U.S. armed forces worldwide and also doubles as the Navy component command of USTRANSCOM; and several smaller "niche" commands, centers, and offices with very focused missions.

Fleet Forces Command also notably includes Task Force 80, which is the designation for the command's major maritime headquarters and task force. Task Force 80 is the lead organization within Fleet Forces Command for all predeployment training, evaluation, and readiness of assigned naval units. The task force includes Strike Force Training Atlantic; Carrier Strike Groups 2, 8, 10, and 12; Expeditionary Strike Group 2; and several smaller squadrons and groups specialized in coastal patrol, riverine operations, and explosive ordnance disposal.

As units of the Navy deploy from the continental United States where they are under the control of Fleet Forces Command and enter an area of responsibility of a unified combatant command and the associated Navy component commander, they are operationally reassigned to the appropriate Navy component and numbered fleet.

United States Pacific Fleet, which is the Navy component of USPACOM, includes the U.S. Third Fleet, which operates in the northern, southern, and eastern Pacific Ocean, as well as along the West Coast of the United States; the U.S. Seventh Fleet, the largest forward-deployed U.S. fleet, which operates in the western Pacific and the Indian Ocean, stretching to the Persian Gulf and including much of the east coast of Africa; and type commands, including Surface Forces Pacific, Submarine Forces Pacific, and Naval Air Forces Pacific.

4-2. The nuclear-powered aircraft carrier remains the principal conventional striking arm of the U.S. Navy. Note the variety of aircraft, hence capability, visible on deck.

United States Naval Forces Central Command, which is the Navy component of USCENTCOM, includes U.S. Fifth Fleet, which operates in the Persian Gulf, Red Sea, Gulf of Oman, and parts of the Indian Ocean, and a number of specific task forces that are not part of the Fifth Fleet.

United States Naval Forces Southern Command, which is the Navy component of USSOUTHCOM, includes U.S. Fourth Fleet, which operates in the Caribbean basin and portions of the Atlantic and Pacific Oceans adjacent to Central and South America. The Fourth Fleet performs a variety of missions, including contingency operations, counter-narcoterrorism, and theater security cooperation activities.

United States Naval Forces Europe-Africa, which serves as the Navy component for both USEUCOM and USAFRICOM, includes the U.S. Sixth Fleet, which operates in the eastern half of the Atlantic Ocean from the North Pole to Antarctica, as well as the Adriatic, Baltic, Barents, Black, Caspian, Mediterranean, and North Seas. U.S. Naval Forces Europe-Africa also includes a number of specific task forces.

Because of their proximity to many of the world's hotspots, the Fifth, Sixth, and Seventh Fleets in the Persian Gulf, Mediterranean, and Far East, respectively, represent the cutting edge of American sea power in these vital regions. Each ordinarily includes one or more amphibious ready groups with embarked marine expeditionary Units (MEUs), task-organized units built around a reinforced Marine infantry battalion.

United States Fleet Cyber Command includes the Tenth Fleet, which has operational control of Navy cyber forces that execute the full spectrum of computer network operations, cyberwarfare, electronic warfare, information operations, and signals intelligence capabilities and missions across the electromagnetic spectrum and the space and cyber domains. Tenth Fleet also coordinates with and supports other fleet commanders, providing guidance and direction to ensure coordinated, synchronized, and effective defense and response capability in cyberspace. Fleet Cyber Command serves as the Navy component command for USCYBERCOM.

The United States Navy Reserve exists to "provide strategic depth and deliver operational capabilities to the Navy and Marine Corps team and joint forces, in times of peace or war." The purpose and organization of the Navy Reserve are described in greater detail later in this chapter.

United States Naval Special Warfare Command serves as the Navy component of USSOCOM. Naval Special Warfare Command provides vision, leadership, guidance, resources, and oversight to ensure component maritime special operations forces are ready to meet the operational requirements of combatant commanders.

Operational Test and Evaluation Force is organized to test and evaluate warfighting capabilities under realistic operational conditions, determining their effectiveness, suitability, and impact on mission accomplishment. Operating at various locations around the world, it includes warfare divisions focusing on surface, undersea, aviation, expeditionary, and C4I (command, control, communications, computers, and intelligence) and space warfare, and a variety of supporting divisions.

418. The Task Force Principle

The task force principle is the name given to the Navy and Marine Corps system of organizing forces for given tasks while preserving a separate administrative organization for training, administration, and housekeeping details. This is the fundamental organizational principle of the nation's naval Operating Forces.

Type Organization. All forces in the U.S. fleets are grouped into the "type organization" of the fleet, which is based on types of ships or forces. Note that the Fleet Marine Force is a type command, since it comprises all Marine Corps tactical units—air and ground—assigned to the fleet. The type organizations are principally responsible to ensure assigned forces are prepared to conduct operations.

Task Organization. The other facet of fleet organization is the "task organization." The task organization conducts operations, using units prepared and provided by the type organization. Taking the Pacific Fleet as an example, it includes several permanent task forces. Certain of these, such as antisubmarine warfare forces, might be task-organized from aviation, surface, and submarine forces to perform a specific task—in this case, to maintain control of the sea.

This system provides for a flexible structure, consisting of fleets further subdivided into forces, groups, units, and elements. Each of these descending subdivisions has a numbered designation and appropriate communication call signs. When a fleet commander receives a task from higher authority, he or she can then assign necessary forces to do the job by creating an ad hoc organization of ships and units as needed. Such a task organization is adaptable to any magnitude of organization, ranging from the campaigns of entire fleets in general war to a single ship on a temporary mission. For example, an LHD (landing helicopter dock) amphibious assault ship might be given a task designation simply to steam across the Chesapeake Bay for a Navy Day visit, and, on conclusion of the job, the task designation would cease.

Within the Seventh Fleet, a typical (hypothetical) task fleet numbering system would be one in which the commander, Seventh Fleet would assign the fleet's major forces to numbered task forces (TFs), such as Battle Force, TF 70; Navy Special Warfare Force, TF 71; Patrol and Reconnaissance Force, TF 72; and so forth. Amphibious forces might be designated Amphibious Force, TF 76, and assigned Marine forces might be designated Landing Force, TF 79.

Within each force, the commander would then assign logical subdivisions of that force as task groups (TGs), such as TG 70.1, Carrier Group; TG 70.2, Gunfire Support and Covering Group; and so forth.

Within each task group, in turn, would be task units (TUs). For example, TG 70.1, Carrier Group, might be divided into TU 70.1.1, Carrier Unit, and TU 70.1.2, Screen Unit.

Note the fashion in which components of a task organization are designated by the addition of decimal separators and successive numbers; this enables you to determine at a glance the place of a given unit in an operational command.

Significance. The simultaneous organization of the fleets by types and task is obviously complex. It is, nevertheless, a system precisely adapted to any given job, large or small, temporary or permanent. Moreover, it is flexible and economical.

SHORE ESTABLISHMENT OF THE NAVY

419. Overview

The Shore Establishment provides support to the Operating Forces in the form of facilities for the repair of ships, aircraft, machinery, and electronics; communications centers; training areas and simulators; intelligence and meteorological support activities; storage areas for repair parts, fuel, and munitions; and medical and dental facilities. The Shore Establishment comprises all field activities of the Department of the Navy, except shore activities assigned to the

Operating Forces of the Navy, including various systems and engineering commands; education and training commands (including the United States Naval Academy); and several other commands, centers, groups, and offices providing specialized services and support, such as the Naval Observatory and Naval Safety Center.

The activities of the Shore Establishment are generally distributed along the coasts where they can best serve the Operating Forces. Many activities for which such proximity to the sea is not essential (notably air, ordnance, and supply) are based inland.

420. Navy Installations Command

Established in 2003, Navy Installations Command is responsible for Navy-wide shore installation management. It serves as a single organization for the management of shore installations that focuses on installation effectiveness and improves the shore installation management community's ability to support the fleet. Commander, Navy Installations Command has overall management responsibility for shore installations and leads installation policy and program execution oversight.

Navy Installations Command is organized worldwide into eleven regionally oriented subordinate commands and activities:

1. Naval District Washington
2. Navy Region Mid-Atlantic
3. Navy Region Southeast
4. Navy Region Northwest
5. Navy Region Southwest
6. Navy Region Hawaii
7. Joint Region Marianas
8. Navy Region Japan
9. Navy Region Korea
10. Singapore Area Coordinator
11. Navy Region Europe, Africa, and Southwest Asia.

Within their geographic areas of responsibility, these commands oversee clusters of naval bases, naval stations, naval shipyards, naval weapons stations, naval air stations, naval air facilities (which are similar to naval air stations but provide fewer capabilities, serve an auxiliary function, or are geographically situated within a sovereign allied nation), and smaller naval support activities, naval fleet support activities, and naval support facilities.

421. Naval Bases and Stations

A naval base or station centralizes, in one command, activities that support the fleet. At each major naval base or station, a single designated officer normally exercises command over all fleet support activities. A naval base or station may include a shipyard and/or an air station. Commanders of naval shipyards are technically qualified officers who are skilled in industrial and matériel management.

Commanding officers of the component activities of a naval base or station receive instructions on support and technical matters directly from the responsible agencies in the Department of the Navy.

422. Naval Air Stations

A naval air station typically comprises the various Shore Establishment activities that furnish aviation logistic support to the Operating Forces of the Navy.

Commanding officers of component activities of naval air stations are subject to the command of their air station commander. As with naval bases and stations, support of such activities stems directly from the Department of the Navy.

COMPONENTS OF THE UNITED STATES NAVY

423. Overview

The United States Navy consists of the Regular Navy and the Navy Reserve.

424. The Regular Navy

The active component of the Navy is referred to as the Regular Navy. Commissioned officers of the Regular Navy (and Navy Reserve) are divided among the line and staff corps (see Figure 4-4).

Line. Line officers exercise military command and are accountable for the exercise of their authority. Among line officers are several types of "line" specialists: naval constructors, naval engineers, and specialists in such fields as intelligence, oceanography, communications, and public information. Only line officers command at sea, and, in general, only line officers exercise command ashore. Members of certain corps, however, such as Medical, Supply, and Civil Engineer Corps, command shore activities and units (such as Seabees) under the cognizance of their respective bureaus. Although, of course, not eligible to command at sea or to command a Navy base or station, Marine officers are nevertheless line officers of the naval service and have been held, legally, to be naval officers.

Medical Corps. This corps is composed exclusively of graduate doctors of medicine who treat the ill, injured, and wounded and administer the hospitals, dispensaries, sick bays, and other medical units of the naval establishment. Medical and dental service for the Marine Corps is provided by Navy doctors, dentists, and hospital corpsmen.

Nurse Corps. Navy nurses are commissioned officers in the Nurse Corps. They serve in hospitals and dispensaries at home and on foreign stations and in hospital ships and transports at sea.

Medical Service Corps. This corps is composed of specialists in optometry, pharmacy, and such allied sciences as bacteriology, biochemistry, psychology, and medical administration and statistics.

Dental Corps. Composed of graduate dental surgeons, this is a separate corps whose members serve at hospitals and dispensaries and on board larger ships. The Dental Corps, like the Medical, Nurse, and Medical Service Corps, comes under the Bureau of Medicine and Surgery.

Supply Corps. This is the business branch of the Navy that administers the Navy supply system and receives and disburses funds for supply and for pay, subsistence, and transportation.

Chaplain Corps. Ordained ministers of various denominations, officers of the Chaplain Corps conduct religious services and promote the spiritual and moral welfare of the Navy and Marine Corps. The chief of chaplains heads the corps. The deputy chief of chaplains also serves as the chaplain of the Marine Corps

Civil Engineer Corps. This corps is composed of formally educated and licensed civil engineers, normally restricted to shore duty, who supervise buildings, grounds, and plants at shore stations, as well as construction of buildings and the layout of shore stations. This corps conceived, organized, and commanded the Navy construction battalions (Seabees), which served so illustriously beside Marines during World War II, Korea, and Vietnam.

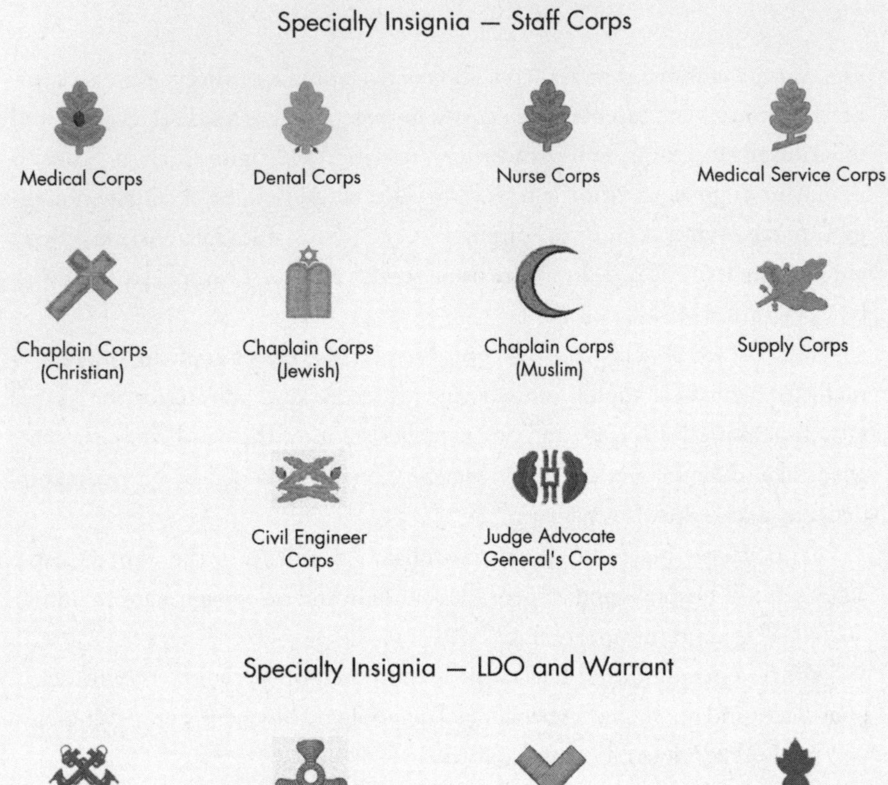

Figure 4-4. Branch and Corps Devices of Commissioned and Warrant Officers of the Navy

Judge Advocate General's Corps. This corps consists of Navy lawyers who have been duly certified to practice and perform staff legal and judicial duties under the judge advocate general and within the system of military jurisprudence.

Warrant Officers. Navy warrant officers possess the most detailed practical knowledge of the complicated mechanisms of our modern Navy and thus provide invaluable technical know-how for the fleet. Despite proposals, based on administrative considerations, that the warrant grades be abolished in favor of limited-duty billets and that no further warrants be issued, it was firmly decided that the Navy warrant officer is here to stay. Warrant grade titles include, among others, boatswain, machinist, electrician, aerographer, photographer, supply clerk, ordnance and mine warfare technician, communications and electronics technician, ship repair technician, equipment and building foreman, bandmaster, medical and dental service warrant, aviation maintenance and operations technician, as well as others (see Figure 4-4).

Enlisted Men and Women. Enlisted men and women of the Navy and Coast Guard are divided into rating groups, as illustrated in Figure 4-5. Just as we expect Navy officers to recognize and identify Marine noncommissioned officers, so should a Marine officer be able to identify Navy petty officers in the various ratings.

425. The Navy Reserve

The Navy Reserve, as the name implies, is the reserve component of the Navy. The purpose, classification, and organization of the Navy Reserve are generally similar to those of the Marine Corps Reserve, discussed in detail in Chapter 7.

Within the structure of the Navy Reserve are three major organizational categories that further define a member's service responsibilities and commitment status: Ready Reserve, Standby Reserve, and Retired Reserve. Each reservist falls into one of these categories based on details such as military experience, military status, and individual situation.

The *Ready Reserve* provides trained officer and enlisted reservists, who, added to qualified personnel from other sources, complete the war organization of the Navy. It represents a pool of trained servicemembers who are ready to step in and serve whenever and wherever needed. It is made up of the Selected Reserve, which includes drilling reservists typically organized into specific units with full-time support (FTS) personnel, and the Individual Ready Reserve

Administration, Deck, Medical, Technical, and Weapons Specialties

Engineering and Hull Specialties

Aviation Specialties

Construction Specialties

Figure 4-5. Specialty Marks of Navy Enlisted Ratings

(IRR), which consists of individuals who have previously served in the Navy's active component or in the Selected Reserve. Officers and enlisted personnel of the Selected Reserve must perform annual training and other duties to keep them ready for immediate mobilization in emergency. FTS personnel perform full-time active duty service that relates to the training and administration of the Navy Reserve program. They may also be assigned to shore activities and commands or operational units. IRR personnel may serve in either an active reserve or inactive reserve status.

The *Standby Reserve* provides a force of qualified and partially qualified officers and enlisted persons who have transferred from the Ready Reserve after fulfilling certain requirements established by law. Most common Standby Reservists are those who have been deemed key civilian employees by a government agency. They will, except on personal application, be called to active duty only for war or a national emergency declared by Congress. While they are not required to perform training and are not part of any specific unit, they do create a pool of trained individuals who can be mobilized, if necessary, to fill manpower needs in specific skill areas.

The *Retired Reserve* includes those who are drawing retired pay or are qualified for retired pay upon reaching sixty years of age. Members of the Retired Reserve are liable for active duty only in time of war or emergency declared by Congress, or when otherwise authorized by law, in the event sufficient qualified personnel are not available in the Ready Reserve and Standby Reserve.

426. Education of Officer Candidates

As with the other services, there are several paths to becoming a candidate for a commission in the Navy.

United States Naval Academy. The Naval Academy was established in 1845 at old Fort Severn, at the mouth of the Severn River in Annapolis, Maryland, to train naval officers.

The strength of the Brigade of Midshipmen is maintained by appointments from senators, congressmen, and territorial delegates; by competitive appointments from regular and reserve enlisted men and women of the Navy and Marine Corps; and by appointments-at-large by the president and vice president. These so-called presidential appointments are made on a competitive basis from among the children of regular and reserve officers, as well as children of any members of the armed forces killed or disabled in the line of duty. In addition, the children of Medal of Honor recipients are admitted to the Academy upon passing the usual mental and physical examinations.

The Academy is commanded by a superintendent of flag rank. The staff includes officers of all the services, as well as civilian professors. The course is four years and leads to a B.S. degree regardless of major.

Since the 1880s, the Marine Corps has each year commissioned a number of Naval Academy graduates as second lieutenants. At present, approximately 20 to 25 percent of the midshipmen per graduating class are permitted Marine Corps commissions; the competition for these vacancies is keen.

Naval Reserve Officers' Training Corps (NROTC). The NROTC offers the opportunity for young men and women to qualify for Navy and Marine Corps Reserve commissions while attending college.

Midshipmen are selected competitively in each state. As NROTC students, they lead the same academic life as college contemporaries, but, in addition to normal studies, they receive professional training in naval science. Midshipmen wear uniforms when engaged in naval duties and receive the pay and allowances of a midshipman. After graduation, the NROTC graduate must normally serve a minimum of four years on active duty as a Navy or Marine officer. Tuition and certain related expenses are wholly paid for by the government.

Besides the foregoing program for candidates, there is also a nonsubsidized NROTC program for college students, which nevertheless does include certain stipends for partial support.

NROTC units are located at more than sixty institutions throughout the country. Individuals interested in this program may find complete information and application instructions by searching online using the keyword "NROTC."

Officer Candidate School. Located at the Naval Training Center, Newport, Rhode Island, the Navy's Officer Candidate School trains young college graduates as Navy Reserve officers. Candidates hold the enlisted grade of officer candidate. They are obligated to serve three years on active duty as commissioned officers after passing the four-month course and to continue in the Reserve a total of six years. Meritorious enlisted men and women selected for integration as regular Navy officers also attend Officer Candidate School.

NAVAL STAFF ORGANIZATION

427. Organization and Functions of an Operational Naval Staff

Naval staffs are organized and function in manners similar to other military staffs, as they, in practice, include personal, executive, and special components.

This discussion of the naval staff system is important because Marine officers serve in some capacity on every significant naval staff. The operational naval staff (as in the amphibious group headquarters) is of primary interest to Marine officers. You will find that other naval staffs, ashore or afloat, are organized along much the same lines, with special functions as appropriate.

Naval staff functions come under two headings: administration, and planning and operations. To carry out these functions, the typical large naval staff is organized much like the Office of the CNO (see Sections 413 through 415). This organization comprises the personal staff and the coordinating staff (which is equivalent to the USMC executive staff).

Personal Staff. The duties of a Navy personal staff are essentially similar to those listed in Section 630 for the Marine personal staff, although titles differ somewhat.

The chief of staff not only carries out the functions the title implies but also is the admiral's personal assistant. He or she is the senior officer on the staff and coordinates all staff activities, thus serving as a member of the coordinating staff as well. In Navy commands headed by officers below flag rank, this billet bears the title of chief staff officer rather than chief of staff.

The flag secretary serves as the admiral's administrative aide and confidential secretary. Like the chief of staff, the flag secretary also has dual status as a member of the coordinating staff, in which he or she heads the administrative section.

The flag lieutenant, in addition to personal services to the admiral, supervises salutes, honors, awards, official calls, uniform, social protocol, and transportation for the admiral and the staff (barge, staff gig, helicopter, and staff cars). The flag lieutenant keeps the staff duty officer, as well as other members of the staff and interested officers of the flagship, apprised of the movements and intentions of the admiral.

Coordinating Staff. The coordinating staff typically comprises four or five sections, each headed by an assistant chief of staff.

The Administrative Section (N-1) is headed by the flag secretary. The section combines in a single entity the shore functions associated with several sections of a Marine Corps staff: Assistant Chief of Staff (AC/S) G-1, staff secretary, adjutant, and legal officer.

The Intelligence Section (N-2) performs naval intelligence functions analogous to those performed by the Marine Corps AC/S G-2 ashore. In some Navy staffs, the intelligence officer likewise has cognizance over public affairs. Marine officers may serve in Navy intelligence sections—primarily in connection with amphibious intelligence.

The Operations Section (N-3) performs planning (N-5 in larger staffs), training, and operations functions comparable to those of the Marine Corps AC/S G-3. In addition, however, the naval Operations Section has responsibility for matters affecting readiness, and, in amphibious staffs, deals with and conducts the ship-to-shore movement. Marines frequently serve in the Operations Section, not only as plans officer but also as military operations officer; both titles are self-explanatory.

The Logistics Section (N-4) has all the functions of the AC/S G-4 section in a Marine Corps staff. In addition, this section plans the availability for overhaul of ships, screens work requests, supervises maintenance, and administers funds for repair and alterations.

The Communications Section (N-6) is sometimes a separate section and sometimes part of the N-1 section. The communications officer not only supervises communications but also controls classified publications for the staff. In amphibious staffs, a Marine communication officer usually forms part of the section.

Specialist Officers. Although the Navy staff organization does not include a special staff as such, it does, of course, have certain specialists who, in effect, comprise a special staff. While the specialties are not as numerous as on a Marine staff, the duties are quite similar. The following specialist officers would be included in the typical Navy staff: weapons officer, air officer, aerological officer, surgeon, supply officer, chaplain, and legal officer.

428. Staff Duty Officer Afloat

Senior line officers (including Marines) take turns as staff duty officer (see Chapter 16) in Navy organizations.

In port, the staff duty officer takes a day's duty, receives routine reports, acts on routine matters in the absence of officers having staff cognizance, regulates the use of staff boats, and tends the side on occasions of ceremony. In an emergency, the staff duty officer must be prepared to make decisions when the admiral and chief of staff are unavailable.

Under way, the staff duty officer stands watch on the flag bridge and represents the admiral in the same way that the officer of the deck represents the captain. The staff duty officer makes routine reports and signals, supervises navigation and station-keeping of the force, keeps the staff log, and oversees the watch on the flag bridge. To perform efficiently, the staff duty officer must keep informed of current operations, expected hazards, conditions of readiness, launching and recovery of aircraft, joining and detaching of units, fueling and provisioning, and so on. The state of relations between the staff and flagship depends in considerable measure on the attitude and consideration of the staff duty officer.

429. Marine Duties on Naval Staffs

Nowhere more than on a Navy staff is a Marine expected to be "soldier and sailor, too." Thus, when assigned to the Navy, never be surprised, regardless of

4-3. The amphibious command ship carries both embarked unit personnel and staff personnel of the flag officer commanding.

what duty you find yourself performing. Your only concern should be to see that that duty is well done, so that as a Marine Corps representative you set an example to your Navy colleagues.

Subject to the foregoing, Marines are usually assigned to one or several of the following staff duties.

Staff Marine Officer. As division, squadron, force, or fleet Marine officer, you exercise staff supervision over Marine personnel and matters within your command. In practice, this boils down to coordination of landing force activities involving Marines, inspection of embarked Marine detachments, advice and assistance as needed for other Marine commanders, and supervision of the flag Marine detachment (or "flag allowance"), if one is provided. Naturally, the staff Marine officer is usually selected to maintain liaison between his or her staff and any Marine or Army staffs in the vicinity. The senior Marine officer on any Navy staff, regardless of other duties, performs the functions just described.

Military Operations Officer. The military operations officer has cognizance over all military operations ashore in which the naval staff may be involved. In essence, the job of the Marine military operations officer is to provide the Navy staff expertise in matters of land warfare and organization.

Combat Cargo Officer. As a member of a Navy staff or ship's crew, the combat cargo officer performs the duties of troop loading, billeting, and landing associated with embarkation functions in the Marine staff ashore.

Other Duties. The foregoing jobs are those to which Marine representatives on Navy staffs are usually assigned. In addition, however (according to your capabilities, experience, and the needs of the organization), you could find yourself performing as security officer, logistics officer, intelligence officer, air officer, or plans officer. In any case, never acquiesce in the bad old practice (still occasionally encountered) of allowing yourself to be assigned duty in a staff section headed by a Navy officer junior to you. Your lineal precedence, based on date of rank, is as binding on a Navy staff as anywhere else.

Under all circumstances, a decisive naval superiority is to be considered a fundamental principle, and the basis upon which all hope of success must ultimately depend.

—George Washington, 1780

5

ROLES, MISSIONS, AND STATUS OF THE MARINE CORPS

Every American respects the Marine Corps, but a surprising number of people are quite hazy on what the Corps really is and does. Every Marine officer should thus possess precise knowledge of and be skillful at explaining the roles, missions, and status of the Corps.

501. Marine Corps Roles and Missions

The Law. The statutes of the United States include many provisions, great and small, that affect the Corps. All these provisions have been codified under Title 10 (Armed Forces), U.S. Code.

The "charter" of the Marine Corps, however, has evolved from three laws: the Act of 11 July 1798, "Establishing and Organizing a Marine Corps"; the Act of 30 June 1834, "For the Better Organization of the Marine Corps"; and the National Security Act of 1947 as amended.

The National Security Act, which unified the armed services, is the controlling military legislation of this country. For Marines, though, the Douglas-Mansfield Bill (Public Law 416, 82nd Congress, 2nd Session) has particular importance. This law amended the National Security Act as it regards the Marine Corps. Its debates and hearings (1951–52) are a trove of information on the Corps.

To summarize, the National Security Act as now amended (see Sections 307 and 401) makes the following provisions for the Marine Corps:

1. It reaffirms the Corps' status as a service within the Department of the Navy.
2. It provides for Fleet Marine Forces, ground and aviation.
3. It requires that the combatant forces of the Corps be organized on the basis of three Marine divisions and three air wings, and sets a peacetime ceiling of 400,000 personnel for the regular Corps.
4. It assigns the Corps the missions of seizure and defense of advanced naval bases, as well as land operations incident to naval campaigns.
5. It gives the Marine Corps primary responsibility for development of amphibious warfare doctrines, tactics, techniques, and equipment employed by landing forces.
6. It seats the commandant of the Marine Corps on the Joint Chiefs of Staff.
7. It affords the Marine Corps appropriate representation on various joint Defense Department agencies, notably the Joint Staff.
8. It assigns the Marine Corps collateral missions of providing security forces for naval shore stations, providing ships' detachments, and performing such other duties as the president may direct.

In taking stock of Marine Corps missions found in law, it is important not to overlook the short phrase "and shall perform such other duties as the President may direct." This phrase, which the Unification Act quotes directly from the 1834 Marine Corps law, stems in turn from similar language in the Act of 1798. It validates in law Marine Corps functions that transcend the Corps' purely naval missions. In mid-1951, the House of Representatives Armed Services Committee highlighted the significance of this clause in a trenchant summary:

> It is, however, the Committee view that one of the most important statutory—and traditional—functions of the Marine Corps has been and still is to perform "such other duties as the President may direct."
>
> The campaign in Korea, in which the 1st Marine Division and the 1st Marine Air[craft] Wing are presently participating, can hardly be called a naval mission. Practically every war involving the United States has found the Marine Corps performing duties other than

naval. Indeed, the first two battalions of Marines raised in this country were raised specifically for service before Boston with General Washington's army.

Many Marine activities in the War of 1812 involved only land fighting; in the 1840s the Marines saw "the Halls of Montezuma" while fighting with the Army in the War with Mexico; in the early 1900s Marine activities in Central America were repeatedly entirely of a land nature; their participation in the fighting in the Boxer Uprising in China in 1900 likewise was of a land nature; certainly when in May 1917 President Wilson ordered the 4th Marine Brigade to serve as part of the Army's 2d Division in the Battles of Belleau Wood, Aisne-Marne, St. Mihiel, Blanc Mont, and Meuse-Argonne, and later in the occupation forces, these can hardly be described as naval missions; nor can the activities of Marine Maj. Gen. John A. Lejeune, in commanding for a time the Army's 2nd Division in France, be called a naval function; nor could the service of Marine aviation in France during 1918 be accurately termed a naval activity.

It is difficult to see how the sending of Marines as the initial force to hold Iceland prior to the last war, until relieved by Army troops, could accurately be called a naval mission; how the reinforcing of Corregidor by the 4th Marine Regiment sent from China just before war broke out, could be accurately termed a naval action; and if the actions of the 1st Marine Division on Guadalcanal, commencing the first American attack of the war on August 7, 1942, can accurately be called a naval action, then in the same fashion the activities of Army divisions in this area must likewise be so termed. It further is worthy of note that on Mindanao and Luzon in the Philippines, in the last ground action against the enemy in World War II, Marine Air Groups 12, 14, 24, and 32, gave close air support to the 24th, 31st, and 41st Infantry Divisions—an activity that appears to the Committee to be only distantly related (if at all) to exclusively naval activities.

The Committee must also call attention to the fact that, after V-J Day, the V Amphibious Corps, USMC, was part of the forces sent to occupy the Japanese Home Islands; the III Marine Amphibious Corps was sent to North China to accept the surrender of Japanese troops there; that a Marine division, with other forces, was kept in China

> until the summer of 1947 during the attempt of the United States to settle civil war between the Chinese Government and Chinese Communists. It is a strained construction, indeed, of military activities to characterize such employment of the United States Marines as essentially naval in character.

In line with the foregoing, Marines have on several occasions been temporarily detached by executive order of the president to service under the secretary of war. The last occasion on which Marines were detached to service under the Army was in July 1941, when the 1st Provisional Marine Brigade in Iceland was assigned to the Army by President Franklin D. Roosevelt. Note the distinction between administrative transfer of Marines to Army duty (which can only be effected by order of the president) and operational attachments under unified command, which occur routinely—as was the case throughout the greater part of the Korean and Vietnam wars, as well as the conflicts in the Persian Gulf and Afghanistan.

So much, then, for the main provisions of law that give the Marine Corps its roles and missions. While those roles are carefully spelled out, the law nevertheless allows employment of Marines anywhere, on any service the president may desire.

Additional Missions of the Marine Corps. In addition to the missions expressly assigned by Congress, the Corps also performs several tasks either assigned by the Department of Defense or in accordance with long-standing custom.

"*The Functions Paper.*" Originally known as "The Key West Agreement" (see Section 401), the Defense Department directive that outlines the functions of that department and of its major components is now usually spoken of as "The Functions Paper." Its main provisions are currently embodied in DODD 5100.01, *Functions of the Department of Defense and its Major Components.* The paper is essentially a compilation of interservice agreements dating from 1948, and revised from time to time, as to how the roles-and-missions provisions of the National Security Act are to be implemented. In addition, the directive establishes a number of service relationships and common functions within the Defense Department, which affect the Marine Corps equally with the other services. Portions of this paper that specifically provide for Marine Corps functions are as follows:

5-1. Marine Corps Forces provide units ready to undertake military missions "in any clime or place."

To maintain the Marine Corps, having the following specific functions:

To provide Fleet Marine Forces of combined arms, together with supporting air components, for service with the Fleet in the seizure or defense of advanced naval bases and for the conduct of such land operations as may be essential to the prosecution of a naval campaign. These functions do not contemplate the creation of a second land Army.

To provide detachments and organizations for service on armed vessels of the Navy, and security detachments for the protection of naval property at naval stations and bases.

To develop, in coordination with the other Services, the doctrines, tactics, techniques, and equipment employed by landing forces in amphibious operations. The Marine Corps shall have primary interest in the development of those landing forces doctrines, tactics, techniques, and equipment which are of common interest to the Army and the Marine Corps.

> To train and equip, as required, Marine Forces for airborne operations, in coordination with the other Services and in accordance with doctrines established by the Joint Chiefs of Staff.
>
> To develop, in coordination with the other Services, doctrines, procedures, and equipment of interest to the Marine Corps for airborne operations.

Although many of the foregoing provisions stem directly from and actually include language of the National Security Act, you should never confuse "The Functions Paper," only a departmental directive, with the National Security Act, which is the law and thus governs in any disagreement. Additionally, it must be noted that the Marine Corps, though repeatedly overruled, has consistently opposed inclusion of the meaningless "second land Army" phrase (see subparagraph 1 in the above-quoted passage) in "The Functions Paper," since nothing could be further from the objectives or interests of the Corps.

State Department Guards. Under authority of the Foreign Service Act of 1946, the Marine Corps has a collateral mission to provide security guards for American embassies, legations, and consulates. For this duty, which demands the highest discretion and trust, the Marine Corps furnishes over a thousand Marines, both officer and enlisted, who are distributed throughout more than 110 State Department overseas posts.

White House Duties. Dating from 1798, the scarlet-coated Marine Band has been styled "The President's Own" because of its privilege of providing the music for state functions at the White House. Similarly, Marines have established and guarded presidential camps at Rapidan, Virginia; Warm Springs, Georgia; Camp David, Maryland; and elsewhere, while Marine helicopters were the first to carry a president and still routinely do so.

Unwritten Missions. Nowhere do the statute books say that the Marine Corps is the national force in readiness, yet our history demonstrates clearly that a fundamental mission of the Corps is and always has been just that. To quote former Assistant Secretary of the Navy John Nicholas Brown: "Readiness, the capacity to move anywhere immediately and become effective, is always needed and at the present juncture of events is especially necessary. This is the daily bread of the Marine Corps."

In close corollary to this traditional mission is the Corps' worldwide service, in times of nominal peace, as "State Department Troops" for enforcement of foreign policy and protection of U.S. nationals or their evacuation, under direction of the Department of State.

502. Status of the Marine Corps

"The Marine Corps is sui generis" ("something entirely of its own sort"), once ruled a federal judge when construing the legal status of the Corps. This is probably the best one-sentence characterization the Marine Corps has ever had.

The Marine Corps is one of the several armed services (Army, Marine Corps, Navy, and Air Force), which, with the Coast Guard (when attached to the naval establishment in time of war), compose the armed forces of the United States. It is important that you be aware of this, since you may sometimes encounter the erroneous term "the three services," which is usually a term of exclusion so far as the Marine Corps is concerned.

Side by side with the Navy, the Marine Corps is one of two military services in the naval establishment, under direct control and supervision of the Secretary of the Navy. Section 503 of this chapter contains a detailed explanation of the relationship of the Marine Corps to the Navy. For the moment, we can let the subject rest with the words of Representative Carl Vinson, distinguished former chairman of the House Armed Services Committee: "The fact is that

5-2. Marine Corps M1 Abrams tanks maneuver across California's Mojave Desert.

the Marine Corps is and always has been, since its inception 175 years ago, a separate military service apart from the United States Army, the United States Navy, and the United States Air Force."

Some account of the evolution of the status of the Marine Corps is useful knowledge for you as a Marine officer.

The Act of 11 July 1798, reconstituting the Corps after its post–Revolutionary War hiatus, provided for a Corps of Marines, "in addition to the present military establishment." In line with this thought, although the Corps' distinct status from the Navy was never questioned, it was nearly forty years before the Corps was firmly dissociated from the Army. During this time, while on shore, Marines (like the British marines) were promoted, paid, rationed, and disciplined under Army Regulations—practices sanctioned not only by custom but also by express rulings handed down from time to time by the attorney general of the United States.

To clarify the status of the Marine Corps, Congress in 1834 affirmed the Corps as a separate service but placed it unequivocally under the Secretary of the Navy and therefore under Navy Regulations "except when detached for service with the Army, by order of the President."

For more than a century, the Acts of 1798 and 1834 governed the status of the Marine Corps. In 1947, the National Security Act became law. This law as amended by Public Law 416 not only spells out the missions of our Corps today but also defines the Corps in declaratory language as one of the four services given statutory missions under the act. In the first years of unification there was some tendency to assume that the National Security Act had intended to tri-elementalize the armed forces on a three-service basis, with the Marine Corps merely a specialist branch of the Navy. This misconception was set at rest with some emphasis in the debate and hearings on Public Law 416, during which Congress avowed that the Marine Corps was not a mere appendage but a service in its own right.

A final and legally definitive ruling on the foregoing point is to be found in House Report 970, 84th Congress. This is the report by the House of Representatives on the codification of Title 10, U.S. Code. This report states: "The legislative history of Public Law 432, the National Security Act of 1947, and Public Law 416 of the 82nd Congress . . . clearly indicates that the Marine Corps is legally a separate and distinct military service within the Department of the Navy, with individually assigned statutory responsibilities, and that the Commandant directs and administers the Marine Corps under delegated command of the Secretary of the Navy."

The status of the Marine Corps can be summed up thus:

1. The Marine Corps is a separate military service possessing distinct statutory roles and missions prescribed by the National Security Act.
2. The Marine Corps is a part of the naval establishment (or Department of the Navy) and comes directly under the Secretary of the Navy.
3. The commandant of the Marine Corps commands the Corps as a whole and is directly responsible to the Secretary of the Navy in a well-defined historical and legal relationship for the total performance, administration, readiness, discipline, and efficiency of the Corps.

503. The Marine Corps and the Department of the Navy

The brotherhood between the Marine Corps and Navy is so longstanding, so close, and so smooth in operation that the casual observer may be readily pardoned the erroneous conclusion that the Marine Corps forms part of the Navy, or vice versa.

As we have seen, this is not the case. To quote General C. B. Cates, nineteenth commandant of the Marine Corps:

> The partnership between the Navy and Marine Corps had its legal birth more than 150 years ago when Congress placed both Services—which were then some 25 years of age—under a newly created Secretary of the Navy. The partnership was a close one initially, and it grew even closer with the passage of time. Today it is so close that only a handful of people—inside the Naval Services as well as outside—realize that technically the Navy and Marine Corps are separate Services under the command of the Secretary of the Navy. Practically speaking, the Navy and Marine Corps have lived, worked, and fought together since their inception.

To understand the place of the Marine Corps in the naval establishment, you must first understand exactly what constitutes the Department of the

Navy, or, as it was called for many years in the past, "the naval establishment." As stated in Navy Regulations, and in Chapter 4 of this *Guide*, the naval establishment (that is, the Department of the Navy) embraces all activities committed to the care of the Secretary of the Navy and thus includes the Marine Corps. This does not make the Marine Corps a part of, but rather a partner of, the Navy proper.

The Marine Corps and Public Law 432. The law that defines the position of the chief of naval operations in the Navy is Public Law 432, 80th Congress (original House of Representatives title, H.R. 3432).

Casual reading of parts of this law by a person not conversant with the intent of Congress in framing it (or of the Navy Department in seeking it) might suggest that this act could be construed as placing the Marine Corps under the command of the chief of naval operations. To save confusion on this, it is enough to quote from an official letter by Secretary of the Navy John L. Sullivan, on 17 December 1947, to General A. A. Vandegrift, eighteenth commandant of the Marine Corps:

> The Commandant of the Marine Corps is informed that it is not the intent of the Navy Department, in seeking enactment of H.R. 3432 [Public Law 432], to alter the Commandant's direct responsibility to the Secretary of the Navy for the administration and efficiency of the Marine Corps.
>
> The Navy Department interprets neither Executive Order 9635 [an earlier directive defining the wartime position of the Chief of Naval Operations] nor H.R. 3432 as interposing the Chief of Naval Operations in the administrative chain of responsibility between the Secretary and the Commandant, or as otherwise modifying the historical relationship between the Secretary and the Commandant.
>
> /s/ John L. Sullivan

The Marine Corps as a Naval Service. Attempts are sometimes made to show that the term "naval service" has a specific organizational meaning that includes both the U.S. Navy and the U.S. Marine Corps, so that together they may be said to constitute one military service—the "naval service." The claim that this term has such a meaning is baseless. Historically, the phrase "naval service" originated as a matter of convenience for the Secretary of the Navy in issuing orders affecting all military personnel under his jurisdiction. It has occasionally been used for comparable specific purposes in statutes, mainly dating years back, dealing with personnel administration or discipline, and with no general or consistent construction or definition of the term in question. That Marines, within the meaning and purposes of these statutes and regulations, are "members of the naval service" has long been accepted without dispute; but, as the codification of Title 10, U.S. Code, underscores (see Section 502), the Marine Corps is a legally distinct and separate military service. Therefore, the best usage when the term "naval service" arises in connection with Marines or the Marine Corps is to pluralize it as "the naval services," since there are always two naval services—the U.S. Navy and the U.S. Marine Corps—within the Department of the Navy, and, when the Coast Guard is assigned in time of hostilities, there are three.

Working Relations between Marine Corps and Navy. Although we have emphasized the legally and essentially separate status of the Marine Corps in the naval establishment, such status does not prevent harmonious working relations between the Marine Corps and the Navy.

5-3. A Marine Corps MV-22B Osprey takes off from Marine Corps Air Station Iwakuni, Japan, in support of earthquake relief efforts. (U.S. Marine Corps photo by LCpl Aaron Henson)

Not only do individual Marines serve as part of Navy commands, and vice versa, but units are likewise freely interchanged. Every Navy staff of any consequence includes one or more Marines, both officer and enlisted, while all major Marine units and stations have Navy doctors, dentists, chaplains, and hospital corpsmen. In addition, Marine Corps Forces include naval gunfire liaison officers—Navy line officers who, as staff officers, help to obtain gunfire support.

Each major combatant ship of the fleet once had a Marine detachment, and major Navy shore stations boasted Marine barracks or detachments for security purposes, although with reductions in Marine Corps end strength this is no longer universally the case. On the other hand, to this day Navy units such as Seabees, naval beach groups, and so on are frequently assigned to Marine Corps Forces.

At higher levels, the Marine Corps Forces (see Section 611) best exemplify the close relationship between the Marine Corps and Navy. Here we have major Marine Operating Forces assigned by the Secretary of the Navy on a continuing basis to duty with the fleets, and, while so assigned, operationally under the CNO, just as much part of a fleet as its ships or aircraft. Side by side with this operational relationship, however, the commandant of the Marine Corps retains full control over the administration, readiness, and military efficiency of the units concerned. And all hands, Marine Corps and Navy, are governed alike by Navy Regulations.

In the words of former Secretary of the Navy Robert B. Anderson, "They are, in every sense of the word, a team."

504. Summary

The missions and status of the Marine Corps are prescribed in the National Security Act as amended. Public Laws 432 (80th Congress) and 416 (82d Congress) supplement and affirm the National Security Act, as does "The Functions Paper" (even though without statutory standing). For a detailed discussion and analysis of the tortured struggle of the Corps to achieve its statutory position, read the lively chapters of Lieutenant General Victor H. Krulak in his *First to Fight*, published by the Naval Institute Press.

The status of the Marine Corps within the Department of the Navy can best be summarized in the words of Vice Admiral O. W. Colclough, while judge advocate general of the Navy: "The Marine Corps has been held for years to be a separate Service, although it operates with the Navy, and under the Secretary of the Navy."

Over and above its usual status and duties within the naval framework, the Marine Corps may be, and frequently has been, assigned other duties and status elsewhere in the executive branch, under the plenary powers that the president possesses with regard to the Corps.

In the vast complex of the Department of Defense, the Marine Corps plays a lonely role.

—The Honorable John Nicholas Brown

6

ORGANIZATION OF THE MARINE CORPS

Major General W. S. "Bigfoot" Brown, one of the Corps' most beloved old-timers, began a lecture at a service school with these words: "Well, gentlemen, they've given me the job of describing the organization of the Marine Corps. This surprised me somewhat, because I never knew we had any organization." Despite this prologue, the Marine Corps does have an organization (see Figure 6-1), and comprehensive knowledge of this organization is one of the first things a Marine officer must acquire.

The Marine Corps, within the Department of the Navy, is organized as a general purpose "force in readiness" to support national needs. Deploying for combat as combined-arms Marine air-ground task forces (MAGTFs), the Marine Corps provides the National Command Authorities (NCA) with a responsive force that can conduct operations across the spectrum of conflict.

601. General Organization and Chain of Command

Two parallel chains of command—service and operational—exist within the Marine Corps. The service chain begins with the president and progresses sequentially through the secretary of defense, Secretary of the Navy, and commandant of the Marine Corps. The operational chain runs from the NCA (see Section 301) directly to commanders of combatant commands (COCOMs) for missions and forces, including Marine Corps forces, assigned to their commands. Marine Corps component commanders provide operational forces to the COCOMs and other operational commanders as required.

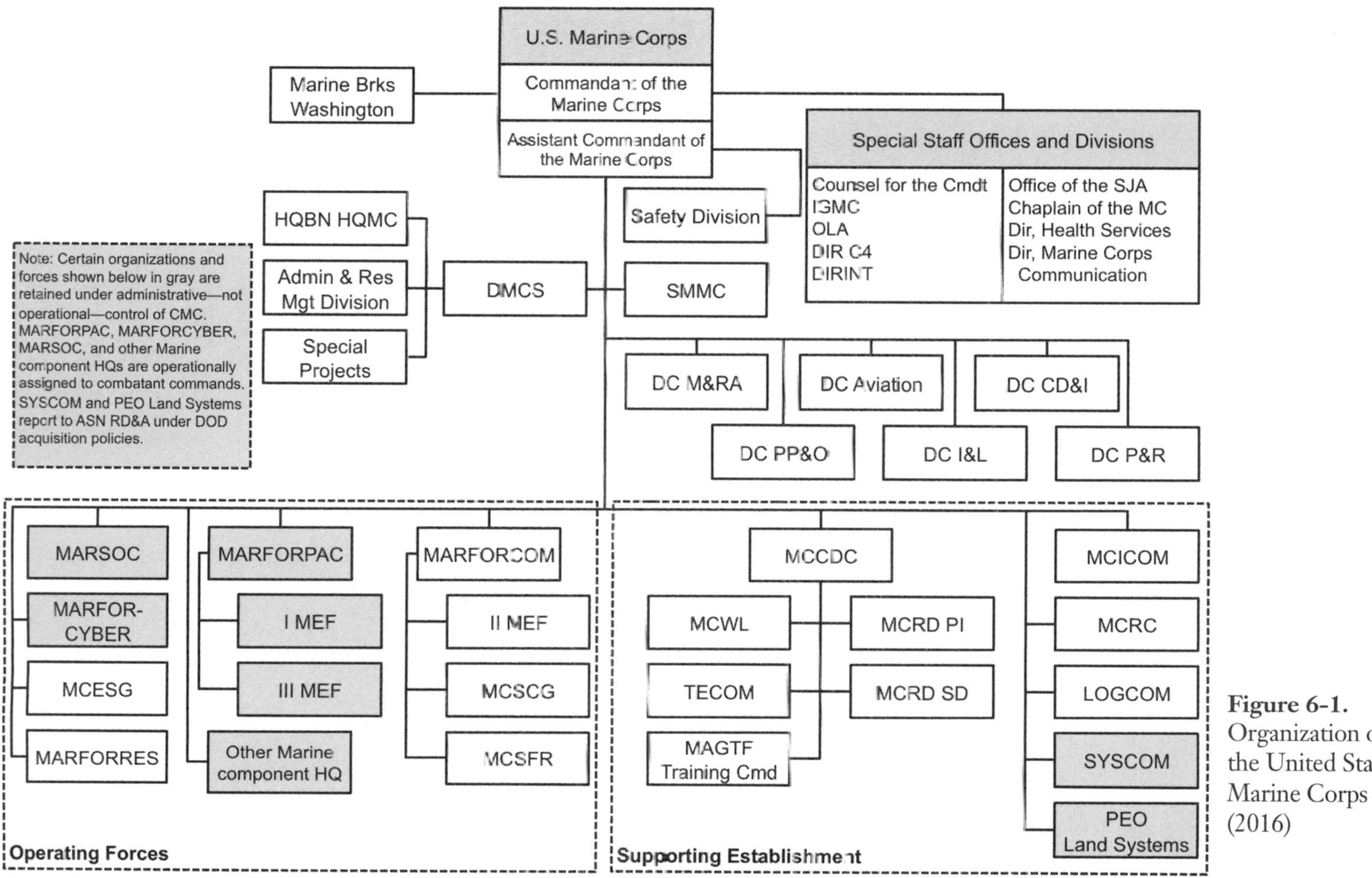

Figure 6-1. Organization of the United States Marine Corps (2016)

The Marine Corps is made up of land combat, combat support, combat service support, and security forces; aviation combat and support forces; and reserve forces. In many ways, the organization of the Corps resembles that of the Navy. The Marine Corps is organized in three broad categories: Marine Corps Headquarters and supporting activities, Marine Corps Operating Forces (both active and reserve), and Marine Corps Supporting Establishment.

Throughout these categories, Marine Corps aviation is included as necessary to carry out the missions of the Corps.

The complete organization of the Marine Corps is detailed in the most current version of Marine Corps Reference Publication 5-12, *Organization of the United States Marine Corps*, which contains an extensive and authoritative discussion of this chapter's topic and is available online.

MARINE CORPS HEADQUARTERS

602. Headquarters, U.S. Marine Corps

Headquarters, U.S. Marine Corps (HQMC) in Washington, D.C., is the executive part of the Corps. HQMC consists of the commandant of the Marine Corps, assistant commandant of the Marine Corps, deputy commandants, staff judge advocate to the commandant, directors, other members of the Navy and Marine Corps assigned or detailed to HQMC, and civilian employees in the Department of the Navy assigned or detailed to HQMC. HQMC is distributed among the Pentagon, Henderson Hall (located on Joint Base Myer-Henderson Hall), Marine Barracks Washington, Marine Corps Base Quantico, and the Washington Navy Yard.

Marine Corps Headquarters is divided (from largest to smallest) into departments, each led by a deputy commandant (DC) in the grade of lieutenant general; divisions, typically led by a major general, brigadier general, or civilian member of the Senior Executive Service; branches, typically led by a colonel or federal civil servant (in the grade of GS-15); sections; and units. Figure 6-1 provides a high-level depiction of the organization of Marine Corps Headquarters together with its relationships with the field activities of the Marine Corps.

Under the authority, direction, and control of the commandant of the Marine Corps (CMC), HQMC prepares for the employment of Marine Corps forces and orchestrates the recruiting, organizing, supplying, equipping, training, servicing, mobilizing, demobilizing, administering, and maintaining of the Marine Corps. HQMC assists in the execution of any power, duty, or function of the CMC. The function, composition, and general duties of HQMC are defined in Title 10, U.S. Code, Subtitle C, Part I, Chapter 506, *Headquarters, Marine Corps.*

603. Commandant of the Marine Corps

The *commandant of the Marine Corps,* reporting to the Secretary of the Navy, leads the Marine Corps, as well as Marine Corps Headquarters. One commandant defined his responsibilities in these simple terms: "I want each of you to feel that the Commandant of the Corps is your friend and that he earnestly desires that you should realize this. At the same time, it is his duty to the Government and to the Marine Corps to exact a high standard of conduct, a strict performance of duty, and a rigid compliance with orders."

Phrasing those responsibilities today, we can say that the commandant is directly responsible to the Secretary of the Navy for the readiness, total performance, and administration of the Marine Corps as a whole, including the Reserve. He commands all Marine forces and activities except those specifically assigned to the naval Operating Forces, unified commands, or elsewhere. For the readiness and performance of those elements of the Marine Corps assigned to the Operating Forces of the Navy, the commandant is also responsible to the chief of naval operations.

With the advice and consent of the Senate, the president appoints the commandant from among the active general officers of the Corps for a four-year term. He holds the rank of general. Under certain conditions, the commandant may be reappointed for more than four years. Archibald Henderson, fifth commandant, has the record—thirty-nine years.

As detailed in Section 409, the principal duties of the commandant extend, but are not limited, to procurement, discharge, education, training (individual and unit), and distribution of the officers and enlisted personnel of the Corps; all matters of command and discipline; and capabilities, requirements, readiness, organization, administration, equipment, and supply of Marine Corps organizations and units. Appendix II contains a list of the commandants from the Marine Corps' inception to the present.

604. Assistant Commandant of the Marine Corps

The *assistant commandant of the Marine Corps* (ACMC) is a general, and the second highest ranking officer in the Marine Corps, who discharges the duties of the commandant during the latter's absence or disability and performs such duties as the CMC may direct. For example, because of the vital importance to the force of operational risk management and safety, the CMC has directed that the ACMC directly supervise the activities of the Safety Division within Marine Corps Headquarters.

605. Director, Marine Corps Staff

The *director of the Marine Corps staff* (DMCS), either a major general or lieutenant general, is the commandant's executive officer. He or she directs, supervises, and coordinates staff activities of Marine Corps Headquarters. In the commandant's absence, the DMCS also performs the duties of the ACMC while the ACMC performs the duties of the CMC.

606. Deputy Commandants

There are six deputy commandants (formerly called deputy chiefs of staff) who lead HQMC departments, most of them situated in the Pentagon, and assist the CMC in managing the day-to-day affairs of HQMC. Their responsibilities within specific functional areas are summarized in the following paragraphs.

The *deputy commandant for manpower and reserve affairs* (DC M&RA), a lieutenant general, has cognizance over matters related to manpower assignment, planning, programming, and budgeting policies; manpower information systems; military and civilian manpower management and administration; equal opportunity policies, programs, and activities; civilian personnel policy; Marine and family programs; the Semper Fit program and exchange services; and assignment and distribution of reserve component military assets. The office of the DC M&RA is situated at Marine Corps Base Quantico, Virginia.

The *deputy commandant for plans, policies, and operations* (DC PP&O), a lieutenant general, is the operations deputy for the CMC; is responsible for coordinating the development and execution of service plans and policies related to the structure, deployment, and employment of Marine Corps forces in general; serves as the focal point for the interface between the Marine Corps and the joint and combined activities of the Joint Chiefs of Staff, combatant commands, and various allied and other foreign defense agencies; has cognizance over unit training and readiness, amphibious doctrine, and other doctrinal and policy matters; and acts for the DMCS in his or her absence.

The *deputy commandant for aviation* (DC Aviation), a lieutenant general, has cognizance over matters related to Marine Corps aviation. The DC Aviation is responsible to develop, integrate, and supervise plans, policies, and budgets for all aviation assets and aviation expeditionary enablers (for example, aviation command and control, aviation ground support, and unmanned aviation systems). On behalf of the CMC, the DC Aviation exercises staff supervision over the activities of Marine Helicopter Squadron One, which provides helicopter transportation and contingency support for the president of the United States, vice president of the United States, members of the president's cabinet, and foreign dignitaries, and supports planning, execution, and reporting for independent operational test and evaluation of helicopters and related systems.

The *deputy commandant for installations and logistics* (DC I&L), a lieutenant general, has cognizance over matters related to logistic plans, policy, and management; contracting policy and contract management; and facilities and installations.

The *deputy commandant for combat development and integration* (DC CD&I), a lieutenant general, commands the Marine Corps Combat Development Command and holds staff responsibility for analysis, development, and integration of Marine Corps warfighting capabilities, including development of future operational concepts and determination of how to best organize, train, and equip the Marine Corps of the future.

The *deputy commandant for programs and resources* (DC P&R), a lieutenant general, has cognizance over Marine Corps fiscal requirements; fiscal planning, programming, and budgeting; and systems and cost analysis. This officer also represents the Marine Corps in certain external functions related to these areas of cognizance.

607. Special Staff and Directors

There are several additional important positions at HQMC with which you should be familiar.

Sergeant Major of the Marine Corps (SMMC). The sergeant major is the senior noncommissioned officer of the Corps and, by virtue of this billet, is senior to all other enlisted Marines. This noncommissioned officer (NCO) advises and assists the commandant in all matters relating to enlisted Marines, as well as other matters within his or her cognizance.

Counsel for the Commandant of the Marine Corps. The counsel, through the main office and field offices, provides comprehensive legal advice and support to the commandant, headquarters staff agencies, and the Marine Corps Operating Forces and Supporting Establishment in the areas of business and commercial law, including environmental law, land use, civilian personnel law, procurement and fiscal law, government ethics, and all other matters under the cognizance of the general counsel of the Navy.

Chaplain of the Marine Corps. The Navy's deputy chief of chaplains serves as chaplain of the Marine Corps, advising the CMC on religious ministry matters in reference to personnel, plans, programs, policies, support, and facilities within the Marine Corps.

Medical Officer of the Marine Corps. This officer advises the CMC and HQMC staff on all matters regarding health care and serves as the functional expert in working with the appropriate HQMC agencies for determining health service and field medical requirements, doctrine, policies, procedures, and programs.

Legislative Assistant to the Commandant of the Marine Corps. This assistant, normally a brigadier general, is the commandant's principal adviser in legislative matters, including liaison with Congress. He or she prepares comments on legislative proposals referred to, or affecting, the Marine Corps (except cases in the province of the DC P&R).

Inspector General. The inspector general (IG) reports to the naval IG, the commandant, and the Secretary of the Navy as a deputy naval IG for Marine Corps matters. It is the inspector general's eagle-eyed responsibility to conduct inspections and investigations as directed by the commandant; to coordinate the readiness programs of the Marine Corps; and to maintain liaison with the inspection agencies of the other defense agencies. It is worth comment at this point that, although an "IG inspection" invariably begets trepidation and soul-searching, the mission of the inspector general is to help and to improve by constructive inspection.

Director, Special Projects. Working under the cognizance of the director of the Marine Corps Staff, this director plans, supports, and conducts events, conferences, symposia, and foreign visits and prepares speeches and articles for the CMC, the ACMC, the SMMC, or as directed by the DMCS.

Director, Headquarters Support. The director has cognizance over administration and management services for HQMC, headquarters security, transportation, internal communications services, and military and civilian personnel for the headquarters.

Director, Command, Control, Communications, and Computers Division. The director, a brigadier general, has cognizance over all Marine Corps automated information systems and programs, command and control systems, and telecommunications and communications security.

Director of Intelligence. The director, a brigadier general, has cognizance over intelligence, counterintelligence, cryptology, and electronic warfare and, as a service intelligence chief, maintains liaison with other government intelligence agencies. He or she also disseminates intelligence information within HQMC.

Director, Judge Advocate Division. The director, normally a major general, serves as staff judge advocate for the commandant and has cognizance over all legal matters (except certain questions of business or budgetary law, which fall to the legal counsel or to the fiscal director).

Director, Office of Marine Corps Communication. The director (formerly the director of public affairs), a brigadier general, heads the Office of Marine Corps Communication. It is his or her delicate, exacting, and sometimes thankless job to represent the Marine Corps to the public. The director is responsible to plan, coordinate, and implement communication strategies designed to build understanding, credibility, trust, and mutually beneficial relationships with domestic and foreign publics. He or she maintains liaison with Defense Department and other government public affairs agencies, and with national public affairs and news media. The director also represents the Marine Corps within the entertainment and publishing industries; manages doctrine, organization, training, matériel, leadership and education, personnel, and facilities issues that affect Marine Corps communication; controls the trademark and licensing activities for the Marine Corps; and exercises staff supervision over Marine Corps field activities that disseminate public affairs information.

Director, Office of Expeditionary Energy. The director of expeditionary energy, a colonel, serves as the CMC's principal adviser on expeditionary energy and resource matters. At its inception, the office was aligned directly under the ACMC. Once the office was well established, however, the director began reporting to the DC CD&I. The director analyzes, develops, and directs the Marine Corps energy strategy to optimize expeditionary capabilities across all warfighting functions.

Director, Safety Division. The director of safety, a colonel, is the senior adviser to the CMC and ACMC for all safety matters and reports directly to the ACMC. The director aims to enhance the Marine Corps' consistent posture of combat readiness by aligning doctrine and policy with risk management principles in order to foster a climate and culture of force preservation.

608. Manpower and Reserve Affairs Department

Of all the agencies in Marine Corps Headquarters, this department has more directly to do with you on an enduring basis than any other throughout your career.

Manpower selects and "procures" you (just as it recruits enlisted Marines). It gives you your commission and administers you from the moment you are sworn in until you rest beneath the trees in Arlington National Cemetery. Manpower assigns you, manages your career, promotes you, and retires you. With one hand, if need be, it disciplines you, while with the other it attends to your welfare. It maintains your records at Marine Corps Headquarters, as it maintains similar records on every officer and enlisted Marine in the Corps. If you become a casualty, Manpower notifies your next of kin, gives you your Purple Heart, and sees that you get the decorations and medals you have earned. Should you have a claim against the government, Manpower adjudicates.

MARINE CORPS OPERATING FORCES

609. Overview

Operating Forces are the heart of the Marine Corps. They provide the forward presence, crisis response, and combat power that the Corps makes available to combatant commanders. The majority of Marine Corps Operating Forces are held in five permanent commands, all headquartered in the United States:

1. U.S. Marine Corps Forces Command (MARFORCOM)
2. U.S. Marine Corps Forces Pacific (MARFORPAC)
3. U.S. Marine Corps Forces Reserve (MARFORRES)
4. U.S. Marine Corps Forces Special Operations Command (MARSOC)
5. U.S. Marine Corps Forces Cyberspace (MARFORCYBER).

Before drilling into the details of some of these commands and discussing how the Operating Forces actually organize to conduct military operations, it is important to introduce the concept of componency.

610. Componency and Marine Corps Components

As discussed in Chapter 3, the president of the United States establishes unified combatant commands to execute broad and continuing missions at the strategic level using forces of two or more military departments. Combatant commands typically have geographic responsibilities (for example, USEUCOM, with responsibility for military operations in the specifically delineated European theater) or functional responsibilities (for example, USTRANSCOM, with responsibility for strategic transportation and distribution supporting the whole of DOD). The combatant commander exercises command authority over his or her assigned forces.

Combatant commands normally include subordinate service component commands (that is, Army, Marine Corps, Navy, and Air Force components). Service component commanders organize their forces to accomplish missions assigned by the combatant commander. Service component commanders normally exercise operational control (OPCON) of forces assigned or attached to their COCOM, or they may be limited under certain circumstances to only tactical or administrative control of these forces. The Marine Corps component commander is responsible to accomplish assigned missions, provide forces, and perform operational-level administrative and logistical tasks on behalf of or in support of assigned or attached Marine Corps forces.

Marine Corps Operating Forces are generally assigned to COCOMs by the Secretary of the Navy through the annual secretary of defense's *Forces for Unified Commands* memorandum, published in the *Global Force Management Implementation Guidance.* With the disestablishment of U.S. Joint Forces Command, some operational forces are retained within the operational control of the services until assigned to a specific COCOM for a specific mission.

6-1. The Marine Corps Forces constitute the cutting edge of America's amphibious assault potential.

611. Marine Corps Forces

The Marine Corps organizes MAGTFs from forces that are organizationally situated within the straightforwardly named Marine Corps Forces (MARFORs) assigned to a specific combatant command, where they function as the service component command, or retained by the Marine Corps under the CMC and available for missions globally. MARFORs constitute a balanced force of combined arms, including aviation. They consist of a headquarters group, comprising command and control, service and support, and other specialized capabilities; one or more Marine divisions or brigades; one or more Marine aircraft wings; and one or more Marine logistic groups. MARFORs are organized, trained, and equipped as Marine air-ground task forces for:

- Service with the unified commands in seizure and defense of advanced bases, and for land operations related to naval campaigns
- Development of amphibious tactics, techniques, and equipment
- Training the maximum number of Marines for war or emergency expansion
- Immediate expeditionary service where, when, and as directed.

Collectively, the active component MARFORs today include three headquarters groups, three combat divisions, three aircraft wings, and three logistic groups. Based on combat experience, the ratio of one aircraft wing to support one Marine division is the fundamental proportion in the Marine air-ground-logistics team.

U.S. Marine Corps Forces Command. The Marine Corps retains control of MARFORCOM, headquartered in Norfolk, Virginia. The CMC, via the Joint Chiefs of Staff global force management process, maintains II MEF and other unique capabilities under the Commander, MARFORCOM.

U.S. Marine Corps Forces Pacific. The Commander, MARFORPAC is assigned to the Commander, USPACOM, functions as the Marine service component commander for USPACOM, and provides I MEF and III MEF to USPACOM. The MARFORPAC headquarters is in Honolulu, Hawaii.

U.S. Marine Corps Forces Reserve. MARFORRES, headquartered in New Orleans, Louisiana, maintains trained reserve units and qualified reservists for active duty service in times of war, national emergency, or in support of contingency operations. The Commander, MARFORRES also functions as the service component commander for USNORTHCOM.

U.S. Marine Corps Forces, Special Operations Command. The Commander, MARSOC is assigned to the Commander, USSOCOM and provides assigned forces to USSOCOM. The MARSOC headquarters is located at Camp Lejeune, North Carolina.

U.S. Marine Corps Forces Cyberspace. Finally, the Commander, MARFOR-CYBER is assigned to the Commander, USCYBERCOM, which is a subunified command under USSTRATCOM. The MARFORCYBER headquarters is situated near Fort Meade, Maryland.

These assignments reflect the peacetime disposition of our Corps' Operating Forces. The majority of the Marine Corps' Operating Forces reside in one of the five aforementioned MARFORs. Marine forces are allocated for contingency planning to the remaining geographic and functional combatant commands: USSOUTHCOM, USCENTCOM, USEUCOM, USAFRICOM, USSTRATCOM, and U.S. Forces Korea (USFK). The secretary of defense provides Marine forces to these commands as required to meet the demands of theater security cooperation, forward presence, and crisis response.

It is worth mentioning here that there are additional MARFORs, but unlike the five already detailed, they are typically headquarters with few, if any, significant forces assigned *on a permanent basis.* These include U.S. Marine Corps Forces South, which is designated as the Marine Corps service component for USSOUTHCOM; U.S. Marine Corps Forces Central Command, for USCENTCOM; U.S. Marine Corps Forces Europe and Africa, for USEUCOM and USAFRICOM; U.S. Marine Corps Forces Strategic Command, for USSTRATCOM; and U.S. Marine Corps Forces Korea, for USFK and United Nations Command.

When Marine Corps units are assigned to the unified commands or to the Operating Forces of the Navy, they report to the senior Marine Corps commander. For the unified command, the MARFOR component commander (COMMARFOR) exercises operational control. That operational control does not include the administration and training responsibilities, which remain under the commandant of the Marine Corps. COMMARFORs have important strategic and budgetary planning activities, under the unified commanders, that contribute substantially to the determination of the size and composition of the Marine Corps' Operating Forces in total.

612. Marine Air-Ground Task Force

The Marine Corps normally organizes and employs its Operating Forces as Marine air-ground task forces, which are integrated, combined arms teams that include air, ground, and logistical units under a single commander, thereby obtaining unity of command and effort. MAGTFs are the fundamental building blocks of the Operating Forces and are the means by which the Marine Corps reliably delivers the National Command Authorities and combatant commanders an operational capability that is rapidly deployable, responsive, versatile, flexible, expandable, and sustainable. MAGTFs are organized, trained, and equipped primarily from the forces of MARFORCOM, MARFORPAC, and MARFORRES. As depicted in Figure 6-2, a MAGTF normally comprises four principal elements: a command element, ground combat element, aviation combat element, and logistic combat element.

The command element (CE) is the MAGTF headquarters. It comprises the commander and a headquarters with an executive and special staff, command and control capabilities, and service support capabilities. The establish-

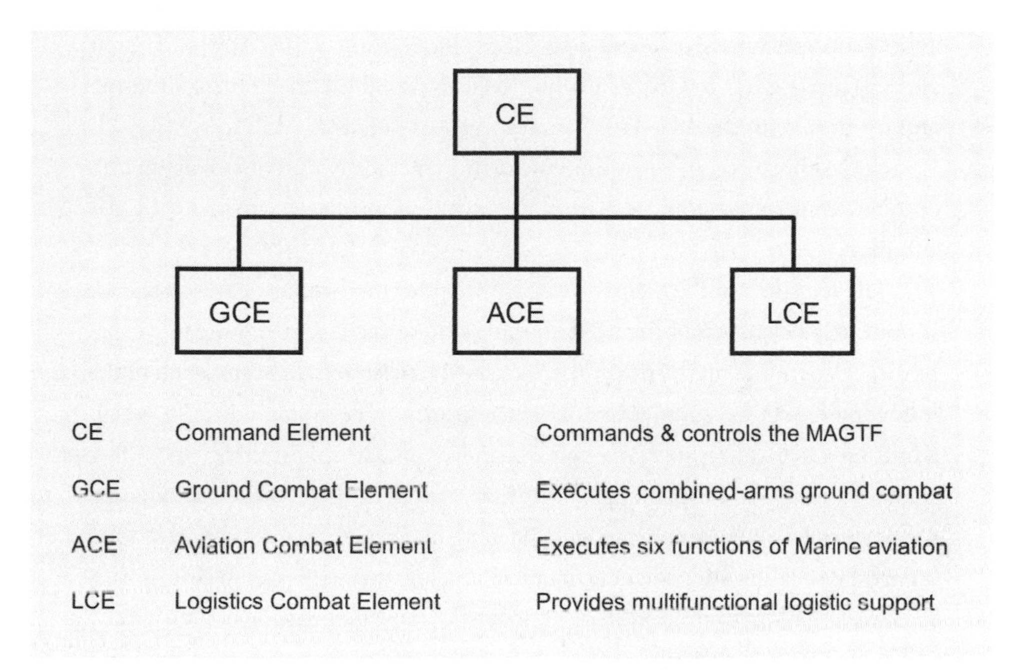

Figure 6-2. Generic Marine Air-Ground Task Force (MAGTF)

ment of a single headquarters over the ground, aviation, and logistic elements provides the command, control, and coordination capability essential for effective planning and execution of operations. In amphibious operations, when Marines constitute the preponderant force, the MAGTF command element serves also as the landing force headquarters. Also capable of operating as the core of a joint task force (JTF) headquarters, the CE enables the MAGTF commander to be appointed JTF or expeditionary strike group commander as well, exercising tactical control over both the embarked MAGTF and the associated elements of other services.

The ground combat element (GCE) is a task organization tailored, as the name implies, for the conduct of ground combat. It is constructed around a ground combat infantry unit and varies in size from a reinforced battalion to a reinforced Marine division or divisions. The GCE also includes appropriate organic combat support and combat service support units. Normally, there is only one GCE in a MAGTF.

The aviation combat element (ACE) is task-organized to fulfill the six functions of Marine aviation. These functions—air reconnaissance, anti-air warfare, assault support, offensive air support, electronic warfare, and control of aircraft and missiles—are provided in varying degrees based on the tactical situation and on the size of the MAGTF. Usually, there is only one ACE in a MAGTF. It includes those organic aviation command (including air control agencies), combat, combat support, and combat service support units required by the situation.

The logistic combat element (LCE) provides the primary combat service support to all elements of the MAGTF in excess of each element's organic capabilities. Depending on the mission, it is task-organized to satisfy any or all of the following functions: supply; maintenance; transportation, including material-handling and landing support; combat and deliberate engineering, including limited construction capabilities; health services, including medical and dental support; military police; automated data processing; personnel services; food services; disbursing support; and financial management. It is capable of providing smaller task organizations for support of MAGTF operations as required.

The Marine air-ground task force is unique to the Corps. It is trained and equipped not only for expeditionary operations and amphibious warfare but also for a variety of combat and noncombat situations. Its structure and its emphasis on strategic mobility make the MAGTF exceptionally useful in a wide array of crises. Its organization by task enables the commander to tailor the force to a specific contingency. The MAGTF can fight well and harmoniously within a joint or combined task force in a land campaign or provide a one-service force of combined arms for a variety of situations.

When employed in other than amphibious operations, MAGTFs are capable of functioning as self-sustaining forces under the operational command of the unified, subunified, or joint task force commander. Their organization and training for amphibious warfare, which the Marine Corps pioneered and continues to perfect, enhance their capability to deploy rapidly by any means.

There are permanent MAGTFs (for example, a standing Marine expeditionary force), but the MAGTF is not necessarily a permanent organization; it is often task-organized for a specific mission and, after completion of that mission, is dissolved in accordance with prearranged plans. A MAGTF headquarters is structured to control whatever forces are assigned; thus, the Marine Corps can rapidly converge forces from any or all of its base locations to form a composite MAGTF without regard for parent administrative organization.

The current and planned uses of Marine air-ground task forces reflect an understanding by the NCA of the unique role expeditionary and amphibious operations can play in a limited or worldwide war. To provide a peacetime presence and rapid response capability that contributes to deterrence and forward defense strategy, Marine expeditionary units (described below) are continuously deployed on amphibious ships in the waters of the Mediterranean Sea, Arabian Sea, Persian Gulf, and Pacific Ocean, and they routinely visit the littoral areas of the Caribbean Sea and Indian Ocean.

Deployed MAGTFs provide the means to rapidly project U.S. power in support of vital U.S. interests anywhere in the world. Able to move on and be supported from the sea, MAGTFs, with associated amphibious shipping and carrier battle groups, are free from dependence on basing or overflight rights and provide an effective force presence without political commitment. During peacetime, they provide assurance to our allies and demonstrate resolve to our adversaries.

To shorten response times, expand strategic options, and reduce strategic life requirements, the Marine Corps has prepositioned equipment and supplies both afloat and ashore in or near potential crisis areas. The prepositioning of matériel for use by MAGTFs led, beginning in the 1980s, to a renewed emphasis on airlifting Marine combat forces to marry up with that equipment, and this deployment option continues to receive emphasis today. Deploying MAGTFs by amphibious warship is often the preferred method; the Marine Corps, however, endorses airlift as an alternative for rapid deployment of its forces in situations permitting nonhostile entry. Additionally, the Marine Corps is beginning to explore the feasibility of deploying Marine forces by multiple means to a "distributed" sea base composed of amphibious warships, combat logistic force ships, and other alternative or nontraditional naval platforms.

Although a MAGTF is a task organization tailored to accomplish a specific mission, there are three standard types of MAGTFs: the Marine expeditionary unit (MEU), the Marine expeditionary brigade (MEB), and the Marine expeditionary force (MEF). There is also the designation of special purpose MAGTF (SPMAGTF) for any unit smaller than the nominal MEU.

Marine Expeditionary Unit. The MEU is the standard, forward-deployed Marine air-ground task force (see Figure 6-3). The MEU's mission is to provide the NCA and COCOMs with a forward-deployed, sea-based, rapid-response

6-2. The MAGTF integrates the power of Marine Corps ground, aviation, and logistic units.

capability to execute a full range of military operations. The MEU is commanded by a colonel. It is a self-contained, general-purpose operating force capable of a range of military missions of limited scope and duration, including selected maritime special operations such as reconnaissance and surveillance; tactical recovery of aircraft and personnel; seizure/recovery of selected personnel or matériel; and visit, board, search, and seizure of vessels. The MEU typically numbers approximately 2,200 Marines and sailors and may be viewed as a forward-deployed extension of the MEB or MEF.

There are seven MEUs: the 11th, 13th, and 15th MEUs are sourced from I MEF; the 22nd, 24th, and 26th MEUs are sourced from II MEF; and the 31st MEU is part of III MEF. These MEUs deploy from their home bases on a rotational basis to conduct forward presence, theater engagement, and crisis response operations in the regions of the Mediterranean Sea, Pacific Ocean, Indian Ocean, or Arabian Gulf. Each MEU is task-organized with up to fifteen days of sustainment and includes:

- A standing CE
- A GCE, known as a battalion landing team, consisting of an infantry battalion reinforced with artillery, reconnaissance, engineer, armor, light armored reconnaissance, and assault amphibian units, and other detachments as required
- An ACE, known as a composite squadron, built around a Marine medium tiltrotor squadron reinforced with detachments from a Marine heavy helicopter squadron, Marine light attack helicopter squadron, Marine attack squadron, Marine unmanned aerial vehicle squadron, Marine air traffic control detachment, Marine wing support squadron, and Marine aviation logistics squadron
- An LCE consisting of a combat logistic battalion organized to provide the MEU's other elements multifunctional combat service support, encompassing supply, maintenance, transportation, engineering, health services, and other services.

The MEU undergoes an intensive twenty-six-week standardized predeployment training program. To gain certification, the unit must demonstrate competence across a range of designated capabilities, be able to plan and execute any assigned mission within six hours of notification, and be able to conduct multiple missions simultaneously.

Embarked aboard the ships of a Navy amphibious ready group, a deployed MEU provides a COCOM or other operational commander with a quick, versatile, sea-based reaction force. In many cases, the MEU embarked on amphibious warships may be the first U.S. force at the scene of a crisis, and it can conduct enabling actions for larger follow-on forces.

Marine Expeditionary Brigade. The MEB is a mid-sized Marine air-ground task force that accomplishes larger, more demanding operational missions than the MEU (see Figure 6-4). The MEB's mission is to conduct major security cooperation operations, respond to larger crises or contingencies, or participate

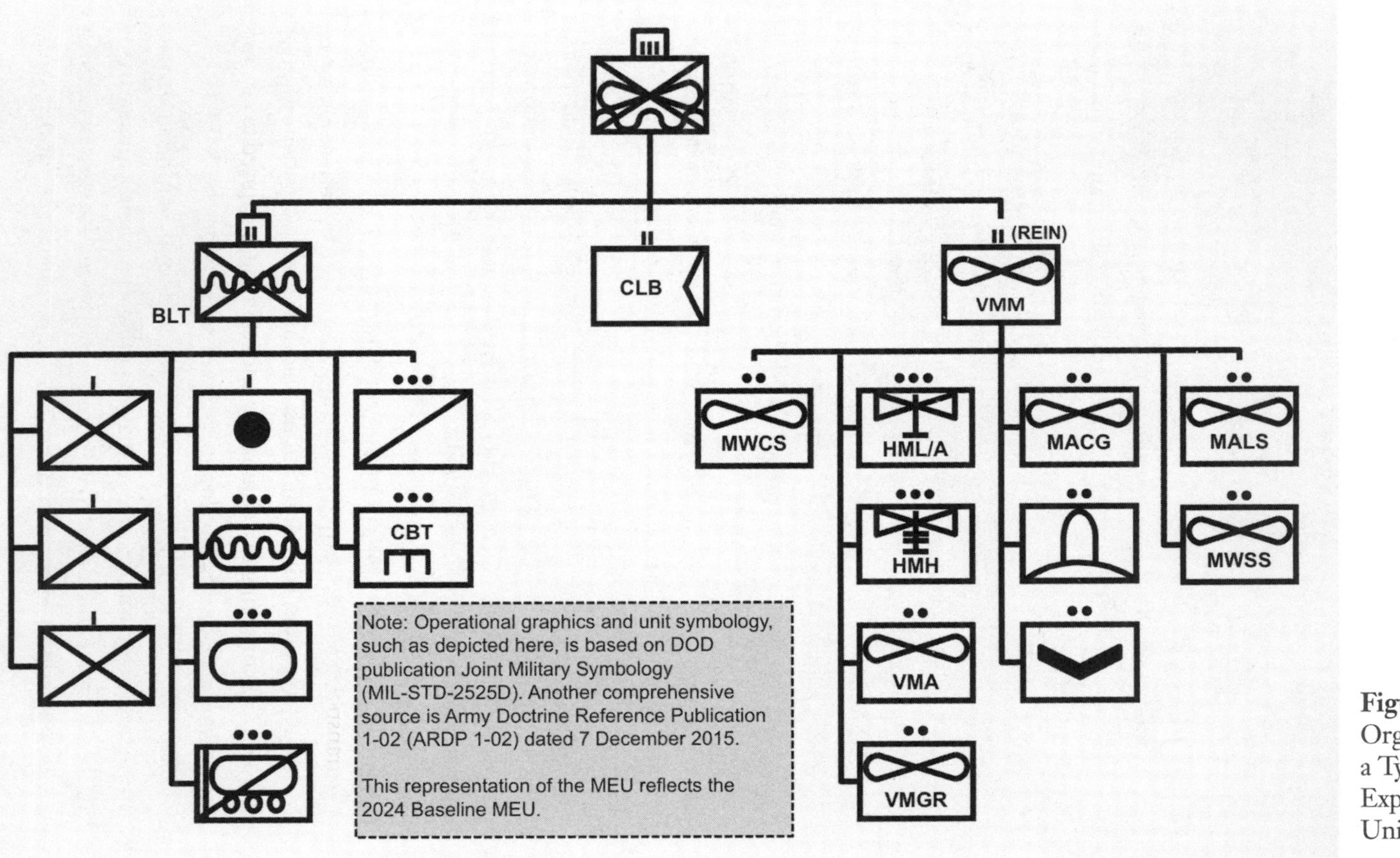

Figure 6-3. Organization of a Typical Marine Expeditionary Unit (MEU)

in major operations and campaigns. A brigadier general normally commands the MEB. Marine expeditionary brigades provide the building blocks for forcible entry and other power projection operations, the landing forces for amphibious assault, and the fly-in echelons that marry up with prepositioned equipment and supplies. Although the MEB varies in composition according to the mission, it typically numbers upward of 15,000 Marines and sailors.

There are three standing MEB command elements: the 1st MEB is embedded in the I MEF staff, while 2nd and 3rd MEBs are stand-alone organizations contained in II MEF and III MEF, respectively. These standing MEB CEs do not all have permanently assigned forces; instead, they maintain habitual relationships with associated Marine divisions, air wings, and logistic groups through planning and exercises. When formed and mobilized, the MEB is capable of full-spectrum operations and self-sustainment for thirty days, and it comprises:

- A CE, which is also uniquely staffed and equipped to form the nucleus of a JTF headquarters
- A GCE, known as a regimental landing team or regimental combat team, depending on the operational situation, and comprising an infantry regiment reinforced with artillery, reconnaissance, engineer, armor, light armored reconnaissance, and assault amphibian units, and other detachments as required
- An ACE, normally known as a provisional air group and consisting of combat assault transport helicopter/tiltrotor aircraft, utility and attack helicopters, fixed-wing attack vertical and/or short takeoff and landing aircraft, fighter/attack aircraft, unmanned aircraft systems, air refueler/transport aircraft, and requisite aviation logistical and command, control, computers, communications, and intelligence capabilities
- An LCE consisting of a combat logistic regiment organized from components of the Marine logistics group to provide the MEB's other elements with multifunctional combat service support, encompassing supply, maintenance, transportation—including landing support for beach, port, and airfield delivery operations—deliberate engineering, health services, and other services.

As an expeditionary force, the MEB is capable of rapid deployment and employment via amphibious shipping, strategic airlift marrying up with maritime prepositioning force assets, or any combination thereof. If the scope of operations expands beyond the capability of the MEB, additional forces can readily deploy to expand to a MEF. Thus, the MEB may become—and is usually regarded as—the forward echelon of the MEF.

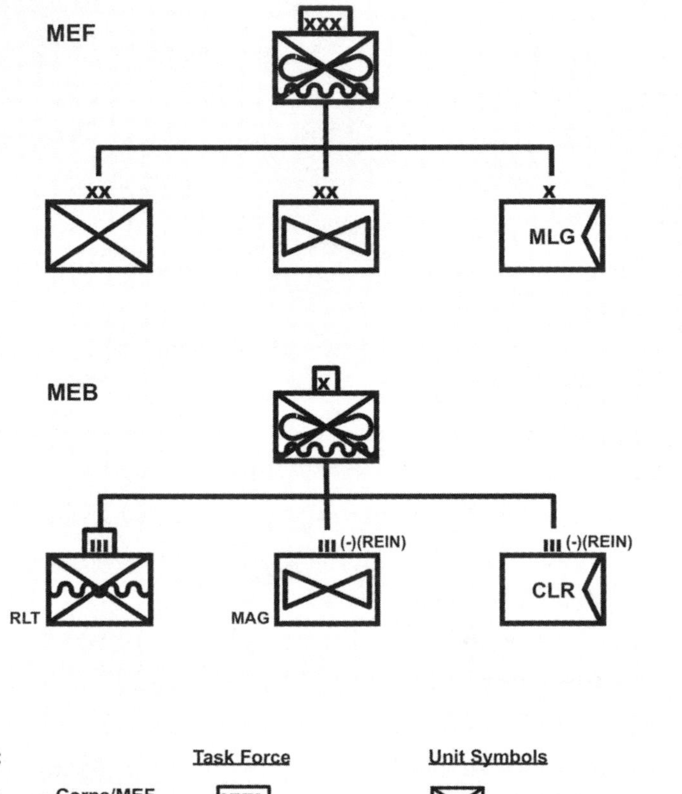

Figure 6-4. Organization of a Typical Marine Expeditionary Brigade (MEB) and Marine Expeditionary Force (MEF)

Marine Expeditionary Force. The MEF is the Marine Corps' largest, most capable, and principal warfighting MAGTF (see Figure 6-4). It is capable of missions across a range of military operations, to include amphibious assault and sustained operations ashore in any environment. The MEF is commanded by a lieutenant general. With appropriate augmentation, the MEF CE is capable of performing as a JTF headquarters. It varies in size, but the MEF can number upward of forty thousand Marines and sailors.

There are three standing MEFs: I MEF, assigned to MARFORPAC and based in southern California and Arizona; II MEF, assigned to MARFORCOM and based in Virginia, North Carolina, and South Carolina; and III MEF, assigned to MARFORPAC and based in Japan and Hawaii. Each standing MEF consists of a permanent CE, including a MEF headquarters group; a permanent GCE, which is one Marine division (MARDIV); a permanent ACE, one Marine aircraft wing (MAW); and a permanent LCE, one Marine logistics group (MLG). These major subordinate commands constitute the primary reservoir of combat, combat support, and combat service support capabilities from which other MAGTFs are sourced.

Special Purpose Marine Air-Ground Task Force. A SPMAGTF is a MAGTF formed to conduct a specific mission, normally when one of the three aforementioned MAGTFs is either inappropriate or unavailable. A SPMAGTF is organized, trained, and equipped to conduct a wide variety of missions that include crisis response, regionally focused training exercises, and peacetime missions.

The MAGTF may be seen as the culmination of over one hundred years of U.S. Marine Corps evolution from a ships' police force to a standing ready force. Its genesis lies in the Huntington Battalion of 1898 (Guantánamo), modified by the development of the air weapon, the Pacific War of 1941–45, and joint forces and combined-arms experiences since the Korean War.

613. Major Subordinate Commands

The Marine expeditionary force is the principal Marine Corps warfighting organization and the principal (though not, as you will see, exclusive) repository of the Marine Corps' Operating Forces. Within each MEF, these forces are held in one of four major subordinate commands (MSCs):

1. MEF headquarters group
2. Marine division
3. Marine air wing
4. Marine logistics group.

Each MSC fulfills a unique role in the MEF and thus has a unique mission and set of characteristics.

6-3. Navy high-speed surface connectors, in this case the landing craft, air cushion (LCAC), impart higher speeds and greater tactical options to the conduct of amphibious operations by MAGTFs.

Marine Expeditionary Force Headquarters Group (MHG). The mission of the MHG is to provide administrative, training, and logistical support to the MEF CE, subordinate MHG units, and, for certain functions, the adjacent MSCs. It provides higher headquarters support to enable the MEF CE to exercise effective command and control of the MAGTF.

Each MEF has one MHG, which consists of a headquarters company and special staff necessary to provide administrative and logistical support; separate communication, intelligence, radio, and law enforcement battalions; an air naval gunfire liaison company (ANGLICO); and an expeditionary operations training group (EOTG). The MHG retains administrative control of the communication, intelligence, radio, and law enforcement battalions; ANGLICO; and EOTG. Operational command of these subordinate battalions is retained by the MEF commanding general, exercised through the MEF CE staff.

Marine Division. The Marine division is the ground combat organization of the Marine Corps. Its mission is to provide forces for amphibious assaults or to execute other operations as may be directed. The MARDIV provides the ground forcible-entry capability to an amphibious task force and conducts subsequent land operations in any operational environment. The division is a balanced force of combined arms, although it depends on the MLG as its primary source of logistic support. Still, the organic capability of the division must be fully understood and used before tapping support from the MLG. In particular, the division possesses significant capabilities in the areas of combat engineer and motor transport support.

Each MEF currently has one MARDIV, although a MEF could feasibly contain multiple divisions. Marine divisions are not identical, but the typical division (see Figure 6-5) consists of a headquarters battalion and three infantry regiments—the division's cutting edge—supported by an artillery regiment and tank, assault amphibian, light armored reconnaissance, reconnaissance, and combat engineer battalions. Today, the Marine Corps includes three active component divisions and one reserve division, but during World War II the Corps reached an all-time high of six divisions.

Because Marine Corps regiments boast rich histories, they merit a brief detour from the discussion of major subordinate commands. Marine divisions contain two kinds of regiments: infantry and artillery. Based on their historical activation and employment, they are numbered as follows:

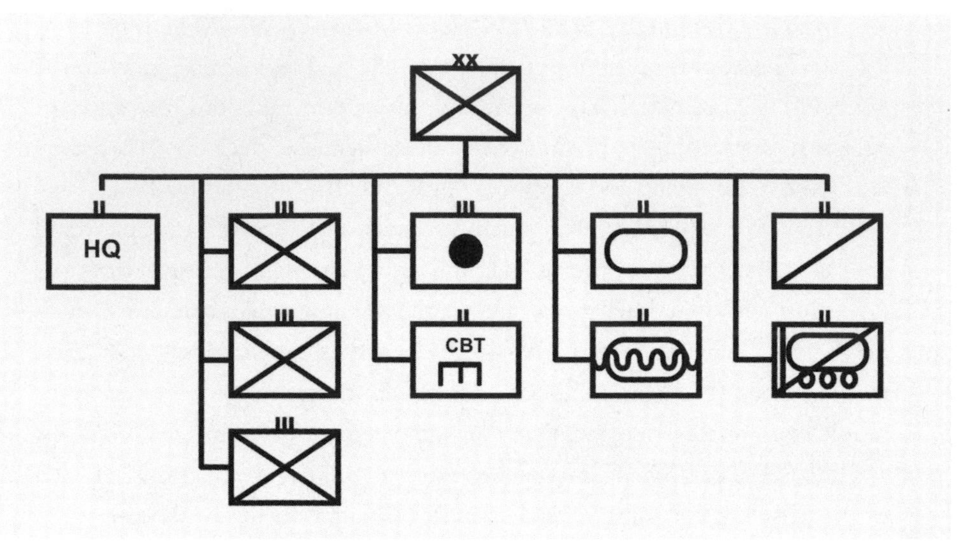

Figure 6-5. Organization of a Marine Division (2016)

- 1st through 9th Marines: infantry
- 10th through 15th Marines: artillery
- 16th through 20th Marines: unassigned (for a period during World War II, these numbers were assigned to Marine engineer regiments that were later disbanded)
- 21st through 29th Marines: infantry.

Not all of these regiments are currently active. The assignment of active regiments to Marine divisions is as follows:

- 1st Marine Division: 1st, 5th, 7th, and 11th Marines
- 2nd Marine Division: 2nd, 6th, 8th, and 10th Marines
- 3rd Marine Division: 3rd, 4th, and 12th Marines
- 4th Marine Division (Reserve Component): 23rd, 25th, and 14th Marines.

The remaining infantry and artillery regiments are inactive. The above alignment, with one exception, reflects the organization for combat of those divisions in World War II. If the numbering at first sight appears illogical, you will find that there are good underlying historical reasons for it in each case.

Marine Air Wing. The MAW is organized to provide flexible and balanced aviation capabilities across the full range of aviation operations, including all of the six functions of Marine aviation: offensive air support, anti-air warfare, assault support, air reconnaissance, electronic warfare, and control of aircraft and missiles.

Each MEF currently contains one MAW. Within the MAW, the basic tactical and administrative unit in Marine aviation is the squadron. Two or more tactical squadrons plus a headquarters squadron, aviation logistic squadron, and wing support squadron constitute the Marine aircraft group. Two or more groups, with a Marine air control group and appropriate supporting and service units, make up a Marine aircraft wing (see Figure 6-6). Today, the Marine Corps includes three active component MAWs and one reserve MAW.

Marine Logistics Group. The MLG provides tactical logistics above the organic capability of supported units to all elements of the MEF. In addition, the MLG serves as the MEF's link to operational- and theater-level logistic agencies capable of supporting the MEF.

Each MEF has one MLG (see Figure 6-7), which consists of a headquarters regiment necessary to provide administrative and logistical support internal to the MLG, as well as selected logistical services externally to the other elements of the MEF; two multifunctional combat logistic regiments, one that focuses on support to the MARDIV and one that provides general support to all MEF elements; and separate, functionally organized engineer support, medical, and dental battalions. In this respect, it is structured to support, in garrison or deployed, a MEF configured around one Marine division and one Marine air wing. All units of the MLG are structured to provide task-organized units to support independently deployed MAGTFs or geographically separated units in garrison.

614. Marine Corps Security Forces

Part of the Operating Forces of the Marine Corps, Marine Corps security forces (MCSF) are organized, trained, and equipped to support combatant commanders and naval commanders by conducting expeditionary antiterrorism and security operations and providing security for strategic weapons and vital national assets. Formerly made up of dozens of Marine barracks and detachments, these declined in number over the years and then reformed in 1986 into MCSF companies, monitored by a single battalion headquarters.

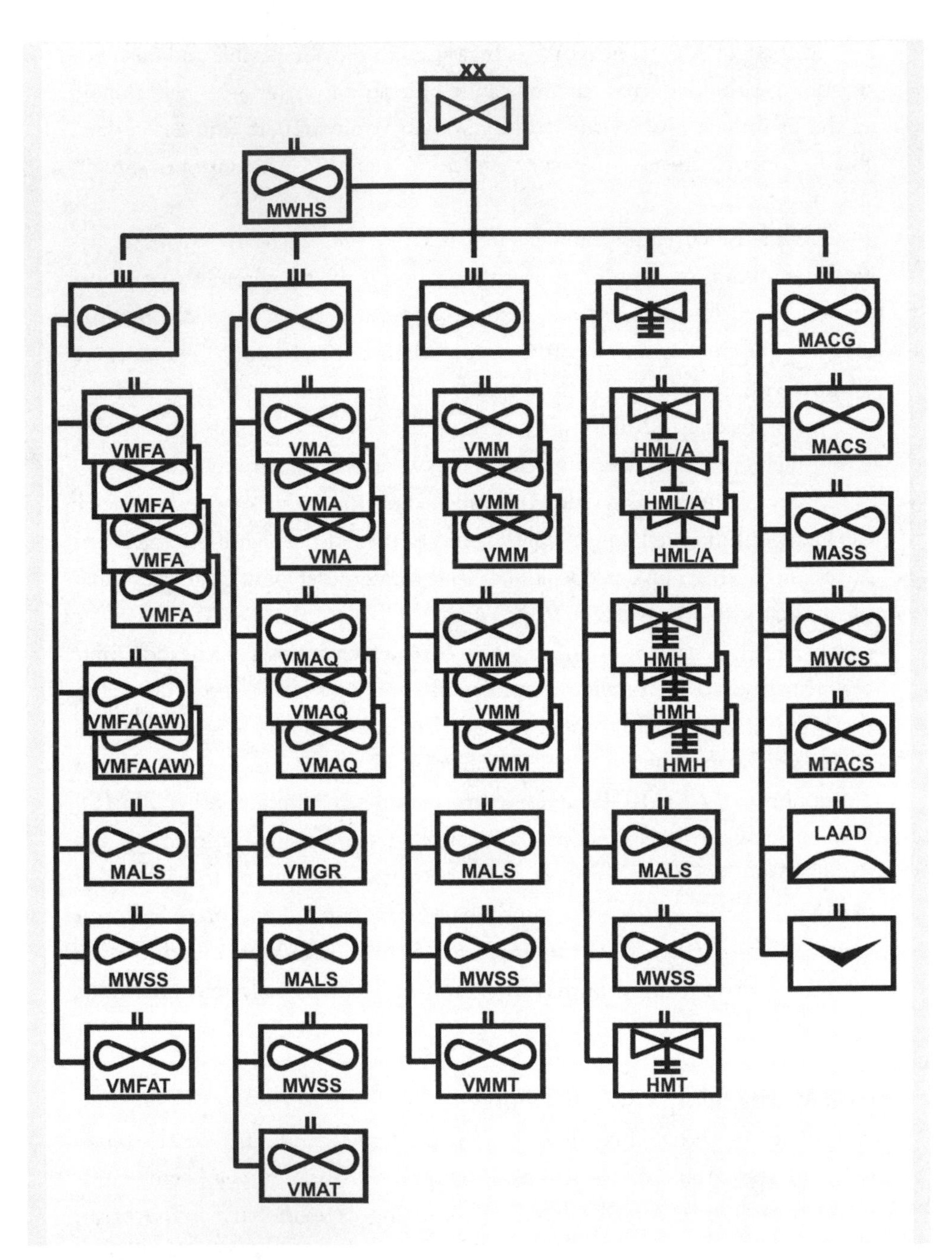

Figure 6-6. Organization of a Marine Aircraft Wing (2016)

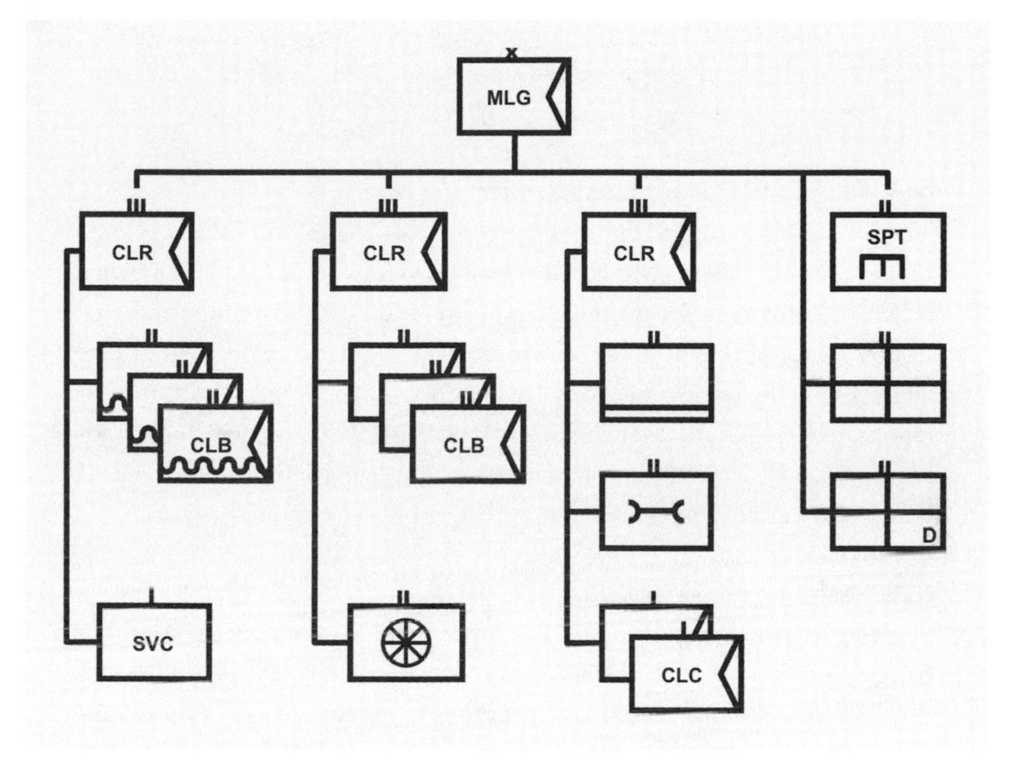

Figure 6-7. Organization of a Marine Logistics Group (2016)

These forces are currently (as of 2016) organized as the Marine Corps Security Forces Regiment under II MEF. Headquartered at Naval Weapons Station Yorktown, Virginia, this unique regiment includes:

- A headquarters company, collocated with the regimental headquarters at Yorktown, Virginia
- A training company, located in Chesapeake, Virginia
- Two MCSF battalions, one based at Kings Bay, Georgia, and the other at Bangor, Washington
- One MCSF company, permanently located at Naval Station Guantánamo Bay, Cuba
- Three fleet antiterrorism security team (FAST) companies permanently assigned within the continental United States (CONUS), two headquartered in Norfolk, Virginia, and one collocated with the regimental headquarters in Yorktown, Virginia

- Three FAST companies forward deployed in support of geographic combatant commanders and stationed in Rota, Spain; Manama, Bahrain; and Yokosuka, Japan.

615. Marine Corps Embassy Security Group

The Operating Forces of the Marine Corps also include the Marine Corps Embassy Security Group (MCESG), which provides, through its detachments, internal security at designated U.S. diplomatic and consular facilities and protection for U.S. citizens and U.S. government property located within designated U.S. diplomatic and consular premises. Aligned under HQMC and reporting to CMC, the commanding officer of MCESG exercises command, less operational supervision, of Marines assigned to Marine security guard detachments around the globe.

616. Seagoing Marines

Standing Marine detachments aboard carriers (and formerly aboard flagships, battleships, and cruisers) ceased to exist as of January 1998. FAST platoons and detachments (see Section 614) now perform, when required, the security mission once accomplished by these "seagoing Marines." Shipboard marines date from earliest antiquity—from the fleets of Hiram of Tyre, and of Greece and Rome, where, respectively, marines were known as *epibatae* and *milites classiarii.* For more detailed information on seagoing Marines, now represented mostly by Marines with embarked MAGTFs, see Chapter 9.

617. Marine Corps Operating Forces on Other Assignment

Because the president can assign Marines to any duty ("such other duty as the President may direct"), Marine Corps Operating Forces can be, and frequently have been, detached for service outside the naval establishment, under unified commands, independently, or even under other executive departments (such as the Marine embassy or mail guards). Command of Marine units not otherwise assigned by the president or the secretary of the Navy remains with the commandant of the Marine Corps.

618. Final Thought on the Operating Forces

Tables of organization (T/Os) spell out the organization of every Marine unit, right down to the individual Marine and his or her duties, rank, specialist qualifications, and personal weapons. Tables of equipment (T/Es) list the organizational equipment required by each unit. When you are assigned to the Operating Forces, know your unit's T/O inside out and acquire more than a nodding acquaintance with your T/E and with the organization of other adjacent and related Marine units with which you are in immediate contact.

MARINE CORPS SUPPORTING ESTABLISHMENT

619. Overview

The Marine Corps Supporting Establishment consists of those personnel, installations, and activities that provide, train, maintain, and support the Marine Corps Operating Forces. The Supporting Establishment thus executes a sizable chunk of the commandant's organize-train-equip mission. This supporting infrastructure includes eighteen major bases and stations in the United States and Japan and all the personnel, equipment, and facilities required to operate them—approximately thirty thousand Marines and sailors. But it is more than just bases and stations; the Supporting Establishment additionally includes all the Marine Corps activities and agencies that support the Operating Forces.

Specifically, the Supporting Establishment includes the following significant commands and organizations, as well as a number of miscellaneous smaller activities:

- Headquarters and Service Battalion, Marine Corps Headquarters
- Marine Barracks Washington
- Marine Corps Combat Development Command, which notably includes the Training and Education Command, Marine Corps Warfighting Lab, Marine Air-Ground Task Force Training Command, and the Marine Corps recruit depots
- Marine Corps Installations Command
- Marine Corps Recruiting Command
- Marine Corps Logistics Command
- Marine Corps Systems Command
- Program Executive Office, Land Systems.

All Marine officers begin their careers as part of the Supporting Establishment in that the first post-commissioning assignment for every officer is

The Basic School, part of Training and Education Command. Later, officers typically return to the Supporting Establishment in between tours in the Operating Forces. Familiarity with the Supporting Establishment is thus useful to every officer.

620. Headquarters and Service Battalion, Marine Corps Headquarters

Situated aboard historic Henderson Hall in Arlington, Virginia, Headquarters and Service Battalion provides operational, administrative, supply, and logistical support for Marine Corps personnel, both military and civilian, assigned within the Washington metropolitan area to Marine Corps Headquarters, other departments and agencies of the federal government, joint and other service schools, as well as Marine Corps personnel within the Washington metropolitan area who are assigned to duty under instruction; hospitalized; awaiting assignment, separation, or transportation; or in a disciplinary status.

The commanding officer of Headquarters and Service Battalion reports to the commandant of the Marine Corps through the director of the Marine Corps staff.

621. Marine Barracks Washington

Occupying a unique place in the Supporting Establishment and in history, Marine Barracks Washington, also known as "Eighth and Eye," is the oldest active post in the Marine Corps. It was founded in 1801 by President Thomas Jefferson and Lieutenant Colonel William Ward Burrows, the second commandant of the Marine Corps. Located on the corners of Eighth and I Streets in southeast Washington, D.C., the Barracks supports both ceremonial and security missions in the nation's capital.

The Barracks is home to many nationally recognized units, including the Marine Corps Silent Drill Platoon, the Marine Band, the Marine Drum and Bugle Corps, the official Marine Corps Color Guard, and the Marine Corps Body Bearers. It is also the site of the home of the commandants, which, along with the Barracks, is a registered national historic landmark.

The Marine Corps Silent Drill Platoon. A unique organization in the Supporting Establishment is the Marine Corps Silent Drill Platoon, a twenty-four-man rifle platoon that performs a unique precision drill exhibition. This highly

6-4. Marines of the Washington Barracks ("Eighth and Eye") parade weekly during summer months at the U.S. Marine Corps War Memorial, Arlington, Virginia. The guard unit remains the standard bearer of the pride and bearing of the Corps.

disciplined platoon exemplifies the distinctive professionalism associated with the Marine Corps. The Silent Drill Platoon first performed in the sunset parades of 1948 and received such an overwhelming response that it soon became a regular part of the parades at Marine Barracks Washington.

The Marine Band. The U.S. Marine Band is also a part of Marine Barracks Washington. This 120-piece military band is not only the best but the oldest (1798) of the armed forces musical organizations. It has the privilege of providing music for all White House and official state functions in Washington, in addition to its normal duties in military parades and ceremonials. By long custom, the director of the band is ex officio musical director of two of Washington's traditional dining clubs, the Gridiron Club (for Washington correspondents) and the Order of the Carabao (military and naval).

622. Marine Corps Combat Development Command

In 1917, the Marine Corps established Marine Barracks, Quantico, where thousands of Marines subsequently trained during World War I. The Marine Corps courses and training activities conducted during World War I assumed more formal status when General John A. Lejeune established the Marine Corps Schools in 1920. Training and innovation continued at Marine Corps Schools through the first half of the twentieth century until the organization was redesignated the Marine Corps Development and Education Command on 1 January 1968. From this tradition, the Marine Corps Combat Development Command (MCCDC) emerged on 10 November 1987, cementing MCCDC's central role in leading the combat development process; developing Marine Corps concepts, doctrine, and capabilities; and training and educating the Corps' Marines.

Today's MCCDC is the intellectual and developmental heart of the Corps. Normally commanded by a lieutenant general, the command serves as the central agency responsible for the training, concepts, and doctrine development necessary for all types of operations by Marine Corps forces. The commanding general also serves as the DC CD&I (see Section 606) and, as such, is also part of the Marine Corps Headquarters staff, charged with the responsibility to lead integration of Marine Corps warfighting capabilities. This arrangement makes MCCDC/CD&I a bit of a hybrid organization—part field command, part headquarters department.

In addition to the general and special staffs typical of a major command, MCCDC/CD&I comprises five significant commands and directorates: Training and Education Command, Marine Corps Warfighting Lab/Futures Directorate, Capabilities Development Directorate, Joint Capabilities Integration Directorate, and Analysis Directorate.

The *Training and Education Command* tends to the responsibilities of the commandant for training and education concepts, policies, plans, and programs—including their execution—regarding the training and education of Marines. The principle subordinate activities include the Training Command (responsible for fifteen formal schools, including Officer Candidates School, Basic School, Weapons Training Battalion, School of Infantry [both East and West], and Expeditionary Warfare Training Group [both East and West], to highlight just a few, and forty-two detachments with other service schools), Education Command (responsible for the Marine Corps University, including enlisted professional military education programs, the Expeditionary Warfare School, Command and Staff College, School of Advance Warfighting, Marine

Corps War College, and College of Distance Education and Training), Marine Corps Recruit Depot Parris Island, Marine Corps Recruit Depot San Diego, MAGTF Training Command (at Twentynine Palms), Center for Advanced Operational Culture Learning, and Marine Corps Center for Lessons Learned.

Of all these institutions, you will most frequently encounter the Marine Corps University as a Marine Corps officer. The president of Marine Corps University serves also as the commander of Marine Corps Education Command, the lineal successor to the fabled Marine Corps Schools. The Marine Corps established its first formal military school in 1891, when the School of Application opened to become the first residential training program for Marine officers. This school evolved into the Officers Training School in 1909 and became the nucleus of Marine Officer Instruction at Quantico following World War I. Realizing the benefits that would be obtained through additional education of officers as they progressed through their careers, additional courses of instruction were created. The first course, called the Field Officers Course, welcomed its first students in October 1920, and the second course, the Company Grade Officers Course, convened its first class in July 1921. These two courses, along with the basic Marine Corps Officer Training School, formed the foundation for what General John A. Lejeune termed "Marine Corps Schools." It was this beginning that formed the basis of the Marine Corps University as it exists today.

The resident schools at Quantico constitute the principal intellectual activity of the Corps. A brief description of these schools follows.

The Marine Corps War College is a top-level school and convenes annually a class of a dozen colonels or lieutenant colonels, including peers from other services.

The Command and Staff College, a nine-month course for majors and lieutenant colonels, is an intermediate-level school. It includes the first phase of joint professional military education in its curriculum.

The School of Advanced Warfighting is a follow-on school for selected graduates of the Command and Staff College course for another year, during which they hone their expertise in operational art and planning. These officers are joined by several of their peers from other service staff colleges.

The Expeditionary Warfare School is a career-level course of instruction for captains. It prepares them for command at the company level and battalion-level staff work in the Operating Forces.

6-5. Essential field skills form an important part of Basic School training.

The Basic School is the place where newly commissioned lieutenants and warrant officers receive their initial training and are made into officers of Marines.

The Staff Noncommissioned Officers' Academy provides advanced NCO training for staff sergeants and sergeants selected for promotion to staff sergeant. The academy also conducts an annual Sergeants Major Seminar. It also validates curricula for similar academies operated at other bases.

In addition to The Basic School, the recruit depots are the foundation of the Corps. "Boot camp" transforms the average young American into a Marine. Highly qualified officers and veteran enlisted drill instructors emphasize the elements of obedience, esprit, and the military fundamentals all Marines must master before taking their places in the fighting elements of the Corps.

The Marine Corps has two recruit depots—at Parris Island, South Carolina, and San Diego, California. Each recruit depot trains and equips the fledgling Marine, or "boot." Recruits from eastern states go to Parris Island, while those from western states go to San Diego. Occasionally in the past, as special conditions have dictated, the Corps has trained recruits at Marine Barracks Washington, as well as at Quantico and Camp Lejeune. After boot camp, the new Marines graduate to advanced individual training at other Marine Corps schools.

Within the Supporting Establishment and connected to MCCDC are several other activities that support the education and training of Marines and merit mention here.

The Library of the Marine Corps provides resources and data to the entire Corps from a building located across the street from the Marine Corps University. It contains a library, archives, telecommunications media, and conference seminar spaces.

The Director of Marine Corps History has cognizance over all Marine Corps historical programs, under the president of the Marine Corps University.

The Director of the Museums Division and the National Museum of the Marine Corps has cognizance over all Marine Corps museums, as well as maintenance of related historical and material references and library functions.

MCCDC/CD&I is, however, much more than Training and Education Command, despite the latter's extensive reach and impact.

The *Marine Corps Warfighting Lab/Futures Directorate (MCWL/FD)* seeks to improve naval expeditionary warfighting capabilities across the spectrum of conflict for current and future Marine Corps Operating Forces. MCWL/FD encompasses five divisions: Futures Assessment, which, as the name suggests, focuses on assessing the future security environment; Concepts and Plans; Wargaming; Science and Technology; and Experiment, which designs, coordinates, and executes live-force experiments of new concepts and technologies.

Capabilities Development Directorate (CDD) operates at the heart of capabilities development, identifying and validating gaps in Marine Corps doctrine, organization, training, matériel, leadership and education, personnel, and facilities and then developing integrated solutions to these capability gaps. Eight integration divisions tend to the key capability development responsibilities carried out by the directorate: Command and Control/Cyber and Electronic Warfare Integration Division, Force Protection Integration Division, Fires and Maneuver Integration Division, Intelligence Integration Division, MAGTF Integration Division, Small Wars Center and Irregular Warfare Integration

Division, Logistics Integration Division, and Maritime Expeditionary Warfare Integration Division. CDD also includes Total Force Structure Division, which is the keeper of the Corps' force structure (simplistically, the tables of organization and equipment for all Marine Corps units), and the Expeditionary Energy Office, which works closely with the combat and technology development communities and serves as the proponent for expeditionary energy in the force development process.

Joint Capabilities Integration Directorate (JCID) is the organization through which MCCDC/CD&I connects to the Joint Capabilities Integration and Development System, which is the formal DOD system that defines and develops acquisition requirements and evaluation criteria for future defense programs. JCID ensures new Marine Corps capabilities are conceived and developed in a joint warfighting context and are ultimately consistent with the integrated joint force.

Enabling and ensuring sound assessment and analysis of potential solutions to capability gaps, *Analysis Directorate* executes and provides oversight for the Marine Corps on all matters pertaining to operations analysis and modeling and simulation. The Marine Corps' service-level activity responsible for studies and analyses, Analysis Directorate serves as the service's lead for modeling and simulation, manages the Marine Corps Studies System, assists the Operating Forces and other Marine Corps agencies with operations analysis support, and represents the Marine Corps at modeling and simulation events across DOD.

623. Marine Corps Installations Command

Marine Corps Installations Command (MCICOM) is, in many ways, the embodiment of the Supporting Establishment. It fashions itself as the "platform" from which the Operating Forces embark on overseas expeditions. It provides, manages, and maintains the training ranges and areas that the Operating Forces use to hone their warfighting skills. And it provides the day-to-day support that is essential to Marines and their families as they live and work aboard Marine Corps installations.

As discussed in Chapter 8, MCICOM oversees base and station operations, develops and coordinates relevant policy, and prioritizes resources for the support of Marine Corps installations. MCICOM is headquartered at the Pentagon, but Marine Corps installations span the globe.

624. Marine Corps Recruiting Command

Headquartered at Marine Corps Base Quantico, Virginia, the Marine Corps Recruiting Command (MCRC) has one of the most challenging missions in the Marine Corps. Accountable to the CMC, the commanding general of MCRC is responsible for the procurement of qualified individuals in sufficient numbers to meet the established personnel strength levels, officer and enlisted, of the Marine Corps, both active and reserve components.

The MCRC divides CONUS into two regions: the eastern recruiting region (covering districts east of the Mississippi River) and the western recruiting region (covering districts west of the Mississippi). The two regions are divided into three districts each, each district comprising several states. The districts are subdivided into recruiting stations located in large metropolitan areas, with smaller recruiting substations covering smaller cities and rural areas. In total, the command has approximately 3,000 recruiters operating out of 48 recruiting stations, 574 recruiting substations, and 71 officer selection sites across the continental United States, Alaska, Hawaii, Puerto Rico, and Guam.

Among a wide range of miscellaneous additional duties, recruiting district directors maintain liaison with corresponding agencies and headquarters of the other three services, state adjutants general, other federal field agencies, schools and colleges, and veterans' associations and military societies.

625. Marine Corps Logistics Command

The Marine Corps' logistic services provide comprehensive support for the Corps. Military logistics is the discipline of planning and carrying out the movement and maintenance of military forces. In its most comprehensive sense, it encompasses those aspects of military operations that involve the design, development, acquisition, storage, distribution, maintenance, evacuation, and disposition of matériel.

From its position in the Supporting Establishment, Marine Corps Logistics Command (MARCORLOGCOM), headquartered at Albany, Georgia, plays a central role in the ongoing logistical support of the Marine Corps. It provides worldwide, integrated logistics, distribution, and supply-chain management; maintenance management; and strategic prepositioning capability in support of the Operating Forces, Supporting Establishment, and other supported units to maximize their readiness and sustainability. According to its strategic plan, MARCORLOGCOM exists to:

- Support Marine Corps Operating Forces with products and services that maximize equipment readiness to go to war, sustain military operations, support redeployment and retrograde, and reset and reconstitute equipment
- Support program managers (notably at the Marine Corps Systems Command and Program Executive Office, Land Systems), who equip the Operating Forces, in the planning and execution of weapon system life-cycle logistics and sustainment support
- Support other customers and DOD worldwide, as required, by being an organization capable of global reach with integrated logistic support.

It is perhaps simplest to provide some insight into what this major Marine Corps command does to support the Marine Corps by describing briefly its organization. MARCORLOGCOM consists of a headquarters element and two or more subordinate commands. The headquarters element includes staff directorates and offices, integrating operations and providing command support, and five distinct centers:

1. Weapon System Management Center provides service-level inventory management and integrates logistic-chain support for ground weapon system and equipment requirements.
2. Maintenance Management Center provides integrated maintenance management solutions in support of ground weapon systems and functions as the link between strategic- and operational-level maintenance planning and the fulfillment of tactical-level maintenance related requirements.
3. Logistics Services Management Center provides program management and integration of support providers for multiple logistic- and supply-chain services that support the Operating Forces.
4. Distribution Management Center provides service-level storage operations of ground weapon systems and collateral material, as well as integrates strategic transportation resources to effect the reliable movement, asset visibility, and accountability of matériel through global distribution networks and nodes.

5. Logistics Capabilities Center manages the Marine Corps' complex logistics-related automated information systems and provides decision support information through data analysis and operations research for MARCORLOGCOM, the Operating Forces, and Supporting Establishment.

MARCORLOGCOM also directs the activities of two permanent subordinate commands. Marine Depot Maintenance Command, headquartered in Albany, Georgia, with industrial production plants in Albany and Barstow, California, rebuilds, modifies, and performs depot-level maintenance on ground weapon systems and equipment. Blount Island Command, located in Jacksonville, Florida, manages, maintains, and provides logistic support for the Marine Corps' strategic ashore and afloat prepositioning programs. In addition, upon Marine Forces request, MARCORLOGCOM provides worldwide supply, maintenance, distribution, and prepositioning support through task-organized contact teams, technical assistance advisory teams, and other logistic support teams, up to a forward-deployed subordinate command.

6-6. The Marine Corps logistic system supports equipment distinctive to the Corps, such as these amphibious assault vehicles, as well as common defense user equipment.

Aviation Supply. You may note that the preceding discussion of Logistics Command has focused on the support of ground weapon systems and equipment. Supporting Marine aircraft and aviation systems is outside the scope of the MARCORLOGCOM mission, and discussing it in any detail is outside the scope of this *Guide.* It suffices to say—and this is a colossal understatement—that Marine aviation supply and support to Marine aviation units are complicated. Marines in aviation units get their clothing, individual equipment, rations, weapons, and pay from the Marine Corps. However, they receive their aircraft, armament, aviation munitions, flight gear, aviation ground support equipment, and most training aids and manuals from the Naval Air Systems Command.

Other Sources of Supply. Through the 1980s and 1990s, the Defense Logistics Agency (DLA) emerged as the overall Defense Department manager of matériel. As America's combat logistics support agency, DLA provides the Army, Marine Corps, Navy, Air Force, other federal agencies, and partner nation armed forces with a full spectrum of logistics, acquisition support, and technical services.

DLA sources and provides nearly all of the consumable items that U.S. military forces need to operate—from food, fuel, and energy to uniforms, medical supplies, and construction material. Among its diverse collection of logistical missions, DLA also supplies nearly 90 percent of the military's spare parts and manages the reutilization of military equipment. And DLA Troop Support Clothing and Textiles provides clothing, textiles, and equipment to U.S. servicemembers and other federal agencies, outfitting every soldier, sailor, airman, and Marine around the world, from their first day of service at basic training to camouflage uniforms worn on the battlefield to service dress uniforms worn in garrison.

DLA and its multiple depots, centers, and activities worldwide are staffed by officers from each of the services. Thus, if you enter the supply field, you may reasonably expect to be detailed at some time to one of these joint agencies.

626. Marine Corps Systems Command and Program Executive Office, Land Systems

Marine Corps Systems Command and Program Executive Office, Land Systems together outfit U.S. Marines with virtually every major piece of equipment and technology they drive, shoot, employ, and wear. Their focus is the

Marine in harm's way, protecting him or her and equipping the warfighter to execute the mission. In a few words, these two organizations of the Supporting Establishment provide the gear that Marines rely on to accomplish their missions.

Marine Corps Systems Command (MARCORSYSCOM). MARCORSYSCOM serves as the Department of the Navy's systems command for Marine Corps ground weapon and information technology system programs. The command's program managers aim to equip and sustain Marine forces with current and future warfighting capabilities. MARCORSYSCOM is organized around nine program managers: intelligence; ammunition; light armored vehicles; command, control, and communications; armor and fire support systems; training systems; information systems and infrastructure; infantry weapon systems; and combat support systems.

MARCORSYSCOM additionally directs the operations of the Marine Corps Tactical Systems Support Activity, which provides test and evaluation, engineering, and deployed technical support for USMC and joint service command, control, computer, and communications systems throughout all acquisition life-cycle phases.

Program Executive Office, Land Systems (PEO LS). PEO LS is a separate command, reporting directly to the assistant secretary of the Navy (research, development, and acquisition), although it works in concert with MARCORSYSCOM. PEO LS encompasses seven program managers: advance amphibious assault; aviation command and control and sensor netting; ground-air, task-oriented radar and ground-based air defense; light tactical vehicles; towed artillery systems; mine-resistant, ambush-protected vehicles; and medium and heavy tactical vehicles.

MARINE CORPS AVIATION

627. The Air-Ground Team

The role of Marine Corps aviation in the air-ground team is to support Marine Corps operations by close and general tactical air support and air defense. Secondarily, Marine aviation may be called on to replace or augment squadrons for duty with the carrier air groups of the U.S. Navy.

The noteworthy characteristic of Marine aviation is that it forms an inseparable part of the combined-arms team (that is, the MAGTF) operated by the Corps. Thus, the special role of Marines in the air is to support their teammates on the ground. The kind of close-air support that Marines are accustomed to demands complete integration of air and ground forces. Pilot and platoon leader wear the same color uniform, share the same traditions and a common fund of experience, and go to school side by side in Quantico. Battlefield and beachhead liaison between air and ground is accomplished by Marine pilots who share frontline fighting positions with the riflemen while directing Marine aircraft onto targets just ahead. This makes for maximum reliance by ground commanders on aviation, and for maximum desire by aviators to assist the ground combat units.

Probably the outstanding demonstration of this tradition in Marine aviation took place during the defense of Wake in 1941. Marine Fighting Squadron 211 provided a heroic air defense of Wake until no more airplanes were left. Then the officers and men of the squadron calmly donned helmets, picked up their Model '03 rifles, and went down to glory as infantry. Twenty-four years later, in Vietnam, a handful of aviation mechanics made similar history when a suicide demolition section of Vietcong sappers rushed the flight line of MAG-16 at Marble Mountain in an attempt to blow up helicopters with satchel charges. As the Vietcong charged, mechanics downed tools, seized their rifles, and killed or wounded every attacker in one blast of well-aimed fire.

628. Organization of Marine Corps Aviation

In many respects, aviation is the part of the Corps that most nearly lives up to Rudyard Kipling's "Soldier and sailor, too," because Marine aviation is very closely related to naval aviation. This relationship stems from not only the long partnership between the Marine Corps and Navy, but also the fact that the preponderance of Marine fixed-wing squadrons are organized and equipped for carrier operations and regularly perform tours of duty afloat. In addition, Marine pilots undergo flight training at Pensacola and earn their wings as naval aviators.

The primary function of Marine Corps aviation is to participate as the supporting air component of the MARFORs in whatever operations they conduct. A collateral function of Marine aviation is to participate as an integral component of naval aviation in the execution of naval functions as directed by the fleet commanders.

6-7. Marine aviation exists to support Marine Corps forces in any operations that they may conduct. Its method of employment stems from the MAGTF doctrine peculiar to the Corps.

The commandant of the Marine Corps controls the administration, individual training, and organization of Marine aviation. The chief of naval operations, however, prescribes (via the commandant) the aeronautical training programs and standards for Marine aviation units. And the aviation matériel used by Marine squadrons comes from the same sources in the Navy as does similar matériel for Navy squadrons.

The organization of Marine Corps aviation resembles the organization of the Corps as a whole:

- Headquarters, in the form of the Aviation Department at Marine Corps Headquarters under the direction of the deputy commandant for aviation
- Operating Forces, in the form of the Marine aircraft wings
- Supporting Establishment, in the form of the air stations and naval aviation depots supporting Marine aviation.

Aviation Department. As the headquarters organization for Marine aviation, this department, under the deputy commandant for aviation, plans and supervises matters relating to the organization, personnel, operational readiness, and logistics of Marine aviation.

Marine Aircraft Wings. Aviation groups and squadrons in the MARFORs are held in the Marine aircraft wing, and they constitute the combatant part of the Corps' aviation organization. These are the Operating Forces of Marine aviation.

6-8. Two F-35B joint strike fighter jets conduct aerial maneuvers over the Atlantic Ocean. (U.S. Marine Corps photo by Cpl N. W. Huertas)

The aviation combat element of the MARFORs includes attack squadrons, fighter-attack squadrons, all weather fighter-attack squadrons, air-control squadrons, aerial refueler squadrons, transport squadrons (tiltrotor, rotary-wing, and fixed-wing), and a variety of headquarters and support squadrons for the groups and wings. The wing is the major tactical unit of Marine aviation, just as the division is the major ground unit. You should remember, however, that the wing is a flexible—not a fixed—organization and that different component organizations can be added or deleted.

Aviation is represented in staff and planning billets throughout the ground organization and through the tactical air control parties that form part of the battalion, regimental, and division headquarters of MARFORs.

Supporting Establishment. The Marine Corps maintains several air stations in order to support aviation units operating ashore. The air stations and facilities of the aviation Supporting Establishment are discussed in Chapter 8.

MARINE CORPS STAFF ORGANIZATION AND PROCEDURE

629. Marine Corps Staff Organization

The general framework of Marine Corps staff organization resembles that employed by the U.S. Army. A complete description of that organization and the associated staff functions can be found in Field Manual (FM) 6-0, *Commander and Staff Organization and Operations*, and it is well worth the effort to make the early acquaintance of this invaluable manual. It perhaps seems odd, at this point, that a guide for Marine Corps officers refers to Army doctrine, but there is a time-honored tradition among Marines of unashamedly adopting best practices, regardless of the source, and Army doctrine in this matter is among the best. Equally important is knowledge of the current edition of Marine Corps Warfighting Publication (MCWP) 3-40.1, *Marine Air-Ground Task Force Command and Control*, which imbeds within several of its chapters and appendices what is effectively the Marine Corps' staff manual.

To suit differing functional needs of the Marine Corps (particularly in amphibious operations), we modify some of the staff functions described in FM 6-0. Moreover, the Marine Corps has evolved several special staff functions peculiar to MARFOR operations that do not appear in FM 6-0. These latter, with other staff functions, are listed below.

Staff Organization. The Marine commander's staff normally consists of three subdivisions: a general (or executive) staff, a special staff, and a personal staff.

As we discuss the staff, one principle should be kept in mind: regardless of how much help the commander receives from the staff, *the commander, and the commander alone, is responsible for all that his or her unit does or leaves undone.* This is a basic principle of command.

General Staff. The general (or executive) staff is a coordinating staff group that plans and supervises all the basic functions of command. In units below divisional or wing level, it is known as the *executive staff*; in divisions or higher headquarters, it is the *general staff*. Except for scale, however, the functions and duties of general and executive staffs are identical.

The basic functions of command are personnel, intelligence, operations and training, logistics, planning, and communications and information systems. These six functions are referred to by number, in the order just given; for example, personnel is "1." If the staff is divisional or higher (a general staff), the numbers are prefixed by the letter "G"; if the staff level is below division or wing (an executive staff), its numbers are prefixed by the letter "S."

The general staff, which is concerned with these command functions, is headed by a chief of staff (or executive officer in units not commanded by a general), who may be assisted by a deputy chief of staff and by a staff secretary; this latter staff officer acts as office manager for the commander, the chief, and the deputy chief of staff. At the major command level, general staff officers are designated as assistant chiefs of staff (AC/S) for their respective functional areas: AC/S, G-1, personnel; AC/S, G-2, intelligence; AC/S, G-3, operations and training; AC/S, G-4, logistics; AC/S, G-5, plans; and AC/S, G-6, communications and information systems (CIS). The commander, assisted by the chief of staff, determines the number, type, and function of general staff sections. If desired, he or she may organize additional principal staff sections on the basis of requirements. Specifics on the organization, functions, and responsibilities of a particular command's staff are normally delineated in that command's published orders, directives, and standard operating procedures (SOPs).

In addition to the "Gs," as the six assistant chiefs of staff are referred to, the staffs of all major commands include a comptroller, or financial management officer, who is considered to be a member of the general staff.

At lower echelons, the executive staff is similarly organized. But executive staff officers are designated S-1, personnel officer; S-2, intelligence officer; S-3, operations officer; S-4, logistics officer; and S-6, CIS officer. Given the military penchant for acronyms and abbreviations, Marines typically refer to these principle staff officers by their alphanumeric moniker. Thus, the unit operations officer is the "S-3," or often simply "the 3."

You will find detailed descriptions of the duties of each of the foregoing officers in the current edition of MCWP 3-40.1, with alternate Army interpretation in FM 6-0.

Special Staff. The special staff includes all the staff who are not members of either the general staff or the personal staff. The special staff is a body of specialist advisers and assistants to the commander who provide technical advice, information, and supervision. Within their respective fields, special staff officers act as advisers, planners, supervisors, and coordinators. They are authorized direct access to the chief of staff or the executive officer and direct liaison with other staff sections in matters of interest to those sections. Special staff officers in some commands or in certain specialties (for example, comptroller or financial management officer) may enjoy direct access to the commander regarding *matters that relate directly to their particular specialties.* However, special staff officers normally operate under the staff cognizance of either the chief of staff/executive officer or a member of the general/executive staff.

These specialists are often organizationally situated in one of the principal staff sections; in some cases, a special staff officer may reside in his or her own separate office and enjoy the support of a number of assistants.

Special staff sections can be organized at will by the commander to fill a particular need (although commanders should be careful to avoid staff "bloat"), or existing sections can be consolidated or inactivated. Thus, the following list of special staff officers is typical rather than fixed (although, in fact, most of these appear in tables of organization and therefore can be considered "normal" for a major Marine headquarters):

Adjutant
Air base operations officer
Air officer
Aircraft maintenance officer
Antiaircraft officer
Antimechanized officer
Fires or artillery officer
Assault amphibian vehicle officer
Aviation electronics (avionics) officer
Aviation supply officer
Chaplain (Chaplain Corps, USN)
Chief air observer
Crash crew officerDental surgeon
(Dental Corps, USN)

Disbursing officer	Embarkation officer
Engineer	Engineering officer
Exchange officer	Explosive ordnance disposal officer
Fiscal officer	Food services officer
Headquarters commandant	Historian
Inspector	Liaison officer
Military government/civil affairs officer	Motor transport officer
Naval gunfire officer	Nuclear, biological, and chemical officer
Ordnance officer	Photographic officer
Postal officer	Provost marshal
Public affairs officer	Shore party officer
Special operations officer	Special services officer
Staff judge advocate	Supply officer
Surgeon (Medical Corps, USN)	Tank officer
Utilities officer	Weather officer

When a command has no special staff representation within a particular specialty or discipline and this command gains an attached unit with that specialty, the attached commander acts as adviser to the gaining commander on matters pertaining to his or her units' capabilities and employment.

Personal Staff. The personal staff consists of the staff officers whom the commander wishes to coordinate and administer directly rather than through his chief of staff. The personal staff thus includes such officers and noncommissioned officers as aides-de-camp, sergeants major, and, for certain purposes, selected members of the special staff, such as the public affairs officer or the inspector.

The relationship between the commander and the personal staff is direct, personal, and confidential. The personal staff performs only such duties as the commander personally directs.

630. Staff Procedure and Relationships

Although this chapter deals mainly with Marine Corps organization, it is impossible to discuss staff organization without a few words on staff procedure and relationships. The fundamentals of staff procedure and relationships are staff supervision and completed staff work.

As a junior officer, you will probably not be assigned to staff duties for a while. Nevertheless, you ultimately face assignment on a staff, and, meanwhile, you will be on the receiving end of staff coordination and supervision. It therefore behooves you to become familiar with the following fundamentals.

Status of the Staff. No staff officer ever exercises command in his or her own right. The orders voiced by a staff officer are those of the commander—whether or not the commander is aware of them at the time when issued. Regardless of how much authority the commander allows the staff, the commander alone retains the responsibility. The commander holds the sack.

Staff supervision consists of advising other staff officers and subordinate commanders of the policies and desires of the commander, interpreting those policies when necessary, and reporting back to the commander the extent and manner in which the policies and desires are being carried out. This supervision does not extend to command.

Completed staff work is the most important working principle of the staff. Completed staff work has been variously defined by many commanders and by official or semiofficial publications. The definition that follows is one of the best and most generally quoted.

6-9. Effective staff work extends through all phases of operations.

Completed staffwork is the study of a problem and presentation of a solution, by a staff officer, in such form that all that remains to be done by the commander is to indicate his approval or disapproval of the completed action. The more difficult the problem is, the greater the tendency to present the problem to the chief in piece-meal fashion. It is your duty, as a staff officer, to work out the details. You should not burden your chief in the determination of those details, no matter how perplexing they may be. You may and should consult other staff officers. The product, whether it enunciates new policy or modifies established policy, should, when presented to the commander for approval, be worked out in finished form.

It is your job to advise the commander what he ought to do, not to ask him what you ought to do. He needs answers, not questions. Your job is to study, write, restudy, and rewrite, until you have evolved a single proposed course of action—the most advantageous course of all that you have considered. The commander then approves or disapproves.

Do not worry your commander with long explanations and memoranda. Writing a memorandum to your chief does not constitute completed staffwork, but writing a memorandum for him to send to someone else does. Your views should be placed before him in finished form, so that he can make them his own views simply by signing his name. In most cases, completed staffwork produces a single document prepared for the commander's signature, without accompanying comment. If the document stands on its own feet, it will speak for itself; if the commander wants further comment or explanation, he will ask for it.

Completed staffwork usually requires greater effort for the staff officer, but it results in greater freedom and protection for the commander. Moreover, it accomplishes two results:

The commander is protected against half-baked ideas, voluminous memoranda, and immature oral presentations.

The staff officer who has a valid, important proposal can more readily find receptive consideration.

> The final test of completed staffwork is this: If you yourself were the commander, would you be willing to sign the paper you have prepared? Would you stake your professional reputation on its being right?
>
> If your answer would be "No," take the paper back and rework it, because it is not yet completed staffwork.

The foregoing should not suggest, however, that the staff officer operates in a vacuum. Properly prepared, he or she understands the commander's method, character, and desires and takes action in that spirit. Commanders give their appreciations of the situation at hand and should indicate their intentions to their staffs. *Staff work therefore reflects the commander's intent* and not the personal whims of the staff officer concerned. When staff officers conceive of other arrangements, they should present them to the commander as clearly identified alternatives. In higher headquarters, this takes the form of a decision brief; at the regimental or small-unit level, the presentation is less formal.

Fighting spirit is not primarily the result of a neat organization chart nor of a logical organization set-up. The former should never be sacrificed to the latter.

—Ferdinand Eberstadt

7

THE MARINE CORPS RESERVE

The Marine Corps Reserve has proved itself repeatedly to be a vital component of the Marine Corps. The highly motivated, well-trained, and characteristically spirited Marine Corps Reserve assists the active component in maintaining its position as the national force in readiness. Over the years, complementary and seamless integration with the active component of the Marine Corps has been a constant aspiration of the Marine Corps Reserve, which distinguishes it from its counterparts in the other services.

701. History of the Reserve

The Marine Corps Reserve came into being in 1916, while Major General George Barnett was twelfth commandant, with an initial strength of three officers and thirty-three enlisted men. Like many other forward steps during the period, the Reserve was, in fact, the product of the foresight and imagination of Barnett's assistant, Colonel John A. Lejeune, who would later become thirteenth commandant. Despite its eventual importance, the Reserve played no significant role in World War I. Indeed, it nearly died on its feet in the early 1920s as a result of fiscal starvation. But for the loyalty and single-mindedness of pioneer reservists of that decade, there might not be a Marine Corps Reserve.

Following enactment by Congress of the Navy Reserve Act of 1925, the Marine Corps Reserve began to come into its own. This legislation for the first time permitted individual training duty with pay, as well as the organization of drilling units in pay status. Training programs were instituted, and units sprang up in 1927. This prosperity was short-lived, however, as the depression years of 1929–33 found the Reserve again without funds. During those lean years, most units continued to drill and train without pay—even buying their own uniforms—and thus again saved the Reserve from oblivion.

It was 1935 before the Reserve was finally able to stand on its own feet. In that golden year, there were three developments: (1) appropriations for training an organized and volunteer Marine Corps Reserve (ground and aviation), which totaled almost ten thousand officers and enlisted Marines; (2) inauguration of the Platoon Leaders Classes in order to obtain a steady input of well-trained, carefully selected junior reserve officers from colleges not participating in Army or Navy Reserve Officer Training Corps; and (3) dawn of the Reserve pilot program for Marine Corps aviation—an extra dividend of the Naval Aviation Cadet Act of 1935.

In 1938, the 1925 Navy Reserve Act was brought up to date by Congress in many aspects—perhaps the most important being the provision, for the first time, of a charter of rights and benefits for the Reserve. Included in this charter were hospitalization, death, and disability benefits; equitable promotion; retirement with pay for active service; and the right to participate in formation of reserve policy.

The solid success of the peacetime Reserve was amply attested in 1939, when individual reservists were brought to active duty after President Roosevelt's proclamation of limited national emergency in September of that year, and a year later in 1940 when mobilization of the remainder of the Reserve brought 15,138 additional Marines to the Colors. The extent to which the Reserve had hewn its place in the Corps was proved in 1945 by the fact that, of 471,000 Marines on active service, the largest number in the Corps' 170-year history, approximately 70 percent were reservists.

Much of the Reserve's effectiveness throughout World War II stemmed from the philosophy behind its mobilization, a philosophy that today is stronger than ever. Although the 1940 Reserve was built around thirty-six hometown battalions and squadrons, each with its own distinctive temper, local associations, and comradeship, Major General Thomas Holcomb, seventeenth commandant, took the position that no Marine, regular or reservist, should, while on active duty, claim any home but the Corps. Thus, as reserve units reached mobilization points, they disbanded and their members simply became individual Marines headed for service in the expanding regular formations of the Fleet Marine Force. To drive home the import of this decision and to emphasize that every man privileged to wear the Eagle, Globe, and Anchor was a Marine, no more and no less, General Holcomb decreed that, except where required by law for administrative purposes, the word "Reserve" and its corresponding abbreviation "R" following the "USMC" would not be used. All hands, reserve and regular, were Marines.

Following World War II, the postwar buildup of its reserves was one of the great achievements of the Corps. Through good leadership (both regular and reserve), through willingness to invest capable personnel in the reserve program, and because of the unflagging loyalty of Marine alumni—"Who ever saw a sorehead ex-Marine?" asked a prominent journalist—the Reserve was in unmatched readiness to back up the attenuated regular Corps when the Korean War flared.

In the field in Korea, as in Pacific battles before then, it was literally impossible to distinguish reservist from regular. Once again, as always, all hands were Marines. Among those who had originally started as reservists, however, it is worth noting that, in World War II and Korea, fifty-seven were awarded Medals of Honor.

Soon after the end of the Korean War, Congress passed legislation (the Reserve Forces Act of 1955) that continues to exercise a profound effect on the reserve components of all the armed forces, including the Marine Corps. This law provided for the so-called Special Enlistment Program whereby young men, after receiving not less than twelve weeks of hard training with and by regular forces, enter the Ready Reserve for a prescribed period of years of obligated service. The Reserve was reorganized on 1 July 1962 to provide a distinct unit mobilization structure, embodied in the 4th Marine Division, 4th Marine Aircraft Wing, and 4th Force Service Support Group. These were to be mobilized and employed as units; however, the Ready Reserve still maintained additional units whose function is to provide trained individual Marines for fleshing out regular and reserve units.

When U.S. forces deployed to the Arabian Peninsula and its seas during 1990–91 for the liberation of Kuwait from Iraqi occupation, Marine Corps forces moved in the vanguard. As the conflict deepened and the eventual campaign took shape, some thirty thousand Marine reservists deployed to augment and reinforce Marine Corps forces and to operate the bases nearly vacated in the United States. The 2002–3 Afghanistan and Iraq operations saw the Corps mobilize some 22,000 reservists by 1 May 2003. A maximum of eight thousand would remain on active duty after March 2004 for augmentation and reinforcement tasks by means of continued call-up and demobilization of reservists.

Today, the Department of Defense Total Force Policy integrates active, reserve, and National Guard forces into all military planning, especially major campaigns requiring more than the forward-deployed segment of the active forces. The Marine Corps reflected this sea change by establishing the position of Commanding General, Marine Forces Reserve to command the Reserve's various major elements under the direction of the commandant.

702. Mission of the Reserve

The mission of the Marine Corps Reserve, both organized reserve units and individual reservists, is to augment and reinforce active component Marine forces in time of war, national emergency, or contingency operations; provide personnel and operational tempo relief for the active forces in peacetime, and provide service to the community.

For decades, the reservist maintained this capability with the stance of the "weekend warrior," drilling monthly on weekends and for two weeks in the summer with his or her unit to maintain the required individual skills and unit capabilities. That routine was judged adequate to provide reserve forces with the capability to mobilize and prepare for eventual operations at the side of active duty forces. Doctrine generally held that a "grace period" of sixty days would ensue while the reservists could prepare for such operations.

Operations at the end of the twentieth century, however, ushered in an era of increasing dependence on the day-to-day readiness of the reservist and quick reinforcement by reserve units. The expenses of maintaining active duty forces, their typical worldwide commitments, and the difficulty of providing certain skills all have demanded an unconditional readiness of the Reserve and an increasing willingness to put it into action in situations short of declared war. Thus, today's reservists train with the knowledge that their commitments to operations might be required in mere days versus months.

Two concepts dominate the doctrine for preparing and deploying the Reserve. *Augmentation* brings units and selected individuals to join the active forces as required for operations, national emergency, or war. *Reinforcement* provides depth, replacement, and capabilities not resident in the active forces for operations, national emergency, or war.

ORGANIZATION AND COMPOSITION

703. Organization of the Marine Corps Reserve

The Marine Corps Reserve today is organized and maintained under the Armed Forces Reserve Act of 1952 (amended in 1955), which superseded the 1938 Navy Reserve Act. This law incorporated the basic principles of its predecessor but modernized the Reserve. Since 1969, legislation has provided annual strength authorizations for the Reserve just as in the case of the active component. In 2016, the authorization for the Marine Corps Reserve stood at 39,600. (This and other laws bearing on the Reserve have been codified under Title 10, U.S. Code.)

Because the Reserve is a component of the Marine Corps as a whole, command and administration of the Reserve stem directly from the commandant. Thus, the departments and offices of Marine Corps Headquarters bear the same relationships and responsibilities toward the Reserve as they do toward the remainder of the Corps.

704. Reserve Branch, Headquarters Marine Corps

The Reserve Branch, situated within Manpower Department, HQMC, serves to monitor the current operations and budget actions of the Reserve for the commandant. The headquarters staff no longer enters directly into the chain of command of the Reserve.

705. Marine Corps Forces Reserve

Reporting to the commandant, the Commanding General, U.S. Marine Corps Forces Reserve exercises command of the elements of the Reserve under the Total Force Concept. With headquarters and staff located at New Orleans, Louisiana, the commanding general exercises command over the 4th Marine Division (4th MARDIV), 4th Marine Aircraft Wing (4th MAW), 4th Marine Logistics Group (4th MLG), Individual Ready Reserve, and Force Headquarters

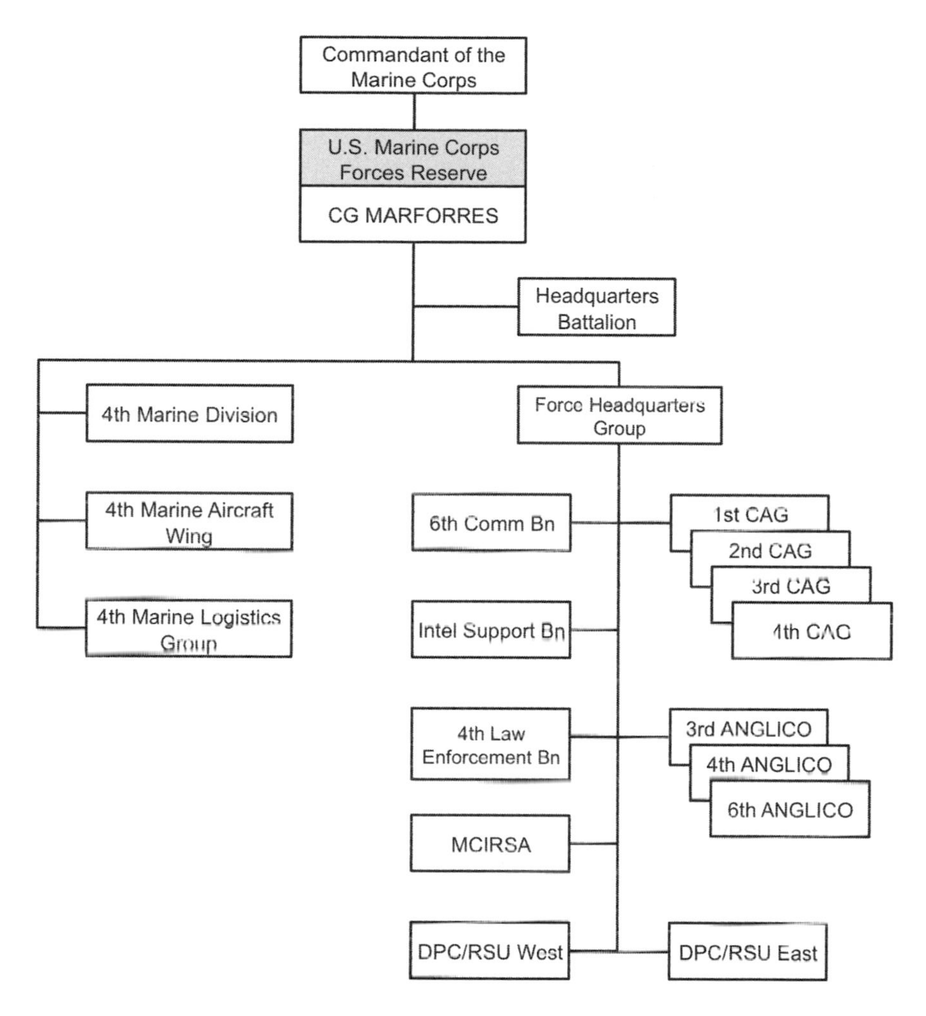

Figure 7-1. Organization of the Marine Corps Reserve

Group, which supports the commanding general's exercise of command and also contains an assortment of units providing functional and specialized capabilities such as supporting arms liaison, civil affairs, and reserve mobilization (see Figure 7-1).

706. Marine Corps Reserve Units

To a greater extent than many Marines realize, the Corps entrusts its readiness to the units of the Selected Marine Corps Reserve (SMCR). They are the backbone of the Reserve and constitute the mobilization backbone of the Corps.

Leaving out the mobilization training units (discussed below), organized units of the Marine Corps Reserve are formed almost entirely from SMCR reservists (see Section 707). Both ground and aviation units are mainly organized at or below the battalion/squadron level. These units parallel—but do not necessarily mirror exactly—prototype units in the active Marine Corps Operating Forces. Thus, in the ground portion of the Selected Reserve, you will find infantry, artillery, armor, assault amphibian, reconnaissance, engineer, signal, and air naval gunfire liaison company units. Reserve aviation likewise follows the active component pattern and includes, in various cities, most of the principal operating units of a Marine aircraft wing: fighter-attack squadrons, transport squadrons, helicopter squadrons, and wing headquarters and service units as well. Reserve logistic units also resemble their active component counterparts.

Because Selected Reserve units follow the active Marine Corps Operating Forces pattern, the administration and functions of these units are carried on in the same way as in similar units in the regular establishment.

Selected ground units are commanded by reserve officers who have been selected for their professional experience and background. Like all commanding officers (COs), they must administer, train, and maintain the readiness of their commands. In addition, however, they must stimulate and promote whatever recruiting is needed to keep their units up to strength. Reserve commanding officers usually serve for a two-year tour, which may be extended to three or more years under certain circumstances. This gives them adequate experience in command and, at the same time, ensures the advantages of healthy rotation.

Aviation units, like ground units, are commanded by reserve officers whose responsibilities are much like those of ground unit commanding officers in the Ready Reserve.

Because of the large amount of technical training, the paramount requirement for safe flight operations, and the quantities of expensive matériel (including aircraft) required by a reserve aviation unit, the inspection-instruction organization (see Section 708) for reserve aviation outfits differs somewhat from that used with ground units.

At the home station of each aviation unit in the Reserve, a parent Marine air reserve training detachment (MARTD) is located. This detachment is commanded by a regular Marine Corps aviator and includes assistant instructors and maintenance crews to support the reserve squadron. The reserve unit's commanding officer comes under the command of the commanding officer of the MARTD.

Staff groups permit drill pay and organized reserve status for more senior reserve officers for whom mobilization requirements exist but who cannot train with other organized reserve units. Staff groups attend paid drills and annual field training.

Mobilization training units (MTUs) are not part of the Selected Reserve but afford training in staff and command functions, ground and air, for reserve officers and enlisted men and women ordinarily not associated with a unit who want to stay with the Corps, keep up professional training, and amass credits for reserve retirement.

A mobilization training unit may be made up of six or more members (officer or enlisted) of any military specialty or combination of specialties. Most MTUs train under a specified syllabus provided by Marine Corps Combat Development Command, but some specialize in given fields when all members hold the same or related military occupational specialties. Each MTU is assigned an adviser, usually the nearest inspector-instructor (see Section 708) or CO, MARTD.

Members of the Reserve who are not affiliated with a unit or who live in a locality without a local unit obtain support and maintain contact with the Corps via the district director's office applicable to the member's geographical region. Those who wish to join the Reserve but have no hometown unit may also obtain advice and help from the district director.

Marine Reserve affairs outside the United States are administered by the Reserve Branch, HQMC.

707. Composition of the Reserve

The Marine Corps Reserve includes individual classes for mobilization planning and assignment that vary according to the preferences and background of the reservist. Thus, the Reserve affords various opportunities for activity, which can usually be adjusted to the desires of anyone qualified to be a Marine. The Marine Corps Reserve comprises the Ready Reserve, Standby Reserve, and Retired Reserve.

The *Ready Reserve* encompasses both reserve units and individual reservists who are liable for immediate active duty during war or national emergency. The Ready Reserve is divided into the Selected Reserve and the Individual Ready Reserve.

Selected Reserve. The Selected Reserve describes the portion of the Reserve that is most ready to reinforce the active component. It is composed of Selected Marine Corps Reserve units, individual mobilization augmentees (IMAs), and members participating in the Active Reserve program.

1. *Selected Marine Corps Reserve Units.* SMCR units include the 4th MARDIV, 4th MAW, 4th MLG, and Force-level units of Marine Forces Reserve. All SMCR units remain under the administrative and operational control of the Marine Forces Reserve commanding general until activated. Reserve end strength varies over time, but SMCR units consist of approximately 17,300 reservists from the 4th MARDIV, 7,200 from the 4th MAW, 7,600 from the 4th MLG, and 14,900 from the Reserve Force Headquarters Group. Currently there are 182 reserve training centers in forty-seven states, Puerto Rico, and the District of Columbia.
2. *Individual Mobilization Augmentee.* IMA Marines are members of the Selected Reserve but are not members of an SMCR unit. They are normally preassigned to an active component unit billet that must be filled to meet the unit's requirements to support mobilization. The IMA program provides a source of trained and qualified individuals to fill a time-sensitive portion of the active component wartime structure.
3. *Active Reserve.* Reservists on active duty with this program normally serve in full-time, active duty billets that support the organization, administration, recruiting, retention, instruction, and training of the Marine Corps Reserve. The program may also permit a Marine reservist to serve on a full-time basis in various billets to help support the active component.

Individual Ready Reserve. Members of the IRR consist of individual Marines who are available for mobilization, have had training, and have previously served in the active forces or in the Selected Reserve. IRR Marines are not actively drilling, nor are they affiliated with the SMCR. A reservist in the IRR falls in one of three categories: (1) reservist who has not completed his or her mandatory service obligation (MSO); (2) one who has completed his or her MSO and remains in the Ready Reserve by voluntary agreement; or (3) one who has not completed his or her MSO (that is, is a mandatory participant), but is transferred to the IRR.

All are deployable. Current law authorizes the president, without a prior declaration of war or a national emergency, to order not more than 200,000 members of the Selected Reserve (of all branches of our armed forces) to active duty for not more than ninety days for purposes other than training.

The second broad category of the Reserve, the *Standby Reserve*, consists of Marines who are unable to meet participation requirements of the Ready Reserve but desire to maintain their affiliation. They may also be bound by a remaining contractual obligation or be officers who have failed to resign their commission. The Standby Reserve is organized into two categories: Standby Reserve–Active Status List and Standby Reserve–Inactive Status List. These reservists are not required to train and are not members of units; however, they are subject to mobilization to satisfy manpower requirements for specific, often unique, skills.

Finally, the *Retired Reserve* consists of Marines who have requested and been approved for retirement. Members of this reserve category may be recalled to active duty under certain, usually rare, circumstances. The four categories of Retired Reserve Marines are Fleet Marine Corps Reserve (FMCR), Retired Reserve Awaiting Pay, Retired Reserve in Receipt of Retired Pay, and Regular Retired List.

RESERVE TRAINING

708. The Inspector-Instructor

To ensure that the Reserve has the benefit of coordinated and professional up-to-date training, advisory personnel from the active Marine Corps are detailed to duty with the Reserve.

Each SMCR unit has a regular Marine officer who is known as the inspector-instructor (I&I). This title describes the job exactly. With the help of a small staff, the I&I must, as instructor, provide training assistance and general guidance to the unit. As inspector, however, he or she must make certain that the unit is up to the standards set by Marine Corps Headquarters. Inspector-instructors for reserve ground, aviation, and service support units are under the direct command of the respective commanding generals of the 4th MARDIV, 4th MAW, and 4th MLG. As seen in Section 706, functions comparable to those of the I&I are performed for reserve aviation units by the CO, MARTD.

The I&I's job (and for that matter, any duty in connection with the Reserve) calls for top-tier leadership, imagination, and tact. Responsibilities are heavy (much heavier than they look on paper). Authority, meanwhile, is slight, as reserve units have their own reservist commanders and staffs. Nevertheless, the job presents great challenges and can deliver corresponding rewards. In most cases, the I&I alone represents the active Marine Corps in the community. The I&I's conduct, example, and loyalty to the ideals of the Corps inform and shape the local community's impression of Marines and, by extension, the whole Marine Corps. The I&I, working with the leadership and members of his or her reserve unit, thus serves as a crucial link between the Marine Corps and the nation's communities from which the Corps draws its support.

709. Training Opportunities in the Reserve

Every Selected Reserve unit must complete a carefully planned annual training cycle. In addition to this unit training program, the individual reservist may avail himself/herself of a wide selection of courses, volunteer periods of training duty, and gratis home study courses (both Marine Corps Schools Extension Courses and Marine Corps College of Distance Education and Training—see Section 1410). Reserve training affords something for every individual's interests and opportunities.

Selected Reserve Training. Training of the average SMCR unit consists of twelve paid weekend drill or flying periods and two weeks' annual active duty training.

Reserve training is as meaningful as human effort can make it. It involves realistic field training, including overnight problems. The amount of air-ground and combined arms training can be considerable, with two or more neighboring units joining in weekend exercises. Selected Reserve artillery units (generally located near Army or Marine Corps bases with range facilities) conduct live firing throughout the year.

7-1. The Marine reservist receives equipment and essential training identical to that operated by active Marine Corps Forces.

The hometown Selected Reserve training cycle culminates annually in two weeks' training by the unit at a Marine Corps base or station. It follows a cycle to include desert, mountain, jungle, amphibious, air-ground, combined arms, and specialist training. When possible, the Marine Corps arranges the movement of Selected Reserve outfits to and from annual training by military airlift or in amphibious shipping. This increases the adaptability, professional know-how, and experience of the units and Marines concerned.

Members of the Selected Reserve receive drill pay for each drill session attended, as well as for summer training. This pay can provide a welcome augmentation for one's primary income.

Individual Ready Reserve Training. Members of the IRR do not have to attend drills but may be required to perform training duty not exceeding fifteen days a year. (Enlisted personnel meeting certain criteria must perform thirty days' active duty annually.) There are also many open opportunities to train with Ready Reserve units or mobilization training units on one's own initiative, with or without pay. Reservists who aim to maintain high levels of professional proficiency and to accrue credits for reserve retirement with pay (see Sections 711 and 712) can keep up to date by periodic spells of training duty and through correspondence courses provided by Marine Corps Combat Development Command's College of Distance Education and Training.

A typical training cycle for an Individual Ready Reservist might include completion of a correspondence course, a two-week reserve summer staff course at Quantico, and perhaps a few days' training duty without pay with a Marine Corps Operating Forces unit, or alternately a Marine Corps base or station, to brush up in a specialty. By remaining professionally up to date, an IRR Marine may earn the opportunity to perform training duty as an umpire during a large training exercise; where qualified, reserve officers are well suited to serve in this capacity.

INDIVIDUAL ADMINISTRATION PERTAINING TO RESERVISTS

710. Transfer into the Marine Corps Reserve

The Armed Forces Reserve Act permits certain members of reserve components of the armed forces to transfer from one service to another. Thus, a member of another reserve component who desires to complete his or her obligated military service in the Marine Corps Reserve may have the opportunity to do so.

Generally speaking, an officer who is not on active duty but does have a remaining period of obligated service in his or her reserve component may be discharged (or resign, if a reserve officer) to accept an appointment in the Marine Corps Reserve. The Reserve Branch, HQMC can provide advice on eligibility for transfer and can assist in the administrative paperwork.

711. Privileges and Perquisites of the Marine Reservist

A Marine recruiting poster, alleged to date from Revolutionary War days, recounts the privileges and perquisites of the Marine of 1776:

> You will receive SEVENTEEN DOLLARS BOUNTY, And on your arrival at Head Quarters, be comfortably and genteelly clothed—And spirited young boys of a promising Appearance, who are Five Feet Six Inches high, WILL RECEIVE TEN DOLLARS, and equal advantages of PROVISIONS and CLOTHING with the Men. In fact, the

> Advantages which the MARINE possesses, are too numerous to mention here, but among the many, it may not be too amiss to state—That if he has a WIFE or aged PARENT, he can make them an Allotment of half his PAY; which will be regularly paid without any trouble to them, or to whomsoever he may direct that being well Clothed and Fed on Board Ship, the Remainder of his PAY and PRIZE MONEY will be clear in Reserve, for the Relief of his Family or his own private Purposes. The Single Young Man, on his Return to Port, finds himself enabled to cut a Dash on Shore with his GIRL and his GLASS, that might be envied by a Nobleman.

Clearly, times have somewhat changed.

Today, the preeminent privilege one gains as a member of the Marine Corps Reserve is the right to wear the Eagle, Globe, and Anchor and call oneself a Marine. But there are other substantial privileges and perquisites, which are summarized below.

Pay. A short but important word, pay is certainly a perquisite of the reservist. For each regular drill or equivalent, one draws one day's pay, according to rank. This also applies to all active or training duty, unless performing these in nonpay status.

Uniforms. Reservists, of course, wear regular Marine Corps uniforms. They are worn, or may be prescribed, during drills and instruction and on other appropriate occasions, such as military ceremonies, military dinners or balls, and similar occasions. When wearing a Marine Corps uniform, it is imperative that a reservist be indistinguishable from the most squared-away active component Marine.

Reserve officers must purchase and maintain their own uniforms, but they receive an initial allowance to help with this expense when first reporting for active duty.

Every reserve officer must possess a required kit meeting minimum requirements but may, in addition, purchase other uniforms, such as dress uniforms and accessories, if one desires them and can find proper occasions to wear them. Marine Corps Headquarters publishes, from time to time, lists of uniforms that reserve officers must have.

It goes without saying—but always bears emphasizing—that wearing Marine Corps uniforms is a privilege, which members of the Reserve have always treasured. When wearing the uniform, reservists must hold themselves accountable to every high standard of the Corps and its discipline.

Clubs and Messes. These centers of Marine Corps social life extend a hearty welcome to the Marine Corps Reserve officer, whether active or inactive. Thus, reserve officers will always find a friendly greeting (and, likely as not, old comrades) in the open mess at the nearest Marine Corps or Navy base or station.

Exchanges and Commissaries. Privileges at military exchanges and commissaries are unlimited for reservists *on drill days.* Commissary privileges are available on a limited basis for those on duty less than seventy-two hours. When a duty period exceeds seventy-two hours, reservists rate the same exchange and commissary privileges as an active duty Marine.

Promotion. Promotion opportunities afford reservists the chance to gain responsibility, expand their contributions to the nation, and, of course, to be eligible for increased retirement pay. (For information on reserve retirement, see Section 712 below.)

Decorations and Medals. Marine reservists may be awarded decorations and medals just as all other Marines—strictly as earned. They are worn on the uniform or, on certain occasions, with civilian clothes in the same way as by regulars (see the current edition of *Marine Corps Uniform Regulations*).

The *Marine Corps Association,* which publishes the professional magazine of the Corps, the *Marine Corps Gazette,* is open to membership by officers and enlisted members of the Reserve. So is the U.S. Naval Institute, which publishes *Proceedings,* the professional journal of the naval services.

Government Insurance Benefits. Marine reservists may qualify for Servicemembers' Group Life Insurance, Veterans' Group Life Insurance, and, for those completing twenty years of satisfactory federal service for entitlement to retired pay, the Reserve Component Survivor Benefit Plan.

Employment Protection. The Universal Military Training and Service Act (Public Law 632, 86th Congress), as amended, protects reservists against loss of seniority, status, pay, and vacation while they are away from their civilian jobs on reserve training duty. Also, reservists who unfortunately become disabled while training and unable to perform the duties of their jobs are entitled to reemployment on other jobs whose duties they may be able to perform. If a reservist is hospitalized incident to training duty, he or she may delay reemployment application for a period up to one year. On the other hand, the law requires the reservist to request leave of absence from his or her employer before going on training duty and to report back to work immediately on completion of training.

In addition to the foregoing, federal employees, if in the Reserve, rate up to fifteen days' extra leave with pay per year to cover periods spent on training duty. They are also protected by law against "loss of time, pay, or efficiency rating" while availing themselves of this additional leave for training. Government-employee reservists ordered to active duty must, by law, be restored to the job they held before being called up.

712. Reserve Retirement

Members of the Marine Corps Reserve are eligible to earn retirement, both honorary (without pay) and with pay. In general, leaving out the Fleet Reserve, the fundamental prerequisite for reserve retirement with pay is twenty or more years' qualifying service (not necessarily consecutive), or twenty years' "satisfactory federal service," not all of which need be active.

Although one may achieve reserve retirement under various provisions of law, the principal one affecting most reservists is a section of Public Law 810, 80th Congress, which makes retirement pay available to all Marine reservists who accumulate sufficient "retirement points" (credit points earned by service, training, and professional military education). The number of retirement points one chalks up also determines the amount of retired pay earned.

Here is a brief description of this retirement system. (Since retirement policies may change from time to time, it is always wise to consult the latest edition of *Marine Corps Reserve Administrative Management Manual.*)

To qualify for reserve retirement, a reservist must earn at least fifty points a year for a minimum of twenty years, but these years need not be consecutive. He or she must earn at least fifty points in a year to have that year count toward reserve retirement. The amount of retired pay one receives is determined by the total number of points accumulated. The number of points earned depends largely on the amount of effort put into training, home study courses, and other types of equivalent instruction: the more one gives as a reservist, the more one receives in return.

After satisfying all the requirements, a reservist normally becomes eligible for reserve retirement pay the first month after his or her sixtieth birthday. He or she may estimate earned reserve retirement pay as follows: (1) divide by 360 the sum of all points earned, (2) multiply the result by 2.5 percent, and (3) multiply this result by the combined annual base pay and longevity pay one would receive if on active duty in the highest grade, permanent or temporary, satisfactorily held during the twenty years' service. The answer is the annual reserve retired pay the reservist will be eligible to receive on attaining the age of sixty.

Amendments to Title 10, U.S. Code created a pair of special cases affecting eligibility for reserve retirement and calculation of reserve retirement pay. First, the law now authorizes a reduction of retirement age for a member of the Ready Reserve (excluding Active Reservists) who serves on active duty for ninety days or more after 28 January 2008. This provision is not retroactive. For each aggregate period of ninety days on active duty in any fiscal year, the eligibility age for reserve retirement will be reduced below sixty years of age by three months. A day of duty may be included in only one aggregate, ninety-day period. In any case, the eligibility age may not be reduced below fifty years of age for a member entitled to retired pay for non-regular service.

Second, Marines who entered service after 7 September 1980 and who elected discharge after completing twenty years of reserve service instead of passing to the Retired Reserve will use the average of the three highest years of basic pay earned during the serving years.

In addition to all the foregoing, physical disability retirement rules that govern regular Marines extend with equal force to reservists who incur service-connected disabilities.

713. Additional Information on Reserve Matters

The Marine Corps Reserve can supply more detailed information on the Reserve, not only to Marines, but also to prospective reservists and friends. The Reserve Branch, HQMC is always glad to answer individual queries and to assist reservists in solving professional problems. However, before contacting Marine Corps Headquarters, it is always wise to search online for a local Marine Corps activity, either regular or reserve. A nearby Marine officer—whether inspector-instructor, NROTC instructor, officer selection officer, or recruiting district director—is always a ready and willing resource, and he or she may be able to provide the best advice on where to find desired information on the Marine Corps Reserve.

In its outstanding service to our Corps, the Marine Corps Reserve has earned the right to be called our "Secret Weapon."

—General Lemuel C. Shepherd Jr.

8

BASES AND STATIONS

Only the globe itself—trademark of Marines—limits the number of places where Marines may serve over the course of their careers.

This chapter explores the major permanent bases and stations of the Corps. These are the places where, between expeditions, deployments, and periods of service at sea, Marines will spend much of their careers honing their craft. In addition, the chapter describes the organization and general conditions at a typical Marine Corps installation, as well as the facilities and services that a typical base or station offers to Marines and their family members.

801. Overview

A variety of major bases and stations form part of the Marine Corps Supporting Establishment and are maintained exclusively for Marine Corps forces. Additionally, Marines in the security forces man several Marine barracks and shore-based Marine detachments at home and abroad.

Except for installations with missions directly reflected in their titles (such as recruit depots or training centers), the Corps has the following kinds of bases and stations.

Marine Corps bases (MCB) and Marine barracks (MB) are the basic permanent installations for support of ground units of the Corps. Both are administratively autonomous and wholly or partially self-supporting. Marine Corps bases, along with similar installations sometimes labeled "camps," are devoted to field training and support of major tactical units, whereas Marine barracks perform security missions.

A Marine Corps air station (MCAS) is the aviation counterpart of a Marine Corps base. Like MCBs, air stations are also permanent, autonomous, and self-supporting. All Marine Corps air stations have a common mission: support of Marine aviation units. When an installation dedicated to supporting aviation units is not self-supporting, it is normally known as a Marine Corps air facility (MCAF).

Marine Corps installations whose focus is to host organizations dedicated to higher levels of support, such as procurement, depot maintenance, and strategic distribution, include Marine Corps logistics bases (MCLB) and Marine Corps support facilities (MCSF).

Finally, there are Marine detachments in several locations. These are the smallest organizations of the Corps that, in some ways, function like installations. A Marine detachment (MARDET), however, depends administratively and logistically on some larger organization (for example, a joint base or a naval station) and often enjoys less permanent status than other Marine activities.

A TYPICAL MARINE CORPS INSTALLATION

802. How an Installation Is Organized

With allowances for different missions, locations, and sizes, most Marine Corps installations follow a similar—though certainly not identical—organization. Figure 8-1 depicts the organization of a hypothetical base or station.

Command. The commanding officer (CO) (if a general, then called commanding general) commands the installation. The CO is responsible for all that the command does or leaves undone.

The executive officer is the line officer next junior in rank to the CO. As the commanding officer's alter ego, the executive officer relieves the commander of administrative detail and succeeds to command in the latter's absence. The extent and character of the duties vary somewhat according to the policies and peculiarities of the CO. On a post commanded by a general, instead of an executive there is typically a chief of staff, and the latter, in turn, may be assisted by a deputy. Given the turnover every two to three years of an installation's active duty leadership, many bases and stations will also have a civilian executive director who provides continuity, as well as specific expertise in the intricacies of installation management.

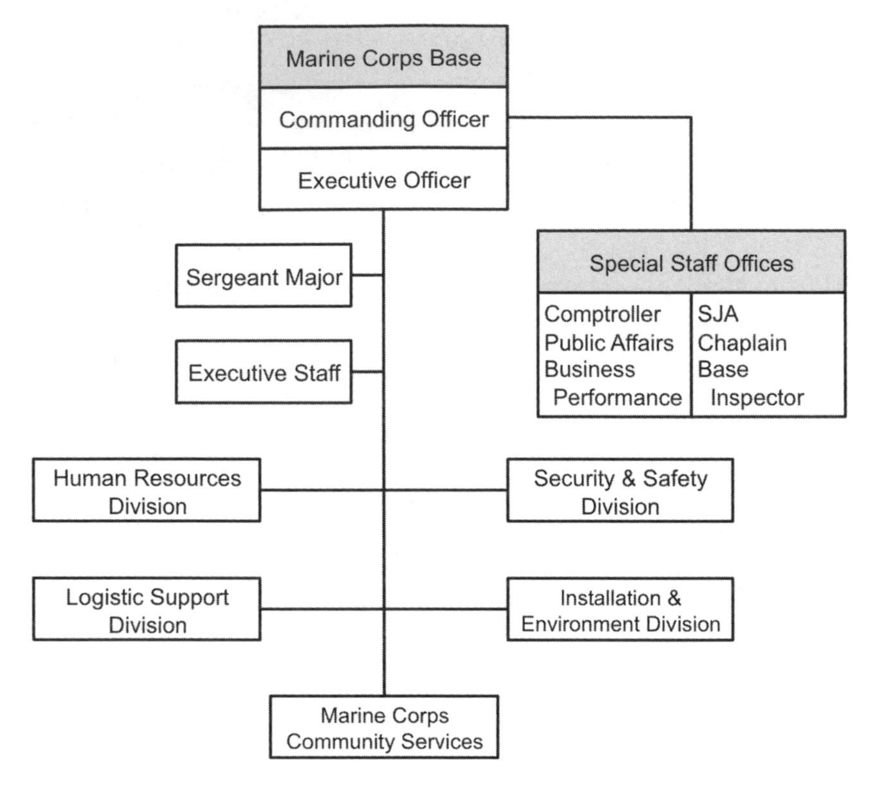

Figure 8-1. Organization of a Typical Marine Corps Installation

Staff. Just as in tactical units, an installation commander is assisted by an executive and special staff much like those described in Section 629. The executive staff typically includes assistants for administration, operations and plans, logistics and facilities (although facilities functions may lie in a distinct staff section), and communications and information systems, which together manage the full range of services that bases and stations must provide. In addition, most have a few special staff functions that differ materially in scale or scope from similar Marine Corps Forces staff jobs, where administrative functions and business operations are not quite so important as on a base or station.

In addition to the command and staff sections, Marine Corps installations typically conduct operations through several subordinate departments, divisions, and offices. These are most often functionally oriented, and their number and configuration vary from installation to installation. The following paragraphs, however, complete the picture of a fairly typical installation.

Security, Safety, and Emergency Services. This department or division normally provides law enforcement and security, fire protection, and emergency medical services to protect life and property, preserve good order and discipline, and promote quality of life. It may also be responsible for management of the installation's safety program, although this function might be organized in a separate installation safety center.

Within this department or division normally resides the *provost marshal.* This is the installation's "chief of police" or "sheriff," responsible for public safety, traffic control, criminal investigation, internal and external security, regulation of pets, and law and order in general. Law-abiding members of the community usually encounter the provost marshal in connection with registration of vehicles, pets, and personal firearms, and when obtaining passes for guests and family members.

Installation and Environment. Often led by an active duty or retired Navy Civil Engineer Corps officer, this department or division plans, oversees, and coordinates the construction, renovation, modernization, maintenance, and demolition of installation facilities and utilities. This organization bears responsibility for minor construction, repair, and upkeep of the physical plant of the base or station, as well as its cleanliness and shipshape appearance. Additionally, it typically manages the installation's environmental programs.

Installation residents are most likely to interact with this organization through a bachelor or family housing office, whose operations usually fall within its purview, or by submitting a request for facility maintenance or repair.

Logistic Support. This department or division of the installation normally provides supply support, which may include military clothing issue and operation of "stores" (commonly called ServMart) that provide office supplies, tools, and other consumables; transportation support, including operation and maintenance of motor vehicles and material handling equipment; and other logistic support. At some bases and station, the logistic support function is part of the installation department or division.

Human Resources. The human resources and administration functions may reside in a department or division of the installation. This is often the case at larger bases and stations with substantial numbers of civilian employees. In other cases, these functions may reside wholly at the staff level within the S-1 or G-1.

Marine Corps Community Services. Every major base or station includes a Marine Corps Community Services (MCCS) department or division, which manages Marine and family programs, recreation and leisure programs, and health and fitness programs and operates the associated facilities and activities. Additionally, MCCS operates retail shopping and service outlets, including the Marine Corps exchanges and annexes, dining establishments, and commercial lodging facilities.

Policies require that MCCS generate revenue to cover its operations, which is to say that most MCCS operations are not supported by funding appropriated by Congress. Instead, retail shopping, dining, and lodging operations—along with some fee-for-service activities—provide the primary revenue supporting MCCS.

Smaller Offices. In addition to the larger department or divisions, most installations include several smaller offices such as the Office of the Comptroller, Office of the Staff Judge Advocate, Office of the Chaplain, Base Inspector's Office, Public Affairs Office (sometimes Office of Community Plans and Liaison with a wider mandate), and Business Performance Office.

Boards and Councils. To advise the commander and sometimes supplement the staff, most installations include one or more standing boards or councils. Some are required by regulations, while others exist to meet local needs. Board and council membership often includes representatives of both the installation staff and the supported community. Typical examples include an exchange council, recreation council, athletic and sports council, school advisory board, and housing advisory board.

803. Facilities and Services

In many ways, an installation resembles a small community. Most if not all the facilities and services you could expect in such a town have counterparts on a Marine installation. Like small towns, however, bases and stations of varying age, locality, and mission exhibit considerable local disparities. Thus, what you find on one installation might not exist, or hardly exists, at another.

One key to gaining the most benefit from the military community resides in the single Marine programs, family programs, and family service centers managed and operated by MCCS at all bases and activities. Family service centers provide a single point of reference for Marines as they change location.

Relocation specialists provide the latest information on new duty stations and civilian communities: housing, child care, schools, employment, vehicle and firearms registration, and non–Marine Corps activities.

The centers offer seminars and orientation courses on the many aspects of family and personal development. Trained counselors and social workers provide guidance and referrals to outside agencies. Courses, home visits, and specialized assistance are available for new and expectant parents. For those families experiencing crises, family advocacy counselors supplement the wide variety of counseling services. Also offered are employment counseling for family members and retirement preparation for Marines, services often not available in communities except at considerable expense. A Marine assigned to another service's installation and his or her family may also use the host command's center.

804. Medical and Dental Care

Virtually every Marine installation includes health-care activities for the health and sanitation of all commands and their members. Normally tenant activities commanded, managed, and operated by the Navy, these activities may range from a dispensary (sick bay) to a clinic (dispensary with limited facilities for inpatient care) or, on the largest installations, a naval hospital that can handle any medical or surgical emergency. Often, a smaller base or station will have a branch clinic that operates as a satellite of a regional naval medical center. For active duty personnel, routine treatment and consultation are afforded daily at "sick call"—a fixed time of day when the sick bay is fully staffed. Emergencies, of course, are dealt with at any time, day or night.

Each installation's health-care activity not only cares for ailments but also wages a ceaseless preventive campaign. All Marines must receive certain immunizations, and every career enlisted Marine and officer must have a thorough physical examination. These examinations are ordered periodically, with the periodicity ranging from one to five years depending on circumstances.

805. Commissary

Most Marine Corps installations host a commissary, the military equivalent of a grocery store or supermarket, which is operated by the Defense Commissary Agency. If not, there is normally one conveniently located at an adjacent base or station. Commissary prices are slightly lower than those charged by grocers in the local community, although so-called big box retailers provide real competition for commissaries, which nevertheless provide good value and win on convenience.

The privilege of making purchases at commissaries is limited to regular and retired personnel, to reservists on active or training duty, and to certain government civilians. Family members of anyone entitled to commissary privileges may also use the commissary. Everyone entitled to commissary privileges must present appropriate identification. Active personnel, as well as retired personnel, are identified by the military identification card, dependents by the identification and privilege card. Use of the commissary is a privilege, not a right, and all purchases must be for your own use and that of your household.

Stock and services available in commissaries vary somewhat according to the size of the installation and the availability of adequate civilian facilities off base. The Defense Commissary Agency has operated all these activities since 1991.

806. Marine Corps Exchange

Marine Corps exchanges (MCX, as they are commonly known) and/or exchange annexes operate at the vast majority of bases and stations. Moreover, these exchange operations, along with the welfare, recreation, and other beneficial activities described below, have been centralized in direction under the MCCS department or division of each installation, and since 1999 they have operated under the headquarters staff cognizance of the deputy commandant for Manpower and Reserve Affairs.

Military exchanges, originally called post exchanges and still called that today on Army installations, go far back into U.S. military history. During the nineteenth century, when the Army pushed our frontier westward, each isolated post had its "post trader," or sutler, authorized to keep store at the post. One of the trader's perquisites was the right of trading with Indians, trappers, and hunters, and from this arose the title "post exchange." After the frontier vanished, the name remained, carrying over from the old Army into the old Marine Corps. In early times, the perquisite of keeping the post trader's stores at the various Marine barracks was awarded to the widow of some officer or senior NCO. The modern post exchange system was established by General

Charles Heywood, the ninth commandant. As part of a Marine Corps–wide rebranding effort beginning in the late 1990s, the Marine Corps exchange system began using the MCX moniker exclusively.

Today's exchange is really the installation's general store. On large bases and stations, it approximates a small department store, but the size of an exchange depends on the size of the installation it serves and the accessibility of civilian shopping centers. Marine Corps exchanges aim to provide military personnel (including family members) convenient retail access, at reasonable prices, to articles necessary for health, comfort, and well being.

Eligibility to shop on base at the exchange, like the commissary, is a privilege that extends only to active or retired service personnel, to their eligible family members and surviving spouses, and to reservists on active or training duty. If in civilian clothes when making a purchase, be prepared to show your ID card. Take note, as well, of the dress code pertaining to both the exchange and commissary and ensure that your family members comply at all times.

The Department of Defense extended, in 2017, limited privileges to all *honorably discharged veterans* to shop online at military exchanges, with the shopping benefit taking effect beginning on Veterans Day in 2017. While shopping privileges exclude the purchase of uniforms, alcohol, and tobacco products, they cover the majority of the online retail environment of the exchange services. This "win-win" policy both recognizes the service of honorably discharged veterans and provides additional financial support to morale, welfare, and recreation programs at military installations.

807. Welfare Activities

In addition to welfare services provided by the chaplain, special services officer, and legal assistance officer, most large posts have representatives of the American Red Cross, Navy-Marine Corps Relief Society, and Navy Mutual Aid Association. The assistance furnished by these groups is described in Chapter 21.

808. Educational Programs and Facilities

Many installations have their own public schools for the children on the installation. In some regions (mostly overseas), these are operated by the highly regarded Department of Defense Education Activity (DODEA), while in other regions schools aboard Marine Corps installations are actually part of a surrounding or adjacent civilian school district. Because of wide variations among school systems, however, you should investigate carefully before you assume that you will find schools that meet your needs at the installation. If overseas where DODEA-operated school facilities are not available, you may collect a modest schooling allowance for each child you place in a local private school of approved standards.

Every post has a free library, open to Marines and their family members. Marine Corps Headquarters provides the books. A few large posts have museums.

Even the smallest station and detachment features an Education Office, charged with providing information on educational opportunities available on and off post, including correspondence courses. Many of these programs lead toward various types of college degrees. The same office will advise you of tuition aid, veteran's assistance, and loan and scholarship programs.

809. Fitness and Recreation

Most posts feature excellent on-station physical fitness, athletic, and recreation opportunities, and the Semper Fit program operated by MCCS offers virtually unlimited opportunities. Facilities for athletic activities and hobbies are open to all. Frequently, instruction in various sports and hobbies will be available at little or no cost, and you and your family would do well to avail yourselves of the opportunity to learn new skills for present and future enjoyment. Depending upon space and demand, Marine Corps bases and stations may have golf courses, tennis courts, marinas, gymnasiums, skeet and small bore ranges, swimming pools, stables, flying fields, and various workshops. Take advantage!

MARINE CORPS INSTALLATIONS COMMAND

810. Overview

Established in 2011 to consolidate and improve the management of Marine Corps installations worldwide, Marine Corps Installations Command (MCICOM) oversees base and station operations, develops and coordinates relevant policy, and prioritizes resources for the support of Marine Corps installations. MCICOM is commanded by a major general, who also functions as the assistant deputy commandant for installations and logistics (facilities) within Headquarters, Marine Corps. MCICOM is located at the Pentagon.

Central reasons for establishing MCICOM included unburdening the Operating Forces from having to manage bases and stations and creating an organization with a singular focus on providing installation support that directly, effectively, and efficiently advances the Marine Corps' warfighting mission. This reorganization enabled operational commanders at all levels to concentrate their efforts on preparing their forces for deployment and employment across the full spectrum of operations.

Marine Corps installations are an essential component of the nation's defense establishment, for they are the "force projection platforms" that enable the readiness, mobilization, training, sustainment, deployment, redeployment, and reconstitution of the Operating Forces.

811. Mission and Organization of Marine Corps Installations Command

The MCICOM mission reads as follows: "As the single authority for all Marine Corps installation matters, MCICOM exercises command and control of regional installation commands, establishes policy, exercises oversight, and prioritizes resources in order to optimize installation support to the Operating Forces, tenant commands, Marines, and family members." MCICOM continually aims to apply its capabilities and capacities to the highest priorities of the operational and training commands located aboard Marine Corps bases and stations.

MCICOM consists of a headquarters situated in the Installations and Logistics Department at Headquarters, U.S. Marine Corps, Washington, D.C., and four subordinate regional commands:

- Marine Corps Installations National Capital Region (MCINCR), located at MCB Quantico, Virginia
- Marine Corps Installations East (MCIEAST), located at MCB Camp Lejeune, North Carolina
- Marine Corps Installations West (MCIWEST), located at MCB Camp Pendleton, California
- Marine Corps Installations Pacific (MCIPAC), located at MCB Camp Butler, Okinawa Prefecture, Japan.

As depicted in Figure 8-2, the MCICOM organization provides for oversight of base and station operations in support of tenant organizations and coordination with both the Marine Forces and key training commands, which fall under the separate cognizance of the Marine Corps Training and Education Command.

MCICOM's more than 33,000 personnel oversee 24 Marine Corps installations, 2.3 million acres of land, and 283 training ranges. Included within these twenty-four installations are eleven air stations, air facilities, and expeditionary airfields. MCICOM also provides operational support aircraft for transporting passengers and cargo in support of contingency operations, training exercises, and operational commanders. To accomplish its mission, MCICOM manages a budget of approximately $2.7 billion each year, providing a broad spectrum of services and support across seven functional areas: command and staff support, installation protection, training and operations support, logistic support, facilities support, information technology, and Marine, family, and community services.

MARINE CORPS INSTALLATIONS NATIONAL CAPITAL REGION

812. Marine Barracks Washington, D.C. 20390

Marine Barracks Washington, located in southeast Washington, D.C., at the intersection of 8th and I Streets and colloquially known as "Eighth and Eye," is the oldest active installation in the Marine Corps. It was established by President Thomas Jefferson and Lieutenant Colonel William Ward Burrows, the second commandant of the Marine Corps, in 1801. "Eighth and Eye" is the Corps' senior installation, both because of its age and because it is home to the commandant. Additionally, it quartered Marine Corps Headquarters throughout its first hundred years.

Marine Barracks Washington is also the "spit-and-polish" installation of the Corps, famous for its weekly Evening Parades, and constructed around a historic barracks square in the heart of southeast Washington.

The Barracks provides ceremonial troops for official occasions in the nation's capital; it supports the U.S. Marine Band and the Marine Corps Drum and Bugle Corps; and its officers and enlisted Marines are assigned to certain special security duties in and about Washington and in the Navy Yard.

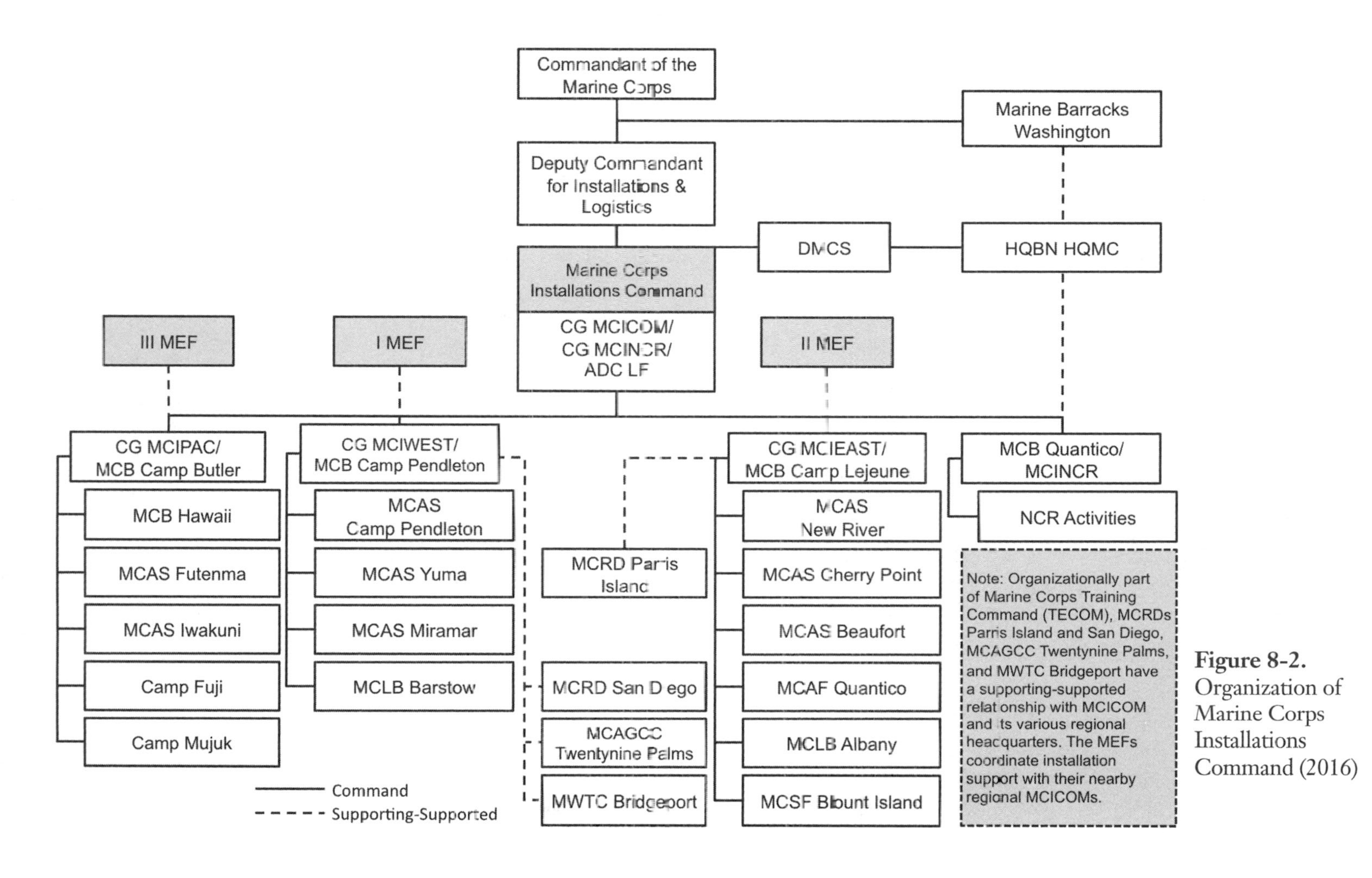

Figure 8-2. Organization of Marine Corps Installations Command (2016)

Administrative details:

Quarters. Center House provides bachelor officer quarters for officers permanently attached. There are no other bachelor officer quarters or family quarters available, although these can both be found at nearby installations managed by the other services.

Schools. In addition to a metropolitan school system, Washington has numerous private and parochial schools. Suburban public schools are adequate, with those in nearby Montgomery Country, Maryland, and Fairfax County, Virginia, generally considered best.

Child Development. The Barracks does not offer child development programs on site; however, typical programs for preschool and school-age children are available at nearby installations such as Joint Base Anacostia-Bolling.

Recreation. Other than the Barracks gymnasium, the only on-post recreation facility at "Eighth and Eye" is Center House, but facilities are abundant in the metropolitan area.

Commissary and Exchange. Commissary privileges are available at various commissaries in the Washington area. An excellent Marine Corps and Army exchange is at Joint Base Myer-Henderson Hall, in addition to the small exchange annexes located at "Eighth and Eye" and Washington Navy Yard.

Neighboring Marine Activities. The Washington area includes Marine Corps Headquarters spread between the Pentagon and Joint Base Myers-Henderson Hall, which supports Headquarters Battalion, HQMC. Both sites are situated in Arlington, Virginia.

813. Marine Corps Base Quantico, Virginia 22134

Marine Corps Base Quantico is, in many ways, the showplace of the Marine Corps. It is located on the Potomac River, approximately thirty-five miles south of Washington, D.C. It is the only base in the Marine Corps to be the site of a national cemetery. Significant tenant organizations aboard the installation include the Marine Corps Combat Development Command, Marine Corps Systems Command, Marine Corps Intelligence Activity (MCIA), Marine Corps

Network Operations and Security Center (MCNOSC), MCAF Quantico, and Naval Medical Clinic. Because of its significant role supporting training, education, and combat development, MCB Quantico is called the "Crossroads of the Marine Corps."

Administrative details:

Quarters. Government quarters are available and sufficient to accommodate all eligible personnel. Off-base housing is available in the surrounding area, north toward Woodbridge and south toward Fredericksburg, with rapid seasonal turnover in rentals. Because of the proximity to Washington, D.C., housing costs are higher than at other Marine Corps bases. Transient and permanent bachelor quarters are available.

Schools. One elementary school, one middle school, and one high school are located aboard MCB Quantico.

Child Development. Two child development centers offer full-day care for children ages six weeks through five years and school age care for children ages six through twelve years. Hourly care is also available.

Recreation. Quantico abounds in recreational opportunities. These include a commissioned officers' mess, eighteen-hole golf course, fifty-meter swimming pool, state-of-the-art fitness center, movie theater, bowling center, auto skills center, marina, base library, intramural athletics, various clubs, and hunting and fishing. Marine Corps Community Services also offers a variety of discounted tickets, tours, and recreational classes. MCB Quantico is also home to the Alfred M. Gray Marine Corps Research Center. Opened in 2006, the National Museum of the Marine Corps is in nearby Triangle, Virginia.

Commissary and Exchange. The commissary and exchange, located together to make parking more convenient, are outstanding. The entire complex is designed like a shopping mall, and the commissary offers shoppers the variety of a major supermarket.

814. National Capital Region Activities

In addition to Marine Barracks Washington and Marine Corps Base Quantico, there are a few other noteworthy Marine Corps activities around the nation's capital. These include:

- Henderson Hall, located on the southern edge of Arlington National Cemetery and named for Brevet Brigadier General Archibald Henderson, the fifth and longest-serving commandant of the Marine Corps. Once an independent Marine Corps installation, Henderson Hall is now part of Joint Base Myer-Henderson Hall.
- Marine Corps Detachment Fort Meade, located in Laurel, Maryland, and host to Marine Corps Forces Cyberspace Command, the service component command for U.S. Cyber Command.

MARINE CORPS INSTALLATIONS EAST

815. Overview

Located aboard MCB Camp Lejeune, MCIEAST is the regional command that oversees the activities of assigned Marine Corps bases and stations located in the eastern United States. MCIEAST develops and implements strategies, plans, and policies for installation management; directs and oversees installation activities; prioritizes allocation of resources; and provides regional services and support through assigned bases and stations to support the Operating Forces and tenant commands and activities. MCIEAST is commanded by a brigadier general, who also serves as the commanding general for MCB Camp Lejeune.

Marine Corps Installations East encompasses a headquarters and seven bases and stations as follows:

- MCB Camp Lejeune, located near Jacksonville, North Carolina
- MCAS New River, adjacent to MCB Camp Lejeune
- MCAS Cherry Point, near Havelock, North Carolina
- MCAS Beaufort, adjacent to Beaufort, South Carolina
- MCAF Quantico, a tenant facility located aboard MCB Quantico in Virginia
- MCLB Albany, located just outside Albany, Georgia
- MCSF Blount Island, located in the vicinity of Jacksonville, Florida.

816. Marine Corps Base Camp Lejeune, North Carolina 28547

MCB Camp Lejeune is the East Coast base for the ground units of the Fleet Marine Force. It accommodates the II MEF Command Element, 2nd Marine Division, and 2nd Marine Logistics Group; 22nd, 24th, and 26th MEUs;

Marine Corps Special Operations Command; several training centers and specialty schools; and the Naval Hospital. It adjoins MCAS New River, home to tilt-rotor and rotary-wing aircraft. Camp Lejeune's neighboring community is Jacksonville, North Carolina.

Administrative details:

Quarters. Government quarters are available and sufficient to accommodate all eligible personnel, occasionally after a moderate waiting period. Since 2007, all family housing is operated as part of a public-private partnership. Prospective and current residents of officer housing aboard MCB Camp Lejeune or MCAS New River should direct housing inquiries to the appropriate private partner: Atlantic Marine Corps Communities (https://www.atlanticmcc.com). Off-base housing is available in Jacksonville and the surrounding environs, with rapid seasonal turnovers in rentals. Transient and permanent bachelor officer quarters are available.

Schools. There are seven schools to serve students in grades kindergarten through high school; these are open to children of service families residing on MCB Camp Lejeune and MCAS New River. Families not on federal property must rely on county or other local schools. East Carolina University operates a branch and an extension division at Camp Lejeune, and major extension universities offer degree programs at the base. Coastal Carolina Community College in Jacksonville offers courses leading to an associate degree.

Child Development. Camp Lejeune's child and youth program offers comprehensive, high-quality child care at multiple locations for infants and children ages six weeks to twelve years.

Recreation. Camp Lejeune boasts ample recreation opportunities. These include a commissioned officers' mess; two eighteen-hole golf courses; multiple swimming pools, fitness centers, and movie theaters; bowling center; auto skills center; marina; base library; intramural athletics; skate park; archery, skeet, and shooting ranges; several recreation centers; hunting and fishing; and an oceanfront for swimming, surfing, and other water sports. Marine Corps Community Services also offers a variety of discounted tickets, tours, and recreational classes.

Commissary and Exchange. The commissary and exchange are excellent and well stocked. The commissary won the 2013 Director's Award for the Best Superstore, awarded by the Defense Commissary Agency. The collocated exchange is configured like a mall, and there are several small exchange annexes to serve outlying areas.

817. Marine Corps Air Station New River, North Carolina 28540

MCAS New River is the East Coast home to Marine Corps tilt-rotor and rotary-wing aviation. It primarily hosts elements of 2nd Marine Aircraft Wing, in particular Marine Aircraft Group 26, Marine Aircraft Group 29, and other units dedicated to aviation support. It adjoins MCB Camp Lejeune, with which it is substantially integrated from a base support perspective, and neighbors Jacksonville, North Carolina.

Administrative details: Although MCAS New River is administratively distinct from MCB Camp Lejeune (the air station has its own commander and staff), the installation support and services are either integrated with or similar to those of the air station's larger neighbor. For an idea of support and services available at New River, refer to the discussion in the preceding section covering Camp Lejeune.

818. Marine Corps Air Station Cherry Point, North Carolina 28533

First commissioned in 1942 as Cunningham Field, in honor of the Marine Corps' first aviator, Lieutenant Colonel Alfred A. Cunningham, and later renamed, MCAS Cherry Point is the largest Marine Corps air station in the world and is one of the best all-weather jet bases. It is home to the 2nd Marine Aircraft Wing headquarters, Marine Aircraft Group 14, Marine Air Control Group 28, the only Marine Corps–operated Fleet Readiness Center, and the Naval Health Clinic.

Administrative details:

Quarters. Government quarters are available and sufficient to accommodate all eligible personnel, with very minimal waiting periods, if any, at Cherry Point. Since 2007, all family housing has been operated as

8-1. Sheltered amid the pines of North Carolina, Cherry Point supports many elements of the 2nd Marine Aircraft Wing.

part of a public-private partnership. Prospective and current residents of officer housing aboard MCAS Cherry Point should direct housing inquiries to the private partner, Atlantic Marine Corps Communities. Private housing is available in adjacent Havelock and nearby Newport, New Bern, Beaufort (pronounced "Bowfort" and not to be confused with Beaufort, South Carolina), and Morehead City. Air station orders require that all newly assigned personnel contact the Military Housing Office for counseling and guidance before entering any agreement, lease, or rental contract for housing, on or off station.

Schools. Although there are no schools aboard Cherry Point, there are five public elementary schools, two middle schools, and one high school in Havelock. Depending on where they choose to reside, Marines assigned to the air station are served by the schools of Craven, Carteret, and Pamlico counties, as well as several parochial school options. The

Joint Education Center provides a wide range of education-related services. Programs ranging from adult high school completion to master's degree programs are offered by Craven Community College and university extension programs.

Child Development. Cherry Point's child and youth program offers comprehensive, high-quality child care at multiple locations for infants and children ages six weeks to twelve years.

Recreation. There are numerous recreation opportunities at MCAS Cherry Point. These include a commissioned officers' mess, eighteen-hole golf course, multiple swimming pools and fitness centers, movie theater, auto skills center, marina, base library, intramural athletics, and hunting and fishing. Marine Corps Community Services also offers a variety of discounted tickets, tours, and recreational classes.

Commissary and Exchange. Cherry Point has a well-stocked commissary and exchange. There is also a pair of exchange annexes.

819. Marine Corps Air Station Beaufort, South Carolina 29906

MCAS Beaufort (pronounced "Bewfort"), home to the Marine Corps' East Coast fixed-wing, fighter-attack aircraft assets, is located in the heart of South Carolina's colorful and historically significant Low Country. It is a major jet base capable of supporting two Marine aircraft groups. It currently hosts elements of the 2nd Marine Aircraft Wing, primarily Marine Aircraft Group 31, and the Naval Hospital. It is also close to MCRD Parris Island, supporting it with military air services.

Administrative details:

Quarters. Government quarters are available and sufficient to accommodate all eligible personnel, with very minimal waiting periods, if any, at Beaufort. Since 2007, all family housing has been operated as part of a public-private partnership. Prospective and current residents of officer housing aboard MCAS Beaufort should direct housing inquiries to the private partner, Atlantic Marine Corps Communities, which operates Tri-Command Communities supporting MCAS Beaufort, MCRD Parris Island, and Beaufort Naval Hospital. Moderately priced private housing is available throughout the northern portions of Beaufort County, although it grows pricier in the environs of Hilton Head. In addition to bachelor officer quarters, the station has one community of quarters at Laurel Bay, five miles west, with 228 sets of officer quarters. All are modern two-, three-, or four-bedroom units.

Schools. There are three federal government schools, kindergarten through eighth grade, at Laurel Bay, open only to children of families occupying Tri-Command government quarters. Otherwise, Marines assigned to MCAS Beaufort rely on Beaufort County public schools or parochial and private schools in the area.

Child Development. The child development center at MCAS Beaufort offers safe, high-quality child care for infants and children ages six weeks to twelve years.

Recreation. Recreation opportunities at MCAS Beaufort are plentiful and well integrated with those of MCRD Parris Island, given the proximity of the two installations. Opportunities include a commissioned officers' mess; eighteen-hole golf course (Parris Island); multiple swimming pools, fitness centers, and movie theaters; auto skills center; bowling center; base library; intramural athletics; and hunting and fishing. Outstanding ocean beaches are near at hand. Marine Corps Community Services also offers a variety of discounted tickets, tours, and recreational classes.

Commissary and Exchange. Air station personnel use the Parris Island commissary. There are two convenient seven-day stores, one on the air station and the other at Laurel Bay. The small Marine Corps exchange is excellent.

820. Marine Corps Air Facility Quantico, Virginia 22134

MCAF Quantico is the home to Marine Helicopter Squadron One (HMX-1), established at Quantico in 1947 as an experimental unit to test and evaluate military helicopters. Founded to develop tactics, techniques, and procedures, as well as to test equipment, HMX-1 is perhaps most widely known for supporting helicopter transport of the president of the United States. In support of this mission, HMX-1 flies either the large Sikorsky SH-3 "Sea King" or the newer, smaller VH-60N "White Hawk"; regardless of the specific aircraft, the helicopter carrying the president always uses the call sign "Marine One."

MCAF Quantico is completely located within MCB Quantico.

Administrative details: As part of MCIEAST, MCAF Quantico is organizationally distinct from MCB Quantico. The air facility, however, is dependent on MCB Quantico for virtually all base support functions. For an idea of support and services available to Marines assigned to MCAF Quantico, refer to the preceding discussion on MCB Quantico in Section 813.

821. Marine Corps Logistics Base Albany, Georgia 31704

MCLB Albany is one of the newer installations of the Corps. The base's principal tenant is Marine Corps Logistics Command, which provides worldwide, integrated logistic support to the Marine Corps. Supported by MCLB Albany, MARCORLOGCOM focuses on supply chain and distribution management, including acquisition, storage, distribution, and disposal of matériel; depot-level maintenance and maintenance management, including rebuilding major weapon systems; and management and maintenance of equipment sets that are strategically prepositioned afloat and ashore in support of the Operating Forces.

MCLB Albany provides the full range of base support to MARCORLOGCOM and several other tenant organizations, including a distribution center of the Defense Logistics Agency. Notably, the base boasts some of the finest storage capability within DOD, encompassing more than 3.8 million square feet of closed storage in nineteen warehouses and more than 7.7 million square feet of open storage lots.

Administrative details:

Quarters. Given the very small active duty population assigned to Albany, there are no bachelor officer quarters. Family housing is available and sufficient to accommodate all eligible personnel, with minimal waiting periods, if any, at Albany. All family housing is operated as part of a public-private partnership. Prospective and current residents of officer housing aboard MCLB Albany should direct housing inquiries to the appropriate private partner: Lincoln Military Housing (http://www.lincolnmilitary.com). There is also a small lodge providing guest accommodations aboard the installation.

Schools. Served by the public school systems of Dougherty and Lee Counties, as well as several private and parochial schools in the area.

8-2. A large live oak tree located just outside Marine Corps Logistics Base Albany's main gate is affectionately known as "Dubber's Oak." The historical landmark is named after Colonel A. E. Dubber, who from March 1951 to July 1955 was in charge of planning and construction of the installation, originally named the Marine Corps Depot of Supplies, Albany, Georgia. (U.S. Marine Corps photo by Nathan L. Hanks Jr.)

Child Development. The child development center offers nurturing, developmentally appropriate care for children from six weeks to twelve years of age on a full-time, part-time, or drop-in basis.

Recreation. Commissioned officers' mess, swimming pool, tennis, bowling, skeet and pistol ranges, movies, intramural sports, and hunting and fishing.

Commissary and Exchange. The commissary and exchange, both medium-sized, more than meet the needs of those stationed at MCLB, and their customer service is outstanding.

822. Marine Corps Support Facility Blount Island, Jacksonville, Florida 32226

Located near Jacksonville, Florida, MCSF Blount Island serves as the hub of the Marine Corps' worldwide prepositioning programs and as the home of

Blount Island Command, which manages these programs in support of the Marine Forces. Both Blount Island Command and the support facility operate with relatively few Marines on staff, relying instead on sizable contingents of federal civil servants and defense contractor partners. As a result, base support at MCSF Blount Island is limited.

Administrative details:

Quarters. Bachelor officer quarters, military family housing, and temporary lodging are available at nearby Naval Air Station Jacksonville and Naval Station Mayport.

Schools. Served by public school systems of Duval, Clay, and Nassau Counties, as well as several private and parochial schools in the area.

Child Development. Child development programs, including child development centers offering full- and part-time care, are available at nearby Naval Air Station Jacksonville and Naval Station Mayport.

Recreation. Nearby Naval Air Station Jacksonville and Naval Station Mayport provide a complete array of recreational opportunities.

Commissary and Exchange. Excellent commissary and exchange services are available at nearby Naval Air Station Jacksonville.

823. Marine Corps Recruit Depot Parris Island, South Carolina 29905

In the mid-1500s, colonial empires clashed on the shores of Parris Island as Spanish and French explorers sought strategic footholds in the New World. Although more than four hundred years have passed, the military tradition continues to be as vital today as it was then. More than one million recruits have been trained on Parris Island since "boot camp" was established there in 1915. Currently, male recruits from the eastern United States and females from throughout the nation are trained at the place "Where the Difference Begins." The depot commanding general, a brigadier general, is also commanding general for the Eastern Recruiting Region.

Marine Corps Recruit Depot Parris Island is not organizationally part of MCIEAST; instead, it is part of Marine Corps Training and Education Command. However, it is discussed here because of its geographic location and the supporting-supported relationship between MCIEAST and MCRD Parris Island.

Administrative details:

Quarters. Refer to the preceding section discussing quarters for MCAS Beaufort.

Schools. There are three federal government schools, kindergarten through eighth grade, at Laurel Bay, open only to children of families occupying Tri-Command government quarters. Otherwise, Marines assigned to MCRD Parris Island rely on Beaufort County public schools or parochial and private schools in the area.

Child Development. The child development center at Parris Island offers safe, high-quality child care for infants and children ages six weeks to twelve years.

8-3. Recruit training at MCRD Parris Island continues to bring the best out of Marines-to-be.

Recreation. Recreation opportunities at MCRD Parris Island are plentiful and well integrated with those of MCAS Beaufort, given the proximity of the two installations. Opportunities include a commissioned officers' mess; eighteen-hole golf course; multiple swimming pools, fitness centers, and movie theaters; auto skills center; bowling center; base library; intramural athletics; and hunting and fishing. There is also a War Memorial Museum. Marine Corps Community Services also offers a variety of discounted tickets, tours, and recreational classes. There is a variety of activities and resort areas in Beaufort County, including historic Beaufort and Hilton Head Island.

Commissary and Exchange. Parris Island has a full-service commissary, and the small Marine Corps exchange is excellent. There are two convenient seven-day stores, one on the depot and the other at Laurel Bay.

MARINE CORPS INSTALLATIONS WEST

824. Overview

Located aboard MCB Camp Pendleton, MCIWEST is the regional command that oversees the activities of assigned Marine Corps bases and stations located in the western United States. Like its counterpart on the east coast, MCIWEST develops and implements strategies, plans, and policies for installation management; directs and oversees installation activities; prioritizes allocation of resources; and provides regional services and support through assigned bases and stations to support the Operating Forces and tenant commands and activities. MCIWEST is commanded by a brigadier general, who also serves as the commanding general for MCB Camp Pendleton.

Marine Corps Installations West comprises a headquarters and five bases and stations as follows:

- MCB Camp Pendleton, wedged between San Clemente and Oceanside, California
- MCAS Camp Pendleton, situated on MCB Camp Pendleton
- MCAS Yuma, adjacent to Yuma, Arizona
- MCAS Miramar, located north of San Diego, California
- MCLB Barstow, just outside of Barstow, California.

825. Marine Corps Base Camp Pendleton, California 95055

"Pendleton" is the prime amphibious training base in the Corps. It serves as the major West Coast base for ground units of the Fleet Marine Force and provides facilities and support for the 1st Marine Division, the 1st Marine Logistics Group, and the Command Element, I MEF. Camp Pendleton also completely envelopes MCAS Camp Pendleton. Recruits from MCRD San Diego complete weapons training at Camp Pendleton's Edson Range and Weapons Field Training Battalion; those who go into infantry attend the School of Infantry at Camp San Onofre after graduation from San Diego. The installation also hosts several other formal schools and smaller organizations. Camp Pendleton is huge—more than two hundred square miles—and geographically diverse, including seventeen miles of undeveloped oceanfront, with coastal mountains and wetlands inland.

The Marine Corps' role at Camp Pendleton history dates from 25 September 1942, when the initial 125,000-acre tract of land was dedicated by President Franklin D. Roosevelt and named in honor of Major General Joseph H. Pendleton. The area where Camp Pendleton is located emerged through Spanish land grants as Rancho Santa Margarlty y Las Flores y San Onofre. Custody of these lands was originally held by Mission San Luis Rey de Francia. It passed through the hands of Don Pio and Don Andres Pico in the mid-1800s, and on through several other owners until the federal government purchased a major portion of the rancho for use as a Marine Corps training base during World War II. The ranch house, in which the rancho owners once lived, is now the residence of the senior commanding general. Nearby are the historic chapel and bunkhouse (now a museum) All three are listed collectively as a national historic site and California state historical landmark.

Administrative details:

Quarters. Camp Pendleton's military housing is managed under a public-private partnership since 2003, and nearly every unit on base was renovated in the ensuing years. There are over seventy-five hundred units located in communities dispersed across the base. The wait for a two-or three-bedroom unit is less than six months, but expect to wait up to a year for four or five bedrooms. Off-base housing is available, but anywhere in the local area is going to be expensive. Before bringing families to Camp Pendleton, it is advisable to contact the Base Housing Office for information. This office can update you on the quarters situation and can, if necessary, help in finding civilian housing.

Schools. Local school districts surrounding Camp Pendleton provide primary and secondary education both on and off the installation. There are five public elementary schools aboard Camp Pendleton: three (North Terrace, Santa Margarita, and Stuart Mesa), offering grades kindergarten through eight, belong to the Oceanside Unified School District and two (Mary Fay Pendleton and San Onofre), offering grades kindergarten through eight, belong to the Fallbrook Union Elementary School District. Depending on housing area assigned, high school students living on base may attend one of three nearby off-base public high schools: Oceanside High School, Fallbrook High School, or San Clemente High School. Parochial and some private schools, together with MiraCosta and Palomar community colleges in the immediate area, offer excellent courses for qualified Marines and their families, as do other colleges in the San Diego area. A number of college and high school completion courses are also offered on Camp Pendleton.

Child Development. Child development centers aboard Camp Pendleton are nationally accredited, facility-based child care services that support the needs of children ages six weeks through five years. Seven separate facilities provide child care and preschool programs for children of military and civilian workers at Camp Pendleton. Distributed conveniently across the base, the centers are open Monday through Friday and offer care on a regular (monthly) and walk-in (hourly) basis. The centers provide cribs and beds, toys, and well-equipped, fenced playgrounds. Enrichment programs are available for all ages. School-aged children may be cared for before and after their school sessions.

Health. Naval Hospital Camp Pendleton is a new medical treatment facility located near the main gate at the south end of the base. The major, forty-two-bed facility is a medium-sized teaching hospital that provides outpatient and inpatient care for active duty servicemembers, their family members, retirees, and other eligible beneficiaries. Outpatient medical care is also offered in five branch clinics, four located throughout the base and one, which caters to family members, located in Oceanside. Additional specialty care is provided at Naval Medical Center San Diego, approximately one hour's drive south from Camp Pendleton or at nearby civilian facilities as needed, and emergency care is available at the hospital on a twenty-four-hour basis.

Recreation. Commissioned officers' mess, with three convenient locations, one with a swimming pool; surfing beaches; freshwater and deep-sea fishing; paintball; skeet and trap; tennis; riding stables; eighteen-hole golf; hunting; additional swimming pools; bowling center; track and field; multiple fitness centers, gymnasiums, and weight rooms; movie theaters; sailing; playgrounds; miniature golf; archery; picnic areas; libraries; hobby shops; intramural sports; and recreation instruction and rental equipment are all available. Youth activity programs are numerous.

Commissary and Exchange. A modern commissary is available in the south near the main gate, with an annex in the northern section. There is a large main exchange opposite the commissary near the main gate, and modern, complete exchange annexes are located within each of the major camps.

826. Marine Corps Air Station Camp Pendleton, California 92055

Established in 1942 as an auxiliary landing field, MCAS Camp Pendleton is completely located within MCB Camp Pendleton. Known also as Munn Field in honor of Lieutenant General John C. "Toby" Munn, the first aviator to command Camp Pendleton, the air station supports the operations of Marine Aircraft Group 39, with several medium tilt-rotor and light rotary-wing aircraft squadrons.

Administrative details: As part of MCIWEST, MCAS Camp Pendleton is organizationally distinct from MCB Camp Pendleton. The air facility, however, is dependent on Camp Pendleton for virtually all base support functions. For an idea of support and services available to Marines assigned to MCAS Camp Pendleton, refer to the preceding discussion on MCB Camp Pendleton.

827. Marine Corps Air Station Yuma, Arizona 85369

One of the newest of the Marine Corps air stations, MCAS Yuma has a 13,300-foot main runway, an instrumented range, and some of the finest flying weather to be found. Covering five square miles of southeastern Yuma, the air station is home to Marine Aircraft Group 13, Marine Aviation Weapons and Tactics Squadron 1, Marine Operational Test and Evaluation Squadron 22, and a number of tenant units involved in aviation, aviation training, and aviation support.

Administrative details:

Quarters. The government housing office provides housing referral services, accepts housing applications, and maintains waiting lists. There are 693 two-, three-, and four-bedroom houses available on the air station designated by various ranks. There are also 128 off-station, two-bedroom apartments, called 16th Street Housing, for E-1 through E-5. There are limited transient accommodations for bachelor officers. The excellent Dos Rios Inn provides temporary lodging.

8-4. This view of the main entrance to MCAS Yuma demonstrates its renowned flying weather.

Schools. Local public and private elementary, middle, and high schools, a junior college, and a college serve those stationed at MCAS Yuma.

Child Development. The child development center is nationally accredited, the first program in the Marine Corps and the third in the Department of Defense to be accredited under new comprehensive and more stringent criteria. Operating on weekdays, it is well equipped and provides a full range of child care and preschool programs.

Health. The Branch Health Clinic Yuma, an extension of the Naval Hospital Camp Pendleton, offers outpatient health care to active duty servicemembers and their families.

Recreation. Commissioned officers' mess; auto hobby shop; bowling; fitness center; library; stables (boarding only); swimming pools; tennis; fishing, camping, and boating at Lake Martinez; and station-operated recreational area.

Commissary and Exchange. Medium-sized and modern.

828. Marine Corps Air Station Miramar, California 92145

Miramar has become one of the Marine Corps' largest aviation facilities, following its reversion to USMC control in the late 1990s. A former cattle and citrus ranch, it first served Army infantry training in 1914 as Camp Kearny. After World War I, Miramar became an auxiliary field for the Navy and an air base for the Marine Corps. When World War II broke out, Miramar quickly expanded. At the end of the war, the Marines moved to MCAS El Toro, and Miramar was developed as a master jet station. After 1973, "Fightertown" was the center of tactical training for the F-14 Tomcat fighters and E-2 Hawkeye airborne early warning aircraft. Highly technical aviation maintenance schools trained men and women to repair and maintain the aircraft. Naval Air Station Miramar reverted to a Marine Corps air station on 1 October 1997, bringing fighter and helicopter squadrons from El Toro and the helicopter-oriented MCAS Tustin.

Today, MCAS Miramar hosts a large complement of the Marine Corps' fixed wing and tilt-rotor aircraft based on the West Coast. It is home to the 3rd Marine Aircraft Wing headquarters, Marine Aircraft Group 11, Marine Aircraft Group 16, and Marine Air Control Group 38, as well as several other tenant organizations.

Administrative details:

Quarters. Family housing at MCAS Miramar has been privatized and is managed, operated, and maintained by Lincoln Military Housing, which offers 592 two-, three-, four-, and five-bedroom homes at Miramar within six communities serving the air station. The government housing office provides housing-referral services, accepts housing applications, and maintains waiting lists. There are permanent and transient quarters for bachelor officers. The Miramar Inn offers modern rooms in a convenient location. There is ample off-station housing, but housing costs in the communities surrounding MCAS Miramar are among the highest in the nation.

Schools. There are no Department of Defense schools located aboard MCAS Miramar. Instead, families assigned to the air station are served by the nearby San Diego Unified School District and Poway Unified School District. Students residing aboard Miramar attend school from kindergarten through twelfth grade in the Mira Mesa Cluster, part of the San Diego Unified School District.

Child Development. The child development center provides weekly care for active duty military and Department of Defense civilian dependents between the ages of six weeks and five years, as well as school-age care up to sixth grade.

Health. Part of the Naval Medical Center San Diego network, a branch health clinic aboard MCAS Miramar offers a wide range of care for active duty personnel and family members. The clinic provides preventive and acute care, while emergency and specialty care is available at the full-service Naval Medical Center San Diego to the south.

Recreation. Miramar offers a variety of recreational activities, including an auto skills center, movie theater, eighteen-hole golf course, parks, outdoor adventure center, paintball park, three full-service fitness centers, and a number of restaurants and clubs for air station personnel. It also features The Great Escape, a facility equipped with billiard tables, ping-pong tables, interactive gaming systems, and a state-of-the-art movie room.

Commissary and Exchange. Large commissary and exchange. There are also several Navy commissaries in the San Diego area, and MCRD San Diego to the south has a large Marine Corps exchange.

829. Marine Corps Logistics Base Barstow, California 92311

Established in 1942, the Marine Corps Logistics Base at Barstow is located to take advantage of a confluence of transportation routes and the Mojave Desert's hot, dry climate, which inhibits deterioration of stored material. Barstow generally supports all Marine organizations west of the Mississippi and in the Far East, operates a central repair shop for all field equipment except aircraft, and stores designated items.

Located midway between Los Angeles and Las Vegas, MCLB Barstow comprises three principal sites. Headquarters, administrative, storage, recreational, shopping, and housing functions are hosted at Nebo, which encompasses 1,879 acres. Yermo Annex spans 1,859 acres and is home to a substantial industrial and storage complex, including a 10-acre repair shop—the largest building in the Marine Corps—and a surrounding 40-acre concrete platform. The third site, numbering 2,438 acres, provides rifle and pistol ranges.

8-5. Only a portion of the industrial sprawl of MCLB, Barstow, can be captured in a single photograph.

Administrative details:

Quarters. MCLB Barstow is one of a few installations with military housing still retained and managed directly by the Marine Corps. The base has fifty married and eight bachelor officer quarters. Although base housing is not mandatory, officers must contact the base housing office before securing off-base housing. Reliable information about off-base housing in the Barstow area is available by contacting the nearby Fort Irwin Housing Referral Office. The Oasis Temporary Lodging Facility offers short-term housing accommodations for military members and their families.

Schools. Public education is provided by Barstow Unified School District, which has six elementary schools, two middle schools, and two high schools. There are also three private elementary schools, and Barstow College, a community college, offers local post-secondary education.

Child Development. A child development center offers quality full-day, part-day, and hourly care for children six weeks to five years of age. School-age care is available for students five through twelve years of age who are enrolled in elementary school.

Health. The Branch Medical Clinic Barstow offers outpatient health care to active duty servicemembers and their families.

Recreation. Consolidated officer–staff noncommissioned officer club, swimming pools, fitness center, tennis, racquetball, nine-hole golf course (located just outside the main gate), bowling center, skeet, and fishing.

Commissary and Exchange. Both are medium sized and well stocked.

830. Marine Corps Recruit Depot San Diego, California 92101

The primary mission of MCRD San Diego is twofold. First is the recruiting of new Marines from the Western Recruiting Region, which is composed of the 8th, 9th, and 12th Marine Corps Districts. Second is the training of Marine recruits using facilities at San Diego and Camp Pendleton, California. Also located at MCRD is the Recruiters' School and the West Coast Drill Instructors' School. The depot is located in central San Diego on the Pacific Highway. The depot commanding general, a brigadier general, is also commanding general for the Western Recruiting Region.

Marine Corps Recruit Depot San Diego is not organizationally part of MCIWEST; instead, it is part of Marine Corps Training and Education Command. However, it is discussed here because of its geographic location and the supporting-supported relationship between MCIWEST and MCRD San Diego.

Administrative details:

Quarters. Except for five sets for key senior officers, there are no government quarters on the depot. Married officers assigned to MCRD San Diego are eligible for family housing located throughout the "constellation" of San Diego naval installations; this housing has been privatized and is managed, operated, and maintained by Lincoln Military Housing. Bachelor officers typically find accommodations off base within the San Diego metropolitan area. There are limited accommodations for transient personnel aboard the compact installation.

Schools. There are no schools aboard the depot, but San Diego has excellent public, private, and parochial primary and secondary schools. Also, there are three major colleges in the city, plus numerous junior colleges.

8-6. Depot headquarters, San Diego, typifies the base's Spanish colonial architecture and atmosphere.

Child Development. The child development center provides weekly care for active duty military and Department of Defense civilian dependents between the ages of six weeks and five years, as well as school-age care up to sixth grade.

Health. Naval Branch Health Clinic provides primary care and dental services to active duty personnel assigned to MCRD San Diego and Marine Corps recruits who are completing initial basic training. Additionally, the clinic completes the comprehensive medical and dental in-processing of recruits, ensuring their individual medical readiness is complete before reporting to the Operating Forces. Family members obtain preventive and acute care at any of several naval branch health clinics in the San Diego area, while emergency and specialty care is available at the full-service Naval Medical Center San Diego.

Recreation. Due to the relatively compact size and urban location of MCRD San Diego, opportunities for recreation aboard the depot are somewhat limited. These opportunities do include a boathouse and marina, fitness center, movie theater, recreation center, and auto skills center. Servicemembers assigned to MCRD San Diego also have access to recreational facilities and programs at nearby naval installations. Additionally, Southern California supplies virtually every type of recreation from swimming to skiing. The commissioned officers' mess is one of the finest and oldest in the Corps.

Commissary and Exchange. MCRD has an outstanding Marine Corps exchange. The nearest commissaries are located at Naval Base San Diego (eight miles distant) and North Island Naval Air Station (nine miles).

831. Marine Corps Air-Ground Combat Center Twentynine Palms, California 92278

With its 932 square miles of area, twice the size of Los Angeles and big enough to encompass Pendleton, Lejeune, and Quantico with room to spare, Marine Corps Air-Ground Combat Center (MCAGCC) is not only the largest installation in the Marine Corps but also a primary training and experimental center for Marine artillery and guided missiles. It is also the location of the Communication-Electronics School and has facilities for most elements of the 7th Marine Regiment (Reinforced). The base also includes the Tactical Exercise

Evaluation and Control Group, which exercises the combined-arms capabilities and readiness of operational units in a live-fire environment.

Like MCRD San Diego, MCAGCC is part of Marine Corps Training and Education Command, not MCIWEST. However, it is discussed here because of the supporting-supported relationship between MCIWEST and MCAGCC.

Administrative details:

Quarters. Housing aboard the base has been privatized and is managed, operated, and maintained by Lincoln Military Housing. Lincoln offers one- and two-story, three- and four-bedroom, duplex-style homes. There are also single-family homes for senior field-grade officers. Lincoln provides overall property management, while the government controls the applications, waitlists, entitlements, Vista del Sol Leased Housing, and other military issues dealing with housing. Bachelor officers stationed at Twentynine Palms typically reside off base. Temporary lodging is available, depending on exercises.

Schools. Students residing on base attend public schools in the Morongo Unified School District. The town of Twentynine Palms has elementary, junior high, and senior high schools, as well as a parochial grade school (through eighth grade). Undergraduate and graduate educational opportunities are available through on-base extension universities.

Child Development. There are three child development centers: one facility provides hourly and full-time care for children from six weeks to three years of age, one provides full-time child care services for children aged six weeks to three years, and one provides full-time and part-time preschool for children aged three to five years. The program also offers school-age care for students through sixth grade.

Health. Serving those residing at the Marine Corps Air-Ground Combat Center and in the surrounding communities, Naval Hospital Twentynine Palms provides comprehensive outpatient and inpatient care, including emergency services, to active duty servicemembers, their family members, and, subject to capacity, retirees and their families.

Recreation. Commissioned officers' mess; four well-configured fitness centers; two swimming pools, including one heated and open year round; intramural sports; skeet, hunting, and fishing; tennis; eighteen-hole golf course; auto skills center; bowling center; paintball park; movie theater; and hobby shop. The base is almost at the epicenter of southern California recreation, and practically any kind of outdoor or indoor recreation is available.

Commissary and Exchange. Both are excellent.

832. Marine Corps Mountain Warfare Training Center Bridgeport, California 93517

The Marine Corps Mountain Warfare Training Center (MCMWTC) is located within the Humboldt-Toiyabe National Forest, twenty-one miles north of Bridgeport, California, and twenty-two miles south of Coleville, California, on Highway 108 in Pickel Meadow. For over sixty-two years, the Marine Corps has conducted training in partnership with the U.S. Forest Service at this location. The training center hosts unit and individual training courses to prepare Marine Corps, joint, and allied forces for operations in mountainous, high-altitude, and cold-weather environments, and MCMWTC develops tactics, techniques, procedures, and specialized equipment for use in mountain and cold-weather operations.

Like MCRD San Diego and MCAGCC Twentynine Palms, the training center at Bridgeport is part of Marine Corps Training and Education Command, not MCIWEST. However, it is discussed here because of the supporting-supported relationship between MCIWEST and MCMWTC.

Administrative details:

Quarters. Lincoln Military Housing manages, operates, and maintains privatized military housing for permanent personnel. Situated approximately twenty-five miles north of MCMWTC, the community is located near Coleville, California, and offers one- and two-story duplex and quadplex homes with two, three, or four bedrooms. Community amenities include a community center, fitness center, swimming pool, and a variety of tot-lots. Temporary lodging is also available at MCMWTC.

Schools. There are no schools at MCMWTC. Servicemembers stationed at Bridgeport typically send their students to the public schools of the Eastern Sierra Unified School District, which includes four elementary schools (kindergarten through eighth grade) and two high schools located in the environs of Coleville and Bridgeport.

Child Development. A child development center is conveniently located in the Lincoln Military Housing complex. It provides full-time, part-time, and hourly care for children aged six weeks to five years. The center also provides before- and after-school care for children five to nine years of age.

Health. Branch Medical Clinic Bridgeport, part of the health network anchored by Naval Hospital Twentynine Palms, provides general wellness care, outpatient care, and basic pharmacy, laboratory, and radiology services for servicemembers and their families. Patients requiring emergency services or specialty care are normally evacuated to civilian hospitals in Carson City, Lake Tahoe, or Reno, Nevada, or, if the situation permits, to Naval Hospital Twentynine Palms.

Recreation. All-ranks club, fitness center, and outdoor recreational services, which offer an extensive selection of equipment rentals to take advantage of the nearby fishing, camping, hiking, backpacking, and skiing opportunities.

Commissary and Exchange. Small commissary near Coleville, California, and small exchange aboard MCMWTC. The Coleville community housing area offers a seven-day store.

MARINE CORPS INSTALLATIONS PACIFIC

833. Overview

Headquartered at MCB Camp Smedley D. Butler in Okinawa, Japan, MCIPAC is the regional command that oversees the activities of assigned Marine Corps bases and stations located outside the continental United States in Hawaii and the Western Pacific. Like its counterparts in CONUS, MCIPAC develops and implements strategies, plans, and policies for installation management; directs and oversees installation activities; prioritizes allocation of resources; and provides regional services and support through assigned bases and stations to support the Operating Forces and tenant commands and activities. MCIPAC is normally commanded by a brigadier general, who also serves as the commanding general for MCB Camp Butler.

Marine Corps Installations Pacific is composed of a headquarters and six bases and stations as follows:

- MCB Camp Butler, located on the island of Okinawa, Japan
- MCAS Futenma, positioned in the southern portion of the island of Okinawa, Japan
- MCAS Iwakuni, situated southwest of Hiroshima on the island of Honshu, Japan
- Combined Arms Training Center Camp Fuji, sited on the southeast slope of Mount Fuji on the island of Honshu, Japan
- Camp Mujuk, located just outside Pohang, South Korea
- MCB Hawaii, situated on the island of Oahu, Hawaii.

834. Marine Corps Base Camp Smedley D. Butler, Japan 96373

MCB Camp Butler is not a single installation; it actually refers to a collection of Marine installations and facilities on the island of Okinawa, including several smaller camps (Camps Foster/Lester, Courtney/McTureous, Gonsalves, Hansen, Kinser, and Schwab). The MCB Camp Butler headquarters is located aboard Camp Foster. The III MEF Command Element, 3rd Marine Division, 1st Marine Aircraft Wing, and 3rd Marine Logistics Group are all headquartered at one of the camps within the Camp Butler complex.

Although not strictly part of the Camp Butler complex, Marine Corps Air Station Futenma, also on Okinawa, shares many services and resources with Butler.

Administrative details:

Transportation. Chartered commercial aircraft, which primarily support the rotation of personnel to and from permanent assignment on Okinawa, use Kadena Air Force Base, while scheduled commercial airlines use Naha International Airport.

Quarters. Marine Corps policy requires all servicemembers permanently assigned to Okinawa on accompanied orders to reside in on-base government housing, which is centrally managed by the Air Force. Additionally, unaccompanied company grade officers (second lieutenant through captain and warrant officer 1 through chief warrant officer 3) must occupy designated bachelor officer quarters. Unaccompanied field-grade officers (majors and above) may decline government quarters, but they must first request approval through their respective chains of command.

There are more than 8,300 housing units, located on seven bases and camps throughout the island of Okinawa. Camps Courtney and McTureous host 12 percent of the housing inventory. Camp Kinser makes up another 12 percent. Twenty-eight percent of the inventory is located aboard Camps Foster and Lester. Kadena Air Base has 48 percent, which incorporates the Camp Shields and Chibana Housing areas. The Housing Management Office on Okinawa has a live-where-you-work policy, which means that the housing office makes every effort to offer members a unit closest to their duty stations. Although off-base rentals are available, some units are old, expensive, and small, and they often lack storage space and modern conveniences.

There are temporary lodging facilities located at several of the camps on Okinawa.

Schools. The Okinawa District of the Department of Defense Education Activity operates thirteen schools (seven elementary/primary schools, four middle/intermediate schools, and two high schools) distributed across Camps Foster, Kinser, Lester, and McTureous, as well as Kadena AFB. Department of Defense schools typically provide a comprehensive, high-quality education.

Child Development. With locations on Camps Kinser, Foster, and Courtney, child development centers offer quality full-day and hourly care for children six weeks to five years old. School-age care is available for children five to twelve years of age who are enrolled in kindergarten through sixth grade. Care is offered during duty hours before and after school.

Health. Naval Hospital Okinawa is the largest overseas hospital in the U.S. Navy. It offers a complete range of medical and dental services through a complex of facilities that includes the main hospital and seven branch medical clinics spread across the island's various camps.

Recreation. Commissioned officers' mess; nine fitness centers; intramural sports; eighteen-hole golf course; auto skills, bowling, and arts and crafts centers; six movie theaters; swimming pools; libraries; skate park; and extensive water sports, including scuba.

Commissary and Exchange. Excellent commissaries are located on Kadena AFB and Camps Courtney, Foster, and Kinser. There are excellent exchanges, operated by the Army and Air Force Exchange Service, with four main stores collocated with the commissaries and eight branch and convenience stores distributed at installations across Okinawa.

835. Marine Corps Air Station Futenma, Japan 96372

The U.S. military originally built Futenma Airfield in 1945 as a site from which to launch B-29 Superfortress strategic bombers to support the planned invasion of mainland Japan. The airfield remained in U.S. Air Force possession until 1957, when it was transferred to the U.S. Navy. The Department of the Navy subsequently developed it into a full-fledged air station for Marine Corps use.

Although the air station's 9,000-foot runway is capable of safely handling the largest commercial and military cargo planes in the world, MCAS Futenma primarily hosts propeller-driven and tilt-rotor aircraft for Marine units on Okinawa. Marine Aircraft Group 36 and Marine Air Control Group 18 are headquartered aboard the air station. Although Futenma can theoretically handle Marine jet aircraft, if they deploy to Okinawa they typically operate from Naval Air Facility Kadena.

Opposition to the U.S. military presence in Okinawa has grown within the local population, and MCAS Futenma has become the focus of much controversy in recent decades. Over the years, there have been several relocation plans developed, modified, and abandoned. As of 2016, the future of Futenma was unresolved, and discussions among the various stakeholders continue.

Administrative details: As part of MCIPAC, MCAS Futenma is organizationally distinct from MCB Camp Butler. However, the air station shares most base support functions and services with Camp Butler, less air station operations, and personnel assigned to the air station have access to the complete range of support and service offered by the Camp Butler complex. For an idea of support and services available to Marines assigned to MCAS Futenma, refer to the preceding discussion on MCB Camp Butler.

836. Marine Corps Air Station Iwakuni, Japan 96310

MCAS Iwakuni is the home station of all tactical jet aircraft units of the 1st Marine Aircraft Wing (whose headquarters is at Camp Butler, Okinawa) and of Japanese naval aviation units as well.

Administrative details:

Transportation. Japan National Railways has outstanding local and high-speed rail service to all points in the main four islands of Japan. Scheduled Air Mobility Command flights handle military traffic directly in and out of Iwakuni, while scheduled commercial flights use Hiroshima Airport (twenty-seven miles distant), with connections for international flights at Tokyo.

Quarters. Besides bachelor officer quarters, Iwakuni has government quarters for officers on accompanied tours. Managed by the Family Housing Office, these include two- and three-bedroom apartments; two-, three-, and four-bedroom townhouses; three-bedroom row houses; three- and four-bedroom duplexes; and three- and four-bedroom single family homes.

Schools. There are two Department of Defense schools located at MCAS Iwakuni: Matthew C. Perry Elementary School (kindergarten through sixth grade) and Matthew C. Perry High School (grades seven through twelve).

Child Development. The child development center offers full-day care for children six weeks to five years of age (not enrolled in kindergarten). Part-day care is offered for those ages three to five. The center additionally offers hourly care. The school-age center offers a variety of planned group and individual activities for children ages five through twelve or those enrolled in kindergarten through sixth grade. The center provides before- and after-school care, extended-break care, to include teacher work days, half days, and winter, spring, and summer breaks for school-age children. The center also hosts a summer program.

Health. Branch Health Clinic Iwakuni, linked to Naval Hospital Yokosuka, Japan, provides primary care, urgent care, flight medicine, and a broad range of standard health services for active duty servicemembers and their family members. Patients requiring emergency services or specialty care are normally evacuated to Naval Hospital Yokosuka.

Recreation. Commissioned officers' mess, fitness center, indoor and outdoor swimming pools, tennis, auto skills center, bowling center, hobby shop, skate park, fishing, and local cultural events.

Commissary and Exchange. Excellent.

837. Combined Arms Training Center Camp Fuji, Japan 96387

Situated at the base of Mount Fuji, Combined Arms Training Center (CATC) Camp Fuji occupies ground that was reportedly used to train samurai warriors long before the Marines arrived. As far back as 1198 CE, the Kamakura Feudal Government trained more than 30,000 samurai warriors on the same ground that Fuji Marines use today. The Fuji Maneuver Area, which consists of the 12,000-acre north area and 22,000-acre east area, is jointly used by U.S. forces and the Japan Ground Self Defense Force (JGSDF). It contains live-fire ranges as well as maneuver areas.

The camp itself is an exclusive-use, full-service, 309-acre U.S. facility designed to support U.S. forces. There is a helicopter runway, which is a joint-use facility shared by U.S. forces and the JGSDF. Camp Fuji has come a long way from the austere training site of the past.

Administrative details:

Transportation. Served by rail (Japan National Railways), bus (local service), and air, via scheduled commercial airlines operating from Tokyo International Airport, commonly known as Haneda Airport or Tokyo Haneda Airport (69 miles distant), and Narita International Airport (112 miles distant). Camp Fuji also operates the Green Line, which provides ground transportation to neighboring military installations.

Quarters. Bachelor officer quarters for unaccompanied officers, as all permanent personnel are assigned to one-year, dependent-restricted tours at Camp Fuji. There is an inn for transient personnel.

Health. Branch Health Activity Camp Fuji, a subsidiary of Naval Hospital Yokosuka, provides basic outpatient care. Specialty and emergency care are available at Naval Hospital Yokosuka, which is located sixty-eight miles away, although particularly critical cases might be treated in nearby Japanese hospitals.

Recreation. Combined club for officers and staff noncommissioned officers, fitness center, athletic fields, tennis, and library. Compared to stateside installations, recreation opportunities at Camp Fuji are somewhat limited; however, the Trips, Transportation, and Recreation Office offers an extensive list of trips and tours throughout mainland Japan. Servicemembers may also take advantage of the recreation offerings at the naval installations at Atsugi and Yokosuka, as well as Yokota Air Base.

Commissary and Exchange. There is a small exchange that provides the basics. The nearest commissary is located at Naval Air Facility Atsugi (forty-two miles distant).

838. Camp Mujuk, South Korea 96218

Camp Mujuk is the only Marine Corps installation in South Korea. It is located about an hour east of Daegu, just outside Pohang, and near the southeastern shoreline. The small installation supports Marines, other U.S. military personnel, and foreign military personnel who deploy to the Korean peninsula for bilateral training and exercises with the Korean armed forces.

Like Camp Fuji, and due to Camp Mujuk's remote location and distance from other U.S. military installations capable of providing services to support families, assignment to Camp Mujuk is a one-year, dependent-restricted tour of duty.

Administrative details:

Transportation. Local rail, bus, and air travel options exist, but servicemembers typically travel via AMC aircraft to Osan Air Base or scheduled commercial airline to Incheon International Airport near Seoul, where they are met by Camp Mujuk staff. That said, those traveling independently to Camp Mujuk via either of these two airports will find a combination of bus and taxi to be the most efficient and cost-effective method.

Quarters. Bachelor officer quarters for unaccompanied officers.

Health. The medical staff aboard Camp Mujuk consists of a single independent duty corpsman. Completing a thorough overseas health screening before assignment to Camp Mujuk is thus absolutely critical and mandatory.

Recreation. Small fitness and recreation centers.

Commissary and Exchange. A very small exchange provides the basics.

839. Marine Corps Base Hawaii, Oahu, Hawaii 96863

In 1994, the Marine Corps consolidated all of its installations in Hawaii. MCAS Kaneohe Bay joined Camp H. M. Smith, Molokai Training Support Facility, Manana Family Housing Area, Puuloa Range, and the Pearl City Warehouse Annex to form a new command, Marine Corps Base Hawaii (MCBH), headquartered at Kaneohe Bay.

The island of Oahu includes several permanent Marine Corps facilities and activities with diverse missions. The headquarters (and nerve center) of all Marine Forces Pacific activities is at Camp H. M. Smith, overlooking Pearl Harbor from the site of the World War II Aiea Naval Hospital. In addition to Camp Smith, there is MCAS Kaneohe, on the "windward" side of the island, home station of the 3rd Marine Regiment, Marine Aircraft Group 24, 3rd Radio Battalion, and a variety of other units. Here, both ground and air units of the Operating Forces train and operate as an integrated air-ground team.

Because of its superb site and outstanding facilities, Camp H. M. Smith is also home to U.S. Pacific Command, which is a tenant activity. Camp Smith is thus the only Marine Corps station that hosts the headquarters of a unified command.

8-7. MCAS Kaneohe Bay, home of the 3rd Marines, lies on the windward side of Oahu.

Administrative details:

Quarters. The Family Housing Department and Hunt Companies, Inc., the Marine Corps' public-private venture partner in Hawaii, provide housing to families of Marines assigned to duty on Oahu and members of other services assigned to MCBH, and Marines stationed at Camp Smith. Marine Corps Base Hawaii's family housing inventory privatized in two phases. Beginning in 2006, the first phase of privatization included 1,175 units. The remaining inventory of 1,142 units privatized in 2007. The base also manages accommodations for bachelor officers and temporary lodging.

Schools. Hawaii Public Schools on Oahu, where most officers are stationed, are organized into three districts: Central, Leeward, and Windward. In most areas, public schools of acceptable quality are located on government property in or near housing areas. Public high schools are also conveniently located but require bus transportation in some cases. Numerous private and parochial schools are available on Oahu and are accessible by bus.

Child Development. Two child development centers provide full-day programs for children six weeks to five years of age. Additionally, there are children and youth programs that provide part-day and full-day child care and education for children six weeks through twelve years of age.

Health. Health services are provided by Naval Health Clinic Hawaii, which is composed of two large clinics: Makalapa at Joint Base Pearl Harbor-Hickam and Kaneohe Bay at Marine Corps Base Hawaii. Other smaller clinics are located at Camp H. M. Smith, Wahiawa, and Barking Sands on the island of Kauai. The Makalapa and Kaneohe Bay clinics provide a wide range of family health services, while the clinic at Camp Smith provides a more limited range of preventive health services aimed at active duty personnel.

Recreation. Oahu and its naval and military installations afford some of the best all-around recreation and liberty in the Marine Corps. In addition to several excellent clubs and messes, the many installations operated by all the military services across the island offer recreational opportunities too numerous to list but sure to satisfy virtually any interest or taste.

Those interested in a Hawaiian vacation on Waikiki Beach at affordable rates should investigate the Hotel Hale Koa (House of Warriors), a government-built, fifteen-story hotel located at Fort DeRussey and open to armed forces personnel and their families. Reservations are first-come, first-served, with active duty people having priority. Another outstanding recreation opportunity lies at the Pacific Missile Range Facility, Kekaha, Hawaii, where the Barking Sands recreational facilities beckon.

Commissary and Exchange. There are several excellent commissaries and exchanges located across Oahu, although prices are higher than on the Mainland.

SMALLER ACTIVITIES AND DETACHMENTS

In addition to the large installations just described, the Corps maintains numerous smaller units, activities, and detachments at various sites around the globe. These generally operate as tenant organizations on another installation or installation complex managed by another service or executive agent.

840. Marine Activities in the Vicinity of Norfolk, Virginia 23551

Although the Norfolk–Hampton Roads area includes no major Marine Corps installations, Camp Allen (formerly Camp Elmore) is located in Norfolk, Virginia, and it is home to both U.S. Marine Corps Forces Command and two Fleet Anti-Terrorism Security Team companies of the Marine Corps Security Force Regiment. Overall, nearly 3,500 Marines reporting to ten local Marine commands call the Norfolk–Hampton Roads area home.

Other Marine commands in the area—many of which are tenants aboard the area's numerous Navy installations—include the Marine Corps Security Cooperation Group, Expeditionary Warfare Training Group Atlantic, various Marine detachments, and the School of Music. Thus, Norfolk and the surrounding area can be considered a Marine Corps station of importance.

Administrative details:

Quarters. Family housing in the Norfolk–Hampton Roads area has been privatized and is managed, operated, and maintained by Lincoln Military Housing. There are four major family communities: Naval Station

Norfolk, Northwest Portsmouth, Little Creek, and Oceana. Additionally, there is a wide range of excellent private housing reasonably priced. Temporary lodging and unaccompanied officer quarters are abundant throughout the area.

Schools. Norfolk has good public, private, and parochial schools—kindergarten through postgraduate.

Child Development. On all the major installations in the area, there are child development centers providing services comparable to those already discussed.

Health. Nationally acclaimed, Naval Medical Center Portsmouth is a state-of-the-art, patient-focused medical center that also boasts premier research and teaching programs designed to prepare new doctors, nurses, and hospital corpsmen for the future. It provides comprehensive health services through the main center at historic Hospital Point and ten branch clinics located throughout the Norfolk–Hampton Roads area.

Recreation. Plentiful in the region. Naval Air Station Norfolk (Breezy Point), has an outstanding commissioned officers' mess, and there are other excellent clubs and messes in the area with recreational facilities of all types. Virginia Beach, adjoining Norfolk, is one of the most attractive shore resorts on the East Coast.

Commissary and Exchange. Excellent and plentiful throughout the area.

841. Marine Corps Embassy Security Group

The Marine Corps maintains Marine security guard (MSG) detachments at designated U.S. Department of State diplomatic and consular facilities around the world. These detachments provide protection to mission personnel and prevent the compromise of national security information and equipment. The Marine Corps has no responsibility in which individual quality and outstanding performance are of higher importance than the MSG program, which the Corps administers and operates for the Department of State.

The Marine Corps Embassy Security Group, which is headquartered at Quantico, Virginia, and commanded by a colonel who reports directly to the commandant of the Marine Corps, exercises command, less operational supervision, over the MSG detachments through nine subordinate regional commands as follows:

- Region 1, including Eastern Europe and Eurasia and situated in Frankfurt, Germany
- Region 2, covering South Asia and the Middle East and based in Abu Dhabi, United Arab Emirates
- Region 3, encompassing East Asia and the Pacific and based in Bangkok, Thailand
- Region 4, covering South America and located in Fort Lauderdale, Florida
- Region 5, covering Western Europe and Scandinavia and located in Frankfurt, Germany
- Region 6, including East Africa and Southern Africa and based in Johannesburg, South Africa
- Region 7, encompassing North Africa and West Africa and situated in Frankfurt, Germany
- Region 8, covering Central Europe and situated in Frankfurt, Germany
- Region 9, covering North America and the Caribbean and located in Fort Lauderdale, Florida.

Under this program, some fifteen hundred carefully selected Marines maintain the internal security of American embassies, legations, missions, and consulates throughout the world. All of these vitally important security posts are under the independent command of staff noncommissioned officers. With the possible exception of recruiting duty and drill instruction at the recruit depots, the Corps has no other program that depends so directly and singly on the loyalty, military character, self-discipline, good sense, and devotion to duty of its noncommissioned officers.

842. Additional Information

While this chapter provides a limited overview of Marine Corps bases and stations, an officer transferring to a new and unfamiliar duty station will desire significantly more detailed information about his or her future professional home. There are several good sources of current, detailed information available online; one is the *My Base Guide* series maintained online by Marcoa Publishing.

Our flag's unfurl'd to every breeze, from dawn to setting sun.

—"The Marines' Hymn"

9

SERVICE AFLOAT

A ship without Marines is like a coat without buttons.

—David G. Farragut

Sea duty, dating from the Athenian fleets of the fifth century BCE and carrying on through Roman times when separate legions of *milites classiarii* ("soldiers of the fleet") were assigned to duty afloat, is the oldest and original duty of marines. In the seventeenth century, when the British and Dutch organized the first modern corps of marines, it was for duty as ships' detachments, and it was for this same purpose that U.S. Marines were first employed. The anchor in our Marine Corps emblem today symbolizes that the Marine is first and foremost a maritime soldier whose natural medium is the sea.

Since World War II and the Korean War, and even more today, the expansion of the Marine Corps, coupled with an increased demand for Marines elsewhere, has unfortunately contributed to the elimination of permanent Marine detachments on Navy ships. As a result, sea duty has virtually disappeared for Marines. That said, should you receive orders to report on board the USS *Bonhomme Richard* (LHD-6) for duty with Combat Cargo, not only are you embarking upon a tour for which previous experience has little prepared you, but also you cannot turn to a contemporary in your outfit for advice. Embarked

Marine units will nonetheless experience service afloat approximately equal to the old sea duty, which remains one of the most rewarding tours that can come your way.

Given that there may be little experience with service afloat among your peers, some research and reference reading is wise. The nominal cost of a current *Bluejacket's Manual* (Naval Institute Press, 2017) and *Watch Officer's Guide* (Naval Institute Press, 2007) will be repaid many times over. In addition, obtain a copy of the invaluable *Naval Ceremonies, Customs, and Traditions* by Admiral William P. Mack and Royal W. Connell (Naval Institute Press, 2004), and locate and review, if possible, the discontinued Marine Corps Education Center Pamphlet 1-17, *Service Afloat.* You may gain a historical perspective from an excellent article on sea duty by Major W. M. Cryan in the September 1961 issue of the *Marine Corps Gazette* and from a similar article in the June 1927 issue by Captain L. C. Shepherd Jr.—still useful and containing much excellent advice. Both articles are in the *Marine Corps Gazette* archives at the Library of the Marine Corps, Alfred M. Gray Marine Corps Research Center, and *Gazette* subscribers may search the online archives at the Marine Corps Association and Foundation web site.

Whether you join a ship as part of the crew, afloat staff, or embarked unit of the Marine Corps Operating Forces, it remains an important mark of your professionalism that you understand the Navy and shipboard life.

THE SHIP AND SHIPBOARD LIFE

901. Reporting Aboard

Although Marines seldom form part of ships' company, they certainly do deploy or "go on float" on board ships of the U.S. Navy. With the continuing deployment of Marine expeditionary units, establishment of the Expeditionary Strike Group concept, and naval integration of tactical aircraft, Navy-Marine Corps integration figures more importantly than ever in today's naval services. Thus, Marine Corps officers and staffs have continued to embark Navy ships for complete deployments, sometimes exceeding six months' duration.

If reporting as an individual, your orders will specify a specific ship and, in peacetime, the port in which you are to meet it. When this is impossible for security reasons, you will be directed to report to some shore command, such

9-1. Sea duty remains the oldest and original duty of U.S. Marines. Seagoing Marines have played traditional roles as prize crews, landing parties, and gunners throughout U.S. history.

as a naval base, a naval shipyard, or a naval district. This headquarters will further direct you where and when to join your ship. Arrive in the specified port at least as early as the night before you are expected to report.

Your ship may be pierside or at anchor. Ships in port but not pierside periodically send boats to the regular fleet landings. Coordinate with the appropriate headquarters to ascertain the schedule for your ship's launch. Plan to have your baggage and yourself at the appropriate pier or landing at least fifteen minutes before the designated time.

After you complete any formalities at the pier or aboard the ship's launch, ensure you pay attention to protocol when boarding your ship. As you reach the top of the gangway or accommodation ladder, come to a halt, face aft, and salute the Colors (if during the hours of 0800–sunset) flown from the ship's stern. Then face and salute the officer of the deck (OOD), saying, "I request permission to come aboard, sir. I am Lieutenant Holcomb reporting aboard for duty."

The OOD will return your salute, probably shake hands and welcome you aboard, and then ask for a copy of your orders for the log. The OOD's messenger or a side boy will escort you below to the command duty officer or a designated representative. You will find the other activities to which you must report much more conveniently located than ashore.

After reporting to the command duty officer, next report to the first lieutenant, or the Marine commander of troops, as appropriate, who will advise you as to subsequent moves. They will ordinarily follow in this sequence:

1. Report to the first lieutenant, the "housekeeper" of the ship, who assigns the rooms, if not already turned over to the commander of troops. You will mess in the wardroom. On nonamphibious ships, the supply officer controls the rooms. On occasion you will work with the supply officer to account for Navy property if placed in your custody.
2. See the mess treasurer and pay your mess entrance fee, known as "the mess share" (see Sections 2209 and 2210).

Plan to make a reporting call on the captain in his cabin within forty-eight hours if you are a senior officer or the commander of troops for embarked units; the officer next in your chain of command will arrange the time, if you ask. Ascertain that the captain is in. Remove your cover before entering the cabin. Be alert for the captain's dismissal; the call will usually last no longer than ten minutes.

902. Ship's Organization

One of your first tasks should be to study the ship's organization. Each ship prepares its own organization book, but all ships have certain essentials in common (see Figure 9-1).

The captain of a naval vessel, the senior line officer assigned to the ship's company, has full command of and responsibility for the ship, and exercises authority and precedence over all persons serving in the ship. Also, the captain is charged with the supervision of all persons temporarily embarked in the ship. The captain's authority, responsibility, and duties are described in *Navy Regulations*, which every officer going to sea should study.

The executive officer (XO) is the executive arm of the commanding officer. As such, he or she is the captain's direct representative and is responsible for the prompt and efficient execution of orders. The executive officer works through the heads of departments, who assist the executive officer in organization, administration, operation, and fighting on board the ship. In addition to these general responsibilities, the XO directly oversees such administrative functions as morale, welfare, berthing, training, personnel administration, religious, and legal matters.

Under the executive officer, the tasks of the ship are divided among the departments and activities and then further subdivided into divisions.

903. Ship's Orientation

Usually in one binder located in the wardroom, you will find the "Ship's Organization and Readiness Manual" (SORM) and "Commanding Officer's Standing Orders" (which are the captain's standing orders to all hands), which contain indispensable information as to the administration of the ship and of the department and division to which you are assigned. The ship's secretary or the aide to the executive officer will issue them. Study them carefully; these regulations will answer many questions and save much embarrassment.

Study the ship's plans, a copy of which can be borrowed from the ship's first lieutenant. Supplement them by a tour of the ship. If no guide is provided for such a tour by new officers, ask your roommate or some friendly officer to show you around. Visit the bridge, forecastle (pronounced "foc'sle"), combat information center, crew's quarters, galley, central control station, plotting rooms, all directors, one mount or turret in each battery, handling rooms, ship control stations, and one engine room.

The Plan of the Day is an important document, issued daily by the executive officer, giving the next day's schedule of routine work or operations and any variations or unusual additions. The Plan of the Day promulgates the orders of

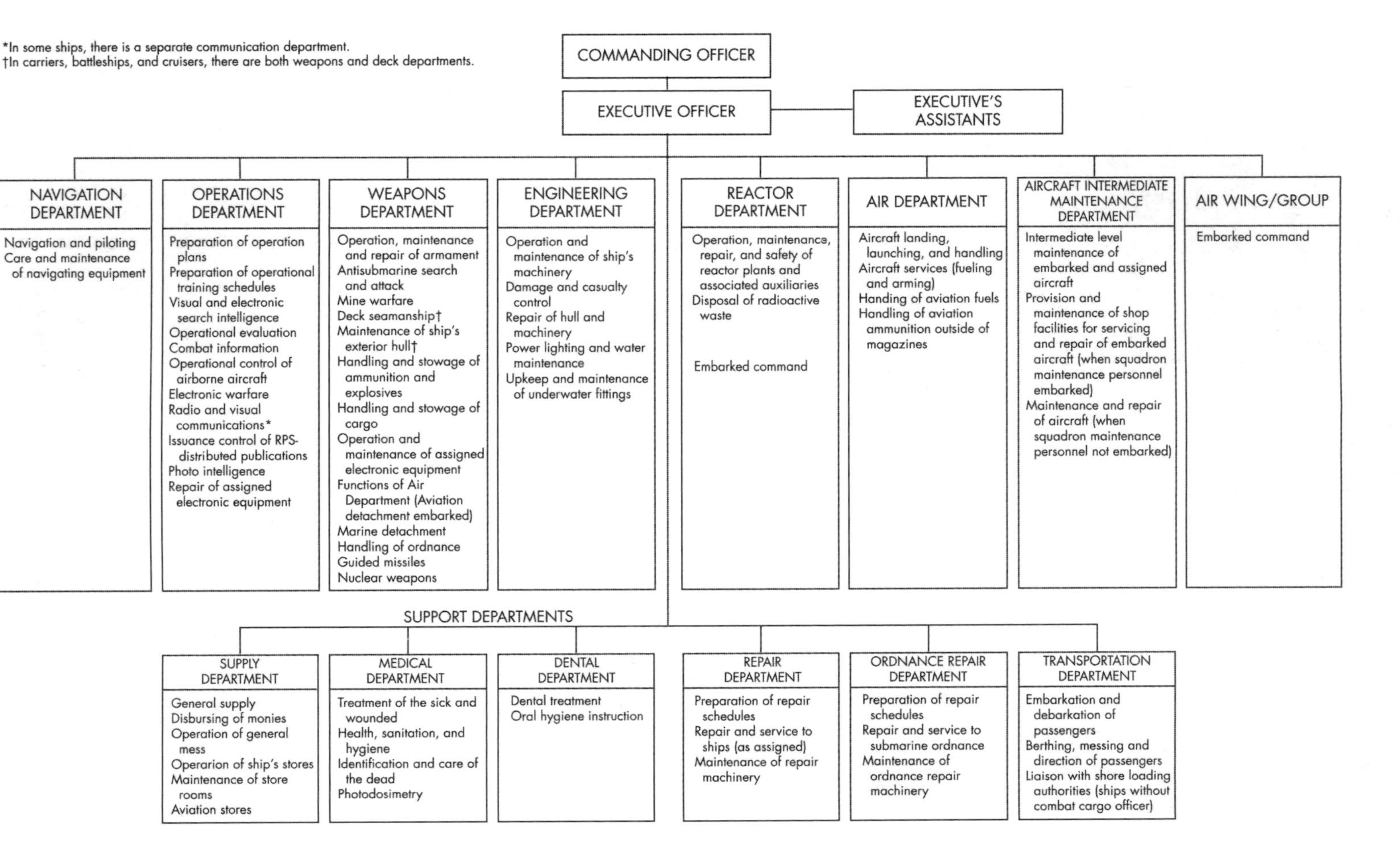

Figure 9-1. Typical Organization of a Large Ship

the day, drills and training, duty and liberty sections, working parties, and movies or recreational events. In recent years, it has become a "for official use only" or sometimes confidential document and cannot be removed from the ship.

The Boat Schedule is promulgated when in port and not lying alongside a dock or pier. Obtain a copy and keep it with you, especially when going ashore.

904. The Quarterdeck

The quarterdeck is a portion of the ship's main deck (or occasionally a prescribed area on another deck) set aside by the captain for official and ceremonial functions. Certain parts of the quarterdeck (usually the starboard side) are reserved for the captain or for an admiral if embarked. The remainder is reserved for the ship's officers. In years past, the detachment parade of the Marines was typically on or immediately adjoining the quarterdeck. The rules, traditions, and etiquette of the quarterdeck are among the most venerable in the service, and their strict observance by all hands is the mark of good sea manners:

- Never appear on the quarterdeck unless in the uniform of the day, except when crossing to enter or leave a boat, or when otherwise required by duty.
- Do not be seen on the quarterdeck with hands in pockets or uncovered, and do not remain on the quarterdeck for any length of time if in civilian clothes.
- Salute the Colors every time you come on board.
- Do not smoke on the quarterdeck until after Evening Colors.
- Do not skylark or engage in recreational sports on the quarterdeck.
- Remain clear of those portions of the quarterdeck reserved for the captain or admiral.

905. The Wardroom

The wardroom is the mess cabin of naval commissioned officers. The term also refers collectively to the individuals who have the right to make use of the space. It provides a place for recreation as well as dining. The wardroom is your home—and your club. It is also used on smaller ships as a meeting or conference room. Here you meet and get to know your fellow officers; it is up to you to make them shipmates.

In Navy messes, tradition is important, and seniority is well recognized. Seats for the captain and executive officer will be designated, usually at the head of the senior table. Some ships may assign seats of other officers such as the supply officer, "Bull" ensign (senior in grade O-1), or "JORG" (most junior O-1).

Unless you are on duty under arms, remove your cover when entering the mess. Although it may seem an anachronism, never unsheathe your sword in a mess. Save your quarrels for elsewhere (see Sections 2209 and 2210).

This does not mean that the silence of a library need be maintained. A noisy mess is often the sign of a happy mess. Between meals, you gather in the wardroom for a moment of relaxation, discussion of problems, watch a video, play a card game, or enjoy a quiet cup of coffee. It is also often a place for fun, on a Mess Night, when spouses and dates are entertained, or on the occasion of a ship's party. It can be all these things, or it can be just a place to eat. It depends upon you and upon the other members of the mess.

Do not loaf about the wardroom during working hours. If you have nothing else to do, catch up on your professional reading and study the ship's organization and regulations. Also be sensitive to the fact that naval officers assigned to ship's company typically work odd schedules due to irregular watches and rarely manage more than six hours of sleep a day. Therefore, they are rarely afforded the opportunity to lounge in the wardroom. As a result, if embarked Marines are regularly socializing in the wardroom for extended periods while they only enter for meals and meetings, there is a possibility that unnecessary tensions may emerge. Awareness of the issue and good manners should be sufficient to head off any unnecessary tensions.

Officers' messes (see Sections 2207 through 2210) are organized as business concerns, with a mess fund to which you contribute your share on joining. Monthly assessments are made, from which costs of food, periodicals, decorations, and other essentials and conveniences are paid. A mess treasurer administers this fund. In addition, on board some ships a junior officer—it could be you—is designated as "mess caterer" and put in charge of menu planning, detailed supervision of meal service, and so on. A good way to get this job is to complain about any of these matters; avoid doing so unless you have better ideas that you would like first-hand experience implementing.

Enlisted mess specialists man the wardroom, "steerage," pantries, and officers' galleys, and they may take care of senior officers' staterooms.

The senior Navy line officer (usually the executive officer) is mess president. Be in the mess before mealtime so that you can take your seat when the "exec" sits down. Typically, upon entering the wardroom after the meal has begun, members ask permission from the most senior officer present before joining a table (although this custom may be dispensed with as impractical on large ships). Etiquette once required that an officer remain seated (unless excused) until the mess president rose. Although this custom is not observed in all ships today, this does not excuse you from showing ordinary politeness and deference.

Wardroom country is "out of bounds" to enlisted persons except when on duty or in special circumstances. Do not use your stateroom as an office. See that enlisted persons have little need to enter wardroom country. When they do, require that they uncover (unless under arms), keep quiet, and refrain from profane language.

906. Wardroom Etiquette

Be punctual for meals. You should be in the wardroom prior to the assigned meal hour. When the commanding officer enters, he will invite all those assembled to eat. If unavoidably delayed, address the commanding officer, express your regrets, and "request permission to join the mess." If the commanding officer is not present, make your request to the senior officer present. If necessary to leave before the senior member has risen, ask to be excused using the phrase, "Request permission to depart the mess."

You should never be on a ship out of uniform unless transiting to/from liberty or for physical training. Do not lounge about the wardroom out of uniform.

Introduce guests to as many wardroom officers as possible, and always to the senior member and those at your own table. Entertain only such guests as your messmates and their families will be happy to meet.

Each guest is considered a guest of the wardroom. Be friendly and sociable with all guests.

Except on mess or party nights, officers' guests should leave the ship by four bells of the first watch (that is, 2200).

Only officers on the sick list may have meals in their rooms. This does not preclude you having a cup of tea or coffee in your cabin when you are working there.

Do not loaf about the wardroom during working hours. It bears repeating: if you have nothing else to do, catch up on your professional reading and study the ship's organization and regulations.

Do not be boisterous in the wardroom; be considerate of your messmates. When a visiting officer enters, introduce yourself, extend the courtesies of the ship, and try to help the visitor in any way you can.

Observe mess rules—for example, not to talk shop at meals, not to talk religion or politics, not to play music during meals—or whatever they may be.

Be just and pleasant in your dealing with mess specialists; make complaints to the mess treasurer.

Do not abuse the privilege of the watch mess specialist by sending him or her on long errands. The watch mess specialist is there to serve all officers.

Gambling, drinking, and possession of liquor or illegal drugs on board ship, except for medical purposes, are serious offenses.

Pay your bills promptly. Within twenty-four hours of reporting, pay the mess treasurer your mess bill and mess share in advance.

When necessary, admit ignorance. Experienced officers respect a frank admission and detest bluff. But endeavor to find out what you did not know.

907. Adjusting to Life at Sea

Your stateroom may be small, or, if large, crowded. Junior officers are usually doubled or quadrupled up. But the commanding officer of an embarked Marine unit is normally assigned his or her own stateroom.

Space will be cramped. You may have an upper bunk, comfortable but not luxurious, a share in a desk with drawers for stowing clothing, a chest of drawers or part of one, and some hanging space. Some rooms have air ports, but most are force ventilated or air conditioned.

Your mess specialist will supply you with bed linen, blankets, and towels and pick up laundry. Deal with the mess specialist tactfully but firmly.

Get to know your roommates, and, if possible, to like them. In cramped quarters aboard ship, it requires a nice adjustment to live in harmony with a number of other positive personalities.

If one of few Marines embarked, you can expect considerable good-natured teasing based on healthy interservice rivalry. Marines at sea traditionally get a certain amount of teasing harassment from Navy shipmates. Remember it is in fun, don't let it get under your skin, and do not hesitate to slip in your own digs as targets present themselves. Make a definite effort to get along. It is a matter of give-and-take; be sure you give more than you take.

MARINE SECURITY FORCE ORGANIZATION

908. Overview

Since their inception, Marine Corps Security Force Regiment (MCSFR) units have conducted the following missions: reinforcement of U.S. embassies, naval station installation security, protection of special weapons, nuclear refueling and defueling security missions, security during Strategic Arms Reduction Treaty inspections, and training in a wide array of antiterrorism and force protection scenarios.

Standing Marine detachments aboard ships disappeared in 1998 and the mission fell to fleet antiterrorism security team companies, platoons, and detachments when required. Under the reorganized concept of fleet security, the FAST companies deploy FAST platoons in support of selected fleet commanders, generally one platoon each for U.S. Naval Forces Central Command, U.S. Naval Forces Europe, and U.S. Pacific Fleet on a six-month rotational basis.

The FAST platoons or their detachments are "task organized security forces to augment Navy security to protect against terrorist acts at designated installations, units, ships, and critical assets, and perform other emergency security operations." Since their first deployment in February 1998, the platoons have conducted installation and airfield security, reinforcement of bombed U.S. embassies, and protected ships and flagships.

When assigned aboard a man-of-war, normally during periods of elevated threat, such security units no longer form part of ship's company, but are embarked as a direct support unit. As such, they report to the commanding officer of the ship to perform assigned missions: security for special weapons, internal security for the ship, and other force protection tasks.

909. The Afloat Detachment Commander

The assignment of shipboard security detachment commander will give you one of the finest opportunities for responsibility and independence that is open to a company grade officer. At sea, you are truly on your own; in general, as long as you discharge your mission responsibilities and tasks detailed in your orders, you will be left alone to get results in your own fashion by both Marine Corps and Navy authorities. Occupying the traditional roles of the Marine shipboard detachments commanders of yore, you could not ask for more.

Moreover, the intimate experience that you gain as to Navy ways, operating procedures, capabilities, and limitations will prove invaluable to you throughout the rest of your career. In later years, as a senior officer, you will find relative ease in transacting Marine Corps business with your Navy counterparts as an old acquaintance. Such rare sea duty should be coveted whenever available.

9-2. Shipboard detachments of Marines still pay traditional attention to the guns. Here, a heavy machine gun is prepared for action on board an aircraft carrier.

The commander of the security force unit will report to the captain of the ship for the efficiency and performance of the detachment. He or she remains responsible to the Marine Corps chain of command for the detachment's personnel administration, training, and the Marine Corps property in his or her charge. The detachment commander may report to the ship's executive officer or a designated ship's department head for specific assignments, augmentation by Navy personnel and equipment, and for the operation of any assigned shipboard systems.

The former duties of shipboard officer or shore patrol officer will normally not be performed by a security detachment commander, except as authorized in orders. However, the detachment commander will still assign detachment personnel to shipboard duties and stations under the ship's *Watch, Quarter, and Station Bill.* This is a chart that lists every person in the ship by name, rank, bunk and locker assignment, cleaning station, watch and liberty section, and battle station. The bill is arranged in standard tabular form and gives a graphic picture of what everyone in the detachment does and when, according to the readiness condition of the ship.

MARINE CORPS FORCES AFLOAT

910. Embarked Marines

With the extinction of seagoing Marine Corps detachments on board Navy ships, the most common type of service afloat for Marine officers comes with the embarkation of your unit for duty with the fleet or for exercises, usually with an afloat Marine air-ground task force or an aircraft squadron ordered to a carrier air group. Such duty reflects the essence of the modern Marine Corps, which has provided landing forces for the fleet throughout our history.

There remains a typical set of misconceptions that can cloud the experience of embarkation for all. This is the notion of some uninitiated Marines that the U.S. Navy exists primarily as a taxi service for Marines and should conduct itself in an appropriately service-oriented manner. At the other extreme are the occasional Navy personnel who think that Marines exist solely to interrupt a ship's routine, clutter spaces, and make a mess of the paintwork on vehicle and cargo areas. Neither concept could be further from the truth. The amphibious force and naval aviation doctrines of the Navy and Marine Corps team provide one of the most striking military capabilities of the history of warfare, primarily through the unique concepts of teamwork, cooperation, and integration that have evolved over decades of training and operations. Your first charge as an officer embarking with your troops must be to create an atmosphere of teamwork and demonstrate the desired symbiotic relationship with Navy counterparts. Accordingly, be prepared to redress ruthlessly all instances of real and pretended friction that can rise from untrained and inexperienced personnel reacting to the obvious conditions of shipboard life.

911. Commanding Officer of Troops

Under *Navy Regulations*, the authority of the commanding officer of a ship governs embarked personnel and units as well. In order to ensure the maximum cooperation and understanding for mutually satisfying results, the commanding officer requires embarked units to organize themselves under a single troop commander, responsible to that commanding officer for all matters pertaining to them.

This commanding officer of troops (more often commander of troops, or COT) therefore functions with respect to the ship's organization as another department head, reporting for the embarked detachments to the commanding officer and executive officer of the ship. Musters, duty assignments, working parties, and the all-important needs of the troops for training and maintenance support on board ship require much attention from the COT. Many of the duties of the COT also approximate those of the commander of the Marine detachments of yesteryear, so your conduct places you equally at the forefront of tradition and an exemplar of Marine Corps virtues to our sister service.

Shipboard collateral duties for Marine officers embarked with their units may include the following: team embarkation officer, ship's platoon commander, troop officer of the day/guard officer, billeting officer, troop mess officer, officer's mess treasurer, and troop communications officer. These and other requirements are made clear by the ship CO before embarkation occurs, mainly through liaison with the advance party that your unit will send to the ship. Your unit will provide a standing working party (ship's platoon), cooks, and messmen on a fair-share basis to assist in the functioning of the ship, which will be your collective home for the period of embarkation.

Your unit also will be responsible for the care and cleaning (but not repair) of the berthing and working spaces assigned. The daily cleanliness of a ship is of paramount concern to all, especially considering the obvious closeness of shipboard life. Do not let your personnel be found lacking. Above all, cultivate the respect of the ship's executive officer by following the standards to the letter and never quibbling over them. Be a good guest, as well as an effective professional. Your conduct, camaraderie, and demeanor should make you indistinguishable from a valued ship's company officer.

Shipboard routine soon becomes second nature to embarked personnel. Training periods and maintenance of troop weapons, equipment, and cargo will take up most of each day, but these will be supplemented as required by ship drills and exercises that, of necessity, must involve you and your Marines. Be familiar with the various watch bills and emergency bills, particularly for general quarters, man overboard, abandon ship, and fires. Learn the rules for movement through the ship during general quarters, and ensure your Marines learn these as well. Learn your way around, and memorize the compartment numbering system in order to locate yourself and ship spaces. Many areas will be designated as "restricted spaces," both to afford requisite security for sensitive equipment and documents and to keep the limited space from becoming overcrowded. These restrictions largely apply to enlisted personnel. Embarked officers should feel free to include these spaces in their familiarization tours, being sure to ask the assigned Navy personnel kindly to explain their duties and the capabilities of their equipment.

912. Guard Duty for Embarked Marine Corps Units

When a Marine Corps unit not part of the ship's company goes to sea, the guard duty required is a combination of that maintained ashore and that required for the exigencies of service afloat.

Bear in mind two principles of command relations: first, the captain of a ship has paramount authority and responsibility for safety, good order, and discipline over everyone embarked in the ship, whether or not under the captain's military command; second, the commander of troops embarked in a ship retains his or her military command authority and responsibility for his or her officers and enlisted persons, subject only to the overriding authority and responsibility of the captain.

Consistent with the foregoing principles, the captain of the ship can call upon the embarked troop units to establish a guard to assist in maintaining the security and safety of the ship by manning such posts as lifebuoy, control of circulation of passengers, and communications, as well as by performing any other necessary guard duties. For internal order, security, and control of embarked units and equipment, the troop commander, with the concurrence of the captain, may establish any posts he or she considers necessary. In general, the troop commander organizes the guard like an interior guard ashore and provides an officer of the day as his or her direct representative for supervising the troop guard and carrying out troop orders, ship's regulations, and special instructions of the ship's captain.

All orders to troops embarked in a ship, including instructions for the troop guard, are transmitted through the commanding officer of troops.

COURTESY, ETIQUETTE, AND HONORS

913. Shipboard Courtesy and Etiquette

On many occasions during your career, you will find yourself serving or embarked in naval vessels, on a Navy staff, as part of the ship's company, or as a passenger. Because of this and because, as a Marine officer, you are a member of the naval services, you must comply meticulously with the courtesies and customs practiced on board Navy warships.

Ladders and Gangways. The starboard accommodation ladder is reserved for officers; if there are two starboard ladders, one ladder may be designated for flag and general officers. The port ladder is for enlisted persons. When a ship is alongside a dock, the officers' gangway usually leads to the quarterdeck; the enlisted's gangway is forward or aft, as the case may be.

Coming on Board and Leaving a Warship. As a Marine officer, whether on duty or as a visitor, you always will be welcome on board a Navy ship. In fact, you should seize every opportunity to visit each type and class of ship so that you may increase your seagoing knowledge. The Navy is rightly flattered by such visits and will do everything possible to make your stay instructive, as well as socially pleasant. Always pay your respects to the senior Marine watch officer when visiting a ship that has Marines embarked.

If the ship is docked, there will be little complication other than perhaps the timing of a visit. If the ship is at anchor in the harbor, obtain permission from the ship's senior officer present at the landing (or from the boat coxswain, if no officer is on hand) to go out in one of the ship's boats. If no boats are at the landing, ask the shore patrol representative when the next boat is due. If you come off in a motor launch loaded with enlisted passengers, you will probably be taken to the port ladder.

Observe boat etiquette. Defer to seniors in the boat, and introduce yourself.

On reaching the quarterdeck, either from the gangway or an accommodation ladder, halt, face aft (or toward the national ensign), and salute the Colors (if displayed). Immediately afterward, render a second, distinct salute to the officer of the deck, and say, "Sir/Ma'am, I request permission to come aboard." When it is time to leave the ship, render the same courtesies in reverse order, saying, "Sir/Ma'am, I request permission to leave the ship" or alternately "Sir/Ma'am, I request permission to go ashore." If you are a member of the ship's company, you report to the OOD as follows: On coming aboard, "I report my return on board, sir/ma'am," and on leaving the ship, "I have permission to leave the ship, sir/ma'am."

Figure 9-2. When Embarking, Junior Officers Board First

Boat Etiquette. When boarding a small boat, juniors embark first and sit forward, leaving the sternsheets for seniors, who embark last (see Figure 9-2). The most senior officer in the boat sits farthest aft, at the centerline, or elsewhere as he or she wishes. When debarking, officers do so in order of rank (see Figure 9-3).

Officers or enlisted persons in the boat rise and salute when a senior officer boards or debarks.

When a boat is crowded, juniors rise and yield seats to seniors. If there are not enough seats, take the next boat.

When another boat passes close aboard with a senior officer embarked and in view, or when a senior officer passes close aboard on shore, the senior officer and the coxswain in each boat render hand salutes (see Figure 9-4). Seated officers do not rise to salute; coxswains rise unless to do so would be dangerous or impracticable.

Figure 9-3. When Disembarking, Senior Officers Are First to Leave the Boat

Marine officers (although line officers) and officers of the Navy staff corps, when senior in a boat, receive and return salutes and are otherwise accorded the deference due individuals of their seniority, but the senior Navy line officer or petty officer in the boat, regardless of how junior he or she may be, is in charge of the boat and is responsible for its navigation and for the safety of personnel and matériel embarked. This is provided by *Navy Regulations* and should be remembered by you as a Marine officer, in case you are inadvertently directed to act as a boat officer.

During Colors, boats under way within sight or hearing lie to or, if necessary, proceed at slowest safe speed. The coxswain (or boat officer, if embarked) stands and salutes unless dangerous to do so. Other persons embarked remain in place and do not salute.

Shipboard Amenities and Saluting. In general, the amenities and rules for saluting set forth in Chapter 11 apply on board ship, but the following special points should be observed.

Personnel at work, at games, or at meals are not required to rise when an officer other than the captain, a flag or general officer, or an officer senior to the captain passes, unless attention is called or when a passageway must be cleared. It is customary for all officers to uncover when entering a sick bay or space in which food is being prepared or served; when a senior officer does so, this indicates that he or she does not desire the people present to be brought to attention.

Figure 9-4. The Coxswain and the Senior Officer in the Boat Render Hand Salutes

Juniors give way to seniors in ships' passageways and particularly when going up and down ladders.

"Gangway!" is a command given by anyone who sees an officer or civilian dignitary approaching a gangway, ladder, or passage that is blocked. Never use "Gangway!" except for an officer or senior civilian. For others, "Coming through!" is appropriate. The senior officer, noncommissioned officer, or petty officer present must clear passage after "Gangway!" has been given.

The ship's captain, any officer senior to the captain, all flag and general officers, the executive officer, and inspecting officers are saluted at every meeting except in officers' country, heads, and messing compartments.

On the first meeting of the day, salute each officer senior to you; thereafter, salutes are dispensed with except when an officer is directly addressed by a subordinate or in the cases of senior officers listed above.

Sentries at gangways salute all officers coming on board or leaving the ship. Sentries posted on the topside also salute officers passing close aboard in boats.

When passing honors are being exchanged between men-of-war or when ruffles and flourishes are sounded on the quarterdeck, all personnel on weather decks, not in formation, come to attention and salute.

Navy (but not Marine) formations on board ship are dismissed with the command, "Post" or "Dismissed" (always issued from attention), whereupon all members of the formation salute, the officer in charge returns the salute, and all hands fall out.

Ship's sentries posted on the dock, when a ship is moored alongside, carry out normal saluting procedures for sentinels ashore.

When Colors go in port and the ship is in port, all hands on weather decks or on the pier (if the ship is berthed alongside) face aft and salute.

914. Display of Personal Flags and Pennants Afloat

On Board Ship. A flag officer or unit commander afloat displays his or her personal flag or command pennant from the flagship but not from more than one ship at a time. If two flag officers are embarked in the same ship, only the senior's flag flies. When a civil official who rates a personal flag is embarked for passage in a naval vessel, his or her flag is flown, but if an officer rating a personal flag or command pennant is also on board, both the officer's flag and that of the civilian are displayed.

In Boats. A flag officer in command, when embarked officially in a naval boat, flies his or her personal flag from the bow. Officers who rate neither display a commission pennant. Officers who rate a personal flag may display a miniature of such flag or pennant from the vicinity of the coxswain's station when embarked on other than official occasions. Civilian officials display their flags, if any, from the bow, if embarked in a naval boat.

915. Official Visits and Calls on Board Ship

Official Visits. Insofar as practical, the same honors and ceremonies are rendered for an official visit afloat as for one ashore. In addition, however, on board ship the compliments mentioned in Section 1120 are added, such as manning the rail and piping and tending the side.

If *Navy Regulations* call for a gun salute on departure of the visitor, the salute is fired when the visitor is clear of the side (to avoid blast), and the flag or pennant (if that person rates one) is hauled down with the last gun of the salute.

Official Calls on Board Naval Vessels. The procedure for receiving official callers on board U.S. Navy ships is more formal than ashore. According to the rank of the visitor, and the occasion, the side may be piped; side boys, guard, and band are paraded; and certain officers attend the side. If you or your ship are on the receiving end of the call, you can find the details (and should check these carefully in advance) in such publications as *Watch Officer's Guide* or *The Naval Officer's Guide*, both of which will be readily available on board, as well as in *Navy Regulations.* For a table of honors to be rendered for the various military and civil officials of the United States and foreign countries, see Chapter 11.

916. Housekeeping Afloat

Much advice and information presented in Chapter 17 applies to Marine units on board ships. The commanding officer of troops thus has additional duty as department head, a status roughly analogous to that of a company commander ashore, although department heads on a carrier or amphibious assault ship may be in the grades of commander or lieutenant commander. The Marines man and maintain certain equipment and have their own part of the ship (where the unit lives, works, and maintains its headquarters—styled, sailor-fashion, as "the Marine office").

The term "housekeeping," however, has no exact equivalent afloat. "Ship's work," or "keeping the ship," includes some housekeeping functions but does not encompass all shoreside connotations of the phrase. In examining housekeeping for Marines at sea, some of the similarities and differences are noted.

Police. "Police," in the Navy sense, means the ship's police force. Under the command master at arms, each division, other than the Marines, details a master at arms whose job is to act as a kind of military policeman in enforcing good order and ship's regulations It is a popular misconception that Marines perform this function and act as "the Navy's police force" on board ship. Nothing could be further from the truth.

Within the Marine unit, however, the term "police" has its normal meaning, as in Section 1701, and the police sergeant performs the duties usually associated with that title anywhere in the Corps.

Subsistence and Mess Management. Like "police" (in the Navy sense), subsistence and food service are functions of the ship's executive officer. The supply officer and assistants perform the duties that ashore would fall to the food service officer, as described in Section 1703. In most ships, a central enlisted mess, called "the mess decks," is operated in a manner resembling a cafeteria. Among enlisted persons, only chief petty officers have a separate mess; Marine gunnery sergeants and above are, for messing purposes, considered to rate as chief petty officers.

Messmen are detailed from privates, privates first class, and, when necessary, lance corporals of the Marine unit on the basis provided by *Navy Regulations.* "Mess stewards" in the Navy are now called "Culinary Specialists." Never detail an NCO as a messman. In recognition of Marines' continuing and important security functions, many ships do not call on the Marine guard for messmen. If you have any latitude in this, make every effort to prevent detail of a Marine for mess duty. If the detachment includes a rated cook, he or she should be assigned to duty in the ship's galley. But never lose sight of the cook as a Marine.

Clothing and Small Stores. Marines may likewise avail themselves—for cash purchases—of the ship's "Clothing and Small Stores," where many items of regulation (Navy) clothing, such as handkerchiefs, socks, and underwear, may be bought at considerable savings over shoreside prices. Obviously, the Marine officers and NCOs must prevent Marines from improper wearing of Navy articles of uniform in lieu of prescribed Marine items of similar type.

Ship's Store. The ship's store is the seagoing equivalent of a navy exchange ashore. The ship's store is operated by the supply officer. It stocks stationery, candy, toilet articles, insignia, and the usual selection of exchange supplies, including, in most ships, "pogey bait" and soda-fountain ("gedunk") delicacies such as are found ashore.

Ship's Welfare and Recreation. On board ship, Welfare and Recreation embraces the gamut of activities associated with Special Services on the beach. Both as individuals and as an embarked unit, Marines take part in the ship's athletic and recreation programs. A ship's special services officer administers the funds for these purposes. Be tactful, but be sure the Marine unit gets its share based on the period of time embarked. This matter includes a deposit of a pro rata share of the store profits to the unit community services or similar welfare and recreation fund before debarking the ship.

917. Shipboard Cleanliness and Upkeep

As its "part of the ship," the Marine unit embarked usually has a berthing compartment, a storeroom, an office, and occasionally topside deck space. The cleanliness and upkeep of these spaces and structures are the responsibility of the Marine unit's CO and ultimately the commander of troops in his or her capacity as a division officer. Each unit performs its own minor repairs; more extensive repair, when needed, is the job of the shipfitters and "repair gangs," based on "work requests" submitted by the COT.

As ashore, your unit will have a police sergeant. Instead of a police shed, though, he or she will have a gear locker. In lieu of a police gang, the police sergeant will levy on every Marine in the unit to keep the ship's "Marine country" a model space, spic-and-span, an example to the bluejackets.

In your responsibility for upkeep and cleanliness of the ship, you should assign certain "cleaning stations" to your NCOs, and, if you are in command, to your junior officer(s) to supervise.

918. Final Thoughts

Glossary for Seagoing Marines. See *Naval Terms Dictionary* for commonly used shipboard terms and phrases that every Marine should know. By using and understanding these, you will prove to Navy shipmates that Marines can be, and are, just as salty as any sailor.

Navy Rating Abbreviations. The Navy's system of ratings (that is, petty officer ranks and specialties) with its many different abbreviations may at first appear confusing but is something seagoing Marines must understand. The *Naval Terms Dictionary,* Appendix B, gives the basic abbreviations and their titles.

. . . that no persons be appointed to offices, or inlisted into said battalions, but such as are good seamen, or so acquainted with maritime affairs as to be able to serve to advantage by sea.

—Resolution of the Continental Congress
to raise Marines, 10 November 1775

10

TRADITIONS, FLAGS, DECORATIONS, AND UNIFORMS

1001. "The Thin Line of Tradition"

The traditions of the Marine Corps, its history, its flags, its uniforms, its insignia—*the Marine Corps way of doing things*—make the Corps what it is and set it so distinctly apart from other military organizations and services.

These traditions give the Marine Corps its flavor and are the reason the Corps cherishes its past, its ways of acting and speaking, and its uniforms. These things foster the discipline, valor, loyalty, aggressiveness, and readiness that make the term *Marine* "signify all that is highest in military efficiency and soldierly virtue."

And remember: whenever the Marine Corps is impoverished by the death of a tradition, you are generally to blame. Traditions are preserved not by books and museums but by faithful adherence on the part of all hands—*you especially.*

MARINE CORPS TRADITIONS AND CUSTOMS

1002. Globe and Anchor

When Major General Smedley Butler (recipient of two Medals of Honor) was a lieutenant in the Philippines in 1899, he decided to get himself tattooed: "I selected an enormous Marine Corps Emblem to be tattooed across my chest. It required several sittings and hurt me like the devil, but the finished product was worth the pain. I blazed triumphantly forth, a Marine from throat to waist. The emblem is still with me. Nothing on earth but skinning will remove it."

Butler was somewhat premature in his last sentence. Within less than a year, during the storming of the Tartar Wall in Peking, a Chinese bullet struck him in the chest and gouged off part of his emblem. The rest of it accompanied him to the grave forty years later.

Whether you are a private or general is secondary compared to the shared privilege of wearing the emblem. The Globe and Anchor—today, often called the Eagle, Globe, and Anchor—is the most important insignia you have.

The Marine emblem (never "logo"), as we know it today, dates from 1868. It was contributed to the Corps by Brigadier General Jacob Zeilin, seventh commandant. Until 1840, Marines wore various devices, mainly based on the spread eagle or foul anchor. In 1840, two Marine Corps devices were accepted. Both were circled by a laurel wreath, undoubtedly borrowed from the badge of the Royal Marines; one had a foul anchor inscribed inside, and the other bore the letters "USM." In 1859, a standard center was adopted—a U.S. shield surmounted by a hunting-horn bugle, within which was the letter "M." From this time on, the bugle and letter "M" without the shield or laurel wreath, were usually worn by Marines on undress uniforms. This type of bugle was

10-1. Today's emblem, the Eagle, Globe, and Anchor, was adopted by Brigadier General Jacob Zeilin, seventh commandant, in 1868.

the nineteenth-century symbol for light infantry or jäger—so called because they were recruited from the ranks of foresters, game-keepers, and poachers, all renowned as skirmishers and riflemen.

In 1868, however, General Zeilin felt that a more distinctive emblem was needed. His choice fell on another device borrowed from the British Marines—the globe.

The globe had been conferred on the Royal Marines in 1827 by King George IV. Because it was impossible to recite all the achievements of Marines on the Corps Color, said the King, "the Great Globe itself" was to be their emblem, for Marines had won honor everywhere.

General Zeilin's U.S. Marine globe displayed the Western Hemisphere (the "Royals" had the Eastern Hemisphere on theirs). The eagle and foul anchor were added, to leave no doubt that the Corps was both American and maritime.

1003. The Marine Corps Seal

The official seal of the Corps, designated by General Lemuel C. Shepherd Jr., twentieth commandant, consists of the Marine Corps emblem in bronze, the

10-2. The Marine badge before 1868 embodied the hunting-horn symbol, traditionally indicative of the light infantry.

eagle holding in his beak a scroll inscribed "Semper Fidelis," against a scarlet and blue background, encircled by the words, "Department of the Navy—United States Marine Corps."

1004. Marine Corps Colors

The colors of the Corps are scarlet and gold. Although associated with U.S. Marines for many years, these colors were not officially recognized until General John A. Lejeune became thirteenth commandant. Today you will see scarlet and gold throughout Marine posts—on signboards; auto tags; bandsmen's drums, pouches, and trumpet slings; military police brassards; officers' hatcords and aiguillettes; and, it sometimes seems, everywhere in sight.

In addition to scarlet and gold, forest green enjoys at least semiofficial standing as a Marine color. During the years since 1912, when forest green was adopted for the winter service uniform, it has become standard for such equipment as vehicles, weapons, and organizational chests and baggage. In addition, forest green is today virtually the distinguishing color of marines throughout the world, being worn as a service uniform by the British, Dutch, Korean, and other corps.

10-3. The Marine Corps seal, designed by General Lemuel C. Shepherd Jr., twentieth commandant, was approved by President Eisenhower in 1954.

Forest green comes from the same source as the light infantry bugle that was once part of the Corps badge. The costume of eighteenth-century huntsmen was forest green. The riflemen recruited from that calling wore green uniforms—a green that survives not only among marines but also in the uniforms of Britain's Rifle Brigade (the "Greenjackets") and India's Ghurkhas.

1005. The Marine Corps Motto

Semper Fidelis (Always Faithful) is the motto of the Corps. That Marines have lived up to this motto is proved by the fact that there has never been a mutiny, or even the thought of one, among U.S. Marines.

Semper Fidelis was adopted as the motto about 1883. Before that, there had been three Marine Corps mottoes, all traditional rather than official. The first, antedating the War of 1812, was *Fortitudine* (With Fortitude). The second, *By Sea and by Land,* was obviously a translation of the Royal Marines' *Per Mare, Per Terram.* Until 1848, the third motto was *To the Shores of Tripoli,* in commemoration of O'Bannon's capture of Derna in 1805. In 1848, after the return to Washington of the Marine battalion that took part in the capture of Mexico City, this motto was revised to *From the Halls of the Montezumas to the Shores of Tripoli*—a line now familiar to all Americans. This revision of the Corps motto in Mexico has encouraged speculation that the first stanza of "The Marines' Hymn" was composed by members of the Marine battalion who stormed Chapultepec Castle.

It may be added that the Marine Corps shared its motto with England's Devonshire Regiment, the 11th Foot, in its day one of the senior infantry regiments of the British army, whose sobriquet was "the Bloody Eleventh" and whose motto was also *Semper Fidelis.*

1006. "The Marines' Hymn" and Marine Corps March

"The Marines' Hymn" is what its name implies, the hymn of the Marine Corps. "Semper Fidelis," one of John Philip Sousa's best-known works, is the Corps' march.

"The Marines' Hymn" (Appendix I) is the oldest of the official songs of the armed services. Every Marine knows the words. The origin of the hymn is obscure. The words date from the nineteenth century, and the author remains unknown. The music comes from an air, "Gendarmes of the Queen," in

Jacques Offenbach's opera *Geneviève de Brabant*, first performed in November 1859. Regardless of its origin, however, *all Marines get to their feet and stand at attention whenever "The Marines' Hymn" is played or sung.*

"Semper Fidelis" was composed by John Philip Sousa in 1888 during his tour as leader of the Marine Band. "Semper Fi," as the troops know it, is habitually rendered for parades, reviews, and march-pasts of Marines.

1007. Birthday of the Corps

The Marine Corps was founded by the Continental Congress on 10 November 1775. The resolution that created our Corps reads as follows:

> *Resolved.* That two Battalions of Marines be raised consisting of one Colonel, two lieutenant Colonels, two Majors, & Officers as usual in other regiments, that they consist of an equal number of privates with other battalions; that particular care be taken that no persons be appointed to office, or inlisted into said Battalions, but such as are good seamen, or so acquainted with maritime affairs as to be able to serve to advantage by sea, when required. That they be inlisted and commissioned for and during the present war with Great Britain and the colonies, unless dismissed by order of Congress. That they be distinguished by the names of the first and second battalions of American Marines, and that they be considered as part of the number, which the continental Army before Boston is ordered to consist of.

Chapter 22 explains how we celebrate the Marine Corps birthday. Although the Marine Corps joins the other services each May in observing Armed Forces' Day, 10 November remains the Marines' own day—a day of ceremony, comradeship, and celebration.

1008. The Mameluke Sword

The sword that Marine officers carry goes back to the *Uniform Regulations* of 1826 (with a hiatus from 1859 to 1875). Records of the day, however, indicate that swords of this pattern were worn by Marine officers before the War of 1812.

The Mameluke sword gets its name from the cross-hilt and ivory grip, both of which were used for centuries by the Muslims of North Africa and Arabia. The Marine Corps tradition of carrying this type of sword dates from

Lieutenant O'Bannon's assault on Derna, Tripoli, in 1805, when he is said to have won the sword of the governor of the town.

Aside from its use on parade, many Marine Corps rituals center about your sword. You wear it when you get married, and you cut your wedding cake with the sword. It is both worn and employed in cake-cutting ceremonies around the world on the birthday of the Corps.

Never unsheathe your sword inside a mess or wardroom. If you do, custom decrees that you must stand drinks for all present. This tradition goes back to stringent rules against dueling in the early days of the Navy and Marine Corps.

1009. "First on Foot, and Right of the Line"

Marines form at the place of honor—head of column or on right of line—in any naval formation. This privilege was bestowed on the Corps by the Secretary of the Navy on 9 August 1876.

1010. "First to Fight"

The slogan "First to Fight" has appeared on Marine recruiting posters ever since World War I.

10-4. Marine Corps recruiting poster, used during and after World War I.

Marines have been in the forefront of every American war since the founding of the Corps. Marines entered the Revolution in 1775, even before the Declaration of Independence was signed. Before declaration of the War of 1812, Marines helped to defend the USS *Chesapeake* against the British. At the outset of hostilities against Mexico, Marines helped to raise California's Bear Flag. Before the Civil War, Marines captured John Brown at Harpers Ferry. They were among the few U.S. regulars who fought in the first Battle of Manassas in 1861. In 1898, Huntington's Fleet Marines were the first U.S. troops to occupy Cuban soil, and Admiral Dewey's Marines were the first to land in the Philippines. Marines were first to land at Veracruz (1914). In World I, the 5th Marines formed part of the first American Expeditionary Force contingent to sail for France. When Iceland had to be occupied in 1941, Marines, the only U.S. troops who were ready, were the first to land. In World War II, at Pearl Harbor, Ewa, Wake, Midway, Johnston Island, and Guam, Marines formed the ready forefront of our Pacific outpost line. At Guadalcanal in August 1942, Marines launched the first American offensive of the war. In the Korean War, the first reinforcements to leave the continental United States were the 1st Provisional Marine Brigade. The first American troops to land in Lebanon in 1958 were Marines. At Santo Domingo, in 1965, Marines were again the first to fight; while, in Vietnam, the first U.S. ground unit to be committed to the war was the 3d Marine Division. In the Persian Gulf War, the Marines opened the ground war.

On this record of readiness, "First to Fight" constitutes the Marine's pride, responsibility, and challenge.

1011. "Leathernecks"

The Marines' long-standing nickname, "Leathernecks," goes back to the leather stock, or neckpiece, that was part of the marine uniform from 1775 to 1875. One historian has written: "Government contracts usually contained a specification that the stock be of such height that the 'chin could turn freely over it,' a rather indefinite regulation, and, as one Marine put it, one which the 'tailors must have interpreted to mean with the nose pointing straight up.'"

Although many justifications have been adduced for the leather stock, the truth seems to be that it was intended to ensure that Marines kept their heads erect ("in battery," the artillery would say), a laudable aim in any military organization, any time.

Descended from the stock is the standing collar, hallmark of Marine blue dress and evening dress uniforms. Like its leather ancestor, the standing collar regulates stance and posture and thus proclaims the wearer as a modern "Leatherneck."

1012. Scarlet Trouser Stripe

Officers and noncommissioned officers have intermittently worn scarlet stripes on dress trousers ever since the early days of the Corps. It is unsubstantiated, even though oft repeated, that the right to wear scarlet stripes was conferred on the Corps as a battle honor after the Mexican War (actually the initial uniform trousers issued after reconstitution of the Corps in 1798 had scarlet piping).

1013. Headgear

Two Marine traditions center on headgear. The *quatrefoil* (the cross shaped braid atop officers' frame-type ["barracks"] cover) has been worn since 1859. The design, of French origin, is a distinguishing part of the Marine officers' uniform.

The campaign cover (years ago called the "field hat") is a broad-brimmed felt hat with a high crown, pinched symmetrically at the four corners. It was the rugged, picturesque expeditionary headgear of the Corps from 1898 until 1942 and became a universal favorite. As a result, although the hat became outmoded during World War II, General Clifton B. Cates, the nineteenth commandant, authorized its use on the rifle range in 1948 and took steps to issue field hats to all medalist shooters in Marine Corps matches. Subsequently, in 1956, General Randolph McCall Pate, the twenty-first commandant, directed that campaign covers be worn by all recruit drill instructors, and the headgear—later copied and adapted by the Army for the same purpose—has become a symbol of Marine Corps recruit training.

1014. Collar Emblems

Although officers have worn collar emblems since the 1870s, enlisted Marines did not rate this privilege until August 1918, when Franklin D. Roosevelt, then assistant Secretary of the Navy, visited the 4th Marine Brigade in France shortly after Belleau Wood. In recognition of the brigade's victory, Roosevelt directed on the spot that enlisted Marines would henceforth wear the emblem on their collars.

1015. Marine Talk and Terminology

The 4th Marine Brigade's admired Army commander at Belleau Wood, Lieutenant General James G. Harbord, was quick to note and record the salty Marine way of saying things:

> In the more than a month that the Marine Brigade fought in and around the Bois de Belleau, I got a good opportunity to get the Marine psychology. . . . The habitual Marine address was "Lad". . . . No Marine was ever too old to be a "lad." The Marines never start anywhere: they always "shove off." There were no kitchens: the cooking was done in "galleys." No one ever unfurled a flag—he "broke it out."

This *Guide* contains a glossary of Marine terms (Appendix VII). Never feel self-conscious about using them. Require that subordinates use them. Accept no substitutes.

1016. "The President's Own"

Founded in 1798 (more than a century before the bands of the other three services), the Marine Band has performed at White House functions for every president except George Washington and was especially sponsored by Thomas Jefferson. Because of its traditional privilege of performing at the White House, the band is spoken of as "The President's Own." President John F. Kennedy epitomized the band's special position when he remarked in 1962, "I find that the only forces which cannot be transferred from Washington without my express permission are the members of the Marine Band, and I want it announced that we propose to hold the White House against all odds, at least for some time to come."

The Marine Band has been present at many of the most memorable and cherished moments in our nation's history, including the dedication of the National Cemetery at Gettysburg when Lincoln gave his immortal address (and his aide-de-camp was Second Lieutenant H. C. Cochrane, USMC). Among the band's many traditions, including leadership for twelve years by John Philip Sousa, is its scarlet, full-dress blouse, the only red coat worn by American forces since the Revolutionary War. (In 1956, the Marine Corps Drum and Bugle Corps was likewise granted the privilege of wearing red coats.)

The Marine Band tours the country each year and has done so ever since Sousa commenced the practice in 1891, although one section of the band always remains in Washington to fulfill its traditional primary mission: "To provide music when directed by the President of the United States, the Congress of the United States, or the Commandant of the Marine Corps."

1017. Evening Parade

From May through early September, a ceremonial Evening Parade is held each Friday evening after nightfall at the Marine Barracks, "Eighth and Eye." This colorful ceremony, executed under searchlight illumination, features the Marine Band, Marine Corps Drum and Bugle Corps, a special exhibition drill platoon, and a battalion of Marines from the barracks. Evening Parades were first held in 1957 after a Marine Corps ceremonial detachment participated in the Bermuda International Searchlight Tattoo and became a fixed Marine Corps custom following similar participation by a larger Marine detachment in the famed Edinburgh Searchlight Tattoo in Scotland in 1958.

Evening Parades are open to the public, and any officer who desires to attend with a reasonable number of guests can usually obtain reserved seats by contacting the Marine Barracks adjutant.

1018. "And St. David"

During the Boxer Uprising (1900) at Tientsin and Peking, the Marine battalion in the international relief column was brigaded with the Royal Welsh Fusiliers (23nd Foot), one of Britain's most renowned regiments. The resulting fellowship between the two organizations is symbolized each year on St. David's Day (1 March, the Welsh national holiday), when the commandant of the Marine Corps and the colonel of the Fusiliers exchange by dispatch the traditional watchword of Wales: "And St. David."

1019. The Commandant's License Plate

If, when in Washington, D.C., you ever bump into a car bearing plate "1775," climb out of the wreckage at attention. That license plate is set aside for the official sedan of the commandant of the Marine Corps.

1020. Rum on New Year's Day

Every New Year's Day since 1804, the Marine Band serenades the commandant at his quarters and receives refreshments in return.

1021. Marine Corps Bulldog

Ever since World War I, the bulldog has been associated with the Corps. An English bulldog has been the official mascot at "Eighth and Eye," and therefore top dog of the Corps, since the 1920s. Prior to World War II, he was always named "Jiggs." Subsequently, however, in an appropriate tribute to one of the Corps' bravest officers, Lieutenant General L. B. Puller, the name has been "Chesty."

1022. Ship's Bell

Most Marine bases, stations, and detachments (and even some camps in the field) have a ship's bell, usually from a warship no longer in commission. The old tradition of striking the bells, following shipboard routine, has fallen into disuse.

1023. Last to Leave the Ship

Marines are always or should be the last—other than the ship's captain—to leave a ship being abandoned or put out of commission. Although the tradition is an old one, it first appears in *Navy Regulations* of 1865: "When a vessel is to be put out of commission, the Marine officer with the guard shall remain on board until all the officers and crew are detached and the ship regularly turned over to the officers of the Navy Yard or station."

1024. Swagger Sticks

The tradition of the swagger stick originated in the British Army and goes as far back as 1790. In the Marine Corps, the stick came into vogue in the latter part of the nineteenth century and was virtually a required article of uniform until World War I. The origin of the swagger stick lay in the whips or batons carried by mounted officers of the eighteenth century. Once carried with relish by many Marine officers, swagger sticks were prohibited in 1960 and adorn only a few mantles in hopes that they might gain favor again.

There was also once in favor a Marine Corps tie with "regimental" colors, scarlet/gold stripes over a forest green background. That tie, and equivalent cummerbund, can be worn at the user's pleasure with civilian attire.

1025. "Tell It to the Marines!"

In his book *Fix Bayonets!* Captain John W. Thomason Jr, gives the generally accepted version of the origin of "Tell it to the Marines!":

> They relate of Charles II that at Whitehall a certain seacaptain, newly returned from the Western Ocean, told the King of flying fish, a thing never heard in old England. The King and court were vastly amused. But, the naval fellow persisting, the Merry Monarch beckoned to a lean, dry colonel of the sea regiment, with seamed mahogany face, and said, in effect: "Colonel, this tarry-breeks here makes sport with us stay-at-homes. He tells of a miraculous fish that foresakes its element and flies like a bird over water." "Sire," said the colonel of Marines, "he tells a true thing. I myself have often seen those fish in your Majesty's seas around Barbados—" "Well," decided Charles, "such evidence cannot be disputed. And hereafter, when we hear a strange thing, we will tell it to the Marines, for the marines go everywhere and see everything, and if they say it is so, we will believe it."

This yarn (for such it is) was for many years credited to Samuel Pepys, although scholars disclaimed it. In *They Never Said It: A Book of Fake Quotes, Misquotes, and Misleading Attributions*, Paul F. Boller and John George assert that the original meaning of the phrase is pejorative to the Marines, implying that they are gullible. And in his "Introduction" to *Semper Fidelis: The History of the United States Marine Corps*, Allan R. Millett includes the Pepys version but also allows that the alternate interpretation, "preferred by everyone but marines," is not very kind to the Marines.

Whatever the truth, the U.S. Marine Corps turned the phrase to its favor in fine Marine fashion when it was incorporated into a 1917 recruiting poster. The poster implied that, when an outrage needs avenging, one should "Tell that to the Marines!" because they will do something about it. In any case, the Marine Corps has embraced the phrase, which is an old one and can be found in print as early as 1726.

1026. At Church Service

Protestant and Catholic services for Marines should always include the Marine Corps Prayer (written at the suggestion of General Shepherd, twentieth commandant, by Bishop Sherrill, former presiding bishop of the Episcopal Church and hero in World War I):

> O Eternal Father, we commend to Thy protection and care the members of the Marine Corps. Guide and direct them in the defense of our country and in the maintenance of justice among nations. Protect them in the hour of danger. Grant that wherever they serve they may be loyal to their high traditions and that at all times they may put their trust in Thee; through Jesus Christ our Lord. Amen.

It is also customary for Marine Corps religious services to conclude with the traditional naval hymn, "Eternal Father, Strong to Save." When no chaplain is available, the commanding officer, following the traditions of the sea, may conduct divine services, hold funerals, and such. When a chaplain is present, some commanding officers may choose to read the lesson, another traditional prerogative of the CO. This is arranged beforehand with the officiating chaplain. It is a good idea to draw your chaplain's attention to the Marine Corps Prayer, above, as some chaplains are unfamiliar with it.

1027. Conduct in Action

Over and above the competence, resolution, and courage expected of every Marine in battle, it is particularly expected that no wounded or dead Marine will ever be left on the field or unattended, regardless of the cost of bringing him in. As for surrender, the Marine Corps code is that expressed by Napoleon: "There is but one honorable mode of becoming prisoner of war. That is, by being taken separately; by which is meant, by being cut off entirely, and when we can no longer make use of our arms."

1028. Marine Corps Museums

"The scrapbook of the Marine Corps," as it was sometimes described, was the Marine Corps Museum. Now rebuilt and rededicated as the National Museum of the Marine Corps and consolidated at Triangle (outside Quantico), Virginia, it remains the central repository of awards, battle honors, historical flags, and other objects of lasting sentimental significance to the Marine Corps. The museum collection documents Marine Corps history from 1775 to the present day. On display is an extensive array of uniforms, weapons, artifacts, equipment, prints, and paintings giving tangible substance to the proud traditions of the Corps. Every Marine Corps officer should become thoroughly familiar with this museum, which now surpasses the best military and naval museums in the United States.

In addition, excellent post museums are located at Camp Pendleton, San Diego, and Parris Island. In Philadelphia, at New Hall, a restored building from pre-Revolutionary days, is an outstanding collection of material dealing with the early days of the Corps and its origins in Pennsylvania. The nearby cruiser relic, USS *Olympia*, contains an exhibit depicting Marines of the Spanish-American War, and the several battleships and aircraft carriers maintained as monuments around the country usually contain exhibits concerning their Marine detachments.

1029. Marine Corps Memorial Chapel, Quantico

The post chapel at Quantico serves, in addition to its regular functions, as the Memorial Chapel of the Marine Corps. Here is kept a "Book of Remembrance" listing the name, rank, and date of death for Marines and members of the Navy serving with the Marine Corps who gave their lives in action in Vietnam and the Afghanistan and Iraq campaigns that began in 2001.

COLORS, FLAGS, AND STANDARDS

1030. Overview

A Parris Island recruit once asked his drill instructor, "Sergeant, who carries the flag in battle?"

Came the unhesitating reply, "Son, *every* Marine carries the flag in battle!"

As the soldier's proverb says, "The flag is a jealous mistress," and any Marine will fight and die rather than permit the National Colors or a Marine Corps Color to be dishonored.

Colors or Standards must never fall into enemy hands. If capture seems inevitable, they should be burned. Unserviceable Colors or Standards, or those from disbanded units, are turned in to the supply system. The latter, in turn, forwards flags of historical value to the Marine Corps Museum, which is the Corps repository for historical flags, as well as for flags and war trophies captured by Marines. Soiled, torn, or badly frayed flags, if not historical, are destroyed privately by burning.

1031. Types of Flags

Marine Corps terms that deal with flags are precise and particular. As an officer, you must learn to distinguish the various kinds of flags and to speak of them in the correct terminology.

National Color or Standard. This is the American flag. When the flag is displayed over Marine or naval bases, stations, or ships, its official title is the *National Ensign.* The national flag carried by Marine organizations is made of silk or nylon and is called the *National Color* (except when borne by a mounted, mechanized, motorized, or aviation unit, when its title becomes the *National Standard*). This technical distinction between a color and a standard also applies to the battle colors and organizational colors described in the following paragraphs.

The National Color is carried on all occasions of ceremony when two or more companies of a unit are present. When not in the hands of troops, the National Color is entrusted to the adjutant. With the Marine Corps Color (discussed below), the National Color is usually displayed in the office or before the tent of the commanding officer. Whenever the National Color is carried in the open, it is escorted by a *color guard* composed of selected Marines, and the Color itself is borne by an outstanding NCO, the *color sergeant.*

The National Ensign, displayed over ships and shore stations, comes in three sizes:

1. *Post flag*: size ten feet by nineteen feet, flown in fair weather except on Sundays and national holidays
2. *Storm flag*: size five feet by nine feet six inches, flown during foul weather
3. *Garrison flag*: size twenty feet by thirty-eight feet, flown on Sundays and national holidays as provided in the *Marine Corps Flag Manual* (but never from a flagpole shorter than sixty-five feet).

For more information on display of the National Color or Ensign, refer to *Navy Regulations* and to the *Marine Corps Flag Manual.*

Marine Corps Colors and Standards. The commandant issues to every major Marine unit or organization a distinguishing flag, which is carried beside the National Color. These unit flags are called *Marine Corps Colors* (or Standards).

A Marine Corps Color bears the emblem and motto of the Corps and the unit title, and follows the color scheme of the Corps, scarlet and gold.

The Marine Corps Color of a Fleet Marine Force unit is called the unit *Battle Color*; the Color authorized for an organization in the Supporting Establishment (such as a Marine barracks) is called the *Organizational Color*. No unit smaller than a separate battalion or regiment receives a Battle Color, nor does a temporary or provisional unit unless specially authorized by the commandant.

Certain organized units of the Marine Corps Reserve are likewise authorized to carry organizational flags of the type just described, but bearing a Reserve designation.

Guidons. These are small rectangular flags, made in the Marine Corps colors, carried by companies, batteries, or detachments, or used as marker flags for ceremonies. *Organizational guidons* carry the Marine Corps emblem and the title of the unit. *Dress guidons* (used as markers) simply bear the initials "USMC."

Personal Flags. Every active general officer in command displays a personal flag. Marine Corps personal flags consist of a scarlet field with white stars, according to the general officer's rank, arranged in the same manner as the stars on Navy personal flags. Regulations governing personal flags are in *Navy Regulations*.

Miscellaneous Flags. In addition to the ceremonial flags just described, the Corps employs several miscellaneous flags and pennants described in the *Marine Corps Flag Manual*. Examples are the United Nations flag, Geneva Convention flag, church pennants, and heat condition flags.

1032. Appurtenances of Flags

The appurtenances of Marine Colors, Standards, flags, and guidons include streamers, bands, cords, tassels, and staff ornaments.

Streamers denote participation in combat or award of a collective citation or decoration conferred on the unit as a whole.

A *silver band* is attached to the staff of a Marine Corps Color or Standard for each streamer awarded.

When the unit or organization does not rate streamers or bands, a *cord* and *tassel*, woven in the Corps colors, are substituted.

The heads of staffs bear the following staff ornaments: Colors and Standards bear a silver lance-head; personal flags, a silver halberd; and guidons, a plain silver cap.

1033. Battle Color of the Marine Corps

The Corps as a whole has one Battle Color called the *Battle Color of the Marine Corps.* This Color is entrusted to the senior post of the Corps, Marine Barracks Washington. Attached to it are all the battle honors, citations, battle streamers, and silver bands that the Corps has won since 1775. At the time of writing, these fifty-four honors included the following:

1. Presidential Unit Citation (Navy) Streamer with six silver and three bronze stars
2. Presidential Unit Citation (Army) Streamer with one silver oak leaf cluster
3. Joint Meritorious Unit Award
4. Navy Unit Commendation Streamer
5. Valorous Unit Award (Army) Streamer
6. Meritorious Unit Commendation (Navy-Marine Corps) Streamer
7. Meritorious Unit Commendation (Army) Streamer
8. Revolutionary War Streamer
9. Quasi-War with France Streamer
10. Barbary Wars Streamer
11. War of 1812 Streamer
12. African Slave Trade Streamer
13. Operations Against West Indian Pirates Streamer
14. Indian Wars Streamer
15. Mexican War Streamer
16. Civil War Streamer
17. Marine Corps Expeditionary Streamer with twelve silver stars, four bronze stars, and one silver "W"
18. Spanish Campaign Streamer
19. Philippine Campaign Streamer
20. China Relief Expedition Streamer
21. Cuban Pacification Streamer
22. Nicaraguan Campaign Streamer
23. Mexican Service Streamer
24. Haitian Campaign Streamer with one bronze star

25. Dominican Campaign Streamer
26. World War I Victory Streamer with one silver and one bronze star, one Maltese Cross, and Siberia and West Indies Clasps
27. Army of Occupation of Germany Streamer
28. Second Nicaraguan Campaign Streamer
29. Yangtze Service Streamer
30. China Service Streamer with one bronze star
31. American Defense Service Streamer with one bronze star
32. American Campaign Streamer
33. European-African-Middle Eastern Campaign Streamer with one silver and four bronze stars
34. Asiatic-Pacific Campaign Streamer with eight silver and two bronze stars
35. World War II Victory Streamer
36. Navy Occupation Service Streamer with Europe and Asia Clasps
37. National Defense Service Streamer with three bronze stars
38. Korean Service Streamer with two silver stars
39. Armed Forces Expeditionary Streamer with five silver stars
40. Vietnam Service Streamer with three silver and two bronze stars
41. Southwest Asia Service Streamer with three bronze stars
42. Kosovo Campaign Streamer with two bronze stars
43. Afghanistan Campaign Streamer with one silver and one bronze star
44. Iraq Campaign Streamer with one silver and two bronze stars
45. Global War on Terrorism Expeditionary Streamer
46. Global War on Terrorism Service Streamer
47. Philippine Defense Streamer with one bronze star
48. Philippine Liberation Streamer with two bronze stars
49. Philippine Independence Streamer
50. French Croix De Guerre Streamer (Fourragère) with two palms and one gilt star
51. Philippine Presidential Unit Citation Streamer with two bronze stars
52. Korean Presidential Unit Citation Streamer
53. Republic of Vietnam Armed Forces Meritorious Unit Citation of the Gallantry Cross with Palm
54. Republic of Vietnam Meritorious Unit Citation Civil Actions Streamer with Palm.

DECORATIONS, MEDALS, AND UNIT CITATIONS

1034. Decorations and Medals

"A soldier will fight long and hard for a bit of colored ribbon," said Napoleon, who originated the awarding of personal decorations.

Napoleon's conqueror, the Duke of Wellington, in turn introduced all-hands campaign medals, the first of which went to British troops who fought at Waterloo.

Both Wellington and Napoleon realized that decorations and medals not only express national gratitude to individuals but also stimulate emulation and esprit in battles to come.

Today, Marine Corps awards fall into three classes: personal and unit decorations; commemorative, campaign, and service medals; and marksmanship badges and trophies. The *Navy and Marine Corps Awards Manual* gives details on all these, together with guidance for anyone who wishes to originate a recommendation that an award be made.

1035. Personal and Unit Decorations

The United States, despite the limitations in Article I, Section 9, of the Constitution, confers numerous military decorations. These range from the Medal of Honor, at the top, to a campaign ribbon in junior position. Certain military decorations are awarded only under special conditions: for heroism only (denoted below by *), for either heroic or meritorious acts (**), or for heroism not in combat (***). In order of precedence, the personal or unit decorations that Marines might receive or might have received are as follows:

- Medal of Honor (Navy)*
- Navy Cross*
- Defense Distinguished Service Medal
- Homeland Security Distinguished Service Medal
- Distinguished Service Medal (Navy)
- Silver Star Medal*
- Defense Superior Service Medal
- Legion of Merit**
- Distinguished Flying Cross**
- Navy and Marine Corps Medal***

- Bronze Star Medal**
- Purple Heart
- Defense Meritorious Service Medal
- Meritorious Service Medal
- Air Medal**
- Joint Service Commendation Medal
- Navy and Marine Corps Commendation Medal**
- Joint Service Achievement Medal
- Navy and Marine Corps Achievement Medal**
- Combat Action Ribbon*
- Presidential Unit Citation*
- Joint Meritorious Unit Award
- Navy Unit Commendation**
- Navy Meritorious Unit Commendation
- Navy "E" Ribbon
- Prisoner of War Medal
- Marine Corps Good Conduct Medal
- Selected Marine Corps Reserve Medal
- Marine Corps Expeditionary Medal
- China Service Medal
- American Defense Service Medal
- American Campaign Medal
- Europe-Africa-Middle East Campaign Medal
- Asiatic-Pacific Campaign Medal
- World War II Victory Medal
- Navy Occupation Service Medal
- Medal for Humane Action
- National Defense Service Medal
- Korean Service Medal
- Antarctica Service Medal
- Armed Forces Expeditionary Medal
- Vietnam Service Medal
- Southwest Asia Service Medal
- Kosovo Campaign Medal
- Afghanistan Campaign Medal

- Iraq Campaign Medal
- Global War on Terrorism Expeditionary Medal
- Global War on Terrorism Service Medal
- Korean Defense Service Medal
- Armed Forces Service Medal
- Humanitarian Service Medal
- Military Outstanding Volunteer Service Medal
- Navy Sea Service Deployment Ribbon
- Navy Arctic Service Ribbon
- Navy and Marine Corps Overseas Service Ribbon
- Marine Corps Recruiting Ribbon
- Marine Corps Drill Instructor Ribbon
- Marine Security Guard Ribbon
- Armed Forces Reserve Medal
- Marine Corps Reserve Ribbon (obsolete)
- Philippine Presidential Unit Citation
- Korean Presidential Unit Citation
- Vietnam Presidential Unit Citation
- Republic of Vietnam Meritorious Unit Citation Cross of Gallantry
- Vietnam Civil Actions Service Medal
- Philippine Defense Ribbon
- Philippine Liberation Ribbon
- Philippine Independence Ribbon
- United Nations Service Medal (Korea)
- United Nations Medal
- NATO Medal for the former Yugoslavia
- NATO Medal for Kosovo
- NATO Medal for Operation Active Endeavor
- NATO Medal for Operation Eagle Assist
- NATO Medal for the Balkans
- NATO Medal for NATO Training Mission–Iraq and International Security Assistance Force
- Multinational Force and Observers Medal
- Inter-American Defense Board Medal

- Republic of Vietnam Campaign Medal
- Kuwait Liberation Medal (Saudi Arabia)
- Kuwait Liberation Medal (Emirate of Kuwait)
- Republic of Korea War Service Medal.

Among the foregoing, the Medal of Honor rates special mention. The Medal of Honor is the highest military decoration conferred by the United States. Ordinarily, it is awarded only for gallantry and intrepidity in combat, at the risk of one's life, above and beyond the call of duty. Since the Civil War, when the award was created, more than three hundred Medals of Honor have been received by U.S. Marines.

Medal of Honor recipients are given the following special privileges and benefits:

- Special Medal of Honor pension of $1,303.51 per month (2017), with cost-of-living increases, in addition to any military pensions
- Ten percent increase in retired pay
- Supplemental uniform allowance for enlisted recipients while still on active duty
- Special entitlement to space-available transportation on military aircraft
- Commissary and exchange privileges (including for eligible dependents)
- Admission for qualified children to any of the U.S. service academies (Naval Academy, United States Military Academy, Air Force Academy, Coast Guard Academy, or Merchant Marine Academy)—without nomination or quota requirements
- Medal of Honor Flag
- Privilege of wearing the uniform at any time provided standards and restrictions are observed
- Interment at Arlington National Cemetery
- Entitlement to special motor vehicle license plates in several states, sometimes with registration fees waived.

Finally, it is a tradition (though not officially recognized) that all hands, regardless of rank, salute a Medal of Honor holder.

1036. Unit Decorations

All top U.S. unit decorations, or "unit citations," as well as several foreign unit citations have been won by Marine Corps units. If you are a member of an organization *when it wins a collective citation*, you are thereafter entitled to wear the citation ribbon or device as a personal decoration.

The *French Fourragère* is the senior unit award (and first collective award) won by Marines. The Fourragère dates from Napoleon's time; it was awarded to the 4th Marine Brigade in 1918 in lieu of awarding all hands the Croix de Guerre. The green and scarlet cord of the Fourragère may still be seen on the left shoulders of members of the 5th and 6th Marines.

The *Presidential Unit Citation* is the highest service unit award. It was also the first American collective award, having been personally instituted by President Franklin D. Roosevelt as a citation for the defenders of Wake (1st Defense Battalion and Marine Fighting Squadron 211) in December 1941. The Presidential Unit is considered to represent unit attainments that would warrant award of the Navy Cross if the recipient were an individual.

The *Distinguished Unit Emblem* was until 1996 the Army and Air Force collective citation roughly equivalent to the Presidential Unit Citation. The Distinguished Unit Emblem has been awarded to several Marine ground and aviation units on detached service with the Army or Air Force.

The *Navy Unit Commendation* ranks next, in the naval service, after the Joint Meritorious Unit Award. Like the latter, the Navy Unit Commendation (NUC) may be won by extremely meritorious service in support of, but not participation in, combat operations. When awarded for combat performance, the NUC is comparable to the Silver Star Medal for an individual; for non-combat meritorious service, this commendation is comparable to the Legion of Merit.

Following the Navy Unit Commendation in precedence is the *Navy Meritorious Unit Commendation.* To be eligible for this award, the unit must have performed service of a character comparable to that which would merit the award to an individual of a Bronze Star Medal in a combat situation or similar achievement in a noncombat situation.

Other unit decorations awarded for collective achievements of valor or merit include the Army Valorous Unit Award, Air Force Outstanding Unit Award, and Joint Meritorious Unit Award (which actually ranks in precedence above the NUC).

1037. Campaign Medals

Campaign or service medals are issued to all hands who take part in particular campaigns or periods of service for which a medal is authorized. In addition to medals for specific campaigns, Marines may be awarded the *Marine Corps Expeditionary Medal* for service ashore on foreign soil, against opposition, for which no other campaign medal is authorized. For similar joint operations in which the Army or Air Force is involved, the *Armed Forces Expeditionary Medal* may be substituted. Campaign medals are often embellished by clasps or bronze stars, which denote participation in specific battles or phases of the campaign.

As a general policy, the Department of Defense does not permit U.S. military personnel to accept service medals from foreign governments. There are, however, exceptions. The *Republic of Vietnam Campaign Medal, Kuwait Liberation Medal (Saudi Arabia), Kuwait Liberation Medal (Kuwait),* and *Republic of Korea War Service Medal* are the only foreign service medals authorized for wear without specific individual authorization. Those who are eligible shall wear these decorations in the manner prescribed in applicable uniform regulations.

In addition to campaign and service medals, certain commemorative medals have been struck to commemorate noncombat but notable achievements, such as polar expeditions or pioneer flights.

1038. Initiating an Award

One of your responsibilities as a combat leader is to see that your Marines are promptly recommended for awards you believe they have earned. During active operations, it is usual for every unit, from battalion up, to maintain a board of awards. The board evaluates and passes on recommendations for decorations that originate within the organization, but you must see that the board of awards receives recommendations promptly and that the recommendations are accurately stated in whatever form may be required.

Few leadership derelictions are more reprehensible than failure to submit proper recommendations for awards, and then to see an award fail because you were too lazy to recommend it in the right form and with the detailed information required.

Standard Marine Corps procedure for initiating awards is described in the *Navy and Marine Corps Awards Manual.*

1039. Wearing Decorations and Medals

The Marine Corps has strict rules that govern the wearing of decorations and medals. These rules are in the *Marine Corps Uniform Regulations.* Some of them follow.

Subject to regulations, you may now accept awards from foreign nations. Most decorations, and all campaign medals, have half-size miniature reproductions known as miniature medals. You wear "miniatures" with evening and mess dress, as well as with civilian full dress or dinner jacket, when appropriate. The Medal of Honor, however, is never represented in miniature, and, when miniatures are worn, the Medal of Honor is suspended in the normal fashion, about the collar.

When medals are prescribed instead of ribbons, unit citations and other ribbons for which no medal has been struck will be worn centered on the right breast.

Marines with eight or more ribbons of any type may wear them in rows of four rather than three, thus avoiding a top-heavy stack. Large medals may not be worn more than seven (five for women) per single row; and miniatures, not more than ten (eight for women). *Marine Corps Uniform Regulations* now detail the manner of wearing and mounting larger numbers of awards by specific numbers and rows.

With every U.S. decoration (and many foreign ones, too) you receive a lapel device for wear with civilian clothes. This may be worn in the left lapel of your civilian suit when you think fit.

Decorations and medals are part of your uniform and must be worn, except that the wear of ribbons on khaki shirts is at the individual's option unless the commander prescribes that ribbons must be worn. If the individual opts to wear ribbons on the shirt, as is typical, there are two permitted options: wearing all authorized ribbons, or wearing only personal U.S. decorations with U.S. unit awards and the Good Conduct Medal. The wearing of campaign ribbons is optional.

Marksmanship badges will not be worn with the evening dress, blue dress "A," blue-white dress "A," camouflage utility, and camouflage maternity work uniforms. Commanders may prescribe marksmanship badges for wear on all other uniforms. Unless otherwise prescribed by the commander, wearing marksmanship badges is at the option of the individual. That said, by current custom, the wear of marksmanship badges is normally confined to the coats of the service "A," blue dress "B," and blue-white dress "B" uniforms. Nor can you wear any ribbon (such as Navy marksmanship ribbons) in lieu of a marksmanship or gunnery badge. Incidentally, you are limited to a ceiling of three badges of your choice, if you rate more than three. The *Marine Corps Uniform Regulations* contain detailed guidance on precedence and placement.

When soiled, faded, frayed, or otherwise unserviceable, the ribbons of decorations and medals should be destroyed by burning, rather than thrown away, not only to prevent reuse by unauthorized persons but also because these ribbons symbolize the bravery, devotion, and sacrifice of U.S. Marines.

Even though entitled to wear foreign decorations or medals, you must always display at least one U.S. medal or award at the same time. And remember that U.S. awards take precedence over foreign awards.

UNIFORMS, INSIGNIA, AND PERSONAL GROOMING

1040. "Well-Dressed Soldiers"

"It is proverbial," wrote one commandant, "that well-dressed soldiers are usually well-behaved soldiers." The Marine Corps has always set course by that axiom and has enjoyed success and repute on both counts.

As a Marine officer, it rests squarely with you to maintain the Marine Corps reputation for smart, soldierly, and correctly worn uniforms.

Marine Corps Uniform Regulations is the "bible" on uniforms, insignia, and grooming. You must know the regulations, set the example by rigid compliance, and enforce the regulations meticulously.

In *Uniform Regulations* you will find two essential compilations: the listing of required articles of uniform for all officers, and the table showing types and combinations of uniforms authorized for officers (see Tables 10-1 and 10-2). They provide a complete checklist of articles (for male officers and female officers, respectively) that should, or should not, be worn as part of each prescribed uniform combination.

1041. Wearing the Uniform

The following paragraphs summarize important rules and information that govern the wearing of Marine Corps uniforms. Once again, details are in the current *Marine Corps Uniform Regulations.*

Uniforms designed to be buttoned *will* be worn buttoned.

Table 10-1. Types and Components of Authorized Uniforms for Male Officers

Designation	*Cap*	*Coat or Jacket*	*Shirt*	*Necktie*	*Trouser/Belt*
Evening dress "A"	Dress	Evening w/strip collar & white waistcoat	White w/pique placket	None	Evening (suspenders optional)
Evening dress "B"	Dress	Evening w/strip collar & scarlet waistcoat or cummerbund (c)	White w/pique placket	None	Evening (suspenders optional)
Blue dress "A"	Dress	Blue w/strip collar	White plain front	None	Sky blue (d) w/web belt or suspenders
Blue-white dress "A"	Dress	Blue w/strip collar	White plain front	None	White w/web belt or suspenders
Blue dress "B"	Dress	Blue w/strip collar	White plain front	None	Sky blue (d) w/web belt or suspenders
Blue-white dress "B"	Dress	Blue w/strip collar	White plain front	None	White w/web belt or suspenders
Blue dress "C"	Dress	Blue sweater (optional)	Khaki long sleeve	Khaki w/clasp	Sky blue (d) w/web belt
Blue dress "D"	Dress	Blue sweater (optional)	Khaki short sleeve	None	Sky blue (d) w/web belt
Service "A"	Garrison/ frame	Green	Khaki long sleeve	Khaki w/clasp	Green w/web belt
Service "B"	Garrison/ frame	Green sweater (optional)	Khaki long sleeve	Khaki w/clasp	Green w/web belt
Service "C"	Garrison/ frame	Green sweater (optional)	Khaki short sleeve	None	Green w/web belt
Utility uniform	Utility	Utility	Green undershirt optional	None	Web belt or martial arts utility belt

a. If required or prescribed.
b. Black gloves always worn or carried with all-weather coat during winter uniform period. Optional when coat not worn.
c. Scarlet waistcoat for general officers only. Scarlet cummerbund for all other officers.
d. Dark blue trousers for general officers.
e. Green scarf optional for wear with all-weather coat/tanker jacket during winter months.

Gloves	*Footwear*	*Outer Coat (a)*	*Insignia Bofs*	*Medals/Ribbons*	*Badges*	*Sword*
White (b)	Black shoes & socks	AWC/ optional boatcloak	Dress collar/cap	Miniature medals	Not worn	Not worn
White (b)	Black shoes & socks	AWC/ optional boatcloak	Dress collar/cap	Miniature medals	Not worn	Not worn
White (b)	Black shoes & socks	AWC/ optional boatcloak	Dress collar/cap	Large medals (ribbons worn per para. 5205.3)	Not worn	(a)
White	Black shoes & socks	AWC/ optional boatcloak	Dress collar/cap	Large medals (ribbons per para. 5205.3)	Not worn	(a)
White (b)	Black shoes & socks	AWC/ optional boatcloak	Dress collar/cap	Ribbons	Optional (a)	(a)
White (b)	Black shoes & socks	AWC/ optional boatcloak	Dress collar/cap	Ribbons	Optional (a)	(a)
(b)	Black shoes & socks	AWC or tanker jacket	Dress cap	Ribbons optional (a)	Optional (a)	(a)
(b)	Black shoes & socks	AWC or tanker jacket	Dress cap	Ribbons optional (a)	Optional (a)	(a)
(b)	Black shoes & socks	AWC (e)	Service collar/cap	Ribbons	Optional (a)	(a)
(b)	Black shoes & socks	AWC or tanker jacket (e)	Cap	Ribbons optional (a)	Optional (a)	(a)
(b)	Black shoes & socks	AWC or tanker jacket (e)	Cap	Ribbons optional (a)	Optional (a)	(a)
(b, d)	Combat boots/socks	AWC (e) or ECWCS	Emblem decal/name & service tapes	Not worn	Not worn	Not worn

Table 10-2. Types and Components of Authorized Uniforms for Female Officers

Designation	*Cap*	*Coat or Jacket*	*Shirt*	*Necktie*	*Skirt/Slacks*	*Handbag/Purse*
Evening dress "A"	Dress	Evening w/ cummerbund (e)	White pleated front	Black	Long black skirt	Black purse
Evening dress "B"	Dress	Evening w/ cummerbund (e)	White pleated front	Black	Long/short black skirt	Black purse
Blue dress "A"	Dress	Blue	White plain front	Scarlet w/skirt, black w/slacks	Blue skirt/ slacks	Black purse or handbag optional
Blue-white dress "A"	Dress	Blue	White plain front	Scarlet w/skirt, black w/slacks	White skirt/ slacks	Black purse or handbag optional
Blue dress "B"	Dress	Blue	White plain front	Scarlet w/skirt, black w/slacks	Blue skirt/ slacks	Black purse or handbag optional
Blue-white dress "B"	Dress	Blue	White plain front	Scarlet w/skirt, black w/slacks	White skirt/ slacks	Black purse or handbag optional
Blue dress "C"	Dress		Khaki long sleeve	Black	Blue skirt/ slacks	Black handbag optional
Blue dress "D"	Dress	None	Khaki short sleeve	None	Blue skirt/ slacks	Black handbag optional
Service "A"	Green service/ garrison	Green	Khaki long or short sleeve	Green	Green skirt/ slacks	Black handbag optional
Service "B"	Green service/ garrison	Green v-neck sweater (optional)	Khaki long sleeve	Green	Green skirt/ slacks	Black handbag optional
Service "C"	Green service/ garrison	None	Khaki short sleeve	None	Green skirt/ slacks	Black handbag optional
Maternity service uniform	Garrison service/ garrison	Green tunic (see para 3016)	Khaki long or short sleeve	Green (a)	Green skirt/ slacks	Black handbag optional
Utility uniform	Utility	Utility	Green undershirt optional	None	Web belt or martial arts belt	Not worn

a. If required or prescribed.
b. Black gloves always worn or carried with all-weather coat during winter uniform period. Optional when coat is worn.
c. Oxford/flats may be worn per paragraph 3010.
d. Green scarf optional for wear with all-weather coat/tanker jacket during winter uniform period.
e. Evening Dress with scarlet waistcoat and plain front shirt worn by general officers.

Gloves	*Footwear*	*Outer Coat (a)*	*Insignia Bos*	*Medals/Ribbons*	*Badges*	*Sword*
White (b)	Black pumps (cloth/suede)	AWC/ optional cape	Dress collar/cap	Miniature medals	Not worn	Not worn
White (b)	Black pumps (cloth/suede)	AWC/ optional cape	Dress collar/cap	Miniature medals	Not worn	Not worn
White (b)	Black pumps (c)	AWC/ optional cape	Dress collar/cap	Large medals (ribbons per para. 5205.3)	Not worn	(a)
White (b)	Black pumps (c)	AWC/ optional cape	Dress collar/cap	Large medals (ribbons per para. 5205.3)	Not worn	(a)
White (b)	Black pumps (c)	AWC/ optional cape	Dress collar/cap	Ribbons	Optional (a)	(a)
White (b)	Black pumps (c)	AWC/ optional cape	Dress collar/cap	Ribbons	Optional (a)	(a)
(b)	Black pumps (c)	AWC or tanker jacket	Dress cap	Ribbons	Optional (a)	(a)
(b)	Black pumps (c)	AWC or tanker jacket	Dress cap	Ribbons optional (a)	Optional (a)	(a)
(b)	Black pumps (c)	AWC or tanker jacket (d)	Service collar/cap	Ribbons	Optional (a)	(a)
(b)	Black pumps (c)	AWC or tanker jacket (d)	Service cap	Ribbons (a)	Optional (a)	(a)
(b)	Black pumps (c)	AWC or tanker jacket (d)	Service cap	Ribbons optional (a)	Optional (a)	(a)
(b)	Black pumps/ oxfords or flats	AWC (d)	Service cap	Ribbons optional (a)	Optional (a)	Not worn
(b)	Combat boots/ socks	AWC or ECWCS	Emblem decal/ name & service tapes	Not worn	Not worn	Not worn

Wear headgear whenever under arms or on watch, except when in a space where a meal is being served or divine service is being conducted, when in quarters (if on watch), or when specifically excused from remaining covered. Remain covered at all times when outside or on topside spaces on board ship. But see Section 913 for further shipboard ground rules.

"Mixed uniform" (components of two different uniforms, worn simultaneously—blue blouse and utility trousers, for example) is *strictly forbidden* unless specifically authorized in *Uniform Regulations.*

Full service "A" uniform (greens), with service coat, may be prescribed for parades, ceremonies, social events, and as the uniform of the day. It is normally worn when reporting for duty, unless otherwise prescribed by the commander. It is normally prescribed for the following official military occasions: (1) when assigned as a member of courts-martial, unless otherwise designated by competent authority; (2) for official visits and calls of, or to, U.S. civil officials, officers of the U.S. Armed Forces, and officials of foreign governments according to *Navy Regulations*; or (3) when visiting the White House at all times, except in a tourist capacity or when an individual is specifically invited on either a social or an official occasion for which another uniform is indicated on the invitation.

A variation of the service uniform, the service "B" uniform is the same as the service "A" uniform except that the service coat is not worn. This uniform may be worn as the uniform of the day and may be prescribed for formations at parades or ceremonies. This uniform will not be worn for formal or semiformal social events.

The short-sleeve khaki shirt with appropriate service trousers/skirt/slacks is designated as the service "C" uniform. It is worn under circumstances similar to the service "B" uniform, particularly in warmer climates.

Blue dress "A" uniform (blues with medals and, when prescribed, sword) may be worn for parades, ceremonies, and formal or semiformal social functions as appropriate to the season or those occasions requiring uniformity with NCOs and below. It is normally worn for the following official military/social occasions: (1) parades, ceremonies, reviews, solemnities, and entertainments when the commander/senior officer present desires to pay special honors to the occasion; (2) official visits of, or to, U.S. civil officials, officers of the U.S. Armed Forces, and officials of foreign governments according to *Navy Regulations*; (3) receptions given by, or in honor of, officials or officers as listed in *Navy Regulations*; or (4) at daytime formal or semiformal occasions.

Blue dress "B" uniform may be worn for parades, ceremonies, informal social functions as appropriate to the season or those occasions requiring uniformity with NCOs and below. It may also be worn as the uniform of the day for those commands that receive the appropriate clothing allowance. Blue dress "B" is normally worn for the following official military/social occasions: official visits of, or to, U.S. civil officials, officers of the U.S. Armed Forces, and officials of foreign governments, according to *Navy Regulations*; and at informal daytime receptions to which a Marine is invited in an official capacity. Dress "B" uniforms consist of the same items as the corresponding dress "A" uniforms, except that ribbons are worn in lieu of medals. Shooting badges may be prescribed.

The blue dress uniform with long-sleeve khaki shirt (without coat) and tie for male Marines or tab for female Marines is designated as blue dress "C." Commanders may prescribe blue dress "C" as the uniform of the day for specified occasions or duties, or for honors, parades, and ceremonies on and off the military activity. The blue dress uniform with short-sleeve khaki shirt (without coat) is designated as blue dress "D." Commanders may prescribe this uniform for honors, parades, and ceremonies where climatic conditions preclude the comfortable wear of the other blue dress uniforms.

The officer blue-white dress "A" and "B" uniforms are prescribed when appropriate to the season for the same types of official military/social occasions for which the equivalent blue dress uniform is prescribed as just discussed. The blue-white dress "A" and "B" uniforms consist of the same items as the blue dress "A" and "B" except the trousers/skirt/slacks are white. The blue-white dress uniform is never worn in ceremonies with enlisted Marines who are not authorized white trousers.

Evening dress is worn on formal evening occasions when civilian full dress is prescribed (such as the Marine Corps Birthday Ball) or on semiformal evening occasions. Evening dress will be prescribed for official or military-sponsored events, either formal or semiformal. Any evening function that you attend as an official representative of the Marine Corps is one for evening dress. Evening dress is an optional uniform for company-grade officers, but its possession becomes mandatory upon promotion to major.

While the boat cloak is optional, male officers should feel free to obtain and, more important, wear this handsome, traditional garment. The boat cloak, made of dark blue broadcloth material lined with scarlet wool broadcloth, may be worn with evening dress and blue dress "A" or "B" uniforms for official and social functions. Female officers may wear the similar dress cape. Neither will be worn when the blue dress uniform is worn as the uniform of the day.

If invited to the White House, check with the aide-de-camp to the commandant, Marine Corps Headquarters, as to the correct uniform and other questions of protocol.

You must buy and maintain in good condition all articles of uniform that the commandant prescribes for officers, as listed in *Uniform Regulations.* You must keep your full assignment of uniforms with you at all times except when in the field.

The law prohibits anyone not in the armed forces from wearing the uniform or any distinctive part thereof (10 U.S. Code 771, 772, 18 U.S. Code 702). This does not apply to retired Marines, who may continue to bear the title and, on occasions similar to active and reserve component personnel, wear the uniform of highest rank held. Persons who served honorably *during wartime* and whose most recent service was terminated under honorable circumstances may wear the uniform in public, but only for military funerals, memorial services, weddings, and inaugurals; parades on national or state holidays; or other parades or ceremonies of a patriotic character in which any active or reserve U.S. military unit is taking part. In other words, *previous service alone* does not grant a universal right to wear the uniform for former servicemembers.

Wearing the uniform is prohibited in connection with nonmilitary commercial or business activities or in any circumstances that might compromise the dignity of the uniform or the Corps.

No Marine (including retired or reserve personnel) may wear the uniform while attending (unless on duty) or participating in any demonstration, assembly, or activity, the purpose of which is furtherance of personal or partisan political, social, economic, or religious issues. In other words, public events of dubious dignity or outright demonstrations and the Marine Corps uniform or emblem do not mix.

Rules on body markings and piercings ebb and flow with the times. By 2007 with increased influence of civilian styles, policies became more restrictive, and they were reinforced to prohibit tattoos or brands on the neck and the head, as well as on the arm and viewable in short sleeves. In 2016, the Marine

Corps published new guidelines, clarifying and easing somewhat the policies governing tattoos and piercings. In all areas of the body, tattoos or brands that are prejudicial to good order, discipline, and morale, or are of a nature to bring discredit upon the Marine Corps, are prohibited. Tattoos, body piercing, and nondental tooth crowns are identified as body art, and commanders are tasked with upholding current regulations regarding eccentric appearance.

1042. Uniform Accessories

Marine Corps uniforms come with far more accessories than comparable civilian attire, and it thus takes some effort before their proper wear becomes habit. The following rules concern the wearing of uniform accessories. Once again, you are wise to refer regularly to the current *Marine Corps Uniform Regulations.*

Belts. Belts are worn with buckle centered and aligned. Belt buckles (except on field equipment) must be brightly polished. Since the introduction of the Marine Corps Martial Arts Program, Marines have the option of substituting a color-coded rigger's belt for the web belt worn with the combat utility uniform. During 2008, this option became a requirement owing to the requirement for all hands to achieve the tan belt during basic training.

Gloves. During the winter uniform period, Marines may wear or carry black leather, vinyl, or cloth (females only) gloves when an outer coat is worn with the service uniform. Black gloves may also be worn or carried with the service "A" uniform or service uniform with sweater or tanker jacket at the individual's option. Local commanders will designate whether gloves will be worn by troops in formation.

Marines may wear black leather gloves with the utility uniform.

White cloth gloves may be worn or carried with evening dress, blue dress, or blue-white dress uniforms during summer and winter uniform seasons. When an outer garment is worn during the winter uniform season, black gloves may be worn or carried. During the summer season, black gloves may be worn or carried when the all-weather coat is worn as the outer garment. White gloves are worn or carried when the boat cloak or dress cape is worn as the outer garment.

Shoes. With the service uniform, Marines must wear approved, commercial black shoes of natural or synthetic leather in semigloss or high gloss (patent) finishes. They must be plain, Oxford-style shoes without fancy stitching. Socks must match shoes in color.

10-5. Marine Corps uniforms are distinguished in their elegant simplicity, smart cut, and the evident pride and bearing of their wearing.

Swords. Swords may be prescribed with all uniforms except evening dress and combat utilities, and they must be carried in line with troops in dress uniforms. Male officers must possess swords, but no longer must have their names engraved on the blade. A Marine officer may carry a parent's sword, provided it is sized correctly.

Jewelry. Marines may not wear jewelry, fobs, pens, or pencils exposed on the uniform, except the following: inconspicuous rings, only one per hand except for engagement and wedding rings, which count as one when worn on a single finger; an inconspicuous wrist watch; a regulation tie-clasp; and sunglasses (conservative design—but may not be worn in line with troops unless by medical requirement).

Women are authorized to wear a single pair of small earrings (one per ear), and they may carry umbrellas when in service or dress uniform.

Mourning Band. You wear the regulation black mourning band on your left arm between the shoulder and elbow when a pallbearer or attending a military funeral in an official capacity, during prescribed official mourning, or for family mourning (optional).

"Sam Browne" Belt. The service, or "Sam Browne," belt is authorized and worn as organizational equipment in organizations when the sword is required for wear or an individual is considered "under arms." Recent change authorizes wear of the belt with all uniforms, with or without service coat.

Religious Jewelry and Apparel. Marines may wear neat and conservative religious jewelry and apparel items as follows: (1) articles of religious apparel that are not visible or apparent when worn with the uniform; (2) visible articles of religious apparel with the uniform while attending or conducting divine services or while in a chapel or other house of worship; and (3) visible articles of religious apparel with the uniform that do not interfere with or replace required uniform articles.

1043. Civilian Clothes

As an officer you are expected to maintain a high standard of civilian dress. Your clothes should be conservative in cut and color, of the best quality, and well maintained.

Never forget, incidentally, that your general neatness and grooming at all times are marked on your fitness report. This includes not only uniform but civilian clothes as well.

When off duty, wear civilian clothes. If on duty abroad, however, be sure to check local directives on wearing of plain clothes. Unless you have permission from the commandant, you may not wear the uniform when on leave outside the United States or its territories.

While dressed in civilian clothes, wear no distinctive articles of the uniform (except items not exclusively military such as sweater, gloves, purse, shoes, socks, underwear, and so forth).

1044. Grooming

The following ten rules guide the maintenance of the professional appearance and good grooming for all officers:

1. Although most military grooming has simply reflected society's standards through history, Marines since the 1950s have stressed neat and close trimming of hair. Although three inches is the maximum permissible length on top for male Marines, hairstyles approaching the maximums are regarded as somewhat foppish by many Marine officers and insubordinate by more than a few others. Therefore, this *Guide* must, in good faith, encourage more junior officers to remain wary and well-trimmed.
2. Keep clean-shaven, except for a mustache, if desired (traditionally, Marines have always rated mustaches, and naval officers, beards, but not the reverse). Eccentricities of mustache will not be tolerated.
3. All leather must be maintained in very high polish.
4. To keep shirt collars trim and neckties in place, wear a collar stay.
5. To make utility trousers look smartest with field boots, turn up the trousers so as to form interior cuffs, and place a blousing band or sleeve garter inside this interior cuff. This produces a neat overhang approximately one inch below the top of the boot. Most Marine Corps exchanges stock bands or garters for this purpose. In a pinch, a strong rubber band or section of inner tube will do the job.
6. Keep the overlap of your khaki web belt within the prescribed 2–4 inches, 2¾–3¾ inches for coat belts.
7. Although your uniforms contain many pockets, the safest rule is to carry nothing in them. Specifically, you should never place anything

in exterior pockets of a dress or service uniform (exceptions: pencil out of sight in a shirt pocket; notebook in hip pocket; wallet and handkerchief kept flat in trouser pockets).

8. At least two weeks before the seasonal change from summer to winter uniform variants and vice versa, break out the forthcoming uniform, have it cleaned and pressed, and check it for completeness and repair.
9. With standing-collar uniforms (as well as evening dress), it is convenient—and military—to carry a handkerchief, if needed, unobtrusively tucked inside your left sleeve; this obviates convulsive dives into the interior of the uniform when a handkerchief is needed.
10. Read and follow the advice on care and marking of uniforms to be found in *Uniform Regulations.*

Old breed? New breed? There's not a damn bit of differences so long as it's the Marine Breed.

—Lieutenant General Lewis B. Puller

This modern tendency to scorn and ignore tradition and to sacrifice it to administrative convenience is one that wise men will resist in all branches of life, but more especially in our military life.

—Field Marshal Archibald Wavell

11

MILITARY COURTESY, HONORS, AND CEREMONIES

MILITARY COURTESY

Military courtesy is the traditional form of politeness in the profession of arms. Though sharing many elements with courtesy in civilian life, military courtesy stems firmly from a traditional code of rules and customs. Just as courtesy in general is said to be "the lubricant of life," so military courtesy helps to ease us along well-worn, tried, and customary paths. Because, by its very nature, the life and discipline of the service are formal, so too is its form of courtesy.

Military courtesy embraces much more than the salute or any other rituals, important as these are. Courtesy is a disciplined attitude of mind. It must be accorded to all ranks and on all occasions. Courtesy to a senior indicates respect for authority, responsibility, and experience. Courtesy toward a junior expresses appreciation and respect for his or her support and for that person as a fellow Marine. Courtesy paid to the Colors and to the National Anthem expresses loyalty to the United States and to the Constitution, which we are sworn to uphold and defend.

Military courtesy is a prerequisite to discipline. It promotes the willing obedience and unhesitating cooperation that make a good unit "click." When ordinary acts of military courtesy are performed grudgingly or omitted, discipline suffers. Discipline and courtesy alike stem from and contribute to esprit de corps. The Marine Corps has always stood at the top of the services by full and willing observance of the twin virtues of soldierly courtesy and discipline.

1101. Conduct toward Members of Other Services

The minutiae of military courtesy vary little from service to service, and from nation to nation. As a Marine (and therefore, as a professional), you must learn the meaning and traditions behind the badges, insignia, and titles of the officers and enlisted personnel of other military services, both American and foreign.

When you go to duty with another service or in another country, make it a particular point to know and, in most instances, defer to the customs and traditions of that service or country (see, for example, Section 1105). On the other hand, never forget that you are a Marine; never feel self-conscious about holding fast to Marine Corps standards of uniform or to the Marine way of doing and saying things.

1102. Military Titles, Phraseology, and Address

Knowing and employing proper military titles and forms of address when interacting with other Marines and members of the other services are a mark of professionalism.

Addressing Seniors. Never forget that "sir" or "ma'am" is an important word in conversation with anyone senior. While you may not be reprimanded on the spot for omission of "sir" or "ma'am," that omission is quickly noted and usually remembered. This norm applies whether in uniform or not, whether on duty or off.

Speaking to Juniors. To help promote subordination and respect among your juniors, address them by their proper titles and their names. Follow the principles laid down in Section 1502, and be wary of overly casual use of first names or nicknames. Formality in speaking to a subordinate is never wrong, whereas informality can be risky and is liable to compromise your position. In particular, never allow casual or even unintentionally disrespectful reference to an absent third person, particularly one senior to one, on the part of one of your juniors.

Shortcuts. It is proper to use shortened titles in conversation or unofficial correspondence. Table 11-1 shows the correct military forms of address on official and unofficial occasions and when dealing with civilians.

Table 11-1. Correct Forms of Address for Naval and Military Personnel

Person Addressed or Introduced	*To Military Personnel*		*To Civilians*	
	Introduce as:	*Address as:*	*Introduce as:*	*Address as:*
Marine, Army, or Air Force Officer	Major (or other rank) Smith	Same	Major Smith[a]	Same
Naval Officer	Captain Smith	Same	Captain Smith[a]	Same
Navy Staff Corps Officer	Commander Smith[b] Chaplain Smith	Same Same	Commander Smith[b] Chaplain Smith	Same Same
Coast Guard and Coast and Geodetic Survey Officers	Same as for same rank in Navy[b]	Same	Same as for same rank in Navy[b]	Same
U.S. Public Health Service Officer (M.D. or D.D.S.)	Dr. Smith[c]	Same	Dr. Smith of the Public Health Service	Dr. Smith
U.S. Public Health Service Officer (Sanitary Engineer)	Mr. or Ms. Smith[c]	Same	Mr. or Ms. Smith of the Public Health Service	Mr. or Ms. Smith
Commissioned Warrant Officer[d]	Chief Warrant Officer Smith[d]	Same[d]	Chief Warrant Officer Smith[d]	Same

Midshipman or Cadet	Midshipman (or Cadet) Smith	Mr. or Miss Smith	Midshipman (or Cadet) Smith	Mr. or Miss Smith
Warrant Officer[d]	Warrant Officer Smith[d]	Same[d]	Warrant Officer Smith[d]	Same[d]
Staff NCO or Chief Petty Officer[e]	Sergeant Major Smith,[e] Master Chief Gunner's Mate Smith	Sergeant Major or Chief	Sergeant Major Smith, Master Chief Gunner's Mate Smith	Sergeant Major or Chief
Noncommissioned Officer or Petty Officer	Corporal Smith or Gunner's Mate Smith	Same	Corporal Smith or Petty Officer Smith	Same
Private or Seaman	Private (or Seaman) Smith	Smith	Private (or Seaman) Smith	Smith

[a] When not in uniform, an officer should be introduced as "of the Navy" or "of the Marine Corps" to distinguish the rank from similar-sounding ranks in the other armed services. Suggested phraseology: "This is Lieutenant Smith of the Marine Corps." Such a form of introduction indicates the officer's rank, service, and the proper form of address.

[b] Add "of the Medical Corps," "of the Civil Engineer Corps," or the other corps when helpful to indicate status of officer. If a senior officer of the Medical or Dental Corps prefers to be addressed as "Doctor," such preference should be honored. Some senior members of the Chaplain's Corps prefer to be addressed by their rank, but it is always correct to address a chaplain of any rank as Chaplain.

[c] In any case where there is reason to believe that the officer's insignia might not be recognized, it is correct to add, "of the Public Health Service," "of the Coast Guard," or "of the Coast and Geodetic Survey."

[d] Male Marine Corps warrant officers appointed in certain occupational fields bear the title of (Chief) Marine Gunner, addressed as "Gunner."

[e] All staff NCOs (that is, those with rank of staff sergeant and higher) are addressed by their particular titles, such as "Gunnery Sergeant Hayes," "Master Sergeant Wodarczyk," or "Staff Sergeant Basilone."

Here are some informalities that usage sanctions.

Medical and dental officers below the rank of commander may be addressed as "Doctor."

Any chaplain may be addressed by another officer as "Padre" and Roman Catholic chaplains of whatever rank (and Episcopal chaplains who so prefer) as "Father."

At one time, custom sanctioned a second lieutenant's being addressed or spoken of as "Mr." or "Ms." But this practice has fallen into disuse. Today, it is normal and preferable to use "Lieutenant," especially in the presence of enlisted people. Do not be surprised to hear warrant officers addressed as "Mr." or "Ms."—especially in the Navy—although addressing them by their proper rank is never wrong.

Lieutenant colonels are commonly addressed as "Colonel."

Generals and admirals, of whatever grade, are spoken to as "General" or "Admiral," respectively.

Where the male officer is addressed as "sir," a female officer may be addressed as "ma'am," or by rank, as "Yes, Major," or "Good morning, Lieutenant."

As an indicator of respect and professionalism, you should address sergeants major and master gunnery sergeants using their complete titles, although after some time working together in a close-knit unit, "Master Gunny" becomes appropriate for the latter.

The first sergeant of a company, battery, or detachment should be addressed by officers of the unit as "First Sergeant." The title "top sergeant" is not used in the Marine Corps. However, officers commonly address master sergeants as "Top" and gunnery sergeants as "Gunny," and neither of these implies any disrespect.

Avoid the unfortunate practice, which has occurred in some instances, of referring colloquially to enlisted Marines as "troopers." This is an Army—not a Marine or Navy—term, going back to horse cavalry, and more recently used to refer to paratroopers. It is inappropriate for Marines (and sounds like the highway patrol). Marines should be referred to collectively as "Marines" or less formally in the traditional Marine usage as "people" (as in the injunction, "You people, square yourselves away").

Address enlisted personnel by rank and last name.

Navy chief petty officers are habitually spoken to as "Chief," although it is wise to address the more senior chief petty officers using the longer forms, "Senior Chief" and "Master Chief," corresponding to their actual grades.

NAVY	MARINE CORPS	COAST GUARD	ARMY	AIR FORCE
W-1 WARRANT OFFICER W-2 CHIEF WARRANT OFFICER	GOLD SCARLET W-1 WARRANT OFFICER GOLD SCARLET W-2 CHIEF WARRANT OFFICER	W-1 WARRANT OFFICER W-2 CHIEF WARRANT OFFICER	SILVER BLACK WO-1 WARRANT OFFICER SILVER BLACK CW-2 CHIEF WARRANT OFFICER	GOLD SKY BLUE W-1 WARRANT OFFICER GOLD SKY BLUE W-2 CHIEF WARRANT OFFICER
W-3 CHIEF WARRANT OFFICER W-4 CHIEF WARRANT OFFICER	SILVER SCARLET W-3 CHIEF WARRANT OFFICER SILVER SCARLET W-4 CHIEF WARRANT OFFICER	W-3 CHIEF WARRANT OFFICER W-4 CHIEF WARRANT OFFICER	SILVER BLACK CW-3 CHIEF WARRANT OFFICER SILVER BLACK CW-4 CHIEF WARRANT OFFICER	SILVER SKY BLUE W-3 CHIEF WARRANT OFFICER SILVER SKY BLUE W-4 CHIEF WARRANT OFFICER
ENSIGN	(GOLD) SECOND LIEUTENANT	ENSIGN	(GOLD) SECOND LIEUTENANT	(GOLD) SECOND LIEUTENANT
LIEUTENANT JUNIOR GRADE	(SILVER) FIRST LIEUTENANT	LIEUTENANT JUNIOR GRADE	(SILVER) FIRST LIEUTENANT	(SILVER) FIRST LIEUTENANT
LIEUTENANT	(SILVER) CAPTAIN	LIEUTENANT	(SILVER) CAPTAIN	(SILVER) CAPTAIN
LIEUTENANT COMMANDER	(GOLD) MAJOR	LIEUTENANT COMMANDER	(GOLD) MAJOR	(GOLD) MAJOR
COMMANDER	(SILVER) LIEUTENANT COLONEL	COMMANDER	(SILVER) LIEUTENANT COLONEL	(SILVER) LIEUTENANT COLONEL

Figure 11-1. Officer Insignia of Rank

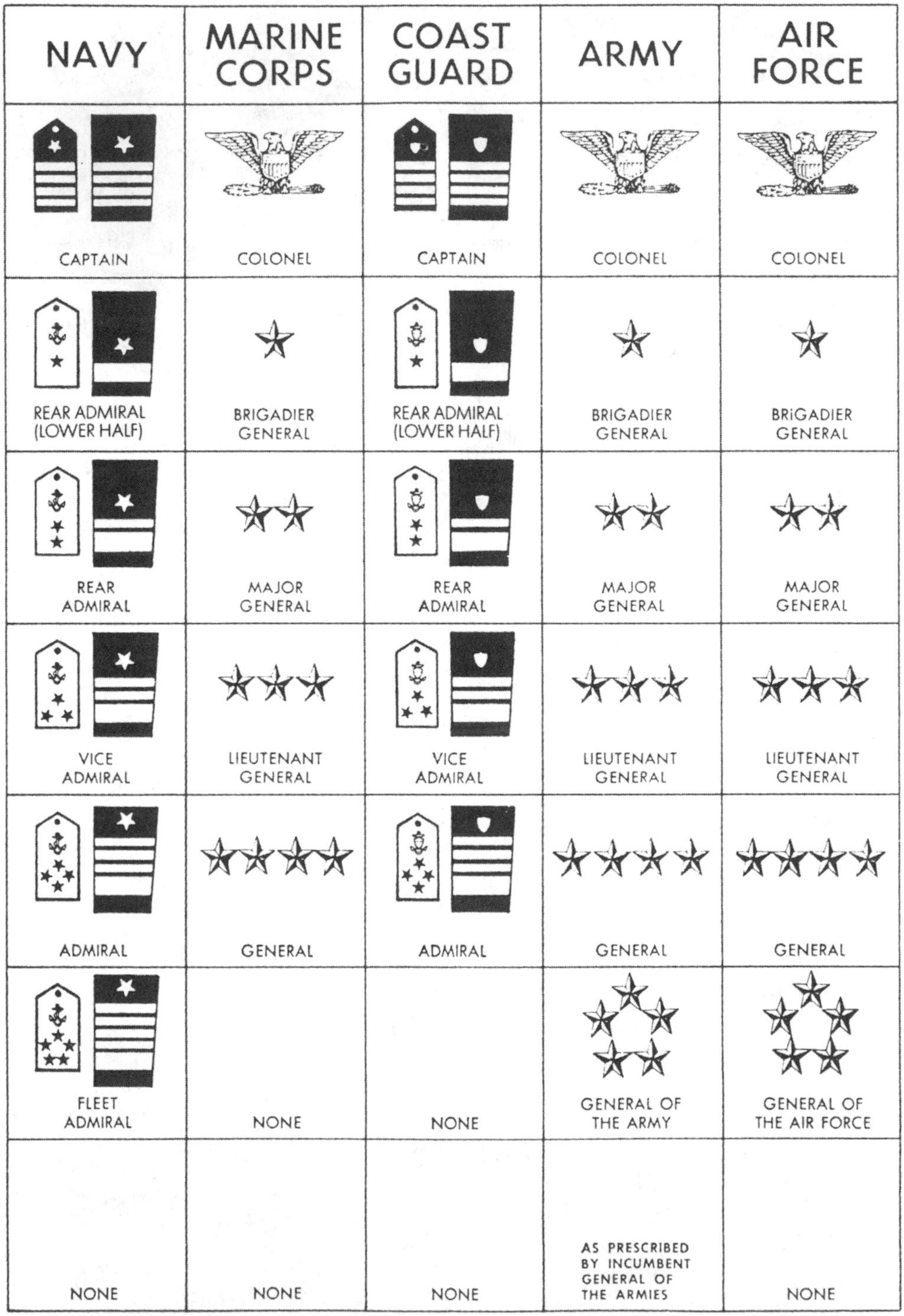

NAVY	MARINE CORPS	COAST GUARD	ARMY	AIR FORCE
CAPTAIN	COLONEL	CAPTAIN	COLONEL	COLONEL
REAR ADMIRAL (LOWER HALF)	BRIGADIER GENERAL	REAR ADMIRAL (LOWER HALF)	BRIGADIER GENERAL	BRIGADIER GENERAL
REAR ADMIRAL	MAJOR GENERAL	REAR ADMIRAL	MAJOR GENERAL	MAJOR GENERAL
VICE ADMIRAL	LIEUTENANT GENERAL	VICE ADMIRAL	LIEUTENANT GENERAL	LIEUTENANT GENERAL
ADMIRAL	GENERAL	ADMIRAL	GENERAL	GENERAL
FLEET ADMIRAL	NONE	NONE	GENERAL OF THE ARMY	GENERAL OF THE AIR FORCE
NONE	NONE	NONE	AS PRESCRIBED BY INCUMBENT GENERAL OF THE ARMIES	NONE

Figure 11-1. Officer Insignia of Rank (*Continued*)

NAVY	MARINES	ARMY	AIR FORCE	
MASTER CHIEF P.O.	SGT MAJOR; MASTER GUNNERY SGT	STAFF SGT MAJOR; COMMAND SGT MAJOR; SPEC 9	CHIEF MASTER SGT.; CHIEF MASTER SGT OF THE AF	E-9
SENIOR CHIEF P.O.	1ST SGT; MASTER SGT	1ST SGT; MASTER SGT; SPEC 8	SENIOR MASTER SGT	E-8
CHIEF P.O.	GUNNERY SGT	SGT. 1ST CLASS; SPEC 7	MASTER SGT	E-7
P.O. 1ST CLASS	STAFF SGT	STAFF SGT; SPEC 6	TECHNICAL SGT	E-6
P.O. 2ND CLASS	SGT	SGT; SPEC 5	STAFF SGT	E-5
P.O. 3RD CLASS	CORPORAL	CORPORAL; SPEC 4	SENIOR AIRMAN	E-4
SEAMAN	LANCE CORPORAL	PRIVATE 1ST CLASS	AIRMAN 1ST CLASS	E-3
SEAMAN APPRENTICE	PRIVATE 1ST CLASS	PRIVATE	AIRMAN	E-2
SEAMAN RECRUIT	PRIVATE	PRIVATE	BASIC AIRMAN	E-1

Figure 11-2. Enlisted Insignia of Rank

Being at ease with the proper military titles and forms of address relies on thorough familiarity with the rank structures of the armed forces and the insignia that denote rank. Insignia of rank appear in Figures 11-1 and 11-2.

In Section 1015, you will find emphasis on the traditional Marine way of saying things, and, in Appendix VII, a glossary of Marine Corps terms. Know, employ, and enforce the use of those terms.

1103. Pointers on Military Etiquette

This subsection compiles a miscellany of Marine Corps and Navy customs, courtesies, and points of etiquette, some written, others unwritten—but all important for you to know and observe.

The CO's "Wishes." When your commanding officer says, "I wish," "I desire," "I would like," or similar expressions, these have the force of a direct order and should be complied with on that basis. Given this custom, commanding officers at every level, including platoon leaders, must take care when expressing their "wishes," lest they find themselves in the predicament of having given an order they did not actually intend.

Accompanying a Senior. The position of honor for one's senior is on the right. Therefore, in company with a senior, you walk, ride, and sit on the left. When entering a vehicle or a boat, juniors embark first and take the less desirable places in the middle or on "jump" or front seats (or forward in a boat); when debarking, the senior leaves first, while juniors follow in order of rank.

When a senior is inspecting, he or she is followed by the immediate commander of the unit being inspected, who remains on the senior's left, one pace to the rear— except that, during inspection of troops in formation, the immediate commander remains on the right of the inspecting officer and precedes him or her while inspecting in ranks. For other pointers on inspections, turn to Sections 1511 through 1515.

Acknowledging Orders. When a Marine officer or enlisted Marine receives orders or instructions, he or she replies, "Aye, aye, sir," or "Aye, aye, ma'am." This phrase, which descends from the earliest days of the Marine Corps and Navy, is used in both services. It means: "I understand the orders I have received, and will carry them out." Never permit a subordinate to acknowledge an order by "Very well," "All right," "Yes," or "Okay."

Mounted Juniors. Mounted juniors dismount vehicles or equipment (or, in days past, horses) before addressing or reporting to seniors, except when in the field. Even then, however, dismount if practical.

Meeting a Senior Indoors. When you meet a senior indoors, in a passageway or doorway, or on a stairway or ladder, give way smartly and promptly. In such an instance, greetings are normally exchanged, initiated by the junior individual.

Senior Entering a Room. When a senior enters a room or passes close aboard unorganized groups either indoors or outside, the senior officer or NCO of the group or groups commands, "Attention on deck!" or simply "Attention!" All hands come to attention and remain so until the senior has passed. If out of doors and covered, all hands salute.

Permission to Speak to Senior Officers. When one of your enlisted people wishes to speak to the company or detachment commander, the enlisted person first obtains the first sergeant's permission (see Section 1502). If he or she desires to speak to an officer of still higher rank or position, the enlisted person must in turn have the company or detachment commander's permission.

Similarly, as a junior officer, you obtain your immediate CO's permission before you seek an official interview with any higher officer. The reason for this is that the first sergeant or CO can probably solve the problem satisfactorily without the matter having to go higher.

Entering an Office. Enlisted Marines entering any office should be required to observe the following procedure, regardless of whether an officer is in the office: knock; enter and stand at attention immediately inside doorway, uncovered (unless under arms); and identify oneself by name and rank, then state one's business.

Although the foregoing sequence is not mandatory for officers, it is a prudent procedure for junior officers to bear in mind, especially when entering the office of one who is appreciably senior. In general, an officer should not "freeze" on entering, however. Having once made an entrance, the junior officer should distinctly come to the position of the soldier (to signify respect for the senior) and then as quickly assume a less formal stance of alert composure.

If you are a smoker, never enter the office of a senior while you are smoking, and do not smoke in the senior's office or presence unless invited to do so.

On the Telephone. Use moderate and respectful tones, and identify yourself and your organization. Be brief. For example, answer a phone call as follows:

"Company B, 5th Marines, Lieutenant Griffith." Never answer by simply saying, "Hello."

Uncovering under Arms. The only exception to the rule that Marines under arms never uncover is at a religious service, such as a wedding, when officers may wear swords and still uncover. You do not unsheathe your sword inside a church, however, unless express authority is granted by an appropriate religious functionary.

SALUTES AND SALUTING

1104. The Military Salute

Saluting is a military custom observed by men and women who follow the profession of arms. It is a matter of pride among Marines, from general to private, to salute willingly, promptly, smartly, and proudly. The good Marine stands out from the other services by a smart, correct, and cheerful salute, which is as much a hallmark of the Corps as the Globe and Anchor. When you salute or receive a salute, you mark yourself as a Marine who has pride in self and Corps.

As a junior officer, you must recognize and teach that the salute is a privilege enjoyed only by military people and is a mutual acknowledgment of comradeship in the profession of arms.

Origins of Saluting. Over the centuries, men-at-arms have rendered fraternal and respectful greetings to indicate friendliness. In early times, armed men raised their weapons or shifted them to the left hand (while raising the empty right hand) to give proof of amicable intentions. During the Middle Ages, knights in armor, on encountering friendly knights, raised their helmet visors in recognition. If they were in the presence of feudal superiors, the helmet was usually doffed. In every case, the fighting man made a gesture of friendliness—the raising of the empty right hand. This gesture survives as today's hand salute, which is the traditional greeting among soldiers of all nations.

Like the original hand salute and doffing of the cap, the discharge of weapons, presentation of arms, and lowering of the point of the sword were all intended to signify good will. In every case, the one so saluting, in good faith, momentarily rendered himself incapable of using his weapon offensively. The descendants of these earlier gestures are the modern sword salute, present arms, and gun salutes.

Whom to Salute. Those entitled to salutes are:

- All commissioned and warrant officers of the Army, Marine Corps, Navy, Air Force, and Coast Guard; of the reserve components of those services; and of the National Guard
- Officers of friendly foreign powers
- By service custom though not by regulation, any high civilian official who is entitled to honors by *Navy Regulations.*

Officers of the same rank may exchange salutes on meeting, although this practice is no longer common. In any case, the first one to recognize the other initiates the salute.

Enlisted Marines salute other enlisted Marines only in formation when rendering reports.

Prisoners may not salute or, for that matter, wear the Marine Corps emblem.

Definitions. The following definitions apply to Marine Corps saluting procedure.

Out of doors means "in the open air; or the interior of such buildings as drill halls and gymnasiums when used for drill or exercises of troops; or on the weather decks of a man-of-war; or under roofed structures such as lanais, covered walks, and shelters open at one or both sides to the weather." It is synonymous with "on the topside" when used afloat.

Indoors means "the interior of any building ashore, other than a drill hall, gymnasium, or armory."

Between decks means "any shipboard space below a weather deck, other than officers' country."

Covered and *uncovered* mean respectively "when and when not wearing headgear."

Under arms is a term indicating that a Marine is carrying a weapon in his hand; is equipped with side arms; or is wearing equipment pertaining to an arm, such as a sword sling, pistol belt, or cartridge belt. Any Marine wearing an "MP" (military police) or "SP" (shore patrol) brassard is considered under arms.

Saluting distance means "the maximum distance within which salutes are rendered and exchanged," prescribed as thirty paces. This figure is considered to be one within which recognition of insignia is possible, and approximately that within which friends or acquaintances can recognize and greet each other. The salute should be rendered when six paces from the person (or Color) to be saluted. If the person or Color to be saluted obviously will not approach within this distance, the salute is rendered at the point of nearest approach.

1105. Hand Salutes

Significance. In some services, the hand salute (Figure 11-3) has been deemphasized almost to the vanishing point, based on an erroneous perception that rendering a salute, rather than being an act of courtesy and soldierly recognition, signifies inferiority and subservience. Nothing could be further from the truth. As in civil life "on the outside," where you show deference and render courtesy to older, more experienced, or more important persons, so, as a junior Marine, you salute first. In returning your salute, the senior in turn salutes you as a fellow in arms. Thus, the exchange of salutes is a two-way street.

The manner and enthusiasm with which you render or receive a salute indicate the state of your training, your individual esprit, the discipline of your outfit, and your quality as a Marine. Correct saluting habits characterize a good Marine.

How to Execute the Hand Salute. Salute only while stationary or at quick time. If you are at the double and must salute or receive a salute, slow to quick time. Stand or walk at attention; head up, chin in, and stomach pulled in. When

Figure 11-3. Hand Salute

halted, come to attention distinctly as a preliminary motion to the salute. Look directly at the person or Color you are saluting. If walking or riding, turn your head smartly toward the person being saluted, and catch that person's eye. Execute the first movement, holding position until the salute is acknowledged or you see that it is not going to be, then complete the salute by bringing your hand down smartly. When doing this, keep your fingers extended and joined, your thumb streamlined alongside—taken together, your hand, fingers, and thumb should form a single, straight "blade." In returning a salute, execute the two counts at marching cadence.

In the Marine Corps and Navy, it is customary to exchange a greeting with a salute. The junior should always say, "Good morning (or evening), sir (or ma'am)," and the senior should unfailingly reply in the same vein—with a smile.

In the Marine Corps and Navy, one does not salute when uncovered— that is, when not wearing headgear. The rare exception to this rule is that the salute *may* be rendered uncovered when, in a special circumstance, not to salute might cause serious misunderstanding or undesired friction. For example, when serving with the Army or Air Force (who *do* salute uncovered), you may, if good judgment and good relations dictate, depart from the naval procedure but beware of adopting the habit. In today's environment of increased "jointness" among the services, knowledgeable Army and Air Force officers are familiar with naval customs concerning salutes and do not normally expect or require Marines to salute when uncovered.

How Not to Salute. A sloppy, grudging salute, or a childish pretense not to notice anyone to whom a salute is due, indicates unmilitary attitude, lack of pride in self and Corps, and plain ignorance.

Never salute with pipe or cigarette in your right hand or your mouth. If you are chewing tobacco or gum, bring your jaws to rest during the exchange of salutes. As under any other circumstances, it is highly unmilitary to be caught saluting with one hand in your pocket, your blouse unbuttoned, or your headgear not squared.

Avoid—and, as an officer, never tolerate—trick salutes. Here are the most common and unacceptable aberrations:

- Right wrist bent
- Left elbow stuck out at exaggerated, unnatural angle

- Palm turned inward, knuckles kept forward
- Fingers on right hand bent and flexed inward
- Right thumb extended away from fingers
- Hips thrust forward, shoulders swayed back.

When you find a Marine doing any of these things, no matter how hard he or she seems to be trying, correct the Marine on the spot, and see that he or she knows and practices the right way to salute.

1106. Rifle Salutes

The rifle salute may be executed from the following positions:

- Right or left shoulder arms
- Order arms
- Trail arms
- Present arms.

Any individual under arms with rifle salutes by one of the foregoing rifle salutes. The only occasion where a hand salute is executed by a Marine with a rifle is at "sling arms."

In its four forms, the rifle salute is rendered as follows under the conditions given:

- *Right or left shoulder arms* is rendered when out of doors at a halt or at a walk.
- *Order arms* is rendered when at a halt, either indoors or out of doors.
- *Trail arms* is rendered when at a walk, indoors or out of doors.
- *Presenting arms* is a special compliment, as a Marine at present arms represents the authority of the nation. The privilege of saluting by presenting arms is reserved for troops in formation and for sentinels on post.

Marines armed with weapons normally carried slung use the hand salute only, and, when so saluting, carry the piece at sling arms, with the left hand grasping the sling to steady the weapon.

1107. Sword Salutes and Manual

You will find the manual of the sword described in *Marine Corps Drill and Ceremonies Manual*, and Sections 1115 and 1116 give further information on the sword. Every Marine officer takes pride in being precise, dexterous, and at ease with the sword (see Figure 11-4).

When armed with the sword, you render or return salutes in the following ways:

- If your sword is sheathed, and you are not in formation, execute the normal hand salute.
- If your sword is drawn and you are halted, either in or out of formation, execute present sword as prescribed in the manual of the sword. If commanding a formation, which will usually be the case if your sword is drawn, bring your troops to attention before you do so.
- If your sword is drawn and you are under way in formation, execute the sword salute, having first brought your command to attention, if necessary.

1108. Individual Saluting Etiquette

Whether to Salute Once or Twice. After an officer has been saluted initially, if that officer remains nearby and no conversation takes place, no further salutes are required.

When a junior is spoken to by, or addresses, a senior officer, he or she salutes initially, and again when the conversation ends or the senior leaves. Throughout the conversation, the junior stands at attention unless otherwise directed by the senior. It should be an instinctive military courtesy on your part, as an officer, to give your subordinates "at ease" or "carry on" during any extended conversation.

Reporting when Indoors. When you report indoors to an officer senior to you, unless under arms, you uncover, place your cover under your left arm, visor forward (or, if a soft cover, hold it smartly in your left hand), knock, and enter when told to do so. Two paces in front of the senior, halt and report, "Sir, Lieutenant Neville reporting." Remain at attention unless told to stand at ease, carry on, or be seated. On being dismissed, take one backstep, halt, and then face about and march out. If under arms, remain covered, and salute on reporting, and again on being dismissed. The latter salute is rendered after completion of your backstep.

After entering, do not report until recognized by the officer and until he or she has completed the business at hand.

The foregoing procedure also applies to enlisted Marines who report to you.

Enlisted Marines Not in Formation. When an officer approaches enlisted Marines who are not in formation, the first to recognize the officer calls the group to attention as soon as the officer comes within ten paces. Out of doors, if covered (as they should be), all hands turn to face the officer and salute when he or she is within six paces. The salute is held until returned. The group remains at attention until the officer has passed or until commanded, "Carry on," which an officer should be quick to do under informal circumstances.

Profit in this by the example of Major General John A. Lejeune, later the thirteenth commandant, during the Meuse-Argonne Battle in 1918. General

Figure 11-4. Sword Salutes and Manual

Lejeune approached a group of Marines, whom an NCO called to attention. As the men sprang to their feet, General Lejeune checked them, saying, "Sit down, men. It is more important for tired men to rest than for the division commander to be saluted."

Overtaking. When you overtake an officer senior in rank proceeding in the same direction, draw abreast on the senior's left, coming to the salute as you do so, and say, "By your leave, sir." The senior officer acknowledges the salute and replies, "Granted." Remember, if approaching at double time, first slow to quick time.

When you overtake a Marine junior to you, pass on the right. As you come into view, abreast, salutes are exchanged.

Indoors. Marines not under arms do not salute indoors. In an office, however, work need not cease when an officer enters unless called to attention, which is normally the case for a commanding officer who enters. When addressed by an officer, the person so addressed should rise.

In the Mess Hall. At meals, do not rise when called to attention but stop eating and keep silent. If spoken to by an officer, an enlisted person gets to his or her feet and stands at attention until placed at ease. If not under arms, be sure to uncover when you enter a galley, mess hall, or ship's messing compartment.

In Sick Bay. Formal military courtesies are neither rendered nor required in a sick bay. Always uncover when you enter a sick bay or ward.

In Vehicles. Except when on board public conveyances, such as street cars, buses, and trains, officers in vehicles are saluted as if afoot. Other passengers salute or return salutes as necessary.

When Mounted. Mounted persons salute in the same manner as if on foot, but salutes are not rendered by anyone standing to or leading a horse. A mounted junior always dismounts before addressing a senior who is not mounted; this rule applies to vehicles as well as horses.

During Games. Games are not interrupted at the approach of an officer. Spectators do not rise or salute unless individually addressed by an officer.

On Guard. Saluting while on guard duty merits special discussion:

- *When armed with the rifle*, sentries salute by presenting arms. A sentry walking post halts, faces the officer being saluted, and comes to the present. If then spoken to by the officer (or by any other person), the sentry executes port arms and holds this position throughout the conversation. If speaking with an officer, the sentry does not interrupt the conversation to salute another officer, unless the officer with whom one is speaking likewise salutes; if so, the sentinel presents arms. At the end of the conversation, the sentry presents arms again. During hours of challenging, the first salute or present arms is rendered when the officer has been duly advanced and recognized, as described in Section 1606.

- *When not armed with the rifle*, a sentry renders hand salutes in the usual way. A sentry armed with a pistol, shotgun, or carbine does not salute during hours for challenging. While challenging, a sentry armed with the pistol remains at raise pistol; one armed with a shotgun or carbine remains at port arms.

If circumstances are such that payment of compliments interferes with a sentry's performance of duty, the sentry does not salute.

Prisoner guards ("chasers") do not salute except when addressed by an officer. If marching prisoners, the chaser halts them and takes necessary precautions for their security before rendering the salute. If armed with the rifle, a chaser executes a rifle salute but does not present arms. Prisoners may not salute at any time. Note that you must never pass between a guard and prisoners, and be sure to correct any guard who permits you or any other person to do so.

When in Doubt. If you are uncertain as to whether a salute is required, always salute. For a properly trained Marine, there should never be any doubt. Should a doubtful situation arise, however, do not go out of your way to avoid saluting. Having made up your mind to salute, do so properly and smartly. Never give a hesitant, half-hearted salute, which suggests only too plainly that you really do not know the score. Remember, it is better to render five unnecessary salutes than to omit one that you should give.

1109. Group Saluting Etiquette

Troops in Formation. Troops in formation salute on command only. Officers and NCOs in command of formations render salutes for their respective units. Before rendering a salute, the person in command brings the unit to attention. Individuals armed other than with a rifle (and officers and NCOs whose swords are not drawn) execute the hand salute.

If an officer speaks to an individual in ranks when the unit is not at attention, the person spoken to comes to attention. At the end of the conversation, the person resumes the position of the remainder of the unit.

Troops at Drill and on the March. Troops drilling do not render compliments. The person in command renders salutes for the unit. An officer in a formation is saluted only if in command of the entire formation, and that officer alone returns all salutes. NCOs in charge of detachments or units do not exchange compliments with other units so commanded, except at guard mounting, when the old and new guards do exchange compliments.

Troops marching at ease or route step are called to attention on the approach of a senior entitled to a salute.

Marine units always begin and end a march at attention. March your unit at attention while within barracks and central areas and on main roads of your post. No matter how tired you are after a day or a night in the field, bring your outfit home with a short, snappy step, pieces aligned, ranks dressed, at regulation cadence, at attention. That is the Marine way.

Groups of Officers. When officers are walking or standing together, or are embarked in a vehicle, all render and return salutes as if each were alone.

Formations in Vehicles. Members of formations embarked, as units, in military vehicles do not salute individually. The senior person in each vehicle renders and acknowledges salutes. Only the hand salute is employed.

Working Parties. The NCO in charge renders salutes for the entire detail. Individuals come to attention and salute if addressed by an officer but do not interrupt work at the approach of an officer unless the detail is called to attention.

While Honors Are Being Rendered. During ruffles and flourishes by the band or field music, while honors are being rendered, the guard presents arms to the recipient of honors. All persons in the vicinity but not in formation come to attention and salute, following the motions of the guard (for example, hand salute on present arms; terminate salute on order arms).

If ruffles and flourishes are followed by a gun salute, persons in the vicinity stand fast at attention until the last gun has fired.

On board ship, all hands on the quarterdeck salute while an officer is being piped over the side. If the guard is paraded, follow the motions of the guard in your hand salute.

At Military Funerals. The basic rule for saluting at military funerals (see Sections 1113 and 1114) is to salute each time the body bearers move the coffin and during volleys and "Taps." If you are wearing civilian clothes, uncover and hold your headgear over your left breast.

During prayers, stand at parade rest without arms, head bowed. During the firing of volleys, come to attention and salute.

Body bearers remain covered, both indoors and outdoors, when carrying the coffin. When the remains are lowered into the grave, body bearers stand at attention, holding the flag waist-high over the grave. The officer in charge of the escort presents this flag to the next of kin after the ceremony.

When a military funeral cortege passes, all hands come to attention and salute the remains, using the hand salute if in uniform, and uncovering in the civilian salute, if wearing civilian clothes.

1110. Saluting the National Anthem

When the National Anthem is played, or "To the Color" is sounded, all military personnel come to attention, face toward the music, and salute. You hold your salute until the last note of the music but remain at attention until "Carry On" is sounded. If the anthem or call is being played incident to a ceremony involving the Colors, face toward the Colors rather than the music.

Troops in Formation. Troops in formation are halted (if on the march) and brought to attention, and the commander salutes, facing in the direction of the unit's original front. If participating in a ceremony that includes rendition of the National Anthem or "To the Color," troops present arms.

Personnel Mounted in Vehicles. During the playing of the National Anthem, all vehicles within sight or hearing of the ceremony stop. Passengers do not debark, but remain seated at attention and do not salute. If the passengers comprise a military detail in an official vehicle, the person in charge debarks, faces toward the flag or music, and salutes.

Personnel on Horseback. Those on horseback halt and salute without dismounting.

Sentries. Sentries halt, face in the direction of the flag or music, and render the hand salute or present arms as appropriate (see Section 1108).

In Civilian Clothes. If wearing plain clothes, face in the direction of the flag or music and come to attention. If wearing headgear, remove and hold it over your left breast with your right hand.

Indoors. When the National Anthem is played indoors, you come to attention and face the music. Only those under arms salute.

Foreign National Anthems. Accord the national anthems of friendly foreign powers the same courtesies as your own.

1111. Courtesy to the Flag

This section confines itself to the courtesies that apply to the National Color (or National Ensign). You will find additional information dealing with flags, Colors, and Standards in Chapter 10, and Section 1118 covers execution of Morning and Evening Colors, the daily ceremonies that take place when the flag is raised and lowered.

Saluting the Flag. Except at Morning and Evening Colors and on board a warship at anchor or pierside, the flag is not saluted when displayed from a mast or flagstaff, nor is any flag saluted unless it is a National Color or Standard as defined in Section 1031. When Colors are encased in a protective cover (and said to be "cased"), they are not saluted. The tenth general order (see Section 1604), which enjoins Marines "To salute all officers, and all colors and standards not cased," has, at times, created some confusion on the issue of saluting the flag; however, there is no routine requirement to salute the National Color when it is flown from a stationary flagstaff, such as in front of a headquarters building.

Colors and Standards not cased and not displayed from a mast or flagstaff (for example, when borne by a color guard) *are* saluted when either you or they approach or pass within six paces. Hold your salute until the Colors have passed or been passed by that distance.

In the field or camp, it is customary to display the National Color and unit Battle Color in front of the commanding officer's tent. According to one's wishes, this may be done every day or only on Sundays and national holidays. All hands who approach within saluting distance (six paces) execute a hand or rifle salute as appropriate, holding the salute until six paces beyond. If a Color sentinel is posted, he or she acknowledges salutes rendered by enlisted Marines; when officers salute the Colors, the sentinel holds his or her salute or present arms until the officer has completed the salute.

Motor Vehicles Passing Colors. When passed by an uncased National Color, all persons embarked in a vehicle remain seated at attention. Vehicles approaching and passing Colors reduce speed; mounted personnel remain seated at attention but do not salute.

Individuals Not in Formation. At the approach of Colors, persons not in formation come to attention, face the Colors, and salute when within saluting distance; if you are passing Colors, continue at attention and salute within saluting distance. Construe this distance literally. Hold your salute and keep your head and eyes turned smartly toward the Colors until they have passed or have been passed by six paces. In civilian clothes, render the civilian salute with headgear held over your left breast.

Dipping the Battle or Organizational Color. In military ceremonies, Battle and Organizational Colors (see Section 1031) are dipped in salute during the playing of the National Anthem or "Retreat" (in place of the National Anthem), "To the Color," or "Hail to the Chief"; when rendering honors to the organizational commander or individual of higher rank; and, during military funerals only, on each occasion when the funeral escort presents arms.

On these occasions, when passing in review, the Battle Color or Organizational Color (but never the National Color) is dipped when six paces from the individual receiving the salute and remains dipped until six paces beyond.

Dipping the National Ensign. The National Color or Ensign is never in any circumstances permitted to touch the ground or deck. At sea, however, it is customary for merchantmen to dip their Colors when passing close aboard a warship, and, in reply, the warship runs her Ensign halfway down and then back up again. This is the only time when a National Color or Ensign may be dipped.

1112. Pointers on Saluting

All salutes received by you must be returned unless you are uncovered or unless both hands are fully loaded or occupied. If you are physically unable to return a salute, you should acknowledge it verbally, and should, if possible, excuse yourself to the individual who rendered the salute. If you are uncovered, or in any circumstance when you cannot render a correct salute, you should, if standing still, come to attention.

When wearing civilian clothes, you should use the civilian salute (headgear held over left breast, in lieu of hand salutes) for salutes to the Colors, salutes to the National Anthem, and salutes during military funerals.

If salutes are to be properly exchanged, both junior and senior must be alert. The junior must spot the approaching senior, and the senior must respond with enthusiasm. The attitude of seniors toward salutes has a profound effect on the spirit with which any salute is rendered. Enlisted persons are discouraged from saluting (and rightly so) if you overlook their courtesy or seem not to observe them. Such an attitude on your part as a Marine officer is discourteous and at times downright insulting.

You can do much to foster correct rendering of salutes by inviting them. A pleasant, direct look at an approaching junior generally puts that person on alert and encourages the junior to salute with goodwill. It is an old trick, when a junior officer seems to need a reminder in saluting manners, for the senior to salute the junior first, with a solicitous greeting, thus extending a courteous reprimand.

In saluting, *do*:

- Begin your salute in ample time (at least six paces away)
- Hold your salute until it is returned or acknowledged
- Look squarely at the person or Colors being saluted
- Assume the position of attention
- Have thumb and fingers extended and joined
- Keep hand and wrist in same plane, not bent
- Incline forearm at 45 degrees
- Hold upper arm horizontal while hand is at salute.

Do not:

- Salute with blouse or coat unbuttoned
- Salute with cigarette, pipe, or cigar in mouth
- Have anything in your right hand
- Have your left hand in a pocket
- Salute when in ranks, at games, or part of a working detail
- Salute at crowded gatherings, in public conveyances, or in congested areas, unless addressing or being directly addressed by a senior
- Salute when to do so would physically interfere with performance of an assigned duty.

One of the most unmilitary habits encountered among some Marines, both while saluting and even in ranks, is the ludicrous habit of leaning over backward (literally) in an effort to stand straight. This swaybacked stance, with stomach and pelvis thrust forward, jaw jutting out, and shoulders too far back, is a caricature of the position of attention. A Marine at attention should stand straight as an arrow, not like a bow.

MILITARY FUNERALS

1113. Overview

Navy and Marine Corps funerals are conducted in accordance with *Navy Regulations* and the *Marine Corps Drill and Ceremonies Manual*, both of which you should check carefully if, in any role other than that of principal, you are to take part in a military funeral. Chapter 21 of this *Guide* contains administrative information on funerals and burials.

Classification. Military funerals are classified:

- By size of escort (depending on rank of deceased) and type of ceremony—for example, full, simple, or modified honors. Some next of kin may wish only gravesite honors or a reduced escort; some may not wish the firing of volleys. Such wishes are, of course, governing.
- By location of military ceremony, that is, church or chapel service (remains received at church and escorted to gravesite); transfer (remains received at station, airport, or cemetery gate and escorted to gravesite); or gravesite (remains conveyed to gravesite by civilian undertaker, with military participation and ceremony at gravesite only).

Uniforms and Equipment. If the organization providing the funeral escort is authorized blues, then the uniforms should be the seasonal blue dress A or B with mourning band on the left sleeve, if available. Otherwise the uniform should be service dress with large medals instead of ribbons, if blouse is worn.

Body bearers should not wear bayonets or scabbards.

For difficult terrain, mud, or foul weather, units and individuals—such as body bearers, music, and firing party—who must leave paved areas may wear shined boots instead of dress shoes.

Officers of funeral escorts wear mourning band and mourning sword knot, as do pallbearers. Noncommissioned officers armed with the sword wear mourning sword knot only (except if acting as pallbearer, when mourning band will also be worn).

When sanctioned by the denomination concerned (as in the case of the Episcopal Church), the officiating clergyman, if so entitled, should wear military ribbons on vestments.

Dependents' Funerals. Military honors (firing of volleys and sounding of "Taps") are reserved for deceased military or former military persons. For the funerals of Marine dependents, body bearers may be assigned and, if desired, the funeral service may be conducted by a Navy chaplain.

Musical Honors. If prescribed by *Navy Regulations*, musical honors are rendered during each transfer of remains into, or from, hearse or caisson to church (or vice versa) and from hearse or caisson to gravesite. Next of kin should have an opportunity to select hymns or funeral music to be played by the band, but the Navy Hymn, "Eternal Father, Strong to Save," always should be included.

Rehearsals and Reconnaissance. Unit rehearsals obviously cannot be conducted at the church or gravesite, although the various evolutions can be adequately rehearsed on the parade ground. Careful but unobtrusive reconnaissance, however, should be conducted by the adjutant (who acts as officer-in-charge unless otherwise prescribed) and by the escort commander. All Marines assigned to funeral details—especially bugler, firing party, and body bearers—must have attained the necessary high standards of individual proficiency in their duties for these occasions.

1114. Funeral Escorts

Officers' Funerals. The basic escort for a deceased officer consists of:

- Escort commander (same rank as deceased, if possible)
- Staff (colonels and flag officers only)
- Band
- Color guard
- Body bearers
- Firing party (eight riflemen with NCO-in-charge)
- Field music
- Personal flag bearer (flag officers only).

Troop escort is as follows for the respective officers.

Major General or Senior: Three ceremonial companies (two platoons of three eight-person squads each).

Colonel or Senior: Two ceremonial companies composed as above.

Major or Senior: One ceremonial company composed as above (escort commander commands company and has no staff).

Company and Warrant Officers: One ceremonial platoon (three eight-person squads; escort commander serves as platoon leader and has no staff).

Enlisted Marines' Funerals. The funeral escort for a deceased enlisted Marine consists of a noncommissioned escort commander (same rank as deceased, or senior), body bearers, firing party (eight riflemen), field music, and, in the case of gunnery sergeants or above, troop escort consisting of a rifle squad.

Simple Honors Funerals. When next of kin does not desire full honors, the simple honors funeral escort, for all ranks, consists of an escort commander (not above rank of captain), body bearers, firing party, and field music.

YOUR SWORD

1115. Rigging Your Sword

Correct wearing of your sword is a point of professional refinement. Derived from "Rig It Right," an excellent article in the *Gazette* (June 1961), by Majors T. N. Galbraith and R. N. Good, here is an account of how you should rig and wear your badge as a commissioned officer.

The first step is to get your sword knot squared away. The way to begin assembly of the knot is to reeve its small end through the eye of the "pommel," slip it back through the two keepers, and hook it to the small metal eye adjacent to the large end. Draw one keeper tight against the pommel, the other over the hook and eye, and you are ready to tie the knot.

Now loop the large end of the knot under the cross guard of the hilt and tie a hitch as shown in Figure 11-5. If you check this diagram closely, you will see that the knot shown is a clove hitch, not the double half hitch specified in regulations. The fact is, a double half hitch will not hold the knot tight to the cross guard, whereas a clove hitch will. Note which side of the clove hitch should face outboard, as depicted in Figure 11-5, when the sword is sheathed and worn.

When the hitch is bent on, draw it taut and, at the same time, work the knot so that the large end does not hang below the upper ring mounting on the scabbard. Depending on the length of your particular knot, the portion from the eye of your pommel to the cross guard will possess some degree of looseness. This is all right: the determining factor is the length of the bight hanging

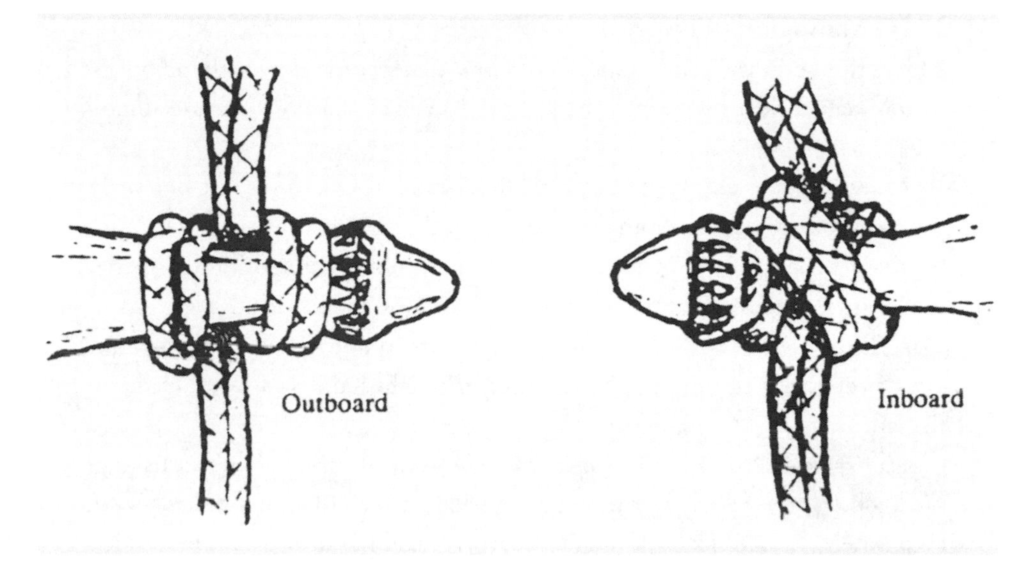

Figure 11-5. Rigging Your Sword

free below the cross guard. If the knot hangs down farther than it should, you may find yourself slapped in the face when you present sword.

Nomenclature of the Sword and Accessories. Attaching the knot may be the most troublesome part of rigging the sword, but the nomenclature of the sword also may be a source of confusion (see Figure 11-6). Sword and scabbard are suspended from the sword sling. If you are wearing a blouse, the sword sling is attached to your Sam Browne belt by the frog or, if with cloth belt, to the shoulder sling; if you are not wearing a blouse, the sword sling is attached to the frog on your belt. In either case, the frog and shoulder sling serve the single purpose of providing a D-ring to which you attach the sword sling.

Attaching Scabbard to Sword Sling. One easy way to attach your scabbard to your sword sling is shown in Figure 11-6. With the sword sling on and its straps hanging free, attach the sling strap snaps to the scabbard rings. Holding the scabbard by its upper ring, give it a half twist toward the body (clockwise) and hang the upper ring over the sword sling hook.

Mourning Knot. Secure the mourning knot to the leather sword knot between pommel and cross guard by doubling the mourning knot in two and passing its two free ends together around the sword knot and through the middle bend, drawing it taut.

1116. Manual of the Sword

This is shown in the *Marine Corps Drill and Ceremonies Manual.* In addition to the manual just mentioned, however, two additional positions are sometimes used.

Standing at Ease. When it is desired to stand at ease or at rest but with sword drawn (as distinct from "Parade Rest"), thus facilitating quick return to the carry for the purpose of giving commands, the old (naval) position formerly used at rest is both military and convenient. Simply stand with the feet apart, as in "Parade Rest," but with the sword blade carried horizontally without constraint across the front of the body, hilt in the right hand and lower blade in the left.

Carrying Sword When Not in Formation. As your sword is not a fishing pole, a hoe, or a golf club, it should be carried and handled in a military way even when you are not in formation and the sword is unrigged. The proper way to do this is to crook your left arm at right angles across the front of your body and to place the sword (sheathed in its scabbard) in the crook, curve of the blade downward and hilt rearward. The sword will ride easily here as long as you hold your forearm steady, and the appearance will be formal and soldierly.

Marching. When under way, with sword drawn, the scabbard will hang and move naturally. Despite jokes to the contrary, it is next to impossible to trip over a scabbard. Few things make you appear more unsure of yourself than clutching at your scabbard while carrying or saluting with your sword.

DISPLAYING THE FLAG

1117. General Concept

Routine Guidelines. Throughout the Navy and Marine Corps, the National Ensign is displayed from 0800 to sunset (except in ships under way, which fly the Ensign continuously). On shore, the flag is flown at base or station headquarters, at other major command headquarters, and/or at the headquarters of the senior when two or more commands are located so close together that separate flags would be inappropriate. Outlying commands or activities display the National Colors in order to make clear their governmental character.

Except when intentionally lowered to half-staff (some may be more accustomed to the interchangeable British term "half-mast," which in American usage refers primarily to the flag's position when flown on board ship), the flag must be "two-blocked" at all times—that is, it must be hoisted and secured at

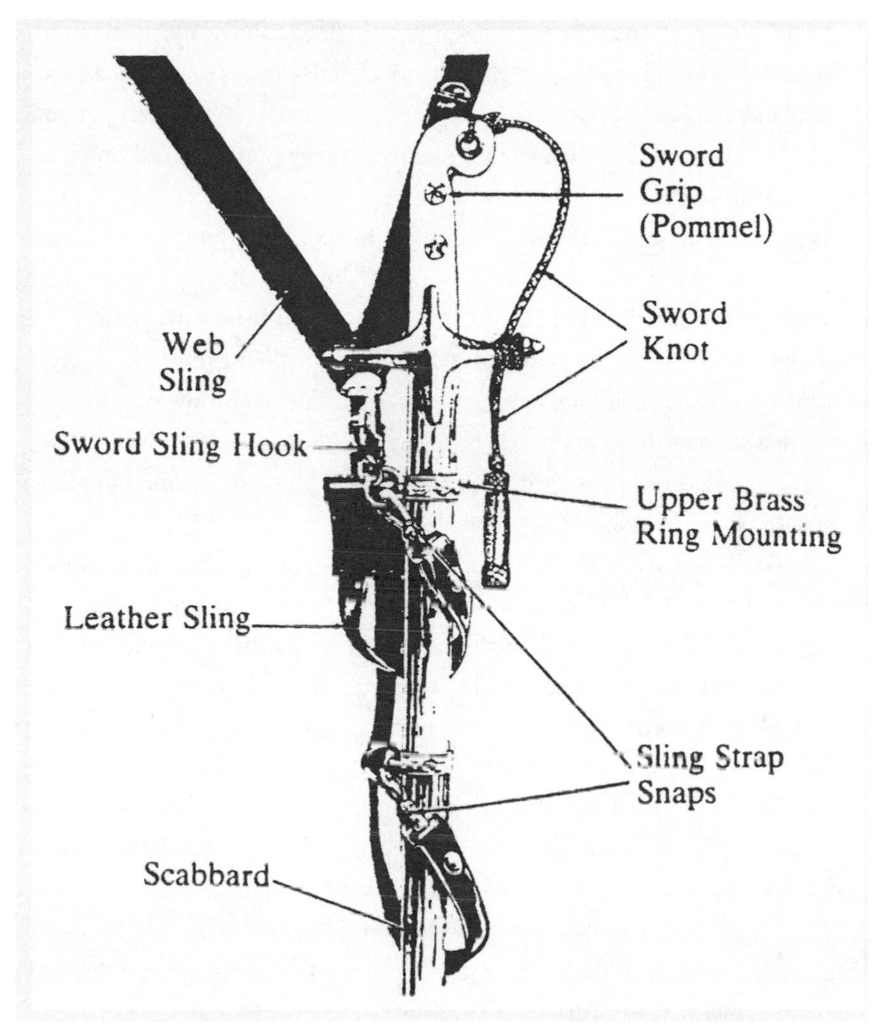

Figure 11-6. Nomenclature of the Sword, Scabbard, and Sling

the very top of the staff, or gaff, since any flag not so secured is technically considered to be at half-staff (see Figure 11-7). Display of the flag at half-staff indicates official mourning. On Memorial Day, the flag is half-staffed until the completion of the required gun salute, or until noon, if no salute is fired.

The position of half-staff is midway between the peak (or truck) and the base of the flagstaff, except when the latter has yardarms or is supported by guys, stays, or shrouds, in which case half-staff is halfway between the peak and the yardarm or the point at which guys, stays, or shrouds join the staff.

The church pennant is the only flag ever flown above the Ensign. It is hoisted at the sounding of "Church Call" for divine services on shipboard, and the National Colors are lowered to a position just under the church pennant. When divine services have concluded, the church pennant is hauled down and the National Colors are "two-blocked."

Colors must never be allowed to become fouled. It is an important responsibility of the guard to prevent this. To avoid fouling, they should be raised or lowered from the leeward side of the pole. Should it become necessary to exchange a set of Colors already hoisted, a new set is first run up on a second halyard (this is why flagpoles have two sets of halyards), and the original set is lowered as soon as the new one has been two-blocked.

It is a recognized international distress signal, afloat or ashore, sanctioned by law, to fly the National Ensign upside down.

In Battle. It is a very old tradition, although no longer prescribed by *Navy Regulations*, that, on joining action, ships break out the National Ensign at the truck of each mast. The spirit of this tradition should be observed on shore. Any position under attack, at which Colors are normally flown, should keep those Colors flying throughout action, night and day, just as the original Star Spangled Banner flew through the night over Fort McHenry at Baltimore (where Marines formed one of the defending units).

Half-Staffing the Flag. First, two-block the flag at the truck (top) of the staff, and keep it there until the last note of the National Anthem or "To the Colors"; then lower it to the half-staff position. In lowering the flag from half-staff, hoist it smartly to the truck at the first note of the music, then lower it in the regular manner, as described in Section 1118.

Displaying the Flag. The National Colors are always on the right (to your left as you face the displayed flags). If other flags are flown from adjacent poles, the American flag will be the first one raised and the last one lowered.

When displayed from crossed staffs, the National Colors are on the right, and the staff is in front of the staff of the other flag with which it is crossed.

When displayed over a street, the blue field (or "union") of the flag should point north on a street running east-west, and point east on a street running north-south.

When used to drape a coffin, the flag should be placed so that the union would cover the head and left shoulder of the body within.

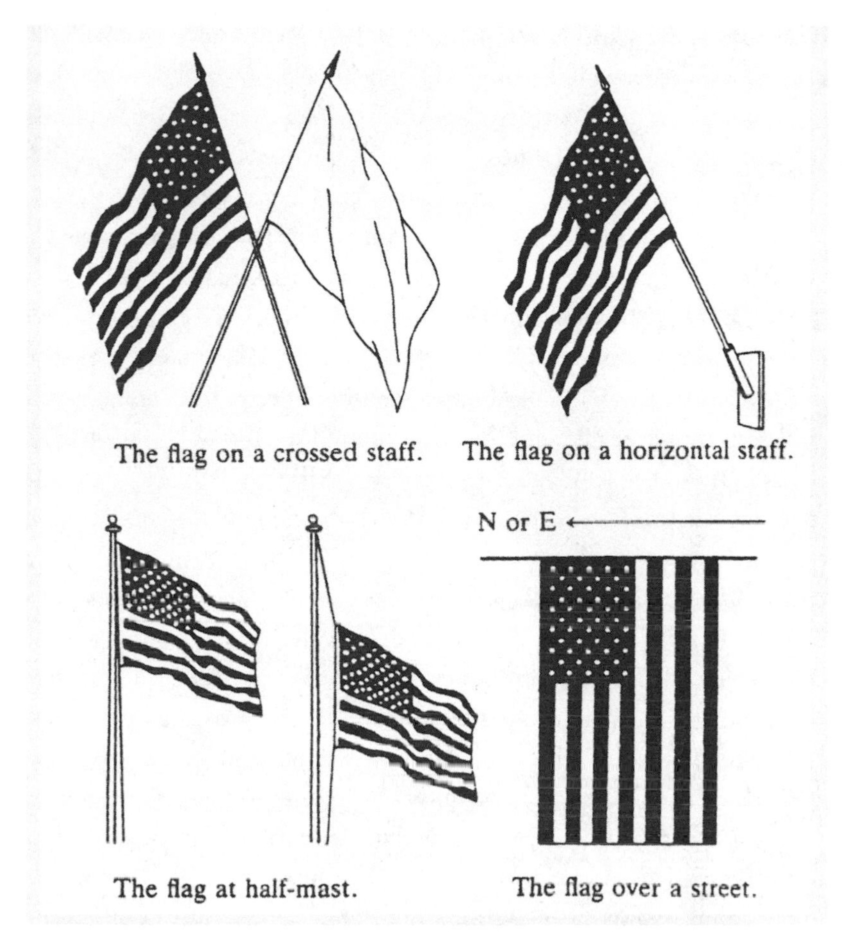

Figure 11-7. Correct Ways to Display the Flag

Foreign Flags. Except in cases of official ceremonies, the carrying of foreign flags by members of the U.S. armed forces is not authorized. An example of an official ceremony would be the arrival or departure of a foreign head of state.

Rulings as to whether given events may be considered official ceremonies should be obtained from Marine Corps Headquarters.

1118. Morning and Evening Colors

Colors are the most important ceremonies of the working day and must be conducted with precision and ceremony. Executing Colors is the responsibility of the guard of the day and should be personally supervised by the commander of the guard (see Chapter 16). Honors to be rendered by individuals and formations are described in Sections 1110 and 1111.

Raising the Flag (Morning Colors). The color guard, a noncommissioned officer and two junior Marines, forms at the guardhouse, with the NCO (carrying the folded Colors) in the center. The color guard marches to the flagstaff, halts, and "bends on" the flag to the halyards. The halyards are manned by the two Marines, and the NCO holds the flag until it is hauled free of his or her grasp. The NCO must see that the Colors never touch the ground. At precisely 0800, the signal to execute Colors is given from the guardhouse by the corporal of the relief on watch. The field music then makes eight bells, and, after the last stroke, the music begins, and the flag is hoisted smartly. When the flag is clear, the NCO comes to hand salute. As soon as the flag is two-blocked, the Marines manning halyards likewise come to hand salute and hold this position throughout the National Anthem or "To the Colors," after which the halyards are triced. In saluting during Colors, members of the Color detail should avoid looking up at the Colors, and should salute in the normal manner and stance.

The guard of the day and band, or field music, parade facing the flagpole. At Morning Colors, following the last stroke of eight bells, attention is sounded by bugle, followed in turn by the National Anthem (if a band is present) or "To the Colors" (by field music). The guard is brought to present arms on the call to attention. If foreign forces are present, the band renders prescribed honors to foreign ensigns after playing the U.S. National Anthem. Hand salutes and present arms end on the last musical note, after which "Carry On" is sounded.

In the absence of a band, "To the Colors" is sounded by field music. If no music is present, the signals for attention, hand salute, and carry on must be given by whistle, which should be regarded as a procedure of last resort. Even if your outfit does not rate or include music, you should make every effort to obtain a bugle and train a nonrated Marine to sound the calls required for Colors. This is where initiative, enterprise, and spirit of "make-do" can show.

Lowering the Flag (Evening Colors). Evening Colors is executed by the same guard detail as Morning Colors, and the ceremony is virtually a reverse performance of the latter. The flag is lowered precisely at sunset, the exact daily time of which should be kept in a table in the guardhouse. Beginning with the first note of the music, the flag is slowly lowered, in time with the music, so that it will be in the hands of the NCO of the color guard as the last note sounds. In the absence of a band, "Retreat" is sounded by field music.

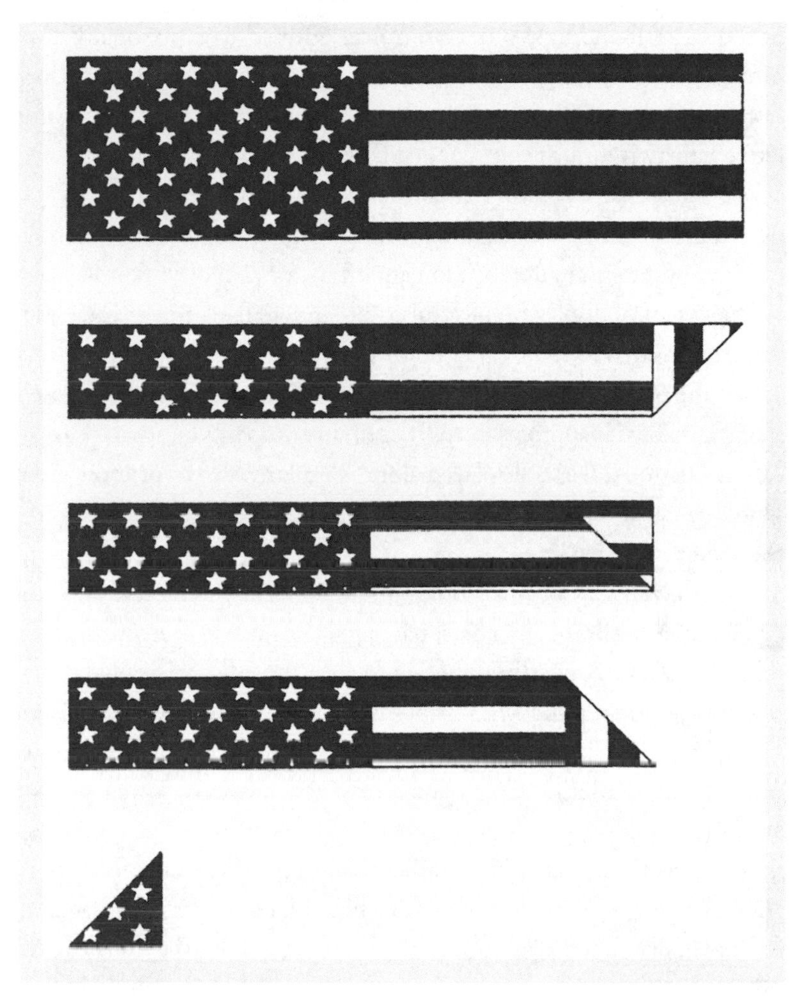

Figure 11-8. Folding the Flag

After being lowered, the flag is folded in the shape of a cocked hat. The correct procedure for folding a set of Colors may be found in Figure 11-8 and should be followed.

Standing lights (such as streetlights and aircraft obstruction lights) throughout the post should not be turned on until after the last note of Evening Colors.

1119. Display of Personal Flags or Pennants

At Commands Ashore. The personal flag or pennant of a general or flag officer is displayed, day and night, in the headquarters area (usually from a staff on the headquarters building). When an officer entitled to a personal flag makes an official visit or inspection at some other activity of the command, the personal flag is hauled down and shifted to the activity that the officer is visiting. If this latter activity is in turn commanded by a flag or general officer, the senior officer's personal flag displaces that of the local commander.

When a foreign ensign or personal flag is displayed ashore during an official visit by, or gun salute to, a foreign officer or civil official, it is broken at the normal point of display of the local commander's flag or pennant, and the latter is in turn shifted to some other point within the command.

If the points of display of two or more personal flags are so close together that it would be inappropriate to fly them in competition, so to speak, the senior officer's personal flag is displayed alone. Similarly, if two or more civil officials who rate personal flags are present officially at the same time, only the flag of the senior is broken.

It is a Marine Corps custom that, on conclusion of a tour in command, a general officer may retain a personal flag.

On Vehicles. Any officer entitled to a personal flag or pennant may display this forward on a vehicle in which the officer is riding officially. Alternatively, one may mount plates, forward and aft, bearing the number of stars appropriate to rank. Marine Corps and Army generals have scarlet plates (but the arrangement of stars on Marine general officers' flags and plates corresponds to that of flag officers of the Navy rather than to that of Army generals). Navy and Air Force flag or general officers have blue plates. A personal flag and a set of such plates are never displayed at the same time from the same car. When the officer who rates the flag or plates is not in the car, the flag should be furled and cased, and the plates cased. This is a point on which drivers should be carefully schooled.

On Board Ship or in Boats. The rules for display of personal flags and pennants afloat are beyond the scope of this *Guide.* It suffices to say that they are complex and precise, and they must be carefully followed. They are given in *Navy Regulations.*

HONORS, OFFICIAL VISITS, AND CALLS

1120. Honors, Official Visits, and Calls

As a junior officer, your first contacts with honors, official visits, and official calls will probably occur on board ship or when you find yourself detailed to command a guard of honor. Like all military etiquette, the subject demands precise attention and compliance with every rule. Because the Marine Corps prides itself on being the most military of the services, make a point to know and observe all the ins and outs of honors and official visits.

The following definitions may be helpful.

Official visit: A formal visit of courtesy that requires special honors and ceremonies.

Official call: An official but informal visit of courtesy that does not require honors or ceremony. Note the distinction between official calls, discussed in this chapter, and personal calls, which are covered briefly in Chapter 22.

Guard of the day: For rendering honors, *Navy Regulations* provides that the "guard of the day" (normally not part of the interior guard, except on board ship) shall be not less than one rifle squad.

Full guard: Not less than one rifle platoon.

Guard of honor: Any guard, not part of the interior guard, that is paraded ashore for rendition of honors. When the interior guard turns out in compliment to an individual, it is spoken of as "the guard," not as a guard of honor.

Compliment of the guard: This honor consists of an interior guard turning out and presenting arms, as a compliment to visiting officers or civilian dignitaries.

Shipboard compliments: In addition to honors by a guard, shipboard compliments may include any or all of the following elements, which are dispensed with ashore:

- Manning the rail on weather decks by the ship's company
- Piping alongside and over the side
- Sideboys.

Because Marines *in a ship's company* are fully occupied with other elements of rendering honors to visitors, these shipboard compliments are performed only by Navy officers and enlisted personnel. Embarked Marines often *do* participate in manning the rail aboard ship.

Honors. Arrangements for rendering honors ashore are usually coordinated by the commanding general's aide. At a station or unit not commanded by a general officer, arrangements are made by the adjutant.

Ashore and afloat, we render the same salutes, honors, and ceremonies, as practical, at Marine Corps bases and stations and in naval ships and stations. Wherever Marines are present, they provide the honor guard. Detailed pointers and procedures on honors are in Section 1122.

It goes without saying that troops paraded as honor guards must be the best. See to it that your guard is correct, snappy, and immaculate—a reflection of the Marine Corps at its smartest.

Official Visits and Calls. Official visits and official calls, as we discuss them here, are paid only by officers in command and are distinct from the personal calls described in Chapter 22.

Generally speaking, official visits are more often paid by commanders afloat, whereas on shore official calls are substituted.

On taking over a command, you must make an official call on the senior to whom you have reported for duty. This call is at the senior's headquarters and is not the domestic "visit of courtesy" that is customary.

In addition, unless the senior indicates otherwise, there are traditionally five other instances when official calls are required:

1. A call by the commander of an arriving unit on his or her immediate superior, if present, and on the senior Marine or Navy officer present
2. A call by commanding officers on an immediate superior in the chain of command upon arrival of the latter
3. A call by an officer, who has been senior officer present, upon that officer's successor
4. A call by the commander of a unit or ship arriving at a Marine Corps installation or naval station, upon the commander of such activity; except that when the arriving commander is senior, the local commander makes the call
5. Calls on high civil officials (state and territorial governors and U.S. diplomatic and consular officials) as prescribed in *Navy Regulations.*

When in the vicinity of a command ashore belonging to another U.S. armed service or to a friendly foreign power, the senior Marine officer present in command arranges with the other commander concerned for an exchange of official visits or calls as appropriate. Check *Navy Regulations* for calling procedure on foreign officials.

When an officer leaves his or her command for an official visit, or returns therefrom, that officer receives the honors prescribed for such a visit, except that his or her own organization remains in uniform of the day and omits gun salutes.

Official calls or visits must be paid expeditiously as they become due, or on the first working day thereafter. They must be returned within twenty-four hours or on the first subsequent working day.

Circumstances permitting, flag officers return in person official visits or calls by officers of the grade of colonel or higher. The chief of staff or deputy commander returns official calls or visits by officers below colonel.

Officers below flag rank return all calls and visits in person.

High foreign officials (other than chiefs of state) return in person visits or calls by a general or an admiral. Otherwise they return such visits by a suitable representative.

Before making or returning an official visit or call, check both *Navy Regulations* and *Marine Corps Uniform Regulations* for the proper uniform. If unable to get access to these publications, or if you cannot find your answer, you will never be far wrong wearing undress blue or blue-white, according to season and climate.

1121. Official Visits and Calls Ashore

Before you make or receive an official call or visit ashore, be sure to have all arrangements taken care of well in advance. This requires liaison between the maker and the recipient of the call, which is up to the aide or the adjutant, as the case may be. Coordinate the following details especially:

- Time and exact place call is to be paid
- Uniform
- Entrance to post, station, and headquarters that caller will use
- Transportation
- Honor guard, if required (see Section 1122)
- Use of calling cards (somewhat archaic, but may still be in fashion in some locales)
- Refreshments to be served, if any
- Specific units, places, or installations to be visited
- Arrangements to break or haul down personal flags or to fire gun salutes.

1122. Procedure and Pointers on Rendering Honors

Preparations. The general's aide (or the adjutant) normally has ample advance notice to prepare for an official visit that requires honors and to notify those concerned. Ashore, the casual or surprise official visit is rare.

When detailed to command an honor guard, you should immediately visit the aide (or report to the adjutant) and obtain all possible information. Check with the bandmaster on the timing of ruffles and flourishes and with the NCO in charge of the saluting battery. If the saluting guns are remote from the honor guard's parade, see that absolutely foolproof communications are established between the parade and the saluting battery. It is elementary, but vital, that the saluting battery knows how many guns are to be fired; also ensure that a standby piece (if available) and spare rounds are in instant readiness to fire in the event of hangfire or malfunctions of a saluting gun.

Make a personal reconnaissance of the honor guard's parade, and know exactly where the guard and band and the recipients of honors are to be posted. Determine what markers and guidons are required, and who will supply and locate them. If possible, give your platoon leaders and leading NCOs an opportunity to look over the ground. If you are going to provide an escort of honor, verify the route of march.

As to the guard itself, spare no effort to make it the finest in the Marine Corps. See that every person is immaculately turned out, that the guard is perfectly sized, and that the entire formation, if possible, is adequately rehearsed. If troops for the guard come from units other than your own, have no hesitation in returning substandard individuals to their units, reporting that you have done this (and why) to the adjutant.

Procedure for Honors on an Official Visit Ashore. The following general procedure can serve as a guide for rendering honors ashore. (Remember, however, that almost every organization has its ground rules and standing operating procedures, and be sure to consult these when preparing to render honors.)

1. Well before the time of arrival of the visiting official, complete the preparations discussed above, parade your guard and band, have the Color detail standing by to break or haul down personal flags involved, and have the saluting battery manned and ready. If possible, especially on a large post, have communications that can apprise you, up to the last moment, of the visitor's movements and approach.

2. When the recipient of honors arrives and debarks from boat, train, car, plane, or helicopter, "Attention" is sounded by bugle. The local commander (or whoever is receiving the dignitary) greets that individual and conducts him or her to the post front and center of the guard.
3. When the official takes post, the commander of the honor guard brings the guard to present arms. All hands in the vicinity, but not those in formation, come to hand salute, following the motions of the guard.
4. When the guard has been presented, and the commander has executed the salute, the band sounds off with ruffles, flourishes, and other musical honors. The personal flag or National Color, as specified for the dignitary, is broken on the first note of the music.
5. The guard is brought to the order after the last note of the music, or when the commander of the guard has exchanged salutes with the official, if there is no music. If a gun salute is rendered, the first gun is fired immediately after the last note of the music, and the guard remains at the present throughout the salute, as do all hands in the official party who hold salutes throughout the gun salute. Persons not in the official party, but in the immediate vicinity, remain at attention during the gun salute. If the National Color, or a foreign flag or ensign, is to be displayed during the gun salute only, it is broken on the first gun and hauled down on the last.
6. On completion of the musical honors or the gun salute, if fired, the honor guard commander brings the guard to order arms, executes present sword to the person being honored, and reports, "Sir, the honor guard is formed." If the personage desires neither to inspect the guard nor that it pass in review, the honor guard remains at attention. For the procedure to be followed for marching the guard in review or for its inspection by the personage, see the *Marine Corps Drill and Ceremonies Manual.*

Honors on Departure from an Official Visit Ashore. In general, departure honors reverse those given on arrival.

1. Departure honors commence when the visiting official has completed personal leave-taking from the senior officer present. Either the latter officer or the aide will signal this to the commander of the guard.

2. Gun salutes, if rendered on departure, must begin before the individual actually leaves (that is, while within earshot). The personal flag, or any national ensign displayed, is hauled down on the last gun.
3. An honor guard is not normally inspected on departure. Hold the guard on parade until the official is out of sight.

Pointers on Honors, Ashore and Afloat. Your "bible" for honors incident to official visits and calls is *Navy Regulations.* The table of honors and ceremonies given here (Table 11-2) is a compilation of the information in those articles, assembled for quick reference. You must also be meticulously familiar with the *Marine Corps Drill and Ceremonies Manual,* which gives detailed instructions for rendering all types of honors.

In addition to guards paraded in receiving the president, any foreign sovereign or chief of state, or member of a reigning royal family, all officers not required elsewhere form on the left of the honor guard, in dress uniform with swords. Troops not otherwise occupied should form on parades adjacent to the guest's route of inspection and also line the route. On board ship, persons not manning the rail fall in at quarters.

Afloat, all ships present, other than the one receiving the president or foreign guest, man the rails and fire the required national salute on the arrival and departure of the distinguished guest.

The officer of the day or officer of the deck attends the arrival and departure of any distinguished visitor, whether or not the visit is official.

Afloat, side honors only (that is, side boys only, no guard or band) are rendered when a general officer, flag officer, or another commanding officer comes on board without flag or pennant flying. If so requested, full honors may be rendered on departure; otherwise, side honors only are again the rule. While side honors are being rendered, all hands on deck and in view of the gangway stand at attention, facing the gangway; they salute as the officer reaches the top of the accommodation ladder or brow, and remain at the hand salute until the end of the boatswain's pipe, following the motions of the side boys.

Honors are dispensed with under the following circumstances:

- When the visiting officer is in plainclothes or visits the post unofficially
- Between sunset and 0800 (except that foreign officers may be rendered honors at any time during daylight)

Table 11-2. Table of Honors for Official Visits

Rank	Arrival on Board or Departure											
		Gun salute								Flag		
Rank	Uniform	Arrival	Departure	Ruffles and flourishes	Music	Guard	Side boys	Crew	Within what limits	What	Which truck	During
President	Full dress	21	21	4	National anthem*	Full	8	Man rail[1,2]	...	President's	Main	Visit
President or sovereign of a foreign country	do.	21	21	4	Foreign national anthem	do.	8	do.	...	Foreign ensign	do.	do.
Member of reigning royal family	do.	21	21	4	do.	do.	8	do.	...	do.	do.	Salute
Ex-president or president-elect	do.	21	21	4	Admiral's march	do.	8	Quarters		National	do.	do.
Secretary of state when acting as special foreign representative of the president	Full dress	19	19	4	National anthem	Full	8	Quarters[3]	...	Secretary's	Main	Visit
Vice president	do.	...	19	4	Admiral's march	do.	8	do.	...	Vice president's	do.	do.
Speaker of the House of Representatives	do.	...	19	4	do.	do.	8	...	...	National	Fore	Salute
Governor of a state of the United States	do.	...	19	4	do.	do.	8	...	Area under governor's jurisdiction	do.	do.	do.
Chief Justice of the United States	do.	...	19	4	do.	do.	8	...	...	do.	do.	do.
Ambassador, high commissioner, or special diplomatic representative whose credentials give him or her authority equal to or greater than an ambassador	do.	...	19	4	National anthem	do.	8	...	Nation or nations to which accredited	do.	do.	do.
Secretary of defense	do.	19	19	4	Honors march†	do.	8	Quarters	...	Secretary's	Main	Visit
Deputy secretary of defense	do.	19	19	4	do.	do.	8	do.	...	Dep. secy.'s	do.	do.
Prime minister or other cabinet officer of a foreign country	Dress	...	19	4	Admiral's march	do.	8	...	...	Foreign ensign	Fore	Salute
Cabinet officer other than secretary of defense	do.	...	19	4	do.	do.	8	...	...	National	do.	do.
Secretary of the Navy	Full dress	19	19	4	Honors march†	do.	8	Quarters	...	Secretary's	Main	Visit
Secretary of the Army or Air Force	Dress	19	19	4	do.	do.	8	...	...	National	Fore	Salute
President pro tempore of the Senate	do.	...	19	4	do.	do.	8	...	...	do.	do.	do.
Assistant secretary of defense	Dress	17	17	4	Honors march†	Full	8	Quarters	...	Asst. Secy.'s	Main	Visit
Under secretary and assistant secretaries of the Navy	do.	17	17	4	do.	do.	8	do.	...	Under or asst. secy.'s	Main	Visit

Table 11-2. Table of Honors for Official Visits *(Continued)*

Rank	Uniform	Gun salute: Arrival	Gun salute: Departure	Ruffles and flourishes	Music	Guard	Side boys	Crew	Within what limits	Flag: What	Flag: Which truck	Flag: During
Arrival on Board or Departure												
Under or assistant secretary of the Army or Air Force	do.	17	17	4	do.	do.	8			National	Fore	Salute
Governor general or governor of territory, commonwealth, or possession of the U.S. or area under the administration of the U.S.	do.		17	4	Admiral's march	do.	8		Area under official's jurisdiction	do.	do.	do.
Committee of Congress	do.		17	4	do.	do.	8			do.	do.	do.
Envoy extraordinary and minister plenipotentiary	Dress		15	3	Admiral's march	Full	8 6		Nation to which accredited	National	Fore	Salute
Minister resident	do.		13	2	do.	do.	6		do.	do.	do.	do.
Charge d'affaires	do.		11	1	do.	do.	6		do.	do.	do.	do.
Career minister or counselor of embassy or legation	do.			1	do.	do.	6		do.			
Consul general or consul or vice consul when in charge of consulate general	do.		11	1	do.	do.	6		District to which assigned	National	Fore	Salute
First secretary of embassy of legation	Of the day with sword					Of the day	4		Nation to which accredited			
Consul or vice consul when in charge of consulate	do.		7			do.	4		District to which assigned	National	Fore	Salute
Mayor of an incorporated city	do.					do.	4		Within limits of mayoralty			
Second or third secretary of embassy or legation	do.						2		Nation to which accredited			
Vice consul when only representative of the U.S. and not in charge of consulate or consulate general	do.		5			Of the day	2		District to which assigned	National	Fore	Salute
Consular agent when only representative of the U.S.	do.						2		do.			
Military and Naval Officers, United States and Foreign[4-7]												
Chairman of the JCS	Dress	19[8,9]	19[8,9]	4	Admiral's march[10]	Full	8	Quarters				
Chief of Staff, U.S. Army	do.	19	19	4	General's march	do.	8	do.				
Chief of Naval Operations	do.	19	19	4	Admiral's march	do.	8	do.				
Chief of Staff, U.S. Air Force	do.	19	19	4	General's march	do.	8	do.				
Commandant of the Marine Corps	do.	19	19	4	Admiral's march	do.	8	do.				
Fleet Admiral or General of the Army or the Air Force	Dress	19	19	4	Admiral's march[10]	Full	8	Quarters				
Admiral or general	do.		17	4	do.	do.	8					
Naval or other military governor, commissioned as such by the president, within area under jurisdiction	do.		17	4	do.	do.	8			For United States officers, personal flag at the main during the salute		
Vice admiral or lieutenant general	do.		15	3	do.	do.	8[11]					

		Arrival on Board or Departure										
		Gun salute		Ruffles						Flag		
Rank	Uniform	Arrival	Departure	and flourishes	Music	Guard	Side boys	Crew	Within what limits	What	Which truck	During
Rear admiral or major general	do.	...	13	2	do.	do.	6	...	...	For officers of foreign nations, the foreign ensign at the fore during the salute		
Rear admiral (lower half) or brigadier general	do.	...	11	1	do.	do.	6	...	...			
Captain, commander, colonel or lieutenant colonel	Undress	...	...	...	...	Of the day	4	...	...			
Other commissioned officers	Of the day with sword	...	...	...	...	do.	2	...	...			
Official not herein provided for	Honors as prescribed by the senior officer present; such honors normally shall be those accorded the foreign official, when visiting officially a ship of own nation, but a gun salute, if prescribed, shall not exceed 19 guns.											
Foreign officer of the armed forces, diplomatic or consular representative in country to which accredited, or other distinguished foreign official	Honors for an official or officer of the United States of the same grade, except, that equivalent honors shall be rendered to foreign officers who occupy a position comparable to Chairman JCS, CNO, Chief of Staff Army, Chief of Staff Air Force, or CMC.											

NOTES

1. All other ships present man rail and fire national salute at official reception or departure of president.
2. For president of United States, president of a foreign republic, foreign sovereign or member of reigning royal family, officers assembled on quarterdeck in full dress, crew man rail, and other officers unemployed formed forward of guard, personnel not occupied fall in at quarters.
3. For others for whom full dress uniform is prescribed designated officers assembled on quarterdeck and formed forward of guard.
4. When side honors only are rendered to a flag or commanding officer, officers and personnel on deck and in view from the gangway shall stand attention facing the gangway, and salute as the officer appears over the side and shall remain at the salute until the end of the pipe.
5. All honors except attendance at the gangway by the officer of the deck, except as social courtesy may demand, shall be dispensed with:
   a. When officers are in plainclothes.
   b. From sunset to 0800 (except that for foreign officers, side shall be piped during daylight).
   c. During meal hours of the crew for officers of U.S. Navy or Marine Corps.
   d. When exercising at general drills or when undergoing Navy Yard overhaul, for officers of USN and USMC.
   e. For ships with less than 180 personnel in the seaman branch, for officers of USN, USMC, USCG, USA, and USAF except when advance notice of an official visit had been recieved.
6. The guard and band shall not be paraded on Sunday for USN, USMC, USCG, USA, or USAF officers.
7. All sentries on the upper deck or in view from outside shall salute all commissioned officers passing them close aboard, in boats or otherwise.
8. If a flag or commanding officer comes on board without flag or pennant flying, only side honors shall be giving unless officer should request full honors on departure. All persons on the quarterdeck shall stand at attention by command without bugle.
9. No officer in civilian clothes shall be saluted with guns or have a guard paraded in his or her honor.
10. Admirals and Marine Corps generals recieve the "Admiral's March"; generals (Army/Air Force) recieve the "General's March."
11. The officer of the deck shall attend at the gangway on the arrival or departure of any commissioned officer or distinguished visitor.

* "Hail to the Chief" may be used in lieu of national anthem on either arrival or departure. When specified by the president, "Hail to the Chief" may be used while the president and immediate party move to or from their places while all others stand fast.

† Honors march is a 32-bar medley in the trio of "The Stars and Stripes Forever."

- During meal hours for the troops (except in the case of foreign officers)
- When a ship is engaged in maneuvers, general drills, or undergoing overhaul in a navy yard, or is in action
- When a unit or post ashore is carrying on tactical exercises or emergency drills
- On Sundays or national holidays (except in the case of foreign officers).

Honors in the Field. Despite the rigors of field service, Marine units make every effort to render appropriate honors even when so serving. The spirit, if not the letter, of the preceding paragraphs must be faithfully observed. It is the distinguishing mark of high-spirited, professional troops that in the face of handicaps and obvious obstacles to smartness, they nevertheless remain smart and military and do the best they can with what they have. Marines in the field may well remember what was said of England's Brigade of Guards: "They die with their boots clean."

For rendition of honors in the field, the most important points are that:

- Marines should be in clean, homogeneous uniforms
- Equipment (especially weapons) should be first-class and serviceable
- Individuals should be smart, alert, and clean
- The place for rendering honors should not be subject to enemy observation
- Military readiness or combat operations should not be interrupted.

POINTERS FOR AIDES-DE-CAMP

1123. Duties and Relationships

Duty as an aide-de-camp (usually short-titled "aide") is one of the most exacting details that a young officer can receive. If you are so assigned, you may take it as a compliment to your military and personal character—a compliment that you must do your best to live up to.

As an aide, you are always on duty, and this duty is always personal and confidential, and always official. Your duties are only such as your general personally directs. On the other hand, if you are to succeed, you must learn quickly to anticipate your general's desires and needs and take care of them without having to be told. No matter what the circumstances, your first thoughts should be for your chief's safety, reputation, convenience, and pleasure. Any duty asked of you should therefore be promptly performed.

Intelligence, tact, loyalty, absolute discretion, and military smartness are the most important characteristics of a good aide, with sensible frankness not far behind. Although, by direction, an aide must often serve as an extra pair of eyes and ears for the general, the aide must avoid becoming a tale-bearer and should, whenever consistent with loyalty and fairness toward the chief, do the utmost to protect other officers' chance indiscretions from reaching the attention of higher authorities.

Aside from your general, the two most important persons with whom you routinely deal are the chief of staff and spouse. Establishment of a cooperative, deferential, helpful relationship with the chief of staff—while being careful never to betray any confidence of the general—is essential.

To sum up, virtually all arrangements that concern the general end up as your responsibilities. Functionally, your job breaks down into scheduling, paperwork, protocol, and personal needs.

Keeping your general on schedule is of overriding importance; it is also one of your most difficult tasks. Remembering that "punctuality is the politeness of kings," you must stay on top of the itinerary or other program for each hour and minute.

At briefings, ensure that the general has good background familiarity with the subject. On visits, see that your chief is prepared for and familiar with the people one can be expected to meet and, where appropriate, with the missions and general situation of units concerned.

Your main job in the realm of paperwork is to keep track of all papers going in or out and, in coordination with the chief of staff, set them into proper priority, depending on deadlines, actions required, and importance.

The responsibilities of protocol and personal needs are covered in subsequent paragraphs.

1124. Travel Arrangements

Before Leaving. Prepare an itinerary, or see that one is prepared, giving hours and modes of arrival and departure at destination and all intermediate stops, and furnish a copy to the chief of staff and any other interested parties.

Obtain a program for each official stop, to include schedule of events, uniforms required, times, and other necessary information. This program, of course, must have been coordinated with the host activity.

Inform your general of the uniforms required throughout the trip.

Obtain your general's orders and transportation requests (if required), and see that transportation is arranged.

Issue instructions for forwarding email or phone messages.

See that all baggage for the official party is suitably tagged and identified. Determine what, if any, papers or files the general will require on the trip and arrange for their handling and stowage, especially that of any classified matter. Additionally, be sure to inventory accessories—spare batteries (if applicable), chargers, adapters for international travel—for cell phones and laptop computer.

To be sure the general can be reached rapidly during any part of the trip, confirm that key command personnel have current cell phone numbers for both you and the general.

During Travel. If traveling commercially, keep timetables handy for your mode or modes of transport (including possible alternatives), and, no matter how you travel, know hours scheduled for arrival and departure. Know places and times for connections.

Prescribe uniforms for aircrew and stewards and ensure that other members of the party are informed as to correct uniform during travel, on arrival, and for scheduled events.

When on board government aircraft, be sure the pilot sends a message ahead, stating the composition of the party, estimated time of arrival, and transportation required on arrival. If traveling commercially, send such a message yourself. Be sure that the host activity is informed if any guests are in the party or of changes in schedule.

Take care of all tickets, baggage checks, baggage handling, and transportation. In this capacity, your first responsibility is to take care of the general's gear and keep track of it at all times. This particularly includes official and classified papers.

Obtain copies of daily papers published at the principal places en route, and see that they reach your chief.

Keep track of time zone changes and the dateline. Remind the general to set his or her watch.

Based on the circumstances, consider taking with you the following: station lists or rosters of officers at activities to be visited; a copy of the "Blue Book"; official and personal stationery and postage stamps as required; notebook, pen, and sharp pencils; a supply of the general's business and visiting cards; ample cash and a supply of personal checks on the general's bank, if you have been granted access to these; cleaning gear; refreshments as may be required; spare insignia and ribbons; and the general's personal flag and vehicle plates (if visiting an activity where such are possibly not available).

Keep a running record by name, rank or title, and address, of all persons to whom "thank you" notes or letters of appreciation should be sent; if you have time, rough out such notes before memory fades.

After Return. Write or prepare, for the general, official and personal letters of appreciation to all who extended special courtesies.

Prepare for the general's signature the itinerary and travel claim, being careful not to omit miscellaneous expenses that can be properly claimed.

Obtain and deliver all personal mail held for your chief.

1125. Duties of an Aide in Garrison

Because you are expected to be the social arbiter and expert on the staff, you should know and possess *Service Etiquette* (by Cherlynn Conetsco and Anna Hart, published by the Naval Institute Press in 2009) and *Naval Ceremonies, Customs, and Traditions* (by Royal Connell and William Mack, also a Naval Institute Press publication from 2004). These books can be relied on for tested and correct advice in virtually any situation involving service social usage or protocol. In addition, you should keep an up-to-date "Blue Book," being careful to annotate all promotions, retirements, changes of status, and yearly promotion zones.

Courtesy and thoughtfulness are indispensable attributes in an aide. You should never be too busy to be courteous to all comers. Especially avoid a nose-in-the-air attitude toward fellow officers.

Stay as much as possible within earshot of your chief.

Make a daily appointment schedule for your chief (and, if the general desires, save it for the record). Keep track of engagements, commitments, and calls to be returned, and remind as necessary.

Whenever anyone calls on the general officially or semiofficially, meet the visitors on arrival and accompany them to departure.

It is not only proper but also completely in order for you to tactfully invite your chief's attention to anything that may be amiss as to uniform or dress, and also to remind the general of any social amenities or courtesies that may have been overlooked. It is up to you to learn your chief's shortcomings and to protect him or her against them.

In cooperation with the chief of staff, supervise the performance of drivers, enlisted aides, and all others who serve the general. Keep them on their toes personally and professionally and weld them into a team. See that the general's office and the outer office are attractive and efficient.

Assist your general and spouse in preparations for all social functions to be given by them. Learn how engaged the general's spouse prefers to be in these functions, and ensure your actions complement his or her efforts in the preparation. Supervise the issuance of all invitations, making sure that dates and times are correct and that the desired uniform or costume is correctly specified, and keep track of RSVPs.

On social occasions, keep close by and see that your general and the persons with whom he or she may be talking are supplied with refreshments. Take post in the receiving line next to your chief, on the approach side. You need not shake hands except with guests you know. The most important thing is to get each name correctly and announce it clearly and distinctly to your chief, even in the cases of people your chief knows well.

Make the acquaintance of aides assigned to other flag or general officers in the immediate area. By close coordination and mutual support, you may be able to prevent many omissions or blunders.

1126. Duties of an Aide in the Field

Your duties as an aide to a general officer in the field are quite different from those in garrison, although the spirit in which they are performed and the basic relationships remain unchanged.

Subject to the general's wishes, you must accompany your chief everywhere. In any case you must always keep a personal situation map and other maps or status boards absolutely up to the minute. Pay particular attention to locations of front lines, of installations to visit, and, above all, of unit command posts. The last information is important not only to the general and driver, but also to you, as the general may often use you to convey personal messages to other commanders.

Be alert as to the military situation and be ready to obtain any information the general wishes, either from staff sections and subordinate headquarters or, if necessary, by personal reconnaissance.

See that your chief's personal wants are cared for. Have arrangements been made for laundry? For keeping weapons and gear in shape? For the fighting position?

Introduce visiting officers, official visitors, correspondents, and other persons having business with the general.

Arrange and control all transportation for the general.

Supervise the general's drivers, orderlies, cooks, and stewards as you would in garrison, but be sure these people are reminded that, in the field, they are combat Marines, too, and must be prepared to defend the general and the area in the event of surprise attack or enemy penetration of the command post area.

Supervise and act as caterer for the general's mess. Be sure that any fatigued, wet, or cold officer or enlisted Marine who sees the general (especially people from frontline units) always gets a cup of hot coffee or other refreshment. Have plenty of coffee for drivers and runners, day or night.

Supervise the security arrangements for the general's area.

Work closely with the headquarters commandant in such arrangements as digging a suitable head, erection of tentage, digging in tents, camouflage of the area, water supply, electricity, and facilities.

Above all, do everything in your power to protect and defend your general, and to shelter the general from unnecessary strain and fatigue.

CEREMONIES

1127. Overview

Ceremonial duties are written deep into our history as a Corps. Marines have always endeavored to excel in this field, and we have good reason to be proud of our record. We should continue so to strive and succeed. Every officer taking part in a ceremony—especially when, as is often the case, little time is available for practice—should realize how broadly revealing of wider professionalism our parade ground performance can be. Precision drill, immaculately turned-out troops, disciplined marching, and fine bearing—all these furnish, for the public to see, evidence of Marine Corps alertness, determination to put out only our best, and pride in Corps and selves. It is no coincidence that among the units and corps famous for ceremonial prowess are also found some of the world's most redoubtable fighting formations.

1128. Types of Ceremonies

The Marine Corps and Navy have eight military ceremonies that may be performed on shore. These ceremonies are in the form prescribed by the *Marine Corps Drill and Ceremonies Manual* and may be modified only when the nature of the ground or exceptional circumstances require that changes be made.

The title and a brief description or discussion of each ceremony follow.

A *review* is a ceremony at which a command or several commands parade for inspection by, and in honor of, a senior officer, or in honor of a visitor or a civilian dignitary. In a review, the individual being honored passes on foot or in a vehicle throughout the formation, which is then marched past the honoree.

Presentation of decorations is the ceremony at which decorations are presented. This ceremony follows, in part, that prescribed for a review; it is noteworthy in that, regardless of rank, the individuals who have been decorated receive the review side by side with the reviewing officer. In modified form, this ceremony can be adapted for such occasions as presentation of commissions or enlisted warrants, commendations, and so forth.

A *parade* is the ceremony at which the commanding officer of a battalion or larger unit forms and drills the entire command and then marches them in review. The battalion parade is the most common form of periodic ceremony, and, under normal garrison conditions in days past, it was traditionally performed each Saturday morning. Together with guard mounting, described below, the parade is probably the most important ceremony for you to know by heart. "Memorize every comma in it!" Captain Lewis ("Chesty") Puller used to enjoin his Basic School lieutenants.

Escort of the National Color is known less formally as "Marching on (or off) the Colors." That is, when the Colors are to take part in a ceremony, be presented to a unit, or turned over to some institution or person for safekeeping, they are ceremonially received and escorted from their place of safekeeping (usually the CO's headquarters), and are similarly returned, by a picked escort. The ceremony for this occasion corresponds somewhat to portions of the famous British ceremony *Trooping the Color* and is derived from that.

Escort of honor is the ceremonial escorting of a senior officer or other dignitary during an official visit or on arrival or departure.

Military funerals are covered in the *Marine Corps Drill and Ceremonies Manual*, as well as in Sections 1109, 1113, 1114, and 2118 of this *Guide*. The ceremonial forms followed in military funerals are among the oldest in the profession of arms; some parts, such as the firing of volleys (originally to frighten evil spirits) can be traced to pagan times.

Inspections, as described in Sections 1511 through 1514, run to all types. The ceremonial inspection of troops in ranks has as its object the general military appearance and condition of individual uniforms and equipment within a command. Officers headed for sea duty should note that personnel inspection on board ship follows considerably different lines and frequently varies from ship to ship. Be sure you know your own ship's ground rules and inspection procedure.

Guard mounting is the ceremony whereby a guard is organized from guard details, is inspected before assuming the guard, and then relieves an outgoing or "old" guard. This is a very old ceremony, portions of which antedate the Revolutionary War and go back to the British Army. Guard mounts may be *formal* or *informal*, according to weather, size of guard, availability of music, or local conditions.

Described in Section 1118, *Morning and Evening Colors* are sometimes regarded as parts of the daily routine. They should, however, be conducted with the same gravity as all ceremonies, if only out of respect to the significance of the daily raising and lowering of the National Ensign.

In addition to the foregoing ceremonies of general character, we employ specific ceremonial forms on the occasion of *change of command*, *relief of the sergeant major*, and for *celebration of the Marine Corps birthday*.

Another form of ceremony not covered in any official regulations is the *tattoo* (sometimes called "searchlight tattoo"). A tattoo is an evening parade conducted under floodlights or searchlights; embellished with traditional, historic, or display drills and special musical features; and usually climaxed by lowering of the Colors, playing of "Taps," and sometimes a traditional evening hymn. Evening parades at Marine Barracks ("Eight and Eye"), though not so entitled, are in fact a form of tattoo.

1129. Precedence of Forces in Parades or Ceremonies

To avoid conflicts at parades or ceremonies, the places of honor are allocated in order of service seniority. Because you may readily find yourself at the head of a Marine detachment in a parade or ceremony, you should know your own place and those of other components relative to your own (Army Regulation 600-25, *Salutes, Honors, and Visits of Courtesy* is a good reference). The precedence of U.S. forces in parades or ceremonies is as follows (reading from the head to rear of column, or from right to left in line):

1. Cadets, U.S. Military Academy
2. Midshipmen, U.S. Naval Academy
3. Cadets, U.S. Air Force Academy
4. Cadets, U.S. Coast Guard Academy
5. Midshipmen, U.S. Merchant Marine Academy
6. U.S. Army
7. U.S. Marine Corps
8. U.S. Navy
9. U.S. Air Force
10. U.S. Coast Guard
11. Army National Guard of the United States
12. Army Reserve
13. Marine Corps Reserve
14. Naval Reserve
15. Air National Guard of the United States
16. Air Force Reserve
17. Coast Guard Reserve
18. Other training organizations of the Army, Marine Corps, Navy, Air Force, and Coast Guard, in that order.

When the Coast Guard is serving as part of the Navy, in time of war or emergency, the precedence of Coast Guard units and personnel shifts to position immediately after Navy units and personnel.

Bear in mind, as a Marine, that although the Air Force is one of the three larger services, it is nevertheless junior in ceremonial precedence to the Marine

Corps. Never accede to erroneous assignment of fourth, or junior, place to Marines, following Air Force units, as is sometimes carelessly done on the basis of size.

The place of honor is the head of column or right of the line, and foreign units should be assigned that post of honor in any American ceremony or procession. Where several foreign units of mixed nationality are present, they should be placed in alphabetical order, ahead of any U.S. forces, if the ceremony is conducted by U.S. forces or on American soil.

The official who organizes and coordinates a street parade or procession is known as the *grand marshal* or, sometimes, the marshal. If your unit is misplaced, this official should rectify the mistake.

1130. General Appearance of Troops and Units

The Marine Corps has long enjoyed a worldwide reputation for smart appearance and soldierly performance of every task. This reputation has been enhanced by continually demonstrating to the American public that our execution of peacetime functions is excelled only by our performance in battle.

During peacetime, the reputation of the Corps is maintained to a considerable degree by creating favorable, highly military impressions in parades, ceremonies, and other functions. It is therefore a responsibility of all officers, and especially commanding officers, that marching units in the public eye fully meet the standards by which the Marine Corps is measured. Those in key positions must have perfect posture; troop leaders must excel in command presence; uniforms and equipment must be outstanding in condition and appearance. All such public appearances should be preceded by ample drill and specific rehearsal as needed.

1131. Pointers on Ceremonies

Know Your Parade Ground. If possible, not only make a personal reconnaissance of the parade ground or area where a ceremony is to be held but also conduct a rehearsal on the ground. At a minimum, be sure your leading NCOs and unit guides know the layout of the ground and how the field is to be marked.

Markers. Dress guidons (see Section 1031) mark the boundaries and the reviewing point for a parade ground. In addition, it is sometimes customary to place small metal discs on the ground to mark the posts of unit guides and other key personnel. The adjutant places markers and guidons, but every officer and NCO must know the system and layout of markers. In addition, guides and leaders should know the lineup of "landmarks" adjacent to and visible from the parade ground, so as to be able to march in exactly straight lines and columns without wavering or falling off to right or left. Guides and leaders should keep their heads up and their lines of sight directly to the front and well out, so as to be able to "navigate" on guidons, markers, and landmarks.

"*Officers Center.*" This challenging precision movement should be gone over until all concerned are perfect. Every individual participant is on display, and this evolution comes at the high point of the parade. Properly executed, "Officers Center" should seem to be the movement of a single Marine. Manuals of sword and guidon count here as at no other time.

Photographers. Photographers, both official and otherwise, can do more to detract from the formality and solemnity of a military ceremony than anyone else. Keep them under strict control, preferably in a suitably located, enclosed vantage point, from which they can get good pictures but will not mar the occasion by capering about.

Cadence. The regulation cadence is 120 steps per minute, and this is the "tempo" at which a military band plays marches. That is, the bass drummer hits the drum 120 times per minute, with a heavier downbeat or thump on the first and succeeding alternate beats. For parades or ceremonies, it makes for smarter appearance to have a short, snappy step and, if possible, a slightly accelerated cadence. Thus, cadence should never fall below 120. When the band is not playing, individual foot movements during a ceremony, notably those by the adjutant when taking post, are traditionally executed at markedly accelerated cadence, with short steps.

Use of Public Address Systems and Amplifiers. In general, except for the largest ceremonies and under special conditions, it is most unmilitary to employ a public address system for commands or other purposes incident to military ceremonies. Regimental and battalion commanders and adjutants should pride themselves on their voice of command and should, if necessary, practice to strengthen and increase its carrying power. Ideally, only the narrator, if the ceremony includes one, will profit from a public address system.

Stepping Off in Time with the Music. Units must step off on the left foot, as is well known, and must accomplish this on command of the leader, and on the first beat of the music—a combination that often defeats inexperienced junior leaders, and one that you, as a Marine, must be prepared to perfect.

One method of achieving this result—which requires briefing your unit and some worthwhile rehearsing—is to give your preliminary command just in advance of the music, and have all hands drilled to step off automatically on the first note of the music, without any command of execution from you; in other words, to *let the first note of the music be the command of execution.* This is particularly effective on parade, after the commands have been given to pass in review.

For guard mounting, and for many other ceremonies where units march onto their parades to music, troops must be brought to right shoulder arms at the first note of "Adjutant's Call" and marched off at the first note of march music. This, too, requires coordination by leader and unit. A recommended sequence for these evolutions—"by the numbers"—is summarized as follows:

1. Bear in mind that Adjutant's Call is a sixteen-beat call, and the first note of march music therefore will be count seventeen.
2. The signal for the first note of Adjutant's Call is given by the drum major, who brings down the baton and can thus be seen by all hands.
3. Give your commands in time with Adjutant's Call, on successive beats as shown in this diagram, in which numbers correspond to beats in the call:

1	2	3	4
Right	Shoul-	der	*Arms*
5	6	7	8
(troops execute the movement)			
9	10	11	12
(pause)			
13	14	15	16
For-	ward	(pause)	*March.*

4. Rehearse this a few times with music, and, in the old Marine phrase, "You've got it made."

Command of Mixed Detachments of Sailors and Marines. When a mixed (or composite) detachment of sailors and Marines is formed for a parade, the Marines occupy their post of seniority and honor at the head of column or on right of line, but the senior line officer present, of the Marine Corps or the Navy, according to date of rank, commands the entire detachment. This rule does not apply when Navy and Marines form separate detachments. It usually occurs when a ship parades as a unit (of which the Marines form part).

Close Order Drill. The object of drill is to teach troops by exercise to obey orders, and to do so in the correct way. For this reason, slovenly drill is harmful. Close order drill is one foundation of discipline and esprit de corps. Well-executed, confident, precise ceremonial close order drill is therefore the foundation of success in ceremonies.

Uniform for Inspections, Parades, and Ceremonies. Where possible, undress or dress uniforms should be prescribed for inspections, parades, and ceremonies. Additionally, swords should be worn on such occasions in preference to pistols and belts. If blues are not authorized for the command, large medals may be prescribed on ceremonial occasions for wear with the service blouse.

Music Played during "Sound Off." At a review or parade, when a foreign visitor or officer of another service is being honored, the march played during "Sound Off" should if possible be one traditional to the officer's country or branch of service. At ceremonies conducted by Marine artillery units, "The Caisson Song" is normally played during "Sound Off." For a parade on the occasion of a Marine's retirement, it is a pleasant and appropriate courtesy to ascertain whether there is any particular march the officer would like to have played on "Sound Off." When several individuals are being so honored, the senior, of course, gets the choice. At the very end of a retirement ceremony, the band should play "Auld Lang Syne."

Law, order, duty and restraint, obedience, discipline. . . .

—Rudyard Kipling, "M'Andrew's Hymn"

PART II

AN OFFICER OF MARINES

12

BECOMING A MARINE OFFICER

An old Marine Corps yarn recounts that a young man from the hinterland, when shipping into the Corps, was asked if he intended to try for a commission.

"I don't think so," the recruit answered. "I'm not a very good shot. I'd better work on a straight salary."

Here are the ways in which you can become a U.S. Marine officer and what happens to you in the process.

There are many ways in which you can obtain a commission. The variety of approaches to officer status in the Corps ensures that the base of experience, background, and education among Marine officers remains broad. It also means that, no matter what your origin, once you qualify for a Marine commission, you stand on equal footing with every other officer candidate, regardless of source or education.

1201. General Requirements to Become an Officer

To be eligible for a commission in the Marine Corps, you must be a U.S. citizen; morally, mentally, and physically qualified; and your application must be approved by Marine Corps Headquarters. If you are already a veteran, you must, of course, have an honorable discharge, and if you are a member of the reserve component of any other service, you must obtain a conditional release from that organization. Under certain limited conditions, officer transfers are authorized from the other services into the Marine Corps; for such transactions, special regulations and procedures apply that are beyond the scope of this chapter.

1202. Roads to Your Commission

To obtain a commission in the Marine Corps, you may follow any one of the several roads subsequently described and later summarized in Table 12-1.

U.S. Naval Academy. Each graduating class from the Naval Academy at Annapolis includes midshipmen who have been selected for Marine Corps commissions. Entrance into the Naval Academy, first step toward a commission via this route, is open to civilian preparatory school and high school graduates and to qualified enlisted personnel from the Marine Corps and Marine Corps Reserve. Information regarding appointment to the Naval Academy can be obtained online (http://www.usna.edu/Admissions). The admissions office can also be reached by phone at (410) 293-1858; however, the Academy encourages use of its online form, so that your question will be routed directly to the appropriate person.

If you are already in the regular Marine Corps or Reserve, consult your commanding officer. In recent years, approximately 20 to 25 percent of each graduating class of midshipmen has been commissioned in the Marine Corps. All USNA graduates have a five-year service obligation.

U.S. Military and Air Force Academies. Limited numbers of graduates of West Point and of the Air Force Academy are also eligible for regular commissions in the Marine Corps, with preference going to former Marines or children of Marines. Information regarding appointment to these academies may be obtained from the Departments of the Army and the Air Force, respectively.

If you are attending an accredited college or are a college graduate, you may enter the Marine Corps as an officer under the following programs.

Naval Reserve Officers, Training Corps. Any college student enrolled either as a scholarship midshipman in the Naval Reserve Officers, Training Corps or as a "college program student, NROTC," can, if selected for the Marine Corps, obtain a commission. The NROTC scholarship midshipman goes to college, when selected and approved, with tuition and mandatory fees paid for by the Navy. He or she also receives an annual $750 stipend for books, all required uniforms, and a subsistence allowance of $250 to $400 per month (amounts as of 2016) during the academic year. Midshipmen also spend summer "cruises" afloat with the fleet and ashore for training at various naval stations. During the summer prior to senior year, every Marine-option midshipman completes Officer Candidate School at Quantico. On graduation from college, with a B.A. or B.S. degree, he or she is commissioned and enters The Basic School (TBS).

A limited number of entry-level NROTC scholarships are earmarked for the Marine Corps. Civilian high school graduates may apply for these through their local USMC officer recruiter, sometimes known as an Officer Selection Officer.

The NROTC "college program student" receives no government financial support, other than a stipend per academic month of $350 in the junior year and $400 in the senior year, but takes the same naval science instruction in college as the scholarship midshipman. If selected for a Marine commission while in college, the contract student spends one summer on a "cruise" at Officer Candidate School (OCS), Quantico. After graduation, he or she is ordinarily commissioned in the Marine Corps Reserve. If you are in NROTC and want to become a Marine officer, see the Marine officer attached to your NROTC unit.

Complete information on NROTC, including application procedures, is available online (http://www.nrotc.navy.mil/index.html).

Platoon Leaders Class. The Platoon Leaders Class (PLC) is a summer officer candidate program designed to train college men and women either as ground officers or as prospective pilots or naval flight officers (NFOs) in Marine aviation. PLC training is limited to two summer periods of six weeks each at Quantico. In the case of college juniors, all training is completed in a single ten-week summer period. At the completion of that training, and upon graduation, you are eligible for commission as a second lieutenant in the Marine Corps Reserve. No uniforms, training, or other work are required of you during the academic year.

To enter PLC, you must be enrolled in an accredited college as a freshman, sophomore, or junior. You must be at least seventeen years old on enrollment and less than twenty-eight on 1 July of the year in which you expect to receive your degree. Upon completion of the first summer training session, applicants may begin receiving a $150 per month (tax-free) stipend. Upon completing their four-year degree, applicants are commissioned as second lieutenants. Unless one accepts tuition assistance under the program (up to $15,600 over three consecutive years), there is no obligation to join the Marine Corps after completion of the course.

If you are headed for law school, you should investigate the special PLC (Law) program, under which individuals who have successfully completed PLC are allowed to remain in law school in inactive status as second lieutenants in the Reserve until they obtain their law degrees and are then brought to complete their required active duty as Marine lawyers. PLCs may also be deferred from active duty to obtain a master's degree in most recognized major fields.

Training consists of a pair of six-week tours (Junior and Senior Course, respectively). During each period, you receive the pay—but not the allowances—of a sergeant.

Training for both ground and aviation candidates is intensive, with initial emphasis on the basic instruction and careful screening required for all Marine officers. Aviation candidates, however, take flight examinations as part of their program, and, if found qualified on graduation, are ultimately sent to flight training on graduation from TBS.

In addition to pay while training and transportation to and from Quantico, you get living quarters, uniforms, and medical and dental care. And during off-duty hours, you have full privileges at the library, exchange, theater, swimming pool, and athletic fields, and, of course, weekend liberty.

Officer Candidate Course. The Officer Candidate Course (OCC) is conducted for college graduates who are over eighteen years of age and less than twenty-eight on 1 July of the year in which commissioned.

The course provides the practical military training needed to qualify for the specialized training to be received as a second lieutenant and, in the case of aviation officer candidates, for flight training. It consists of ten weeks of intensive training at Quantico, Virginia. Upon successful completion of this course, you are commissioned a second lieutenant.

In addition to the training already described, OCC and PLC candidates, after being commissioned, attend TBS at Quantico before being assigned to a specialty school or unit. Aviation officer candidates, if found qualified, go on from TBS to between fifteen and eighteen months of preflight and flight training in commissioned officer status.

The Marine Corps pioneered the award of officer commissions to meritorious enlistees long before the practice was accepted among the other three services. In the Marine Corps, the door remains open through several programs.

12-1. Marine officers are commissioned from a variety of sources, with the universal goal of providing leadership to U.S. Marines.

Enlisted Commissioning Program (ECP). Enlisted Marines enter ECP through a competitive application process while they are on active duty. Applicants must be at least twenty-one years of age but not over thirty, have completed at least one year of active duty, have one year of enlistment remaining, and have qualifying test scores on the Scholastic Aptitude Test. They must have obtained a BA or BS degree. Successful applicants receive orders to OCS and receive their commissions upon its completion.

Marine Enlisted Commissioning Education Program (MECEP). Like ECP, enlisted Marines enter MECEP from active duty through a competitive application process. Applicants must be at least twenty-one years of age but not over thirty, be a sergeant or above, and have qualifying Scholastic Aptitude Test scores. Under this program, qualified enlisted Marines are assigned to a special preparatory course and then to college, during which they remain on active duty and draw full pay and benefits. On successful completion of college, preceded by summer officer candidate training, they receive commissions as second lieutenants in the Marine Corps Reserve.

Warrant Officer. Exceptional noncommissioned officers may compete for appointment as warrant officers (WOs) in specialized fields. Because qualifications for WO vary appreciably from time to time, the requirements for such appointments are not summarized here.

Limited Duty Officer (LDO). Warrant officers of the Marine Corps may apply for LDO commission in specialized fields, such as administration, intelligence, infantry, logistics, artillery, engineers, tanks, amphibian tractors, ordnance, communications, supply, food, motor transport, and aviation (see Section 1807).

Temporary Officer. In addition to the established programs shown in Table 12-1 and described so far, authority exists in law to issue temporary commissions as second lieutenant and above to selected warrant officers and enlisted Marines in order to meet pressing or particular needs. Individuals so commissioned as temporary officers retain their permanent grades and status and revert thereto when the requirement for their services in the advanced rank ceases. Temporary officers have been commissioned during all twentieth-century wars, up to and including Vietnam. As in the case of LDOs and WOs, programs and requirements are variable.

Former Regular Officers. Former regular officers of the Marine Corps who have not attained their thirtieth birthday at time of appointment and who resigned from the Corps in good standing may be reappointed with the approval of the Secretary of the Navy. Former officers of the other armed forces may, within certain limits, be appointed by transfer in the Marine Corps Reserve, but under no circumstances in a grade higher than that held in the former service.

1203. Officer Candidate School

In obtaining your commission via PLC, NROTC, MECEP, or through any of the inputs that lead you to the Officer Candidate Class, you will receive pre–Basic School instruction while assigned to Officer Candidate School. Conducted at old Brown Field, Quantico's original air station and later the immediate post–World War II site of The Basic School, this rigorous training is primarily concerned with imparting to officer candidates the knowledge required of the basic enlisted Marine, while at the same time rigorously screening all candidates to be sure they are officer material. In effect, OCS is an officer candidate's boot camp, and a very exacting one.

Table 12-1. Avenues to a Career as a Marine Officer

Program or Source of Input	*Age Limit*	*Education Requirements*	*Open to*	*Leads to*
U.S. Naval Academy		Graduation from USNA	Midshipmen USNA	2d Lt. USMC
U.S. Military of Air Force Academies[1]		Graduation from USMA or USAFA	Cadets USMA or USAFA	2d Lt. USMC
NROTC (Marine Option NROTC Scholarship Program)	Be 17 but not 21 years of age by 30 June of the year entering college	B.A. or B.S. degree[2]	NROTC midshipmen	2d Lt. USMC
NROTC (College Program)	Be 17 but not 21 years of age by 30 June of the year entering college	B.A. or B.S. degree[2]	NROTC midshipmen	2d Lt. USMC
Platoon Leaders Class (Ground or Aviation)	Be at least 17 years old and less than 28 (27 1/2 for aviation) at time of appointment to commissioned grade	B.A. or B.S. degree[2]	College freshmen, sophomores, juniors[1]	2d Lt. USMC
Officer Candidate Course	Be at least 20 but less than 28 (27 1/2 for aviation) at time of commissioning	B.A. or B.S. degree	Regularly enrolled senior in good standing, or a graduate, of an accredited institution granting a 4-year baccalaureate degree in a field other than medicine, dentistry, veterinary, pharmacy, chiropody, hospital administration, optometry, osteopathy, or theology[3]	2d Lt. USMC
Marine Corps Enlisted Commissioning Education Program (MECEP)	Be at least 20 but less than 26 years old by 1 July of the year entering college	B.S. degree[2]	USMC enlisted, with GCT 120 or higher and 6 years' obligated service	2d Lt. USMC

Table 12-1. Avenues to a Career as a Marine Officer (*Continued*)

Program or Source of Input	*Age Limit*	*Education Requirements*	*Open to*	*Leads to*
Enlisted Commissioning Program	Be at least 19 1/2 and less than 27 1/2 on date of application	High school graduate (or GED certificate issued by State Department of Education) and have satisfactorily completed not less than 1 year of unduplicated college work at an accredited institution.	Private and above, USMC and WACR with GCT of 120 or higher and at least 12 months remaining on current enlistment and who have completed recruit training	2d Lt. USMC
Limited Duty Officer	WO applicants who have a minimum of 10 and a maximum of 20 years' active service and who have not reached their 46th birthday by 1 January of the fiscal year in which the appointment is to be made	EL 110 (ASVAB)	Permanent warrant officers in grades W-2 through W-4	1st Lt. USMC
Warrant Officer	Must be of an age to allow 30 years' total active service by age 62	GCT 110 or higher	Sergeant or above with 5-12 years' active service. COs may recommend waivers for preeminently qualified NCOs with up to 14 years of service	Warrant Officer (W-1) USMC

[1] Military Academy and Air Force Academy graduates may by law be commissioned in the Marine Corps, but the Departments of Army and Air Force will only grant approval in exceptional cases.

[2] Successful college graduation and completion of program are prerequisites for commissioning.

[3] Aviation candidates must meet flight physical standards and will be sent to flight training on completion of required ground training. Current regulations require all to attend Basic School prior to reporting for flight training.

(To be eligible for any program, you must be able to meet the general requirements stated in Section 1101.)

1204. Becoming an Officer

No matter how you earn your appointment as a Marine officer, the day finally arrives when you are to be sworn in as a second lieutenant.

Your commission and orders will be forwarded to your commanding officer (if you are already in the service in some capacity) or to a Marine activity near your home for presentation. The swearing-in ceremony and required administrative steps will ordinarily be taken care of by the presenting officer. Bear in mind, however, that pay and allowances do not begin for officers until they are sworn in and commence active duty, nor can you assume title and status as an officer until you have taken your oath and formally accepted your appointment. *You should therefore seek to be sworn in at the earliest opportunity.*

Of that oath, one of the Navy's greatest and best-loved fighting admirals, Arleigh A. Burke, once wrote:

> It is a responsibility that should not be taken easily. And its phraseology is disarmingly simple. When an officer swears "to support and defend the Constitution of the United States against all enemies, foreign and domestic"—he is assuming the most formidable obligation he will ever encounter in his life. Thousands upon thousands of men have died to preserve for him the opportunity to take such an oath. What he is actually doing is pledging his means, his talent, his very life, to his country. This is an obligation that falls to very few men.

The U.S. Supreme Court has more succinctly ruled that "the taking of the oath of allegiance is the pivotal fact which changes the status from that of civilian to that of soldier."

As you raise your right hand and stand at attention to take your oath, you are at a turning point in your life. In a matter of seconds, you will become an officer in a Corps whose valor, renown, and honor are second to none. From the moment you complete your oath "*to support and defend the Constitution of the United States of America against all enemies, foreign and domestic,*" you are a lieutenant of Marines responsible to the president and your superior officers, and fully amenable to military justice. It is a great moment.

1205. Your Commission

After you are sworn in, you receive your commission. A *commission* is the formal written authority, issued in the name of the president of the United States, which confers on you your rank and authority as a Marine officer. It is signed by the president and by the Secretary of the Navy and is issued under the seal of the Department of the Navy and countersigned by an officer at Marine Corps Headquarters, normally the commandant. Your commission states your rank and the date from which it is effective (your date of rank, so-called) and enjoins "those officers and other personnel of lesser rank" to obey any lawful order you may give. You receive a new commission for each rank to which you are promoted.

1206. "Special Trust and Confidence"

Before you file away, or even frame (as many do), your first commission, reread and reflect upon its opening phrase: *Know ye, that reposing special trust and confidence in . . . .*

With these words, the president of the United States certifies, via the Secretary of the Navy, that you, as a commissioned officer, have been set apart from your fellow citizens as one in whom "special trust and confidence" are placed. On the basis of this special trust, you as an officer are granted special privileges; on the same basis, you are subject to special responsibilities and obligations. In the words of the old French phrase, *noblesse oblige*, literally meaning "nobility obligates." This conveys the idea that nobility extends beyond mere entitlements and requires the individual who holds such status to fulfill certain responsibilities, particularly in leadership roles, and to exceed minimal standards of conduct, performance, and appearance.

In specific implementation of the foregoing, the *Marine Corps Manual* states: "The special trust and confidence which is expressly reposed in each officer by his commission is the distinguishing privilege of the officer corps." As a commissioned officer, you should be vigilant to discharge and, where necessary, enforce performance of all responsibilities, and thereby merit and guard the privileges.

1207. The Basic School

The orders that accompany your appointment and initial commission will direct you to proceed to Quantico, Virginia, and report as a student at The Basic

School, sometimes simply called Basic School. The mission of TBS reads: "Train and educate newly commissioned or appointed officers in the high standards of professional knowledge, *esprit de corps*, and leadership to prepare them for duty as company-grade officers in the operating forces, with particular emphasis on the duties, responsibilities, and warfighting skills required of a rifle platoon commander."

Ordinarily, your orders specify a date by which you must report. *It is vital that you comply carefully with your orders, and, above all, that you report on time*, normally between 0700 and 1700 on the designated date. There is no poorer way to start a Marine career than by being late for TBS!

In reporting, be guided by Sections 1301 and 1302 of this *Guide*. These give the procedure for joining a new station. When first reporting to Basic School, you will wear the service "A" uniform, if you have it from prior service, or a well-fitting and pressed business suit.

Hints on Reporting to Basic School. You are specifically not required to possess any articles of uniform upon reporting, aside from any issued at OCS and your commissioning uniform. You should, however, take care that your hair is closely trimmed and that you present a neat appearance. Be sure your state of physical fitness matches or exceeds that from your officer entry program days! Before reporting, log on to the TBS web site on the Internet, find information about the school, read the current commander's intent of the commanding officer, peruse the TBS reading list, and begin to absorb it. The web site also has copies of all student handouts in electronic form. Forewarned is forearmed!

You should have enough money available for living and other expenses until your first payday, which will be about three weeks after you join. Joining instructions that accompany your orders will suggest minimum amounts of cash that single or married new lieutenants should have.

Travel light and bring little baggage, as stowage space is limited.

Outside working hours, like any other officer, you may wear civilian clothing. This, however, must conform to accepted standards within the officer corps: clothes of eccentric design or color are not tolerated. As a minimum, you should have one suit, of conservative cut and color (charcoal gray and navy blue are best options), as well as sports attire.

Except for commissioning uniforms, camouflage utilities, and working uniforms, do not purchase or contract for uniforms before you report to TBS.

Warrant officers, on the other hand, are encouraged to have a complete set upon reporting. Year after year, students report with uniforms and accessories bought in good faith, only to find them ill-fitted, nonregulation, and far too costly. Beware of high-pressure uniform salesmen and so-called package deals for uniforms. One of the first items of business after you join will be a uniform orientation session conducted by the school. Only after that should you begin acquiring your uniforms. Note that during the first few weeks of TBS, you will be required to purchase the Marine Corps blue dress uniform to wear at Basic School's Marine Corps Birthday Ball. This uniform can cost upward of $800. Ensure that you have a plan to finance this purchase at the outset.

The Basic School, the oldest Marine Corps school, is an institution whose importance to the Corps is equaled only by that of the two recruit depots. TBS traces its history to 1 May 1891 when, as the "School of Application," it was founded at Marine Barracks Washington by Colonel Charles Heywood, ninth commandant of the Corps. At various times the school has been located at Annapolis, Maryland; at Port Royal, South Carolina (later to become famous as Parris Island); at Norfolk, Virginia; at Philadelphia Navy Yard; and, finally, at Quantico.

Today, Basic School is located approximately twelve miles from the main-side area of Quantico. The school's headquarters is located at Camp Barrett, one of the outlying camps of Quantico's Guadalcanal area, which constitutes the greater part of the 57,000 acres of the training reservation.

No matter how you earned your commission, your first assignment as a second lieutenant will be as a student in the Officer Basic Course, a course of approximately twenty-eight weeks' duration. In addition to the Officer Basic Course for newly commissioned second lieutenants, Basic School conducts a Marine Warrant Officer Basic Course for newly appointed warrant officers.

When you report to TBS, you will turn in your orders to the personnel officer, who will then assign you to a student company. The average class is made up of a company of about 250 students, including young officers from various allied countries around the world. The company is commanded by a major, with a captain as executive officer and captains and senior lieutenants as staff platoon commanders. Upon reporting to your company commander, you will receive an orientation on the course: what will be expected of you and what you can expect from the school. You will be assigned to a platoon and quarters. You will then be issued your field equipment, individual weapons, and textbooks for your forthcoming courses. You will do theoretical work in the classroom and then go to the field and work it out practically. About one-half of your training is in the field, and about one-fifth of this takes place at night.

Basic School curriculum, including intense and rugged fieldwork, provides graduates with a foundation of leadership and professional knowledge upon which they may build their careers. While the curriculum emphasizes the skills needed to lead an infantry platoon, lessons here apply to Marine officers in every leadership role. Training progresses through four phases. The first focuses on the individual technical and tactical skills required of an officer. In the second and third phases, you will build on these skills and prepare to lead by example in command of a platoon. Finally, in the fourth phase, you will study the strategic organization that makes the Marine Corps our nation's expeditionary force in readiness and will prepare to apply your leadership skills in action.

Within the foregoing academic framework, the objectives of Basic School are twofold: first, to instill the Marine Corps attitude and, second, to teach new lieutenants the basic professional techniques that a Marine officer must know. In other words, it is up to TBS to make a Marine officer of you. The extent to which the school succeeds, however, is largely up to you. Officer students who do not measure up to the standards set for Marine officers are dropped from Basic School, their commissions are revoked, and they are returned to civilian life. Remember that, at Basic School, you are under continual, experienced observation.

Immediately after TBS, every officer goes to follow-on training in some specialty school or course—for example, flight training—to qualify the officer in his or her new military specialty. Rarely, a few officers will receive orders from TBS directly to their first unit, where they will commence work while awaiting a seat at their specialty school. Officers with an infantry (03) military occupational specialty remain at Quantico for additional advanced infantry training. Thus, in all, your professional apprenticeship, including Basic School, lasts a minimum of six months.

Quarters. Bachelor officer quarters (BOQ) for the officer students at TBS are found in O'Bannon and Graves Halls. These quarters are not luxurious, although you will find them clean and quite comfortable. This BOQ also houses Basic School's dining hall and bar, a snack bar, television lounge, library and reading room, and reception room. Married students who are accompanied by their spouses will find housing on or off base; however, when in training they will be assigned a room as a "Brown Bagger." "Brown Baggers" will use their assigned room to store field equipment, organizational gear, and uniforms.

Heywood Hall is the main administration building of Basic School. Adjoining Heywood Hall are four modern, air-conditioned classrooms with a total seating capacity of 1,150 students. Conveniently located between these classrooms is the snack shop.

Additional facilities at Camp Barrett include a small Marine Corps exchange, barber shop, snack bar, post office, gymnasium, outdoor theater, chapel, armory, additional classroom facilities, gas chamber, combat conditioning facilities, clinic, and a lighted playing field for baseball, softball, or football.

HINTS FOR NEW OFFICERS

1208. What to Do, Not to Do, and Some Pointers

As a Marine officer, you represent the Corps. Conduct yourself with dignity, courtesy, and self-restraint.

Avoid any show of self-importance. Do not bluster, especially toward civilians or enlisted personnel.

Be wary of situations beyond your depth. A new lieutenant is not expected to be all wise. You are expected to keep your head and to possess enough common sense and knowledge of your own limitations to prevent you from overextending yourself. As a new second lieutenant, you should normally avoid making an assertion the begins with the phrase, "In my experience." At all costs avoid the impression of a brash young know-it-all.

Something else will be expected of you: *not to make the same mistake twice*, particularly after having been told about it by a senior. Learn to accept criticism positively and with grace.

On joining a new organization, you will be closely looked over by all hands, officer and enlisted. The first impressions can make (or break) you. Be natural and courteous, prompt and punctilious, "squared away" in uniform and deportment.

From the moment you become a Marine, you should cultivate the habit of punctuality. Along with discipline, dedication, obedience, and loyalty, it should be a matter of pride never to be late. *Always be five minutes early* for any formation or professional commitment.

Avoid the habit of complaining or whining, and avoid those who do. Refrain from criticizing unless you are ready and able to provide a better solution. By the same token, cultivate the habit of optimism. An optimist is like a breath of fresh air and cheers all with whom he or she comes into contact. One of the great sayings of the greatest of all naval officers, Lord Nelson, was, "I am not come forth to find difficulties, but to remove them."

Be industrious and persevering, attentive to duty, and attentive to essential detail. Whether ashore or afloat, in garrison or in the field, the best officers are those who possess powers of acute observation, and, having those powers, know how to use them. Akin to observation are the power and habit of forethought.

Learn to control and to hide your feelings. In addition to being alert, always try to look alert.

Whatever you do, do thoroughly, and do it with enthusiasm and imagination. Do not confine yourself to doing only what you are told to do. Do more than you are told to do. And bear in mind that it is the smart, quick, and, if possible, cheery voice that gets the job done and urges others to prompt action.

If you are asked a question and are unfamiliar with the answer, do not bluff. The proper answer from a young officer in such circumstances is, "I'll find out."

Do not procrastinate. When you have a job to do, do it at once. If you have several items to be accomplished, prioritize and do the important thing first. If you find yourself stymied, do not shove the matter aside or report back that you cannot do it—try some other way, and keep on trying. Remember that, in the service, it is results that count and that if you can acquire the reputation of a capable officer, you are on your way to success.

Always give thought to the service reputation that you build and acquire day by day. An officer's reputation for character and efficiency is his or her vested capital. Take this away, and the officer's usefulness is gone. And remember, you cannot fool your contemporaries. Working closely together, officers soon learn the ins and outs of each other's lives and character.

Personal appearance is most important in the service, and although most young officers must and should economize wherever possible, purchasing inferior uniforms is a false economy of the worst kind. The only way to economize on uniforms and equipment is to get the best and then take meticulous care of them. Economize on your bar bill rather than your tailor's bill. Nobody in the world looks shabbier than a shabby officer. Male officers should never appear unshaven after the start of the workday.

Military bearing is equally important. Stand straight. Keep your hands out of your pockets. Never chew gum or smoke in public while in uniform.

Keep fit. The Marine Corps will help you with this by periodic physical fitness tests and by vigorous training all year, but fitness is a continuous matter and must be a continuous concern to every officer. No Marine can afford to become fat.

Briefcases and backpacks should never be carried slung over a shoulder while in uniform (there is an exception for a military issue backpack, in which case it may be worn as intended using both shoulder straps); carry them in you left hand. And as a general rule, avoid carrying packages when in uniform.

As you acquire clothing, mark each article as laid down in *Marine Corps Uniform Regulations.* Stencil your baggage and personal kit appropriately. Inside each piece of baggage, stencil or affix the same information in a permanent manner. You can purchase clothing-marking sets at the Marine Corps exchange. Once deployed to or off foreign shores and using field or ships' laundry services, it is too late to mark your clothing properly.

In your relations with your fellow officers, avoid joining factions or, if there are any bad feelings between others, avoid taking sides. Do not gossip; gossip always finds its way back. Only say of a fellow officer who is absent what you would say to his or her face.

Never, under any circumstances, speak ill of the Corps, or of your own organization, in the presence of enlisted Marines, civilians, or members of the other services. Before you voice any criticism, however merited or carefully thought out, be sure it cannot be construed by outsiders so as to derogate the Corps. By the same token, avoid criticizing other units or services, at least in public.

Conduct all your business through proper channels. "Channels" is a highly important word in the service. The phrase, "Go through channels," which you will hear repeatedly, simply means, "Don't go over people's heads." In giving instructions or in doing or getting things, be careful not to go over someone's head or infringe on his or her areas of responsibility. This is a sure way to trouble in the service.

Now that you are a Marine yourself, keep your eyes open for likely recruits and for potential officers among your friends. Such individual recruiting of new Marines by convinced and loyal old Marines is one of the principal ways in which the Corps maintains its quality.

When answering a phone call at work, answer up smartly, in Marine Corps fashion, with your name and rank: "Lieutenant Burrows," not "Hello." When you make a call, identify yourself immediately: "This is Lieutenant Wharton, Marine Corps." Be sure to add "Marine Corps." It prevents mix-ups with the other services.

Since you are now a member of the most professional of the services, you should join the Marine Corps Association and subscribe to the professional journals listed in Appendix III. If you intend a career, you should by all means immediately join the Army and Navy Club in Washington, while you can still do so as a newly commissioned officer without payment of initiation fees. See Section 2213 for details.

Know where to find information. Find time to go through all the basic professional publications, page by page—read *Navy Regulations, Marine Corps Manual, Marine Corps Uniform Regulations, Marine Corps Drill and Ceremonies Manual,* and, of course, all the basic Marine Corps doctrinal publications and reference manuals relating to Marine weapons and basic tactical principles. Basic School will direct your attention to the most important provisions in all the foregoing, but, by going through these publications on your own, you will learn where to find information that lazy or inattentive young officers will say is not included in the manuals.

Get into the habit of being systematic and methodical. In Lord Chesterfield's words, "Dispatch is the soul of business, and nothing contributes more to dispatch than method. Fix one certain day and hour in the week for your accounts, keep them together in their proper order, and you can never be much cheated." By so doing, you will be able to accomplish two or three times as much as an equally capable but unsystematic officer.

As an officer embarking on your new career, you should do everything possible to match your living arrangements to your new position as an officer of Marines. This should not be misconstrued as encouraging extravagance, but your pay is given you for a purpose, and you owe it to the service to dress and live, however simply, like an officer.

If you do not have one already, open a checking account with a substantial bank, preferably one with branches located near naval installations around the

12-2. Rigorous training and critical evaluation remain the hallmark of Marine Corps officer schools.

country and accustomed to handling officers' accounts on a worldwide basis. This will help avoid the administrative burden of continually opening and closing bank accounts as the transfer from duty station to duty station. Begin systematic savings with your first paycheck, aiming for a minimum of 10 percent of gross pay throughout your career. Take out life insurance immediately (see Chapter 21).

Be extremely circumspect in any kind of financial transactions with fellow officers. "Neither a borrower nor a lender be" is golden advice; be not a cosigner either—many an officer has discovered that his or her signature on a "friend's" note has resulted in the loss of both the friendship and the amount of the loan. Other than in the line of duty, you are prohibited by *Navy Regulations* from any pecuniary dealings with enlisted persons, and this prohibition must be strictly observed.

Do not intrude among enlisted persons. They are entitled to privacy among themselves as you are. Do not enter noncommissioned officers' messes except by specific invitation of the senior NCO present or for official unit functions. If you have been commissioned from the ranks, remember this prohibition now that you are an officer. You cannot turn back the clock.

An officer is much more respected than any other man who has as little money.

—Samuel Johnson

It's not hard to be an officer, but it's damn hard to be a good officer.

—Gunnery Sergeant Daniel Daly

13

NEW STATION

No statistician has ever totaled the endless adages about the importance of good beginnings, but one thing is certain: as far as your Marine Corps career is concerned, all of them are true.

The instant you show your face on a new station, you come under close observation and appraisal. And when you report for duty on your first station—whether in garrison, in the field, at sea, at school, or beyond the seas—you begin to lay the foundation of the service reputation that will make or break your future.

How you conduct and carry yourself; how you wear your uniforms; how you behave; how much you know, pretend to know, or do not know—by all these details you are judged.

1301. Preliminaries

After completing Basic School and military occupational specialty (MOS) training, you will have received your primary MOS (see Chapter 14) and orders to your first station. In the majority of cases, this will be a unit in the Marine Corps Operating Forces. You also will have been authorized some delay in reporting, which will give you an opportunity to catch your breath after training and to square yourself away for further adventures. If you are ordered to one of the Marine divisions or aircraft wings, your first assignment will be predetermined by your MOS. If, however, you are ordered to a non–Operating

Forces unit or command, it is good practice to write ahead in order to introduce yourself and to assist your new commanding officer in deciding where and how to employ you to greatest advantage. A good example of such a letter (which should be formal but unofficial) follows:

> 10 March 2015
> Chief of Staff
> Marine Corps Recruit Depot
> San Diego, California 92140
>
> Dear Sir (or Madam):
>
> I have just received orders to report to the Recruit Depot not later than 20 June 2015. My present intention is to arrive in San Diego on the 18th and report for duty at 0800 on the 19th.
>
> I am married but have no children, and my wife will remain on the East Coast for the time being until I have an opportunity to find suitable housing and get settled in whatever duties may be assigned me.
>
> Although commissioned under the NROTC program, I have had three years' enlisted service in the Marine Corps, including one year with the rifle range detachment at Camp Lejeune, and believe I could do well on the range or with any of the recruit battalions.
>
> Having had no previous duty at San Diego, I would appreciate it if I could be sent any orientation or general information literature as to the base, together with any particular instructions you may have for me.
>
> I am looking forward to this tour of duty with pleasure and hope I may render useful service.
>
> Very respectfully,
> Wharton Burrows,
> 2ndLt USMC

Remember you will be reporting in to your new station or unit in the service uniform (normally service "A," although some commands direct the wear of a different uniform when first reporting for duty). This requires prior planning on your part to ensure that you have a complete uniform while traveling between duty stations. You should also have enough uniforms (for example, utilities) so you can go to work immediately if the need arises. In no case should you ship all your uniforms and assume they will be ready and waiting at your new station.

It has become a standard practice to call the adjutant or executive officer of the new unit to which an officer will be assigned, particularly when the battalion is already known. If there are multiple officers proceeding to the same unit, as may happen after completing a course, they should make a concurrent call, so as to conserve the time of the officer thus contacted at the new organization.

Frequently, the unit will assign an inbound officer a sponsor, usually an experienced officer of the same grade, MOS, and marital status. This officer can provide much helpful information on the unit's schedule, assist with settling into a new base, and otherwise orient the incoming officer on arrival. Almost all bases and stations operate home pages on the Internet, and these remain excellent sources of information. Links to these and more can be found at the official Marine Corps web site (http://www.usmc.mil).

1302. Reporting on Board in Garrison

There are as many ways to report in to a new station as there are individuals. During your career, you will see them all: the procrastinator, tearing out in a taxicab five minutes before midnight on the last day his orders allow; the travel-worn parents with house trailer, children, and wilted clothes; the careful officer who arrives two days early and scouts the lay of the land before reporting.

Without considering the trouble in store if you miscalculate your reporting date or if you arrive late for any cause, legitimate or not, you may be sure that last-minute arrival is a risky business, and one that can start you out off balance. So allow ample time, whatever else your personal logistics call for.

Let us assume, then, that you have budgeted "proceed, travel, and delay" (if any), that you have arrived at a city adjoining your first station, and that you are there in plenty of time—at least a day to spare.

So here you are, at the threshold of your first station.

Put on your best civilian clothes (or, if you prefer, service "A"). Get a haircut. Drive out to the base, show your identification card (or orders, if you have not yet been issued an ID card) to the sentry at the main gate, and ask the sentry to direct you to the adjutant's office for the command you will be joining. The adjutant is the staff officer who traditionally receives newcomers to the command. Large bases and stations (such as Camp Lejeune), which include several commands, now have a joint reception center or personnel administration center where all company officers report initially. After leaving the reception center, you proceed as described herein, reporting to the adjutant of the command to which you have been assigned.

Before you enter the adjutant's office, knock (or hesitate in the doorway until invited in), and have your orders handy. Introduce yourself informally; "Sir, I'm Second Lieutenant Nicholas. I have orders to report in tomorrow, and would like to find out where and when I report, the uniform, and any information you may have on my assignment."

The adjutant probably will have advance information of you and will know a good deal about your immediate future. In any case, the adjutant will look over your orders and, unless extremely busy, chat a few minutes, if only to size you up and get you off to a proper start.

Find out the exact time and place for reporting, the name and title of the officer to whom you report, and the required uniform. This last information allows you to visit the Marine Corps exchange to purchase any uniform items you may have overlooked.

Usually an officer reports for duty at the commencement of office hours, or at such other time during the forenoon as the commanding officer desires. This information can be ascertained in advance of reporting. If, in order to comply with the letter of orders, you must report at night or after working hours, the officer of the day or staff duty officer will receive you, log you in, and, if necessary, provide overnight accommodations. Next day, you then report formally to your new commanding officer.

From the moment you step on board, you must be alert, fit, and ready to do whatever may be required—and do it instantly.

Your service "A" uniform should be freshly cleaned and pressed. Your shoes should shine, your brightwork gleam. Your hair should be cut and your face newly shaven. Check to make sure that pockets are buttoned and that all insignia are in place and correct. Look yourself over in the mirror for a last-minute check.

With you should be your original orders with a half dozen copies, personal records, and miscellaneous papers that have to do with the day's business (documentation of travel expenses, check-in sheet, information booklet, and so on).

If you are staying off base and have no personal transportation, or if you arrive by train or air, you are normally authorized to take a taxi and claim reimbursement on your travel orders. Alternately (rarely in the United States but more common overseas), you may telephone the installation and ask for the motor transport dispatcher. Identify yourself, explain that you are reporting under orders, and ask that transportation pick you up and drive you to headquarters. Be sure to tell where you are and who you are (so that the driver will know whom he or she is to look for) and emphasize that you are traveling under orders. Have the dispatcher tell you when you may expect to be picked up.

Once on board, enter your command's headquarters and present yourself at the time and place previously ascertained, if you have conducted a preliminary reconnaissance; if you are in any doubt, report to the adjutant. He or she will take your orders and have them endorsed. The adjutant will show you to the office of the commanding officer or executive officer (if reporting to a large installation or major command, possibly the chief of staff, the deputy chief of staff, or the G-1).

On cue from the adjutant, step smartly into the office, uncovered, halt at attention two paces before your senior's desk, and say, "Sir, Second Lieutenant Zeilin reports on board for duty." *Do not salute*; Marines do not salute uncovered or indoors (except when under arms).

The officer to whom you are reporting will then have you sit down, put you at ease, and chat with you a few minutes, both as a matter of courtesy and to fix you in mind. Do not get flustered; answer questions briefly and directly, and sit erect without slouching or fidgeting. The end of the interview usually will be indicated by instructions that you report to some lower headquarters or commence the prescribed check-in procedure. Unless you are urgently needed, your commanding officer will almost always ask whether you have had time to "get squared away" and will allow you reasonable opportunity to attend to such personal matters as housing, administration, and the like.

After you leave, retrieve your orders with their reporting endorsement. You will need them all day.

If you have not already arranged for quarters, this should be an early step in the reporting process. At large bases, there is usually a housing office, which not only assigns government quarters but also can give you leads on off-base housing. Because government quarters are assigned (with few exceptions) on a first-come, first-served basis, present yourself immediately to the person who runs the quarters list, and see that your name is placed on that fateful roster, which determines when you move in. (Typically, housing offices today permit you to apply for quarters as soon as you receive orders to your new station, and your control date on the quarters list is determined by the date of detachment from your previous station; it is, of course, in your interest to verify that this is correct.) Before making any arrangements, let alone signing leases, for off-base housing, be sure to get your change-of-station orders endorsed to the effect that public quarters are not available. If you lease "ashore" before getting an endorsement, you may find yourself being moved into quarters anyway and, in any case, losing your quarters allowance.

Once you have gotten yourself housed, the finance office or section will be your destination. Ask for the NCO or officer who handles officers' pay accounts. Here you will provide certain personal information and data and here, also, the NCO will likely audit your personnel records with you to ensure all information is accurate and updated. In addition, the finance office will help make arrangements to pay you whatever travel allowances are due—a much-needed bonus that helps bring your finances back to level after the expenses of travel.

With orders endorsed, quarters arranged, and pay in your pocket, you will be ready to claim whatever baggage and effects you may have shipped from your home or former station. The traffic (or distribution) management office (TMO or DMO) takes care of this by holding your gear until you report in and claim it. Again, your orders are necessary. You are entitled to temporary storage of your effects. If your baggage and effects have not arrived, leave word with TMO where you wish to be notified when your gear gets in. TMO will deliver it to government quarters or to any point off base within a reasonable radius. After that, it is your problem.

Under most circumstances, military health records are mailed between military treatment facilities when you transfer, although there are exceptions (for example, when traveling overseas on permanent change of station or transferring to a remote duty station). If you hand-carried your health records, you should next leave them at the clinic, aid station, or sick bay that will provide your health services. Find out where this is before you leave station or unit headquarters. If your new station has a standard check-in procedure for officers newly reporting, the check-in sheet will tell you where to find the sick bay. With health record in hand, enter and ask for the records office. Here a Navy hospital corpsman will accept your health record, enter you on the records, and, likely, audit your record to verify that you are up to date on your immunizations. If you need dental work or any routine medical assistance, now is the time to make your needs known.

By the time you have covered the rounds just described, you will more than likely be ready for a bite to eat. This can usually be obtained at the commissioned officers' mess. If you are pressed for time, most Marine Corps exchanges have a short-order restaurant or food court; here you can eat on the run—less elegant, perhaps, but enough to sustain you through the day. Lunch at the mess, however, will enable you to take care of another traditional obligation, that of joining the mess. Here you may activate your membership, pay dues if necessary, and ascertain the privileges and obligations of the mess.

Last, but by no means least, if driving your own car, present yourself to the provost marshal and have your car registered. Marine Corps installations require that privately owned vehicles carry a proper state registration, be insured according to state laws, and be able to pass safety examinations. Nothing can be more troublesome than not being able to meet installation requirements for registration of a car; without registration, you may be required to park outside the installation and walk from there. Advance precautions to have your car in good shape and fully insured can save you days of walking, plus much vexation. Never park in a space reserved for someone else. Such spaces are usually marked by signs or numbers painted on the curb or road surface. Few events annoy a senior more than to find his or her space preempted by a junior.

1303. Shaking Down

As you settle into your outfit and assignment, your success will depend largely on your common sense, application, willingness to learn, and skill in human relations. Here, however, are a few tips:

- Learn quickly to associate as many names, faces, and jobs of the officers and enlisted Marines about you as you can. Study your Marines' records (which include background information).
- Read bulletin boards—not only the current, but all the past accumulation that most bulletin boards display; it may be old hat to the unit's plankowners, but it is background to you.

- Find out the mission of your organization if you were previously unable to do so.
- Study the tables of organization and equipment for your organization. The S-1 and S-4 can provide these.
- Study your organization's general orders and standing operating procedures. You can get copies from your first sergeant.
- Read installation regulations; they can keep you out of much trouble.
- Learn the geography of your installation and training areas by map and personal reconnaissance. "I'm a stranger here myself" is a poor reply for an officer to give.
- Above all, strive to know your Marines. As you begin this ceaseless and vital Marine Corps task, crack open your copy of the *Marine Corps Manual* and read the article entitled "Relations Between Officers and Men."

1304. Orienting Yourself

As you shake down, the sergeants in your unit can be a new lieutenant's best professional friends. Both parties observe proper military courtesy and maintain mutual respect.

An officer—especially a new one—should never be too stiff-necked or proud to learn from anybody who knows more about a particular subject.

Some commanding officers work out an informal orientation dealing primarily with internal administrative matters—mess, supply, paperwork—for new junior officers. If nothing of the kind is directed, you may find it desirable, after touching base with your captain, to take care of the following priorities:

1. Ask the first sergeant to assemble copies of standing orders and manuals you ought to read—and read them carefully. Make friends with, and respect, the first sergeant.
2. Go to the supply room and find out the basics of obtaining, caring for, and accounting for supplies, equipment, and other property. There is a lot to learn about these topics. Find out how weapons are safeguarded and about ammunition stowage. (Incidentally, refamiliarize yourself with safety regulations.)
3. Visit the battalion or other mess that feeds your unit. Catch the mess sergeant at a slack time and ask how the mess and galley are operated,

how rations are drawn, and how the mess force is handled. Although most Marine Corps mess halls are operated by contractors today, this action bears special importance if your unit does operate or have responsibilities for the mess hall, as it will then become part of your duties as officer of the day to monitor. In fact, study the orders governing your duties as officer of the day (staff duty officer if more senior) well before you stand such duty for the first time.

Besides all the foregoing, read up on your job. Use the fine professional manuals, from the Marine Corps and other services, that bear on your duty and unit. You will be surprised how soon you become recognized as professionally qualified.

REPORTING IN THE FIELD

1305. Actions upon Arrival

Although reporting in the field is now somewhat rare, the circumstances under which you might join your first command in the field are as various as the world's geography and climate. A force on occupation duty leads a different life from a Marine division or aircraft wing at the peak of a campaign. And joining an embarked Marine expeditionary unit during deployment presents its own set of challenges. Nevertheless, in preparing for field duty, here are some useful rules.

Get all the briefing you can, especially from those who have recently returned. Accept only guardedly advice or information from anyone who has not been on the spot recently. Find out, if you can:

- The local climate
- The uniforms worn and also whether these uniforms may be procured after you arrive or whether they should be brought with you
- The correct email address and mailing address, which will enable correspondence to meet you rather than lag weeks behind
- Local shortages or hard-to-get items—these are the things you will want to have with you.

Do not tarry in moving forward. The "pipeline" affords many delays. Overcome them, and press forward to your destination.

Travel lightly. For a junior officer this usually means some combination of military rucksack, seabag, and hanging bag; briefcase or helmet bag; and little more. Keep your baggage tagged with your name, unit, and destination.

Keep your travel orders and service records on you. Get a notebook and pencil, and keep them handy.

Try to reach your destination with two or more hours of daylight to spare. Night is no time for strangers to be stumbling about a new unit. When you report in, follow the procedure described in Section 1302 as closely as circumstances permit. As soon as operational circumstances allow and administrative formalities are complete, you should immediately:

- Find out where and when you wash, sleep, and eat
- Ascertain immediately the likelihood of enemy attack and the degree of readiness being maintained; this includes blackout rules and where and when you wear sidearms and personal protective equipment, as well as what to do if an enemy attack takes place
- Learn the password and countersign and the location of mine fields and entanglements.

1306. Taking Command in the Field

If you are taking over a command, especially one in contact with the enemy, you must do the following:

- Understand your mission and know the degree of readiness required of your unit.
- Meet your subordinate leaders, so that you can identify them and they can identify you. Meet your leading NCO and keep him or her with you.
- Walk your front lines or perimeter. Locate your unit's boundaries on the ground. Identify adjacent units. Inspect individual positions. Locate the enemy. Show yourself to your Marines.
- Inspect your unit's weapons and equipment. If the situation permits, hold emergency alerts and battle drills.
- Check your interior and exterior guard and security.
- Verify your communications. Be sure you are familiar with all emergency signals.

- Ascertain plans for and amount of supporting arms available. Know how to obtain them.
- Check your supply situation. This includes, at minimum, ammunition, water, and rations—"beans and bullets," the old phrase puts it.
- Make a thorough sanitary inspection, covering heads, urinals, garbage and trash disposal, and water supply. Field hygiene is vital to unit readiness. Do not overlook general policing of your area.
- Know how to get medical assistance and how to evacuate casualties.
- And, finally, remember that you can count on the Marines around you, just as they are depending on you.

OVERSEAS TRAVEL AND FOREIGN STATIONS

1307. Overview

About a fifth of your career (other than expeditionary or war service) is spent on foreign stations.

You probably will be visiting a country that is new to you. You may miss some conveniences and facilities to which you are accustomed at home. Language, customs, national characteristics, and living habits may well differ markedly from your own.

Learn to view foreign usages and characteristics with understanding and enthusiasm and without arrogance, insularity, or provincialism. If only for the success of our missions overseas, Marines must earn the friendship of the people in whose countries we serve. Self-discipline, courtesy, tolerance, generosity, and good humor are the best ambassadors.

Finally, remember Laurence Sterne's dictum on foreign travel: "An Englishman does not travel to meet English men." When abroad, meet the people and live the life of the country where you are stationed. Otherwise you might just as well never leave home.

1308. Personal Effects

One thing you must bear in mind: even though ordered to sea or foreign service in one part of the world, you may suddenly find yourself on the way to some place quite different. Thus you must select wardrobe and personal effects that, with minimum weight and bulk, keep you prepared for duty anywhere—from the Arctic to the Caribbean, or from Asia to Alaska.

Your maximum personal travel baggage should typically comprise seabag, hanging bag, and briefcase. You may allow yourself additional baggage when the mission requires that you travel with substantial tactical and organizational equipment. To be absolutely sure none of your essential gear goes adrift, there is but one safe rule, as voiced by a well-seasoned old-timer in the Corps: "Sit on your baggage and keep your orders in your pocket."

Common sense and the advice of fellow officers who are familiar with your destination are the surest guides on what to take overseas. Regardless of destination, however, never be without a complete service uniform (with garrison cap, to save space) and accessories, at least one set of utility clothing, field boots, rainproof parka, and regulation raincoat.

Do not take valuable papers, such as insurance policies, car titles, or deeds; irreplaceable jewelry; or anything else you cannot afford to lose. Leave such items in a safe deposit box. And be sure your spouse's or next of kin's power of attorney contains authority to get into the safe deposit box. Consult Section 2115 for further information.

1309. Moving Family Overseas

Overseas travel of your family on an accompanied tour via government transportation is usually contingent on your having adequate housing (or good assurance thereof) for them at the destination.

When possible, the Marine Corps tries to arrange for you and your family to travel together to an overseas station. If there must be delay and separation before the overseas area commander allows your family members to join you, the Corps will do its level best to get them moving quickly.

Get the latest information on living conditions in the overseas area, including climate, housing, food, education, shopping, recreation, and health care. Such data will help you decide what to take. Chapter 8 provides some details on overseas installations to which Marines are most often assigned, but this type of information is perishable, so check your destination installation's home page for the latest information.

1310. Preparations for Travel Overseas

Planning for, traveling to, and settling in at a new station overseas can be a daunting prospect, especially for the less traveled. Take the following preparations seriously.

Passports. You and each member of your family will require passports, unless you are ordered to one of a few areas where this rule is waived. Your change of station orders will normally include instructions that you obtain an official passport, and the duty station you are leaving should have an office (normally the office that also issues ID cards) that will usually obtain it with minimum delay. It is also advisable to obtain a standard tourist passport. Apply to one of twenty-seven State Department regional passport agencies located around the country in major metropolitan areas—or, if no other source is at hand, apply to the designated clerk at the nearest branch of the United States Post Office. Regardless of what agency you deal with, have the following items with you when you apply:

- Birth certificates for yourself and family members
- Evidence of naturalization if you or your family members are not native U.S. citizens
- Old passport or, at a minimum, the number(s) of past U.S. passports held
- Your ID card and other supporting identification
- Two passport-size photos, full-face and uncovered, of each person.

Visas. Be sure you have all visas required by countries en route and at your destination. Again, your most reliable source is the Manpower Department, Marine Corps Headquarters through your command's personnel officer or adjutant. The Department of State maintains an informative web site (https://travel.state.gov/content/travel/en.html) with a vast amount of information for overseas travelers, including a "Visa Wizard." The nearest consulates of the countries on your itinerary can also, of course, answer your questions and issue visas when needed. Remember that you cannot get a visa until you have your passport.

Physical Examinations and Immunizations. You and your family members must have physical examinations and complete certain immunizations before going overseas. The requirements for both vary from time to time. Have your immunizations recorded and certified on the appropriate international certificate of inoculation and vaccination, and be sure that every shot is recorded in your health record. Otherwise, you may find yourself getting a double dose of inoculations every time you step ashore.

You can get the necessary physical examinations and immunizations from your medical officer. If your family members are moving alone from an area without a Navy surgeon nearby, have them consult the nearest armed forces medical facility. Under outpatient provisions for family medical care, they may alternately receive examinations and immunizations from civilian sources.

Medical service for families is usually variable overseas. So is dental service. This largely explains why some overseas assignments carry restrictions of dependent family members. Both you and your family should make every effort to be in top health before going overseas.

Baggage. Before you pack, contact your local TMO/DMO to confirm your weight allowances for overseas assignment—that is, how much baggage may accompany you and how much you may ship—as well as what items may accompany you and the precise address to which baggage must be shipped. Mark and tag your gear clearly and indelibly. It is wise to put a copy of your basic orders inside each piece of baggage.

Forwarding Mail. Find out your new email address and mailing address in advance and submit address changes, via the Internet if possible, to all correspondents, businesses, and publications with which you have relationships. If updating addresses online is not an option for a particular correspondent or business, send change-of-address cards, which are usually available from your unit mail clerk or the nearest post office branch. If you are not sure of your new addresses, wait until you arrive, then handle the changes without delay.

When stationed in a foreign country, have your magazines, parcels, and any dutiable articles sent to you via the nearest Fleet Post Office (FPO) or Army Post Office (APO). This not only gets you domestic rather than appreciably higher overseas subscription rates but enables you to receive stateside parcels without the red tape of foreign customs.

1311. On Foreign Station

Here are some final considerations as you anticipate your overseas assignment.

Arrival. Because you are traveling under orders (and with an official or perhaps a diplomatic passport), you will have few, if any, problems with foreign customs or immigration authorities. You probably will be met by some representative of the military community that you are joining. The commander responsible for your area or port of entry will try to move you expeditiously to your destination. If delay is unavoidable, the commander will normally arrange accommodations. But keep in touch with the officer you are relieving (if you know him or her)—that is the person directly interested in your safe and speedy arrival.

Language. Where your duties make it desirable, the Marine Corps makes every effort to give you language training before sending you to a foreign billet. Your spouse should also enroll in some type of language instruction. Your young children will have the opportunity to pick up the language of the country soon enough from other children, through recreational opportunities, and perhaps even in school. To enable them to learn the country and its ways, as well as the language, give serious consideration to enrolling the children in local schools, if this is safe and feasible. In certain overseas areas where there are no U.S. schools operated by the Department of Defense Education Activity, the Department of Defense will pay all or part of the cost of private schooling in eligible local schools for your children. This is an opportunity you should not overlook.

Regardless of whether you are in a U.S. service community or on detached service alone, you will be working with the citizens of the country where you are serving, and you must perfect your command of the local language. Some commands maintain language tutors and conduct regular classes. If you cannot avail yourself of them, you can almost always hire your own tutor for a nominal fee. Educate the entire family. The ability to speak the language vastly extends your opportunities and earns the respect of all with whom you deal.

Sanitary Precautions. Depending on the country, sanitation and public health abroad may not attain the levels to which you have been accustomed at home. Gain an understanding of the local public health situation as soon as you arrive. Take nothing for granted. Be especially careful against insect-borne and enteric diseases. Maintain current immunizations. If circumstances demand it, drink only pasteurized or boiled milk and water that has also been boiled. Avoid raw fruits and vegetables unless you are quite sure "night soil" is not used as the local fertilizer. Make your own ice at home, using pure water. Your medical officer can advise you on what you can get away with and what you must watch.

Shopping. The "bargains" you and your spouse may find on foreign station will sometimes seem unbelievable. If you do not know quality, values, and the local market, take along a friend who does.

Look into the foreign exchange, currency, and tax situations. Find out where you can get the best legal rate of exchange (although your hotel will almost always change money, hotels usually charge a commission or give you a poor rate). In some countries, dollar purchasers are accorded purchase-tax exemptions; in others, some types of currency are more readily negotiable and thus get better rates of exchange. Know these fine points and take advantage of them. On the other hand, never demean your country or your Corps by black marketeering. This sort of thing is emphatically not done by Marines and is sternly dealt with in the few cases that arise. If you know quality, style, and value, a relatively small outlay may obtain furniture, linens, rugs, silver, chinaware, and other fine goods you might never be able to afford at home.

Take it easy at first, however. Look for a while, then buy. Do not bypass your military exchange. Purchase through an exchange gives you some assurance of quality and equity in price. Often, in fact, exchanges can do better than you as an individual because of mass purchasing and bargaining experience.

Well begun is half done.

—Horace, Epistles, I

14

THE PROFESSION OF ARMS

Military professionals exist to provide effective armed forces to the nation for use as an instrument of policy. In peacetime, this mission demands that an officer exert every effort to ready and prepare the military organization to fight a war that he or she hopes will never be fought. That feature leads to the salient way in which the profession of arms stands apart from all others. Although the armed forces use many terms in common with the learned professions—rights, duties, rewards, and privileges—only the profession of arms carries the obligation to surrender life itself if duty so demands. That liability is not often called upon in time of peace, but Marines of every epoch have faced considerable violence and borne many casualties in operations short of war.

Order distinguishes the profession of arms. Because the military operates by applying force, even violence, toward the resolution of a political question, properly vested authority exists at all levels of the military structure. On the other hand, one cannot say that initiative and latitude are not offered to the officer. The increasingly complex and sophisticated skills that a Marine must acquire through the period of active service exert a fascinating challenge for those intent upon mastering the nuances of military science. Many officers remain Marines simply because of the satisfaction gained in attaining a high degree of expertise in association with a like-minded cohort.

The professional officer continually seeks education and increased levels of qualification. Unlike other professions where a lengthy period of initial education qualifies a practitioner for life, the military professional's initiation merely suffices for the apprentice years. Thereafter, the officer returns to school frequently for specialist, technical, command, and staff courses. Perhaps up to one-fifth of an officer's career will be spent studying, expanding one's experiences, and preparing for greater responsibilities. This amount far exceeds the preparation for law and significantly exceeds that for medicine. In addition to formal courses, the officer reads relevant periodicals and books and seeks out ideas and innovative methods in an ongoing process to acquire knowledge and extend abilities.

14-1. Teamwork, dedication, esprit . . . the way of the Marine.

In fact, the skills required for military purposes know no real bounds. The Marine Corps encourages intellectual endeavors of all sorts and frequently provides time and funds in their support. Officers may work toward a doctorate in physics or master a foreign language. The Corps can and will make direct use of such qualifications. There also seems no doubt that learning to paint, ski, sail, ride, play a musical instrument, or climb mountains will prove of benefit to the Corps, indirectly if not directly. As long as you strive to improve your military skills, your fellow officers will respect and support your most eccentric hobbies and activities. This freedom of individual expression, in the midst of an ordered world, features in no other line of work but the military. The Corps remains necessarily a closely knit group with high values, fairness, and consistency. People are at the heart of the profession of arms.

1401. A Balanced Career

If you aim for the top, you must have a balanced career. A well-rounded career guarantees decisiveness, judgment, steadiness, and practicality at the top. Raw material for these attributes is found in most officers. But the extent to which you develop those qualities results largely from the kind of career you pursue.

You should seek the following for a balanced Marine career:

- Experience in command
- Professional education
- Duty with the Operating Forces
- Combat experience
- Joint staff and high-level experience.

As you proceed from duty to duty, remember that it is the commandant who assigns you, but it is still your career. You must monitor it intelligently without earning the pejorative label "careerist"—one whose offense is placing career before Corps. Watch your career as anxiously as a chemist compounding a critical formula. Your career is your critical formula.

1402. Assignment and Detail

The right balance in your career results largely from assignments, or "details," as they are sometimes still known in the Marine Corps. Your assignments send you to school, overseas, and to the Operating Forces and determine which of the thousand-and-one Marine jobs you fill. Thus, a balanced career can be attained only through a sound pattern of assignment. It is one of the important functions of Marine Corps Headquarters to see that, during the first twenty years of service, every officer gets assignments designed to develop his or her potentialities, to afford equal opportunity for advancement, and to qualify the officer for command responsibility appropriate to rank.

Figure 14-1 represents the "typical career pattern" often spoken of by career counselors. Too many variations exist to speak realistically these days of such patterns. Typically, a ground officer will serve in some sequence such as Marine Forces, non–Marine Forces, career-level school, and staff duty as a captain, followed by more Marine Forces, non–Marine Forces, and staff tours intermingled with intermediate and perhaps top-level schools and high-level staff duty as a field grade officer. Aviation officers tend to spend much more time in flying tours and comparatively less time on staff duty than do ground officers.

Managing your career while at the same time meeting the needs of the Corps is the job of the Officer Assignment Branch (Code MMOA), Marine Corps Headquarters. The "monitors" distribute officers to all Marine commands immediately subordinate to Headquarters. These commands in turn assign you according to your experience and military specialty.

Assignments are classed as follows:

- *Command*: duty as commanding officer or executive officer of any Marine organization
- *Staff*: duty on the general, special, or executive staff of any organization above company or squadron level
- *Instructor*: duty on the staff or as an instructor at any U.S. or foreign military school
- *Student*: duty under instruction at any school
- *Joint service assignment*: duty on the staff of a joint command or component of the Department of Defense
- *Special duty*: a range of varied and miscellaneous duties, such as sea duty, supply duty, duty as an aide-de-camp, and duty involving flying.

The normal tour for Marine officers on duty ashore is three years, although the demands of the service sometimes require departure from this or any other standard duration of tour.

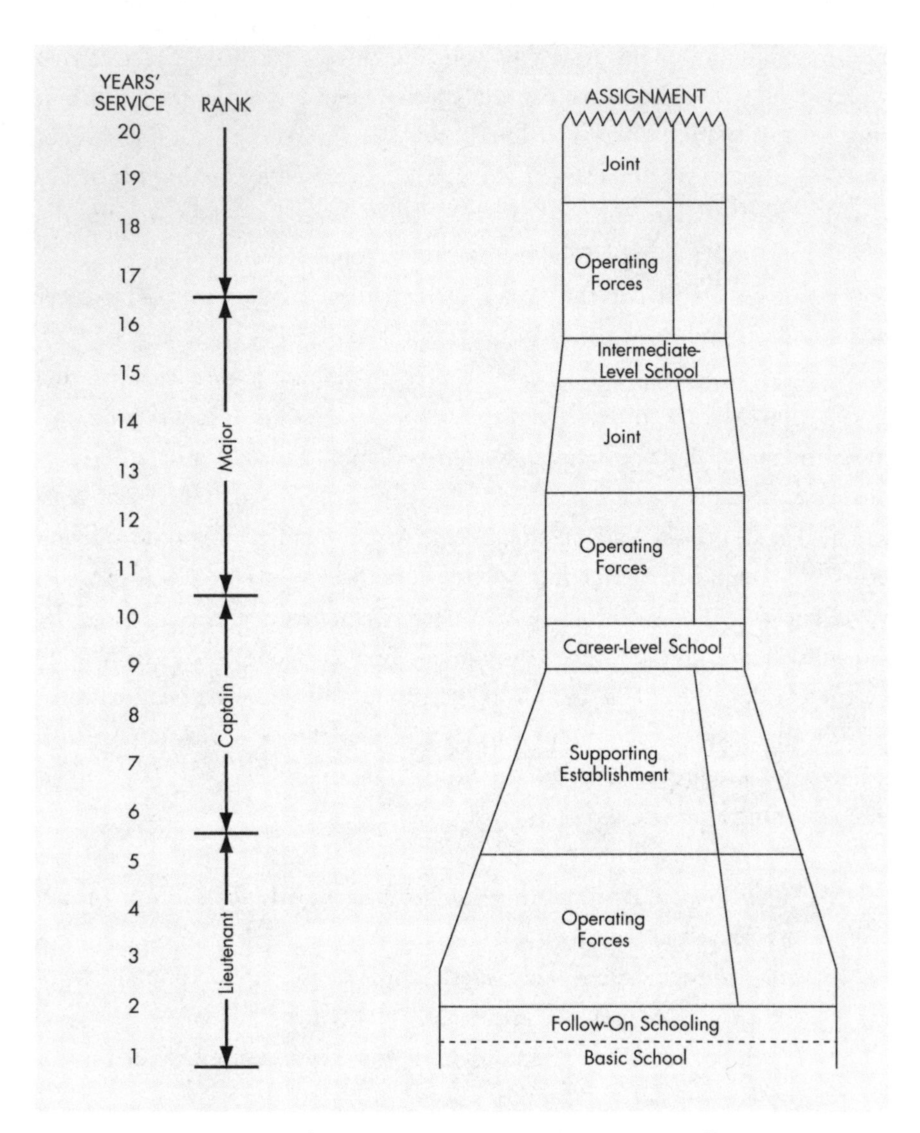

Figure 14-1. Typical Assignment Patterns for Marine Officers

Overseas (and certain other) tours are classed as either "unaccompanied" (without family) and "accompanied" (with family). It is reasonable to anticipate one accompanied foreign tour during your career and about three unaccompanied.

Although it is up to Marine Corps Headquarters, and every commanding officer, to balance your assignments, the fact remains, as has been emphasized, that it is your career. This is well recognized, and you have ample opportunity to put your wishes for assignment on record.

On each fitness report, you state your preference for your next duty, and your reporting senior must in turn give his or her own recommendation as to what assignment should be made. In addition, any officer may write an official letter (usually an administrative action form) to the commandant to request a future assignment.

There are several factors involved in determining who moves where: date of last unaccompanied overseas tour, school requirements, moves precipitated by school and/or unaccompanied tour completions, career development, time on station, and, of course, special requirements—the exceptional cases—as well as economy. Timing and individual availability for assignment also bear heavily on final decisions.

You can generally expect to be assigned to overseas unaccompanied tours on the basis of your date of return from previous unaccompanied duty relative to all other officers of your grade and military occupational specialty (see Section 1405).

The normal process of detailing officers to the various billets of the Corps revolves around annual preparation of "slates," or lists showing the assignments in each rank that are planned for the forthcoming year. Based on a normal three-year turnover, about one-third of the officer corps should be transferred each year. But because some billets have shorter tours than three years, a larger percentage usually moves.

Slating is essentially a cross-matching of Marine Corps officer requirements (based on tables of organization, approved manning levels, school quotas, and so on) with officers available for transfer in a given calendar year. The decisions on individual assignments in each case are based on optimum career pattern (including need for schooling); individual qualifications (such as MOS, college degree, language skill); present station (to avoid costly, time-consuming cross-country or Atlantic to Pacific moves); and, of course, the individual's requests.

Over and above all the foregoing, the factor of overriding importance in slating (and thus in shaping careers) is performance. No matter what duty you have had in the past, the singular consideration that will shape your future assignments is an established record of and reputation for consistently high performance across the range of your career.

You often hear it loosely said that "nobody pays any attention" to individual officers' requests. This is not true; contrary to all rumor, the Officer Assignment Branch does have a heart.

The core of the process lies with carefully selected officers at Marine Corps Headquarters called monitors (or, in Navy parlance, "detailers"). The responsibility of a monitor is to assign officers under his or her cognizance in the most efficient manner to meet the needs of the Marine Corps. At the same time, your monitor tries to harmonize your best interests and expressed desires with the requirements of the Corps—not an easy job.

To accomplish the above, the Marine Corps maintains an open door policy, in which informal, frequent contact between individual officers and their respective monitors is encouraged. You can always email, call, or, when in the Washington metropolitan area, visit your monitor. In addition, the Manpower Department tries to have selected monitors visit major commands and schools on the East and West coasts each year, together with a special trip to the Western Pacific.

So never hesitate to make your desires known, especially when you feel your career might be broadened by some assignment that may seem professionally necessary to you, such as in a particular Marine Forces unit or schooling. If you pass through Quantico, stop by the Manpower and Reserve Affairs Department and consult your monitor. Fortunately, the Corps is small enough to accommodate its own needs and the desires of its officers pretty consistently. But you must do your part.

1403. Initial Detail

Undoubtedly, one of your major concerns is where you will be detailed upon graduating from Basic School. In virtually all cases, lieutenants and warrant officers graduating from Basic School are immediately ordered to follow-on training to qualify them in their MOSs. They are then ordered to their new permanent stations or organizations. The following paragraphs describe the steps and procedures leading to assignment of your MOS and first permanent duty station.

Early in the course, you will have a chance to submit a form showing your preference for duty. Here you indicate, in order, choices of occupational field (see Section 1405), preferences of geographic area, and any reasons to support these choices. Your company officers recommend, assign, and endorse this form, affixing your leadership and academic grades and their appraisal of your attitude, motivation, and general value to the service. The form then goes to the Officer Assignment Branch, HQMC.

The ground officer assignment section controls the detail of officers into the occupational fields. Just before receipt of Basic School preference statements, the monitors review their respective quotas based on projected requirements. On arrival of the preference forms, the monitors consult and tentatively select candidates for their respective occupational fields.

How do Basic School staff and monitors make up their minds? As to occupational field, the monitors' choice depends on several factors:

- Current requirements of the Marine Corps
- Previous military education and experience
- Civilian education and experience
- Your desires
- Basic School staff recommendations.

Concerning geographic area, you will be ordered where the Marine Corps needs you, with your preference taken reasonably into account if possible. In any case, however, you can usually expect orders to the Marine Corps Operating Forces.

1404. Initial and Permanent Precedence

Every new second lieutenant is assigned a date of rank. Those with the same date of rank are assigned temporary initial precedence (see Section 1809), which governs their seniority until publication of the first lineal list, or "Blue Book," after they have finished Basic School. At this time, their names are rearranged in permanent precedence within groups having the same date of rank, according to Basic School standing.

1405. Your Military Occupational Specialty

As you look down a roster of officers, you may at first be puzzled to see an entry such as this: 1STLT JOHN HEYWOOD 0802/0840/0803.

Those mysterious numbers listed after the rank and name, you will soon realize, are individual identifying badges worn by today's Marines. Those four-digit numbers indicate the MOSs of the individual concerned.

Your *primary MOS* describes your primary specialty and, by extension, the type of unit you are considered primarily qualified to command; your *secondary MOS* may indicate additional specialty skills and other command qualifications or staff qualifications.

The MOS system thus provides the Marine Corps with a running inventory of talent and indicates at a glance the professional qualifications of each officer and enlisted Marine. For example, returning to Lieutenant Heywood, just mentioned, a translation of the entry would run as follows:

1STLT JOHN HEYWOOD: rank and name
0802: field artillery officer
0840: naval surface fires planner
0803: targeting effects officer.

Obviously, those MOSs and the skills they represent are extremely important to you. When you report to a new station, those numbers generally determine your assignment because every position, or "billet," in the Marine Corps carries the MOS appropriate to that billet.

When you report to Basic School, you are classified as a basic officer. You retain this classification only until basic training is completed and the Marine Corps has had the opportunity to size you up. Before you leave Basic School, you are normally assigned a *primary* MOS by the commandant of the Marine Corps in one of the following fields of specialization:

- Personnel and Administration (that is, Adjutant): Occupational field 01
- Intelligence: Occupational field 02
- Infantry: Occupational field 03
- Logistics: Occupational field 04
- Communications: Occupational field 06
- Field Artillery: Occupational field 08
- Engineer: Occupational field 13
- Tank/Assault Amphibian: Occupational field 18
- Ground Supply: Occupational field 30
- Financial Management: Occupational field 34
- Public Affairs: Occupational field 43

- Legal Services (that is, Judge Advocate): Occupational field 44
- Military Police: Occupational field 58
- Aircraft Maintenance: Occupational field 60
- Aviation Supply: Occupational field 66
- Air Control/Air Traffic Control/Antiair Warfare: Occupational field 72
- Pilot/Naval Flight Officer: Occupational field 75.

If you later qualify for other fields, you receive secondary MOSs to denote this fact. As you acquire staff specializations (for example, as a force deployment and planning officer; chemical, biological, radiological, and nuclear defense officer; or civil affairs officer), these are reflected by secondary MOSs.

Every Marine officer below colonel (regular and reserve), as well as every enlisted Marine, is classified under this system. Once you have your primary MOS, it can be changed only by the commandant. Should you feel that you have not been correctly classified in accordance with your skills or experience, or wish to qualify in a new field, you may so request in an official letter to the

14-2. An officer will spend almost a third of his or her career working within a primary occupational specialty, such as field artillery, the 08 occupational field.

commandant, who then approves or disapproves the change you desire, taking into consideration the needs of the Corps, your skills, and your wishes.

One word of caution: Although your MOS labels you for certain duties and patterns of assignment, never let that MOS be a pair of blinders. Avoid overspecialization in fact or attitude. Remember that every Marine, regardless of MOS, must always be prepared for all duties appropriate to his or her rank. The genius of the Corps lies in the fact that Marine officers have never let themselves be "jurisdictionalized" into competing branches or watertight professional cliques.

You are, first and foremost, a line officer of Marines; secondary to that, you pursue a major professional specialty. Command and leadership are the only universal military occupational specialties of all Marine officers and NCOs.

1406. Assignment of Female Officers

Successive revisions of Title 10, U.S. Code, have provided an integrated career for male and female officers through the grade of general. In 1981, the lineal lists of male and female officers merged, and all were selected for promotion under direct competition among contemporaries. In 1994, policy changes removed the former restrictions on women serving in combat units, in combat aircrews, and on board combatant ships. Until 2015, policy stipulated that women could serve in all units except those primarily concerned with "engaging the enemy on the ground with individual or crew served weapons, while being exposed to hostile fire and to a high probability of direct physical contact with the hostile force's personnel." This translated into assignment policies that permitted women to be assigned to any occupational field except 03, 08, and 18. During 2015, changes in America's political and cultural climates crossed a threshold, and the push to open all MOSs to women gathered momentum. Although implementation plans for opening the 03, 08, and 18 occupational fields to women are a work in progress, it appears that women will soon be eligible to join men in the Marine infantry, artillery, and armor disciplines.

Pregnancy may not bar assignment or retention of women in the Marine Corps. Those who become pregnant have the option to remain on active duty or be discharged. If they elect to remain on active duty, they are treated the same as their male counterpart parents in terms of assignments. There are no special considerations based solely on the fact of family responsibilities.

A request for separation by reason of pregnancy may be denied if a woman has incurred an additional active duty obligation following receipt of special compensation, funded education, or advanced technical training, or when she serves in an MOS requiring her retention based upon the needs of the service. A request for separation will be considered under any of the above conditions if the woman can show overriding or compelling factors of personal need.

1407. Professional Schools

You cannot overemphasize the importance of professional education.

In school, you learn from the hard-won experience of others, and you develop your own professional skills. The schooling you pursue and your application to professional studies probably exercise more immediate leverage on your career than any other factors.

Levels and Types of Schools. Professional schools are classified by instructional level as being resident or nonresident; as being of general curriculum or specialized; and as being Marine schools or schools of other services.

The levels of Marine officer schooling are *Basic* (followed immediately by follow-on training in MOS), *Career-Level, Intermediate,* and *Top.* Section 1408 contains typical examples of professional schools sorted by level.

So far as numbers permit, it is Marine Corps policy that every permanent unrestricted officer goes to school at each level through intermediate. You may not attend two schools on the same level. For the top-level schools (such as the

14-3. Throughout your career, you must hold tactical and technical proficiency as the greatest of your personal goals.

National Defense University), only the most qualified officers are selected. If you aspire to attend such a school, you must accumulate a record of performance that competes favorably with your equally ambitious fellow officers.

In addition to resident schooling, the Marine Corps encourages all officers to enroll in nonresident (online or extension) courses. You can pursue these on your own time, thus adding to your professional knowledge and better preparing yourself for resident instruction when the time comes. It is the advice of many successful officers that, during your first fifteen years of service, you should always be enrolled in some course (see Section 1410).

Schooling Outside the Corps. Many Marine officers attend schools conducted by other U.S. services and foreign nations. This ensures a wide base of professional thinking throughout the Corps and fosters insight by Marines into every aspect of the profession of arms—land, naval, and air.

It is a Marine tradition, which you should never forget, that when you attend the school of another service or country, you should return at or near the head of the class, or—as is said half-jokingly—not return at all.

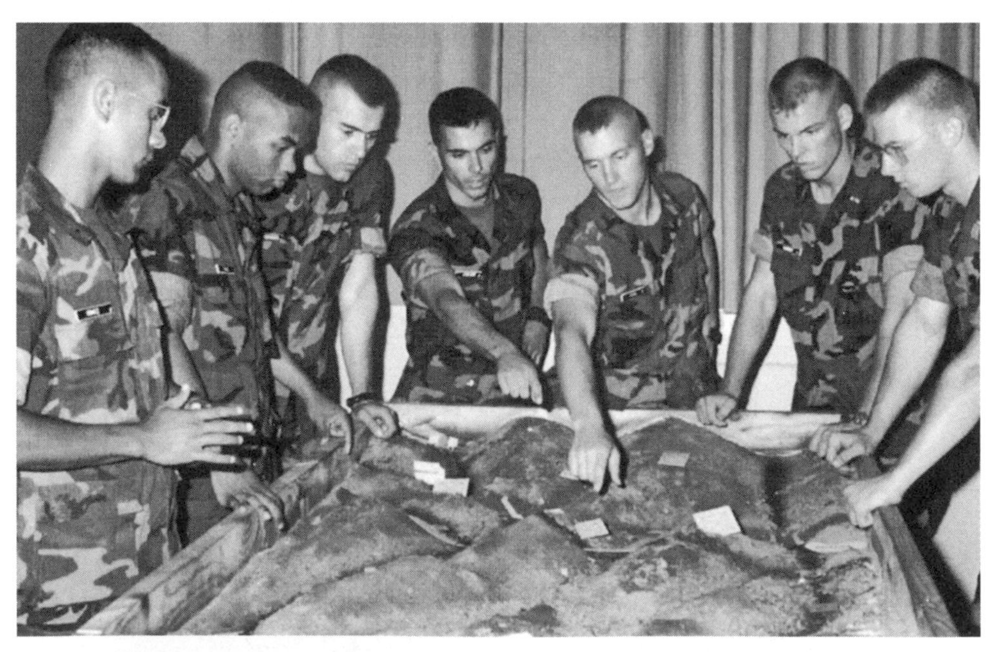

14-4. Basic School provides entry-level professional education and training.

Marine Corps Schools. Although many Marines attend school outside the Corps, the Marine Corps University at Quantico provides the bulk of the professional education for Marines. At Quantico are schools from basic through top levels, together with several specialist schools. Quantico's students come from all officer ranks of the Corps, from other U.S. services, and from numerous foreign countries. Quantico is the goal of every Marine officer who wants to make the most of his or her career. For more information about the schools, read Sections 622 and 1207.

1408. Resident Schools

A "resident school" is one that you attend in person, as distinguished from a "nonresident school," whose instruction is distributed by correspondence or the Internet. Marine officers attend resident schools at Quantico, the majority of the schools run by the other services, a number of civilian schools, and a few schools conducted by foreign countries. The list varies from time to time, and Marine Corps Headquarters periodically lists each course or school open to officer or enlisted Marines.

Here are typical courses and schools that you might attend. You may find names of still more in the current directive on this subject and in the annual naval messages announcing board results.

Basic Level:

Basic School, Quantico, Virginia

Career Level:

Expeditionary Warfare School, Quantico, Virginia
The Infantry School (USA), Fort Benning, Georgia
The Field Artillery School (USA), Fort Sill, Oklahoma
The Engineer School (USA), Fort Leonard Wood, Missouri
The Armor School (USA), Fort Benning, Georgia
The Signal School (USA), Fort Gordon, Georgia

Intermediate Level:

Marine Corps Command and Staff College, Quantico, Virginia
Command and General Staff College (USA), Fort Leavenworth, Kansas
College of Naval Command and Staff (USN), Newport, Rhode Island

Air Command and Staff College (USAF), Maxwell AFB, Alabama
Joint Forces Staff College, Norfolk, Virginia
Joint Services Command and Staff College, Shrivenham, England
NATO Defense College, Rome, Italy

Top Level:

Marine Corps War College, Quantico, Virginia
Army War College (USA), Carlisle Barracks, Pennsylvania
Naval War College (USN), Newport, Rhode Island
Air War College (USAF), Maxwell AFB, Alabama
National War College, Washington, D.C.
Dwight D. Eisenhower School for National Security and Resource Planning, Washington, D.C.
British Imperial Defense College, London, England
NATO Defense College, Rome, Italy.

Occasional assignments are made to other foreign schools at intermediate and top levels in Spain, France, Norway, Germany, Australia, and Japan, and others according to current bulletins. Additionally, each year there are several fellowships with graduate-level programs at various U.S. universities and Washington-area think tanks that qualify as top-level schooling.

Generally speaking, the duration of resident courses increases with the level of the school. In quiet times, instruction is more leisurely, whereas during war or emergency, courses are compressed to the maximum extent. The average length of a peacetime resident course is from seven to nine months.

The resident schools of the Marine Corps at Quantico are open without distinction to all commissioned line officers, both ground and aviation.

1409. Flight Training

If you have an urge to fly, if you can pass the searching battery of physical and psychological tests, and if you are a lieutenant with less than three years of service, under age twenty-seven when you apply, and a Basic School graduate or student, you may apply to Marine Corps Headquarters and be assigned as a student naval aviator or naval flight officer. Initial flight training is conducted at NAS Pensacola, Florida. It does not count as schooling on any of the levels described above, and whether you succeed or not does not debar you from normal schooling to which your rank and length of service otherwise entitle you. Once you complete flight training and are given your wings, you will be assigned to duty in an aviation unit, probably in an Operating Forces unit.

1410. Distance Learning

In years past, Marines could pursue professional education and development by correspondence course—a course of study in which students and instructors or administrators communicate by mail. The Marine Corps Institute (MCI) at Marine Barracks Washington administered the Marine Corps' correspondence courses until 2015. MCI was the oldest correspondence school for the U.S. armed forces, having been founded in 1920 to permit World War I Marine veterans to complete interrupted education. Over the years, it changed from a general, semi-academic correspondence school to one that focused primarily on the professional development of enlisted Marines. In 2015, the Marine Corps transferred the distance education mission and functions to the College of Distance Education and Training (CDET) at Marine Corps University (MCU), Quantico, Virginia.

The mission of CDET is to design, develop, deliver, evaluate, manage, and resource distance learning products and programs across the Marine Corps' training and education continuum. Through a variety of distance-learning delivery systems, CDET provides distance education and training opportunities for all Marines, government employees, and family members. CDET's online learning management system, MarineNet, provides education to all Marines wherever they are stationed. Additionally, the college's worldwide seminar program supports the professional military education (PME) distance education programs (DEPs) through a network of satellite campuses and learning resource centers.

All Marine Corps distance education is free of charge to Marines and Navy personnel serving with the Corps. In addition, Marine officers are eligible to take similar courses conducted by the U.S. Naval War College, Newport, Rhode Island, and, if no equivalent Marine distance education course exists, similar instruction offered by the Army and Air Force war colleges and the National Defense University.

The following personnel are eligible for enrollment in MarineNet courses:

- Marines of any rank on active duty
- Marines reservists of any rank (provided that the courses requested are commensurate with the rank of, and are appropriate for, the individual reservist)
- Family members of Marines
- Retired Marines, members of the Fleet Marine Corps Reserve, and disabled former Marines
- Eligible members of other armed services (as determined by the service concerned)
- Civilian employees of the Marine Corps.

The College of Distance Education and Training also distributes officer PME through its distance education programs. The Expeditionary Warfare School Distance Education Program (EWSDEP) provides Marine captains career-level professional military education and training in command and control, MAGTF operations ashore, and naval expeditionary operations. This enables them to command or to serve as a primary staff officer in their MOS, integrate the capabilities resident within their element of the MAGTF, integrate their element within the MAGTF, and understand the functioning of the other elements of the MAGTF. The Command and Staff College Distance Education Program (CSCDEP) provides graduate-level education to develop critical thinkers, innovative problem solvers, and ethical leaders who will serve as commanders and staff officers in service, joint, interagency, and multinational organizations confronting complex and uncertain security environments. Officers interested in enrolling in EWSDEP or CSCDEP should pursue enrollment through MarineNet.

CDET does not offer any top-level school programs; however, there are distance education programs available that offer Marine Corps officers a unique opportunity for high-quality nonresident education. Nonresident top-level schools open to Marine officers include the Army War College and the Air War College.

Naval War College. The College of Distance Education (CDE) represents the Naval War College's outreach program. It exists to provide executive-level education to officers of the various military services and to senior Department of Defense and other federal employees. CDE offers three delivery methods: faculty-led evening seminars, a web-enabled program, and a CD-ROM–based correspondence program. These courses largely mirror the program of study offered to resident students at the Naval War College's Newport campus. If you wish to enroll, or if you seek further information, visit the CDE web site or contact the College of Distance Education directly by email.

Other Service Courses. If you want to take a correspondence course offered by the Army, Navy, Air Force, or Department of Defense for which the Marine Corps does not have an equivalent, apply directly to the school of interest.

For younger officers of marked ability, the White House Fellows Program is worth looking into. In this program, officer college graduates (age twenty-three through twenty-six), as well as civil servants, educators, and journalists, are given a year of first-hand, high-level experience in the workings of the U.S. government at the White House and Cabinet level.

1411. College Degree Program

One of the basic educational goals of the Corps is that any officer who does not have a baccalaureate degree will be offered the opportunity to earn one.

Officers who have completed two or more years' undergraduate work are eligible for the college degree program (sometimes referred to as "Operation Bootstrap") for not more than twenty-one months' residential instruction at an approved institution. In this program, you are ordered in a duty status to the institution in question. You receive normal pay and allowances but in turn meet the various academic fees and expenses out of pocket. (Most tuition and other academic expenses normally can be funded through the individual officer's Veterans Affairs entitlements.) To be selected, you may be in any grade, as a permanent regular officer, from warrant rank to that of lieutenant colonel (although it is exceedingly rare today that a senior commissioned officer would not have received already his or her degree). Applications must reach Marine Corps Headquarters at least six months before the start of the college term specified by you. Special consideration is given to officers who have demonstrated interest and accomplishment in off-duty educational programs.

1412. Special Education and Advanced Degree Programs

The Corps has three programs in which officers can be encouraged and assisted to obtain advanced degrees above baccalaureate level.

The tuition aid program is a strictly do-it-yourself arrangement on your own time while continuing to perform regular duties, but the Marine Corps pays 75 percent of tuition costs.

In the special education program (SEP), officers study in a variety of disciplines for periods up to twenty-four months. Chosen curricula are tailored to billet needs of the Corps and may or may not lead to an advanced degree. (Officers, however, are at liberty to take on extra course loads, which, taken with the prescribed curriculum, would earn a degree.) All tuition and related expenses are paid by the Marine Corps while you continue in pay status.

The advanced degree program (ADP) is essentially a higher-level version of "Bootstrap." An officer, paying his or her own educational expenses, gets eighteen months in which to gain an advanced degree while continuing to receive regular pay and allowances. Again, in most cases, GI Bill entitlements cover academic expenses.

Typical, though by no means inclusive, of fields open to officers in the SEP and ADP are applied mathematics (statistics); aeronautical engineering; communications engineering; computer engineering; computer science (technical); defense systems analysis; education, curriculum, and instruction; electronics engineering; management; financial management; operations analysis; and public relations/journalism.

Selection for SEP and ADP is made on application to the commandant, by a Headquarters Marine Corps selection board.

In addition to all the organized, formal schooling just described, there remains a place for the traditional battalion or squadron officers' school, conducted by the commanding officer and best-qualified officers of the unit. A well-tested arrangement is to hold it each Friday afternoon, followed immediately by a happy hour.

1413. Professional Reading

Great military leaders throughout history have recognized the importance of continuous reading in the profession of arms. Wrote Napoleon Bonaparte: "Read and re-read the campaigns of Alexander, Hannibal, Caesar, Gustavus Adolphus, Turenne, Eugene, and Frederick. Make them your models. This is the only way to become a great general and to master the secrets of the art of war."

A few officers attain high rank without having mastered the history of war, but they are few indeed. The habit of systematic, planned reading of history, biography, and literature enables you to live up to your profession and to apply the lessons of the past to the future. Remember Metternich's remark: "The past is chiefly useful to me as the eve of tomorrow—my soul wrestles with the future." Professional reading means more than studious application to field manuals and the regulations by which we steer our course. This type of reading should be taken for granted. So should the reading of service journals. Professional reading even transcends military matters (remember Clemenceau's barbed dictum: "War is too important a matter to be left to the generals"). Your professional reading ought to embrace military and naval history and biography, U.S. and world history, literature, international affairs, economics, and psychology.

This sounds like a large order. It will not seem so large once you begin. The most important part of a professional reading program can be summed up in one verb: Read!

Right now, subscribe to your professional journals: the *Marine Corps Gazette*; the U.S. Naval Institute *Proceedings*; and—for current service news—the widely read and well-informed *Marine Corps Times*. If you have a bent for military history, take *The Journal of Military History*. Additionally, there is now an assortment of cutting-edge online journals focused on military and national security issues that merit a look.

Look over the suggested list of books in Appendix III that every officer should know, and start reading them. Better still, start acquiring them. Both the Naval Institute and the Marine Corps Association, incidentally, sell current books to members at discounts of 10 to 20 percent. If you want a more extensive compilation of outstanding professional books, look for the recommended reading list for Marine and Navy officers on the web site of the Naval War College, Newport, Rhode Island.

The Commandant's Reading List has fostered unit libraries and reading seminars to assist Marines in reading two to four of the listed titles each year.

A final must are the high-quality Marine Corps operational histories prepared by the History Division, Marine Corps Headquarters and University. Every officer should know them.

So now it is time to build your professional library and get in the habit of reading professional journals. The Marine Corps packs and ships your professional library from station to station at no charge against your weight allowance and at no cost to you.

1414. The Service Author

Every officer with professional ideas worth expressing should support his or her service journals by contributing. There are three good reasons why you should do this. First, you support the publications that spread military knowledge and raise professional standards; second, you give readers the benefit of your ideas and experience; and third, you acquire a service reputation for professional keenness.

It is widely believed that elaborate and drastic regulations hamper an officer who chooses to write for publication. This is certainly not the case for reputable journals such as *Proceedings* or the *Gazette.* Additionally, online journals focusing on national security and military affairs such as *War on the Rocks* and *Task and Purpose* offer welcoming venues for military writers. Be aware, however, that material prepared by active officers for outside publication may require clearance by the Secretary of the Navy and by the Department of Defense. It is usually wise to consult your security manager and staff judge advocate before submitting a manuscript for publication.

In any case, you cannot reveal classified information in an article for publication any more than you can disclose the same information in a letter or in careless conversation. Nor can you represent that you are an official spokesman of the Marine Corps or the Department of the Navy, or give such an impression. Finally, whatever you write for publication should constitute a constructive contribution to the primary missions of the Department of Defense.

If you are ever in any doubt as to the classification or general propriety of an article or manuscript, you may always submit it to the director of the Office of Marine Corps Communications (formerly Public Affairs), Marine Corps Headquarters, who will advise you as to its suitability for publication.

1415. Public Speaking

Distinct, forceful speech is an essential quality for a successful officer. Public speaking ability is a primary tool of leadership. Because a large part of your career will be devoted to explaining, announcing, and teaching, you should learn at least the fundamentals of speaking technique—and the sooner, the better.

Some believe that public speaking ability is a magic gift, bestowed on some but denied to others. This is far from true. Public speaking, like the technique of shooting a rifle, can readily be—and must be—learned. Good speakers are made, not born.

But how do you become a good public speaker? What individual qualities do effective military speakers cultivate and possess?

Be purposeful. You must have a clear view of your objective—that is, of what you are trying to put across. You must be able to balance the speaking time allocated to the various aspects of your topic against achievement of your objective. Avoid digression into irrelevancy.

Know your stuff. You must have a thorough grasp of your subject, backed up, if possible, by practical experience. Conversely, avoid, if you can, having to talk about matters in which you lack experience.

Prepare. Even if you have all the knowledge, skill, and experience needed to put your subject across, there is no shortcut in preparation. Choose the right approach and method of presentation; arrange your material in logical phases, each one followed by a summary; if you are instructing, use visual aids to help your audience see your points. Psychological studies show that 75 percent of all we learn is taken in through the eye, whereas only 13 percent comes through hearing and the rest through other senses.

Be enthusiastic. Enthusiasm is as infectious as boredom. It is the driving force of a good speech or lecture. But your enthusiasm must be balanced and seasoned. If you make your listeners feel that you are a fanatic with a wild gleam in the eye, they will discount what you say and soon become bored. And enthusiasm unseasoned by intelligence and humor soon exhausts the hearer.

Cultivate a dramatic sense. Do not be content with dull, stodgy presentations; instead, cultivate what show business people call "sense of staging." Get in touch with the mood of your audience. Use variety of pace, surprise, and emotional and dramatic appeal to drive home your points. If you can tell a funny story well, do not be afraid to use it. But do not indulge in a gag just for the gag's sake. Remember also that there are other (and usually more effective) ways to introduce a subject than by telling an irrelevant "funny" story.

Have a confident, easy manner. Give your listeners confidence in what you say by having that confidence yourself. Speak clearly and distinctly. Remember that distinctness of speech stems from distinctness of ideas. One way to maintain a confident, easy manner is to stick with language in your "comfort zone." Do not be flowery.

Have the right approach. Your particular approach should be determined by the nature of the audience. Regardless of the kind of audience you face, however, avoid the following:

- Flippancy. A flippant speaker displays disrespect for his subject and usually for the audience also.
- Cheap humor and vulgarity. Do not play the clown to get a cheap laugh. Vulgarity offends most listeners and, if repeated, bores all. By cheapening your remarks, you cheapen yourself and the Marine Corps.
- Slangy diction. Judiciously used, slang can be quite effective. But if you use slang indiscriminately, you lose your effect and grate on the audience's nerves.
- "Big words" and pedantry. Overuse of technical terms or of involved, long-winded constructions wraps your subject in a fog. Five-dollar words used merely for effect do not impress your listeners with anything but your stuffiness.

14-5. The officer, above all else, must be a skilled teacher and be able to communicate concepts at many levels of knowledge.

Make the most of your voice and body. Voice is your basic weapon. To exploit your voice, develop power, distinctness, and variety of delivery. Your body supports your voice through erect, confident posture, natural movement, meaningful gesture, and eye contact with every listener. Make it a rule to look every listener in the eye while you speak to a group.

1416. Public Affairs

Intelligent and candid relations with the public form an important part of every Marine's career, from private to general, regardless of specialty.

The Marine Corps has long benefited from an aggressive and positive public affairs program, in which attention is drawn to the mission, capabilities, and security that the nation derives from the Corps' existence. Public affairs specialists assist commanders in handling community and media relations to present and explain Marine Corps activities in order to broaden the public view of the Corps. In many cases, this means that prompt attention is paid to good and bad news so that the unsparing eye of the citizenry will see that the Corps measures up to the high standards of discipline, devotion to duty, individual smartness, and valor—hallmarks of the Corps.

In spite of your not being a public affairs specialist, know that your every action in public view will enhance or degrade the carefully won reputation the Corps enjoys today. The Corps' best advertisement is the individual Marine. Deal truthfully, pleasantly, and respectfully with the public and its media representation. Be aware of what the public affairs program has outlined for appropriate remarks to the press and public. The Corps belongs to the nation, and your individual contribution, however isolated, will only enhance public knowledge and appreciation.

The future success of the Marine Corps depends on two factors: first, an efficient performance of all the duties to which its officers and men may be assigned; second, promptly bringing this efficiency to the attention of the proper officials of the Government, and the American people.

—John A. Lejeune

When I give you the word, together we will cross the Line of Departure, close with those forces who choose to fight, and destroy them. Our fight is not with the Iraqi people, nor is it with members of the Iraqi army who choose to surrender. While we will move swiftly and aggressively against those who resist, we will treat all others with decency, demonstrating chivalry and soldierly compassion for people who have endured a lifetime under Saddam's oppression. . . . fight with a happy heart and a strong spirit. . . . carry out your mission and keep your honor clean.

— James N. Mattis, 2003

15

LEADERSHIP

Service—in peacetime, and especially in wartime—makes great demands on the mental, moral, and physical strength of the individual Marine. In battle, character traits weigh more heavily than intellectual acuity. Even in this age of highly developed technology, it is still humans who must stand the test. Leadership thus assumes extraordinary importance, for it convinces the Marine of the necessity of service and encourages faithful performance of duty. The Marine's readiness to serve and, in wartime, to risk his or her life closely relates to the integrity of the nation and the survival of its free and democratic order.

The foundations of an individual's performance as a Marine are discipline, courage, self-assurance, a sense of duty, and cooperative thinking. These qualities support the Marine as he or she endures hardships and strives to accomplish the mission. Establishing such foundations remains the salient objective of leadership. Of them, discipline plays the indispensable role in maintaining the combat power of a unit. Undisciplined behavior must be countered immediately and appropriately. In well-disciplined units, a sense of comradeship emerges, and soldierly values—such as confidence and unselfishness—predominate. It is the duty of commanders at all levels to gain the trust of subordinates and establish solidarity in their units. This is accomplished primarily through the demonstration of knowledge and wisdom, example, fairness, patience, and thoughtfulness, as well as through the administration of appropriate strictness.

Most destructive to comradeship are misguided ambition, selfishness, and insincerity. A unit that has grown together into a "band of brothers" will be able to withstand severe stress.

All leaders, regardless of their fields or styles of leadership, share one characteristic—confidence, in themselves and in their cause. A person gains self-confidence by surmounting difficulties through intelligence and judgment. That confidence transmits itself to others and is a source of inspiration to Marines serving under that individual. The leader also understands the obligation to look after those in the command. The more arduous their situation, the more intensely subordinates must feel that their commanders—their leaders—are vigilant on their behalf. Again, this relates to the feeling of comradeship that should pervade a unit, holding true up, down, and across the ranks. This is one reason it is nearly always a mistake to break up a unit, particularly in combat.

In wartime, troops face enormous psychological pressures brought on by the force of the weapons being used against them, by disruption of communications and isolation from other friendly forces, and by rumors planted by the enemy. The natural fear resulting from any of these causes can escalate into unrestrained, unreasoning, and self-destructive fear—panic. All signs of panic must be nipped in the bud by the commanding officer before losing influence over the troops. But before the situation reaches a point where a commanding officer must use drastic measures to quell the first signs of panic, he or she can follow a course of action that can help prevent it. By providing the unit with up-to-date, factual, and objective information and by reiterating that their fight is meaningful and their political and military leadership sound, the commander can psychologically equip the troops to withstand the pressures of war.

This chapter describes characteristics, techniques, and procedures that contribute to effective leadership. As you peruse these paragraphs (or any text on leadership), remember that the royal road to leadership is not merely to read, but rather to lead.

THE MARINE LEADER

1501. Attributes of a Marine Leader

Major General John A. Lejeune summarized the attributes of a Marine leader: "The young American responds quickly and readily to the exhibition of qualities of leadership on the part of his officers. Some of these qualities are industry, energy, initiative, determination, enthusiasm, firmness, kindness, justness, self-control, unselfishness, honor, and courage."

Although Lejeune's list can scarcely be improved, it is worth amplifying and explaining.

The contagion of example is the central thought in General Lejeune's passage. It is not enough that you merely know a leader's qualities and not enough that you proclaim them; you must *exhibit* them. To exact discipline, you must first possess self-discipline, and to demand unsparing attention to duty, you must spare none yourself.

15-1. Marine officers must offer their skills and knowledge in a tactful, understanding, and cooperative fashion to allies and officers of other services.

Much of the power of example, in turn, stems from "command presence," or the kind of military appearance you make. *Command presence* is the product of dignity, military carriage, firm and unhurried speech, and self-confidence. Command presence is one useful adjunct of leadership that can be systematically cultivated. "Spit and polish" alone should not be confused with command presence.

Resolution and tenacity—an unfaltering determination to achieve the mission assigned to you—are the fuel of leadership.

Ability to teach and speak usually denotes an effective leader and enhances whatever latent leadership talents you possess. Cultivate this gift at every opportunity. It is a lever that can decisively influence your career.

Protection and fostering of subordinates distinguish Marine Corps leadership. Leaders assume responsibility for their subordinates' actions (their mistakes, too) and see to it that credit is received where it is due. Leadership means looking out for your people.

Encouragement of subordinates is a tradition of Marine leadership. Give subordinates all the initiative and latitude they can handle. Encourage them in professional studies and reading. Make sure they seek professional schooling.

Professional competence may not make your Marines like you but will surely elicit their respect. "You can't snow the troops" is an old Marine saying. If you are professionally able, your enlisted Marines will be the first to get the word. Conversely, they will be mercilessly quick to spot a fraud. Demonstrate competence and keenness as an officer, and your Marines will be content to be led by you. Never be ashamed to be known as a "hard charger," as long as your aim is the best interest of the Corps.

Here is a classic remark by one of the Corps' hardest-charging generals, Graves B. Erskine: "The first thing, a man should know his business. He should know his weapons, he should know the tactics for those weapons, and he should not only be qualified for the grade he is assigned to, but at least for the next higher grade."

Education contributes to professional competence. Education and study give you technical proficiency, help you think clearly, enable you to express yourself, and command respect from all.

Physical readiness, though not an end in itself, is essential for every Marine and thus doubly so for every leader. Unless you can confidently face your physical fitness test, you are not fit for active command.

The *spirits of "can-do" and "make-do"* are as old as the Corps itself. To do the best you can with what you have, to do it promptly, cheerfully, and confidently, marks you as a leader in the best traditions of the Marine Corps. The world is divided into "can-do" and "can't-do" types. Be sure you are in the former class.

Adaptability marks a seasoned Marine. As a leader, keep loose; roll with the punches. Cultivate that most admirable trait, "grace under pressure."

Devotion to the Marine Corps and its standards begets equal earnestness and devotion from subordinates. Take the Marine Corps and its time-honored ways with full seriousness, and so will your command. That is the Marine Corps attitude.

As both summary and comment on the foregoing, here is a thought-provoking list of attributes. How do you measure up?

Serious	Competent	Inventive
Disciplined	Aggressive	Austere
Loyal	Knowledgeable	Purposeful
Authoritative	Tenacious	Compassionate
Courageous	Proud	Sensitive
Tough	Resolute	

Based on the views and example of one of the Marine Corps' foremost leaders, Lejeune, the foregoing is a somewhat historical but timeless discussion of leadership. It is meant to supplement, not supplant, formal teaching on leadership within the Marine Corps. Every Marine officer must also know, embrace, and embody the Corps' leadership traits: justice, judgment, dependability, integrity, decisiveness, tact, initiative, endurance, bearing, unselfishness, courage, knowledge, loyalty, and enthusiasm.

YOU AND YOUR SUBORDINATES

1502. Dealing with Subordinates

Whether your subordinates are officers or enlisted Marines, support and back them to the hilt. They will turn to you for encouragement, guidance, and support. Never let them down. Nothing should ever be "too much trouble" if it is needed for your outfit. Protect, shelter, and feed them before you think of your own needs.

Demand the highest standards and never let those standards be compromised. Field Marshall Erwin Rommel stated this in slightly different words: "A commander must accustom his staff to a high tempo from the outset, and continually keep them up to it. If he once allows himself to be satisfied with norms, or anything less than an all-out effort, he gives up the race from the starting post, and will sooner or later be taught a bitter lesson."

Live, lead, and exercise command "by the book." Let this be understood by your Marines.

Keep *responsibility* centralized—in you. Decentralize *authority*. Give subordinates wide authority and discretion. Tell them what results you want, and leave the "how" to them. Never oversupervise.

Avoid overfamiliarity of manner or address. If you have feet of clay—and most humans do have some weakness or character flaw—overfamiliarity with subordinates is the surest way to reveal it.

Develop genuine interest in your Marines as individuals. Study each personality. Seek out background information from service records. Learn names, and address your Marines by proper names. Never let any Marine picture himself or herself as "a mere cog" in the machine. No Marine is a cog.

In your daily exercise of command, avoid the "hurry-up-and-wait" tendency that characterizes ill-run commands. That is to say, think twice before you apply pressure to speed up something if the result is simply that your people will have to stand around waiting at some further stage. Do not get them out unduly ahead of time for formations and parades, especially if every other echelon has added its few minutes of anticipation, too. And always be on time and on schedule as far as you yourself are concerned. One of the most basic rules of military courtesy is to never keep the troops waiting.

Respect the skill and experience of your NCOs. Learn from the wisdom of NCOs, but never let them snow you. Do everything in your power to enhance the skill, prestige, and authority of NCOs, except at the expense of your own authority. In public, address NCOs by name and rank. In private, you may call them by their last names only. *Never address an enlisted person by his or her first name or nickname.*

Be accessible to any subordinate who wishes to see you. It is a tradition of the Corps that any enlisted Marine who desires an interview with the commanding officer must obtain the first sergeant's permission. It is equally a tradition of the Corps that permission is unhesitatingly given unless the Marine is drunk or flagrantly out of uniform. In connection with such requests, you should give your first sergeant direct and positive instructions that he or she must report to you, the commanding officer, every complaint received from an enlisted Marine. Most of these need never come to your attention otherwise or in any official form, but this rule helps to avert trouble before it becomes serious.

1503. Issuing and Enforcing Orders

"Promulgation of an order represents not over 10 per cent of your responsibility. The remaining 90 per cent consists in assuring through personal supervision on the ground, by yourself and your staff, proper and vigorous execution." So wrote General George S. Patton on the subject of orders. Issuing and enforcing orders constitute one of the main functions of an officer.

Before you issue an order, ask yourself if it can be reasonably carried out. If, in the circumstances, an order cannot be executed as given, it should not be given.

Never give an unlawful order—that is, an order that contravenes law or regulations or demands that your subordinates break the rules. A good test of a lawful order is, "Could a subordinate be court-martialed for failing to comply?"

Issue as few orders as necessary. Keep them concise, clear, and unmistakable in purpose. Anything that can be misunderstood, will be.

Never contravene the orders of another officer or NCO without clear and pressing reason. If possible, make this reason evident when you countermand the order in question. If orders to you conflict, seek guidance or obey the last one.

When you have once given an order, be sure it is executed as you give it. Your responsibility does not end until you have assured yourself that the order has been carried out. Never shrug off half-hearted, perfunctory compliance. "If anyone in a key position appears to be expending less than the energy that could properly be demanded of him," wrote Rommel, "that man must be ruthlessly removed."

An order received from above should be passed on as your order and should be enforced as such. Never evade the onus of an unpopular directive by throwing the blame on the next higher echelon.

15-2. The peculiarities of aircrew and flight leadership place special demands on officers in aviation fields.

It cannot be too often repeated that when you issue an order, make clear what you want done and who is to do it—but avoid telling subordinates how it is to be done. Remember the old promotion examination question for lieutenants, in which the student is told that he or she has a ten-person working party, headed by a sergeant, and must erect a seventy-five-foot flagpole on the post parade ground. Problem—How to do it? Every student who works out the precise calculations of stresses, tackle, and gear, no matter how accurately, is graded wrong. The desired answer is simple: The lieutenant turns to the sergeant and says, "Sergeant, put up that flagpole."

1504. "R.H.I.P."

As an officer, you are generally entitled to take precedence ahead of your juniors and all enlisted persons. This privilege is admitted in the service proverb "Rank has its privileges," or R.H.I.P. Just when and where you "pull rank," though, is a matter of some delicacy.

Generally speaking, you should assert your privilege when your time is circumscribed by duty or when failure to do so would demean your status as a commissioned officer. For example, an officer should not waste his or her own time and the government's by falling in line behind privates in a clothing storeroom or hesitate to claim the attention of an administrative functionary hemmed in by enlisted persons. Conversely, in situations where all persons are equal, take your place with the others regardless of rank. In the mess, at the barber shop (unless there is an officer's chair), at the post exchange, or at games, avoid taking advantage of rank.

Finally, every Marine officer pulls rank in reverse when it comes to looking out for the troops. In the field, before you yourself eat, every enlisted Marine must have had a full ration. Before you take shelter, your Marines must have shelter. "There is no fatigue the soldiers go through," said Baron Friedrich von Steuben in 1779, "that the officers should not share."

MILITARY DISCIPLINE

1505. The Object and Nature of Discipline

Effective performance by Marines in combat is the direct result and primary object of military discipline. Discipline may be defined as prompt and willing responsiveness to orders and unhesitating compliance with regulations. Since the ultimate objective of discipline is effective performance in battle, discipline may in a very real sense spell the difference between life and death (or, more important to the Marine, between victory and defeat). It is that standard of deportment, attention to duty, example, and decent behavior that, once indoctrinated, enables Marines, alone or in groups, to accomplish their missions.

To many persons, discipline simply means punishment. In fact, discipline is a matter of people working well together and getting along well together—and, even if there be a lack of harmony among them, discipline is a means of cementing them as a fighting organization. In the Marine Corps, as in any military organization, it is necessary for people to do certain things in prescribed ways and at given times. If they do so, we say they are well disciplined.

Discipline exists in everyday life: people obey traffic lights, pay greens fees, go in through marked entrances and out through exits. Nevertheless, military discipline differs fundamentally from the disciplines of civilian life, because a Marine, having taken an oath to serve an allotted time, is committed to his or

15-3. Marine leaders command from the front of their units, share hardships, and demand the utmost efforts of their subordinates.

her duty while a civilian worker is free to quit a job at any time. For this reason, "management," a popular word in the civilian sector, is an impoverished one in military circles compared with "leadership."

1506. The Basis of Discipline

The best discipline is self-discipline. To be really well disciplined, a unit must be made up of individuals who are self-disciplined. In the ultimate test of combat, the leader must be able to depend on the Marines to do their duty correctly and voluntarily whether anyone is checking on them or not. If time and the situation permit, you should make known to your subordinates the reasons for a given order because this knowledge will increase the desire of your people to do the job and will enable them to do it intelligently. You must know what you want of your people, let them know, and then demand it of them.

1507. Characteristics of Effective Discipline

Until severely tried, there is no conclusive test of discipline. Troops remain relatively undisciplined until physically and mentally exerted (a fact that shapes much of the programs of recruit and officer training). No body of troops could possibly enjoy the dust, the heat, the blistered foot, and the aching back of a road march. Nevertheless, hard road marching is a necessary and sound foundation for the discipline of combat troops. The rise in spirit within any unit, which is always marked when Marines rebound from a hard march or after a record day, does not come from a feeling of physical relief but from a sense of accomplishment.

Another key factor in sound discipline is consistency and firmness. You cannot wink at an infraction one day and put a person on the report for the same offense tomorrow. You must establish and make known your standards of good discipline, and be consistent—firmly consistent—every day.

Discipline imposed by fear of punishment will inevitably break down in combat or any other severe test. If you threaten your troops, discipline will also break. Discipline will not break under stress, however, if troops understand why they are enduring hardship and danger.

PRAISE AND REPRIMAND

1508. Occasions for Praise

A basic rule is to *praise in public and reprimand in private.*

Never let a praiseworthy occasion pass unmentioned. This means more than the occasional back-pat. Here are ways in which you can make the most of opportunities to praise subordinates.

Promotion. When an officer is promoted (although regulations no longer so require), he or she should be sworn in at Office Hours (see Section 1510) by the senior Marine officer present. Administration of the oath adds greatly to the solemnity of the occasion and enables the officer to reaffirm the original oath taken on receiving his or her first commission. If practical, the spouse and children should be invited. All fellow officers who can be spared should attend.

The officer administering the oath should always give a set of insignia to the individual being promoted—if possible, a set of his or her own insignia from an earlier rank, a gift that is always appreciated.

Enlisted promotions are effected by presentation of the individual's warrant for the next higher rank. This should be accomplished at a formation. If a parade or other formation cannot be arranged, the person should receive the warrant from the commanding officer at Office Hours, in the presence of his or her immediate commanding officer and first sergeant. If enlisted offenders are to appear at the same Office Hours, parade them in the rear, in order to give them occasion to reflect on "the other side of the coin."

Under no circumstances should a Marine be called into the company office and receive the warrant from the first sergeant or clerk. This is the wrong way and reflects directly on you if you permit such procedures.

Reenlistment. When a number of Marines ship over on the same day, arrange a formation in their honor. Otherwise, individuals should be shipped over at Office Hours. If practical, make this the occasion for a day off—and, if warranted and possible, there is no better moment to effect a promotion. Nothing starts a new cruise so handsomely as another chevron.

Presentation of Decorations. The *Marine Corps Drill and Ceremonies Manual* describes the ceremony for presenting decorations. Even at some inconvenience to the unit, decorations—particularly those earned in combat or awarded for heroic action—should be presented with utmost formality at a parade or review, as laid down in the book. Avoid the easy solution of calling in the Marine to Office Hours and presenting the medal with a handshake. The fundamental purpose of awards is to inspire emulation. To do this, you must present medals or commendations in the presence of all members of the command or unit.

A modified version of the awards ceremony can serve equally well for such occasions as presentation of Good Conduct Medals, civilian commendations, commissioning of meritorious NCOs as warrant officers or second lieutenants, and so on.

In combat, when an award can be made immediately, it is sometimes effective for a senior commander to visit the recipient at the unit, call together comrades, and give the medal on the spot. With decorations, even more than other rewards, "he gives thrice who gives quickly." As a combat leader, be alert for every deserving act, especially by an enlisted Marine. Know the criteria and

Marine Corps standards for every award, and how to initiate proper recommendations (see Section 1038).

Retirement. The honorable retirement or transfer to the Reserve of any officer or enlisted Marine should be habitually effected at a parade or review. In the case of an officer, it is also appropriate for the officers of the unit to "dine out" at a mess night, as described in Section 2203.

Completion of Distance Learning Course. Any Marine who completes a distance learning course should receive the diploma from the commanding officer at Office Hours or formation.

1509. Reprimand

One basic rule of reprimand has already been stated—*do it in private.*

A second rule is found in the Marine proverb: "Never give a Marine a dollar's worth of blame without a dime's worth of praise," which is to say that it can useful, when feasible, to begin and end a reprimand on a positive note.

And avoid collective reprimands, let alone collective punishments. Nothing so rightly infuriates an innocent person as to be unfairly included in an all-hands blast or all-hands punishment.

Before you issue reprimand or censure, be sure that an offense or dereliction of some kind has been committed. This is basic. You cannot call down a Marine just because you do not like "the color of his or her eyes." Before chastising any individual, ask yourself if what that person has done, pushed to the limit, would sustain charges under any article in the Uniform Code of Military Justice. This can save you much embarrassment and injured innocence at the hands of sea-lawyers, while it sometimes cuts the other way to protect a subordinate against hasty rebuke when not warranted.

Know what you intend to say before you launch into reprimand. A sputtering, inconclusive rebuke only makes an officer look silly.

Avoid uncontrolled anger, profanity, or abuse. Many experienced Marines, both officer and NCO, know how to vent anger into indignation. Make this your object but at all costs avoid "acting tough."

Never make a promise or threat that you are not capable of fulfilling, or that you do not intend to fulfill. Never bluff, or you will be called in short order.

Like reward, the effectiveness of admonishment is in direct proportion to its immediacy. When you spot something amiss, take corrective action at once.

Never let a wrongdoing Marine slide by with the thought, "Well, he/she is not one of my troops. Let his/her own outfit handle it." *Every* U.S. Marine is one of *your* troops.

If you have occasion to correct a Marine not under your command, find out who the Marine is and see that his or her commanding officer knows about it. This will be appreciated by the CO who is just as anxious as you are to have his or her Marines up to snuff. Moreover, the derelictions of an individual are the responsibility of the immediate senior. A Marine with a dirty rifle is a black eye for the squad and fire-team leader; a Marine in your platoon who fails to salute is a discredit to your leadership. Napoleon's dictum, "There are no bad regiments—only bad colonels," applies with equal force to fire teams, squads, platoons, companies, and battalions as well.

1510. Office Hours

Office Hours, the Marine Corps equivalent of Captain's Mast, is the occasion when the commanding officer awards formal praise or blame, hears special requests, and awards nonjudicial punishment. As pertains to military justice, detailed treatment of Office Hours procedure and nonjudicial punishment is contained in Chapter 20.

Remember that Office Hours is a ceremony, and that much of the desired effect depends upon the manner in which it is conducted. And when you hold Office Hours, do so with the greatest respect for each person's individuality. Not only must the punishment fit the crime, it must fit the person. Never let anyone leave Office Hours with a sense of injustice or frustrated misunderstanding.

A special and important variation of Office Hours is Request Mast, an occasion set aside for individuals who may have special requests or grievances that they wish to present to the commanding officer. It is one of the responsibilities of command to keep this opportunity open to any Marine who, *in good faith,* wishes to utilize it. In holding Request Mast, one important point to remember is that the individual is entitled to complete privacy. Unless requested otherwise, you should see Marines alone, and should take all necessary steps to avoid any prejudice to their interests that might arise out of a bona fide complaint or special request.

INSPECTIONS

1511. Inspections

Inspections are one of the most important tools of leadership and command. Throughout your Marine Corps career, you will be continually inspected or inspecting. Inspections serve two purposes: first, to enable commanding or superior officers to find out conditions within an organization; and second, to impart to an organization the standards required of it.

There are several types of inspection, varying from inspection of personnel in ranks to inspections of matériel, supplies, equipment, records, and buildings. Each inspection has a particular purpose, which the inspecting officer will keep foremost in mind. Thus, it is up to you to ascertain or forecast the object of the inspection and to prepare yourself and your command accordingly. For example, if the inspection is to deal with the crew-served weapons and transportation in your unit, it does no great good to emphasize clean uniforms and haircuts at the expense of matériel upkeep. On the other hand, good-looking vehicles do not excuse greasy, worn clothing at a personnel inspection.

1512. Preparation for Inspection

Once you know the purpose of an inspection, you must prepare your outfit. The best way to do this is by putting yourself in the inspector's shoes. Be sure your leading NCOs also understand the "why" of the inspection so that they can cooperate intelligently in "getting tuned to concert pitch." Many an inspection crisis has been averted by a quick-witted, loyal NCO with a ready answer.

While your unit prepares for inspection, move about with a leading NCO, usually your police sergeant and/or first sergeant depending on the nature of the inspection. This enables you to see that preparations are what you want, and it reminds your people that you have direct interest in the hard work they are engaged in. It also lets you discover weak spots in good time.

Time preparation for inspection so that everything is ready about thirty minutes before the appointed hour. This gives your Marines a final opportunity to get themselves ready. It also gives you a margin to handle last-minute emergencies.

Ten minutes beforehand, have your responsible subordinates standing by their respective posts, or, if the inspection is to be in formation, have your troops paraded, steady and correct. You yourself should be either at the head of them or at the entrance to your area, poised to meet the inspecting party. As a platoon leader, you should have your platoon sergeant and guide assist you in the inspection. If you are the company commander, you should have your first sergeant and gunnery sergeant in your inspection party. One of these NCOs should have a notebook and pencil ready to take notes. The police sergeant should have a flashlight. All rooms, compartments, sheds, and so forth should be unlocked and open.

When the inspecting party arrives, salute and report your unit prepared for inspection. Post yourself at the left rear of the inspecting officer. Answer questions calmly and with good humor. Avoid alibis. Remember, there is only one inspector and you should take no actions or make comments yourself, except to attend the inspector. Do not reprimand your troops during inspection for shortcomings the inspection brings out. It is your outfit; the shortcomings are yours. Be alert for the inspecting officer's comments. These prepare you for the next inspection.

Afterward, if results have been notably good or notably poor, assemble your people and tell them about it. Give every Marine a personal stake in the success of each inspection.

1513. Conduct of the Inspection

Nothing else can raise the standards of a command like an intelligent program of inspection, carefully followed up. Some officers unwisely discount the value of formal inspections, saying that they result in unbalanced, artificial impressions, and that COs ought to observe informally in order to find out "real" conditions. While it is certainly true that every CO must keep on the move and keep his or her eyes open, the periodic formal inspection is vital because it requires all hands to overhaul their areas of responsibility. Moreover, formal inspection is the only way to determine accurately the degree of progress being made by a unit.

Before conducting an inspection, you, like the unit being inspected, must also make careful preparations. There are at least seven considerations that should guide every inspector:

1. Know what you intend to concentrate on—in other words, the purpose of the inspection.

2. Have a planned route and sequence of inspection designed to cover the entire unit and area.
3. Organize your inspecting party. This should include one Marine to take notes, one with flashlight, plus the requisite specialist talent (such as hospital corpsman, technicians, and so forth) needed to advise and assist.
4. See that you and your party are perfectly turned out and neatly uniformed. Inspections also operate in reverse.
5. Be up to date on details of maintenance and function of any matériel you are to inspect. If matériel is on the program, leaf through the appropriate technical manual, which will contain a checklist for inspection. Become familiar with the nomenclature, functioning, and maintenance indicators associated with the equipment. When you inspect, do so impartially and pleasantly. Avoid a fault-finding spirit; the object of inspections is to help and inform, not to antagonize. Praise individuals when you properly can. As you uncover defects, be sure that the responsible individuals understand what you have discovered and why it constitutes a defect.
6. Inspect yourself. Never walk in front of another Marine to inspect at less than your best. The Marines you look at are inspected once, by you. All of them, on the other hand, inspect you as you pass down the ranks. Do not be found lacking.
7. Inspect in cadence and at attention. Have a leading NCO—sergeant major or first sergeant—precede you.

Finally, regardless of the purpose of the inspection, never overlook the individual Marine. See that he or she is smart and military. Look the Marine in the eye. Make the Marine feel that he or she is the ultimate object, and that you are deeply interested in him or her as a person and a Marine.

1514. Inspection Follow-up

An inspection loses value if you fail to follow it up. This is the main reason for keeping careful notes on the comments of the inspecting officer.

Inspection notes should be disseminated to everyone concerned, broken down into items for corrective action, so that they can serve as a checklist. When you reinspect, review previous inspection notes as a guide for follow-up. On the receiving end, you can use past notes to prepare for future occasions. It is a grave reflection on you as a leader if the same defects continue to show up on consecutive inspections.

1515. IG Inspections

Via the long-standing previous title, "the adjutant and inspector," the inspector general of the Corps can trace roots back to 1798. Today, the IG's job is to assist and examine by periodic inspections the effectiveness of Marine Corps commands in terms of ability to carry out their missions; unit leadership, economy, policies, and doctrine; work and health conditions; and discipline.

After a visit to a command by an IG team, one of three grades is awarded: satisfactory, noteworthy, and unsatisfactory. Although it may seem difficult for a unit under such searching inspection to believe, the IG is there to help: inspections are always a search for causes, not an inventory of symptoms.

OTHER ASPECTS OF LEADERSHIP

1516. Weapons Proficiency

A Marine leader has few better ways of setting the right example to his or her troops than by maintaining high proficiency with infantry weapons—notably, the rifle and pistol. Marines respect a good shot and an officer who is handy with small arms. Do your best each year when you go to the range. Every enlisted Marine will be watching to see how you do. Make yourself a model of marksmanship technique. Demand no special favors: behind a rifle, on the firing line, all Marines are equals. Clean and maintain your own weapon, pick up your own brass, keep your own scorebook, and keep your mouth shut.

Never violate a safety precaution. Remember the shooter's proverb: "There is no such thing as an accidental discharge."

Although you will never match your best enlisted Marines, seek knowledge and skill in firing and employing crew-served weapons, such as machine guns and assault and antitank weapons.

1517. Looking Out for Your Marines

In the final analysis, the essence of Marine leadership is looking out for your people.

For the sake of your unit, you must be tireless, you must be imaginative, you must be willing to shoulder responsibility. Their well-being must be your first preoccupation. Their interest and advancement must be always on your mind. Looking out for your Marines demands that you hold several questions foremost in your mind:

- Are they comfortably clothed, housed, and sheltered?
- Are they well fed?
- Are they getting their mail?
- Is their pay timely and accurate?
- If sick and wounded, can they rely on help?
- Are they justly treated?
- Are they trained to accomplish their mission?
- Are you available to everyone who needs counsel?
- Are you alert to help each one in his or her career?

As an officer, you demand a great deal of your Marines. But they, in fact, demand much more of you. If you let down one of your Marines, you are letting down the entire Corps.

The general must know how to get his men their rations and every other kind of stores needed in war. He must have imagination to originate plans, practical sense and energy to carry them through. He must be observant, untiring, shrewd, kindly and cruel, simple and crafty, a watchman and a robber, lavish and miserly, generous and stingy, rash and conservative. All these and many other qualities, natural and acquired, must he have. He should also, as a matter of course, know his tactics; for a disorderly mob is no more an army than a heap of building materials is a house.

—Socrates

For if the trumpet give an uncertain sound, who shall prepare himself to the battle?

—I Corinthians 14:8

16

ON WATCH

One of the most stirring guard orders ever received by U.S. Marines was issued on 11 November 1921 by Navy Secretary Edwin Denby, himself a former Marine. The nation was in the grip of a crime wave, which had been highlighted by armed robberies of the U.S. Mail. Four days before Secretary Denby penned his letter of instruction, the president had directed that the Marine Corps take over the job of safeguarding the mail, and fifty-three officers and twenty-two hundred enlisted Marines were already on watch in post offices, railway mail cars, and postal trucks throughout the country. "To the Men of the Mail Guard," wrote Edwin Denby:

> I am proud that my old Corps has been chosen for a duty so honorable as that of protecting the United States mail. I am very anxious that you shall successfully accomplish your mission. It is not going to be easy work. It will always be dangerous and generally tiresome. You know how to do it. Be sure you do it well. I know you will neither fear nor shirk any duty, however hazardous or exacting.
>
> This particular work will lack the excitement and glamor of war duty, but it will be no less important. It has the same element of service to the country.
>
> I look with proud confidence to you to show now the qualities that have made the Corps so well-beloved by our fellow citizens.

> You must be brave, as you always are. You must be constantly alert. You must, when on guard duty, keep your weapons in hand and, if attacked, shoot and shoot to kill. There is no compromise in this battle with the bandits.
>
> If two Marines, guarding a mail car, are suddenly covered by a robber, neither must hold up his hands, but both must begin shooting at once. One may be killed, but the other will get the robber and save the mail. When our men go in as guards over mail, that mail must be delivered or there must be a Marine dead at the post of duty.
>
> To be sure of success, every Marine on this duty must be watchful as a cat, hour after hour, night after night, week after week. No Marine must drink a drop of intoxicating liquor. Every Marine must be most careful with whom he associates and what his occupations are off duty. There may be many tricks tried to get you, and you must not be tricked. Look out for women. Never discuss the details of your duty with outsiders. Never give up to another the trust you are charged with.
>
> Never forget that the honor of the Corps is in your keeping. You have been given a great trust. I am confident you will prove that it has not been misplaced.
>
> I am proud of you and believe in you with all my heart.
>
> /s/ Edwin Denby

Mail robberies ceased within a matter of days after Secretary Denby penned his order, and not a single piece of mail was lost to a robber while Marines stood watch.

1601. Watchstanding

The Importance of Guard Duty. In the Marine Corps and Navy, the safety and good order of the entire command depend on those who stand guard. Thus, watchstanding is your strictest routine duty. The importance of guard duty is underscored by the fact that sleeping on watch can be punished by death in time of war and by heavy penalties in peacetime.

In addition to combat missions, the Marine Corps is the combat security force for the naval establishment and is thus responsible for the good order and protection not only of its own bases and stations but also, when assigned (see Section 614), of naval stations and vessels. As a Marine officer, you are therefore expected to be an authority on watchstanding and guard duty, as well as a model watch officer, ashore or afloat.

The Corps' motto, *Semper Fidelis*, never demands more than when you are on guard. Marines maintain four kinds of guard: an exterior guard ashore, an interior guard ashore, a ship's guard afloat, and special guards.

An *exterior guard* is maintained only in combat or when danger of attack exists. An exterior guard protects the command against outside attack and is organized and armed according to the tactical situation.

Interior guards have the fourfold mission of protecting life, preserving order, enforcing regulations, and safeguarding public property.

Ships' guards carry out the same general missions afloat as interior guards do ashore but differ in details of organization and duty because of shipboard conditions.

Special guards include all guards organized for special purposes (for example, train or boat guards and so on). Additionally, most posts having custody of special weapons have a separate main guard for that purpose alone, leaving other normal security functions at the installation to the main guard.

In addition, Marines frequently perform military police and shore patrol duties for the regulation and assistance of Marines and sailors on liberty.

Status of Marines on Watch. Any Marine on guard, whether officer or enlisted, represents the commanding officer. In the execution of orders or the enforcement of regulations, the Marine guard's authority is complete. When you receive a lawful order from a member of the guard, comply without hesitation and ask your questions afterward. Remember that an armed sentry has full authority to enforce instructions.

THE INTERIOR GUARD

1602. The Interior Guard

The interior guard—established to protect life, preserve order, enforce regulations, and safeguard public property—derives its authority directly from the commanding officer. Figure 16-1 shows the organization of a typical interior guard. The guard comprises a main guard and, when needed, special guards.

1603. Duties of the Guard

The duties of the guard (and the CO's responsibilities in connection with the guard) are as follows.

The commanding officer establishes the guard and sees that it functions properly. Either the CO or a representative (usually the executive officer or adjutant) receives the daily reports from, and relieves, the officers of the day, examines the guard book, and issues whatever special instructions may be needed.

The *staff duty officer* (or, in some places, command duty officer) may be required at a large organization or installation where subordinate or tenant commands maintain separate guards. The staff duty officer coordinates subordinate guards and acts for the commander in an emergency.

The *officer of the day* (OD) supervises the main guard, executes all orders that pertain to the guard, and is responsible that the guard performs effectively. While officer of the day, you are the direct representative of the commanding officer.

The *commander of the guard,* a staff NCO, is responsible for the proper instruction, discipline, and performance of the guard. A commander of the guard is usually required only for a large guard.

The *sergeant of the guard,* whatever his or her actual rank, is the senior NCO of the guard. The sergeant of the guard assists the commander of the guard, or, if the guard does not include one, performs the latter's duties. The sergeant of the guard supervises the enlisted members of the guard and is responsible for government property charged to the guard.

Nonrated members of the guard are organized into three reliefs, each of which includes a sentinel for each post and one supernumerary and is commanded by a *corporal of the guard.* The corporal of the guard instructs and supervises the relief, which takes its successive turn on guard throughout the tour of duty.

1604. Duties and General Orders for Sentinels

The sentry is the workhorse of the guard. The universal respect accorded a U.S. Marine sentinel is based on that person's high military efficiency and the fact that he or she is habitually armed and prepared to defend his or her post and person in the execution of orders. A sentinel's duties are to carry out the general

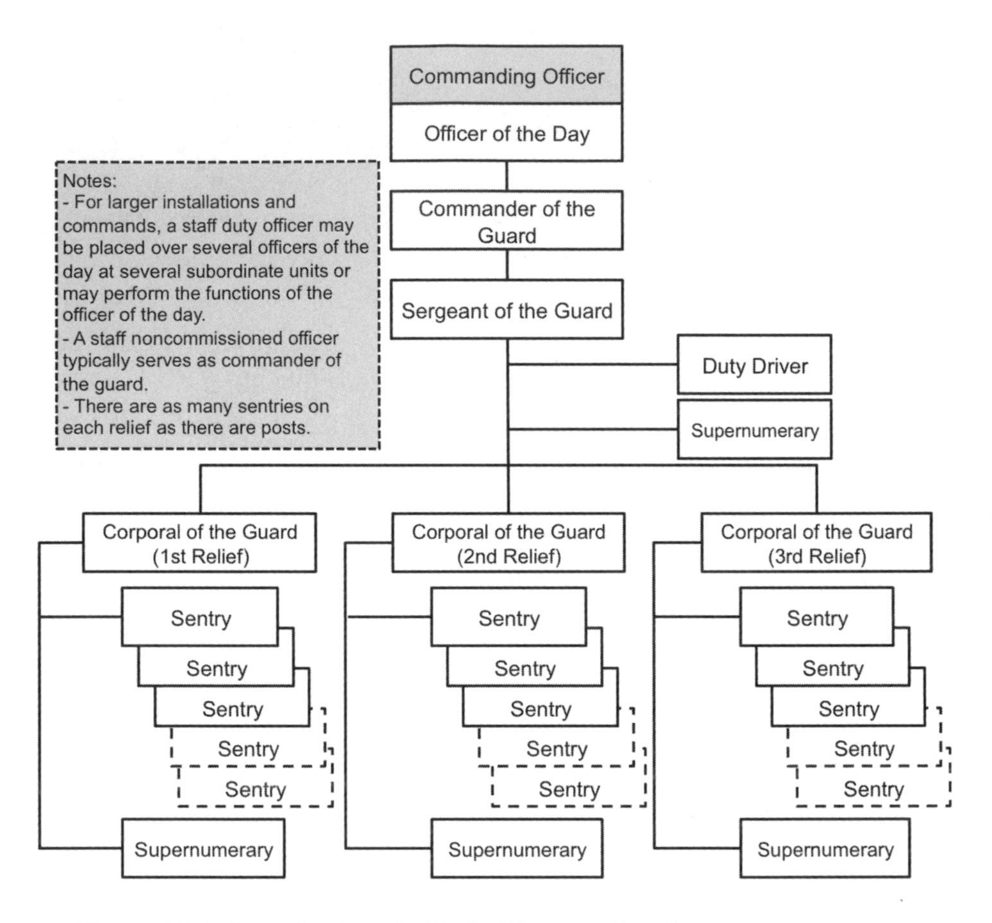

Figure 16-1. Organization of a Typical Interior Guard

orders for a sentinel on post, as well as special orders applicable to the particular post. Every Marine, officer or enlisted, must know the eleven general orders by heart:

1. To take charge of this post and all government property in view.
2. To walk my post in a military manner, keeping always on the alert, and observing everything that takes place within sight or hearing.
3. To report all violations of orders I am instructed to enforce.
4. To repeat all calls from posts more distant from the guardhouse than my own.
5. To quit my post only when properly relieved.

6. To receive, obey, and pass on to the sentry who relieves me, all orders from the commanding officer, officer of the day, and officers and non-commissioned officers of the guard only.
7. To talk to no one except in line of duty.
8. To give the alarm in case of fire or disorder.
9. To call the corporal of the guard in any case not covered by instructions.
10. To salute all officers, and all Colors and Standards not cased.
11. To be especially watchful at night, and, during the time for challenging, to challenge all persons on or near my post, and to allow no one to pass without proper authority.

In addition to routine sentry duties, nonrated members of the guard are assigned to certain special duties, such as the following.

Guardhouse Sentinel (Post No. 1). If one is assigned, the sentinel assists the corporal of the guard in carrying on guardhouse routine. Your guardhouse sentinel should be picked for intelligence, reliability, and smartness.

Main Gate Sentinel. This sentinel ensures that only authorized persons enter or leave the post through the main gate; he or she also directs traffic and assists visitors. Your main gate sentry stands watch in the show window of the station; therefore, select the sentry for soldierly appearance, judgment, and thorough knowledge of the post. The main gate is a spot for outstanding Marines.

Supernumerary. One additional sentry stands by as a supernumerary to replace anyone who must be relieved. The supernumerary can be kept busy as a messenger and general assistant in the guardhouse.

Driver. A motor transport operator or licensed incidental driver is assigned to the guard to drive the guard vehicle. Always keep the driver up to standard in uniform and appearance; it is a notorious and shameful failing among guard drivers to lag behind the rest of the guard in this respect.

The general policy of the Marine Corps is that all sentries will be armed. Detailed safety instructions, as well as restrictions on the use of the weapon, should be known to all members of the guard, from OD to sentry. Improper or careless use of firearms is an extremely serious matter.

The security environment both at home and abroad is markedly more complex today with the expanded reach of international criminal and terrorist organizations; advent of so-called lone wolves, often inspired by ideologies spread by social media; and proliferation of advanced technology and increasingly lethal weaponry. Although certainly not the only novel security challenge in this environment, the active shooter is of particular concern to members of an interior guard who may be first on the scene. An active shooter is an individual actively engaged in killing or attempting to kill people in a populated area, such as on a base or station. Sentries must be well trained to identify an active shooter situation, take appropriate immediate action, and coordinate with specialized response teams, if any, when they arrive. For such situations, vigilance, clear procedures, and thorough training are keys to their successful resolution.

1605. Daily Guard Routine

The daily routine of an interior guard varies somewhat according to the wishes of the commanding officer and the size and missions of the post. But, in the main, guard duty runs as follows.

The normal tour is twenty-four hours. Anyone detailed for guard duty must be on board and fit for duty at least four hours before commencement of the tour.

Details for guard duty should be published well in advance, by written order, and should specify uniform and equipment, together with any other information not covered in standing orders. *Officers detailed for guard duty must be notified in person or by written order, preferably both.* This is the adjutant's responsibility. The adjutant also keeps the officer-of-the-day roster, which determines the order in which officers stand watch.

A tour on guard begins in formal situations with *guard mounting,* when the old (outgoing) and new (incoming) guards are paraded and inspected. After guard mount, old and new officers of the day and sergeants of the guard relieve each other, whereupon the officers of the day report to the commanding officer, and the new officer of the day assumes duty.

The guard's routine includes execution of Colors, posting and relief of sentinels, supervision of meal formations, and rendition of honors to the commanding officer, visiting officers, and civilian dignitaries.

Each relief normally stands watch for four hours before turning over to the next relief. Thus, in a twenty-four-hour tour, each relief stands a total of eight hours on watch—four by day and four by night.

1606. Challenging and Countersign

"Halt! Who goes there?" the traditional *challenge*, has been employed by Marines since 1775. As an officer, you should know exactly how to challenge and reply because a faulty challenge or reply may not only embarrass you but in combat can also cost one's life.

The challenge is used at night or in low visibility to identify anyone approaching a sentinel.

On hearing any suspicious noise, the sentinel brings his or her weapon to a ready position and commands, "Halt! Who goes there?" The person challenged halts and then identifies himself or herself either by a password or by some such answer as "Friend" or "Officer of the day." The sentinel replies, "Advance, friend, and be recognized." The person is allowed to approach near enough to the sentinel to be recognized and is halted again, at which time the sentinel examines the person. When satisfied, the sentinel commands, "Pass, friend"; or, if being visited by the officer of the day, reports, "Post Number *X* secure, sir/ma'am."

It is extremely important, not only as military etiquette, but for your own safety, to reply audibly and promptly when challenged and to comply exactly with the sentry's orders. The sentry is the person behind the weapon. You are in front of it.

Challenge and countersign (sometimes called the "password") are used to distinguish between friend and enemy. In the use of this procedure, which takes place only when prescribed by the commanding officer, the person or party approaching a sentry is challenged in the usual way, as described above. Then, after advancing the person for recognition, the sentry repeats the secret challenge, an agreed code word to which the person being challenged must respond with the countersign, a second code word that validates the reply. Challenge and countersign change daily and must be kept from the enemy at all costs.

OFFICER OF THE DAY AND COMMANDER OF THE GUARD

1607. Officer of the Day

Because OD duties will take up much of your energies as a company officer, this section discusses the responsibilities of that job. In addition to what you read here, however, you must be thoroughly familiar with the *Interior Guard Manual*, as well as base, station, and unit standing orders that deal with guard duty.

1608. Duties of the Officer of the Day

As officer of the day, you must attend to several routine duties. More important, however, as the CO's representative, you must be ready to act promptly and sensibly in any contingency not covered by the letter of your orders.

Inspect each relief of the guard by visiting sentinels at least once while that relief is on post. One inspection must take place between midnight and reveille. When visiting sentinels, cover the following points:

- Verify that the sentinel is on post, alert, in correct uniform, and correctly armed and equipped.
- Question the sentinel on special orders, checking particularly that the sentinel knows the limits and designation of the post; the location of fire-fighting gear on the post, and how to sound a fire alarm; any recent changes in special orders for his or her post; the reason the post is required; and restrictions, if any, on use of a weapon.
- Verify that the sentinel knows verbatim, and understands, the general orders for sentinels. Have the sentinel repeat several and explain them in his or her own words.

Supervise and coordinate the inspections to be made by your commander of the guard and sergeant of the guard. See that these do not conflict with or duplicate yours.

Take immediate steps, in an emergency, to protect life and public property and to preserve order. As soon as the situation permits, report what has happened and what you are doing about it to the commanding officer (or to the executive officer, or staff duty officer if your command has one).

Always inform the guard where you can be reached when not in the guardhouse. If possible, leave a telephone extension.

Abstain from alcohol throughout your tour.

Unless otherwise authorized, *remain fully clothed* at all times. This enables you to turn out immediately in case of fire or other emergency. Nothing can get an OD into more trouble than arriving late and drowsy at the scene of trouble.

Inspect galleys and messes, in accordance with local orders, at each meal during your watch.

Finally, *review the OD logbook before guard mount and correct any mistakes.* In it, log the times when you visited sentries, together with any other information you think proper to place on record. Then attest to the correctness of the entire report by signing the logbook, which constitutes your official report.

1609. Relieving as Officer of the Day

After guard mount, old and new officers of the day both report to the executive officer (or another staff officer as designated by command policy) for relief and posting.

March in, at attention, covered and wearing side arms (as prescribed by command policy), and halt in front of the executive officer (old officer of the day on the right). You both salute together. Thereupon the old OD says, "Sir/Ma'am, Lieutenant Smith reports as old officer of the day," and hands the logbook to the XO. The latter reads the report, asks any questions that come to mind, and comments as necessary. Then the XO informs the old officer of the day, "You are relieved." Thereupon the old OD salutes and withdraws. Then the new officer of the day again salutes, and says, "Sir/Ma'am, Lieutenant Jones reports as new officer of the day." The executive officer gives the new officer of the day instructions, whereupon the latter salutes and withdraws.

All movements during relief and posting as officer of the day are carried out at attention and in cadence. If an emergency strikes between guard mount and the time when you report to the XO, the senior of the two ODs takes charge of both guards, old and new.

1610. Duties of the Commander of the Guard

As you have seen, the duties of commander of the guard are carried out by the sergeant of the guard if no separate commander of the guard is detailed. Regardless of whether performed by a staff NCO or an NCO, the duties listed here constitute a useful checklist by which, as officer of the day, you can ensure that your guard is running smoothly. The commander of the guard:

- Informs the officer of the day of any orders that have come from anyone other than the OD and passes on to his or her relief all instructions and current information
- Sees that the guard is properly instructed and that it performs properly
- Ensures that the guard performs its duties with the prescribed uniforms and equipment

- Makes certain that all inspections (by both the commander or the guard and sergeant of the guard) are carried out on time and as directed by the OD
- Sees that sentinels are relieved, Colors executed, the proper bugle calls sounded, bells struck, and guard routine followed
- Ensures that legible copies of general and special orders for each post are mounted both in the guardhouse and under shelter on each post
- Inspects guardhouse and brig thoroughly at least once during your tour
- Inspects each relief of the guard while it is on post and, just as the officer of the day, makes one inspection of sentinels between midnight and reveille
- Parades the guard for inspections as required
- Reports to the officer of the day if any member of the guard takes sick, quits his or her post, or has to be relieved for any reason
- In emergency, turns out the guard, sounds the appropriate call or alarm, and promptly notifies the officer of the day
- Detains any suspicious persons, reporting the circumstances to the OD
- Writes his or her report in the guard book and, at the end of the tour of duty, presents the logbook to the OD.

Additionally, the commander of the guard must send help immediately if any sentry calls, "The guard!" This is the SOS for a sentinel on post.

Duties relating to Colors are traditionally of sacred importance. The commander of the guard must make up the details to execute Morning and Evening Colors, attend Colors to be certain that this ceremony is correctly performed, and ensure that the Colors are properly stowed and are handled only in performance of duty (see Sections 1117 and 1118). Additionally, he or she must report to the OD if a set of Colors is unserviceable.

Finally, like the officer of the day, the commander of the guard must also keep the guard informed of his or her whereabouts whenever out of the guardhouse—if possible, by providing a telephone number.

1611. Hints for the Officer of the Day

Of all officers, you are the one who can least tolerate any discrepancy or violation of orders. *Never overlook a dereliction or infraction*, however minor. Be especially alert for:

- Unmilitary behavior
- Marines out of uniform
- Traffic offenders
- Safety hazards
- Unsanitary, unusual, or unsightly conditions
- Security of restricted areas.

Keep meticulously informed on the movements and whereabouts of the commanding officer and the executive officer. Try to see the post as it would appear through their eyes and act accordingly.

Be meticulous in bearing and conspicuous by your neatness when on watch. A neat OD has a well-turned-out guard. Keep your leather shining. Polish your brightwork. Wear your best uniforms. Set an example for the whole command.

No matter how many times you have stood watch before, review the guard orders as soon as you take over. Changes have a way of sneaking in without warning. "That isn't the way it used to be" is no excuse.

Prevent your guard from idling. See that it is instructed in guard orders and routine, and especially in safety precautions. More so-called accidental discharges of firearms take place during guard duty than anywhere else. Sad but true, the overheads of many guardrooms are pockmarked by 9mm bullet holes.

See that reliefs and sentinels are posted in military fashion, by the book.

Keep an eye on the Colors. Such avoidable fumbles as Colors unwittingly hoisted upside down have, on occasion, provided the hapless OD with several days' enforced leisure. Never allow Colors to become fouled or snarled about the pole or halyards.

Visualize every emergency that could happen during your watch. Decide now what you will do. What if fire breaks out? A serious automobile accident occurs? Electric power or utilities fail? Disaster occurs in a nearby community? Is there a bomb threat or terrorist threat? Know your answers in advance.

If serving as staff or command duty officer for a base or station, visit the main gate during rush hours. Let yourself be seen, and let the main gate guards know you are on hand to back them up.

Be unfailingly courteous, especially to civilians and visitors. The good name of the installation and, in fact, the Marine Corps is in your hands when you are on watch.

Avoid making your rounds surreptitiously. Being seen is one of the main functions of the officer of the day.

Enforce orders to the hilt. If an order is unwise, impractical, or out of date, the best way to get it modified is to enforce it and to report that you are doing so. Never slough over an order because you think it is a "dead letter."

Avoid personal dealings with drunks. Let enlisted members of the guard deal with them while you keep in the background. This will not only save you potential embarrassment but may also save the drunken person from some offense much more serious if done toward an officer. But never allow a drunk to be roughly treated, and, above all, *never detain a supposed drunk without medical examination.* It is easy to confuse seeming intoxication with the symptoms of serious head injury.

Be immediately accessible at all hours. Do not let members of the guard, however well meaning, interpose themselves between you and any sober caller, whether in person or by telephone. You never know who may be calling.

16-1. The guard must never be relaxed. In 2005, Marines man a vehicular checkpoint in Iraq.

Finally, run your guard the way you know it should be run. You have the responsibility, backed up by almost unlimited authority. If the guard is below standard, you have only yourself to blame.

MILITARY POLICE AND SHORE PATROL

1612. Concept of Patrols

Whenever enlisted men go ashore on liberty, it is customary to provide military police, whose job is to:

- Assist the civil authorities in dealing with members of the armed forces
- Maintain discipline and good behavior among Marines and bluejackets ashore, and get them back in good order
- Aid and safeguard personnel on liberty in every possible way.

This duty is described as military police when performed by a Marine organization; when a ship or Navy shore station provides such a guard, it is known as shore patrol. Embarked Marines or Marines assigned to tenant organizations aboard naval stations often participate in shore patrol with their Navy brethren. Shore patrol routine and duties are covered in the *Navy Shore Patrol Manual*. In a few places where large military populations are present from all services, a joint patrol is sometimes organized and titled "armed forces police detachment."

Never resist, obstruct, or fail to cooperate with a shore patrolman or an MP, even if he or she comes from the Army or Air Force. Under joint regulations, MPs and SPs have all-service authority, with power to enforce any lawful acts or instructions. If you have any complaints, make them through military channels to the proper superior authorities.

1613. Hints on MP and SP Duty

When assigned to MP or SP duty, remember that you are functioning as a *military* police officer. Do not assert police authority over civilians. That is a job for the civilian police. By the same token, keep your charges reminded that they are Marines, first and foremost, and police only in a secondary and qualified sense. Do not tolerate any symptoms of "lawman" or highway-patrol swagger on the part of any of your Marines.

Never imbibe alcohol while on MP or SP duty. It is a long-standing naval custom that the least evidence that an MP or SP has partaken of alcohol while on duty demands a court-martial.

Make yourself and your MPs or SPs conspicuous. This helps to hold down violations and gives assurance to all that the situation is well in hand.

If possible, have medical assistance ready at hand. Should your patrol not include a doctor or corpsman, know where you can get medical aid without delay.

Get on easy working terms with the local police. Cooperate sincerely with them, and they will do the same with you. Be unfailingly courteous toward civilians.

If in a foreign port, obtain a trustworthy interpreter who knows the local customs. Try to select enlisted Marines who know the language.

Let your enlisted people deal with drunks. Be sure to arrange a medical examination of any seemingly intoxicated prisoner.

Handle prisoners "by the book." Allow no undue force, "third degree," or abusive behavior toward a prisoner, no matter how he or she provokes you. Unauthorized treatment of a prisoner is unworthy of a Marine officer.

Avoid disorderly public scenes, prolonged disputes, or heated brawls. Get troublemakers back to headquarters and deal with them in private.

Know your orders, *Navy Regulations*, and Uniform Code of Military Justice, down to the last comma.

Above all, exercise common sense and tact. It is your job to prevent trouble as well as to quell it. When you see a Marine or bluejacket in difficulty, ask yourself, "How can I help this person?"

A Marine on duty has no friends.

—Marine Corps proverb

Duty is the great business of a sea officer; all private considerations must give way to it, however painful it may be.

—Horatio Nelson

17

HOUSEKEEPING

In military parlance, the term "housekeeping" connotes the humdrum but necessary stewardship of administration, services, and maintenance that a unit requires for day-to-day existence. Housekeeping thus embraces such matters as police and maintenance; supply and property; food services; military exchange; morale, welfare, and recreation; and such essentials as clothing, equipment, transportation, and pay. Afloat, housekeeping focuses especially on cleanliness and upkeep.

The organization where housekeeping is below par finds itself perpetually beset with irksome disorders and nagging minor problems. Streamlined and effective housekeeping is a prerequisite to tactical efficiency so that the unit can pursue its military missions unhampered by distracting administrative demands.

1701. Police and Maintenance

Police and maintenance are the janitorial side of administration. "Police" has to do with tidiness and good order; "maintenance" means upkeep. Every organization or unit has at least some responsibilities for police and maintenance. Except on large installations or in major commands, both functions normally come under a single officer. The following discussion applies most directly at the company, battalion, or squadron level.

Every unit, afloat or ashore, designates a *police sergeant*, a noncommissioned officer who supervises cleaning details, trash collection, minor repair, and upkeep. Despite the title, the police sergeant may be any rank from corporal up. This NCO should be selected by virtue of cost-consciousness, powers of observation, forceful character, ability to work independently, ingenuity, and tinkering bent. The police sergeant is the key person in your unit's housekeeping setup.

The police sergeant's workshop is known as "the police shed." This is anything from a storeroom to a separate building that houses tools, scrap materials, cleaning gear, paint, and salvaged items, which an energetic police sergeant will habitually recover wherever found adrift. As can be realized, the police shed, properly administered, may resemble a miser's lair.

The labor force for police details comes from varying sources. Except in small organizations, the police sergeant has one or more assistants, ordinarily jackleg artificers known collectively as "the police gang." The police gang is supplemented by working details—sometimes prisoners from the brig, more often those awarded extra duties at Office Hours. Much of the effectiveness of extra duties as a disciplinary measure depends on the personality and executive abilities of the police sergeant. If the supply of malefactors is inadequate, the first sergeant supplies working parties from those available. Needless to say, close liaison should be maintained among the first sergeant, the police sergeant, and the gunnery sergeant.

When police and maintenance efforts bulk sufficiently, a unit, base, or station maintenance officer or public works officer (see Section 802) is detailed. The duties, on enlarged scale, are much the same as those of the police sergeant. Whenever the commanding officer conducts an inspection, he or she is accompanied, among others, by the maintenance officer (if there is one) and the police sergeant.

1702. Subsistence and Mess Management

"An army travels on its belly," wrote Napoleon, and so does the Marine Corps. There is no more direct way to the heart of a Marine than through the stomach. This being the case, every officer will benefit by some familiarity with the rules and arts of food service management, which are set forth in the *Marine Corps Manual* and presented in greater detail in the *Marine Corps Food Service and*

Subsistence Manual and current Marine Corps order on consumer-level supply policy.

Today, most fixed mess operations are contractor operated; still, a word is in order to describe how messes are organized because a commander's responsibility for the mess can never be delegated. The term "mess" refers to the enlisted dining facility, where enlisted members of the command are fed, rather than any of the various types of officers' mess. Marine Corps messes today mainly operate on a cafeteria system.

The dining facility and its management represent one of the most important responsibilities of command. The commanding officer must ensure without fail that the troops are served meals that, in the traditional officer-of-the-day logbook phrase, are "well served and well prepared, of good quality, and sufficient in quantity."

On large installations with several separate messes, and in Marine divisions and aircraft wings, a consolidated food service system is employed. This simply means that all messes are centralized for operations under a single food service officer; that central storage is provided for perishables, dry stores, and other mess supplies; and that messes typically support multiple units in a designated area of the installation. In addition, the food service officer supervises training of mess personnel, advises the CO and supply and commissary officers on mess matters, and systematically inspects all messes. On small posts, there is often no food service officer, and the responsibilities may fall to the supply officer or another officer as a collateral duty. For that matter, on many small posts, Marines eat in the Navy mess.

The food service officer is a specialist, but *unit mess officers* are not—and that is where you come in. Every unit with its own mess (for example, a field mess) has a mess officer, usually a lieutenant. This officer in turn has a noncommissioned assistant, the mess sergeant, who is a specialist. The quality and standing of any given mess usually reflect the energy, imagination, and capability of the mess officer and mess sergeant, working as a team.

You may be a unit mess officer at some time in your career, and the experience will be invaluable in preparing you for command. Thus, you should know how a typical mess is organized and how it operates.

The *mess sergeant* is the leading NCO of the mess. This billet demands a capable executive, a good cook, and an efficient culinary planner.

The *chief cook* is senior cook in the galley force and supervises the cooks in preparation of food.

The *chief messman*, usually an NCO, is in charge of messmen. He or she is responsible for the cleanliness of the galley and mess hall. The chief messman is a key billet assignment. Although most tables of organization do not contain a chief messman billet, you should nevertheless try to find the right person and detail that individual permanently. A slipshod mess hall manned by idle, unclean messmen usually can be traced back to an inefficient chief messman.

The *storeroom keeper* assists the mess sergeant by keeping the galley stores and provisions.

Cooks are divided into watches, regulated by the chief cook. Each watch should be headed by a rated cook, known as the "cook on watch." Depending on the size of the galley and galley force, the cook on watch may be assisted by other cooks or by "strikers," as apprentice cooks are known. Messmen who show a bent for cooking are sometimes assigned as strikers.

Messmen are the "hewers of wood and drawers of water" for the mess. Messmen serve food, wash dishes, wallop pots, police the mess hall and galley, and function as the mess sergeant's labor force. On posts where civilian messmen are not authorized, messmen are detailed monthly from the nonrated Marines of the command, in accordance with the *Marine Corps Manual*. The normal assignment of messmen is one for every twenty-five to thirty members of the command. An NCO should never serve as a messman (except as chief messman).

1703. The Unit Mess Officer

The duties of the unit mess officer are as prescribed by the commanding officer. If you are detailed as unit mess officer, immediately look up appropriate references in the *Marine Corps Manual*, *Marine Corps Food Service and Subsistence Manual*, and Marine Corps order on consumer-level supply policy. Despite some variations from unit to unit, all unit mess officers should make frequent spot checks and inspections of the galley and mess hall, paying particular attention to:

- Personal cleanliness of cooks and messmen (clean, regulation clothing; clean hands and fingernails; obvious general health)

- Cleanliness and good order of cooks' and messmen's quarters, including condition of weapons and individual equipment
- Contents of garbage cans (to eliminate waste and to spot badly prepared food)
- Good order and sanitary condition of storerooms and "reefers" (look especially for signs of spoilage or evidence of rodents or insects)
- Cleanliness of mess halls (properly washed dishes and utensils, immaculate decks and tabletops, condiments covered)
- Sanitary garbage stowage and disposal.

Attend at least one meal daily. Attend breakfast at least once a week. See that food is served hot and appetizingly and that there is enough for all. Enforce wearing of the prescribed uniform by troops being fed.

Subject to unit policies and space constraints, provide separate messing sections in the general mess for officers, when they are subsisting in the mess; for staff NCOs; for sergeants and corporals; and for nonrated enlisted. Special tables for staff NCOs and sergeants and corporals—screened off, if possible are most important and should be provided whenever physically possible.

Stand by the mess and galley area for all inspections by the commanding officer. Have your mess sergeant and chief messman with you.

Be prepared at all times (especially if responsible for an Operating Forces mess) to take the field and serve rations under field conditions.

See that no Marine ever goes hungry or misses a meal because of a conflict of duties. This means that special servings, both group and individual, may be frequently required for those on watch and for drivers, travelers, and the like. Indoctrinate your mess force that any Marine who has unavoidably missed a meal must receive hot chow and hot coffee, day or night. A proper galley has hot coffee available to all comers, all the time.

1704. Clothing Your Marines

Instructions for wearing the uniform and specifications of all articles of uniform are found in *Marine Corps Uniform Regulations.* Procurement, issue, and inspection of clothing are covered by *Individual Clothing Regulations.*

It is your responsibility, as a Marine officer, to see that every Marine under your command is always properly uniformed and always possesses the required regulation clothing correctly marked.

Every unit has periodic *clothing inspections* for all hands. When inspecting, ensure that:

- Each person has the required quantities of clothing
- Clothing is marked as required by *Marine Corps Uniform Regulations,* bearing correct name and rank insignia
- Clothing is in the hands of the person whose name appears thereon
- Clothing is serviceable or that there is evidence that any unserviceable items are being replaced.

Whenever a Marine is transferred or joins, the platoon leader should hold an individual clothing inspection.

Special clothing, such as cooks' and messmen's uniforms, cold-weather gear, flight gear, and chemical warfare clothing, is organizational property and issued to individuals on receipt, like equipment. If someone loses clothing, the Marine must then replace it by cash purchase. At stated intervals, each Marine receives a *clothing replacement allowance,* a pay-record credit to permit replacement of worn-out items. If a Marine needs clothing but does not have enough money, the issue is made and checkage entered against future pay. This system makes it impossible for a Marine to have an excuse for not having required and serviceable uniforms. It is your responsibility to make this system work.

1705. Supervision of Uniforms

Here are time-tested ways to keep your Marines properly uniformed:

- Carry out frequent, systematic clothing inspections with careful follow-up of deficiencies. This means keeping written individual records.
- Place full-length mirrors in passageways and exits of barracks and in headquarters entrances to encourage the habit of self-inspection.
- Rotate the command through various uniform combinations on successive days or at troop inspections.
- Obtain cleaning, washing, and pressing equipment (irons and ironing boards) for squad rooms and barracks.
- Inspect unit laundry rooms to ensure that washers and dryers are in good working order and the spaces are in a good state of police.

Overall, inculcate officers and NCOs with their responsibility to enforce proper wearing of the uniform by Marines at all times. You have no excuse for disregarding a breach of uniform regulations with the famous last words: "He/she isn't one of my Marines. It's up to that Marine's outfit to police its own." When you encounter an individual out of uniform, require immediate correction. If the violation is egregious, report the incident to the Marine's organization commander.

1706. Individual Equipment

In addition to uniforms, every Marine is issued a weapon and individual combat equipment (once called "782 gear" or "deuce gear" from the original custody receipt form). It is one of your first responsibilities to see that the arms and equipment of your Marines are on hand, ready, and serviceable.

17-1. Officers must ensure that equipment and weapons are properly maintained and accounted for. The battlefield is unforgiving of neglect.

Upon joining the unit, a Marine is issued a rifle or pistol. It is up to that Marine to keep that weapon (or its successors) in top condition, since all will have to depend upon it in combat. Even when temporarily armed with other organizational weapons, the Marine is responsible for that individual weapon's safekeeping and maintenance. A Marine's rifle is a mirror of its owner; the rifles of a platoon or a detachment are the mirror of the platoon leader or detachment commander.

In addition to the weapon, a Marine's *individual combat equipment* (ICE) comprises other items that one needs to fight and survive in the field. The major items of individual equipment are load-bearing equipment, cartridge belt, ammunition pouches, canteens, canteen cup, first-aid packet, poncho, helmet, helmet cover, bayonet, and entrenching tool. Marines obtain their ICE from a contractor-run issue facility, which operates under the Consolidated Storage Program managed centrally by MARCORLOGCOM. These facilities are strategically located at Marine Corps bases, stations, and base clusters around the world. In addition to ICE, the issue facility also issues and recovers chemical, biological, radiological, and nuclear defense equipment; special training allowance pool gear; and soft-walled shelters and camouflage netting.

Your responsibility for your troops' equipment is similar to your responsibility for their clothing. It is a matter of constant supervision and inspection. Remember that each item of equipment is government property, bought and paid for by the taxpayers—including you and the Marine who carries it. Field service and combat consume equipment, and this is to be expected. What is not to be expected, and will not be tolerated in the Marine Corps, are carelessness and negligence toward the weapons and equipment on which Marines' lives depend.

1707. Pay

Detailed information on pay is contained in Chapter 19. From a housekeeping point of view, interest lies in the command responsibilities involved in paying the troops. These responsibilities are simple.

The most important responsibility of a commanding officer, as far as pay is concerned, is to see that Marines are paid correctly. When a Marine finance officer is present, this will present fewer problems. For outlying detachments, or for units dependent on other services or on visiting finance officers, the problem sometimes requires close supervision.

Officers have the duty of advising their people in money matters and of encouraging them to save and to take advantage of the opportunities that the government provides.

1708. Property

Handling and accounting for public property consume much of the energy of the Marine Corps. The golden rules on property are found in the current Marine Corps order on consumer-level supply policy. You, and every officer in the Corps, should be familiar with these rules and definitions, the most important of which are summarized in the following paragraphs.

Anyone who possesses government property or who commands those who possess it, whether it is in use or in storage, has *responsibility* for that property, whether or not that individual has signed a receipt for it. Responsibility—in the supply sense—means the obligation of anyone who is required to have personal possession of, or supervision over, public property, to ensure that it is procured, used, and disposed of only as authorized. When you have public property in your custody, you assume, as a public trust, responsibility that this property will be utilized only as authorized by law or regulations.

The commanding officer of any base, station, or unit, however, has *command responsibility* over all the public property of the command. It is the CO's job to ensure that all such property is safeguarded, maintained, and accounted for. An officer has *accountability* (and is known as an *accountable officer*) when specifically detailed to duty involving pecuniary responsibility for government funds and property. An accountable officer—as distinguished from a *responsible officer*—must keep formal records and stock accounts subject to audit by higher authority.

As you can see, virtually every Marine officer has some type of responsibility for government property, whereas relatively few officers are accountable. It is unlikely that you will become an accountable officer unless you specialize in supply; you may well be a responsible officer tomorrow.

1709. A Responsible Officer's Duties

As a responsible officer you have certain basic obligations with regard to public property.

You are personally (and pecuniarily) responsible for all nonexpendable property issued to you. You are also responsible that all nonconsumable but expendable property issued to you be used only for the purposes authorized. Most such items, like 782 gear (see Section 1706), which, owing to its nature, may often be in short supply and is always pilferable, require control by individual memorandum receipt.

You must inspect your property frequently to ensure serviceability, safekeeping, and proper use. At least quarterly, you must take physical inventory and adjust discrepancies with the accountable officer (usually the unit's supply officer).

You must possess in serviceable condition all equipment shown on your unit's allowance list. The allowance list for a unit is prepared by the supply officer and contains all items allowed for the organization by tables of equipment and tables of allowance and any supporting allowance items except repair parts.

You must keep records reflecting the status of equipment and property for which you are responsible. The principal document for this purpose is normally a consolidated memorandum receipt (CMR), a computerized print-out that the accountable officer produces for you.

It is desirable that you designate in writing at least one representative, officer or enlisted, who is authorized to receipt for property in your name. An officer representative is known as the "property officer," and an NCO as the "property sergeant."

Turn in to the appropriate supply agency any property grossly in excess of authorized allowances or not needed for fulfillment of your missions.

When relieved by another officer, you must conduct a joint inventory, normally using your CMR, and adjust any discrepancies with the accountable officer. Your relief must then sign for all nonexpendable property carried on the CMR and any other equipment custody records. If you are relieving, and circumstances prevent joint inventory and immediate signature, you are nevertheless responsible for all property on hand. Before you sign any equipment custody records, however, be sure to make an immediate inventory of all property.

Ensure that your officers and enlisted persons are instructed in the care, use, and maintenance of government property and that all hands are totally cost-conscious. The persons you select for safekeeping property—your property sergeant, in particular—must be chosen with great care. Do not entrust keys of storerooms or chests to others without providing for officer supervision.

1710. Expenditures of Property

Even with the most careful stewardship, property wears out and supplies are expended. The Marine Corps recognizes this; the supply system permits expenditure of matériel, and there are procedures for fixing responsibility for unusual or improper loss or damage to government property.

Nonconsumable expendables and consumables are expended on issue by the supply officer. Thus, no formal accountability exists for these items. Nevertheless, you must ensure that there is sufficient control over such matériel to guarantee proper use as well as ordinary economy.

If nonexpendable property is unavoidably lost or destroyed, this fact should be brought immediately to the attention of the supply officer, who may drop the property, with the approval of the commanding officer, through a special adjustment to the account.

If culpability or negligence is the suspected cause of loss of a nonexpendable item, an investigation should be held to determine the exact circumstances surrounding the loss (find details in the current Marine Corps order on consumer-level supply policy).

Checkage of individual pay is a means by which the government recovers the value of lost, damaged, or destroyed property from anyone who acknowledges responsibility therefor. An individual cannot be compelled to reimburse the government but can be subjected to disciplinary action, which most Marines are anxious to avoid.

1711. Hints on Property

In addition to the advice in the current Marine Corps order on consumer-level supply policy, a few hints on the management of your property are in order.

Maintain good, friendly relations with your accountable officer. Keep that officer candidly informed on the state of your property account. Though you may have shortages, the accountable officer in turn may have overages. Share your problems.

Keep in touch with salvage and reclamation activities—for example, the nearest branch of Defense Logistics Agency Disposition Services. It is often possible to adjust an awkward debit balance through assists from reclamation.

Look and plan ahead. Nothing is worse than getting caught short because of the lack of ordinary foresight.

Be cost-conscious. The money available to your unit is not limitless, and supplies cost your unit money.

Follow through. Your responsibility does not end with the placing of requirements for matériel with the supply officer. It ends only when the items in question are physically either in the hands of the user or in your storeroom. As the Duke of Wellington wrote in 1810: "It is very necessary to attend to all this detail and to trace a biscuit from Lisbon into a man's mouth on the frontier and to provide for its removal from place to place by land or by water, or no military operations can be carried out."

Take pains to determine and enforce responsibility for government property among your subordinates. When one of your Marines loses or damages property, institute pay checkage against that person. This not only reimburses the government for the loss and thus clears your books, but it also reminds all hands that property is to be respected and cared for.

Keep a neat, uncluttered storeroom. Allow no "grab-bag" accumulations in dark corners. Inspect your storeroom frequently—and unannounced.

Finally, remember the old tongue-in-cheek saying that supposedly covers every known category of government property: "If it's small enough to pick up, turn it in; if you can't move it, paint it."

1712. Morale, Welfare, and Recreation

Morale, welfare, and recreation (MWR) concerns—once commonly called "special services"—embrace a number of nonmilitary Marine Corps Community Services (MCCS) activities within the Marine Corps, chief among which is unit recreation. Remember, however, that no matter what machinery may be set up for MCCS purposes, nothing can supersede or diminish the commanding officer's paramount responsibility to lead, care for, counsel, and educate those under command.

The mainstay of the base, station, or unit MWR program is the recreation fund, which provides for the recreation, amusement, and welfare of all hands. Each battalion has an area coordinator who, along with the MWR officer, holds responsibility for the administration of these funds. The recreation fund obtains income from exchange system profits and the central MCCS fund. Recreation funds are "non-appropriated funds." Some latitude exists in spending them for items not covered by official grants but nevertheless desirable for the welfare and morale of the command. Some examples of allowable expenditures include athletic equipment; athletic and marksmanship prizes; dances, picnics, and parties for the unit; and washers, dryers, irons, and televisions for the barracks.

Before seeking to make a purchase from the recreation funds, consult your area coordinator and MWR officer, not only to ensure that your project has authorization but also to preclude a prohibited transaction.

The MCCS division of your base or station also provides health, fitness, and recreation activities and facilities for use by you and your family.

1713. Transportation

Every unit, station, or base that has vehicles includes a motor transport officer, who, under the S-4, is responsible for the upkeep and operation of the unit's transportation. The motor transport force is made up of drivers and mechanics. Motor transport operations are supervised by a noncommissioned dispatcher, who assigns vehicles to particular runs and keeps the unit's transportation operating in accordance with policy and regulations. When you need transportation, you normally contact the dispatcher, the "front man," so to speak, of the motor transportation organization, although many organizations will have more specific procedures for arranging transportation.

When dealing with drivers and transportation, keep the following pointers in mind.

Cars and drivers are for official business; use them accordingly. However, commanding officers, senior staff officers, and aides-de-camp frequently have cars and drivers assigned for official use as required. Misuse of government transportation is a serious matter.

If you are the senior officer in an official vehicle, you are responsible for its safe operation and proper employment. If the driver breaks rules, you are responsible. Never, except in an emergency, order a driver to transgress a regulation or safety precaution. If you do, be ready to explain.

You cannot drive a Marine or Navy vehicle without a government motor vehicle operator's license. In addition, some commands require a unit driver's license. Other commands prohibit any officer from driving official vehicles except in emergency.

When duty requires a driver to make a run during meal hours, it is your responsibility to see that arrangements are made to feed that Marine (not just a sandwich or snack, but a proper hot meal). Always ask your driver if he or she has been fed, and see the matter through. If you are not satisfied, call the dispatcher or, if necessary, the motor transport officer. In extreme cases, you may have to arrange directly with the mess sergeant. Regardless of how you do it, see that your driver is fed.

Avoid keeping vehicles waiting. Send them back to the motor pool, with instructions to return at a specified time (or call when you need a return trip). When using an official vehicle in connection with an official social function, avoid having your driver wait outside at your pleasure. Be meticulously punctual; keep to schedule.

Play fair with the dispatcher, and the dispatcher will play fair with you. Require drivers to be military and correct in manner and uniform. When not otherwise employed, see that the drivers perform routine checks, upkeep, and maintenance on their vehicles, regardless of whether they are normally assigned to you or not.

If you are concerned with motor transport operations, "safety" and "preventive maintenance" are key words.

Let all things be done decently and in order.

—I Corinthians, 14:40

18

OFFICERS' INDIVIDUAL ADMINISTRATION

Although a few administrators may convey the reverse impression, there is nothing inherently complicated or darkly mysterious about individual administration. This term merely comprises a number of administrative matters that concern you personally: your record, rank, promotions, retirement, official correspondence, leave, and liberty. Pay and allowances, and official travel, closely related, are covered in Chapter 19.

To give you working familiarity and ready reference with military administration, and to prevent its seeming a black art known only to a chosen few, become familiar with *Navy Regulations, Department of the Navy Correspondence Manual, Marine Corps Manual,* and pertinent Marine Corps orders—and let individual administration serve and help but never get the better of you.

OFFICERS' RECORDS

1801. Your Official Record

Throughout your career, documents and correspondence concerning you accumulate at Marine Corps Headquarters. These become part of your official record. The vital importance of your official record to you and your career cannot be overstressed. The entries in your record form the basis of your service reputation.

Your official record in Washington comprises a multipart, electronic administrative record; an official military personnel file, also in electronic form; and certain additional files, some of which may be kept by the judge advocate general of the Navy. You have access to the majority of your record via secure login to Marine Online.

The administrative portion of your record includes the following major components:

- The *basic individual record (BIR)* contains information relating to your service "contract," including your commissioning source, date of entry into service for pay purposes, date that any obligated service ends, and so forth; service information, including current grade, date of rank, MOS, information on your current tour and combat tour(s), etc.; and personal information, such as home of record, country of origin, citizenship, blood type, current contact information, current billet and duty status, and information on your dependent family members.
- The *basic training record (BTR)* documents your current unit and annual training status and contains your career service training and education records, including selected special training records; education records, documenting military and civilian schools attended and formal MOS and PME courses completed; foreign language training; martial arts training; and miscellaneous test scores.
- The *chronological record* is a record of your career assignments, sorted chronologically and listing the units or organizations you have been assigned to, your primary duty at each, and any additional remarks.
- The *individual medical record* summarizes some important information from your more comprehensive health records, which are kept separately in both physical and electronic form by Navy medicine. In particular, this record provides current status of key immunizations, physicals, and required periodic health assessments.
- The *record of emergency data (RED)* contains current information on marital status, spouse, children, and next of kin, as well as essential addresses, phone numbers, and notification instructions, if any. *It is vitally important to keep your RED completely accurate and up to date.*

This administrative portion of your official record also includes some additional minor sections further addressing education, operational cultural information (that is, foreign language skills and test results, self-professed language skills, and self-reported unofficial foreign travel), and pay amounts and leave balances.

The second major part of your official record, your *official military personnel file (OMPF)*, is a document collection that serves as your record of performance from initial entry through final separation. The OMPF is divided into sections:

- Official military photograph used by promotion selection and command screening boards
- Master Brief Sheet summarizing your record of performance
- Performance evaluations detailing your performance in each assignment
- Commendatory/derogatory information encompassing personal awards, school transcripts, and other items
- Reporting Senior and Reviewing Officer profiles that provide a cumulative snapshot of how you have performed these responsibilities as you evaluated the performance of your subordinates.

Marine Corps Headquarters (Code MMRP) recommends that you perform a self-audit of your OMPF in advance of a scheduled performance counseling interview, in preparation for any selection board, and in advance of contacting customer service (Code MMRP-20) to review your record. The web page that serves as the table of contents to your OMPF provides a link to instructions on performing a self-audit.

Updating Your OMPF. There are several ways to update your OMPF:

Email: This is the preferred and fastest way to update your OMPF. Again, the web page that serves as the table of contents to your OMPF provides current instructions and email addresses that you should use depending on your needs and circumstances.

In person: You may drop off update material at the MMRP customer service window located on the first deck of Building 2008 at Marine Corps Base Quantico, Virginia.

Mail: You may mail update material to Headquarters U.S. Marine Corps (MMRP-20), 2008 Elliot Road, Quantico, VA 22134-5030. If board eligible, you should indicate on the outside of the envelope: "Update material for the FYxx (insert board name)."

To streamline the process of updating your OMPF, you should format every document you submit as a single-sided, black-and-white, multipage document (documents scanned at a resolution of 200 dots per inch work best). Each page in the document must contain the individual's grade, full name, and EDIPI number (found on the back of the ID card). Documents submitted without an EDIPI number run a high risk of not being added to the OMPF. Color documents and documents taken with a smart phone will not be processed.

Finally, there are a few additional files that are part of your official record. The *confidential file* contains any correspondence to or about an officer that must be kept in a confidential status. Few officers have material on confidential file.

Proceedings of courts or boards that affect your record are filed by the judge advocate general (JAG) of the Navy. You may examine these records in the JAG files. If unfavorable, such matter is referred to you before being filed.

The only persons who enjoy access to your record are you (via Marine Online); your personal representative, armed with proper proof; designated headquarters personnel; and, when authorized by the Secretary of the Navy, the courts. No person (including you or your agents) without proper authority can withdraw official records and correspondence from the files or destroy them.

Make it a habit to review your record at Marine Online at least annually.

Without vicious intent, some officers have added to their records by their reporting officials—perhaps by carelessness or misdirected intentions—an accumulation of minor lapses that prove as detrimental to their service reputations as serious missteps.

It is important, in closing this topic, to emphasize that adverse matter cannot be placed in your official record without your knowledge and must always be referred to you for statement. If you wish to give your side of the matter, you may do so; if you have nothing to say, you so state in writing. In either case, the adverse matter goes back to the commandant of the Marine Corps, via the reporting officer and thence through normal channels. Whether favorable or unfavorable, correspondence once rightfully included in your record cannot be removed without authorization by the Secretary of the Navy.

1802. Your Personal Record

The only administrative records that physically accompany you now throughout your career, as distinct from records filed in Washington, are your *officers qualification record (OQR)*, *health record*, and *dental record*.

Your OQR contains, at a minimum, a NAVMC 763 (Appointment Acceptance) (essentially the officer version of a contract), NAVMC 118(3) (Chronological Record), NAVMC 118(11) (Administrative Remarks), record of emergency data, and Servicemembers Group Life Insurance Beneficiary Election Form. In addition to this, if the officer is a "Mustang" (prior enlisted), his or her enlistment contract(s) and DD Form 214 are in the OQR. A NAVMC 10922 (Dependency Affidavit) is also included for married officers.

Your health and dental records are opened by the Navy's Bureau of Medicine and Surgery and contain a summary of your health history prior to accession, the results of your physical examinations, and the medical history of every ailment that befalls you during your career.

1803. Your Personal File

The day you are commissioned, start a personal file. This should contain, in one folder, all original travel orders and, in another, all official correspondence from, to, and concerning you. In addition, remember that some unofficial emails, letters, or notes you write or receive are just as important to your career as the official ones. And depending on your experiences and achievement, your writings and musings during your career may interest a wider audience. The Marine Corps Archives at the Alfred M. Gray Marine Corps Research Center encourages retired officers to donate personal files and papers to the Marine Corps Archives.

1804. Fitness Reports

Fitness reports provide the periodic documentation of your professional performance and character for the Marine Corps performance evaluation system (PES). The system provides for the reporting, recording, and analysis of the performance, potential, and professional character of all Marines in the grade of sergeant and above. The fitness report form, when properly completed, constitutes the principal record of your performance of duties and conduct for a designated period of time. Linked together, these reports assist selection boards of all varieties in determining which officers are best suited for the services desired. They also provide the commandant and staff with information as to your desired duty assignments and locations for the future.

The authoritative source for complete information on this topic is the *Performance Evaluation System (PES) Manual.*

Completed and maintained electronically, the fitness report form (NAVMC 10835) consists of several distinct sections as follows:

- *Section A* contains administrative information including information that identifies you individually; describes your unit and duty assignment; denotes the occasion of and period covered by the report; lists your most recent physical fitness score, small arms qualifications, and preferences for future assignments; and identifies your reporting senior, normally that officer next above you in your chain of command (unless he or she is of the same grade), and reviewing officer, normally the officer to whom your reporting senior reports. It remains your responsibility to provide the report to your reporting senior with the information in this section correctly stated.
- *Section B* contains a complete description of your billet, focusing on key functions and responsibilities. This section is technically the reporting senior's responsibility, but many reporting seniors will have you prepare a draft, which they will refine.
- *Section C* lists your key accomplishments in the billet during the period covered by the report. Again, your reporting senior will often expect you to prepare a draft of this section.
- *Sections D through H* are used by the reporting senior to rate your personal attributes in categories (for example, "Mission Accomplishment," "Leadership," "Intellect and Wisdom") of particular interest to the Marine Corps. For each category, your reporting senior matches his or her appraisal of you to a provided word description. Elaboration, if needed, is added at the bottom of each section or to a later section.
- *Section I* calls for "Directed and Additional Comments." Your reporting senior uses this section to add his or her own concise, personalized

word picture of you, which is mandatory; any additional comments needed to elaborate on ratings of your personal attributes (Sections D through H); and any other comments or information needed to complete the evaluation.

- *Section J* contains the reporting senior's signature (and yours if the report contains adverse material).
- *Section K* contains your reviewing officer's marks and comments evaluating your performance and character, in particular placing your reporting senior's evaluation in a broader context. The reviewing officer also affixes his or her signature in this section.
- *Section L* is purely administrative. It merely indicates if there is addendum material included.

General officers are evaluated by letter reports, annually for brigadier generals.

Your fitness reports obviously will constitute a running record of your performance of duty throughout your career, as seen through the eyes of your various commanders and supervisors. It is the most vital single source of your personal and professional record. It will merit your attention and review through your last day of service.

Occasions for Reports. There are thirteen occasions when a fitness report must be prepared on Marines in the grades of sergeant through colonel:

1. Grade Change
2. CMC Directed
3. Change of Reporting Senior
4. Transfer
5. Change of Duty
6. To Temporary Duty
7. From Temporary Duty
8. End of Service
9. Change in Status
10. Annual (Active Component)
11. Annual (Reserve Component)
12. Semiannual (lieutenants only)
13. Reserve Training.

The annual fitness report periods (ending on the last day of the months given in Table 18-1) for Marines vary by grade, corresponding to the needs of the promotion boards.

Reporting Senior. Normally, the reporting senior is the first commissioned or warrant officer (civilian GS-09 or above under certain circumstances) in the chain of command who is senior to the Marine reported on. Such a senior may be in the same grade as the Marine reported on if that officer is the commanding officer or officer-in-charge, or has the specific authorization of the reviewing officer. The performance evaluation system values the reporting senior's viewpoint as the best position from which to observe a Marine's performance and the officer as the person most responsible for setting the Marine's daily tasks and the standards to which they are performed.

Reviewing Officer. The reviewing officer next receiving your fitness report is normally that officer (or civilian in grade GS-12 and above) next senior in the chain of command to the reporting senior. The reviewing officer occupies a critical link in the system by ensuring adherence to the stated regulations and exerting the leadership, supervision, and detached point of view to obtain unbiased and accurate reports. The reviewing officer bears ultimate responsibility for the accuracy, completeness, and correctness of the fitness report. Errors by either the Marine reported on or the reporting senior are returned to them for correction. The reviewing officer completes portions of the reviewing officer certification to indicate agreement or disagreement with the report. Written remarks, based upon the reviewing officer's personal knowledge of the Marine, are encouraged, especially to determine the Marine's potential to serve

Table 18-1. Fitness Report Periods by Grade

Grade	*Active Component*	*Reserve Component*	*Active Reserve*
Colonel	May	July	July
Lieutenant Colonel	May	June	June
Major	May	September	June
Captain	May	September	June
First Lieutenant	October and April	October	October
Second Lieutenant	January and July	April	N/A
Warrant Officers	April	October	October

at a higher grade and also the Marine's general value to the service, in comparison with the other officers of the same grade serving with the reviewing officer. Remarks must be provided to clarify disagreement with the reporting senior or, in the case of adverse reports, to adjudicate the respective positions of the Marine and the reporting senior.

Initial reports on Marines joining the organization within ninety days of the end of the fitness report period are normally omitted (annual) or completed as "not observed" (all other occasions). This rule is excluded when, in the view of the reporting officer, sufficient observation occurred and the report provides important information to the commandant and remains fair to the Marine thus observed. A typical case would be during high-intensity or combat operations where close, daily, and detailed personal observation occurs.

Adverse reports contain any one of several possible ratings or phrases reflecting unsatisfactory performance and require special handling in addition to the normal processes. Generally, any of the following cases would constitute an adverse report:

- A report of failure of physical fitness testing or weight control program
- Any rating of "adverse"
- Any comments in Section I of a derogatory nature, comments on failures, unsatisfactory performance of duty or on a required program of training or education, or comments of a failure to measure up to norms and expectations
- Similar adverse material contributed by the reviewing officer.

The revised performance evaluation system introduced in 1999 greatly altered the scope and nature of fitness reports, their completion, and handling. After the first major overhaul in several decades, the revised system reduces the amount of writing and limits the scope of evaluation to assigned duties and tasks. It virtually eliminates gratuitous or freewheeling commentary, which in the past contributed to an acknowledged "inflation" and distortion of the system's goals. The new system permits the use of automated technology, which greatly enhances the quality of procedures, processes, and accountability.

Under the revised system, the reporting seniors and reviewing officers are themselves "rated" with a profile revealing their tendencies in marking fitness reports. Marines will always receive a copy of the report as written by the reporting senior, and adverse reports will be referred back to the subject officer now by Headquarters Marine Corps for final comment, rather than attaching it to the initial report at the unit level. Reviewing officers must make an evaluation of all officers of the same grade as the subject officer, if known, within that officer's command.

Records. A few months after you have seen your fitness report online, you will receive a computer-generated receipt from HQMC that contains a recapitulation of the tabulated markings. Keep this in your personal file and verify its later transfer to your Master Brief Sheet. The latter is mailed annually to all officers and can be requested at will from the HQMC Career Counseling Section (Code MMOA-4).

With the migration online of Marine Corps personnel records and administrative systems, including performance evaluation, you can audit your performance record at any time. Look at your trends, as displayed in the reports, and objectively strive to improve the weaknesses reported by your seniors, many of which you share with most other officers. If you desire professional help in interpreting or planning your career, seek the guidance of the HQMC Career Counseling Section, via appointment. That section's counselors have the advantage of knowing how the other officers of your grade and year group are performing and can advise you in clear and dispassionate terms.

In the event that, after all interviews and reviews of your record have been accomplished, you believe a report reflects errors or injustice on the part of the reporting senior or reviewing officer, you have the final recourse of an appeal to the Board for Correction of Naval Records (BCNR) of the Department of the Navy. Any officer seeking such redress should obtain first the advice and recommendations of the HQMC Career Counseling Section before presenting the petition. The procedure proceeds as follows: The petitioner fills out the appropriate application form for correction of error or injustice, attaching copies of fitness reports, amplifying statements, and supporting evidence as applicable. Before reaching the actual board, however, the petition for redress must receive a review by the performance evaluation review board (PERB) of the relevant service, in this case the Marine Corps. If the PERB agrees with the petition, the records will be amended or removed without further authority to meet the applicant's requirements. If the PERB recommends the retention of the records, then the BCNR takes the matter for consideration. This three-member board will recommend, based upon a majority vote, the final actions to be taken by the Secretary of the Navy. A final report of the BCNR to the petitioner will report the decision of the secretary and the actions, if any, taken with respect to the petitioner's records.

1805. Marking Fitness Reports

Because fitness reports are decisive in the career of a Marine, the preparation of a fitness report is one of the most weighty tasks you will ever perform and an opportunity for you to contribute materially to the overall improvement of the Marine Corps. Instructions governing fitness reports are found in pertinent Marine Corps orders, most notably the *PES Manual*, which you should review before you complete a report or a recommended report.

The suitability of an officer or noncommissioned officer for future assignments, selection, or retention is based in large degree on the evaluations made by reporting seniors. For most officers and noncommissioned officers in today's large services, there is little else on which decisions can be based.

Performance appraisal should be a continuous process rather than an intermittent one performed only at fitness report time. Shortcomings should be pointed out as they arise—not saved up. Counseling policy, now distinct from performance evaluation, requires you to sit down periodically with the Marine reported on and candidly discuss his or her general performance and personal qualities. This is not always an agreeable session for either party, but it is a responsibility of leadership at every level.

You must therefore prepare fitness reports carefully, impartially, and with a full appreciation of the task at hand and the responsibility that goes with it. A report that is unduly negative or fails to accent the positive might cost the Marine Corps a fine officer or noncommissioned officer. On the other hand, your failure to point out weaknesses can cause the selection and promotion of a Marine unsuited for higher rank at the expense of one who is. Reporting seniors can virtually ensure selection or force the separation of a given individual. Thus, as a reporting senior, you can add luster to a career or destroy it. This is a burden officers must bear with utmost care.

Put aside prejudice or partiality as you evaluate. Compare the Marine being reported on with others of the same rank and experience. Consider fully the circumstances and context of the reporting period. Guard particularly against the attitude of the moment; you are grading an individual's total performance during the whole period covered. Make initial drafts of the report, then review it for consistency and fairness. Enter the final marks on the form, and type the comments.

Bear in mind that any group contains a few individuals at the top and bottom, respectively, who stand out favorably or unfavorably. The majority represents a fairly level standard of performance in between. If you find that your ratings tend to put most officers at the top or at the bottom, be quite sure you can justify this departure from the normal distribution (as you are specifically required to do in the case of certain outstanding or unsatisfactory marks). Remember that most officers are average officers, or nearly so. It is the easy way out to give high ratings to all officers, rationalizing that "everyone does it." But overrating an average officer leaves no scope for the brilliant one.

Do not hesitate to use the "not observed" rating for any characteristic for which your observation has truly been too limited to warrant sound evaluation. An overall report of "not observed" may be provided if you have had less than ninety days' observation of the Marine reported on, except in the cases of lieutenants or persons returning from temporary duty or changing status, in which cases the observation period must be less than thirty days. An "observed" fitness report can also be written on an officer or NCO of the Marine Corps Reserve on active duty for training for twelve to thirty days. If you feel that you can make a normal observed report of less than ninety days, other than in the preceding occasions, you may do so but will be required to justify that action. In contrast to earlier systems, a "not observed" report may still reflect certain mandatory comments, such as failure to complete a course, failure to pass the physical fitness test, or placement on the weight control program.

The final written section of the new fitness report, "Section I—Directed and Additional Comments," carries somewhat less weight than the former "Section C," a single space furnished for all written comments. Because the new report contains sections on the billet description, billet accomplishments, and an evaluation of some thirteen attributes among four categories, comments in this section must be clear, objective, and to the point—not an attempt to provide superlative descriptions and superfluous statistics to enhance one's image.

In Section I, you must include mandatory comments to provide a word picture of the Marine reported on for all observed reports. While these comments must be concise, they should provide a more complete and detailed evaluation of the individual's professional character. You may also address any entry made in Sections A through H or as you deem appropriate. Next, you will insert the phrase "directed comments" and/or "additional comments" and under each heading supply objective, clear, and concise statements either required by the evaluation system (refer to the *PES Manual*) or considered necessary by you to complete an accurate picture of the officer or NCO you are evaluating.

PROMOTION AND PRECEDENCE

1806. The Marine Corps Promotion System

The Marine Corps and Navy share a system of officer promotion that has been under continuous evolution since 1915 and, in recent years, has served as a model for the other services. Under this system, officers who are judged "best fitted" are selected for advancement, while those least fitted are passed over and must ultimately retire. Determination of who is best qualified for promotion is accomplished by boards of senior officers, known as selection boards.

Promotion never comes automatically. To qualify for promotion, you must not only perform effectively and loyally in your present rank, but you must also develop and prove your capacity to handle the increased responsibilities of higher rank. And you must excel in ways that best satisfy the needs of the Marine Corps.

1807. Officer Distribution

The Defense Officer Personnel Management Act of 1981 provides officer promotion machinery for the Army, Marine Corps, Navy, Air Force, and Coast Guard. The Navy and Marine Corps provisions are generally similar. One of the most important things that this law does is to establish certain categories of officers for promotion purposes. It also regulates the number of officers who may be assigned to each grade. This is known as "officer distribution" and determines how many vacancies for promotion each rank contains.

Officer Categories. All Marine officers are line officers. Some commissioned officers, however, are designated "restricted in the performance of duty," in contrast to all other Marine officers, who are described as "unrestricted officers."

Existing law provides for two categories of restricted officers: permanent regular limited duty officers and permanent warrant officers. All other officers in the Corps are considered for promotion and assignment purposes as not being restricted in the performance of duty.

Limited duty officers are former warrant or noncommissioned officers who have been commissioned for duty in the particular fields in which they have specialized, such as administration, ordnance, motor transport, and so on. If the officer so applies, and is judged to be qualified, an LDO may be designated as an unrestricted officer, and the limited duty designation ceases.

Like limited duty officers, warrant officers are also appointed for duty in particular fields and are thus restricted to performance of duty in the appropriate field. Warrant officers selected from certain "line duty" MOSs carry the title of "Marine gunner" and wear the gunner's bursting bomb insignia. The occupational fields from which Marine gunners are usually appointed are 03 (infantry), 08 (field artillery), 18 (tank/assault amphibian), 25 (communications), and MOS 4915 (range officer).

Reserve officers, unless on active duty with the regular establishment, are selected separately. If on active duty with the regular establishment, reserve officers are selected and promoted along with regular contemporaries. The Marine Corps has a continuing requirement for reserve officers on active duty beyond their obligated service and now offers them a career program comparable to that of regular officers.

Distribution of Officers by Grade. The number of officers who may be promoted above first lieutenant depends on the authorized numbers for each grade. These ceilings are computed by Marine Corps Headquarters and approved by the Secretary of the Navy, and they vary periodically with the laws that establish the authorized strength of the Marine Corps. To provide some insight, Figure 18-1 provides the grade distribution of active duty officers in the Marine Corps in early 2016.

If the Secretary of the Navy decides that fewer officers than those computed are required in any grade, the secretary can establish that lesser figure as the authorized number for that grade.

Limited duty officers are not "additional numbers," but the actual number of LDOs may not exceed 3.64 percent of the total number of unrestricted officers at each grade.

Grade	Number	Percentage
Warrant Officer	2,102	10.04
Second Lieutenant	1,880	8.98
First Lieutenant	3,609	17.25
Captain	6,759	32.30
Major	3,875	18.52
Lieutenant Colonel	1,925	9.2
Colonel	693	3.31
General Officer	83	0.40
Total	**20,926**	**100.00**

Figure 18-1. Active Duty Officer Distribution by Grade (2016)

General Officers. Examining all provisions of the Officer Personnel Act dealing with general officers demands an extensive and even technical understanding of officer personnel management and is thus beyond the scope of this *Guide*. However, awareness of the following highlights is worthwhile:

- Law limits the number of four-, three-, two-, and one-star generals on active duty in the Marine Corps.
- The commandant and assistant commandant of the Marine Corps are four-star generals. A Marine as chairman of the Joint Chiefs of Staff or commander of a combatant command also would be a four-star general.
- Lieutenant generals in the Marine Corps typically fill the positions of deputy commandant at Marine Corps Headquarters; commanding general, MARFOR; commanding general, MEF (commanding general, II MEF, a two-star as of 2016, is an exception); and, when assigned, certain deputy commander and principal staff officer billets at certain major joint commands.
- Major and brigadier generals typically serve as commanders, deputy commanders, and principal staff officers at divisions, wings, and other major Marine Corps commands, and at lesser joint commands and task forces.

1808. Promotion Procedure

Promotion to first lieutenant is by seniority on completion of twenty-four months' service in grade. From captain to major general, inclusive, promotion is by selection. The standard of selection is "best fitted"; eligibility requirements, selection procedures, and so forth are the same for all.

Eligibility for Selection. You become eligible for selection when, approximately, you have completed years of service as follows: first lieutenant, two; captain, four; major, ten (plus or minus one); lieutenant colonel, sixteen (plus or minus one); and colonel, twenty-two (plus or minus one). Note that wartime exigencies can drop as much as two years from these criteria, as happened for 2007–2008 promotions.

Eligibility for selection does not necessarily mean you enter a promotion zone, as described below. Once you become eligible, though, your eligibility for promotion continues, regardless of failure of selection, as long as you remain on active duty.

Mechanics of Selection. Each selection board receives the names and files (see Section 1801) of officers who are eligible for consideration. In addition, each board is informed of the names of the eligible officers who constitute the primary promotion zone for that grade. Whenever a selection board convenes, the Secretary of the Navy determines how far down the eligible list the board must go in making selections to ensure a satisfactory flow of promotion.

Beginning with the most senior officer of the grade under consideration who has not previously failed to be selected, the promotion zone goes down to the last unrestricted officer needed to maintain the flow of promotion "up or out," as determined by the Secretary of the Navy.

A separate promotion zone is established for limited duty officers, and the selection board is allocated separate quotas of limited duty vacancies to be filled by selection. These officers are considered only upon their specialist qualifications. They do not compete for selection with unrestricted officers.

Any officer eligible for selection may forward to the president of the board a letter inviting attention to any matter of record that the officer deems important in his or her case. This, however, is a privilege that should be exercised with the utmost prudence. Do not rock your boat.

All officers senior to or in a promotion zone "fail of selection" (that is, are "passed over") if not recommended for promotion. The effects of failing of selection, in terms of mandatory retirement, are covered in Section 1811.

Except for LDOs, a selection board must go below the promotion zone, among the eligibles, and select outstanding officers for accelerated promotion. But no officer below the promotion zone is considered passed over, even if an officer junior to him is selected for accelerated promotion, and not more than 10 percent of the total number of officers whom the board is authorized to select may come from below the zone, except in the case of colonels and brigadier generals being considered for the next higher grade.

Once selected, your name is submitted by the board to the commandant, Secretary of the Navy, and finally the president. If, as is usual, all names are approved, you are then promoted, subject to Senate confirmation, according to vacancies.

Selection Boards. Marine selection boards usually consist of at least nine active or reserve officers and are convened by the Secretary of the Navy annually. The board is usually balanced in numbers of ground and aviation officers with representation of service support MOSs, and, if LDOs and reservists are to be considered by the board, it includes one of each as members.

No officer may be a member of two successive boards for the same grade. This ensures that eighteen different officers must pass on your case before you twice fail of selection.

Members of selection boards are sworn to act without prejudice or partiality and, like members of a court-martial, may not disclose their deliberations. Specifically, their sworn duties and obligations are as follows:

- To recommend the best-fitted officers for promotion
- To give equal weight with line duty in the Operating Forces to equally well-performed duty in the Supporting Establishment, or duty in any technical specialty
- Not to consider as prejudicial the fact that an officer under consideration may have been previously passed over
- Not to select more officers than the number set by the Secretary of the Navy (but the board need not select the full number if there are insufficient qualified names under consideration).

Effecting Promotions. When selected for promotion, your name goes on a promotion list in normal order of seniority. As vacancies occur, you are then promoted. All officer promotions, regular and reserve, however, are subject to such physical, mental, moral, and professional qualifications as the Secretary of the Navy may prescribe. On promotion, you rate the pay and allowances of the higher grade from the date of the appointment.

1809. Precedence

Precedence is your right of seniority over other officers, based on grade and on the date of your appointment within a grade. The rank and precedence of officers on active duty is shown in numerical order in *The Combined Lineal List of Officers on Active Duty in the Marine Corps*, otherwise known as the "Blue Book." Your date of rank is also stated on your commission. Although complex methods previously determined the order of precedence of officers appointed to the same date of rank, today, class standing at Basic School remains the sole criterion for that order, which will change thereafter only as officers are selected, "deep selected," or passed over for promotion.

Your Social Security number serves, in effect, as your service number instead of the "file number" every officer used to have. In addition to the Social Security number, every Marine officer has a number in grade, which is his or her number, in order of precedence within grade, in the "Blue Book." Your number in grade gives an exact indication of your precedence.

Precedence of officers of different services is in accordance with their relative grades and, within grade, in accordance with respective dates of rank, the senior in date of rank taking precedence. Among officers of different services of the same relative grade and the same date of rank, precedence is determined according to the time each has served on active duty as a commissioned officer.

RETIREMENT AND SEPARATION

1810. Basics

Retirement is removal from active duty following completion of certain service and longevity requirements, after which the retired officer receives retired pay. Although no longer on duty, a retired officer remains a member of the Marine Corps, retains his or her rank and status as an officer (being entitled to all military courtesies of that rank), and may under certain conditions be recalled to active duty.

In contrast, *separation or discharge* is an absolute termination of officer status. Depending on the character of discharge, the officer being separated may or may not receive lump-sum separation pay. A form of separation distinct from retirement, *resignation*, is total, voluntary separation from the service. There is also a disability severance pay for persons holding less than twenty years' service. *Revocation of commission* may separate any officer who has been on continuing active duty for less than three years as a commissioned officer in the Marine Corps or Navy. An officer whose commission is revoked does not receive any advance pay or allowances or separation pay.

1811. Involuntary Retirement and Separation

Except for physical reasons, you retire upon reaching a certain age, on completing certain periods of service, or after failure of selection for promotion.

Retirement Based on Age. Officers still on the active list must retire at age sixty (sixty-two in the case of flag officers), unless the president in a particular case defers retirement. Such retirement may not be deferred beyond age sixty-four.

Retirement Based on Length of Service. Lieutenant colonels and above must serve three years in grade to retire at that grade. The Marine Corps grants waivers to this rule under certain rare circumstances. The following paragraphs summarize general length of service restrictions by grade.

Major generals (as well as lieutenant generals) normally retire within a month of the date that they complete five years' service in grade and thirty-five years' commissioned service. They may stay on active duty from year to year if so recommended by a board convened for the purpose and approved by the secretary of the Navy.

Brigadier generals retire within a month of the date that they complete thirty years' service or five years in grade.

Colonels retire within a month of the date that they complete thirty years' total commissioned service, if they have twice failed for brigadier general, or the date that they complete five years' service in grade.

Lieutenant colonels retire within a month of the date that they complete twenty-eight years' total commissioned service, if they have been passed over for colonel.

Majors retire within a month of the date that they complete twenty years total commissioned service, if they have twice been passed over for lieutenant colonel. They have to retire six months after their second failure, though present policy continues them to twenty years' service, provided no more than six years' continuation is thus required.

Captains and *first lieutenants* who are twice passed over for major and captain, respectively, are honorably discharged (not retired) six months following the second failure, with separation pay based on length of service. An LDO, however, has the option of reversion to prior enlisted status.

Warrant officers who are twice passed over for promotion to the next higher permanent warrant grade, and decline reversion to enlisted status, are discharged with separation pay if they have less than eighteen years' active service since initial appointment as a warrant officer; if warrant officers so passed over have eighteen but less than twenty years' service since the original appointment, they will be retired (unless picked up in the interim) two months after completing twenty years. Any regular warrant officer who has at least twenty years' active service in the armed forces will be retired at age sixty-two, or, short of that age, on completing thirty years' active service in the armed forces.

Limited duty officers, if not otherwise subject to retirement, must retire after completing thirty years' active Marine Corps or Navy service.

Selective Early Retirement. Defense Department policies authorize the services to convene boards to select officers for retirement in advance of the statutory limits of service. Such measures seek to retain the desired annual vacancies in grade and allow promotion opportunities for juniors at the desired rates (see Section 1807). The boards convene when directed by the service secretary and have the same composition normally as the board convened to promote to the next higher grade. Officers so selected will be retired on the date seven months after the board's results are approved. Such officers who choose to retire before the seven months elapse are considered "voluntary" retirements. Normally, such boards perform their duties only in time of forced personnel reductions by the services.

Officers Reported as Unsatisfactory. If at any time before completion of twenty years' service, your name comes before a selection board in normal course and you are specifically reported by that board to be unsatisfactory in performance of your duties, you are honorably discharged with separation pay (not retired) on 30 June following approval of the report by the president. An LDO so reported has the normal option of reverting to his or her former status. Do not confuse this procedure with being passed over (which is bad enough).

Revocation of Commission. The Secretary of the Navy may revoke the commission of any officer who has less than three years' continuous service. Discharge of this type does not include separation pay. The most usual causes for revocation of commission are academic failure at Basic School, general low-caliber or unsatisfactory performance of duty, or temperamental unsuitability.

1812. Voluntary Retirement

After a regular or reserve officer completes twenty years' active duty in the Marine Corps, Army, Navy, Air Force, or Coast Guard (including reserve), ten years of which must have been active commissioned service, he or she may, at the discretion of the president, retire with the highest grade satisfactorily held, as determined by the Secretary of the Navy.

When an officer has thirty year's active service, he or she may retire with 75 percent of active duty base pay.

Retirements take effect on the first day of the month after the Secretary of the Navy approves the request, *except* in cases of voluntary retirement in which a later date has been approved.

If you are considering voluntary retirement or are subject to involuntary or statutory retirement and you have any doubt as to your physical qualification for release from active duty, obtain a preliminary physical examination *six months ahead of the estimated retirement date.* If a disability is discovered at this time, you might be eligible for physical retirement. Information as to your physical condition must be received by Headquarters Marine Corps in time to modify action on your retirement papers.

After the president or Secretary of the Navy approves a request for retirement, or approves involuntary retirement proceedings, and the retirement has become effective, there is no process of law whereby the retired status can be changed except through disciplinary action or because of physical disability incurred subsequently while serving as a retired officer on active duty.

1813. Disability Retirement

Disability retirement is governed by Title 10, U.S. Code. Its important provisions are summarized below.

A *temporary-disability retired list* exists in each service, to which are transferred individuals whose physical condition prevents proper performance of duty but who may yet recover. Pay on the temporary-disability retired list may be either 2.5 percent of active duty pay per year for the number of years of service, or the percentage of disability fixed; but retired pay may not be less than 50 percent or more than 75 percent of active duty pay. Disability retirement pay is tax-exempt.

Persons whose disability is less than 30 percent may instead be discharged with separation pay.

If you are on the temporary-disability retired list, you must have a physical examination at least every eighteen months, for not more than five years. During that time, if your disability becomes permanent and is 30 percent or more, you are permanently retired for physical disability. If, upon examination, you are again found physically fit while on the temporary-disability retired list, you may, at your own consent, be reappointed to the active list in a rank not below that held when you went on the temporary-disability retired list. If you do not wish to return to active duty or are not qualified for duty but are still rated less than 30 percent disabled, you may be separated from the service, with separation pay.

If you are hospitalized for more than three months, a clinical board (or board of medical survey) at the hospital considers your case and usually recommends that you be (1) returned to duty, (2) given further treatment, (3) ordered to limited duty and reexamination after a stated period, (4) given sick leave and reexamination thereafter, or (5) ordered before a Marine Corps physical evaluation board (PEB).

You may waive the right to appear in person, but should be very wary of this unless the medical evidence in your case is uncomplicated and the result certain. You should also have counsel.

Appearance before the board requires less than a day; final action is taken by the Secretary of the Navy. If you are incapacitated but do not require hospitalization, you may take leave or be assigned to temporary duty. If found qualified for continued active duty, you are ordered back to duty. If retired, you must complete travel home within one year from the date of retirement, in accordance with *Joint Travel Regulations*. You may choose any residence desired, even overseas, without regard to your current address of record held at Headquarters.

The report of a PEB is extensively reviewed in the Navy Department. The final reviewing authority is ordinarily the judge advocate general of the Navy. Retirement takes effect on the first day of the month after the secretary approves.

If you have less than eight years' active service and if disability is less than 30 percent, the PEB must determine whether your disability is the proximate result of active service. If the board so finds, you may be discharged with separation pay. Eight years or more of active service is normally considered sufficient to judge the disability at proximate result of military service.

CORRESPONDENCE AND MESSAGES

1814. Official Correspondence

Both Marine Corps and Navy employ the same forms and procedures for official correspondence. These are prescribed in the *Department of the Navy Correspondence Manual*, *Navy Regulations*, and the *Marine Corps Manual*. "Correspondence" embraces letters, endorsements, memoranda, electronic mail (both formal and informal), and facsimile transmissions. Correspondence is filed and maintained in accordance with the *Department of the Navy Records Management Manual*.

As an individual, you may originate official correspondence that pertains to you personally (including any recommendations for improvement or innovation that may benefit the Marine Corps). Correspondence affecting a command as a whole can be originated only by, or in the name of, the commanding officer.

Official correspondence must be conducted through channels and must be promptly forwarded. Failure to do so (if in proper form and language) is a very serious dereliction.

Avoid unnecessary, verbose, imprecise correspondence. Joseph Pulitzer's rule for the staff of the old *New York World* applies with considerable force to military correspondence: "Accuracy, brevity, accuracy!"

During the past decade, government correspondence has grown less precise and less effective. Vague expressions, superlatives, affectations, jargon, and clichéd prose have become commonplace, replacing, in many cases, clear and understandable terms. Complex language is used, not because it contributes to clarity, but because it makes the user feel self-important. It is not consistent with the character of the Marine Corps or with efficiency to dilute correspondence with unmilitary expressions or unnecessary language. Bumper-sticker phrases have no place in Marine Corps documents; leave them to the bumper stickers.

You will find admirable advice regarding official correspondence, and military writing in general, in the *Navy Correspondence Manual.* Read and heed.

1815. Official Letters

According to the nature of the correspondence, official letters may follow either the naval form (which is used throughout the naval establishment) or the business form. Examples and detailed instructions covering both forms can be found in the *Navy Correspondence Manual.*

Hints for Official Letter Writers. Sooner or later, every officer serves as a staff officer, and writing is an essential survival skill during such duty. In addition to taking the initiative and following through, which are keys to success in any Marine Corps assignment, writing *well* will distinguish you from your peers. Here is some advice for preparing official naval correspondence.

Until you are quite familiar with the prescribed forms for official correspondence, do your writing within arm's reach of the *Navy Correspondence Manual.* See that your unit clerks do likewise. And keep an up-to-date dictionary at hand. English is a delightfully idiosyncratic language, filled with exceptions, contradictions, and even perhaps confusion. Sometimes words sound the same but mean different things, and sometimes words are spelled the same but sound differently and mean different things; for example, there's a difference between "led" (led), "lead" (led), and "lead" (led). The dictionary is your friend.

Avoid pointless letters. Correspondence with higher authority should be confined to specific requests, reports, and concrete recommendations.

One letter should normally deal with one subject only. Cover separate subjects to the same addressee by separate letters. Answer official letters by letter, not by endorsement on the letter received, unless specifically directed to do so.

Write in concise, unadorned, direct, and clear language. Generally, use short sentences and paragraphs. Use the passive voice sparingly ("Please arrange the following," not "It is requested that the following arrangements be effectuated"). Do not be afraid to use the first person.

Be as temperate and courteous in correspondence as you would be in discussing the subject face to face with your correspondent.

Organize your facts and ideas before you write. The standard sequence for a staff study or estimate is a good one for almost any kind of official correspondence:

1. Statement of the problem
2. Facts bearing on the problem
3. Discussion
4. Conclusions
5. Recommendations.

Do not send official letters to other officers in the same command. Correspondence within units and headquarters should be by memorandum.

Block out important official letters in double-spaced rough draft. This permits you to make legible corrections and interlineations.

Use "Marine" or "Marines," "officer," "enlisted person," or "all hands" instead of the more generic and bureaucratic "personnel" or "members" wherever possible in official correspondence or directives.

In expressing time, use the naval twenty-four-hour system and never add the superfluous word "hours"—write "1230," not "1230 hours."

Always choose a short, simple word over a long one. Write "pay," "help," "mistake" instead of "compensation," "assistance," "inadvertency." Here are a few examples of gobbledygook, jargon, and canned language excerpted from a sampling of official correspondence. We would all be better off if most of these were never written again:

above-named personnel
as appropriate
appraise—where "apprise" is intended
at the earliest practicable moment
considered opinion
definitive—where "definite" is meant
deobligate
effectuate
finalize
firm up

forward—where "foreword" is intended
formalize
frame of reference
full impact
in conformance with
infeasible of accomplishment
in light of the foregoing
interface incompatibility (except in information management)
lead, the bluish-white lustrous metal that is very soft, highly malleable, and a relatively poor conductor of electricity (with symbol Pb and atomic number 82)—as a misspelling of "led," the past participle of the verb "to lead"
logisticswise
management—as a substitute for "command" or "leadership"
marshall—as a misspelling of "marshal"
materially impaired effectiveness
maximize
outload, offload, onload—"load" and "unload" work fine
personnelwise
pertinent facts
preventative—as "preventive" will do (the extra syllable adds nothing)
pursuant to
rendered mandatory
salient data
thorough and complete investigation
top management
unprecedented—as a substitute for "unusual."

1816. Official Mail

Official correspondence may be mailed with official franked envelopes bearing an official return address and the notation *Official Business* in the upper left-hand corner. As an officer, you are entitled to use such envelopes for correspondence that clearly involves government business and for government parcels within prescribed weight limits. Be scrupulous in exercising this privilege. Remember you also are a taxpayer.

1817. Personal Correspondence

Because you change stations every few years, keeping correspondents advised of your correct mailing address can be quite a problem. Change your address with your regular correspondents online if possible, or get change-of-address cards from your mail clerk or station post office and send them every time you are detached. For guidance of your family or parents at your permanent home address, postal laws and regulations permit postage-free forwarding of any class of mail addressed to a member of the armed services, if marked, "Change of Address Due to Official Orders, Postal Reg. 157.9."

Fleet Post Office and Army Post Office. Mail may be sent to units and persons afloat or overseas at domestic postage rates via East Coast and West Coast military postal centers. This privilege merits your use, as it saves you and your correspondents considerable money in postage charges, especially for publications and parcels. Units that deploy or are at sea receive their mail via the tracking and routing efforts of military postmasters in the shortest time possible.

Generally speaking, if a ship or Marine Corps deployed unit is on the East Coast, the Atlantic, Europe, or Africa and adjacent waters, its mail goes via FPO AE or APO AE (plus zip code), with domestic postage charges to New York. Ships and units in the Pacific, Far East, or Indian Ocean receive mail via FPO AP or APO AP (plus zip code) with domestic charges paid to San Francisco or Seattle. A ship or station based in one geographic area, but deploying temporarily to another, will retain its original address, even though the postmasters will route the mail through different theaters. Finally, be aware that current postal privileges allow free mailing of letters and small parcels *within* a given postal theater, by writing "MPS" in the corner normally reserved for stamps. Be sure to obtain specific instructions, however, before attempting to use this procedure.

SECURITY OF INFORMATION

1818. Operational and Personal Security

After taking your oath and becoming a new Marine officer, in your new life and status you receive access to information not generally available to civilians. One of your most important responsibilities then becomes the safeguarding and proper use of this information in such a way that it can never fall into the hands of enemies of the United States. Remember that, war or peace, the battle for information goes on continually. Our success in this battle will determine whether the odds of physical combat are on our side or our enemies' sides.

Indiscreet conversation and personal letters constitute great menaces to security. Guard against unthinking discussion of classified "shop talk," even with your family and friends. Avoid loose talk in public places. When you are on the telephone, you can never tell who may be listening. Automatic self-censorship is a responsibility of all Marines.

1819. Security of Classified Matter

Classified matter is anything—either information or matériel—that, in the public interest, must be safeguarded against unauthorized or improper disclosure. *Navy Regulations*, as well as the *Department of the Navy Personnel Security Program* and the *Department of the Navy Information Security Program*, contains detailed instructions that must be followed to the letter when you handle classified matter. The security of classified matter is the security of the United States.

Classifications. The categories of security classification are *Top Secret*, *Secret*, and *Confidential*. In addition, regulations classify certain information regarding nuclear weapons and related subjects as *Special Information.* It is up to the originator of matter—if so authorized—to assign it the appropriate classification, and he or she, as well as higher authorities, may reclassify it when appropriate. Reclassification can involve either "upgrading" or "downgrading."

Handling of Classified Matter. The precautions regarding preparation, marking, custody, handling, transmitting, storage, disclosure, control, accounting for, and disposal of classified matter may be found in the references at the beginning of this section, and, of course, you must follow them to your utmost. If, however, you find yourself in a situation where you cannot physically comply with certain of these rules, you are bound simply to do your utmost, in common sense and zeal, to safeguard whatever may be entrusted to you. Should you have reason to believe classified information has been compromised, through your fault or anyone else's, you must inform your security manager or commanding officer at once.

No one, regardless of rank, position, or clearance level, is automatically entitled to knowledge or possession of classified matter. Such information goes only to those who *need to know.*

LEAVE AND LIBERTY

1820. Leave of Absence

Subject to the needs of the service, leave of absence provides time off for mental and physical relaxation from duty and gives you the opportunity to settle your affairs when the time comes for change of station. Every officer on active duty accrues leave at the rate of thirty days a year (that is, 2½ days per month).

Your commanding officer sometimes cannot grant every officer all the leave he or she rates without jeopardizing the readiness of your command. Whatever leave is not taken "goes on the books" until you have a maximum of sixty days' unused, or accrued, leave. Earned leave that accrues above sixty days must be automatically dropped on 30 September each year, and when you retire. As you approach retirement, under certain circumstances it may be beneficial to let leave accrue to a minimum of thirty days, since you receive a lump-sum payment for such accrued leave when you retire. Short of final years, however, take leave as you can; regular leave keeps you sharp for the next mission. And you can never recover the unused leave days that are dropped each 30 September.

Leave of absence, or more simply and commonly *leave,* describes authorized vacation or absence from duty, as distinguished from liberty, which is merely authority to be away from your place of duty for short periods and is not charged to leave.

Accrued leave is the unused leave to your credit "on the books" each 1 October. You cannot bank up more than sixty days' accrued leave, except in extraordinary circumstances when authorized by Marine Corps Headquarters.

Annual leave is leave taken as routine vacation from duty. Annual leave is limited to your total accrued leave plus up to forty-five days' advance leave, with approval, but may not exceed periods of sixty days.

Sick leave is given to convalescents on recommendation of the medical authorities or to repatriated prisoners of war. Sick leave does not count against accrued leave.

Emergency leave may be granted to help alleviate some personal emergency, such as death or serious illness in the immediate family. Emergency leave is charged against accrued leave and may not exceed 105 days.

Excess leave is leave in excess of all your accrued leave plus forty-five days' advance leave. Avoid taking excess leave when you can possibly do so because your pay and allowances are checked while you are on excess leave.

Earned leave is the term used to describe the leave potential of an individual at any given date during the fiscal year. Earned leave is calculated as follows. From the amount of accrued leave, subtract whatever leave has been taken since the outset of the fiscal year to the date in question. To that remainder add the amount of leave earned since the beginning of the fiscal year. Earned leave may exceed sixty days during the fiscal year but will always be cut back to sixty days at the beginning of the new fiscal year.

Advance leave is an accounting term to describe leave granted in advance of accrual.

Delay in reporting is leave authorized to be taken after detachment from one permanent station and before reporting to another. It is normally charged against your leave balance.

Graduation leave is granted to officers newly commissioned from one of the service academies (not to officers from any other source). It is thirty days, not chargeable to the officer's leave account, and you must take it prior to reporting to the first permanent duty station (ordinarily Basic School) or CONUS port of embarkation if ordered to permanent duty beyond the seas.

1821. Computing Leave and Delay in Reporting

No small amount of low-order bookkeeping and finger counting centers on the average officer's calculation of leave and delay. The calculations are, however, relatively straightforward.

Your day of departure on leave, normally after 1600, counts as a day on duty (and hence is not charged as leave). If your commander authorizes a departure earlier than 1600, the day still counts as a day of duty, not as a day of leave.

If you return after the beginning of working hours on shore station or on board ship, the calendar day of return counts as a day of leave. For leave-accounting purposes, the beginning of the formal workday varies by command, but it is typically 0700, 0800, or 0900. If you return after the designated start of the workday, your day of return counts as a day of leave. If, however, you return before working hours, the calendar day of return is a day of duty. All the days in between count as days of leave.

Finally, regulations require Marines to begin and end leave periods at or in the vicinity of their duty locations. They also prohibit the combination of leave periods with liberty periods. The implications of these regulations for computing leave periods are somewhat nuanced. Check with your adjutant or personnel officer for clarification.

1822. Leave Requests and Records

Requesting Leave. When you want leave, give your immediate supervisor or commanding officer advance notice. Some organizations have an annual leave plan that permits all officers to book leave well in advance. After you have informal approval for your projected leave, submit a leave request via Marine Online to the officer who is authorized to grant leave—usually your battalion commander, squadron commander, officer in charge, or one of their designated subordinates such as the executive officer, adjutant, or personnel officer. Your leave request should include the number of days and type of leave desired, the number of days' leave you have already taken during the fiscal year, your address while on leave, whether you are a member of any court or board, and any other pertinent information or special justification for the request.

If approved, your leave request is returned by electronic endorsement, which you then print and keep with you throughout your leave.

Officers are typically entrusted to sign themselves out on and in from leave by annotating their leave papers directly. Some commands may require them to report the start and end of leave with a telephone call to the officer of the day or S-1.

Address During Leave. It is your responsibility to keep your command apprised of your address at all times while on leave. If your plans change, inform your command by telephone. If you are touring, set up a number of check-in points, such as hotels where you expect to stay or homes of friends or relatives. You have no leg to stand on if, while on leave, your command tries to communicate with you and cannot reach you. The ubiquity of cell phones today has made this responsibility easier to fulfill.

Your Leave Record. Every officer has a leave record (part of the leave and earnings statement, or LES) on which all leave taken is debited and all leave earned is credited each month. This record is compiled and kept current by the headquarters that administers you, but it is your responsibility to see that your leave record is correct.

1823. Foreign Leave

Foreign travel while on leave is subject to certain controls and restrictions for reasons of personal and operational security. In general, Marines desiring to take leave or travel outside the United States, or outside the territory or foreign country of current assignment, must obtain approval from their commanding officers; there are, however, exceptions for visits to certain foreign areas specified from time to time in current directives, for which blanket authorization is granted.

Marines going on foreign leave may travel, on a space-available basis, in government aircraft. Unless you are specifically authorized to wear a uniform while on foreign leave, you must wear civilian clothes.

1824. Liberty

Liberty is local free time, within limits, that does not count as leave. Normal weekends are considered periods of liberty. Liberty may also be granted at any time for up to forty-eight hours. If the period includes a legal holiday, any commanding officer can extend a "forty-eight" to a "seventy-two."

Commanding officers so authorized by the commandant may grant ninety-six-hour liberty, which normally encompasses a weekend. But, as previously mentioned, liberty cannot be used as a device to extend leave.

Unless you have specific permission to the contrary, while on liberty you must remain within the general vicinity of your duty station. Almost all bases, stations, and units have standing orders that designate "liberty limits"—normally functions of the length of the liberty period—beyond which ordinary liberty does not extend. The purpose of this is to prevent Marines from going so far afield that they cannot count on returning safely within the prescribed time.

IDENTITY DEVICES

1825. ID Card

The armed forces identification card, or ID card, is the most important identifying document you have. Today's ID card, a common access card (CAC) identical for active duty and inactive reserve forces, features bar coding, a magnetic strip, and an embedded integrated circuit chip. It identifies you as a Marine officer and must be safeguarded with great care. The Marine Corps issues retired

Marines a simple green photo ID card. Loss of an ID card is serious and must be reported immediately because the cards are controlled items.

Carry the card at all times, and never surrender it. If somebody asks you to surrender your ID card in exchange for a temporary pass or badge—for example, to access a building or space—they are doing so in violation of regulations; after showing them your CAC, politely offer them another form of identification to hold "hostage." The ID card is not a pass, but an identifying device.

1826. Identification Tags

Every Marine on active duty is issued two "dog tags" for identification should he or she be killed or wounded in action. These tags are items of equipment. When not required to be worn, they must remain in your possession. Note that both tags must be worn, when tags are required.

1827. Official Photograph

An official photograph is part of your official record at Marine Corps Headquarters. Prior to any consideration by a regular promotion board or other board, you must submit an official photograph. This photo cannot be more than six months old when the board convenes. This is then filed in your official record. Considering its purpose, you should take care to look your best. See your adjutant or consult current directives to determine the uniform, pose, and data desired. If your board is about to convene, arrange for the current photo to be transmitted directly to the Promotion Branch (HQMC Code MMPR-1).

1828. Dependents' ID Cards

Your spouse and each family member over age ten are entitled to an armed forces dependent's card. This card, like your ID card, is an identity device and does not in itself entitle the bearer to anything. It ordinarily serves, however, to establish identification for medical care, military exchange, and similar privileges extended to dependents.

My Lord—If I attempted to answer the mass of futile correspondence that surrounds me, I should be debarred from all serious business of campaigning.

I must remind your Lordship—for the last time—that so long as I retain an independent position, I shall see that no officer under my command is debarred, by attending to the futile drivelling of mere quill driving in your Lordship's office, from attending to his first duty—which is, and always has been, so to train the private men under his command that they may, without question, beat any force opposed to them in the field.

—Letter attributed to the Duke of Wellington

19

PAY, ALLOWANCES, AND OFFICIAL TRAVEL

A Marine Corps anecdote relates that, during the early days of World War II, a lofty-minded civilian visited Guadalcanal. During his tour, war aims were mentioned. Addressing Lieutenant Colonel L. B. Puller, one of the most hard-bitten professionals on the island—or, for that matter, in the Marine Corps—the visitor inquired, "And what, colonel, are you fighting for?"

Colonel Puller reflected for a moment, then answered, "$649 a month." It is immaterial whether you are inclined to this view or to the sentiments of George Washington, who shared his thoughts on remuneration with Congress upon his appointment as commander in chief in 1775: "As to pay, I beg leave to assure the Congress that, as no pecuniary consideration could have tempted me to accept this arduous employment at the expense of my domestic ease and happiness, I do not wish to make any profit from it." The importance of knowing about pay and allowances is self-evident.

Every member of the service is normally paid twice monthly based on *grade* and *length of service.* Regardless of whether your grade is temporary or permanent, you are paid at the rates prescribed for that grade.

The military term for your pay is *military compensation.* The military equivalent of a civilian salary includes basic pay, quarters allowance, subsistence allowance, and, often overlooked, the federal income tax advantage deriving from tax-exempt allowances. Your basic pay is the core of your military compensation, and it is a function of your pay grade and longevity—that is, the length of your service creditable for pay purposes. You also normally enjoy a modest cost-of-living increase to basic pay each January, in line with pay levels in the private economy.

Besides regular pay, just described, officers whose duties or status so qualify them are entitled to incentive and special pay, including flight pay (see Sections 1908 and 1909).

MILITARY COMPENSATION

1901. Pay System

Marines, both active and reserve, are paid through a centralized, automated Marine Corps total force system (MCTFS). A prospective replacement under final review, the Defense Integrated Military Human Resource System (Personnel and Pay), constitutes part of an integrated armed forces pay and personnel system.

Under MCTFS, a master pay account is maintained for each Marine by the Defense Finance and Accounting Service. For your use, DFAS produces a monthly leave and earnings statement from information in your master pay account, available to you online (https://mypay.dfas.mil/mypay.aspx). Your LES reflects what you are due, tax withholding, leave balance, and any deductions, and it forecasts the amount payable for the next two paydays.

By Department of the Treasury mandate, all Marines receive their semimonthly pay by electronic funds transfer, or "direct deposit," to their designated bank account.

1902. Service Creditable for Pay Purposes

In determining your length of service for pay purposes, you receive credit for all service, active or inactive, in the Marine Corps, Navy, Army, Air Force, Coast Guard, the reserve components thereof, and the National Guard. In addition, credit is given to Marines for service in the Nurse Corps of the Army, Navy, and the Public Health Service, and reserve components thereof. Credit is also allowed for service as an officer, deck officer, or junior engineer in the National Oceanic and Atmospheric Administration. Active service in the appointive grade as aviation cadet and officer candidate (Platoon Leaders Class) may be counted as service for pay purposes.

Service not creditable for longevity increases is service as cadet or midshipman; service in inactive National Guard, or in State, Home, or Territorial Guard; service in ROTC; and time spent in voided fraudulent enlistment.

You count, in the computation of basic pay, the total of all periods authorized to be counted in any of the services.

1903. Family Members

Although basic pay is not affected by marital status or family members, some allowances do vary according to your family size. The law defines family as:

- Your spouse (whose dependency is presumed)
- Unmarried children under age twenty-one (twenty-three if enrolled in higher education), or over age twenty-one if handicapped and incapable of self-support
- A parent (or one who has stood in loco parentis), if chiefly dependent on you for over half support
- Stepchildren and adopted children, if dependent.

Except for your spouse or unmarried minor children, you must be able to prove dependency for any persons for whom you claim allowances.

1904. Subsistence Allowance

Every officer on active duty receives a basic monthly subsistence allowance (known officially as *basic allowance for subsistence*, or BAS), regardless of his or her family status. The law exempts subsistence allowance from income tax.

1905. Quarters Allowance

Quarters allowance (known officially as *basic allowance for housing*, or BAH) comes in many forms to satisfy various housing situations that occur among servicemembers. In general, you are entitled to an amount of BAH that is a function of duty location, pay grade, and whether you have dependents. Under most circumstances, you receive BAH for the geographic location where you are stationed, not where you live. Additionally, you may be entitled to different BAH amounts if you are residing separately from your dependents. This occurs, for example, if you are assigned to an unaccompanied overseas tour or have a dependent child that resides with a former spouse. The rules regarding these situations can become quite complex. Consult your local finance office if you are in one of these situations.

If you are on permanent duty within the fifty states and are not furnished government quarters, you are entitled to BAH, calculated based on your dependency status, pay grade, and permanent duty station's zip code. If stationed overseas, including U.S. protectorates, and not furnished government quarters, you are entitled to an overseas housing allowance (OHA), calculated based on your dependency status, pay grade, and permanent duty station. If serving an unaccompanied overseas tour, you normally rate BAH at the "with dependents" rate based on the zip code where your spouse or family actually resides, plus OHA at the "without dependents" rate if you are not furnished government quarters overseas.

If you live in quarters managed under the public-private venture program, which operates at many U.S. installations, you remain entitled to and continue to receive quarters allowance. Under normal circumstances, you in turn surrender this same amount to the private partner (for example, Lincoln Military Housing) in a manner similar to paying rent.

Officers without family members who do not qualify for a full quarters allowance because they are at sea or living in government quarters are entitled to a partial quarters allowance.

While on authorized delay or in transit between permanent stations, you rate quarters allowance, as well as for the interval between the date when sworn in and reporting for first duty.

If uncertain about your entitlement to quarters allowance, consult your unit's personnel officer or the local finance office. Inattentive or careless officers have unwittingly drawn quarters allowances exceeding their entitlements and, after several months or even years, found themselves deeply indebted to the federal government.

The law exempts quarters allowance from income tax.

The Defense Travel Management Office maintains a handy online BAH calculator that will help you verify your entitlement to quarters allowance at your present or any future duty station. To find it, search "BAH calculator."

1906. Family Separation Allowance

If your dependents are not authorized to live with you at or near your permanent duty station, whether inside or outside the United States, you may be entitled to *family separation allowance* (FSA) payable at the rate of $250 per month (2016).

FSA is intended to provide compensation for added expenses incurred because of an enforced family separation under one of the following circumstances:

- Transportation of dependents is not authorized at government expense, and the dependents do not live in the vicinity of your permanent duty station.
- Transportation of dependents is authorized at government expense, but you have elected an unaccompanied tour of duty because a dependent cannot accompany you to the permanent station due to certified medical reasons.
- You are on duty aboard a ship, and the ship is away from the homeport continuously for more than thirty days.
- You are on temporary duty away from the permanent station continuously for more than thirty days, and your dependents are not residing at or near the assigned temporary duty station.

In addition, you may be entitled to FSA if your dependents are evacuated from a danger area and they temporarily occupy government quarters at a safe haven area.

1907. Uniform Allowances for Officers

All Marine officers, regardless of source of commission or previous enlisted status, are entitled to an *initial uniform allowance.* Except as noted below, the initial uniform allowance is payable only once to an officer:

- Upon first reporting for active duty (other than for training) for a period of more than ninety days
- Upon completing at least fourteen days of active duty or active duty for training as a member of a reserve component
- Upon completing fourteen periods of inactive duty training as a member of the Ready Reserve
- Upon reporting for the first period of active duty required of a member of the Armed Forces Health Professions Scholarship Program.

Upon transfer to a different reserve component that requires a different uniform, a reserve officer may receive another initial uniform allowance. Regular officers may not receive this allowance when transferring to another military service.

Civilian clothing allowances for officers depend on an assignment to a high-risk area, certified as such by the Department of State or Department of Defense. In such a case, where officers wear civilian clothing for all or a substantial part of their duties, a one-time allowance is paid for the two- or three-year tour length.

The subject of uniform allowances remains complex. For the final word, consult *DOD Financial Management Regulations, Volume 7A.*

1908. Special and Incentive Pay

Basic pay and allowances are only a part of military compensation. Many Marines qualify for various special and incentive pays that are part of the Marine Corps' recruitment and retention efforts. Some of these compensate Marines for assignment to hazardous or difficult duty conditions. Examples include additional pay for undertaking an aviation career, maintaining needed foreign language proficiency, or performing hazardous duty in obedience to competent orders.

Current law authorizes more than sixty special and incentive pays, although not all may be available to Marines. By way of example, the following hazardous duties currently rate incentive pay:

- Duty involving parachute jumping as an essential part of military duty
- Duty involving frequent and regular participation in flight operation on the flight deck of an aircraft carrier or ship other than aircraft carrier from which aircraft are launched
- Duty involving the demolition of explosives as a primary duty (including training for such duty)
- Duty inside a high- or low-pressure chamber
- Duty as a human acceleration or deceleration experimental subject
- Duty as a human test subject in thermal stress experiments
- Duty involving the servicing of aircraft or missiles with highly toxic fuels or propellants
- Duty involving fumigation tasks utilizing highly toxic pesticides
- Duty involving laboratory work utilizing live dangerous viruses or bacteria

- Duty involving handling of chemical munitions
- Duty involving maritime visit, board, search, and seizure operations
- Duty involving use of ski-equipped aircraft on the ground in Antarctica or on the Arctic ice pack.

You may not receive hazardous duty incentive pay for more than two purposes at the same time.

In addition to hazardous duty incentive pay, Marine officers frequently qualify for two other types of incentive pay:

- Career sea pay (CSP) compensates persons assigned to a ship performing missions while primarily under way. Payment ranges from $50 to $150 per month depending on pay grade. (More than thirty-six months entitles you to CSP premium.)
- Foreign language proficiency pay (FLPP) provides up to $1,000 (see the current Marine Corps order on this program for detailed information) per month for persons demonstrating and maintaining proficiency in one or more foreign languages, validated by examination on an annual basis. Only those assigned to billets requiring language proficiency or holding an MOS that requires language skills will receive FLPP.

Special and incentive pays such as these are normally *not* exempt from income tax.

1909. Flight Pay

To qualify for flight pay (or, as it is now technically termed, "aviation career incentive pay," or ACIP), you must be designated as a student naval aviator or student naval flight officer, or rated as naval aviator or naval flight officer, and be assigned to an aviation unit having aircraft. During your first twelve years' service, besides having a minimum number of operational flying assignments, you must also meet annual and semiannual prescribed minimum required flight hours. After your initial twelve years in flight status, your continued qualification to fly for pay depends on satisfactory passage of "gates" set by law, which are contained in *Department of Defense Financial Management Regulation, Volume 1-16*. Determining continued entitlement to ACIP beyond twelve years is somewhat complex, but the *Marine Corps Assignment, Classification, and Travel System Manual* (ACTSMAN) contains two handy flow charts to aid in understanding the process.

1910. Advance Pay

An advance of pay (a "dead horse" in slang) incident to a permanent change of station (PCS) provides funds to meet the extraordinary expenses of a government-ordered relocation. It assists with out-of-pocket expenses that exceed or precede reimbursements incurred during a PCS move, which are not typical of day-to-day military living.

You may draw advance pay up to 90 days prior to departure from the old permanent duty station until 180 days after reporting to a new permanent station, provided the orders are not incident to separation from the service or trial by court-martial. Temporary duty en route is no bar to drawing advance pay. The amount advanced normally does not exceed one month's pay, but with approval you may draw as much as three months' basic pay (less income tax, deduction for Social Security, and indebtedness to the government).

1911. Midshipmen and Cadets

Academy midshipmen and cadets at the other service academies receive $1,027.20 per month (as of 2017) in basic pay, from which several mandatory fees are deducted. They receive rations in kind or commuted rations at rates periodically fixed by regulations.

1912. Pay of Enlisted Personnel

The monthly basic pay of enlisted personnel of the Marine Corps, Navy, Coast Guard, Army, and Air Force may be found in current pay tables and is the same, grade for grade, in all services.

Under certain circumstances, enlisted Marines may be authorized a subsistence allowance in lieu of rations in kind at a current rate determined by law and regulation. Regulations give commanding officers some latitude in authorizing this allowance.

In general, enlisted Marines are entitled to a quarters allowance, with or without family, under the same conditions as officers.

Leave rations are granted to enlisted Marines on leave (if they are not furnished rations in kind) at the current BAS rate.

1913. Enlisted Clothing Allowances

An initial, in-kind clothing allowance is granted to each enlisted person. Six months after assignment to active duty, a monthly basic clothing replacement allowance accrues to each enlisted person. The first payment of this allowance is made on the Marine's enlistment anniversary month after completing one year of uninterrupted service. After three years of service, an increased standard clothing maintenance allowance accrues.

1914. Reenlistment Bonus

The purpose of this bonus is to encourage enlisted Marines, particularly those with costly or specialized skills, to reenlist. To provide you an idea of the magnitude of this bonus, Marines who were reenlisting during fiscal year 2016 after completing their first enlistment (known as first-term Marines) in one of twenty-five high-demand military occupational specialties were eligible for "shipping over" bonuses ranging from $12,000 to $56,000. Including those with lesser bonuses, there were, in total, fifty-five specialties offering first-term reenlistment bonuses in 2016. Be aware of current reenlistment bonuses so that you can intelligently advise your Marines and promote their reenlistment.

1915. Retired Pay

Retired pay refers to and consists of the retainer received by an officer on the retired list. In contrast, separation pay is a lump-sum payment made to an officer involuntarily discharged from the service, based on 10 percent of active duty pay for each year of commissioned service. No allowances are paid to retired officers.

Computation. Originally, retired pay was based on the active duty pay of the grade in which an officer was serving at the time of retirement, plus periodic increases thereafter. Except for physical disability retirement, retired pay was computed by multiplying 2.5 percent of the officer's active duty base pay at time of retirement at twenty or more years by the number of years' service creditable for pay purposes, the total not to exceed 75 percent of such basic pay.

Marines entering service after 7 September 1980 may retire after twenty years of service and receive a monthly retainer based on 50 percent of their averaged high three years of pay, plus 2.5 percent for each additional year served after twenty. Those entering after 1 August 1986 can also retire after twenty years of service and receive payment based upon 50 percent of their high three years of pay. This last category of retiree, however, may elect the REDUX retirement system as an alternative and receive a career retention bonus of $30,000 at year fifteen, then retire after twenty years of service on a basis of 40 percent of high three years of pay plus 3.5 percent of each additional year served after twenty. A significant feature of the REDUX scheme comes with a recompilation of retirement pay at age sixty-two. Essentially, the high-three and REDUX program salaries are equalized at this point. However, subsequent cost of living adjustments are reduced for the REDUX participant.

Persons retiring on or after 1 January 2007 may receive credit for years of active service in excess of thirty years, under conditions authorized during a period designated by the secretary of Defense for such purposes. In theory, this new act provides for computing retired pay percentages from 75 to 100 percent of active duty basic pay (Paragraph [3], Section 1409[b], Title 10, U.S. Code, as amended).

In 2015, the *Military Compensation and Retirement Modernization Commission* called for yet another revision to the military retirement system and, at writing, Congress was considering the proposal, which amounted to a hybrid retirement system combining features of traditional military retirement pay and civilian-style, defined-contribution plans (that is, 401[k] retirement plans).

Retired Pay Accounts. DFAS Retired and Annuitant (R&A) Pay manages pay accounts for all military retirees. DFAS is an agency under the Office of the Secretary of Defense. R&A Pay establishes, maintains, and pays military retirees and their surviving spouses and other family members.

Income tax continues to be withheld on retired pay except for physically disabled officers wholly exempt from payment of income taxes. Unless otherwise requested, all allotments are automatically continued when you retire.

1916. Settlement for Unused Leave

Each member of the Marine Corps or Marine Corps Reserve having unused leave to his or her credit on discharge or separation from active duty is compensated for such unused leave on the basis of basic pay. Payment is made for a career total up to sixty days' unused leave. Thus, as retirement approaches, some may consider it advantageous to keep the maximum accrued leave on the books.

TRAVEL BY MILITARY PERSONNEL

1917. Travel Orders

Travel status is travel away from your duty station, under orders on official business. When you apply for reimbursement for travel performed, or for transportation for travel to be performed, you must have travel orders.

Authority to issue travel orders rests with the commandant, who delegates this authority to certain commands.

All travel orders normally contain the following nine items:

1. Marine's name
2. Reference to authority other than the commandant
3. The place or places to which the Marine is ordered to travel
4. The date on which the Marine will proceed
5. The delay authorized in reporting, if any
6. The modes of transportation authorized
7. The duty (official/public) to be performed
8. The person to whom the Marine shall report (if so required)
9. The accounting data for cost of travel.

Omission of any of these items can delay reimbursement and might cause rejection of a travel claim as invalid. Be sure you understand your orders before departure, and carry them out exactly.

It is important to understand terminology in your orders that affects the timing—what is known as "proceed time"—on which you must execute travel. The dates when you must comply with travel orders, and when you must report, depend on certain phraseology that always appears in orders. Check to see which of the following expressions appears, then govern yourself accordingly.

"*Proceed.*" If your orders have no limiting date and no haste is required in execution, you are directed simply to "proceed." You are allowed four days' proceed time before commencement of travel (unless you have also been granted delay in reporting).

"*Proceed without Delay.*" When haste in execution is demanded, you are directed to "proceed without delay." You are allowed only forty-eight hours' proceed time before commencement of travel.

"*Proceed Immediately.*" When maximum haste is required, orders are worded "proceed immediately." In this case you rate only twelve hours' proceed time before commencement of travel.

A number of additional ground rules apply to computation and availability of proceed time when travel orders require temporary or temporary additional duty (TAD) or are received while on such duty. For these rules, consult the *Marine Corps Assignment, Classification, and Travel System Manual.*

You should be familiar with several types of travel orders.

Permanent Change of Station. This includes transfer from one permanent station to another; travel to first duty station after appointment; call to active duty; change in home port or home yard of a ship (for family members); and travel home from last duty station upon retirement, separation, or relief from active duty.

Temporary Duty (TD). This is duty at a place other than permanent station, under orders that direct further assignment to a new permanent station. While on temporary duty—as distinguished from *temporary additional duty*—you have no permanent station.

Temporary Additional Duty. This includes travel away from permanent station, performance of duty elsewhere, and return to permanent station.

Blanket or Repeat Travel Orders. These are temporary additional duty orders issued to individuals for regular and frequent trips away from permanent duty stations in connection with duty.

1918. What to Do about Your Orders

Upon receipt of orders (this is written to apply specifically to temporary additional duty orders, as these are the most frequently encountered), here are the steps to follow:

1. On receiving orders, read them through and check the following points:
    a. Correct rank, name, Social Security number, and MOS
    b. Departure date
    c. Place or places to be visited
    d. Whether you are to report to a given headquarters or command
    e. Mission you are to accomplish
    f. Security clearance

   g. Modes or options of transportation
   h. Whether the orders are signed
   i. First (receiving) endorsement completed
   j. Statement on requirement to use government quarters and meals.
2. If your orders appear incorrect, or if it appears that you cannot carry them out as directed, return them immediately to the issuing officer with an explanation of the difficulty.
3. Check out before departing and check in on return with your adjutant/S-1, or possibly the Installation Personnel Administration Center depending on duty station policies, during working hours, or with the officer of the day or staff duty officer at all other times.
4. If your orders so direct, you will have to report to some other headquarters or command (these are known as "reporting orders"—those not requiring you to report to anyone are known as "nonreporting orders"). When your TAD is completed at the distant place or station and before returning, be sure your orders are endorsed and signed, stating the time and date you reported, the date your TAD was completed, and the availability or nonavailability of quarters and messing facilities.
5. If your orders do not direct you to report (that is, are "nonreporting") and if you intend to claim full per diem, and if your TAD at a place is twenty-four hours or longer, you must obtain a certificate of endorsement from the command representative at that place, to the effect that government quarters and mess were not available for your occupancy while there on TAD, assuming that was the case. This entitles you to a higher per diem to cover your lodging expenses.
6. If, while away from your parent command, you find you cannot carry out your orders as written without incurring additional expense, or if some unforeseen contingency arises that is not provided for in the orders, request instructions by telephone (which can be reimbursed at government expense) or email before proceeding further. Reimbursement for unauthorized additional expenses or unauthorized travel might be denied if prior approval from the command is not received.
7. If orders specify travel by government aircraft where available, you must use government air unless a transportation officer certifies that government air transportation is not available. Under current regulations,

government air is considered "available" if there is a scheduled government plane departing for your destination within forty-eight hours of the time you plan to leave. If no special mode of transportation—or some other option—is specified in your orders, take your choice but aim to make it one that is most economical for your command.

8. Keep an accurate itinerary and a record of authorized travel expenses for which you can claim reimbursement (see Section 1921).
9. Turn in your orders for return endorsement and then complete your travel claim within five working days after your return to home station.

1919. Travel Time

Travel time allowed in connection with permanent change of station is either the actual time required or "constructive travel time," whichever is less.

Actual travel time is computed in whole days regardless of the length of time actually spent traveling in any given day. This requires completion of an itinerary showing all stops of one calendar day or more.

Constructive travel time for commercial transportation is one hour for each forty miles of travel by rail or bus, with a proportionate part of one hour allowed for any fraction of forty miles; and one hour for each five hundred miles of air travel, with similar proportionate allowances for fractions of five hundred miles. One day of travel time is allowed for each eighteen hours of commercial constructive travel time.

Constructive travel time for travel by privately owned vehicle (POV) is based on one day for each three hundred and fifty miles and for any fraction above fifty miles (that is, 350 miles = 1 day, 400 miles = 1 day, 401 miles = 2 days).

Regardless of the actual sequence of travel, constructive travel time is computed in order of POV, commercial surface, and commercial air. It is computed on the basis of the official distance between the points of duty contained in the *Defense Table of Official Distances* (DTOD).

Regardless of the mode or modes of transportation, only one day of travel time is allowed if the ordered travel is four hundred miles or less.

Government and commercial vessel travel time is the actual time required to complete the trip.

Proceed, delay, and travel time are covered in detail in Chapter 4 of the ACTSMAN. There are few parts of the ACTSMAN more important for a young officer to know thoroughly.

1920. Travel Guidelines

The guidelines and norms for official military travel are complex and vary somewhat with the type of travel you are executing, but here are some of the highlights.

On *permanent change of station*, except when traveling in a group or with troops, you normally enjoy some flexibility for travel within the United States. When executing PCS orders, you may elect one of the following modes of transportation (listed from most common to least common):

- Privately owned vehicle, which entitles you to mileage expense at a prescribed rate
- Common carrier transportation (scheduled air, rail, or bus) on government travel request (GTR), which means the government procures the ticket(s) at no expense to you
- Government or government-contracted transportation, if available, which the government funds directly
- Common carrier transportation at your initial expense (when authorized and quite rare), which means that, after you submit your travel claim, the government reimburses you the authorized expense of the ticket(s) you purchase.

When executing PCS travel by privately owned vehicle, the authorized travel days are calculated using 350 miles per day (based on the DTOD distance between the authorized points). One travel day is allowed for each 350 miles of official distance of ordered travel. If the excess distance is 51 or more miles after dividing the total official distance by 350, one additional travel day is allowed.

For travel in connection with TD, reimbursement for travel is generally similar to PCS as shown above.

For travel under TAD orders, which permit per diem reimbursement, transportation is normally furnished in kind or by transportation request, and reimbursement is at specified per diem rates. If, for whatever authorized reason, you opt not to accept transportation in kind or by transportation request and travel by POV, you will be reimbursed for the actual cost of the conveyance or at a given prescribed rate per mile for the official distance. If travel by POV is authorized and used—as more advantageous to the government—you are entitled to a different mileage rate.

If the TAD orders authorize you to travel by private conveyance (normally when it is advantageous to the government), you are entitled to travel time for the actual time necessary to make the trip within certain parameters. In this case, the authorized travel days are calculated using 400 miles per day (again based on the DTOD distance between the authorized points). One travel day is allowed for each 400 miles of official distance of ordered travel. If the excess distance is 1 or more miles after dividing the total official distance by 400, one additional travel day is allowed. When the total official distance is 400 or fewer miles, only one day of travel time is allowed. If POV use is for the traveler's convenience, the traveler is only authorized one travel day (based on a typical flight time of one day) for each leg.

When orders direct a specific mode of transportation but you perform travel via another mode, including privately owned conveyance, for your own convenience, you will not be entitled to reimbursement of full mileage expense, or to a monetary allowance in lieu of transportation, unless the authority responsible for furnishing the transportation requests certifies that GTRs were not available or the mode of transportation directed was not available at the time and place required in time to comply with the orders.

In all cases, travel time in excess of that authorized by the directed mode in your orders is chargeable as annual leave.

1921. Reimbursement of Travel Expenses

The law provides for reimbursement of authorized travel expenses for military personnel and, when applicable, their authorized dependents who travel by private conveyance, bus, rail, or aircraft. The allowances for travel are computed based on some combination of actual expenses, mileage rates, and/or per diem expenses. Basically, the regulations authorize reimbursement of four broad categories of travel expenses:

1. *Transportation* expense covers the expense of your conveyance from origin to destination (and return, if applicable), and it is provided for by transportation in kind, transportation by GTR (for example, a plane ticket procured on your behalf by the government), reimbursement thereof when you purchase it yourself (if authorized), or a monetary allowance in lieu of the cost of transportation based on distance in official mileage tables (normally when you use a POV).

2. *Lodging* expense covers your cost of overnight lodging for the nights authorized, which must fall within strict guidelines for reimbursement. Rates of reimbursement vary by locale.
3. *Meals and incidentals* expense covers your expenses for daily meals and certain minor expenses while traveling, and it is based on established per diem rates that also vary by locale.
4. *Reimbursable* expenses include certain expenses (see Section 1923) that do not fall in the above-listed categories but are authorized, such as fuel expense for an authorized rental vehicle, and which normally require receipts.

The term *per diem* is generally understood to comprise lodging expense and meals and incidentals expense.

The regulations governing authorization for and reimbursement of travel, as well as the actual rates of reimbursement, are contained in the *Joint Travel Regulations* and *Marine Corps Travel Instructions Manual.* Check with your local finance officer for guidance, as the regulations can be complex, and claiming reimbursement for unauthorized expenses can land you in trouble.

1922. Per Diem Allowances

These are designed to offset the cost of lodging, meals, and incidental expenses incurred by a member while performing travel away from the permanent duty station or while changing duty stations. You get per diem for temporary additional duty or temporary duty, including periods of necessary delay while awaiting transportation and at ports during permanent change of station.

In the United States. Per diem policies and rates within the United States are given in *Joint Travel Regulations* (JTR). Where government quarters and/or mess are available, the allowance is reduced proportionately. If you claim maximum per diem, you must secure a certificate from the local commander that government quarters and/or mess were not available.

Outside the United States. Per diem allowances vary widely from country to country and are subject to frequent change. They are discussed in Chapter 4 of the JTR.

The Defense Travel Management Office also maintains current per diem information and rates on its web site (http://www.defensetravel.dod.mil/), which is a great resource.

1923. Reimbursable Expenses

Certain travel expenses, described above among the four main categories of travel expenses, are separately reimbursable. Although the following is not an exhaustive list, these include:

- Taxi fares or other local transportation between places of abode and terminals, and between terminals when free transfer is not included; also taxi fares between terminal and place of duty
- Fees for checking baggage and excess baggage, when approved
- Fares and tolls
- Official telephone calls
- Registration fees at technical, professional, or scientific meetings and so forth, when approved
- Passport and visa fees, including cost of photographs required in connection therewith, and cost of traveler's checks
- Entry fees, port and airport taxes, and embarkation or debarkation fees upon arrival or departure from foreign countries
- Incidental expenses that can be justified as necessary for mission accomplishment.

On all the foregoing items, you may be required to produce receipts in order to support claims in excess of $75. If in doubt on any point, consult the JTR as well as your finance officer. If you and the finance officer disagree as to whether a given item is reimbursable (or if you differ on any computation of pay and allowances), you have the right to submit a claim for adjudication by the comptroller general. The finance officer will explain how to go about this.

1924. Travel Advance

Before departure under orders on permanent change of station, you may, if you request, draw an advance on mileage allowance, known as a travel advance. An advance of per diem on TD or TAD orders is also considered a travel advance. However, advances are no longer extended to individuals who are required to possess and use the Government Travel Charge Card, which includes most officers. Do not confuse these advance payments with a "dead horse," described in Section 1910.

1925. Travel Claim

After reporting at your new station and *getting your orders endorsed*, present your original orders with the appropriate number of complete copies (usually between two and five), to the designated administrative NCO, who will help you prepare and submit your claim for mileage (if applicable), per diem, and other reimbursable expenses on your orders. You must normally submit your completed claim within three working days, depending on local policy. You must file a claim even if you have drawn an advance.

1926. Travel in Government Conveyance

Travel by government aircraft or any other government conveyance is travel in kind. You rate per diem at the prescribed rate. On extended navigational flights for proficiency purposes, if authorized at your request, no per diem is payable.

TRAVEL BY FAMILY MEMBERS

1927. Travel by Family Members on Permanent Change of Station

The government pays authorized travel expenses for family members on permanent change of station.

If you are not traveling by private vehicle, it is simplest to obtain tickets for family members by government transportation request. You may, however, transport family members at your own expense, *although this is unusual, and it is wise to seek authorization before doing so.* You claim reimbursement for your family's travel expenses afterward at prescribed mileage and per diem rates within certain maximum ceilings.

In the event you plan to marry while en route to a new duty station (for example, en route to your first station after graduating from Basic School), your proceed time, leave, and excess travel time are added to your date of detachment to determine the effective date of your orders for the purpose of entitlement to dependent's travel. *It will be to your advantage to discuss this with your finance officer and ask for his or her advice.*

Claims for reimbursement must be signed by you unless you are in a casualty status. When family travel is incident to your having been reported as a casualty, the claim will be signed by the senior family member.

TRANSPORTATION OF HOUSEHOLD GOODS

1928. Shipment of Household Goods

Household goods include baggage, clothing, personal effects, and professional books, papers, and equipment. Not included, however, are most vehicles, pets, and articles not belonging to your family.

You may ship household goods at government expense (including packing, crating, unpacking, uncrating, drayage, and hauling as necessary) on permanent change of station, within weight allowances, under the following circumstances:

- Entrance into the service, or orders to more than twenty weeks of active duty
- Orders to sea or duty overseas, where family may not follow
- Permanent change of station orders while on active duty
- Orders to duty under instruction of twenty or more weeks' duration
- Orders to or from prolonged hospitalization
- Honorable separation or retirement
- Death on active duty, or reported dead, missing, or interned
- Transfer between ships having different home ports
- Orders changing home port of ship to which attached
- Transfer between ship and shore station, where shore station is not ship's home port.

But shipment is not authorized in the following circumstances:

- Before receipt of orders, unless specially authorized by competent authority
- If separation is other than honorable, or if transfer is incident to trial
- For change of station by reservists on duty for less than six months.

There is also a "do-it-yourself" household-goods shipment program under which you move your own effects by commercial or rental vehicle and are paid up to 75 percent of what it would have cost the government to ship the goods. Before doing this (which requires specific authorization), you should get the advice of your traffic management officer. Based on the experience of some officers, this is not the money-making prospect that it might, at first, seem.

1929. Weight Allowance

There are limits, based on pay grade, to the amount of household goods that you may ship at government expense. Current tables of weight allowances show the maximum weight of household goods that may be shipped by you on either permanent or temporary change of station. To illustrate, the 2017 weight allowances for a second lieutenant were 10,000 pounds (without dependents) and 12,000 pounds (with dependents). Remember that the government ships professional books, papers, and equipment (defined in Section 1936) without charge to your allowance.

On permanent change of station, you may ship "by expedited mode" (in most instances, simply a phrase for express shipment) up to one thousand pounds net weight, if shipped via commercial air, of personal property classified as unaccompanied baggage. This shipment should include only high-priority items necessary to permit you to carry out your duties or to prevent undue hardship to you or your family, and the net weight is charged against your total weight allowance. This type of shipment is invaluable for uniforms (but be sure to hand-carry a complement of essential uniforms you will need) and effects required immediately after reporting.

Household goods in excess of weight allowance may be shipped, but excess costs will be charged to you. Be careful; these excess costs can mount quickly. Remember, however, that weight allowances shown are net; that is, they do not include packing materials.

1930. Storage of Household Goods

Temporary Storage. You are entitled to temporary storage at government expense for up to ninety days in connection with any authorized shipment of household goods. Under certain conditions arising from circumstances beyond your control—such as unavailability of quarters at the new station, arrival of your effects before you do, early surrender of quarters, and so forth—competent authority may authorize an additional ninety days' storage. This added time in storage is not automatic; to arrange it, you should consult your traffic (or distribution) management officer.

Nontemporary Storage. The term "nontemporary storage" refers to storage for longer periods, typically in the range of six months to three years. There are many situations under which an officer may be entitled to nontemporary storage of household effects, not exceeding prescribed weight limitations. Because the length of storage at government expense varies and you are subject to excess costs for storage beyond the authorized time limit, you should check with the traffic management officer. Among the most common situations under which you are entitled to nontemporary storage are the following:

- Temporary duty pending detail overseas
- Change of station from within the United States to outside the United States
- Permanent change of station with temporary duty en route
- Retirement, discharge with severance pay, or reversion to inactive duty with readjustment pay (up to one year's storage allowed)
- Assignment to government quarters.

Prohibited Articles. You may not store automobiles, flammables, ammunition, or liquor.

1931. Dislocation Allowance

When an officer with family has completed a permanent change of station move, he or she gets a dislocation allowance (DLA) to help pay the numerous extra expenses of relocating a household. DLA is payable only once in any fiscal year, except by special authorization or when the officer is ordered to or from a course of instruction. It is not payable on orders to or from active duty. An officer without family is authorized DLA on permanent change of station if not assigned government quarters at the new post.

1932. Trailer Allowance

An officer on a permanent change of station is entitled to a trailer allowance for transportation within the United States of a "house trailer," if owned, for use as living space. Trailer allowance therefore means the moving or transporting of a trailer at government expense or subject to reimbursement. If you elect to claim trailer allowance, you cannot claim dislocation allowance or transportation of household goods. Always consult your installation's traffic management officer and your finance officer before taking any action in transporting your trailer.

1933. Household Goods Loss, Damage, and Transit Insurance

You may suffer loss or damage to your personal property during shipment; this is an unfortunate risk inherent in military service and changing duty stations. If your property is lost or damaged, there are provisions for you to file a claim directly with the carrier. The carrier's maximum liability for loss or damage on a shipment is the greater of $5,000 or $4 per pound times the weight of the shipment, up to a maximum amount of $50,000. Although the development of the Internet-based Defense Personal Property System in recent years has somewhat improved the moving experience and claims process, collection of claims against a carrier remains a complicated, time-consuming, often frustrating, and sometimes fruitless process. Thus, where the value you set on your household goods exceeds the carrier's liability, you may be wise to purchase additional protection in the form of a commercial transit insurance policy.

Should you take out such a policy, be careful to find out exactly what type of coverage you are getting. It is well to note, for example, that most such policies expire when your effects are delivered. Thus, when effects are delivered by van to a warehouse for temporary authorized storage, your policy will very likely expire as soon as the goods are accepted by the warehouse unless you have made special arrangements to extend your coverage. Further, reimbursement on such policies is computed on the ratio of the declared value of your shipment to the amount of insurance purchased. For example, if you state that your effects to be covered are worth $4,000 but only insure for $2,000, the insurance company will pay only $50 for an item worth $100. A personal property insurance policy, for a few additional dollars, may prove more comprehensive.

Ultimately, if you are unhappy with the resolution offered by the carrier, you have the option to transfer your claim for lost or damaged household goods to the regional military claims office with responsibility for your new duty station.

1934. Check-Off List for Shipping Household Goods

The following short paragraphs summarize key things you should do and think about when you ship household goods (HHG).

Read carefully the "It's Your Move" pamphlet, which should be available from your traffic management officer or the Defense Personal Property System web site.

Have enough certified copies of your orders (usually ten copies for each shipment). Then see your traffic management officer at least three months before you plan to move. Earlier is better if you are contemplating a summer move. If your orders are "short-fused," see your traffic management officer within a day or two of receiving them.

Tell the traffic management officer if you have professional books and papers to be shipped so that they may be weighed separately and packed without being charged against your weight allowance.

If you plan to depart for your new station before your household goods are shipped, designate your spouse or someone you trust *completely* as your agent when you arrange your move; leave or send this individual enough certified copies of orders to initiate shipment; and also consider leaving him or her a *limited* power of attorney or written authority to make the shipment.

If you have high-value items to be shipped, inform your traffic management officer so that special arrangements can be made.

Get all possible information about your housing situation at the new station before you request shipment of your goods.

Request storage at point of origin (your old station) whenever you are in doubt as to where to ship your goods (up to ninety days of storage on either end).

If goods go by van, be sure to get a copy of the inventory sheet from the driver.

Never sign a blank "certificate of packing," which the driver might present you.

If your orders are modified or canceled, or a change of destination of the shipment is desired, notify your traffic management officer immediately.

Get from your traffic/distribution management office the estimated time of arrival of your goods at destination, as well as the destination TMO/DMO telephone number.

Be at home on the day of the expected move.

If possible, turn over all your household goods for the same destination at the same time, except items to be shipped by express.

Let the movers know about fragile items, such as chinaware and delicate glassware.

Keep nonperishable food supplies together for proper packing.

Walk through every room of your home and check in every drawer, cabinet, and closet before releasing the movers.

Make arrangements for receipt of your household goods at destination. If you cannot be there yourself, check with your TMO to find out whether storage is authorized. In cases of direct delivery by van, you or your agent must be at the new home to receive it. Plan in advance where (in what room) you want your items to be placed.

Here is a summary of things not to do.

Do not request shipment to some place other than your new station without finding out first how much it will cost you.

Do not contract for shipment with commercial concerns unless you have been authorized in writing to do so by your traffic management officer.

Do not be upset if the movers do not show up at your quarters exactly at the appointed hour. It is hard to schedule a move by the minute.

Do not try to get special services from the carrier until after you have checked with your traffic management officer.

Do not, in general, disassemble or pack anything yourself in preparation for your move. Leave this to professional packers. Usually commercial firms will not pay claims on items they did not pack. Any exceptions to this general rule should be covered with you when you arrange your shipment.

Finally, although Marines have scant option as to when they move, the best time of year to schedule movement of household effects is from October through May (a period when only about 30 percent of all moves take place). In any given month, according to the Defense Department's Military Surface Deployment and Distribution Command, which is responsible for the Defense Personal Property Program, the best time to move is between the third and twenty-fifth of the month. In other words, if you want better, quicker, more careful handling of household effects, do not move in the summer or at the end of a month—if you have a choice.

1935. Household Goods Defined

Household goods are items associated with the home and all personal effects belonging to a member and dependents on the effective date of the member's permanent change of station or temporary duty orders that legally may be accepted and transported by an authorized commercial transporter. In addition to clothing, furniture, and other normal household items, these personal effects include:

- Professional books, papers, and equipment (PBP&E) needed for the performance of official duties at the next or a later destination (PBP&E is not calculated in the Marine's weight allowance and therefore must be weighed separately and identified on the inventory at origin as PBP&E)
- Spare POV parts and a pickup tailgate when removed
- Integral or attached vehicle parts that must be removed due to their high vulnerability to pilferage or damage (for example, seats, tops, winch, spare tires, portable auxiliary gasoline cans, and miscellaneous associated hardware)
- Consumable goods for members ordered to certain locations specified in JTR, Appendix F
- Vehicles other than POVs, such as motorcycles, mopeds, hang gliders, golf carts, jet skis, and snowmobiles (and/or their associated trailers)
- Boats (and/or their associated trailers)
- Ultralight vehicles (defined in 14 CFR §103 as being single occupant, for recreation or sport purposes, weighing less than 155 pounds if unpowered or less than 254 pounds if powered, having a fuel capacity not to exceed 5 gallons, airspeed not to exceed 55 knots, and power-off stall speed not to exceed 24 knots)
- Utility trailers, with or without tilt beds, with a single axle, and an overall length of no more than twelve feet (from rear to trailer hitch) and no wider than eight feet (outside tire to outside tire). Side rails/body may be no higher than twenty-eight inches (unless detachable) and ramp/gate for the utility trailer, no higher than four feet (unless detachable).

Household goods do not include:

- Personal baggage when carried free on commercial transportation
- Automobiles, trucks, vans, and similar motor vehicles; airplanes; mobile homes; camper trailers; horse trailers; and farming vehicles
- Live animals including birds, fish, and reptiles
- Articles that otherwise would qualify as HHG but are acquired after the effective date of the PCS order

- HHG for resale, disposal, or commercial use
- Privately owned live ammunition
- Hazardous articles, including explosives, flammable and corrosive materials, poisons, and propane gas tanks (see DOD 4500.9-R, *Defense Transportation Regulation,* Part IV, *Personal Property,* for examples of hazardous materials).

Note that if returning from foreign shore-duty overseas, your legitimate household goods are allowed to enter the United States duty-free.

1936. Professional Books, Papers, and Equipment

Professional books, papers, and equipment merit further discussion because failure to properly identify and account for PBP&E can contribute to exceeding your weight allowance. PBP&E are articles of HHG in a member's possession needed for the performance of official duties at the next or a later destination. Examples include:

- Reference material, which may be used in professional education, development, and/or writing
- Instruments, tools, and equipment peculiar to technicians, mechanics, and members of the professions
- Specialized clothing such as diving suits, astronauts' suits, flying suits and helmets, band uniforms, chaplains' vestments, and other specialized apparel that is not normal or usual uniform or clothing
- Individually owned or specially issued field clothing and individual combat equipment
- An official award given to a member by a service (or a component thereof) for service performed by the member in the member's capacity or by a professional society or organization or by the United States or a foreign government for significant contributions in connection with official duties
- Personal computer and accompanying equipment used for official government business (that is, laptop, CPU, monitor, keyboard, mouse, one printer, and one set of small computer speakers).

Excluded from PBP&E are sports equipment and office, household, or shop fixtures or furniture (such as bookcases, study/computer desks, file cabinets, and racks), even though perhaps used in connection with the PBP&E.

1937. Excess Charges

Knowing and adhering to your applicable weight allowance are vitally important, as costs can mount rapidly. Gaining at least a basic understanding of your entitlements associated with PCS is equally important. The member is financially responsible for all transportation costs as a result of:

- Exceeding the authorized weight allowance
- Transportation between other than authorized locations
- Transportation of articles that are not HHG (see definition of household goods in Section 1935)
- Transportation in more than one lot (other than an unaccompanied baggage shipment authorized to be transported separately from the HHG shipment, transportation of shipment to storage when authorized, and expedited transportation of items of extraordinary value when authorized)
- Special services requested by the member (for example, the cost of increased valuation liability)
- Transportation-related costs that are incurred by the government due to negligence by the servicemember or the servicemember's agent (for example, attempted pickup and/or delivery charges).

ALLOTMENTS AND TAXES

1938. Allotments

As a matter of convenience and to facilitate regular monthly payments, you may make allotments of your pay for certain purposes. When you make an allotment, your pay is checked that amount, and the Marine Corps transfers it monthly to the designated recipient. Individuals can start and stop allotments conveniently themselves using the MyPay web site.

You may grant allotments to a bank and to pay life insurance premiums. You may also make allotments for purchase of U.S. Saving Bonds or other investment purposes. Allotments are credited on the last day of the month of checkage.

You should register an allotment for support of your family as soon as you are ordered overseas so that your family can rely on uninterrupted support—especially if you are headed for combat.

1939. Income Tax

Your basic pay and any special pays are taxable income, subject to federal and state withholding tax at its source. Not taxable, however, are disability retired pay and most allowances, including quarters, subsistence, and family separation allowances. Tax exemptions for Marines and sailors serving in combat zones during hostilities are covered below in Section 1941.

Marine Corps withholding tax procedure provides that the finance officer establishes your withholding rate, based on your rate of pay; this rate changes when your pay changes. Tax deductions are checked on your pay record in the same fashion as allotments. At the end of the year, DFAS furnishes you a withholding statement, through MyPay, to be filed with your income tax return. You in turn must inform the personnel officer of your tax exemption status by filing a W-4 form, so that the correct rate is applied.

When hospitalized in a naval hospital as a result of wounds, disease, or injury *incurred while in a combat zone*, you may, if certain conditions are met, exclude from taxable income a certain portion of your pay, which is known as "sick pay." Check with your legal assistance officer (or that of the naval hospital) to determine eligibility. This can be a substantial tax benefit and should not be overlooked.

1940. Social Security Tax

Social Security coverage extends to Marine officers on active duty and requires the withholding of Social Security deductions from pay. These taxes are computed on your base pay for grade and length of service and are deducted at rates prescribed by law.

The amount subject to withholding and the amount of tax withheld are reflected on the Internal Revenue Service W-2 form furnished to you by DFAS at the end of each year, as well as your monthly LES.

1941. Combat Pay and Tax Exemptions

Combat pay (technically termed "hostile fire pay") is provided for all military personnel serving within geographic limits established by the secretary of defense during hostilities and meeting certain criteria of exposure to hostile fire or enemy action. This pay is the same for all grades and is taxable to the same extent as other pay. The rate is currently $225 per month (2016). Your finance officer can advise you as to eligibility.

Income tax exemption for officers and enlisted persons serving in combat areas may be placed in effect by executive order of the president. This exemption extends to all military pay of enlisted men and warrant officers. For commissioned officers, the amount of pay eligible for combat zone tax exclusion equals the sum total of the monthly basic pay for highest enlisted pay grade plus the amount of hostile fire pay that the officer rates for the qualifying month. Here again, your finance officer can advise you as to eligibility and the precise provisions of the effective executive order. Note that the geographic areas of this tax exemption bear no relation to, and do not necessarily coincide with, the combat pay geographic limits mentioned above.

If love of money were the mainspring of all American action, the officer corps long since would have disintegrated.

—*The Armed Forces Officer*, 1950

20

MILITARY JUSTICE

This chapter contains a general description of the system of military justice in force in the U.S. Marine Corps and, with minor differences, throughout all the U.S. armed forces. This chapter is not intended as an exhaustive review or as a source of legal authority; it merely covers some major points in military law. Because the military justice system is complex, technical, and, at times, inflexible, there can be no substitute for consultation with a knowledgeable individual. Should a substantive or procedural question arise, refer to your staff judge advocate or legal officer.

Military law governs individual conduct and performance of duty in the naval services. It also provides means—nonjudicial punishment and trial by court-martial—for enforcing the rules. As a Marine officer, you must be familiar with military law and its sources. It is part of the tradition of Marine Corps discipline that legal proceedings are conducted expeditiously, firmly, and expertly. Marine officers are frequently called upon to perform various legal functions, and they must set an example with their competence and knowledge.

2001. Sources of Military Law

The sources of military law include the Constitution of the United States, the Uniform Code of Military Justice (UCMJ), and other acts of Congress. The implementation and administration of these laws in the military are accomplished by the president, who has promulgated the *Manual for Courts-Martial,*

United States (2016 edition) (MCM), as amended, and the Secretary of the Navy, who has promulgated the *Manual of the Judge Advocate General* (JAGMAN). These two manuals constitute the primary sources of military law that applies to the Navy and Marine Corps. You must be generally familiar with these publications and pertinent general orders.

Other sources of military law include decisions of the Court of Military Appeals and Navy–Marine Corps Court of Military Review; directives from the president, secretary of defense, Secretary of the Navy, and commandant of the Marine Corps; and customs and usage of the service.

2002. Civil and Military Law

In addition to being subject to the federal and state laws that bind all citizens of the United States, members of the armed forces are subject to a second body of law and a separate jurisprudence. This body of law includes the statutes and regulations setting forth the rights, liabilities, powers, and duties of officers and enlisted persons in the military services. Thus, members of the armed forces may be brought before civil or military tribunals and are generally answerable to both bodies of law. Breaches of the peace and other minor offenses by service personnel that violate both civilian and military law will often be tried by court-martial, although this does not exclude exercise of civil jurisdiction as well. When an offense violates state, federal, and military law at the same time—for example, a serious crime, such as murder—the authority that first obtains control over the offender may try him. Just as civil courts may not interfere with military courts (other than by writ of habeas corpus), neither do military authorities have the power to interfere with civil courts.

A member of the Marine Corps accused of an offense against civil authority may, upon proper request, be delivered to the civil authority for trial. Regulations promulgated by the Secretary of the Navy covering this are found in the JAGMAN.

In foreign countries, Marines are subject to the laws of those countries and may be tried and punished by foreign authorities. In certain countries, the United States has "status of forces agreements," which, among other things, prescribe conditions under which U.S. military personnel may be delivered to local authorities for trial in local courts (or, alternatively, tried by U.S. military courts). These agreements vary from country to country.

2003. Uniform Code of Military Justice

On 5 May 1950, the Uniform Code of Military Justice (hereafter abbreviated as the UCMJ or simply the Code) was approved by President Harry S. Truman. The authorities that administer military justice under the present revised Code are shown in Figure 20-1. The following paragraphs describe some of the basic principles, provisions, and features contained in the Code.

Instructions and Publication. Certain articles of the Code must be carefully explained to every enlisted person entering active duty, then again after six months, and also when reenlisting. A complete text of the Code must be available to every person on active duty in the armed forces of the United States.

At frequent intervals, the "punitive articles" (those dealing mainly with offenses and punishments) must be published to troops and posted so that the crew of a naval vessel and the personnel of shore stations may read them. This is known—in the old Navy phrase—as "reading the Rocks and Shoals."

Jurisdiction. All persons in the armed forces are subject to the Code. Reciprocal jurisdiction between services is provided, but the exercise of jurisdiction over a member of another service is limited to those circumstances prescribed by the president in the *Manual for Courts-Martial,* that is, when a joint service command is specifically authorized to refer such cases or when manifest injury to the armed forces will result from the delivery of the accused to the accused member's service.

Rights of the Accused. In addition to the constitutional rights enjoyed by all American citizens, an accused person under the Code has (1) the right to be warned before interrogation of any suspected offense; (2) the right to a preliminary investigation before trial for an offense; (3) the right to challenge members of the court, both for cause and peremptorily; (4) the right, if convicted, to testify under oath or to make an unsworn statement to the court regarding extenuating or mitigating matters; (5) the right to forward a brief of matters that should be considered in review of the case; and (6) the right to counsel at specified stages of the foregoing proceedings.

Rights of the Victim. In addition to the constitutional rights enjoyed by all American citizens, a victim of an offense under the Code has (1) the right to be reasonably protected from the accused; (2) the right to reasonable, accurate, and timely notice of hearings, courts-martial, and public proceedings relating to the offense, as well as of the release or escape of the accused from confinement; (3) the right not to be excluded from any public hearing or proceeding

	Nonjudicial: Commanding Officer's Office Hours		Judicial: Court-Martial, General	Judicial: Court-Martial, Special	Judicial: Court-Martial, Summary
Members	Art. 15 By commanding officer	Art. 15 By officer in charge	Art. 16 Five or more members plus a military judge	Art. 16 Three or more members plus a military judge	Art. 16 One commissioned officer
Convening Authority			Art. 22 (1) President of the United States (2) Secretary of a department (3) Commander in chief of a fleet, CO of a naval station or larger shore activity beyond limits of United States (4) CG of a Marine Corps division, separate brigade, separate wing, etc. (5) COs designated by the secretary of a department or the president.	Art. 23 (1) Persons who may convene a general court-martial. (2) CO of any naval or Coast Guard vessel. (3) CO of any independent Marine Corps unit where members of that corps are on duty (4) COs and OsINC designated by the secretary of a department	Art. 24 (1) Persons who may convene a general or special (2) CO or OINC when empowered by the secretary of a department.
Jurisdiction	Art. 2 Officers and any other personnel in his or her command	Art. 2 Enlisted personnel under his or her charge	Art. 18 All persons subject to the code for all offenses made punishable by the code.	Art. 19 All persons subject to the code for any non-capital offenses made punishable by the code; further for capital offenses under such regulations as the president may prescribe.	Art. 20 All enlisted personnel subject to the code for any non-capital offense made punishable by the code unless accused objects to trial thereby, in which case trial may be ordered by special or GCM.
Punishments and Limitations	Art. 15 PUNISHMENTS INCLUDING ADMONITIONS OR REPRIMANDS AS FOLLOWS Officers and Warrant Officers 1 Restrictions to limits, with or without suspension from duty, for 30 days (60 days if by flag/general officer) 2 Arrest in quarters for 30 days (if imposed by flag/general officer in comd) 3 Forfeiture of 1/2 pay for 2 months (if imposed by flag/general officer in comd) 4 Detention of 1/2 pay for 3 months (if imposed by flag/general officer in comd)* Enlisted 1 Three days' confinement on bread and water or diminished rations (if imposed on a man attached to or embarked in a vessel) 2 Thirty day's correctional custody (limited to 7 days if imposed by officer below Maj/LCdr). 3 Forfeiture 1/2 pay for 2 months (limited to 7 days' pay if imposed by officer below Maj/LCdr). 4 Reduction to next inferior rating (if imposed by officer below Maj/LCdr) or reduction to lowest or intermediate pay grade (by LCdr/Maj or above). Reduction may only be accomplished from grade within promotion authority of officer imposing punishment, and no person above E-4 may be reduced more than one grade.** 5 Forty-five days' extra duties (14 days if imposed by officer below Maj/LCdr). 6 Sixty days' restriction to limits with or without suspension from duty (4 days if imposed by officer below Maj/LCdr). 7 Detention of 1/2 pay for 3 months (14 days if imposed by officer below Maj/LCdr).*		Art. 18 Any punishment not forbidden by code including death when specified. President may prescribe limitations.	Art. 19 Any punishment not forbidden by code except death, dishonorable discharge, dismissal, confinement in excess of 12 months, hard labor without confinement in excess of 3 month's forfeiture of pay exceeding 2/3 pay per month or forfeiture of pay for a period exceeding 12 months. A BCD may be adjudged only if complete record of proceedings and testimony before the court has been made.	Art. 20 Subject to presidential limitations any punishment not forbidden by code except death, dishonorable or bad conduct discharge, dismissal, confinement in excess of one month, hard labor without confinement in excess of 45 days, restriction in excess of two months, or forfeiture of pay in excess of 2/3 pay for one month.
Qualifications of Members			Art. 25 Any officers on active duty shall be eligible to serve on all courts-martial. Any warrant officer on active duty shall be eligible to serve on general and special courts-martial for the trial of any person except an officer. Any enlisted person on active duty who is not a member of the same unit shall be eligible to serve on general and special courts-martial for the trial of any enlisted person if prior to the convening of the court the accused personally has requested in writing that enlisted persons serve on it. Upon such request the membership must include at least one-third enlisted personnel.		

*The president has excluded use of this punishment.

**The secretary of the Navy has limited reduction to one pay grade.

Figure 20-1. Administration of Military Justice under the Uniform Code of Military Justice

relating to the offense, except under certain specific circumstances; (4) the right to be reasonably heard at a public hearing, sentencing hearing, or public proceeding relating to the offense; (5) the reasonable right to confer with counsel representing the government at any public hearing or proceeding relating to the offense; (6) the right to receive restitution as provided by law; (7) the right to proceedings free from reasonable delay; and (8) the right to be treated with fairness and with respect for the dignity and privacy of the victim of an offense under the Code.

Review and Appeals. The Code establishes elaborate machinery and channels for review and appeal of courts-martial. In all cases the convening authority (that is, the commander, at a given level, empowered to send a case to a court-martial) must take action to approve, remit, or suspend an adjudged sentence. The convening authority may not, however, adjust any findings of guilt for felony offenses where the sentence is longer than six months or contains a discharge; nor may the convening authority change findings for any sex crime, irrespective of sentencing time.

The accused may waive appellate review by higher authority. If not waived, the case may be reviewed by various officers in the chain of command; by *Courts of Military Review* (composed of three or more officers or civilian lawyers qualified to practice before federal courts or before the highest court of a state); by the *judge advocate general of the Navy*; by the *Court of Military Appeals* (a court composed of five civilian judges); and by the U.S. Supreme Court.

Approval. Sentences of death must be approved by the president. Sentences dismissing an officer, cadet, or midshipman must be approved by the Secretary of the Navy. Sentences to a dishonorable or bad-conduct discharge are not executed until appellate review is completed and the trial case affirmed by the Court of Military Review (unless appellate review has been waived).

Legal Duties. Officers who perform legal duties include the following.

The *staff judge advocate* is the senior Marine officer lawyer, certified in accordance with the Code, who performs the staff legal duties of a command.

A *judge advocate* is a Marine officer lawyer certified in accordance with the Code to perform duties as trial and/or defense counsel. In addition, the judge advocate is authorized to review trial records of summary, special and general courts-martial.

A *military judge* is a judge, appointed by the judge advocate general of the Navy, who serves on general and special courts-martial in a capacity similar to that of a civilian judge. If the accused requests and the military judge consents, a military judge may sit as a one-officer court-martial to determine the issue of guilt or innocence and adjudge sentence if found guilty.

An *initial review officer* is a disinterested and detached officer who reviews command decisions to confine individuals prior to trial by court-martial. Not later than seven days after imposition of pretrial confinement, the initial review officer must determine whether confinement will continue or the Marine will be released.

A *legal assistance officer* is a Marine officer lawyer designated by the commander to give legal advice to members of the command on personal legal problems involving civilian law generally.

A *legal officer* is an officer (nonlawyer) designated by a commanding officer to perform legal duties, of purely military nature, within the command. This officer does not render legal assistance (see above) but can answer questions regarding the Code.

2004. Common Offenses and the Small Unit

The Punitive Articles. Articles 77–134 of the Code ("the Rocks and Shoals") divide punishable offenses into three general groups: (1) crimes common to both civil and military law, such as murder, rape, arson, burglary, larceny, sodomy, and frauds against the United States; (2) purely military offenses arising out of military duties and having no counterpart in civilian life, such as desertion, willful disobedience of lawful orders of superior officers and noncommissioned officers, misbehavior before the enemy, and sleeping on watch; and (3) a general group of offenses based on two articles that do not specify any particular acts of misconduct but cover a variety of transgressions harmful to the service in general terms.

Article 133, the first of these last two articles, applies only to officers and midshipmen. It makes punishable "conduct unbecoming an officer."

The second, Article 134, applies to all persons who are subject to military law. Offenses punishable under this article include disorders and neglects prejudicial to good order and discipline, conduct tending to bring discredit upon the armed forces, and crimes and offenses covered by federal laws other than the Uniform Code of Military Justice. This general article ensures that there will be no failure of justice simply because an offense is not specifically mentioned in an article of the Code.

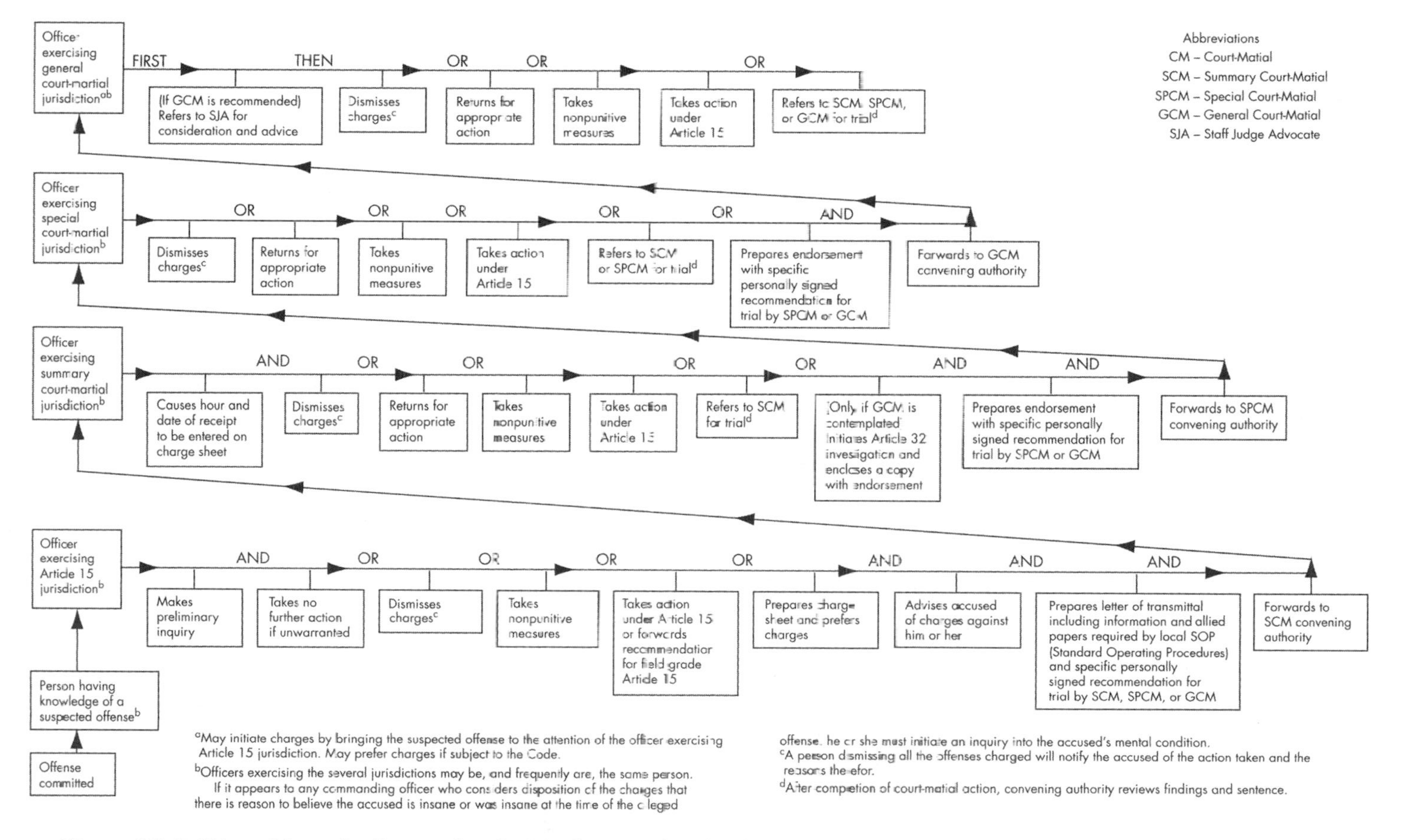

Figure 20-2. Disposition of a Case under the Uniform Code of Military Justice

Among the foregoing punitive articles, the following are most frequently violated:

- 85: Desertion
- 86: Absence without leave
- 87: Missing ship or unit movement
- 92: Failure to obey order or regulation
- 107: False statements
- 108: Military property of United States—Loss, damage, destruction, or wrongful disposition
- 111: Drunken or reckless driving
- 112a: Wrongful use, possession, etc., of controlled substances
- 113: Misbehavior of a sentinel or lookout
- 120: Rape, sexual assault, and other sexual misconduct
- 121: Larceny and wrongful appropriation
- 128: Assault
- 132: Fraud against the United States
- 134: General article (conduct to prejudice of good order and discipline; scandalous conduct).

Offenses in the Small Unit. As a company-grade officer, you should familiarize yourself with the most commonly encountered offenses, mainly order violations, which arise within the platoon, company, or battery:

- 86: Absence without leave
- 89: Disrespect toward superior commissioned officer
- 90: Assaulting or willfully disobeying a superior commissioned officer
- 91: Insubordinate conduct toward warrant officer, noncommissioned, or petty officer
- 92: Failure to obey order or regulation
- 112a: Wrongful use, possession, etc., of controlled substances
- 113: Misbehavior of a sentinel or lookout (most often, drunk or asleep on watch)
- 121: Larceny and wrongful appropriation
- 128: Assault.

With increased emphasis on preventing and combatting sexual assault and sexual harassment in all its forms in the military, it is worth highlighting several changes to the Code over recent years. These changes affect Article 120, covering rape, sexual assault, and other sexual misconduct, and Article 125, covering forcible sodomy. Those accused of violating either of these two articles must appear before a general court-martial; there is no opportunity to be tried at a summary or special court-martial. Those found guilty of rape, sexual assault, or forcible sodomy now are subject to mandatory minimum punishments, including dishonorable discharge for enlisted personnel and dismissal for officers. Prior to the *National Defense Authorization Act of 2014*, which enacted these changes, there was a five-year statute of limitations on rape and sexual assault cases under Article 120; now, there is no such limit. Finally, Congress also repealed the offense of *consensual* sodomy under Article 125 to bring the article in line with Supreme Court rulings.

To deal effectively with all of the offenses encompassed by all the punitive articles, you should familiarize yourself with the elements that form each, together with the possible defenses against such charges. Otherwise, you cannot effectively use the Code as a tool for maintaining effective discipline.

2005. Investigations, Warnings, and Evidence

Criminal investigations of felonies and other serious offenses are normally performed by the Naval Criminal Investigative Service (NCIS). Some serious and less serious offenses may be investigated by the Criminal Investigation Division of an installation's provost marshal office or by a duly appointed member of the command. There are two types of investigations relating to offenses that are frequently performed within the chain of command: preliminary inquiries (preliminary to an Article 15 hearing, see below) and Article 32 investigations, which are preliminary to a general court-martial. Since the latter must normally be performed by a judge advocate, detailed discussion of Article 32 investigations lies beyond the scope of this *Guide*.

Preliminary inquiries are a common occurrence within units and should thus be understood by all officers. Typically, within the Marine division, a company commander who receives a report of misconduct directs that a preliminary inquiry be conducted by an officer or staff NCO of the command. The purpose is to provide the CO with sufficient information so that he or she can intelligently dispose of the case. Depending on the CO's wishes, the inquiry may be oral or written.

What you are looking for in a preliminary inquiry boils down to three elements: (1) Has any offense chargeable under the Code been committed? (2) Who committed it? (3) What is the gravity of the offense in light of the circumstances?

Your job is not to perfect a case or "hang" an accused but to collect all evidence, favorable or unfavorable, to enable your commander to dispose of the matter.

A preliminary inquiry is inherently informal. It is up to you to go out and get the information. Likely places to start include the logbook of the officer of the day, military police "blotter," civilian police, hospitals and dispensaries, judges advocate, and witnesses otherwise identified. What you learn should be distilled into findings of fact, together (if requested by the CO) with any opinions or recommendations arising out of the inquiry.

Warnings. Because both the Constitution and Article 31 of the Code protect a Marine from being forced to incriminate himself or herself, every accused or suspect must be fully warned of certain rights. Such a warning should inform the individual of the following:

- The nature of the offense of which the individual is suspected
- That the individual has an absolute right to remain silent
- That any statement made may be used against the individual in any subsequent trial or proceeding
- That the individual has the right to consult a lawyer and have counsel present during all questioning and that he or she may seek counsel's advice before answering any question
- That the individual may obtain a civilian lawyer at his or her own expense
- That if the individual cannot afford or does not desire civilian counsel, he or she may have a military lawyer at no cost
- That the individual may discontinue an interrogation at any time at his or her own option.

Evidence. Without attempting to summarize the laws of evidence, which are precise and complex, it is enough to say that even junior officers should be familiar with them for two reasons: (1) evidence that is obtained in any manner contrary to law generally cannot be used against an offender; and (2) much evidence is originally uncovered, either at first instance (for example, by an OD) or during preliminary inquiry, by junior, nonlawyer line officers—that is, you. Thus, the admissibility (which is to say, the usability) of evidence often depends on correct decisions at the outset, based on your knowledge of the rules.

Two kinds of searches that frequently turn up evidence are the limited search of an individual and the immediate area, incident to a lawful apprehension based upon probable cause, and a search authorized by a commanding officer on probable cause of areas within the command (for example, a barracks). The laws of search, which are part of those of evidence, are also precise and complex, and you should be acquainted with them. Many an otherwise well-founded case has failed because an officer has conducted an overly broad or otherwise improper search, which in turn denies admissibility of evidence so obtained.

NONJUDICIAL PUNISHMENT

2006. Convening Nonjudicial Punishment (CO's Office Hours)

Commanding officers and officers-in-charge are authorized by Article 15 to impose nonjudicial punishment (at "Office Hours" in the Corps, "Captain's Mast" in the Navy) upon members of their command. Under Article 15, a commanding officer is defined as a commissioned or warrant officer who, by virtue of rank and assignment, exercises primary command authority over a military organization or prescribed territorial area, which under pertinent military directives is recognized as a command. Under the law, distinctions are made between officers in command, with progressively increased limitations on their powers, as follows. Flag and general officers in command and officers having general court-martial jurisdiction have the greatest scope of nonjudicial punishment. Among commanding officers not in the foregoing class, those of or above the rank of major/lieutenant commander have considerably increased authority over that possessed by COs of company grade and officers-in-charge (see Figure 20-1).

Nonjudicial punishment is a disciplinary measure more serious than administrative corrective measures but less serious than trial by court-martial. Nonjudicial punishment provides an essential and prompt means of maintaining good order and discipline and also promotes positive behavior in Marines without incurring the stigma of a court-martial.

Preliminary Report and Investigation. The customary procedure for putting a Marine on report is as follows.

An officer may submit a report against a Marine directly to the executive officer or adjutant of the command concerned. Otherwise a written report is sent up the accused's chain of command to the executive officer or the adjutant, giving the name of the offender, the offense charged, the name of the individual making the charge, and any witnesses.

The executive officer or adjutant makes, or causes to be made by the offender's company commander, the provost marshal, or other responsible person, a thorough investigation of the charges. (See Section 2005 for details on the conduct of the preliminary inquiry, or investigation into an offense.) For company-level proceedings, see Figure 20-3.

At company level each morning, the first sergeant informs the commanding officer of Marines placed on report during the preceding day. At battalion level, this is done by the executive officer or adjutant.

Officer offenses, when they occur, are by custom the province of battalion commanders or higher. They are dealt with by special reports and handled separately and privately.

Unit Punishment Book (UPB). Every unit whose commander has Article 15 powers must keep a Unit Punishment Book, which is simply a record of each case considered at Office Hours. The UPB also records each individual's acknowledgment that he or she has been apprised of the individual's rights under Articles 15 and 31 and his or her waiver of right to trial by court-martial. The first sergeant or sergeant major takes care of this prior to Office Hours and obtains the individual's initials in the appropriate spaces in the UPB. At this time, the accused is also told that, although he or she has no right to legal representation at Office Hours, the individual may obtain a personal representative to speak in his or her behalf and also call witnesses and cross-examine witnesses against the accused.

The UPB is an important administrative record, which is liable to inspection at any time, incident to a case, or by higher authority or the IG. A sloppy or improperly kept UPB can get you into trouble.

2007. Office Hours Procedure

Office Hours, as we have seen, is the Marine Corps equivalent of Captain's Mast. Like Mast, Office Hours can be, and frequently is, devoted to nondisciplinary matters such as praise, special requests, and the like. Here, however, we are concerned only with the legal and disciplinary aspects of Office Hours. Bear in mind that Office Hours is not merely an administrative procedure but also a ceremony intended to dramatize praise and admonition. Like any ceremony, it should be dignified, disciplined, especially set apart in the daily routine, and carefully planned (see also Section 1510).

Office Hours should be:

- Held at a set time and in a set place, usually the office of the commanding officer
- Attended by immediate commanding officers and first sergeants (or platoon sergeants if within a company) of those required to appear, whether for praise, reproof, or request
- Supervised by the adjutant and sergeant major if at battalion level, otherwise by the company first sergeant
- Held in full, immaculate uniform of the day.

Every officer attending Office Hours should review the cases of personal concern. If one of your Marines is up, take a careful look at the Marine's service record and talk with the squad leader and platoon sergeant. Assure yourself that your Marine is in tip-top condition as to uniform, cleanliness, and military demeanor. If you yourself hold Office Hours, be sure to review the service records and individual cases before you call in the individuals concerned. This does not mean that you should prejudge the case in any sense of the word. However, it does ensure that you focus your thoughts on the Marine and on the case.

Under the provisions of Paragraph 4, Part V, of MCM, a Marine receiving Office Hours has the right to personally appear at the hearing or waive appearance and submit written matters for the CO's consideration. To make an impression on the Marine, the CO may desire that the Marine be present for the hearing or at least for announcing punishment, even when appearance has been waived. In such cases, the Marine will be ordered to be present but cannot be forced to participate in the proceedings.

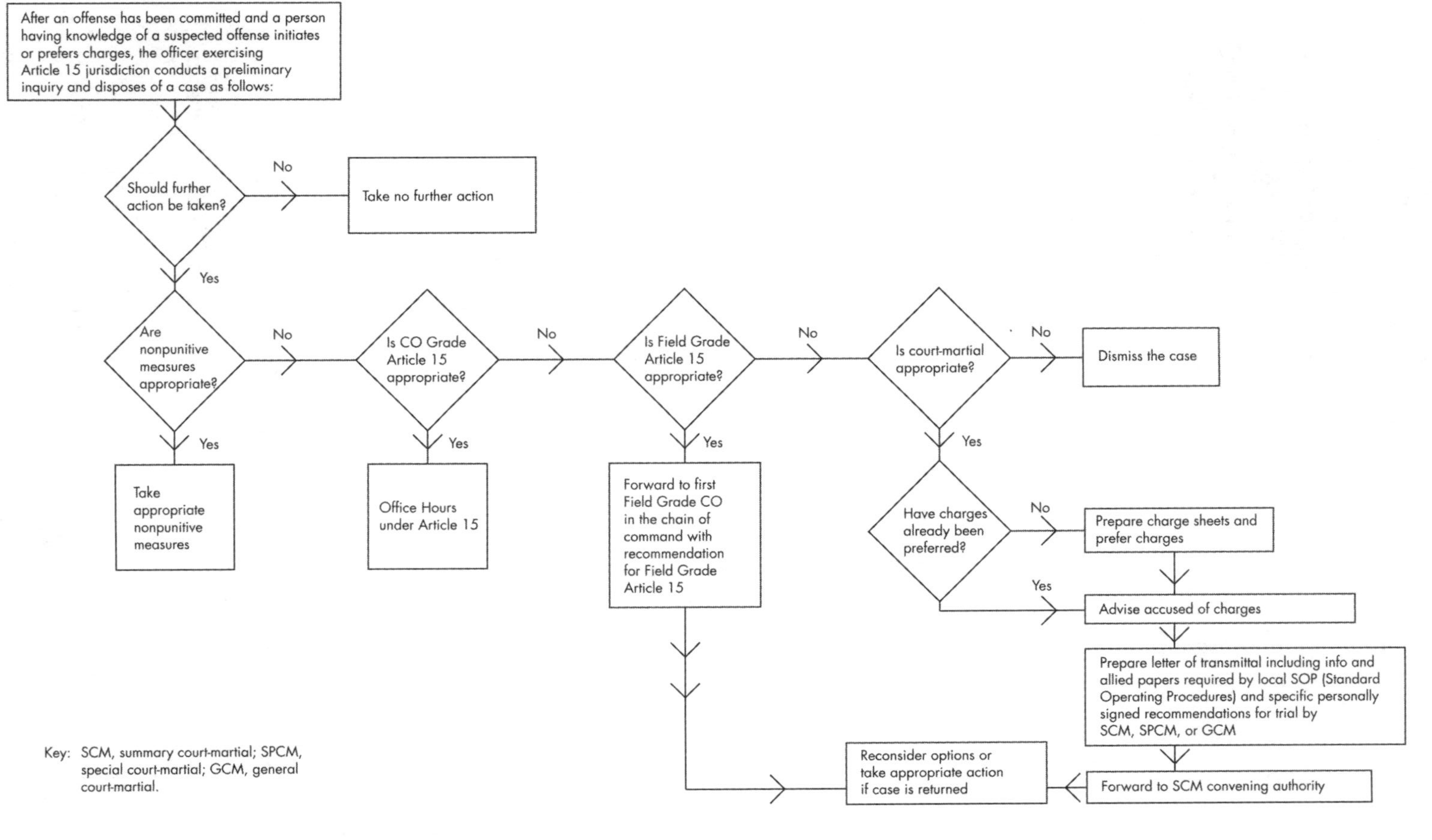

Figure 20-3. Decision Flow Chart for Company Commander's Disposition of an Office Hours Case under Article 15, Uniform Code of Military Justice

Here is a typical Office Hours procedure.

1. Ten minutes before the scheduled time, the sergeant major (or first sergeant, if a company-level proceeding) assembles all who are to appear, together with any enlisted witnesses and the respective first (or platoon) sergeants, who bring the service records (if these are not already in the hands of the sergeant major). At the same time, immediately subordinate commanders and any officer witnesses report to the adjutant, who conducts the officers into the commanding officer's office, where they are then seated.
2. At the appointed time, the adjutant (or company executive officer) stands on the left of the commanding officer with relevant documents; these should be opened and tabbed appropriately for ready reference. First (platoon) sergeants stand in a group to one side. The sergeant major (first sergeant) conducts in the first accused and reads aloud the charge or report against the accused, while the adjutant (company executive officer) places the documents before the CO. The accused stands uncovered and at attention throughout, one pace in front of the commanding officer's desk.
3. After the charges have been read, the CO must be satisfied that the accused understands his or her rights under Articles 15 and 31, UCMJ, and, as a matter of prudence, should again warn the Marine as follows: "Private, you do not have to make any statement regarding the offense of which you are accused or suspected. I must warn you that under Article 31 of the Code any statement made by you may be used as evidence against you in a trial by court-martial. Also that, if you so desire, you have the right to a trial by court-martial rather than accept nonjudicial punishment here at Office Hours. Do you understand? What have you to say?" This gives the accused a chance to tell that individual's side of the case if desired. Witnesses may be called—usually the reporting officer and witnesses to the offense. The accused must not be compelled to make a statement, nor does the accused have to admit guilt or produce evidence.
4. After all explanations have been heard and the commanding officer has considered the report of preliminary investigation, the CO has four courses of action (see Figures 20-2 and 20-3):

- Dismiss the accused, either accepting the explanation or giving a warning.
- Award nonjudicial punishment.
- Order the accused to be tried by special or summary court-martial (or recommend such trial, if the CO is not authorized to convene these courts).
- For a very serious offense, order or recommend that an investigation be conducted under Article 32 to determine whether the accused should be tried by general court-martial. An Article 32 or pretrial investigation must be conducted before a case can be referred to a general court-martial.

5. At the conclusion of the hearing, the sergeant major (first sergeant) commands, "About, FACE. Forward, MARCH." On the command, "MARCH," the person marches out of the office, and the process is repeated in the next case.

When meritorious cases (such as presentation of Good Conduct Medals, promotions, or special commendations) are involved, disciplinary cases should first be paraded in the rear of the CO's office, to watch the meritorious proceedings. They are then marched out and individually brought in again as described above.

2008. Appeal from Nonjudicial Punishment

When nonjudicial punishment is imposed at Office Hours, the Marine must be informed of the right to appeal the punishment to the next immediate superior in command if he or she feels that the punishment is unjust or that it is disproportionate to the offense. This appeal must be in writing and must be presented within five days. A Marine who has appealed may be required to undergo any punishment imposed while the appeal is pending, except that if action is not taken on the appeal within five days after the appeal was submitted, and if the Marine so requests, any unexecuted punishment involving restraint or extra duty will be stayed until action on the appeal is taken. The immediate superior in command (or the officer who imposed punishment) may, at any point, suspend probationally any part of the unexecuted punishment or remit, mitigate, or set it aside.

2009. Limits of Nonjudicial Punishment

At Office Hours, under Article 15, the commanding officer may impose, in addition to or in lieu of admonition or reprimand, one or certain combinations of the sentences outlined below.

Upon *officers and warrant officers*:

1. By any commanding officer: restriction to specified limits, with or without suspension from duty, for not more than thirty consecutive days
2. If imposed by an officer exercising general court-martial jurisdiction or an officer of general or flag rank in command:
   - arrest in quarters for not more than thirty consecutive days
   - forfeiture of not more than one-half of one month's pay per month for two months
   - restriction to specified limits, with or without suspension from duty, for not more than sixty consecutive days.

Upon *other military personnel of the command*:

3. By any commander:
   - if imposed upon a person attached to or embarked in a vessel, confinement on bread and water or diminished rations for not more than three consecutive days
   - correctional custody for not more than seven consecutive days
   - forfeiture of not more than seven days' pay
   - reduction to the next inferior grade, if the grade from which demoted is within the promotion authority of the officer imposing the reduction or any officer subordinate to the one who imposes the reduction
   - extra duties, including fatigue or other duties, for not more than fourteen consecutive days
   - restriction to specified limits, with or without suspension from duty, for not more than fourteen consecutive days.
4. If imposed by a commanding officer of the grade of major or lieutenant commander or above:
   - if imposed upon a person attached to or embarked in a vessel, confinement on bread and water or diminished rations for not more than three consecutive days

- correctional custody for not more than thirty consecutive days
- forfeiture of not more than one-half of one month's pay per month for two months
- reduction to the lowest or any intermediate pay grade, if the grade from which demoted is within the promotion authority of the officer imposing the reduction or any officer subordinate to the one who imposes the reduction, but enlisted members in pay grades above E-4 may not be reduced more than one pay grade, except that during time of war or national emergency this category of persons may be reduced two grades if the secretary concerned determines that circumstances require the removal of this limitation
- extra duties, including fatigue or other duties, for not more than forty-five consecutive days
- restriction to specified limits, with or without suspension from duty, for not more than sixty consecutive days.

Although the law permits reduction of more than one pay grade, Navy Department regulations provide that no person can be reduced more than one grade at a nonjudicial punishment. Even more important as far as Marines are concerned, *no staff NCO may be reduced nonjudicially at Office Hours under Article 15 of the Code, except by the commandant,* as the commandant is the only one who has the authority to promote a staff NCO.

On the point as to who may impose commanding officer's punishment aboard ship, only the captain has such power over members of the ship's company (the Marine detachment included), even though the title of the CO, Marine detachment, is also that of commanding officer. On the other hand, the disciplinary authority of the commanding officer of an embarked, separate organization of Marines (a floating battalion, for example) remains unaffected whether afloat or not, insofar as members of the CO's command are concerned.

Office Hours punishment is not considered as a conviction insofar as the offender's record is concerned. Remember, also, that under no circumstances may an offender awarded extra duty be placed on guard to work it off. And do not forget to keep the unit record of nonjudicial punishment as required by the Code and departmental regulations.

NAVAL COURTS-MARTIAL

2010. Summary Courts-Martial

Summary courts-martial may be convened by any person who may convene a general or special court-martial, the commanding officer of all battalions and squadrons, and the commanding officers or officers-in-charge of any other commands, when empowered by the Secretary of the Navy.

A summary court-martial (SCM) consists of one commissioned officer, whenever practical not below the rank of captain, USMC, or equivalent. This officer will be of the same armed force as the accused, although the Navy and the Marine Corps are considered the same service for this purpose. When only one officer is attached to a command, the commanding officer will conduct the summary court-martial, in which case no convening order is required. The summary court-martial officer is not sworn but performs his or her duty under the overall sanction of the oath of office.

Commissioned officers, warrant officers, cadets, midshipmen, and those accused of capital offenses cannot be tried by summary court-martial. Witnesses testify under oath. Examination is conducted by the summary court-martial officer. Rules of evidence are binding. A finding of guilt at a summary court-martial is not recorded as a federal criminal conviction; thus, it is aimed at promptly addressing relatively minor offenses.

Right to Counsel. The accused at a summary court-martial does not have the right to counsel. If the accused hires civilian counsel, that counsel will be permitted to represent the accused if it will not delay the proceeding unreasonably and if military exigencies do not preclude it.

Limits of Punishment. Summary courts-martial may adjudge any sentence not in excess of confinement at hard labor for one month, forfeiture of two-thirds pay per month for one month, and reduction to pay grade E-1. Within specified guidelines, restriction for up to sixty days, hard labor without confinement for forty-five days, or three days on bread and water may be substituted for or combined with hard labor with confinement at hard labor or each other. Enlisted Marines above pay grade E-4 will not be reduced more than one pay grade and cannot be adjudged confinement or hard labor without confinement. An admonishment or reprimand may be adjudged in all cases.

Objection to Trial by the Accused. No person may be tried by summary court-martial over his or her objection. Each person must consent to the trial or the case is returned to the convening authority for further action.

Record. The record of a summary court-martial is written on a standard record of summary court-martial form (DD Form 2329). Detailed instructions and examples of the record of trial are found in the MCM. The accused has seven days after the sentence is announced to submit matters to the convening authority. The convening authority can then act to approve or disapprove the findings and sentence, subject to the previously discussed constraints. An entry reflecting trial by SCM is also made in the Marine's service record book.

2011. Special Courts-Martial

Special courts-martial may be convened by any of the officers shown in Figure 20-1 and, specifically insofar as the Marine Corps is concerned, by any officer with general court-martial authority; any general officer in command; commanding officer of any battalion or squadron; directors of Marine Corps Districts; commanding officer of any Marine brigade, regiment, detached battalion, or corresponding unit; commanding officer of any aircraft group, separate squadron, station, base, or Marine barracks; commanding officer of any independent Marine Corps unit or organization where members of the Corps are on duty; any inspector-instructor; and any other CO or officer-in-charge when so designated by the Secretary of the Navy. A special court-martial may try officers or enlisted persons for any offenses (except capital) that the convening authority deems appropriate.

A special court-martial is composed of a military judge, optionally with not less than three members, who may be commissioned officers, warrant officers, or (if the accused is an enlisted person and so requests) enlisted persons of any of the services, including members of the National Oceanic and Atmospheric Administration and the Public Health Service, when assigned to and serving with the armed forces. An accused has the option in both general and special courts-martial to request trial by military judge alone, in which case the judge alone hears arguments, adjudges guilt, and hands down the sentence. In this case, there are no other members of the court.

When a full special court-martial sits, the function of the members (sometimes called "the panel") is to determine guilt or innocence and adjudge sentence, if the accused elects sentencing by members after the findings are announced. The senior member of the court, usually a major or higher—even though no longer presiding (which is the judge's duty)—is called the president.

The *trial counsel* conducts the prosecution's case; the *defense counsel* acts as defense attorney for the accused. In the naval services, a reporter transcribes the testimony and keeps the record under guidance of the trial counsel. The bailiff acts as guard and messenger and, if need be, escorts the accused.

If an accused enlisted person requests in writing that enlisted members be included in the special court-martial trying the case, at least one-third of the members must be enlisted, unless that many cannot be obtained. Enlisted members cannot be from the same unit as the accused. When enlisted members cannot be obtained, the trial may still be held, but convening authority must give the reasons in writing. No member of a court-martial should be junior to the accused, and warrant officers or enlisted persons may not, under any circumstances, sit as members for the trial of a commissioned officer. While the law provides for a variant form of special court without military judge and with diminished powers, it is the policy of the Marine Corps that all Marine special courts shall have military judges and full powers. For that reason, this *Guide* omits other references to the lesser type of court.

2012. General Courts-Martial

The highest naval court, the general court-martial, may be convened by the president; the Secretary of the Navy; the commandant of the Marine Corps; the commanding generals of the Fleet Marine Forces; the commanding general of any corps, division, aircraft wing, or brigade; the commander of a fleet; the commanding officer of a naval station or large shore activity beyond the continental limits of the United States; any general officer or immediate successor in command of a unit or activity of the Marine Corps; and such commanding officers as may be authorized by the president and the Secretary of the Navy. General courts may try anyone who is subject to the Code and award any punishment authorized by law (see Table 20-1).

Composition. A general court-martial is composed of not less than five officers (one-third enlisted members, if an enlisted accused so requests). A military judge serves with each general court-martial. The president should be a senior officer. Unless unavoidable, all members should be senior to the accused.

Investigation of Charges. Charges may not be referred to a general court-martial unless they have been formally investigated or such investigation has been waived by the accused. This investigation may be ordered by the court-martial convening authority. The officer conducting the investigation must, with rare exception, be a judge advocate, preferably a field grade officer possessing substantial legal training and experience. The investigating officer's job is neither to build up nor to whitewash a case, but simply to ascertain the facts thoroughly and impartially under Article 32 of the Code.

Proceedings. A general court-martial is conducted with special military formality. The military judge presides, while trial counsel prosecutes and defense counsel defends.

Although special courts have jurisdiction to try officers, by custom of the Marine Corps, officer cases are reserved for general court-martial. Article 66 requires automatic review by the courts of criminal appeals only in cases that include death, dismissal, a dishonorable or bad-conduct discharge, or confinement for two years or more. In cases involving confinement for six months

Table 20-1. Court-Martial Punishments

Type of Punishment	*General Court-Martial*	*Special Court-Martial*	*Summary Court-Martial*
Bad conduct discharge (enlisted only)	Yes	Yes	No
Confinement	Yes	Yes (enlisted only; not in excess of 12 months)	Yes (enlisted only below 5th pay grade; not in excess of 1 month)
Bread and water*	Yes	Yes	Yes
Death	Yes	No	No
Dishonorable discharge (warrant officers and enlisted only)	Yes	No	No
Dismissal (officers only)	Yes	No	No
Fines	Yes	Yes	Yes
Forfeiture	Yes	Yes (not in excess of ⅔ pay per month for 12 months)	Yes (not in excess of ⅔ of 1 month's pay)
Hard labor (without confinement–enlisted only)	Yes (not in excess of 3 months)	Yes (not in excess of 3 months)	Yes (not in excess of 45 days; only enlisted below 5th pay grade)
Life imprisonment	Yes	No	No
Loss of numbers, lineal position, senority	Yes (seniority only)	No	No
Reduction of officer	No	No	No
Reduction to lowest enlisted grade	Yes	Yes	Yes (only enlisted below 5th pay grade)
Reprimand	Yes	Yes	Yes
Restriction to limits	Yes (not in excess of 2 months)	Yes (not in excess of 2 months)	Yes (not in excess of 2 months)

*Subject to various administrative limits; enlisted personnel only.

or more, but less than two years, an accused may petition for review. All cases involving a sentence to death must be approved by the president before that portion of the sentence is executed. Dismissal of a commissioned officer, cadet, or midshipman may be approved and ordered executed only by the secretary of the service concerned or designated under secretary.

2013. Duty as a Court Member

Second lieutenants rarely serve as court members, but first lieutenants and captains often do. Despite the importance of this duty, no special preparation is required. Your one big responsibility as a member is to be there, smartly turned out in the prescribed uniform, prepared to look and be alert. From the time court convenes until it finally adjourns, no matter how pressing your regular duties may be, your duty as a member is primary and comes first.

As trial progresses, the military judge will explain all applicable points of law. Your job is to listen to the evidence adduced by both sides, determine the facts fairly and impartially, and then apply the law, on which the judge will have instructed you, to the facts as you see them. Every member has an equal vote regardless of grade. You may not divulge your deliberations.

2014. Role of Counsel

Counsel on both sides before Marine Corps courts-martial must be qualified judge advocates.

Trial counsel prosecutes cases for the government, but he or she is more than a prosecutor; the trial counsel has a responsibility to help the court develop the truth and safeguard the rights of the accused. You will often have dealings with trial counsel in preparation for cases in which you may have conducted an inquiry or investigation or may be called as a witness.

Defense counsel conducts the defense, to which every accused is entitled. It is the duty of defense counsel:

- To undertake the defense regardless of personal opinion as to the guilt of the accused
- To disclose to the accused any interest the defense counsel may have in connection with the case, or any ground of possible disqualification, and any other matter that might influence the accused in the selection of counsel

- To represent the accused with undivided fidelity
- Not to divulge the secrets or confidences of the accused.

2015. Arrest, Restriction, and Conditions on Liberty

When charged with an offense, anyone subject to the Code may be subjected to pretrial restraint (moral or physical restraint) as follows: conditions on liberty, restriction in lieu of arrest, arrest, or confinement. These are administrative acts, not punishment.

Conditions on liberty are imposed by orders directing a person to do or refrain from doing certain acts.

Restriction in lieu of arrest is the restraint of a person by oral or written orders directing the person to remain within specified limits. A restricted person shall perform full military duties unless otherwise directed.

Arrest is the restraint of a person by oral or written orders directing the person to remain within specified limits. A person in the status of arrest may not be required to perform full military duties.

Confinement is physical restraint depriving a person of freedom.

Pretrial restraint should be no more rigorous than the circumstances require. Pretrial restraint is not punishment and should not be used as such. Personnel should not be placed in confinement pending trial by court-martial unless it is foreseeable that the individual will not appear at trial or will engage in serious criminal conduct, and that less severe forms of restraint are inadequate. Personnel in pretrial confinement may not be subjected to punishment (including hard labor). Additionally, a command representative must visit them periodically to ascertain their condition and see to their needs.

An officer under arrest must remain within the limits assigned; an arrested officer cannot officially visit the commanding officer or other superior officer unless summoned or on approval of a written request for a meeting.

An officer under arrest should not ordinarily be deprived of the use of any part of the ship or station to which the officer had access before arrest. But, on board ship, if suspended from duty, an arrested officer may not visit the ship's bridge or quarterdeck, except in case of danger to the ship.

You should distinguish between pretrial restraints, which are discussed, and the officer punishment, awarded by a commanding officer, of restriction to limits, suspension from duty, or arrest in quarters—all generically known in the naval services as "hack." An officer in such status is spoken of as being "in hack" or "under hack" (see Section 2009).

Physical Restraints. As an officer of the day, you will occasionally have the decision of arresting, apprehending, or confining enlisted people, and, on rarer occasions, of applying such physical restraints as irons or even straitjackets, the use of which is carefully restricted by *Navy Regulations* and other instructions.

On probable cause to believe that an offense has been committed, any of the following may apprehend (arrest) any enlisted person: officers, warrant officers, noncommissioned officers, and enlisted personnel on duty as military police. As OD, you may apprehend and also confine. Orders for confinement, which you may receive from a commanding officer, may be oral or written, direct or conveyed through a staff officer.

You (as an OD) are required by the Code to accept any prisoner brought to you by a commissioned officer with a signed, written report of an offense. Not later than your relief as officer of the day, you must report to the commanding officer the full details of any such confinements.

Instruments of restraint (handcuffs, for example) can never be used for punishment. They are authorized only for safe custody and no longer than is strictly required to prevent escape during transfer; on medical grounds certified by the medical officer; or, by order of the CO or officer-in-charge, to prevent a Marine from injuring himself or herself.

RELATED ADMINISTRATIVE PROCEEDINGS

2016. Administrative Investigations

It is important to be familiar with several forms of administrative investigation (sometimes called "JAG Manual investigations") convened by commanders under the regulations of the *Manual of the Judge Advocate General.*

These proceedings perform no direct judicial function and are in no sense the trial of an issue or of an accused person. They are convened and conducted to inform the convening authority of the facts involved. The court of inquiry is the most formal fact-finding body and is used for the most serious matters: for example, loss of life under peculiar circumstances; a serious fire; loss, stranding, or serious casualty to a ship of the Navy; or major loss or damage to government property.

In case of loss of life, a medical officer should be a member of the court of inquiry or investigation. The investigating body must determine, if possible, whether death was caused through the intent, fault, negligence, or inefficiency of any person in the naval services. No opinion will be expressed, however, regarding the misconduct and line-of-duty status of an individual in the report of investigation of his or her death or any endorsement thereon.

It is also important to be aware that, in addition to the administrative investigations (described below) governed by the JAGMAN, other investigations may be required by other regulations. These investigations have different purposes, and both JAGMAN investigations and other investigations may be appropriate under certain circumstances. Examples of investigations required by other regulations include:

- Investigations conducted by an inspector general
- Investigations of aviation mishaps
- Investigations concerning security violations, in particular those that may involve the compromise of classified information
- Safety and mishap investigations
- Investigations conducted by NCIS.

The important thing to remember here is that, to avoid potential conflicts among investigations, commanders must be aware of the conduct of adjacent or parallel investigations and coordinate appropriately.

Under the JAGMAN, there are three types of administrative investigations: courts or boards of inquiry, litigation-report investigations, and command investigations.

Court or Board of Inquiry. The court of inquiry and the board of inquiry are formal fact-finding bodies in the naval services. Courts and boards of inquiry use a hearing procedure and should be reserved for the investigation of major incidents or serious or significant events.

Courts of inquiry have the following characteristics:

- Convened by a general court-martial convening authority or other person designated by the Secretary of the Navy

- Convened by written appointing order, which should direct that all testimony be taken under oath and all open proceedings, except counsel's argument, be recorded verbatim
- Consist of at least three commissioned officers as members with appointed legal counsel and other advisers as needed
- Follow a hearing procedure
- Designate as parties to the proceeding persons subject to the UCMJ whose conduct is subject to inquiry
- Designate as parties to the proceeding persons subject to the UCMJ or employed by and who have a direct interest in the subject under inquiry
- Have the power to order military personnel to appear, testify, and produce evidence, and the power to subpoena civilian witnesses to appear, testify, and produce evidence.

Courts of inquiry return findings of fact and do not express opinions or make recommendations unless required to do so by the convening authority.

Boards of inquiry have the following characteristics:

- Convened by a general court-martial convening authority
- Convened by written appointing order, which should direct that all testimony be taken under oath and all open proceedings, except counsel's argument, be recorded verbatim
- Consist of one or more commissioned officers as members with appointed legal counsel and other advisers as needed
- Follow a hearing procedure
- *May* designate as parties to the proceeding persons whose conduct is subject to inquiry or who have a direct interest in the subject of the inquiry
- *Do not* possess power to subpoena civilian witnesses unless convened under Article 135, UCMJ, but can order naval personnel to appear, testify, and produce evidence.

Do not confuse reports of such proceedings (or of individual investigations) with certain reports required by *Navy Regulations* or with reports of investigations conducted by the inspector general.

Litigation-Report Investigation. Commanders use a litigation-report investigation to investigate an incident or event that has the potential to result in claims or civil litigation against the Department of the Navy for damage to real or personal property, personal injury or death caused by Navy personnel acting within the scope of their employment, or on behalf of the Department as an affirmative claim for damage caused to Department property by non-DON personnel or caused by DON personnel not acting in the performance of their duties. The primary purpose of a litigation report is to document facts and gather evidence to protect the legal interests of the Department and the United States.

It is enough to be aware of this type of administrative investigation, as you are unlikely to encounter a litigation-report investigation early in your career.

Command Investigation. A command investigation functions as a tool to gather, analyze, and record relevant information about an incident or event of primary interest to the command. Most investigations will be of this nature. It is an informal proceeding conducted by one or more officers, and it is ordered by any commander with Article 15 powers. Save that it is nonpunitive and thus outside the disciplinary process, it is not unlike the preliminary inquiry into an offense, described earlier in this chapter.

Though an informal proceeding, a command investigation is not a minor affair. For example, an important part of any investigation dealing with death, injury, or individual performance of a Marine (for example, a serious traffic accident involving a government vehicle) is to determine whether it took place in line of duty or involved individual misconduct. Such findings have wide repercussions in subsequent handling of claims against the government, determinations by the Department of Veterans Affairs, and so on. For this reason, the responsibility of an investigation is heavier than may at first seem to be the case.

The conduct of a command investigation may well be one of your earliest legal assignments on your own, so it behooves you to handle it in competent fashion.

Lost, Damaged, or Destroyed Government Property. A common form of investigation often falling to junior officers is an investigation into the loss, damage, or destruction of government property. When such an investigation falls to your lot, it is imperative that you first consult the current Marine Corps order on consumer-level supply policy, which supplements the JAGMAN with much special information.

2017. Administrative Discharge Boards

These boards, convened by officers with general court-martial jurisdiction, hear cases of individuals whose separation from the Corps by administrative discharge (as distinct from a punitive discharge) has been recommended. The *Marine Corps Separation Manual* requires that the board consist of at least three officers, one of which must be field grade. Junior officers may serve as board members and frequently have to appear before such boards as witnesses.

In general terms, the board, like an investigation, seeks to determine facts and, based on these, recommends either that a Marine be retained in the Corps or that he or she be given an administrative discharge of a character and type recommended by the board.

Law is a regulation in accord with reason, issued by a lawful superior, for the common good.

—Thomas Aquinas, *Summa Theologica*

PART III

PERSONAL, FAMILY, AND SOCIAL MATTERS

21

PERSONAL AND FAMILY MATTERS

Your first responsibilities as a Marine officer are to country and Corps. Hardly second, however, are your responsibility to your family and your responsibility to organize your affairs so that they can continue undisturbed through all the ups and downs and sudden turnings in a service career.

Sudden death is only one contingency you must anticipate. What if you are captured? Prematurely retired? Ordered overseas where your family cannot follow?

Reflect on these possibilities. Put your house in order. Keep it in order.

FINANCIAL MATTERS

2101. Overview

Under the selection system of promotion and owing to the rigors of military service, most officers retire between the ages of forty-five and sixty, and all must retire by age sixty-two. Thus, a service career is shorter than that in any other profession. Today's laws have considerably lessened assurance of adequate retirement income, even for the physically retired. If you are over age fifty or physically disabled when you retire, your prospects for employment are regrettably poor. For all these reasons, you must lose no time in laying the foundations of a balanced estate—an estate that reflects well-planned objectives; that is built on a prudent insurance program, wise investments, and property ownership; and that affords protection against the unexpected.

2102. Survivor Benefits

Current laws, which took effect in 1957 and have since been amended and extended, provide a greatly improved structure of benefits for eligible survivors of all officers and enlisted Marines who die on active service or after separation from active service if, in the latter case, death results from a condition incurred or aggravated on active service. These benefits are described in this chapter as follows: federal government life insurance; Social Security; Survivor Benefit Plan (SBP); death benefits (including back pay, death gratuity, dependency and indemnity compensation, pension for non–service-connected death, compensation for unused leave); and, finally, other benefits.

2103. Life Insurance

From the moment you take out life insurance, you create a cash estate of the amount of that policy, an estate whose proceeds are not taxable under the inheritance laws of most states. Life insurance provides an estate while you are in a low income bracket and before you have had time to accumulate sizable savings, and it protects the future of your spouse and family during your younger years against the occupational hazards of your profession. Finally, certain types of life insurance give a modest return on your investment and can help maintain your standard of living after retirement.

This section does not advocate one type of insurance over another; it merely aims to summarize several life insurance options that the informed officer might consider.

Broadly speaking, there are two categories of life insurance: permanent life insurance, which provides insurance for the entire life of the insured party, and term life insurance, which insures an individual for a defined period of time, the "term." Each of these categories contains a number of variations.

Whole life insurance is basic permanent insurance. It covers the insured for his or her entire life. This type of policy includes a cash-value component that grows tax deferred at a contractually guaranteed rate. The premiums are usually level for the life of the insured, with part of the premium applying to the insurance portion of your policy, part covering administrative expenses, and the balance contributing to the investment, or cash, portion of the policy. The death benefit is guaranteed for the insured's lifetime.

Universal life insurance, which is sometimes called flexible premium or adjustable life, is another form of permanent life insurance. Like whole life, it provides cash-value benefits based on prevailing rates of return. The principal feature distinguishing this policy from whole life is that the premiums, cash values, and the level of insurance protection may be adjusted up or down according to the insured's changing needs.

Variable life insurance is similar to whole life, though more complicated. It combines whole life's traditional protection and savings features with the growth potential of investment funds in lieu of the savings component.

Variable universal life insurance is still more complex, for it combines features of universal life insurance and variable life insurance. In somewhat simplified terms, it provides the insured the flexibility of selecting and adjusting insurance premiums, death benefits, and investment choices. Be aware that, under these types of policies, the policy owner bears significant investment risk, and the death benefit may rise or fall depending on the performance of the underlying investments.

Term life insurance, the second broad category, is the most economical and straightforward form of insurance. Term life insurance pays a clearly stated amount on the death of the insured, but it is distinguished from permanent insurance in that it provides coverage only during a clearly defined, but fixed, period of time—typically from one to thirty years. Nor does it include a cash-value component. Term life is particularly useful when the period of needed protection is known and limited and when the funds available to pay premiums are limited, as premiums for term life insurance are the among the lowest available. Premiums for term life insurance increase (in most cases) at the end of each five years, and they can become virtually prohibitive at age seventy.

Level term life insurance is characterized by a fixed death benefit and a guaranteed premium for specified periods—the longer the guarantee, the higher the premium. These policies are normally renewable at the end of the term, but at increased premiums as the insured ages.

Another variation of term life insurance, *decreasing term life insurance,* combines a level premium with a decreasing death benefit over time. Individuals often use this form of term life insurance to protect mortgage debt by roughly matching the declining death benefit with the declining mortgage liability, thus enabling the policy's beneficiary to pay off a home mortgage upon death of the insured.

Finally, *annual renewable and convertible term insurance* is one of the more complex forms of term insurance. It normally protects the insured for a single year, but permits him or her to renew the policy at higher premiums for successive periods thereafter without the need to resubmit evidence of insurability. The policy holder may also convert these term policies into permanent life insurance under specified terms.

Your Life Insurance Program. A sound life insurance program varies with income, age and number of your children, your own age, and your probable number of years remaining on the active list. Periodically, you must overhaul your program and consider carefully the number of years your children will remain dependent, their educational requirements, your outside income, your spouse's employment capabilities, your income after retirement, and any experience qualifying you for civil employment.

Consider the needs of your family five, ten, and twenty years from now and your probable income. Think about retirement income, education, and cash for the down payment on a house. Contrary to some opinion, not all permanent policies are bad; they can satisfy certain needs efficiently and effectively. In some instances and for certain needs, term policies are the ideal choice.

Life insurance is a complicated but necessary financial instrument that protects family members and loved ones. Selecting life insurance is a very personal decision, and you would be wise to carefully assess your insurance needs and then research and understand your options before selecting an insurance product. If you find this important task daunting, it may be wise to consult a financial professional who takes seriously a *fiduciary duty* to provide advice in your best interest.

But, first, consider joining the *Navy Mutual Aid Association*, which is a mutual, nonprofit, tax-exempt, voluntary membership association of sea-service personnel and their families. Navy Mutual offers life insurance and other financial products to its members. The association gives more than helpful assistance to beneficiaries of its members. Details on Navy Mutual are given below and in Section 2105.

Only second to Navy Mutual, you should also consider the *Group Insurance Plan of the Marine Corps Association (MCA)*, which pays an active duty death benefit up to $500,000. Details on the MCA Group Benefits Plan are given below.

At least every five years, review your program. You may well find that changes in income or employment and a different family situation indicate modifications. Look through a sound guide on insurance.

Government Life Insurance. Military service entitles you to *Servicemembers' Group Life Insurance* (SGLI), which provides term life insurance in $50,000 increments up to the maximum of $400,000 in addition to any other government insurance carried, for all persons on active duty. Your pay is checked monthly for this coverage, and you are covered for the full amount until and unless you cancel all or part of your coverage, or until (as the law permits) you convert SGLI into VGLI (see below) upon separation or retirement, with the ultimate option of further conversion into permanent protection, *without medical examination,* provided by a commercial insurance company. Death claims are handled by Marine Corps Headquarters and by the commercial company that is the prime insurer.

Veterans' Group Life Insurance (VGLI) is a five-year nonrenewable term policy that has no cash, loan, paid up, or extended values. VGLI automatically covers Marines who are separated or retired (or reservists released from active duty over thirty days). VGLI takes effect at the end of the 120-day free coverage under SGLI following separation or retirement as above, only if payment for at least the first month of the required premium has been made before the end of the 120-day SGLI free period. Depending on age, monthly VGLI premiums vary and must be paid directly to the Office of Servicemembers' Group Life Insurance. Detailed information is available online (http://www.benefits.va.gov/insurance/vgli.asp) or by contacting the office directly.

At the end of its five-year term, VGLI may be renewed or converted to an individual insurance policy with an eligible company *without medical examination,* as noted above.

On government insurance matters, refer to the *Handbook for Retired Marines,* published by Headquarters, U.S. Marine Corps, and frequently updated.

Navy Mutual Aid Insurance. The Navy Mutual Aid Association (https://www.navymutual.org) is a nonprofit association that offers quality life insurance to members at close to net cost, helps members obtain all government benefits to which they are legally entitled, and educates members and their families on matters of financial security. Individuals in the following categories are eligible for membership: active duty servicemembers, those recently separated honorably from active duty (within 120 days of separation), military retirees, members of the Reserve or National Guard, and employees of the U.S. Public Health Service or National Oceanic and Atmospheric Administration. Also, honorably discharged veterans residing in any of the following states are eligible for membership: Arizona, Connecticut, Florida, Hawaii, Maryland, North Carolina, Oregon, Rhode Island, South Carolina, Texas, and Virginia. Rates are minimal for three coverage plans, although there are several term and permanent plans worth investigating.

On receipt of notice of your death from the Navy Department, the association pays 10 percent of the death benefit, up to $10,000, to your beneficiary overnight; the remainder of the benefit will be paid in accordance with the desires of the beneficiary. Navy Mutual will also render help to your surviving dependents in settlement of all other claims. Perhaps the most important service of this kind performed by the association is the assistance provided in securing service-connected compensation for spouses, children, and dependent parents of deceased members of the association (see Section 2125). In the event compensation is disallowed initially (as sometimes happens), the association provides, without charge, competent legal representation before the Veterans Administration Board of Appeals, in order to obtain the best possible settlement. Every Marine officer should be a member of Navy Mutual. *Attend to this now.*

Marine Corps Association & Foundation (MCA&F) Group Benefits Program (https://www.mca-marines.org and http://www.mcainsurance.com) incorporates term insurance plans and other beneficial programs designed and operated by Marines. It is open to any member of the MCA&F, if under age eighty. Depending on the plan chosen and on the age of the insured, benefits may go as high as $500,000. Rates are very competitive. One of the attractive features of this plan is that, unlike most group insurance products, you may, after separation or retirement, continue your low-cost protection until age seventy so long as you retain MCA membership (another good reason to take the *Gazette*).

Notes on Life Insurance. If you hold it, do not let government insurance lapse. In service or out, it is the best insurance you can get.

Do not take out insurance haphazardly. Include it as part of a comprehensive personal financial plan.

Do not overload yourself with insurance against remote dangers, but be sure your policies protect against all expected military hazards. Many insurance companies have restrictions, sometimes included in the proverbial "fine print," as to war, flying hazards as pilot or crew of a military aircraft, and so on.

Keep your listed beneficiaries up to date. Name contingent beneficiaries. Remember to include the phrase "or to the survivor or survivors thereof," which covers most eventualities. If a beneficiary dies, make a prompt change in beneficiary. Consider the effect if both you and your beneficiary should die in the same accident.

Review settlement arrangements with your insurance agent or broker periodically to ensure that they are adapted to your present circumstances.

Will your spouse have funds immediately after your death? Navy Mutual is splendid for this purpose.

Pay premiums by allotment. Regulations permit indefinite allotments for insurance premiums that continue after retirement. Payment by allotment prevents lapse of policies.

Do not place all your insurance with a single company. Protection is enhanced by diversification among several good companies, although this does complicate the bookkeeping.

If you have your policy made payable to your estate, payment of proceeds will be delayed until completion of administration. This could be costly and reduce your estate, while delaying benefits to your dependents.

Although insurance is something you should attend to promptly, perform your due diligence and be wary before you sign insurance contracts. Be extremely cautious in dealing with companies and insurance agents who hover about newly commissioned lieutenants. Deal with sound, well-known companies, and select an agent with discrimination.

2104. Social Security

Contributory Social Security coverage is extended to all hands in uniform. Your contribution is made through an automatic checkage of a percentage of your basic pay. In addition to your military retirement pay, assuming you complete a military career, and any disability compensation paid by the Veterans Affairs, Social Security provides monthly income for:

- You, as early as reaching age sixty-five (or age sixty-two, if you apply to receive the smaller payments due at that time)
- Your spouse, if you die and your minor children remain in your spouse's care
- You, your spouse, and children, if you should be totally disabled
- Your spouse, if not entitled earlier, on attaining age sixty
- Your children under age eighteen, or older if incapable of self-support, after your death or while you are disabled
- Your dependent parents.

The payments for a family group may go as high as the legal maximum even though you have only paid into the Social Security program through taxation of your basic pay for a few years. The amount of your Social Security benefits is determined by your "average monthly wage" during the years you were contributing. The exact amount differs in almost every case and must be worked out. If you are eligible for any of the Social Security benefits just mentioned, you must apply for them; benefits are not paid automatically. You must file an application and it must be in the hands of the Social Security Administration (or with a U.S. Foreign Service officer, if outside the United States) before it can pay you. File immediately when you become eligible because back payments are limited by law. The local post office can furnish you with the address of the nearest Social Security district office. You should get in touch with the district office a few months before reaching your full retirement age, or when your spouse reaches age sixty, or at any time if you become disabled. When you die, your next of kin should check with the Social Security office to see if there is an entitlement to survivor's insurance.

You need not have wage credits for military service added to your record currently. These credits are recorded when a claim is made for retirement or survivor's insurance payments.

Your Social Security number is important for both you and your family to know, and it must, of course, accompany claims or inquiries. Moreover, it is used for several military administrative purposes and is used by the Internal Revenue Service in connection with all your tax returns and related records. Record it in your safe deposit box and with any emergency papers you keep, such as insurance policies and so forth.

To assist in computing where you stand under Social Security, the Social Security Administration encourages every insured individual—you—to request a Statement of Wages every three years from the Social Security Administration. There are also calculators available online (https://www.ssa.gov). In this way you can determine whether the records are complete and you are getting credit for all earnings on which Social Security tax has been paid.

You can get full information on these and other matters of interest by searching online, applying to the nearest Social Security Administration office, and usually from your unit personnel officer. Before retirement, investigate your Social Security rights and credits, and be sure your spouse is acquainted with his or her rights under this law.

2105. Insurance Death Claims

Government Insurance Death Claims. If you were on active duty, your beneficiary will be mailed forms by the Department of Veterans Affairs. The VA is notified by Marine Corps Headquarters; no further proof of death is required. Your beneficiary must fill out the form and return it.

If you were retired or separated from the service, however, your beneficiary should apply to the nearest VA regional office for necessary forms or see the legal assistance or personal affairs officer at the nearest Navy or Marine Corps installation; if these are inaccessible, the beneficiary should seek assistance from his or her nearest state or other service organization. Proof of death must be furnished; the beneficiary should get certified copies of the public death record, coroner's report, death certificate of attending physician, or death certificate of naval hospital.

Because of a backlog of VA claims in central and regional offices, there may be appreciable delay before payment. Navy Mutual, if you are a member, can keep claims moving.

The beneficiary should hold your government policy until the claim is paid; it should not be sent with the claim.

Commercial Insurance Policy Death Claims. The beneficiary should consult local representatives of each company or write directly to the head office. The following actions are required:

- Give insured's name.
- Give insurance policy numbers.

- Request necessary forms to make a death claim.
- Return by *certified mail* the completed forms, with return receipt requested.
- Send a certified copy of the death certificate, or affidavit of death as described above, or, if death occurred at sea or abroad, a certified copy of the official notification of death.

You should list the commercial insurance companies that insure your life in the record of emergency data section of your computer file at Marine Corps Head-quarters. Headquarters will notify the companies in case of death. Most companies accept such notification as proof of death.

Some companies require submission of the policy before paying the claim. Your insurance agent will assist your beneficiary with this paperwork.

Navy Mutual Aid Association. Deaths occurring on active duty or at a naval hospital are reported to Navy Mutual via official channels. In case of death occurring elsewhere or under circumstances wherein an official death message may not have been sent to the Navy Department, the next of kin should notify Navy Mutual via the most rapid means. As previously noted, 10 percent of the death benefit up to $10,000 will be paid overnight to the beneficiary, and the rest of the benefit will be paid in accordance with the desires of the beneficiary. A letter containing details of what must be done, enclosing all forms to be signed, is sent to your beneficiary at once. Navy Mutual also notifies any civilian insurance companies with which you may be insured of your death and the address of your next of kin. The finance officer holding your accounts is notified of your death and the name and address of next of kin for the purpose of expediting payment of arrears of pay, unused leave compensation, and death gratuity, if eligible.

In general, it is unwise for your family to put claims for government benefits in the hands of private attorneys, as this may simply cause unnecessary delay and will certainly entail added expense.

2106. Survivor Benefit Plan

The SBP provides survivor income of up to 55 percent of your retired pay to your surviving spouse and dependent children.

In the past, surviving members of a retired Marine's family often found themselves with little or no income after the retiree's death. The SBP fills that gap; until the plan's enactment, retired pay ended with the retiree's death, unless he or she had elected to take part in the old Retired Servicemen's Family Protection Plan, known in turn originally as the Contingency Option Act.

You will be automatically enrolled in the SBP with maximum coverage when you retire, if you have a spouse or dependent child at retirement time, unless you specifically elect a lesser coverage or decline participation, *with concurrence of your spouse*, before the day you become entitled to retired pay.

If you have no spouse or dependent child when you retire, you may either join the plan then by naming someone else as beneficiary or begin participation later if you acquire a spouse or child after retirement, but within one year of acquiring said family members.

The cost of SBP will be checked from your retired pay (6.5 percent of insured portion).

Because the government pays a substantial part of the SBP costs, your loss of retired pay for participation might be considerably lower than if you had purchased the same commercial coverage at retirement time.

SBP survivor benefits are based on your retired pay at time of death, or escalated base amount, not that initially received or elected when you began.

The decision whether to elect the SBP is a big one. It is a complement to life insurance, not a substitute (it is taxable as an annuity, you have no equity in the plan, and you cannot cash it in or borrow against it). Whether it is best for you depends on your personal situation. Basically, if you have a long life expectancy on retirement and are well fixed with adequate life insurance and a solid estate, the plan has the disadvantages that you will probably receive reduced retired pay for many years, your surviving spouse may remarry (at which time payments cease unless remarriage is after age fifty-five) or die soon (at which time payments cease), and he or she would receive little benefit. On the other hand, if you are in such poor health that you cannot obtain additional insurance, it could be an excellent means of augmenting insurance and other survivor benefits, at a relatively small cost, and should be carefully pondered.

2107. Other Kinds of Insurance

Automobile Insurance. Your car can cause you much grief if not properly insured. Many states and all Marine Corps installations require public liability and property damage insurance before you can obtain required registrations for your car.

Auto insurance is available to cover liability for bodily injury; property damage; medical payments; collision or upset; fire and lightning; and transportation, theft, windstorm, earthquake, explosion, hail, or water damage. Liability awards for bodily injury and property damage are very high and are rising. Your insurance agent can recommend how much coverage you should carry in each category. Collision or upset coverage is also very expensive; you should therefore take out a "deductible" policy (for example, $500 deductible for each accident, as nearly every accident now costs that much or more). This protects you against heavy damage to, or total loss of, your car.

Personal Property Insurance. Personal property (clothes, jewelry, silverware, furniture, computers, and so on) should be covered against fire, theft, and breakage or other damage at home or during transportation. Inexpensive "floater" policies for officers are written by many companies.

Fire Insurance and Personal Liability Insurance. Take out fire insurance on any house or other real property you own. Another valuable coverage is personal liability insurance, which protects you against claims for injuries by persons visiting your home or by workmen; damage done by pets, children, spouse, or self (usually including damage arising out of sports); and damage done to the property of others by such accidents as falling trees or fire originating on your property. This insurance is inexpensive but invaluable when trouble comes.

One highly regarded underwriter is United Services Automobile Association (USAA), San Antonio, Texas, an association of servicemembers who mutually insure each other against automobile liabilities and loss incurred to personal effects. USAA (https://www.usaa.com) has grown to offer a full range of competitive financial products.

2108. Real Estate

While you are young, with small income and few obligations, it is probably better to rent quarters for your family. As you get older and have children, you may agree with many officers that it is advantageous to own your own home. Marines have some advantage in this, as there are a few localities where they may be ordered to duty over and over again. For example, a ground officer would serve most stateside duty in the vicinity of Camp Lejeune, Camp Pendleton, and Washington-Quantico; an aviator would have maximum service in the vicinity of Miramar, Yuma, Cherry Point, Beaufort, and Washington-Quantico.

Some officers find it financially advantageous to buy a house where they have duty and are not assigned quarters, then sell or rent when ordered to other shore duty, or else leave the family in their own home while on sea or expeditionary service. Although absentee landlord is certainly a difficult role, it is worthwhile to have a home available when you return, and you can approach retirement with something besides canceled checks and rent receipts. When retirement comes, you have an asset that will permit you to buy a house wherever you decide to settle, if the city where you already own a house does not suit you. And if you die on active duty, your family will have a home or an income from the real estate you leave.

Consider carefully the terms of ownership of any real property before the deed is prepared. Joint ownership or transfer of property to your spouse by deed may offer material advantage to your estate. Leave with your valuable papers a list of your real estate holdings that gives the description and location of all holdings; location of deeds, mortgages, or other papers; and original cost, depreciated cost, estimated present value, and present ownership status.

If you do rent housing, you should insist on a "military clause" in the lease. This clause generally states that the tenant may terminate the lease subject to payment of a certain sum and allows the tenant to end the lease on thirty days' written notice to the landlord, for any one of several reasons, such as permanent change of station or release from active duty. Your legal assistance office can give you desired wording and other details.

2109. Control of Property

An individual may use or control an estate himself or herself or through an agent acting under power of attorney. Remote control of one kind or another is often necessary during a service career.

Joint Ownership. To facilitate use of property and to provide for its disposition on death, an individual may arrange for most property to be held in joint tenancy (with spouse or other beneficiary) with right of survivorship, thus enabling the joint tenant to use and control the property jointly during the individual's lifetime and, after his or her death, to obtain full title as survivor. Property held jointly cannot be disposed of by will if your joint tenant survives you, but it is wise to include provision for its disposal should your joint tenant die before you do.

The advantages of joint tenancy are less expense, less inconvenience, and less time required to dispose of property after a death. But there are also disadvantages. Be aware, too, that the provisions of the Servicemembers' Civil Relief Act (SCRA) exempting military personnel from state or municipal taxation where they are temporarily stationed do not apply to your spouse's interest in property.

Real estate is not the only property that can be held in joint tenancy. Joint bank accounts and joint ownership of securities, with right of survivorship, have some advantages.

Note that joint ownership of government savings bonds, if held in safekeeping with the Treasury Department, does not necessarily ensure flexibility. Such a bond cannot be withdrawn by a joint owner unless the purchaser has registered with the safekeeping agency a sample of the co-owner's signature, along with written authority to withdraw the bond.

Automobiles. Joint ownership of the family car also has advantages. Serious loss may result if your spouse or another family member drives your individually owned car after your death. The best plan is to hold the title to the car in joint tenancy. The certificate of title and the insurance policy should bear the names of the joint owners.

Although joint ownership of automobiles is desirable, your spouse's interest in this personal property is taxable. Payment of taxes in a state where you live temporarily can be avoided under the SCRA, if the car is registered in your name alone, in your own state of legal residence. A power of attorney to your spouse, however, will enable him or her to transfer title, secure registration, sell, or buy a car during your lifetime.

Joint Bank Accounts. If suddenly ordered to expeditionary service or upon sudden death, an officer who carries a bank account in his or her own name only may deprive the family temporarily of access to funds at a time when they are most needed. Investigate the advantages of joint accounts—at least during times when you are separated from your family.

2110. Investments

The complexity of the financial environment, particularly in light of the many new investment instruments that have become available, may initially prove overwhelming to you. In investments, as in your military career, you must remain informed and consistent in your approach. A good place to begin your familiarity with the world of investment is the library or bookstore, where generally accepted references can help you to navigate the reef-strewn waters of high finance.

Investments should be viewed as a part of a well-conceived and comprehensive personal financial plan (see Figure 21-1). Your aim should be threefold: to save a portion of your income (5 to 10 percent is a good starting point), beginning early in your career and increasing the share saved as your income progresses; to preserve what you have saved by investing conservatively; and to select investment vehicles that have a record of providing a positive, long-term return on your capital. The old adage that it is tough to make something out of nothing is never more applicable than in the area of investments.

2111. Borrowing Money and Loans

Because the first few years of a junior officer's career may well be spent paying off debts, it may be wise to underscore Shakespeare's advice, "Neither a borrower nor a lender be," if you can help it. Avoid loan sharks, and equally avoid

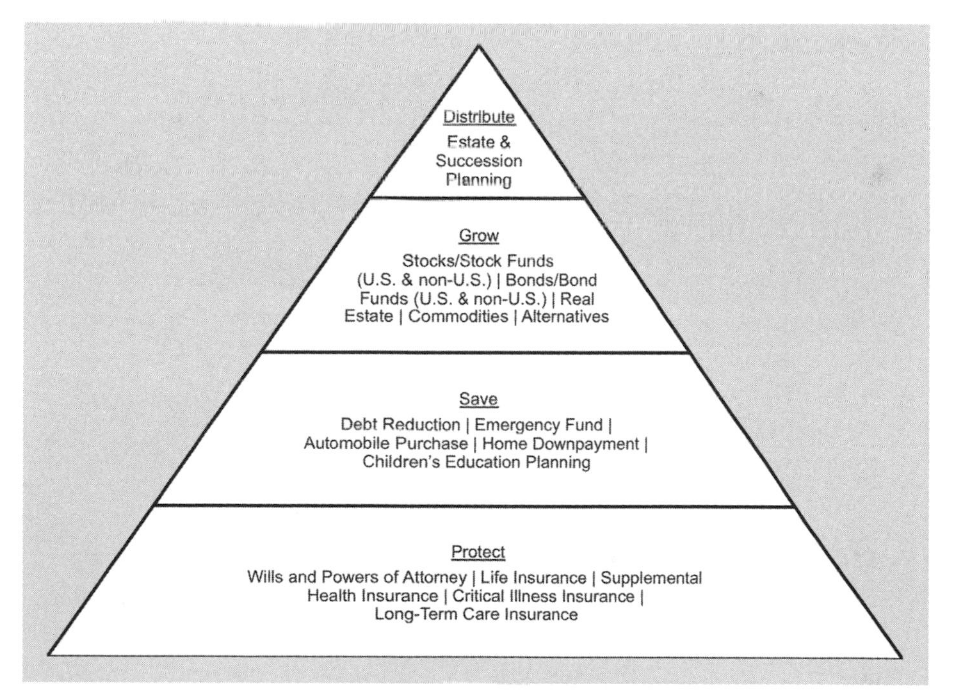

Figure 21-1. Personal Financial "Pyramid"

private loans to fellow officers, however deserving the case may appear; particularly avoid acting as cosigner to any note—this makes you just as liable as the borrower.

Interest Rates. The amount of interest you pay on a loan is a matter of vital concern and often a source of confusion. This is because most lenders charge different rates from those they quote. There are four ways of quoting interest: monthly (for example, 1 percent per month); add-on rate (6 percent per year); discount rate (6 percent per year); and simple annual rate (6 percent per year). Only the last—simple annual interest—is quoted in true terms.

To convert quoted rates to simple annual interest, and thus to true interest, multiply a monthly rate by 12, and multiply an add-on or discount rate by 2.

Whenever you borrow, ask what kind of interest is being charged—add-on, discount, monthly, or simple. Convert the quoted rate to true annual interest. Then compare interest costs and other charges to determine which lender offers you the best terms.

It is also important to understand the difference between annual percentage rate (APR) and annual percentage yield (APY). The former, APR, is the simple annual rate of interest without taking into account the compounding of interest within the year. The latter, APY, accounts for the effects of compounding and rises as the compounding period shortens. This difference has important implications for borrowers, who actually pay back their loans at the latter rate. For example, a borrower with a loan at 5 percent APR actually pays 5.06 percent APY if compounding is semiannual; 5.09 percent APY, quarterly; and 5.11 percent APY, monthly.

If you need credit, investigate the Navy Federal Credit Union or Marine Federal Credit Union. Both for borrowing and saving, whether by mail or in person, these nonprofit organizations are tailored to the needs of the young officer—charges are comparatively low and interest earned on deposits is generous. Navy Federal Credit also covers loans with life insurance at no extra cost, which is of great benefit to a young officer.

2112. Servicemembers' Civil Relief Act

Building on the Soldier's and Sailor's Civil Relief Act of 1940, civil protections for military personnel were completely revised and updated in the SCRA of 2003. It is designed to relieve officers and enlisted servicemembers from worry over certain civil problems and obligations.

The SCRA temporarily suspends enforcement of some civil liabilities of military personnel on active duty if your inability to meet your obligations results from your military status. Additionally, the act protects personnel from a form of double taxation that can occur when they have a spouse who works and is taxed in a state other than the state in which they maintain their permanent legal residence. The law prevents states from using the income earned by a servicemember in determining the spouse's tax rate when they do not maintain their permanent legal residence in that state.

Legal advice is necessary in any application of the SCRA because of the many technicalities. The act is designed to provide a shield against hardship; *it is not a device to evade civil liabilities.* Information and advice may be obtained from your legal assistance officer, who is located at the legal services center at your base or station.

FAMILY MATTERS

2113. Medical Care for Family Members

Medical care for service families and for retired officers and their families is provided by the government on a space-available basis in military health-care facilities. TRICARE is the military health insurance program that provides for medical care and hospitalization of military family members. A small fraction of the typical annual cost of a dependent family member's medical care and hospitalization is borne by the individual service family or individual through an annual premium payment and "co-pays" for some procedures.

Eligibility. Virtually all family members (spouse and unmarried children under age twenty-one—subject to a few exceptions) of Marines on active duty are eligible for civilian medical care and care in military medical facilities. In order to receive such care, however, armed forces personnel first must enroll their families in the Defense Enrollment Eligibility Reporting System (DEERS). Check with your personnel officer or, on larger posts, the DEERS Office for appropriate forms and actions. You should update your family's enrollment in this system immediately when you have a change in family status. Do not put this off, as your family cannot be treated without DEERS certification.

Retired officers and their dependents likewise have such eligibilities, but under differing provisions (see Section 2127). If you die, whether on active duty or after retirement, your surviving dependents remain eligible for care at armed forces or U.S. Public Health Service medical facilities (subject to availability of space and staff), as well as for certain civilian medical care and hospitalization.

Civilian Medical Care. Under TRICARE (http://www.tricare.mil), civilian semiprivate hospitalization, outpatient care by civilian facilities, routine doctor visits, prescribed medicines, laboratory and X-ray tests, rental sick-room equipment, artificial limbs and eyes, and so forth are available to family members of active duty Marines on a cost-sharing basis. For active duty servicemembers, there are basically three plans to choose from: TRICARE Prime, TRICARE Standard, or TRICARE Extra. In general, depending on the plan you select, you pay some combination of a minimum annual fee per person or family, co-pays per visit, and/or cost-share per medical service or procedure. Given the differences in cost, flexibility, and level of service among the plans, it is wise to consult a TRICARE benefits adviser when selecting a plan.

A program of financial assistance is also provided for active duty personnel whose spouses or children are mentally or physically handicapped. This program authorizes diagnostic services, treatment, and use of private nonprofit and nonmilitary institutions for such handicapped family members, with you (the sponsor) paying a varying amount according to rank and the government paying the remaining portion of the cost up to a given maximum.

Medical Care at Service Facilities. When medical staff, space, and facilities are available, the Navy Medical Department will provide the following care for your family:

- Diagnosis
- Treatment of acute medical or surgical conditions, contagious diseases, and acute emergencies of any kind
- Immunization
- Maternity and infant care.

All care received for and during a pregnancy that results in hospitalization is considered, for payment purposes, as part of that hospitalization, and oral contraceptives are considered to be prescription drugs.

Family members (including parents, if legally dependent upon you) are normally able to receive outpatient services—those medical services provided without hospital admission. Virtually all medical activities on board military installations in the continental United States and outlying stations have dependent outpatient service.

The extent and quality of medical services for family members vary widely with the limitations of local dispensaries, or hospitals, and with the medical workload as a whole. Isolated outlying stations may provide more basic medical and dental services, relying on a regional medical center for comprehensive care.

In some regions, available health services are coordinated among various government health providers. In effect, you and your family may be assigned to a specific primary clinic for all outpatient and referral services. Consult your unit or base medical department or retired affairs office, as appropriate, to obtain information on local procedures.

On outlying stations, in addition to the service medical care noted above, dental care frequently can be provided to family members, subject to limitations of workload and facilities, provided adequate civilian dental services are not available. The government will also, in appropriate cases, provide transportation for family members from outlying stations where medical care is inadequate to centers where proper care can be provided (with round-trip expenses for attendants when they are found to be required).

A few cautionary words are in order on the subject of family medical care.

First and foremost, the medical needs of military personnel are the primary concern of the Medical Department. This means that care for family members takes second place and always gives way, when conflict arises, to military medicine functions. That said, the medical needs of family members will be met; it is just that the arrangements may not always be optimal.

Second, although members of the Marine Corps and Navy receive free dental care, dependents do not (except on remote, overseas stations or as otherwise required in connection with medical or surgical treatment). As compensation, you are offered the TRICARE Dental Program, a government cost-sharing program equivalent to TRICARE.

Third, to receive medical assistance from any Navy (or armed forces) establishment, your family member must possess and present a family member identification card (see Section 2114 below). Obtain these cards and have each family member carry a card.

Finally, if you wish, and can afford the more personal attentions of a private practitioner and civilian hospital, you are free, at your own expense, or under certain TRICARE plans when applicable as just noted, to obtain such services.

2114. Identification and Privilege Cards for Family Members

The Department of Defense issues (on application) a standard Identification and Privilege Card (Form DD 1173) for family members (except children under age ten) of all active duty personnel. This card is essential to enable your family to use the medical facilities, commissary, exchange, and other services provided at military installations. It is honored on not only Marine and Navy bases and stations but those of the other services as well. As soon as you have family members, you are required to apply to your commanding officer for their identification and privilege cards and DEERS enrollment.

LEGAL MATTERS

2115. Powers of Attorney

A power of attorney authorizes someone else, your "agent," to act in your name in the same manner and extent as you yourself could act. This power permits your agent to do only acts expressly stated therein.

When you are on expeditionary duty "beyond the seas," a power of attorney enables your family to carry on your affairs without interruption. Thus, when ordered overseas, you should consider whether to execute a power of attorney covering your affairs generally and particularly with reference to reimbursements from the United States. If you wish to include authority to transact business in general, consult the legal assistance officer to ensure that the power is legally sufficient but not needlessly broad.

Whether general or limited, you should verify that your power of attorney includes the following phraseology, or something reasonably similar:

> To execute vouchers in my behalf for any and all allowances and reimbursements payable to me by the United States, including, but not restricted to, allowances and reimbursement for transportation of family members or shipment of household effects as authorized by law or Navy or other regulations; to receive, endorse, and collect the proceeds of checks payable to the order of the undersigned drawn on the Treasurer of the United States for whatever account, and to execute in the name and on behalf of the undersigned, all bonds, indemnities, applications, or other documents, which may be required by law or regulation to secure the issuance of duplicates of such checks, and to give full discharge of same.

Such a power of attorney for governmental transactions should be executed in the presence of required witnesses and acknowledged before a notary public, or, if outside the United States, by any officer of the United States authorized to administer oaths. Your unit adjutant is normally vested with notary powers. For purposes other than those given, each specific power must be mentioned to be effective.

Bear in mind that not everyone needs to execute a power of attorney, as it can be a dangerous tool in the hands of the uninitiated or untrustworthy.

2116. Will

Considering the occupational hazards of our profession, it is important that you have a will. A will simplifies settlement of your estate, reduces expenses, conserves assets, and enables your last wishes to be carried out.

Definitions. A *will and testament* is the legal document by which an individual leaves instructions for disposition of property after death. A holographic will (rare today) is one that has been entirely handwritten and signed by the testator.

A *testator* is a person who leaves a will. An *intestate* is a person who dies without a will.

Settling an estate is a general term used to denote the entire process of collecting assets, filing inventories and accounts, paying claims, distributing assets in accordance with the will or laws of descent and distribution, and filing final accounting with the court.

An *executor* is appointed by your will to execute its provisions after your death. If you die intestate, the court appoints an administrator, who discharges the duties of an executor in settling the estate.

A *codicil* adds to, or qualifies, a will; it revokes the will only to the extent that it is inconsistent therewith. Will and codicil are construed together. A codicil is drawn in the same way as a will. When possible, the best procedure is to make a new will rather than to add a codicil to an old will.

Probating a will is the process of presenting the will for record to the proper authority in the county where the deceased had legal residence.

Before Making a Will. Analyze your estate; estimate state and federal taxes, and plan to minimize them. Then, if not sooner, confer with a competent legal adviser. See your legal assistance officer or a member of the local bar for this advice. It is well at this time to discuss, and preferably put in writing, the lawyer's expected charges for settling the estate.

Confer with the trust officer of your bank for help with administering expenses and taxes.

Provide liquid assets in your estate to meet taxes.

List the property that you cannot dispose of freely—property limited by joint tenancy, community property, your share of trust funds, life insurance already assigned to individuals, and so on—and put down opposite each the amount that you are entitled to distribute:

- Cash
- Real estate
- Securities
- Life insurance payable to the estate
- Business interests
- Automobiles in your name
- Household furniture and furnishings that are not community property
- Personal effects
- Other property.

Estimate expenses and debts to be paid from your estate:

- Expense of last illness
- Funeral expenses
- Unpaid household bills
- Personal debts
- Mortgage or notes payable (just your share, if joint)
- Expense of administering estate
- Taxes, such as real estate, estate, and inheritance.

Be careful in making cash bequests; if your estate decreases, you may cut off residual legatees with little or nothing.

For a small estate, it is probably best for husbands and wives to make the other the executor of each other's estate. For a large estate or a complicated will, give consideration to your bank as executor or coexecutor. The trust department of a bank has officials trained to handle large or complicated estates; a bank is a continuing institution; a bank is financially responsible; a bank has a fiduciary responsibility to act in your best interests; a bank receives no more for its services than an individual. Seek advice from your lawyer and banker.

When your executor has accepted the assignment, discuss your plans, go over your affairs—and take him or her into your confidence.

If your estate is within the amount exempt from a tax, a simple holographic will may be adequate, although this is scarcely necessary given the ease of preparing wills aided by modern computer software. Your lawyer can express your thoughts and wishes in legal language; he or she can give you advice that will help ensure a well-planned estate.

File the original of your completed will in your safe deposit box or other secure location (or with the Navy Mutual Aid Association, if you belong), but be sure that your spouse and your executor possess copies of your latest will and know the location of the original.

During your lifetime, you will probably make a new will several times. Certain milestones indicate when to reconsider your will and bring it up to date:

- Change of legal residence
- Removal of executor to another state or his or her death
- Radical change in your estate
- Sale of property mentioned in your will
- Major changes in tax laws
- Marriage, divorce, or remarriage
- Birth or death of child
- Death of spouse.

It is wise, in any case, to review your will every few years, and you should check it on changing legal residence (not change of station) to another state, as the provisions of your will may not be legal in that state and your executor may not be able to function there.

2117. Drawing a Will

A will must be in writing, but no particular form is required if its wording intelligently expresses your intent.

If you dispose of real property, your will must be made in accordance with the law of the state where the real property is located. If you dispose of personal property, your will must be made in accordance with the law of the state in which you are a resident. If both real property and personal property are disposed, your will must conform to the laws of all states among which the property is distributed.

The number of witnesses required for a will varies from none (for a holographic will) to three; *have three witnesses* to your will, and be safe. Sign in their presence, so that they see you sign and understand that it is your will you are signing. Witnesses, then, in your presence and in the presence of each other, sign the attestation. Be sure that none of the witnesses is mentioned in the will; attestation by an interested witness may invalidate the will, or the witness may lose a legacy. Witnesses should write their places of residence opposite their signatures. Because the authenticity of signatures must be proved in court at the time of probating, take care to select witnesses who will be available.

A Simple Will. To illustrate, the following short form of a simple, holographic will was used years ago by some officers:

> All my estate I devise and bequeath to my wife, for her own use and benefit forever, and I hereby appoint her my executrix, without bond, with full power to sell, mortgage, lease, or in any other manner dispose of the whole or any part of my estate.
>
> John Wharton (Seal) (Date)
>
> Subscribed, sealed, published, and declared by John Wharton, testator above named, as and for his last will in the presence of each of us, who at his request and in his presence, in the presence of each other, at the same time, have hereto subscribed our names as witnesses this (date) at the City of Washington, in the District of Columbia.
>
> (Signatures and addresses of witnesses, preferably three in number. Be sure that the word "Seal" is written in parentheses after each signature, as shown above.)

A Simple Codicil. If possible, write a codicil on the same sheet of paper as the will; if written on a separate sheet, fasten the two together securely. Here is a simple form of codicil:

I, John Wharton, of Washington, District of Columbia, make this codicil to my last will dated (date), hereby ratifying said will in all respects save as changed by this codicil. Whereas, by said will I gave Robert Anderson Wharton, my son, a legacy of $5,000, I now give him a second legacy of $10,000, making $15,000 in all.

(Then follow the testator's signature and seal, the attestative clause, and the witnesses' signature and seals.)

If you decide to modify your will, once it is executed, do not make alterations or interlineations. Consult your legal assistance officer on what to do.

Probate. If executed according to law of your legal domicile, a will made anywhere in the world will be admitted to probate in the jurisdiction of your domicile without question.

Probate establishes the validity of the will and evidences the right of beneficiaries to succeed to title to property in the estate. The place of probate is usually the county and state in which you are domiciled at the time of death; the will must also be probated in any other county and state where you own real property.

DEATH AND BURIAL

2118. Burial Arrangements

When Death Occurs Near a Navy or Marine Activity. When a Marine officer on active duty dies at or near his or her station, the commanding officer takes charge and arranges for local burial or for shipment of the body at government expense. (For burial in Arlington National Cemetery, see Section 2120 and the *Marine Corps Casualty Assistance Program.*)

In case of death in a naval hospital, the hospital authorities handle the arrangements.

Death at a Remote Place. When an officer on active duty dies at some distance from a Marine Corps installation, naval station, or hospital, the next of kin should contact the nearest Marine Corps or Navy activity for aid. If unable to contact a local activity, he or she should telephone the deceased's commanding officer or Marine Corps Headquarters, Washington, D.C., giving the deceased's full name, rank, and Social Security number; the date, place, and cause of death; and the place where burial is desired. Request instructions as to burial arrangements and give the address to which a reply may be sent.

Death in a Naval, Military, or Veterans Hospital (while in Inactive Status). Where death of a veteran or a retired or inactive officer occurs in a naval or military hospital or in a facility, the hospital authorities will make necessary arrangements upon request of the next of kin.

The Navy Mutual Aid Association has an outstanding pamphlet, *What to Do Immediately in Case of Death,* which is available on request. Obtain a copy of this and keep it with your important papers, as it is a complete checklist of essential information and actions required.

2119. Burial Allowances

The expenses of burial or shipment of the remains of Marine officers who die on active duty that are borne by the surviving spouse or another individual may be reimbursable. When the place of death is remote from a Marine Corps or naval station or hospital, the surviving spouse or individual is well advised to consult carefully with the casualty assistance calls officer (CACO), whom the Marine Corps will assign. When it is impossible to obtain instructions from the CACO or other Marine or Navy authorities, the surviving spouse or individual may employ a local funeral director, or, if necessary, arrange shipment of the body to the place of burial, but in such cases he or she should obtain itemized bills and receipts. Authorized categories of expenses are described below. Because the precise allowances can change, it is best to consult the CACO, who will have access to the prevailing reimbursable amounts listed in the *CACO Guide to Benefits and Entitlements.*

Primary Expenses. Allowances will normally cover reasonable costs for removal of remains, embalming, casket, clothing, dressing, cosmetic/restorative procedures, permits, air tray, cremation, urn, and engraving.

Secondary Expenses. Allowances will normally cover reasonable costs for professional services, facilities, staff, church, limousines, gratuities, obituary notice, memorial items, one grave space, cemetery labor, headstone or marker, vault/outer enclosure, and columbarium.

Reimbursable amounts differ based on the following factors:

- Interment in a private cemetery
- Interment in a national cemetery

- Direct disposition to a national cemetery
- Cremation
- Whether there is government involvement with burial in a national or private cemetery.

Transportation Expenses. Subject to limits, the cost of transportation is normally reimbursed in addition to primary and secondary expenses.

In the case of an honorably discharged, inactive, or retired veteran, the VA pays burial allowances, which are flat-rate monetary benefits that are generally paid at the maximum amount authorized by law for an eligible veteran's burial and funeral costs. The allowed amounts depend on whether or not the death is considered "service connected," whether the veteran was hospitalized in a VA medical facility at time of death, and when the veteran died.

As of 2017, the maximum burial allowance for service-connected death is $2,000. If the veteran is to be buried in a national cemetery, the VA may reimburse some or all of the costs of transporting the deceased veteran's remains.

The burial allowance for non–service-connected death is $300. Additionally, the VA will pay $749 for a burial plot. There are slightly higher non–service-connected burial allowances payable if the veteran was hospitalized by VA at the time of his or her death.

Generally, no expenditure is authorized for shipping the remains of an officer who dies on inactive duty, such as in a retired status. However, if the death occurred while the officer was properly hospitalized by VA, or under VA-contracted nursing home care, some or all of the costs for transporting the remains may be reimbursed.

There is no interment expense for burial in one of the many national cemeteries situated around the country.

If funeral expenses have been paid, claim for reimbursement should be submitted in writing with the assistance of the assigned CACO, stating name and rank of deceased, date and place of burial, and enclosing itemized bills in triplicate, receipted to show by whom payment was made, and the dates when rendered. If funeral expenses have not been paid, unpaid bills in triplicate are forwarded as above. (All claims for burial expenses must be submitted within two years after permanent burial or cremation.)

If remains are claimed at the place of death for private burial, and the service of the government is refused, the next of kin thereby relieves the government of any obligation for funeral or transportation expenses.

2120. Place of Burial

You may be buried at the place of death, in a private cemetery near your home, or in an open national cemetery. Leave written instructions as to your choice. If burial is to be in a national cemetery, the funeral director should contact the superintendent of the national cemetery selected; if your family lives near the selected national cemetery, the next of kin may request burial directly from the cemetery superintendent.

Remains are cremated only on written request from the next of kin.

Arrangements for burial at sea may be initiated via either Marine Corps Headquarters or local naval authorities. Burial at sea is not a right but a privilege, which might not be feasible to accord. Expenses incurred for delivery of remains to point of embarkation aboard a naval vessel must be paid by your survivors.

Military Funerals, Arlington National Cemetery. Funeral arrangements for burial in Arlington National Cemetery are made with the superintendent by the shipping activity, funeral director, or next of kin. Headquarters Marine Corps can make hotel reservations for family and friends, meet trains or planes, explain the different types of military funeral, and assist in selection of honorary pallbearers and furnish their transportation. Headquarters Marine Corps will also put the surviving spouse in touch with the Navy Mutual Aid Association (if deceased was a member) or another organization that can assist in preparing applications for pensions, compensation, or other claims on the government.

After the next of kin has received confirmation from Arlington of the request for burial, he or she should contact the office of the Superintendent of Arlington (and also pass the information on to Headquarters Marine Corps), stating the number in the funeral party, the means of transportation, the date and hour of arrival, and whether local transportation and hotel reservations are required.

When you think of burial, remember that Quantico now has a national cemetery, which ought to be considered as a special place for our own in the Corps.

2121. Other Information

Funeral Flag. A U.S. flag accompanies the remains and may be retained by the family. When death is remote from a naval or Marine activity, the postmaster of the county seat may furnish a flag.

Honors. When practical, and if requested, full military honors will be provided at the funeral of an officer (see *Marine Corps Manual*). But at cemeteries remote from both Marine Corps installations and Marine Corps Reserve activities, military honors are not always practicable, and relatives must make their own arrangements for funeral services. Veterans organizations usually can assist.

Gravestones. The government will provide a standard white headstone inscribed with the name, grade, and branch of service of the deceased. If burial is in a national cemetery, do not order a private monument until the design, material, and inscription have been approved by the National Cemetery Administration. The superintendent of the national cemetery concerned should be informed of plans for the headstone when you apply for the burial lot; many national cemeteries allow private markers only in certain areas.

Government headstones are provided for officers' dependents buried with the sponsor in national cemeteries.

Transportation for Family. One person may escort the body of an officer who dies on active duty to the place of burial. The escort may be a relative or friend (not in the service), with the government providing transportation in kind. If private burial is desired, a military escort usually accompanies the remains.

Household Effects. The household and personal effects of an officer who dies on active duty may be shipped from the last duty station or place of storage to the place the next of kin selects as home. Arrangements are made in the usual manner with the local traffic or distribution management officer, but shipment must take place within a year of death.

Death Certificates. For a death on inactive duty, the funeral director will obtain as many certificates as may be requested, at a nominal cost ($1 to $2 each, depending on the locality). They are needed for each insurance company, for the will, for each claim, for Marine Corps Headquarters, for the pay office carrying your accounts, and for the transfer of each security held in joint ownership. For deaths on active duty, Marine Corps Headquarters furnishes five copies of the official Report of Death, which will serve as a legal death certificate. Additional copies may be obtained on request.

The next of kin should also ask two officers or other friends, who knew the deceased, to identify the remains. These witnesses will then be prepared, if required, to furnish the affidavit of death sometimes demanded by commercial insurance companies.

Burial Privileges for Family Members. If a family member of any Marine on active duty dies at or while traveling to or from the place of active duty, certain government allowances are payable for transportation of remains.

SURVIVOR BENEFITS AND ASSISTANCE

2122. Death Benefits

Back Pay. Pay and allowances to the credit of a deceased are payable to the persons designated to receive them on the record of emergency data section of the computer file at Marine Corps Headquarters. If the deceased did not make such a designation or if the person designated dies first, this payment is made to the surviving spouse or, if predeceased, to the children, then the parents. Headquarters Marine Corps will send the necessary form to the person(s) eligible to receive this payment.

Compensation for Unused Leave. Your spouse or estate is eligible to claim and receive compensation for any unused leave to your credit, should you die on active duty.

Death Gratuity to Active Personnel. When death occurs on active duty, $100,000 is payable in a lump sum to the spouse of the deceased, or, if predeceased, to children; if he or she is not survived by children, then to any parents or brothers and sisters so designated. Payment to the spouse or children is mandatory and is not affected by designations. This gratuity cannot be checked to liquidate overpayment or any debt to the United States, and it is nontaxable. In most cases, payment should be made within twenty-hour hours after receipt of notification of death. In all other cases, Headquarters Marine Corps will institute the claim for death gratuity to the eligible beneficiary upon notification of death of a Marine; therefore, it is not necessary for your next of kin to request this benefit. In case of financial distress, your spouse may apply to the nearest Marine command for help. The Navy-Marine Corps Relief Society will also help with either a grant or loan (see Section 2125). The death gratuity just described is also paid if death occurs within 120 days after retirement or separation from the service, provided death is due to disease or injury incurred or aggravated while on active duty.

Dependency and Indemnity Compensation (DIC). DIC is a tax-free, monthly monetary benefit paid to eligible survivors of servicemembers who die in the line of duty or eligible survivors of veterans whose death resulted from a service-related injury or disease. The surviving spouse and/or children must meet certain eligibility requirements published by the VA, and they will have to submit proof of eligibility when they apply.

Eligible survivors may apply for DIC in a variety of ways:

- Consult the CACO, who will assist in completing and submitting the Application for Dependency and Indemnity Compensation, Death Pension and Accrued Benefits by a Surviving Spouse or Child (VA Form 21-534)
- Work with an accredited representative or agent
- Go to a VA regional office and obtain the assistance of a VA employee
- Complete VA Form 21-534 and mail it to the Pension Management Center that serves the state or region.

Based on 2017 figures, the VA pays DIC to the surviving spouse at the monthly rate of $1,257.95. This amount is increased by $311.64 per child for each dependent child less than eighteen years of age. Eligible survivors are entitled to additional amounts if they meet certain criteria.

2123. Other Benefits

Hospital and Medical Care. Dependent parents, spouses, and children under age twenty-one of deceased Marines are eligible for certain civilian medical care on a cost-sharing basis and, in general, for admission to armed forces hospitals. They may receive outpatient medical service where such service is available.

Exchange and Commissary Privileges. Armed forces exchange and commissary privileges are available to the families of Marine Corps personnel upon presentation of a valid identification and privilege card. Before going overseas, be sure that these ID cards are current for each family member and that those over ten years of age have their own cards.

Educational Assistance for Children of Marine Corps Personnel. From time to time, the Department of the Navy publishes a list of schools, colleges, universities, and other organizations that grant concessions and scholarships to service children.

Navy Relief Educational Loans. The Navy-Marine Corps Relief Society (see Section 2125) offers interest-free loans and grants ranging from $500 to $3,000 per academic year for undergraduate/post-secondary education at an accredited two- or four-year educational, technical, or vocational institution in the United States. This financial assistance is available for children of active duty, retired, or deceased sailors and Marines; and for spouses of active duty and retired sailors and Marines. Information may be obtained from the Navy-Marine Corps Relief Society.

Family Educational Assistance. Administered by the VA, this program provides up to thirty-six months of schooling for spouses of deceased veterans, spouses of living veterans, and children of either (ages eighteen to twenty-six) when death or total, permanent disability arose from service. Spouses and children of Marines who were missing in action (MIA), prisoners of war (POWs), or forcibly detained or interned by a foreign power for more than ninety days are also eligible.

In certain cases, children with disabilities may begin special courses as early as age fourteen. In most cases, a child's eligibility ends with the twenty-sixth birthday.

Generally, eligibility for a spouse extends to ten years from the veteran's date of death or total, permanent disability, whichever is later. For spouses of MIAs or POWs, eligibility extends to ten years from the date the servicemember was so listed.

Naval Academy Preparatory Scholarships. The U.S. Naval Academy Foundation awards preparatory school scholarships to enable high school seniors who are the children of active, retired, or deceased Marine Corps, Navy, or Coast Guard personnel to prepare for entrance to the Naval Academy.

Employment. Important civil service preferences are granted to surviving spouses, not remarried, in connection with examinations, ratings, appointments, and reinstatements under civil service and in connection with government reductions in force. Those interested should contact the U.S. Office of Personnel Management for information.

2124. Marine Corps Casualty Procedures

The Marine Corps notifies the next of kin recorded on your record of emergency data in case you are seriously injured, wounded, killed, or missing. Your next of kin is kept advised of your condition while you are on the critical list.

When an officer dies or is missing in action, a casualty assistance calls officer is appointed from a nearby Marine Corps organization to provide advice and assistance to the survivors. It is the CACO, usually accompanied by a chaplain and perhaps another command representative, who makes personal notification of the death or missing status. In the ensuing weeks, the CACO meets periodically with the next of kin and outlines rights and benefits of survivors, helps prepare claims, and so forth.

Chaplain. The survivors of a deceased Marine (active or retired) should not fail to seek assistance from the chaplain of the nearest Marine Corps or naval activity. Not only can chaplains minister spiritually at this difficult time, but they are also ready to help with burial arrangements, transportation, and all the problems that arise after the death of a Marine. Chaplains may assist the CACO with arrangements for burial in government or civilian cemeteries and upon request will normally conduct the funeral service, unless the next of kin prefer other arrangements.

Marine Officials. The nearest Marine commanding officer, recruiting officer, or inspector-instructor is competent and glad to assist families of deceased Marines with their problems.

2125. Aid from Organizations

Several organizations offer advice and assistance to families of deceased Marines.

American Red Cross. This organization assists families with all types of government claims, as well as other problems. Proof of dependency is necessary; family members should consult the Red Cross field director at the nearest base or station or the Red Cross chapter in their town.

Navy Mutual Aid Association. In case of death of a member, the secretary of the association should be the very first resort. Navy Mutual (https://www.navymutual.org) can be depended upon to handle all matters pertaining to pensions and other government claims.

Navy-Marine Corps Relief Society. This organization provides aid to members of the naval services and their dependents. Aid includes financial assistance (loan or grant); services of a Navy Relief nurse; help with transportation and housing; information about dependency allowances, pensions, and government insurance; location of and communication with naval personnel; and advice about community services. Apply to the local branch or through the national office (http://www.nmcrs.org).

Tragedy Assistance Program for Survivors (TAPS). This program began as a group of bereaved military families who lost their loved ones in a military plane crash in Alaska in 1992. Formally founded in 1994, TAPS employs best practices found in peer-based support programs to assist anyone who is grieving the death of someone who died while serving in the military, regardless of where they died or how they died. Grief counseling, case work, peer mentors, and care and support groups are a few of the services TAPS offers. Contact information for TAPS is available online (http://www.taps.org).

United Service Organizations (USO). Known for its centers at transportation hubs providing respite to traveling servicemembers and its entertainment programs for those deployed, the USO also supports families of deceased servicemembers. The USO often assists by making special travel accommodations for grieving families in transit at its airport centers around the world. The organization also supports families through partnerships with organizations like TAPS. Contact information for USO is available online (https://www.uso.org).

Veterans' Groups. The Military Officers Association of America, American Legion, Veterans of Foreign Wars, Disabled American Veterans, Military Order of the World Wars, Marine Corps Scholarship Foundation, and other veterans' groups may also render aid to survivors of Marine veterans.

RETIRED OFFICER BENEFITS

2126. Overview

When you retire, you rate various Marine Corps benefits and perquisites. In addition, you may be entitled to various veterans' benefits if you apply for them. Some of these have already been mentioned, and this section sums up the most important ones. In connection with most veterans' benefits, it is important to know that, although your retired pay is taxable, it is not classed as "other income," and thus does not bar you from receipt or limit the extent of benefits for which you are otherwise eligible, except that, if you receive disability compensation from the VA, your retired pay is reduced by the amount of the VA disability payment.

2127. Medical Care and Hospitalization

As a retired Marine, you benefit from several health-care alternatives. These include TRICARE, VA-provided medical benefits, and other supplemental health-care insurance options.

TRICARE for Retirees. Retirees and their authorized family members remain eligible to use military treatment facilities, depending on availability, and civilian health-care facilities under TRICARE. TRICARE eligibility remains in force until you are sixty-five years of age. Upon reaching age sixty-five and becoming eligible for Medicare, TRICARE ends and you become eligible for TRICARE for Life, a supplemental insurance program.

For information on TRICARE or TRICARE for Life, contact a beneficiary service representative or health benefits adviser at your nearest military treatment facility.

TRICARE currently offers retirees three health-care options:

1. *TRICARE Prime*: This is a health maintenance organization–style managed-care program. Retirees are required to pay an annual enrollment fee. They and their eligible family members are assigned a primary care manager, who determines the most appropriate, available source of care at either a military treatment facility or a civilian network provider. They pay little or no co-payment, and they are usually not required to file claims for their care.
2. *TRICARE Extra*: This is a preferred provider organization–style program. Retirees need not enroll; however, retirees and their eligible family members must obtain care from a TRICARE network provider. Retirees will be responsible for paying the annual deductible and cost shares at a reduced rate. The network provider will file the health insurance claims.
3. *TRICARE Standard*: This is a fee-for-service option. There is no annual enrollment fee, but it requires an annual deductible and cost shares, ranging from 20 to 50 percent, *after* the deductible has been reached. Under TRICARE Standard you are responsible for filing your claim.

Retirees should contact a health benefits adviser or beneficiary counselor and assistance coordinator at a nearby military treatment facility or stop by a TRICARE Service Center for more assistance.

U.S. Department of Veterans Affairs Health Care. Retired Marine officers continue to be eligible for VA medical care. The Veterans Health Administration is America's largest integrated health-care system with over 1,700 health-care sites, serving more than eight million veterans each year.

Obtaining VA-provided medical care requires enrollment. VA operates an annual enrollment process. It is wise to plan ahead, because the enrollment process can be lengthy, as VA evaluates a variety of factors during the application verification process when determining a veteran's eligibility for enrollment. Once a veteran is enrolled, however, he or she remains enrolled in the VA health-care system and maintains access to VA health benefits.

This may be a good option if there is a well-regarded VA medical center nearby.

TRICARE Retiree Dental Plan. The TRICARE Retiree Dental Program (TRDP) provides comprehensive dental coverage for retirees and their family members. Under contract with the U.S. Department of Defense, the Federal Services division of Delta Dental Plan administers the TRDP.

The TRDP is a voluntary dental benefits program with enrollee-paid premiums.

Covered services under the TRDP are offered throughout the fifty states, most territories of the United States, and Canada.

Finally, *a word to the wise*: At the time of retirement, when your active duty health record is closed out, make a copy for personal retention in case of future VA claims or whenever you need attention from any other medical facility.

2128. Veterans' Benefits

As a veteran of military service, whether in time of war or peace, you have certain privileges and benefits. Although some of these are subject to expiration, Congress adds others from time to time. The following are the most important current benefits.

Department of Veterans Affairs. The VA offers a multitude of benefits to persons honorably discharged from the armed forces: special care and pensions for the physically and mentally impaired; hospital and domiciliary care; vocational rehabilitation; family benefits, including financial and education support; loans or loan guarantees for acquiring homes or farms and their upkeep and improvement; home remodeling for the disabled; nursing home care; alcohol and drug rehabilitation; counseling services; and burial and funeral expenses. Consult your nearest VA field office. Once you are admitted to any program, including active duty VA loans and educational benefits, retain your VA file number for easy access to all future transactions.

Educational Assistance. The VA provides education benefits to eligible servicemembers, veterans, and certain dependents and survivors. You may receive financial support for undergraduate and graduate degrees, vocational and technical training, licensing and certification tests, apprenticeships, on-the-job training, and more.

There are several educational programs sponsored and supported by the VA for which you may be eligible.

Post-9/11 GI Bill. The Post-9/11 GI Bill provides to eligible servicemembers and veterans up to thirty-six months of education benefits. Post-9/11 GI Bill benefits may include financial support for school tuition and fees, books and supplies, and housing. Eligible veterans may also receive reimbursement for license or certification tests (such as broker, private investigator, and CPA), national tests (for example, Scholastic Aptitude Test, College Level Examination Program, American College Testing, Graduate Management Admission Test, and Law School Admission Test), or assistance for apprenticeships or on-the-job training. A one-time payment to support relocation from certain rural areas to attend school is also available.

Each type of benefit, such as tuition or books, has a maximum rate. Based on the length of your active service, you are entitled to a percentage of the maximum total benefit.

Montgomery GI Bill. The Montgomery GI Bill–Active Duty (MGIB-AD) provides eligible veterans up to thirty-six months of financial assistance for educational pursuits, including college, vocational or technical training, correspondence courses, apprenticeships or on-the-job training, flight training, high-tech training, licensing and certification tests, entrepreneurship training courses, and national examinations. Generally, your MGIB-AD benefits are paid directly to you on a monthly basis.

You may be eligible for MGIB-AD benefits while on or after separating from active duty. To receive benefits after separating, you must have received an honorable discharge. You generally have ten years from your last date of separation from active duty to use your MGIB-AD benefits.

Reserve officers are eligible for different VA educational benefits. They should investigate the VA benefits web site for the most up-to-date information.

2129. Travel on Government Aircraft

Retired officers, and family members when accompanied by the sponsor, may travel, space available ("Space-A"), in government aircraft both within the continental limits of the United States and overseas. To arrange this, check with the operations section at the Air Mobility Command terminal from which you wish to depart. AMC passenger terminal personnel are in the best position to provide the most current information about AMC policies, procedures, routes, schedules, and waiting lists.

Be aware that there is no guaranteed space for any Space-A traveler. The Department of Defense is not obligated to continue an individual's travel or return him or her to the point of origin or any other point. Travelers must have sufficient personal funds to pay for commercial transportation to return to their home or duty station if Space-A transportation is not available. Such travel is a privilege, not an entitlement.

Retired officers and accompanying family members who desire to travel Space-A may register to do so at passenger terminals from which they plan to depart; registration may be submitted in person or by fax, email, Internet, or mail. On the day of the desired flight, all passengers are required to be ready for travel at the designated "show time." To be considered travel ready, each prospective passenger must have all required documentation (with ID card and, of course, passport, visas as required, and immunization record if required) and checked baggage; all accompanying family members must be present.

Routes and schedules vary, so you will need to contact the various AMC terminals directly for the latest Space-A travel opportunities. Still, if your destination is the Pacific or the Far East, the AMC terminal at Travis AFB, California, is perhaps the best option, although other west coast terminals such as Joint Base Lewis-McChord, Washington, may provide travel options. For Japan and Alaska, travelers have found flights at Lewis-McChord and the AMC terminal at Seattle-Tacoma International Airport, Washington. For the Mediterranean or Latin America, the AMC terminal at Joint Base Charleston, South Carolina, has traditionally been a good source. And for Europe, the terminals at Joint Base McGuire-Dix-Lakehurst, New Jersey, and Dover AFB, Delaware, have been good options.

Space-available travelers—especially retirees who travel with the lowest priority—are subject to being "bumped" by official travelers and travelers on emergency orders at any point en route. Baggage is limited to sixty-six pounds. Finally, it bears repeating that that Space-A travelers must have sufficient ready cash to proceed via commercial means if "bumped."

Detailed policies and procedures are available on the AMC Travel web site (http://www.amc.af.mil/amctravel/).

DIVORCE

2130. Divorce

The decision to dissolve a marriage is an intensely personal one. Because of the structure of dependency benefits, however, an officer seeking separation or divorce needs to keep the commanding officer advised of administrative or social changes and needs to inform and provide documents to unit administration.

Separation does not usually involve changes in dependency, but *divorce* does. In a divorce, identification cards must be recovered, your former spouse must be removed from DEERS, and your remaining dependency obligations must be certified. This means recertifying any children or other legal dependents in DEERS and submitting a copy of the divorce decree and any accompanying support agreement to Headquarters Marine Corps. These may serve as references in case the government has to adjudicate elements of the decree. You should seek the most competent legal advice you can afford, so that an equitable arrangement can be determined as soon as possible. Then adhere to your legal obligations so that the Corps need not intervene in your personal affairs and finances.

If you are facing divorce, you should be aware of the potential impact of *garnishment.* The Social Services Amendment of 1974, Public Law 93-647, Section 459 authorized garnishment of active duty and retired pay to meet the obligations of alimony and child support. Garnishment was limited two years later under Public Law 95-30, Section 509 to either 50 or 65 percent of the individual's aggregate disposable earnings received from the federal government, depending on whether the individual had remarried. A valid court order must be issued to garnish pay, naming the agency required to effect the garnishing and stipulating enforcement of child support or alimony obligations. Commanders are then required to forward such orders to the finance center for action. Part 6, Chapter 1 of *DOD Financial Management Regulation, Volume 7B*, provides a detailed explanation of garnishment policies and procedures.

In addition to support requirements, a divorced officer also faces possible division with a former spouse of military retired pay as property. The 1981 McCarty decision by the Supreme Court ruled that such pay was not subject to division as property, in effect safeguarding military pensions of those divorced before the date of the decision, 26 June 1981. But Public Law 97-252, effective 1 February 1983, contains a Former Spouse Protection Title that permits state courts to consider dividing military disposable retired pay as property between parties in a divorce regardless of the number of years the couple was married. Remarriage of the ex-spouse does not necessarily cause termination of the award. The title also extends health and commissary and exchange privileges to ex-spouses married during at least twenty years of active service.

The lesson of the foregoing paragraphs should be clear: if ending a marriage, seek the best legal advice and consider the local laws and customary judgments most carefully before proceeding.

Foreign Divorces. Medical care, quarters allowances, and other dependents' benefits have been denied in the cases of military personnel who have obtained foreign divorces, usually Mexican, and later attempted to marry some other person. You have the responsibility of preventing members of your command from the often tragic difficulties that can result from foreign divorce entanglements.

Three things come not back: the arrow that is flown,
the spoken word—and lost opportunities.

—Omar Ibn, 581–644

22

MARINE CORPS SOCIAL LIFE

There was once an era when officers and their families lived, worked, and socialized within a rather insulated community of fellow servicemembers. Most officers and families lived on board bases, and the nearby civilian communities offered less in the way of social attractions than did the bases. With the coming of World War II, the military services expanded, and the separate military and civilian societies became more intertwined. In the postwar period, the larger peacetime military establishment and frequent expansions during the conflicts of the second half-century brought that old insular military society to a gentle close. Today, military officers live, commute, and mix freely with their civilian counterparts. The demands for recreation and social activities have far outstripped the capacity of the bases.

There still remain many enjoyable trappings of that old military society to enjoy and to share on occasion with your civilian friends. This chapter contains some useful information covering those traditional activities. A few have become extinct for practical purposes but are retained here for reference in the event that they could be revived in isolated instances or celebrated in a foreign country in which you serve.

As you become a Marine and join the corps of officers, you also must be prepared to share the time-honored and pleasant social traditions of your Corps. As you do so, remember one thing above all: the phrase "an officer and a gentleman/lady" is a current one in the Marine Corps. It means what it says.

2201. Helpful References

This chapter is not intended to cover completely etiquette and protocol for Marine officers but simply to deal with the military and more especially the Marine aspects of service social life. For more general reference, consult the latest editions of the following publications:

Service Etiquette (Naval Institute Press). This classic is a sound general guide, indispensable in certain matters.

Social Usage and Protocol Handbook: A Guide for Personnel of the U.S. Navy (Department of the Navy). This government publication, for many years withheld from general circulation by DON civil servants, is a comprehensive, useful *vade mecum* within its limits. Any officer going on attaché, military assistance group, or naval mission duties should obtain a copy.

Protocol for the Modern Diplomat (Department of State). Although not specifically designed for the military community, this remains a useful compilation containing many excellent suggestions and much good advice.

SOCIAL OCCASIONS

2202. Marine Corps Birthday

As every Marine knows, the Corps was founded on 10 November 1775. From that day to the present, 10 November has been the climax of the Marine Corps year, the top social occasion of the Corps.

The birthday of the Marine Corps is celebrated officially and socially by all Marines throughout the world. Not only do Marine units carry out the prescribed ceremony, but wherever one or more Marines are stationed—on board ship, at posts of other services, even in the field—10 November is celebrated.

How a Command Observes 10 November. For a Marine command, the birthday includes prescribed or customary features, which are observed as circumstances permit. For Marines with other services, many of these items cannot be fulfilled exactly, but this list may serve as a guide:

- A troop formation (preferably a parade and cake-cutting ceremony) for publication of the article from the *Marine Corps Manual* (see Appendix V). The uniform should be a blue dress A (which includes large medals) or an authorized variation thereof that is appropriate to the climatic conditions. If blues cannot be worn, the service uniform is appropriate. On board ship, hold a special formation of all Marines and get permission from the captain to pipe the birthday article over the public address system. If you are with some other service and only a few Marines are present, you may defer publishing the article until the evening social function.

- Holiday rations, which should include a main course of roast beef or steak, accompanied by a lobster tail or shrimp
- Maximum liberty and minimum work consistent with the missions of the command
- A birthday ball for officers and one for enlisted Marines. At each, a cake-cutting ceremony takes place. Circumstances sometimes dictate (for example, at smaller commands) a single, all-hands ball.

Any training or instruction scheduled for 10 November should emphasize the traditions and history of the Corps.

The Birthday Ball. It is up to you to celebrate the annual birthday ball with pride, forethought, and loving care. Every Marine command must have one. If on detached service away from the Corps, the senior Marine officer present must make every effort to arrange a suitable birthday ball, and it is up to every Marine to chip in to support it.

The birthday ball is formal, which means evening dress for officers who possess it, or blue dress (with large medals) as a substitute. Those who are not required to possess either evening dress or blues wear service uniform.

The birthday ball is a command performance. Unless duty prevents, you attend. If resources permit, distinguished civilian guests and officers from other services should be invited, but not too many. Be sure that retired Marine officers and any Marine officers present from other countries are included.

Appendix VI describes the procedure for a birthday ball ceremony. This procedure, of course, is a guide, and details may vary according to facilities, numbers of officers and guests, and local traditions. There is only one ironclad rule for the birthday ball: Make it a good one.

2203. Mess Night

A mess night (also called a "guest night" or a "dining-in" in some circles) is a formal military dinner with a set agenda attended by all members or by the

22-1. Cutting the birthday cake is the highlight of the traditional birthday ball.

officers of a command or unit. A variation of the mess night, a "dining-out" includes spouses and often omits some of a mess night's more formal and traditional elements.

Mess nights may be held on special anniversaries, such as that of a battle in which the unit has participated, to recognize officers being detached, or to honor a distinguished guest or guests from another unit, service, or country. By custom, attendance is considered obligatory.

In the U.S. armed forces, mess nights date back to the Army's regimental messes of the pre–World War I days and to the days of the wine mess in the wardroom afloat, which ended abruptly in 1914 when Secretary Josephus Daniels imposed prohibition on the Navy. In this early era of a small Marine Corps with only several hundred officers, the only permanent Marine officers' mess was at "Eighth and Eye," where in the Old Center House (torn down in 1908) the officers of Headquarters and the Barracks had their mess nights. Happily, the custom continues in today's successor Center House, as elsewhere.

Chapter 8 of the *Social Usage and Protocol Handbook* provides a useful, official discussion of the major features of a mess night.

Preparations. The first step in preparing for a mess night is to designate the officer who will act as vice president. In some units, the vice president is traditionally the junior lieutenant present. However, it is good practice to rotate the post among all company officers on board so that all may gain experience. In any case, the function of the vice president, at least beforehand, is to undertake all preliminary arrangements—guest list, seating diagram, and menu, all to be approved by the mess president; catering details; music; decorations; and so forth. The success of the evening depends on the vice president, who is typically addressed as "Mister Vice" or "Madame Vice" as appropriate.

Subject to local or unit customs and to facilities that are available, here are specific arrangements that should be made for a mess night:

1. After approval of the guest list, invitations should be prepared and mailed or delivered at least two weeks in advance of the mess night. Each guest, regardless of organization or of sponsoring officer in the host unit, is a guest of the mess and should be so treated.
2. The table is set with complete dinner service—wine glasses, candles, and flowers. Unit or command silver (if maintained) should be used.
3. Unless the commanding officer desires to preside, a field-grade officer—often the executive officer—is detailed as president of the mess for the occasion; a company-grade officer acts as vice president.
4. Uniform is evening or mess dress, blue dress A, or blue-white dress A. Civilians invited to a mess night should wear full dress with miniature medals if uniform is evening or mess dress; dinner jacket with miniatures, if blues or blue-whites.
5. The National Color and the Marine Corps Color are placed behind the president's chair. Guidons and drums may also be used as decorations.

6. The mess president sits at the head of the table, the vice president at the foot. Other guests and members take seat by rank (as in the wardroom on board ship), except that guests of honor are on the right and left of the president. A seating diagram should be posted in advance, and place cards and menu cards prepared. All preliminary arrangements are supervised by the vice president.
7. If available, a three- or four-piece military string orchestra should be detailed to provide dinner music. The orchestra should know the national anthems and regimental marches of guest officers. If suitable "live" music is not available, a good-quality public address system with taped or recorded selections will serve as a substitute. The musical program should be checked and timed by the vice president and should always include "Semper Fidelis" and the regimental march of each guest.
8. In some messes and commands, the custom of emulating the Continental Marines endures by drinking toasts in rum punch rather than port. Here is the mix for "1775 Rum Punch": four parts dark rum, two parts lime juice, one part pure maple syrup. Add small amount of grenadine syrup to taste. Ice generously and stir well. The maple syrup was originally used during the Revolution because of the British blockade that cut off supplies of West Indies sugar cane.

Procedure. Officers assemble in an anteroom thirty minutes before dinner for cocktails and to greet guests. This should be the occasion for all officers to speak to guests and make them feel welcome. It is also the opportunity for each officer to pay respects informally to the senior officers present, COs especially. Dinner is announced in accordance with local custom. In some messes, "Semper Fidelis" is played; elsewhere, Officers' Call is sounded followed by a march (when drum and bugle corps is available, "Sea Soldiers" is a suitable march); still another variation is to play "The Roast Beef of Old England" (known and used in the "Old Navy" as "Officers' Mess Gear") on fife and drum. Whatever the signal, officers and guests proceed to their places. Each guest should be escorted by a member of the mess. A brief grace is said by the chaplain, if present; otherwise, by the president. Officers then take seats. The ranking guest, seated at the mess president's right, is served first, then the president, and so on counterclockwise without further regard to seniority. Appropriate wines are served with each course. There must be no smoking during dinner, and no officer may leave the table until after the toasts, except by permission from the president. (If for any reason, official or otherwise, you arrive late, you should express your regrets to the mess president before taking your seat.)

After dessert, there is a short concluding grace, the table is cleared, and port decanters and glasses are placed on the table in preparation for a series of formal toasts. The port passes clockwise until all glasses are charged. When the decanter (or both decanters, if two are used) has completed the circuit, the president raps for silence. If a foreign officer is present, his or her head of state is toasted first; otherwise, toasts begin with the president of the United States. To begin, the president rises, lifts a glass, and says, for example, "Mister (or Madame) Vice, His Majesty, King _____ of _____." The vice president then rises, glass in hand, waits until all have risen, and gives the toast. "Gentlemen, His Majesty, King _____ of _____." The orchestra plays the appropriate foreign national anthem, following which all say, "King _____ of _____," drink, and resume seats. Good-natured conversation may resume. After about a minute, the president again raps for silence, the senior foreign officer rises, and says "Gentlemen, the president of the United States," and the orchestra plays the National Anthem. If no foreign guests are present, the president makes the first toast to the president of the United States. Subsequently, there is a series of additional formal toasts, which may depend on the occasion or circumstances surrounding the mess night. Normally, designated members of the mess offer formal toasts in pre-planned succession, with each toast seconded by the vice president in the aforementioned fashion. If the guest of honor is from another service, a toast to that service is in order.

After the formal toasts, coffee is typically served, the smoking lamp is lighted, and the president rises and introduces the guest of honor, who then addresses the mess. If the impending departure of an officer occasions the mess night, the commanding officer makes brief, usually humorous remarks, whereupon the officer being honored replies in the same vein. In some messes, the orchestra remains and plays the regimental march of each guest, during which the individual stands. After this, or whenever the orchestra is released, the president may send for the orchestra leader and offer a drink.

Following speeches, the president may open the floor to informal toasts offered by members of the mess. During this period, any member of the mess who wishes to initiate a toast rises and addresses the president. On being recognized, the member briefly presents his or her rationale for the toast, ending with the words of the proposed toast. Inspired wit and subtle sarcasm are much appreciated in these toasts. If the president deems the toast justified, he or she will direct the vice president to second the toast in the same manner as in the formal toast.

The concluding toast is always to the Marine Corps, during which, if music is available, "The Marines' Hymn" is played. The wording of this toast should be, "Mister (or Madame) Vice, Corps and Country," and the custom has grown up (proposed long years ago by Colonel A. M. Fraser) that the vice president reply in words taken from a Revolutionary War recruiting poster of the Continental Marines—"Long live the United States, and success to the Marines!"

Before leaving the subject of toasts, note that toasts may be divided into four classes, and that they are given in the following order:

Toasts of Protocol:	Toasts to foreign governments or chiefs of state and toast to the president of the United States
Official Toasts:	Toasts to other services, military organizations, government departments, agencies, or institutions
Traditional Toast:	"Corps and Country"
Personal Toasts:	Toasts to individuals (distinguished guests, officer being dined out, and so on).

With the exception of the evening's final toast, formal and informal toasts are not "bottoms up." Do not be caught in the position of having an uncharged glass!

The traditional toast ends the formal part of the evening. At this point, the president announces, "Ladies and gentlemen, will you join me in the bar?" and the senior officers rise and depart the dining room, following which the remaining members of the mess adjourn individually to the bar and anteroom, where songs may be sung and games played. All hands should remain until the ranking guest and the commanding officer leave, after which anyone may secure at discretion.

Circumstances frequently do not permit a mess night with all formalities as to uniform, catering, and table service that are outlined herein, or all of them might not be desired. This should not deter an organization from making the effort. The idea is to do the best you can with what you have, and let the spirit of the occasion take care of the rest. Do not, in particular, let yourself be overcome or stultified by the apparent formality of mess nights; the object is the pleasure and comradeship of all hands. Reports that a few commands have actually rehearsed mess nights, if true, make the occasion ridiculous. A mess night is not a minuet.

The costs of a mess night, like other "chip-in" Marine Corps social functions, should be prorated by rank so that officers who make the most, pay the most. Here is a version of the famous Schatzel formula for prorating costs by rank (see Table 22-1); it appears complicated but is actually quite simple.

This formula is also useful to calculate cost shares for the annual Marine Corps birthday ball, and might be adapted for use when planning an all-hands ball.

As to timing, it is better not to schedule mess nights too regularly. It is much preferable that officers begin asking when the next one will take place. Thus, a mess night will be looked forward to with anticipation and never become a burden.

Table 22-1. Prorating Event Costs by Rank

Grade	*Base Pay*	*Number Participating*
Colonel	x	δ
Lieutenant Colonel	y	σ
Major	z	λ
Captain	a	Φ
First Lieutenant	b	Δ
Second Lieutenant	c	μ

$$K = \text{total cost of the function}$$
$$E = x\delta + y\sigma + z\lambda + a\Phi + b\Delta + c\mu$$

Colonel share = Kx/E
Lieutenant Colonel share = Ky/E
Major share = Kz/E
Captain share = Ka/E
First Lieutenant share = Kb/E
Second Lieutenant share = Kc/E

2204. Military Wedding

As a Marine officer, you enjoy the privilege of having a military wedding. A military wedding is simply a formal wedding with traditional service embellishments. The following paragraphs describe the characteristic features and ground rules of a military wedding.

Uniform. Marine members of the wedding party wear blue dress A with sword. Dress A uniforms call for medals, not ribbons. If the weather requires, wear boat cloak rather than overcoat if available. Even though wearing sword, and thus under arms, the bride and groom should not wear gloves, whereas the ushers should wear gloves throughout the ceremony.

Needless to say, all servicemembers of the wedding party wear the same uniform. If officers from other services are included, they wear their nearest equivalent uniform. For an evening wedding, evening dress is worn. Civilian members of the wedding party wear civilian formal.

Wedding Party and Ushers. Since your wedding is to be military, members of the wedding party and ushers may be regular or reserve officers. Inactive reserve officers may don uniforms for the occasion. It is usual for ushers to be the same rank as the bride or groom, although this is not mandatory. The senior usher coordinates or signals for movements by the ushers and for the arch of swords.

The best man looks out for the groom. Although a brother or close friend customarily performs this function, it is permissible and considered a nice compliment for a male officer to ask his immediate commander (if close in rank and on those terms) to be the best man. Under analogous circumstances, a female officer could appropriately ask her immediate commander to be the maid/matron of honor. In any case, however, your CO and fellow officers should be invited to the wedding, and all will attend.

In the unlikely event the wedding takes place away from the bride's home, and her parents or near relatives cannot attend—as is sometimes the case in the service—it is appropriate for the commanding officer or other senior officer to give away the bride.

The Clergy. You may choose either a chaplain or a civilian member of the clergy. A chaplain performs the ceremony in uniform or in vestments, according to the customs of the denomination. In some denominations (such as the Episcopal Church), ministers, whether chaplain or civilian, are permitted to wear military ribbons on their vestments, and will do so if you request. The best man should see to this. If your wedding is an evening affair, it is appropriate for the clergyman to wear miniature medals on a civilian coat at the wedding reception.

Do not pay a chaplain for officiating at a military wedding. If you have a civilian clergyman, follow civilian custom regarding fees. Again, this is something the best man traditionally handles. The same applies to fees for an organist and music at the church.

Wedding under the Colors. If you wish, and your denomination permits, the National Color and Marine Corps Color of your unit may be crossed above and in the rear of the chaplain, or displayed during the ceremony in the chancel of the church. This is known as "a wedding under the Colors." It is an old tradition, signifying your spouse's acceptance into the Corps.

Handling the Colors for this ceremony is the responsibility of the senior usher, who, with designated ushers, receives the Colors (cased) from the adjutant, places them before the ceremony, and removes, cases, and returns them immediately afterward.

Wedding Present from the Unit. The officers of the bride's or groom's battalion, squadron, or headquarters or service school classmates if at school when married—traditionally present the couple with a piece of silver plate, such as a silver tray, water pitcher, or cocktail shaker, which is appropriately engraved. With the advent of gift registries, they may want to consider selecting a gift from the registry. Some units have a standard type of wedding gift, which it is the duty of the adjutant to procure, engrave, and collect for. A typical inscription for a piece of silver plate might read: "From the Officers of the 1st Battalion, 5th Marines."

If the wedding takes place at a school, it is up to the senior Marine officer in the class to arrange this wedding present.

Arch of the Swords. This is probably the best-known feature of a military wedding. It is carried out in this fashion: After the ceremony, the senior usher forms the ushers in column of twos and places them immediately outside the exit of the church, facing inboard. As the newly married couple passes through the portal, the senior usher gives the preparatory command, "Officers, draw," pauses briefly, and then commands, "Swords." At the command of execution, ushers carry out only the first count of the movement and leave their swords raised, with tips touching, to form an arch under which the couple passes. After the newlyweds have passed, swords are returned on command by the senior usher.

22-2. Social occasions can provide enrichment of the military professional's life.

Cutting the Wedding Cake. The wedding cake is cut by the bride and groom together, using the sword. If two Marine Corps officers are marrying, it is proper to use the senior's sword. After the cake has been cut, the best man proposes a toast to the bride and groom, and, as the guests drink, the orchestra plays "Auld Lang Syne."

2205. Calls

The exchange of calls once received emphasis in military society far exceeding that on the "outside." Although at first glance a bit ritualistic, they did serve to break down barriers of seniority, widen one's circle of acquaintances, and disclose mutual interests that might otherwise have gone unnoticed. The Marine Corps far exceeds the size that it was in earlier times when tradition held that Marines all knew one another. Calling has declined in the same manner that the old isolated military posts and their insular societies have expired. Instead, the function formerly served by calls is largely accomplished during a "hail and farewell," a periodic command gathering during which the CO introduces newly joined officers and their families and recognizes the contributions and achievements of officers departing for a new permanent posting. If only for historical interest, it is worth briefly discussing calls here, especially in the event that you serve in a foreign country still observing this practice.

Calls are of two kinds—official and personal. You will find the former covered in Sections 1120 and 1121. Official calls are rendered only between commanding officers, officers of state, and officers' messes. Personal calls are exchanged among officers and their families.

Although service customs govern personal calls, some commanding officers have special preferences as to when and how calls are paid. Thus, before making any calls, check with the adjutant, and, if necessary, with the general's aide (or, if serving with the Navy, the flag lieutenant) in order to find out the local policies. Twenty minutes (or "one drink") is the accepted duration of a formal personal call.

2206. Hail and Farewell

A hail and farewell is an informal command gathering at which the commanding officer welcomes—or "hails"—officers and their families who have recently joined the unit and bids farewell to departing officers and their families. It is a casual social event that builds camaraderie within the command and, among other aims, accomplishes what personal calls formerly accomplished. It also provides the opportunity to publicly recognize the service to the command of departing officers and their families. Although a hail and farewell ought to be an enjoyable event you attend enthusiastically, you should consider it a place of duty unless you are otherwise engaged in a time-sensitive mission or task important to the command.

Although there is no fixed periodicity for a hail and farewell, commands commonly hold them quarterly. If held more frequently, the event may be perceived as burdensome. When less frequent, they often fail to serve their purpose: newly joined officers are no longer "new," and departing officers may depart without appropriate recognition from the command.

Likewise, there is no prescribed format for a hail and farewell. There are as many styles of hail and farewell as there are commands and commanders. The one overarching rule is that they should be casual, enjoyable gatherings that renew the bonds of camaraderie and friendship among the unit's officers and their families. Here are a few ideas to consider should you be involved in planning a hail and farewell:

- Hold the event at a convenient, pleasing location. The officers' club or lounge is an ideal venue.
- Consider the schedules of those to be hailed and bid farewell—officers and their families—when selecting date and time. It is often a good idea to schedule the hail and farewell during the latter part of the workday on a Wednesday or Thursday, although consideration in scheduling should also be given to the needs of working spouses and school-age children.
- The executive officer must ensure all officers attend.
- For attire, uniform of the day normally suffices.
- Allow some time for libations and socializing before commencing the informal agenda of the hail and farewell.
- Hails are brief introductions by the CO of the new officers. When bidding farewell to an officer, the CO will normally speak a bit longer on the contributions and achievements of the departing officer and, if applicable, spouse, and then turn the floor over to the departing officer for brief remarks.
- Depending on the size of the unit, a well-run hail and farewell need last no more than one or two hours.
- It is a failure of leadership when an officer is permitted to depart for a new posting without a proper "farewell."

Typically, the executive officer or adjutant will help orchestrate a hail and farewell. The adjutant is additionally responsible for procuring mementos for departing officers, if this is a command practice.

CLUBS AND MESSES

2207. Commissioned Officers' Messes

Every base or station has a commissioned officers' mess in some form. The mess acts as a social focus for the officers and spouses of the installation, it serves meals, and it sometimes provides accommodations for visiting officers.

Today, the commissioned officers' mess is most often referred to as "The Club" or "The Officers' Club." Like any club, the mess is a private association operated for the convenience of its members on Marine Corps bases and stations by Marine Corps Community Services, a department or division of the installation. Although you are not automatically a member of every commissioned officers' mess at every station just because of your rank and status, it is nonetheless habitual to extend privileges of a station mess to any visiting officer and family. At your home station, you are automatically a member of the commissioned officers' mess upon payment of the required membership fees, if any (in fact, membership fees are rare today), but you may be denied the privileges of the mess if you abuse them.

2208. Officers' Clubs and Bachelor Officer Quarters

Clubs and unmarried or bachelor officer quarters, when available, have three main functions: social recreation, meal service, and housing for bachelor, temporary bachelor, and visiting officers. Any officer assigned temporarily or permanently to a BOQ normally pays a fixed charge to take care of cleaning services, linen, and so forth. In certain BOQs with messing facilities, officers living therein pay for and take meals at given rates on a menu catered by the base officers' club. In a few cases (for example, Camp Barrett at Quantico), the base central mess operates the officers' dining facility and serves (and charges for) the basic ration, which is habitually a good one. Where a BOQ does not have a messing capability, you may take your meals at the officers' club (or possibly in an officers' section of a unit mess hall).

Closely related to the BOQ are its derivatives, MOQ and TOQ. An MOQ is a married officer quarters, usually an apartment building, and TOQ stands for transient officer quarters.

2209. The Wardroom Mess

A wardroom mess is a commissioned officers' mess on board ship. The wardroom is the common room, recreational space, and dining room for the officers of a man-of-war. The wardroom mess is the organization through which the ship's officers cater their meals and meet most of their social and recreational needs while on board. Like any closed mess, the wardroom mess is a private association whose operation is paid for by members. Because wardroom messes fulfill essential functions of feeding and accommodation, they receive some government support. You will find notes about wardroom mess etiquette in Chapter 9. If you are going to sea duty, be sure to look up these rules—and observe them.

2210. Mess Etiquette

Before leaving the subject of clubs and messes, here are some general rules of conduct and etiquette that have always maintained the tone and correctness of Marine officers' messes.

Remember that the mess belongs to the members who support it. As a guest, defer to their ways and rules; as a member, assume responsibility for it and support it as your mess.

Dress conservatively and correctly at the club. You cannot go wrong, ordinarily, if you wear full uniform of the day or complete civilian clothes. What is considered appropriate civilian attire at the officers' mess varies around the country and around the world; clubs in Hawaii and on the West Coast tend to be more casual; clubs on the East Coast and overseas, less casual. The dining room in an officers' mess may require more formal attire than an adjacent officers' lounge. Most messes publish and post their uniform rules. You, your guests, and your family members must abide by them if you expect to use the club.

If your officers' mess still maintains member accounts, pay your bills promptly, sign chits legibly and accurately, and always be sure your checking account is in shape to meet any checks you write. The officers' mess is founded on the proven concept that a Marine officer's word or signature is his or her bond. Dishonorable disregard of your obligations as an officer will destroy your personal standing, weaken your mess, force irksome restrictions on other members, and bring swift retribution, which will mar your record.

Tip mess employees as you would in a civilian restaurant or bar, unless the mess rules specify otherwise.

When you are a guest in a club or mess—unless the place accepts cash or credit cards—do not attempt to offer drinks to others, as settling your bill will be awkward. If you are on temporary additional duty and thus become a member of the mess, however, you are expected to pay your fair share. If, as a member, you see a strange officer alone in your mess, introduce yourself and extend hospitality; remember that a guest of any officer is a guest of the mess.

When you bring guests to the mess, be sure they are those you would entertain in your own home or introduce, as your friends, to the commanding general and spouse.

Whether in a private club or a service mess, remember that an officer of Marines is well mannered. If in doubt as to some nicety or ground rule, be gracious. You will never go far wrong.

WASHINGTON DUTY

2211. White House and Diplomatic Functions

The White House is a focus of social and official Washington. Some officers on duty in Washington may expect to be entertained at the White House, and a few are detailed to additional duty as Marine aides-de-camp at the executive mansion.

Because a White House invitation constitutes a presidential command, it takes precedence over any other social commitment, previous or not. If you receive a White House invitation, consult one of the aides to the commandant at Marine Corps Headquarters. The aide will tell you the uniform and give you whatever briefing may be in order.

Second only to White House functions in their requirement for fine attention to dress and etiquette are those conducted by the diplomatic corps.

Uniform is ordinarily worn for official parties at embassies or legations or those given by a military or naval attaché. The general rule is: blues for afternoon receptions and cocktail parties; evening dress for formal evening parties, black or white tie.

When at a foreign diplomatic party, be alert for and familiar with foreign badges and insignia of rank and with their national anthems. On occasions of this kind, your dignity, courtesy, and smartness set you apart not only as a Marine but as a representative of the United States.

Service Etiquette is an invaluable reference if your duties immerse you in the Washington social scene.

2212. Recreation in the Washington Area

Private Clubs. The Washington area boasts two of the foremost military and naval clubs in the country: the Army and Navy Club (the "Town Club") and the Army and Navy Country Club (the "Country Club").

The Army and Navy Club, located on historic Farragut Square in Washington, is one of the senior private clubs in the United States, and it provides all amenities (including rooms for members and guests). The "Town Club" is a traditional meeting place for officers and their friends. The Army and Navy Country Club, in Arlington, Virginia, overlooking the city, is one of the coolest summer spots in the metropolitan area and a country club of first rank (with a first-rank golf course).

Both the Town Club and Country Club allow newly commissioned officers to join, as nonresidents, with greatly reduced entrance fees. If you fail to take advantage of this privilege at the outset of your career, you must later buck waiting lists and pay relatively large initiation fees, which may make it impossible for you to be a member of these fine clubs. Membership on these terms is one of the best bargains open to a new officer; lose no time in taking advantage of it.

MARINE CORPS SOCIAL CUSTOMS

2213. Standing Social Customs

Certain social customs are observed throughout the Corps and deserve mention here.

Wetting Down Your Commission. Whenever you are promoted, you are obligated to hold a "wetting-down party." At this affair, your new commission (which was traditionally displayed at some conspicuous but safe vantage point) is said to be "wet down." When several officers are promoted together, they may join in a single wetting-down party.

Cigars. If you are a new parent, it is common and appreciated to distribute cigars or candy to all officers and staff NCOs of your unit.

Five Aces. Any officer who rolls five aces when throwing dice for refreshments in a mess is obliged by tradition to buy a complete round of drinks for all the messmates present. In large messes, this custom is eased to the extent that you have to buy drinks only for your own party.

Entering a Mess Covered. Unless you are on duty and under arms, if you enter a mess covered, you are liable to buy all present a round of drinks. Most messes adhere to and post the old rule: "He who enters covered here buys the house a round of cheer." In fact, some even have a bell and lanyard that may be rung by anyone present who spots an offender against this rule, thus signaling a free round.

Placing Your Cover on the Bar. Those who place their headgear on the bar are also liable to buy the house a round of drinks.

Drawing Your Sword in a Mess. The seagoing rule that any officer who unsheathes a sword in the wardroom must buy a round also applies on shore, if you are so unwary as to draw sword in any public room of an officers' mess. The custom goes back to the days of dueling, when this was one method of cooling off hotheads and restricting indiscreet sword play.

Welcome on Board. Whenever a new unit arrives at an installation, or a transport brings in an appreciable number of Marines or Marine families, the local Marine commanding officer or representative, together with the nearest military band if feasible, greets the newcomers.

Send Off. When a unit or draft leaves, the commanding officer, band, and friends see them off. If the move is routine, the band plays "Auld Lang Syne" as aircraft embarkation is completed, the transport casts off her last line, or the train gets under way. If the unit is bound for war or expeditionary service, "The Marines' Hymn" is the send-off. In either case, the departing unit should be played down to the airfield, dock, or loading platform by "Semper Fidelis."

Special Courtesy to Commanding Officers and Senior Guests. At any social functions—cocktail parties and receptions especially—you have certain special obligations to your commanding officer and spouse and to the guest of honor, if any. On your arrival (or on the CO's arrival, if later than yours), both you and your spouse should make it a point to approach and speak to the CO and spouse as soon as practicable. This is known as "making your number." Except when absolutely necessary, you should not depart before your CO and the guest of honor do so. If you must leave early, however, express your regret to your CO and ask permission. It is a mark of poor military courtesy and social manners if either you or your spouse fails to observe these courtesies.

2214. Social Dos and Don'ts

Common sense, tact, and ordinary courtesy are the fundamentals of social success in the Marine Corps. For fine points and unusual situations, you may wish to refer to the tested references listed in Section 2201 or some other recognized social guide such as *Emily Post's Etiquette* (18th edition). The following pointers are supplementary, therefore, but worth your perusal.

When you are on a base or station, on board ship, in uniform ashore, or otherwise recognizable as a Marine officer, your conduct must be impeccable. "If you must raise hell," runs an old Marine proverb, "do it at least a mile away from the flagpole."

It was once written, "The ideal income is a thousand dollars a day—and expenses." Obviously you do not stand much chance of attaining this on service pay, although a few inexperienced or improvident officers try to live as if they had it. You cannot fool anybody as to how much you make, so live within your income.

"Good clothes open all doors"—be sure yours are correct both for style and occasion. And always check to see which uniform is prescribed before you attend a social function.

"Whoever gossips to you will gossip of you" and "It is easier to be critical than correct"—avoid criticism about other officers, and never vent destructive criticism of your service, your unit, or your superiors.

Never serve bad liquor—"Use hospitality to one another without grudging."

Be punctual. It is never wrong to arrive exactly on time for a social function, although it is sometimes considered a courtesy to the host or hostess to arrive perhaps ten minutes after the appointed start time. For large cocktail parties, dances, and receptions, you may arrive not later than a half-hour after the announced time. For seated meals, it is best to be exactly on time. "Punctuality is the politeness of kings."

Do not load down social conversation with technical language or with labored application of Marine Corps terms to civilian matters. On the other hand, as a professional, learn the talk and nomenclature of the Corps. Use precise terms to convey precise meanings. Avoid undue shop talk and thus avoid the character whom Joseph Addison so well described: "The military pedant always talks in a camp, and is storming towns, making lodgements [sic] and fighting battles from one end of the year to the other. Everything he speaks smells of gunpowder; if you take away his artillery from him, he has not a word to say for himself."

At a mess or at any official function, politics, religion, and sex are discussed (if at all) only with the greatest discretion. Whatever you do, never speak ill of your Corps or of any fellow officer in the presence of outsiders, civilians, or members of any other service. And remember always, insofar as public utterances are concerned, an American soldier has no politics and espouses no political party or cause.

Polite society is no place to play "the tough Marine." Courtesy and personal modesty are never more becoming than in an officer. Rudeness, abruptness, gory tales of blood and thunder, and coarse language usually show up the greenhorn or counterfeit, and certainly the ill-mannered. "The bravest are the tenderest; the gentlest are the daring."

Remember that your spouse does not and cannot wear your rank. Be certain that he or she understands this quite clearly and does not exhibit a tendency to dominate the juniors or subordinates. This will only belittle your rank in the eyes of others. Insist, however, that your spouse receive due courtesy from all.

"Be prepared" is just as good a social motto for Marine officers as for Boy Scouts. Before you attend any social function, ascertain the dress, whether there will be a receiving line, who will receive, when the line closes, and who of importance to the Marine Corps may attend. All these are the essential elements of information that help place you at ease and prepare you for any social eventuality.

Teach me to be obedient to the Rules of the Game.

Teach me to distinguish between sentiment and sentimentality, admiring the one and despising the other.

Teach me neither to proffer nor to receive cheap praise.
If I am called on to suffer, let me suffer in silence.
Teach me to win if I may; teach me to be a good loser.

Teach me neither to cry for the moon nor to cry over spilt milk.

—Lines framed in his cabin by King George V of England, while serving as a naval officer

We are all members of the same great family. . . . On social occasions the formality of strictly military occasions should be relaxed, and a spirit of friendliness and good will should prevail.

—John A. Lejeune

APPENDIX I
"THE MARINES' HYMN"

From the Halls of Montezuma
To the shores of Tripoli,
We fight our country's battles
In the air, on land, and sea.
First to fight for right and freedom,
And to keep our honor clean,
We are proud to claim the title
Of United States Marine.

Our flag's unfurl'd to every breeze
From dawn to setting sun;
We have fought in ev'ry clime and place
Where we could take a gun.
In the snow of far-off northern lands
And in sunny tropic scenes,
You will find us always on the job—
The United States Marines.

Here's health to you and to our Corps
Which we are proud to serve;
In many a strife we've fought for life
And never lost our nerve.
If the Army and the Navy
Ever look on Heaven's scenes,
They will find the streets are guarded
By United States Marines.

APPENDIX II

COMMANDANTS OF THE MARINE CORPS

Major Samuel Nicholas, 1775–81
Lieutenant Colonel William Ward Burrows, 1798–1804
Lieutenant Colonel Franklin Wharton, 1804–18
Lieutenant Colonel Anthony Gale, 1819–20
Brigadier General Archibald Henderson, 1820–59
Colonel John Harris, 1859–64
Brigadier General Jacob Zeilin, 1864–76
Colonel Charles G. McCawley, 1876–91
Major General Charles Heywood, 1891–1903
Major General George F. Elliott, 1903–10
Major General William P. Biddle, 1911–14
Major General George Barnett, 1914–20
Major General John A. Lejeune, 1920–29
Major General Wendell C. Neville, 1929–30
Major General Ben H. Fuller, 1930–34
Major General John H. Russell Jr., 1934–36
Lieutenant General Thomas Holcomb, 1936–43
General Alexander A. Vandegrift, 1944–47
General Clifton B. Cates, 1948–51
General Lemuel C. Shepherd Jr., 1952–55

General Randolph McC. Pate, 1956–59
General David M. Shoup, 1960–63
General Wallace M. Greene Jr., 1964–67
General Leonard F. Chapman Jr., 1968–71
General Robert E. Cushman Jr., 1972–75
General Louis H. Wilson Jr., 1975–79
General Robert H. Barrow, 1979–83
General Paul X. Kelley, 1983–87
General Alfred M. Gray Jr., 1987–91
General Carl E. Mundy Jr., 1991–95
General Charles C. Krulak, 1995–99
General James L. Jones, 1999–2003
General Michael W. Hagee, 2003–6
General James T. Conway, 2006–10
General James F. Amos, 2010–14
General Joseph F. Dunford Jr., 2014–15
General Robert B. Neller, 2015–

APPENDIX III
READING FOR MARINES

I want Marines to read beyond the list, too, especially paying attention to current events, science and technology, and what our potential adversaries are up to around the world.

—General Robert B. Neller,
37th Commandant of the Marine Corps

Marines and other artisans of war justly find perplexing the prospect of future war, for which they are charged to prepare. The answers to questions of who, when, where, and to what aim will not grow less elusive in the future—of this we can be certain. One method of preparing for the future increasingly espoused by Marines lies in general reading in the only laboratory the soldier has, the study of the social sciences. This appendix suggests books and journals that will benefit you as a Marine and as a professional soldier. Any such listing is bound to be arbitrary; many of the thousands of other writings on the military art will certainly prove enjoyable and beneficial as well. I have tried to suggest works of significant breadth and quality that remain available in bookstores, although some may be difficult to locate.

The reader will notice immediately a dearth of autobiography and biography, a field so obvious and rich as to defy selecting a few. In addition, you should read the excellent official histories of the Marine Corps and U.S. Army dealing with World War II, Korea, Vietnam, Afghanistan, and the Gulf Wars. The official World War II histories of the United Kingdom, Canada, Australia, and New Zealand also make remarkably fine reading.

The works suggested in this appendix are meant to complement those on the Commandant's Professional Reading List (CPRL). The books on the CPRL are selected specifically to promote critical thinking and professional development at each rank, whereas the reading recommended here offers the Marine officer a broad and perhaps timeless perspective on the profession of arms. In any case, the Commandant's Professional Reading List is the current assemblage of "must-reads" for Marines, and you must quickly gain familiarity with it and use it to guide your professional reading. The Library of the Marine Corps maintains the current CPRL online at its research portal.

Without further qualification, here are more than eighty books, grouped into nine categories, that cannot fail to improve your insight and skill as a professional.

GENERAL SURVEYS

Bernard Brodie, *Strategy in the Missile Age* and *War and Politics*

Martin van Creveld, *Supplying War: Logistics from Wallenstein to Patton* and *The Transformation of War*

Paul Fussell, *Wartime: Understanding and Behavior in the Second World War*

John W. Hackett, *The Profession of Arms*

Basil H. Liddell Hart, *Strategy*

Michael Howard, *War in European History* and *Studies in War and Peace*

Allan R. Millett, *Semper Fidelis: The History of the United States Marine Corps*

Michael A. Palmer, *Command at Sea: Naval Command and Control since the Sixteenth Century*

Peter Paret, *Makers of Modern Strategy from Machiavelli to the Nuclear Age*

Barry R. Posen, *The Sources of Military Doctrine: France, Britain, and Germany between the World Wars*

Theodore Ropp, *War in the Modern World*

Russell F. Weigley, *The American Way of War: A History of United States Military Strategy and Policy*

CAMPAIGNS AND TACTICS

Rick Atkinson, *An Army at Dawn: The War in North Africa, 1942–1943,* and *Crusade: The Untold Story of the Persian Gulf War*
Correlli Barnett, *The Desert Generals*
Antony Beevor, *Stalingrad: The Fateful Siege, 1942–1943*
Robert A. Doughty, *The Breaking Point: Sedan and the Fall of France, 1940*
John A. English and Bruce I. Gudmundsson, *On Infantry*
John Erickson, *The Road to Stalingrad: Stalin's War with Germany*
Bernard B. Fall, *Street Without Joy: The French Debacle in Indochina*
Richard B. Frank, *Guadalcanal: The Definitive Account of the Landmark Battle*
David M. Glantz, *Colossus Reborn: The Red Army at War*
Michael Gordon and Bernard Trainor, *Cobra II: The Inside Story of the Invasion and Occupation of Iraq*
John Hackett, *The Third World War: The Untold Story*
Don Higginbotham, *The War of American Independence*
Wayne P. Hughes, *Fleet Tactics and Coastal Combat*
Stanley Karnow, *Vietnam: A History*
John Keegan, *The Face of Battle: A Study of Agincourt, Waterloo, and the Somme*
William S. Lind, *Maneuver Warfare Handbook*
Charles B. MacDonald, *Company Commander*
Allan R. Millett, *Their War for Korea: American, Asian, and European Combatants and Civilians, 1945–1953*
Alan Moorehead, *Gallipoli*
Samuel Eliot Morison, *The Two-Ocean War: A Short History of the United States Navy in the Second World War*
Edgar O'Ballance, *No Victor, No Vanquished: The Yom Kippur War*
Qiao Liang and Wang Xiangsui, *Unrestricted Warfare: China's Master Plan to Destroy America* (trans. Lenni Brenner)
Erwin Rommel, *Attacks*
Gunther E. Rothenberg, *The Art of Warfare in the Age of Napoleon*
Cornelius Ryan, *A Bridge Too Far* and *The Longest Day*
Hew Strachan, *The First World War*
Russell F. Weigley, *Eisenhower's Lieutenants: The Campaigns of France and Germany, 1944–1945*
Gerhard L. Weinberg, *A World at Arms: A Global History of World War II*
H. P. Willmott, *Empires in the Balance: Japanese and Allied Pacific Strategies to April 1942*

AMPHIBIOUS WARFARE

Joseph H. Alexander and Merrill L. Bartlett, *Sea Soldiers in the Cold War*

Merrill L. Bartlett, *Assault from the Sea: Essays on the History of Amphibious Warfare*

Jetek A. Isley and Philip A. Crowl, *The U.S. Marines and Amphibious War: Its Theory and Its Practice in the Pacific*

LEADERSHIP

Al Kaltman, *Cigars, Whiskey, and Winning: Leadership Lessons from General Ulysses S. Grant*

John Keegan, *The Mask of Command*

Stanley McChrystal, *Team of Teams: New Rules of Engagement for a Modern World*

Barry Strauss, *Masters of Command: Alexander, Hannibal, Caesar, and the Genius of Leadership*

TECHNOLOGY AND INNOVATION

Bernard Brodie, *Sea Power in the Machine Age: Major Naval Inventions and Their Consequences on International Politics, 1814–1940*

Bernard Brodie and Fawn M. Brodie, *From Crossbow to H-Bomb: The Evolution of the Weapons and Tactics of Warfare*

William H. McNeill, *The Pursuit of Power: Technology, Armed Force, and Society since A.D.1000*

Williamson Murray and Allan R. Millet, *Military Innovation in the Interwar Period*

SOCIAL AND POLITICAL

John L. Esposito, *Unholy War: Terror in the Name of Islam*

David Fromkin, *A Peace to End All Peace: The Fall of the Ottoman Empire and the Creation of the Modern Middle East*

Mike Gravel, *The Pentagon Papers: The Defense Department History of United States Decisionmaking in Vietnam*

Morris Janowitz, *The Professional Soldier: A Social and Political Portrait*

Paul Kennedy, *The Rise and Fall of the Great Powers*

Henry Kissinger, *Diplomacy*

Bernard Lewis, *The Shaping of the Modern Middle East*

Hans J. Morgenthau, *Politics among Nations: The Struggle for Power and Peace*

CLASSICS

Julius Caesar, *The Civil War of Caesar*
Karl von Clausewitz, *On War* (ed. Peter Paret and Michael Howard)
Flavius Josephus, *The Jewish War*
T. E. Lawrence, *The Seven Pillars of Wisdom*
Alfred Thayer Mahan, *The Influence of Sea Power upon History, 1660–1783*
Tacitus, *The Annals of Imperial Rome*
Thucydides, *History of the Peloponnesian War*
Mao Tse-Tung, *On Protracted War*
Sun Tzu, *The Art of War*
Xenophon, *The Persian Expedition*

MISCELLANEOUS

Arthur S. Collins Jr., *Common Sense Training: A Working Philosophy for Leaders*
Victor H. Krulak, *First to Fight: An Inside View of the U.S. Marine Corps*
S. L. A. Marshall, *Men against Fire: The Problem of Battle Command in Future War*
John G. Meyer, *Company Command: The Bottom Line*
Sam C. Sarkesian, *Combat Effectiveness: Cohesion, Stress, and the Volunteer Military*
Edwin H. Simmons, *The United States Marines: A History*

FICTION

Philip Caputo, *A Rumor of War*
Jaroslav Hasek, *The Good Soldier Schweik*
Ernest Hemingway, *For Whom the Bell Tolls*
Bill Mauldin, *Up Front*
Erich Maria Remarque, *All Quiet on the Western Front*
Michael Shaara, *The Killer Angels*
John W. Thomason Jr., *Fix Bayonets!*
James Webb, *Fields of Fire*

Most of these books can be obtained through the Marine Corps Association Bookstore or the U.S. Naval Institute, with discounts offered to members. Many may also be available through online sellers such as Amazon. For discount offers and sales, query the Military Book Club, Edward R. Hamilton

Bookseller, P.O. Box 15, Falls Village, CT 06031 (www.militarybookclub.com). For out of print military history titles, try The Military Bookman at Chartwell Booksellers, 55 East 52nd Street, New York, NY 10055 (or browse online, www.militarybookman.com) or Antheil Booksellers, 2177A Isabelle Court, North Bellmore, NY 11710. Perhaps the finest collection in the world is offered, at no mean price, by Francis Edwards Antiquarian Booksellers, which is now part of Hay Cinema Bookshop, Ltd. at The Enterprise Park, 2 Forest Road, Hay-on-Wye, HR3 5EH United Kingdom (www.francisedwards.co.uk).

PROFESSIONAL JOURNALS

Air & Space Power Journal
Joint Force Quarterly
Journal of Military History
Marine Corps Gazette
Military Review
Naval War College Review
Parameters
PRISM
Proceedings

More expensive, but useful, are the following:

Jane's Defense Weekly
Jane's International Defense Review
Military History Quarterly
Royal United Services Institute Journal

All military laws and military theories which are in the nature of principles are the experience of past wars summed up by people in former days or in our times. We should seriously study these lessons paid for in blood, which are a heritage of past wars.

—Mao Tse-Tung, 1936

APPENDIX IV
FELLOW MARINES

The bonds of comradeship-in-arms that knit together many of the corps of marines in today's world remain unusually strong. As a member of the world's largest (though not the oldest) of these military organizations, you should know of the other sea soldiers serving under foreign flags. Many of these—the older corps in Europe and the Latin American and East Asian corps of marines and naval infantry—enjoy long-term relations with the U.S. Marine Corps, and the respective commandants have exchanged messages and visits over the years.

This appendix includes information, as known, on some of the other such corps, many of which had been regarded as "on the other side," depending on the varied courses of diplomacy.

THE ROYAL MARINES

I never knew an appeal to their courage or loyalty
that they did not more than realize my expectations.
If ever the hour of real danger should come to England,
the Marines will be found the country's sheet-anchor.

—Admiral Lord St. Vincent

Britain's Royal Marines, elder brothers of the U.S. Marine Corps, were 111 years old in 1775 when our own Corps was founded. From inception, the infant

American Corps was modeled after its illustrious British prototype, and many of the traditions of our Corps today can be traced to the Royal Marines.

As a result, despite early "quarrels" (as in 1775, at Bunker Hill, and in 1814, when Royal Marines burned Washington after the Bladensburg fight), the camaraderie between U.S. and British marines is a tradition of both corps, and knowledge of the Royal Marines is part of every U.S. Marine's fund of information.

The Royal Marines perform much the same duties as U.S. Marines, with certain variations. As is the case for one of our Fleet Marine Force commanding generals, the Commandant General, Royal Marines, serves as a "type commander" under the fleet commander of the Royal Navy. The fleet commander, under the present system (since 1993), delegates full command of the Royal Marines to the commandant general, who also has the right of direct access to the First Sea Lord, equivalent to the CNO of the U.S. Navy, on regimental matters of the Royal Marines.

The roles of the Royal Marines include the following: providing an amphibious commando brigade (with supporting army, navy, and air force personnel and units) capable of worldwide deployment, as well as for traditional infantry tasks; detachments for navy ships and certain shore stations; special forces, such as the Special Boat Service; a special unit to protect nuclear weapons and sites; maritime counterterrorism; the Royal Marine Band; and other missions as the Navy Board may direct.

The uniforms of the Royal Marines are much like our own. Aboard ship and on certain shore duties, they wear blues. Their ranks, rank insignia, and field undress uniforms are those of the British Army, but the color of the service uniform is forest green. All Royal Marines wear a blue beret as one type of headgear, but members of commando units wear green berets, because green has always been the traditional commando color.

The official colors of the corps are scarlet, yellow, green, and blue. These colors appear on the Royal Marines necktie, which is worn with civilian clothing by all members of the corps.

Although Royal Marine officers wear British Army rank badges, they are promoted and paid under the naval system. An officer can expect to be promoted to captain at about age thirty and would then receive the pay of a lieutenant commander in the Royal Navy or an army major. Further promotion depends upon selection, with up to 60 percent of the captains reaching major at an average age of 37.5 years. A lieutenant colonel equates to a naval captain and a colonel to a captain of six years' seniority. As with the British Army, the grade of brigadier is an appointment position for a colonel, with two- and three-star grades the same as in other services.

The "Birth of the Corps Day," which corresponds to our 10 November, is 28 October of each year. The Royal Marines were organized in 1664.

The sovereign, or a member of the royal family, is captain-general of the corps. At present, this ceremonial post is filled by the Duke of Edinburgh, husband of Queen Elizabeth II.

The principal stations of the Royal Marines are the major barracks (Stonehouse) at Plymouth; Commando School, Bickleigh; Infantry Training Center, Lympstone; Amphibious School, Poole; and a recruit depot and school of music at Deal.

Although U.S. and British marines have served side by side on many occasions, both corps particularly cherish associations stemming from the Boxer Uprising and the Korean War. In the Boxer Uprising, U.S. Marines and Royal Marines formed the backbone of the band of Western troops who defended the Legation Quarter in Peking throughout a long and bloody siege in 1900. In addition, in the International Brigade, which finally relieved both Peking and Tientsin, U.S. and British marines were formed side by side. Fifty years later, a Royal Marine commando was attached to the 1st Marine Division in Korea and served with the division throughout the Chosin Reservoir campaign.

Finally, it is interesting to note that the Royal Marines conducted the first carrier-based helicopter assault landing ever executed in combat at Suez in 1956.

ROYAL NETHERLANDS MARINES (*KORPS MARINIERS*)

The *Korps Mariniers*—as the Dutch Marines are officially entitled—was founded on 10 December 1665 in the Dutch Wars, which caused the British to form the Royal Marines. One of the most important early operations of the Netherlands Marines was the amphibious raid up the Thames in 1666, one of the few occasions when foreign troops have landed in Great Britain since the Norman Conquest. Subsequently, the *Korps Mariniers* performed normal sea duty and garrison duty throughout the Dutch empire. During World War II, when

Holland was overrun by the Germans, several thousand Dutch Marines were trained at Camp Lejeune as the basis for reconstitution of the corps, and the relationship between our two corps has since been close. *Qua Patet Orbis* ("To the Ends of the World") is the Dutch Marines' motto; their uniforms, both service and dress, are similar to those of the Royal Marines and of the U.S. Marine Corps.

Today, the *Korps Mariniers* numbers about 2,300 and continues to serve as an integral part of the Royal Netherlands Navy. It provides detachments for ships and naval stations and takes responsibility for the physical, military, and ceremonial training of all Navy personnel. Dutch Marines are specially trained to execute special maritime operations, amphibious landings, and expeditionary land operations with light infantry units. The *Korps Mariniers* includes a deployable, brigade-level command element, two combat groups, a surface assault and training group, a sea-based support group, and maritime special operations forces. The 1st Marine Combat Group is the main contribution of the Royal Netherlands Marines to the United Kingdom/Netherlands Landing Force. Some four hundred Dutch marines guard installations in the Netherlands Antilles and Aruba. There is also a "special assistance unit" for counterterrorism tasks.

The headquarters of the corps is in Rotterdam, with principal barracks there and on the island of Texel. Amphibious training is conducted on Texel.

SPANISH MARINES (*INFANTERÍA DE LA MARINA ESPAÑOLA*)

Dating from the *Tercios de la Armada Naval* of Spanish Armada days and earlier, Spain's *Infantería de la Marina* can claim four centuries of service. Its men fought at Lepanto in 1571 and with the Armada in 1588; defended Cartagena in 1741; took Sardinia in 1748; and served gallantly in the Peninsular War, Cuba, the Philippines, Guam, Morocco, Cochin China, the Spanish Civil War, and the Sahara (Ifni).

The missions of the Spanish Marines are to guard ships and stations and maintain trained expeditionary forces.

The *Infantería de la Marina* today maintains *Agrupaciones* (light infantry battalions) at El Ferrol, Cartagena, Cádiz, Las Palmas, and Madrid. Each contains an expeditionary company in addition to guard companies. The *Tercio de la Armada* is a marine expeditionary brigade maintained at San Fernando (Cádiz) for duty with the fleet. It is collocated with the development and education center. The Major General Commandant has his office and staff in the Navy Headquarters, Madrid.

Spanish Marine officers' uniforms are those of the navy, with distinguishing badges; enlisted Marines wear dress blue similar to those of the Royal Marines, and combat/utility uniforms resembling those of our own Corps. The emblem of the *Infantería de la Marina* is an anchor (up-and-down) with crossed rifles, surmounted by the crown of Spain.

The Spanish Marines' motto is "Valiant on Land and Sea." Since 1701, the traditional colors of the corps have been red and blue. As in the case of our own Corps, Horse Marines are both a tradition and a joke with the Spanish, dating from the fact that, during the nineteenth-century guerrilla operations in Cuba, "Navy Cavalry" mounted units were formed of Marines. The birthday is celebrated on 26 February for this, the oldest corps of marines in the world.

ARGENTINE MARINE CORPS

The origin of the Argentine Marines dates to 1807 when a naval battalion was organized to defend Buenos Aires against British attack. Subsequently, during Argentina's War of Independence, marines served on board warships and conducted landing operations. In 1879, a Marine artillery battalion was formed, to man coast defenses at Argentina's seaports and naval bases. In 1947, following World War II, the corps was reorganized along modern amphibious lines, and a U.S. Marine adviser was provided. However, he did not accompany the battalion that spearheaded Argentina's seizure of the Falklands/Malvinas Islands by amphibious assault in 1982.

The major operating units of the Argentine Marine Corps include base security units, infantry battalions assigned to the fleet amphibious brigade and the southern district, plus additional battalions and groups of commandos, field artillery, antiaircraft artillery, coastal defense artillery, amphibious vehicles, and service support troops.

The uniforms and ranks of the corps are similar to those of our own. The annual birthday ceremonies are held on "Day of the Marine Corps," 19 November.

BRAZILIAN MARINE CORPS (*CORPO DE FUZILEIROS NAVAIS*)

The *Fuzileiros,* as the Brazilian Marines are known throughout Brazil, date their lineage back to the Portuguese Marines, which were founded in 1797. Units of this organization first came to Brazil in 1808, and 7 March, the date of their landing, is the birthday of the corps in Brazil, which was then an overseas dominion of Portugal and subsequently separated amicably from the mother country.

Brazilian Marines fought in their country's wars throughout the nineteenth century, including major riverine operations along the River Paraguay. The most recent expeditionary service of the *Fuzileiros* was as part of the Inter-American Peace Force, which kept order in the Dominican Republic for fifteen months in 1965 and 1966, side by side with U.S. Marines during part of that time.

The Brazilian Marine Corps is divided into operating forces (which include a Fleet Marine Force and security forces) and a supporting establishment, which functions in the same way as our own. The Fleet Marine Force includes a naval division of three infantry battalions, plus one each of armored vehicles, field artillery, antiaircraft, and headquarters troops. In support, there are also a logistics group and a special operations battalion. The security forces include base garrisons and a group or battalion in eight of nine naval districts. The *Fuzileiros'* headquarters and FMF are located at Rio de Janeiro.

COLOMBIAN MARINE CORPS

The first combat landing by Colombian Marines took place on 11 November 1811, less than a year after their organization during their country's War of Independence. Throughout the nineteenth century, the corps had its ups and downs, but it was permanently constituted as amphibious and expeditionary troops in 1937. Ever since 1948, during Colombia's prolonged struggle to defeat banditry, the corps has been continually engaged in riverine, amphibious, and pacification duties. Like our own Corps, the Colombian Marines carry out operations in both the Atlantic and the Pacific. The corps includes twenty-one infantry, riverine, and commando battalions organized in four tactical brigades. Many of its officers today are graduates of the Basic and Expeditionary Warfare Schools and Command and Staff College at Quantico, and many of its NCOs are also graduates of U.S. schools.

VENEZUELAN MARINE CORPS

The Venezuelan Marine Corps was formed on 22 July 1822—as in the case of most of the other South American Marines—during its country's War of Independence. During the nineteenth century, however, it became inactive, and it was not officially reconstituted until 11 December 1945.

The missions of the Venezuelan Marines include amphibious operations, counterguerrilla and pacification duties, and naval base security. The corps regularly conducts battalion-level landing exercises, and over a third of its officers are graduates of U.S. Marine Corps schools.

The Venezuelan Marine Corps fields four amphibious brigades, a riverine brigade, two riverine border brigades, a special operations battalion, a brigade of engineers, a field artillery group, and a communications battalion, plus supporting logistic units. Naval Police fall under the command of the Venezuelan Marine Corps, as do naval base security units. All these units have been active in Venezuela's defense against guerrillas and bandits.

REPUBLIC OF KOREA MARINE CORPS (ROKMC)

The Korean Marine Corps, which has fought side by side with U.S. Marines in two wars—Korea and Vietnam—was founded on 15 April 1949 at Chinhae, destined to become the Quantico of Korea. In less than two years, the 1st Korean Marine Regiment had become an integral part of the 1st U.S. Marine Division and played an outstanding part in the three years of hard fighting.

The primary mission of the ROKMC is to conduct amphibious landings as part of the national mobile striking force and to serve as a portion of the national force in readiness. In addition, like our Corps, it performs security duty for the naval shore establishment and is responsible for the development of amphibious warfare doctrine, tactics, techniques, and materiel.

The ROKMC is organized into two divisions and one brigade, together with supporting forces. In addition to maintaining a brigade in the mainline of resistance at Kimpo, the ROKMC has two main bases, Chinhae and Pohang. Marine garrisons or security units are found at Seoul, Paeng Yong Do, Cheju-Do, Pusan, Muk-Ho, Inchon, and Mokpo. In 2016, the Ministry of Defense announced the creation of a new "Spartan 3000" brigade numbering—not coincidentally—3,000, which would remain on constant alert, ready for employment in any part of the Korean Peninsula within twenty-four hours in case of external aggression.

The uniforms of the ROKMC are similar to those of the U.S. Marine Corps. The official color of the ROK Marines is scarlet. The creed of the corps, which serves as its motto, is as follows:

Loyal to the nation
Be ever victorious
Unite as a family
Honor is worth more than life
Love your fellow countrymen.

ROYAL THAI MARINE CORPS

The Royal Thai Marine Corps was formally organized on the U.S. Marine Corps model on 30 July 1955, but it also traces its modern existence to 1932, with historical antecedents to 1824. Its missions are amphibious operations, base defense, counterinsurgency, and support of the Royal Thai Army. Naval ranks and titles are used throughout the corps. Combat operations include the 1941 conflict with France, border conflicts with Cambodia since 1961, insurgency actions throughout the 1970s, and action against a Vietnamese incursion in 1985.

Thai Marine operating forces consist of a combat division and a security regiment.

Sattahip, on the Gulf of Thailand, is the main base of the Thai Marines, but Chanthaburi, near the Cambodian frontier, is the secondary base. In addition to being headquarters for the corps, Bangkok is also the home station for a Marine garrison.

FRENCH MARINES (*FUSILIERS MARINS*)

In contrast to the Anglo-American evolution, French Marines started out as sailor-infantrymen rather than soldiers of the sea. This was the inspiration of Cardinal Richelieu, as he founded the Sea Company in 1622 for landing party duties in the French Navy and raised a full regiment in 1627, the official year of origin. The *Regiment de Marine* became the *Fusiliers Marins* by an imperial decree of 5 June 1856, which confirmed their status as seagoing specialists. They have fought in all the modern conflicts of France, with particularly distinguished service in the world wars and in Indochina. Today, the operating forces have formed seven companies of *fusiliers marins* and two larger groups for the security of the large bases of Brest and Toulon and other facilities, and five commando companies of *commandos marine* based at Lorient, with one company detailed to its submarine at Toulon. Other marines serve in the school, also at Lorient.

These *fusiliers* must be distinguished from other troops often reported as "French Marines." The latter are the former colonial infantry of the French Army that guarded and fought in the outposts of the French empire, most of which were administrated by the Navy Ministry. In the modern order of battle of the French Army, these *Troupes de Marine* units formed motorized and parachute battalions of the 9th Marine Division, redesignated the 9th Light Armored Marine Brigade in 1999. They are modern army units, not designed for service with the French Navy. They still bear some traditions of their naval origins, however, referring to their infantry troops as *marsouins*, or "porpoises."

PORTUGUESE MARINE CORPS (*CORPO DE FUZILEIROS*)

The Portuguese Marines trace ancestry to a shipboard corps formed in 1585 to serve guns on board ship, defend the coast against pirate attacks, and serve in the royal guard.

With continuous service since 1621, the *Fuzileiros* have been integral to the Portuguese Navy and use naval ranks and service uniforms. The corps' most intensive period of service came during the frustrating 1961–75 insurrectionist wars in the colonies of Guinea, Angola, and Mozambique, where some thirteen thousand men saw action.

Today, Portuguese Marines comprise two battalions, one to guard ships and stations and one to provide a landing battalion for the Navy, based in Lisbon.

RUSSIAN MARINES

The turbulent history of the Russian Marines began, as with many other modern trends, with Peter the Great. Soviet practitioners used the term "naval infantry" loosely for large detachments of sailors thrown into land battles, as well as specialized permanent troops. Peter, from the start, plainly titled his marines *Morskoi Soldaty*, or sea soldiers, and assigned them to sea regiments, beginning in November 1705. By 1715, experience gained in campaigns against Sweden caused him to more than double the force to five large battalions. Steady growth under Peter's successors came to an abrupt halt when Napoleon's invasion caused a permanent transfer of all the sea regiments to the Russian Army.

Not until the early 1960s did the Soviet Union reestablish the naval infantry. Each of the four Soviet Navy fleets received base security units and a landing battalion. A later expansion created a combined arms brigade in each fleet, complete with armored vehicles and heavy weapons. The Russian Republic continues to operate the naval infantry on a reduced scale commensurate with fleet operations.

ECUADORIAN MARINES

Founded officially on 12 November 1966, after a four-year trial period, the *Cuerpo de Infanteria de la Marina* of Ecuador guards the naval base of Guayaquil, provides an amphibious spearhead, and assists in internal security.

CUBAN MARINES

Even newer than the Ecuadorian corps is the elite Cuban naval infantry. First noticed in 1979 in a naval parade, the contingent has not exceeded one thousand men. It provides a motorized amphibious battalion for operating forces and has security and special operations elements as well.

THE MARINE CORPS IN CHINA

Moving to the other side of the globe, the question of Chinese sovereignty, the "One-China" principal, and the "One-China" policy are among the more complex and debated geopolitical issues of the day; thus, there is no simple and straightforward discussion of Chinese Marines. Given this state of geopolitics, it is unsurprising that there effectively remain two Chinese Marine Corps, separated by tradition, politics, and the Taiwan Strait. Both Chinese corps can trace lineage to the earlier Chinese Marines of 1917, with antecedents dating to 1433.

Taiwanese Marines

Although no longer recognized diplomatically by the United States, Taiwan, formally the Republic of China, continues to field one of the largest Marine Corps in the world. Founded on 16 September 1947 in the midst of the Chinese Civil War, the Taiwanese Marines (also ROC Marines) expanded under U.S.

assistance after 1951 and oriented themselves to the USMC organization of their advisers. After the tough Kinmen Island defense of 1958, the Taiwanese Marines settled into a taut peacetime training and readiness regimen that continues today.

With a Fleet Marine Force of three brigades, one amphibious armor group, and one amphibious reconnaissance and patrol unit, plus security and support units, the Taiwanese Marine commandant exercises command from Tsoying, with another major installation located at Fang-Shan. The colors are scarlet and gold.

Chinese Marines

Still somewhat obscure are the size and composition of the Marine Corps of the People's Republic of China, which operates under the somewhat awkwardly translated moniker "People's Liberation Army Navy Marine Corps," or PLAN Marine Corps. But with a six-thousand strong brigade assigned in 1980 to Hainan Island in peacetime and the continuing modernization of the Chinese fleet, it is conceivable that it could rival the size and status of its island counterpart. A second brigade of six thousand marines was established in the Guangzhou military region in 1990, and reports in early 2017 indicate that China has plans to expand the PLAN Marine Corps to number one hundred thousand. Considered elite troops in China, PLAN marines typically perform two principal missions: spearheading amphibious operations and garrisoning island chains.

The PLAN Marine Corps celebrated its twenty-fifth birthday in 2005. This suggests no such corps in China prior to 1980.

APPENDIX V

ARTICLE 38, *MARINE CORPS MANUAL*, 1921

Every 10 November, the central part of the ceremony to celebrate the Corps' anniversary is the publication to all hands of Article 38, *Marine Corps Manual*, 1921, which was written especially for this purpose by John A. Lejeune, the thirteenth commandant. While this text and its introduction are found in the *Marine Corps Manual* today, it is reproduced here as a matter of convenience for those who do not have a *Manual* within easy reach.

> On November 1st, 1921, John A. Lejeune, 13th Commandant of the Marine Corps, directed that a reminder of the honorable service of the Corps be published by every command, to all Marines throughout the globe, on the birthday of the Corps. Since that day, Marines have continued to distinguish themselves on many battlefields and foreign shores, in war and peace. On this birthday of the Corps, therefore, in compliance with the will of the 13th Commandant, Article 38, United States Marine Corps Manual, Edition of 1921, is republished as follows:
>
> "(1) On November 10, 1775, a Corps of Marines was created by a resolution of the Continental Congress. Since that date many thousand men have borne the name Marine. In memory of them it is fitting that we who are Marines should commemorate the

birthday of our Corps by calling to mind the glories of its long and illustrious history.

"(2) The record of our Corps is one which will bear comparison with that of the most famous military organizations in the world's history. During 90 of the 146 years of its existence the Marine Corps has been in action against the Nation's foes. From the Battle of Trenton to the Argonne, Marines have won foremost honors in war and in the long era of tranquility at home, generation after generation of Marines have grown gray in war in both hemispheres, and in every corner of the seven seas that our country and its citizens might enjoy peace and security.

"(3) In every battle and skirmish since the birth of our Corps, Marines have acquitted themselves with the greatest distinction, winning new honors on each occasion until the term 'Marine' has come to signify all that is highest in military efficiency and soldierly virtue.

"(4) This high name of distinction and soldierly repute we who are Marines today have received from those who preceded us in the Corps. With it we also received from them the eternal spirit which has animated our Corps from generation to generation and has been the distinguishing mark of the Marines in every age. So long as that spirit continues to flourish Marines will be found equal to every emergency in the future as they have been in the past, and the men of our Nation will regard us as worthy successors to the long line of illustrious men who have served as 'Soldiers of the Sea' since the founding of the Corps."

The inspiring message of our 13th Commandant has left its mark in the hearts and minds of all Marines. By deed and act from Guadalcanal to Iwo Jima, from Inchon to the Korean Armistice, from Lebanon to Taiwan, the Marines have continued to epitomize those qualities which are their legacy. The success which they have achieved in combat and the faith they have borne in peace will continue. The Commandant and our many friends have added their hearty praise and congratulations on this, our _____ birthday.

APPENDIX VI
BIRTHDAY BALL CEREMONY

The following paragraphs outline the sequence of events for conducting the Marine Corps birthday ball ceremony in a medium-sized command with drum and bugle corps (or at least a field music) and an orchestra available. Bear in mind that this is a guide and may be modified according to local resources and traditions. This outline does not include provisions for separate narration, although a narrator may easily be included, as has become customary.

- At H–15 minutes, drum and bugle (D&B) corps sounds *Officers' Call.*
- Adjutant (who acts as announcer) requests that officers and guests clear the floor for the ceremony. Floor Committee places line and stanchions (if used) to define ceremonial aisle and area.
- At H–5, the D&B unit, color guard, and honor guard form at exit, prepared to march on. For an officers' birthday ball, honor guard consists of two officers of each grade; at small posts, where the ball is an all-hands event for the whole command, honor guard consists of two lieutenants, two staff NCOs, two sergeants, and two corporals. All honor guard members are covered and wear Mameluke or NCO sword as appropriate.
- At H–1, adjutant takes post on floor, adjacent to exit, and, at H-hour, when all hands are posted, commands, "Sound *Adjutant's Call.*"

- D&B sounds *Adjutant's Call,* then marches up the aisle to designated post, playing "Foreign Legion March" or "Sea Soldiers." When D&B halts, historical pageant, if any, commences. At conclusion of pageant—or next event, if no pageant—orchestra plays "Semper Fidelis."
- On first note of "Semper Fidelis," honor guard steps off.
- Honor guard, junior rank in lead, proceeds up the aisle two abreast, each pair at six-pace intervals. At six paces inside hall, senior person in leading pair commands, "Officers, Halt." Without further command, pair faces outboard, takes three paces, halts, and faces about. Six paces farther, the next junior pair repeats this evolution, etc. In each case the only spoken command is "Officers, halt," the remaining movements being executed simultaneously in cadence without command. Throughout the posting of the honor guard, all pairs execute their movements precisely in sync. When the honor guard is posted, the orchestra stops playing.
- D&B sounds *Attention.*
- Senior Marine commander and the guest(s) of honor (the official party) enter and march up aisle, face about, take post at head of aisle near abreast of senior pair of honor guards, and receive honors (if a flag or general officer is present) from D&B.
- Orchestra commences "Stars and Stripes Forever." Color guard enters from exit and marches up aisle, halting abreast of next senior pair of honor guards. Music ceases when color guard halts.
- Adjutant, from original post at rear, proclaims, "Long live the United States, and success to the Marines!"
- D&B plays "To the Color." All covered officers come to hand salute. Colors then take designated post.
- Fanfare by D&B.
- Orchestra commences "The Marines' Hymn." Birthday cake is wheeled in from exit by four-person cake escort, followed by the adjutant. Cake is posted abreast of second senior pair of honor guards. Cake escort takes post in rear of cake.
- Adjutant steps front and center between cake and official party.
- Senior Marine commands, "Publish the Article."

- The adjutant then publishes Article 38, *Marine Corps Manual*, 1921, and resumes post.
- Senior Marine steps forward to make remarks, followed by remarks, if any, by honored guest.
- At conclusion of remarks, oldest and youngest Marines present step forward and take position next to the guest of honor. Next, adjutant steps forward and hands senior Marine an unsheathed Mameluke sword (previously placed on cake table), with which senior Marine cuts cake while orchestra plays "Auld Lang Syne."
- Senior Marine then presents cake slices in sequence to the guest(s) of honor, oldest Marine present, and youngest Marine present, giving a brief introduction of the latter two in the process if not introduced by a narrator. When the honored guest is senior to the senior Marine (for example, an ambassador, Secretary of the Navy, etc.), he or she may be asked to cut the cake by the senior Marine, who then introduces the youngest and oldest Marines, who in turn receive slices from the honored guest.
- Cake escort then retires cake to a flank, where it is received by waiters.
- D&B commences "Semper Fidelis." Senior Marine and official party march off and then proceed to head table or box.
- Color guard marches off, immediately followed by the honor guard in reverse sequence (senior pair leading). As the rear rank of honor guard comes abreast of next pair, the senior of that pair commands, "Forward, march," and the pair marches three paces inboard face toward the exit (i.e., right and left respectively) and steps off without further command in time with the music. The D&B marches off at six paces behind final pair of honor guards. On passing through exit, each D&B player mutes instrument so the music will seem to fade away in the distance.
- Floor Committee removes line and stanchions. D&B ceases playing, and ceremony is ended.

APPENDIX VII
GLOSSARY

This glossary contains a compilation of terms both historically and currently peculiar to the Marine Corps. Certain terms might be recognized as being shared with the other services; in such cases, however, the terms have been incorporated here by virtue of long inclusion as part of the Marines' distinctive vocabulary.

The authoritative source for all military terminology, abbreviations, and acronyms is Joint Publication 1-02, *Department of Defense Dictionary of Military and Associated Terms*. It is worth familiarizing yourself with this document. Marine Corps Reference Publication (MCRP) 1-10.2 (formerly MCRP 5-12C), the *Marine Corps Supplement to the Department of Defense Dictionary of Military and Associated Terms*, complements the *DOD Dictionary*, and you should also know how to access a copy of this official compendium of Marine Corps terminology.

COMMON TERMS, PHRASES, AND USAGES

Airdale: Aviator.

All hands: All members of a command; everybody.

Ashore: (1) On the beach, as differentiated from on board ship; (2) any place off a Marine Corps or government reservation.

Aye, Aye, Sir/Ma'am: Required official acknowledgment of an order, meaning, "I have received, understand, and will carry out the order or instructions."

B&W: Solitary confinement on bread and water, now only authorized on board ship; sometimes spoken of as "cake and wine."

Barracks cover (or **cap**): Frame type, visored headgear, so called because this type of cover was traditionally prescribed for organizations not part of the Operating Forces.

BCD: Bad-conduct discharge; also known colloquially as the "Big Chicken Dinner."

Bend on: To tie on, attach, or affix; from the nautical term "halyard bend," which is a hitch-style knot used to attach the end of a rope at a right angle to a cylindrical object such as a beam.

Binnacle list: List of Marines placed on light duty by the surgeon; in old days, it was posted on or near the binnacle.

"Blue Book": *Combined Lineal List of Officers of the Marine Corps on Active Duty*; also the *Register of Commissioned and Warrant Officers of the U.S. Navy and Marine Corps*; so called because in the days before electronic publications it was bound in a blue cover.

Blues: Dress or undress blue uniform.

Boondockers: Field shoes or boots.

Boondocks: Woods, jungles, faraway places; semifacetiously defined as "that portion of the country that is fit only for the training of Marines."

Boot: A recruit, or more generally any new person of very limited experience.

Boot camp: Recruit depot.

Break out: (1) To unfurl; (2) to remove from storage; (3) to arouse.

Brig: Place of confinement aboard ship or ashore at a Marine Corps or naval station; the base or station prison.

Brig rat: One who has served much brig time; a habitual offender.

Brig time: Confinement.

Bulkhead: (1) A wall; (2) to complain against or asperse a superior while superficially pretending not to.

Campaign cover: Broad-brimmed felt hat with four-dent crown, formerly worn by the Marine Corps on expeditionary service, but now worn only at rifle ranges and recruit depots; also known colloquially as a "Smokey the Bear" cover; years ago, called a "field hat" in the Marine Corps, but the Army term for similar headgear appears to have been adopted and adapted.

Cannon-cocker: Artilleryman.

CG: The commanding general.

Charger: Highly motivated, aggressive Marine (short for "hard charger").

Chaser: An escort, sometimes armed, for a prisoner or detail of prisoners (short for "prisoner chaser").

Checkage: Process of electronically drawing payment from a servicemember's pay account in reimbursement for items lost, meals provided, or other services provided by the government.

Chew out (or **on**): Reprimand severely.

Chief messman: Permanently detailed assistant to the mess sergeant, in charge of all messmen and responsible for the police and good order of the mess hall.

Chit: Acknowledgment of indebtedness to a mess; a receipt or authorization; in general, a small piece of paper.

Chopper: Helicopter.

Chow: Food, rations.

Chow down: To eat heartily.

Chow hound: One who appreciates food.

Class VI: Technically, personal demand items in the military supply system, but commonly used in reference to alcoholic beverages of any kind.

Clutch: A serious, sudden emergency.

Clutched up: Nervous, panicky.

CMC: Commandant of the Marine Corps.

CO: The commanding officer.

Color sergeant: A distinguished noncommissioned officer given the privilege of carrying the National Color and of commanding the color guard.

Communicator: Officer or enlisted man assigned to or specializing in communication duties.

Company-grade officer: An officer of grade second lieutenant through captain; also normally covers the first three grades of warrant officer.

Corpsman: Enlisted servicemember of the Navy Hospital Corps.

Cover: A Marine cap or hat; headgear.

Crummy: Untidy or unclean in person or uniform.

Crying towel: A towel said to be employed by those with many troubles or complaints to wipe away their tears; a crying towel is said to hang in every chaplain's office.

Cumshaw: (n) Something free, gratis, obtained at no cost; (v) to obtain something at no cost or with no accountability in the supply system.

Cut it: See **hack it**.

D&D: Drunk and disorderly, an entry formerly made on the liberty list beside the name of anyone returning from liberty in that condition.

DD: Dishonorable discharge.

Deck: (n) The floor, the surface of the earth; (v) to knock down with one blow.

DI: Recruit depot drill instructor, ordinarily an experienced drillmaster.

Dinged: Hit, as by a bullet; to be *dinged* by enemy fire.

Doc: Navy hospital corpsman.

Doggie: Enlisted Army soldier; diminutive for "dog-face."

Dope: (1) Information; (2) sighting and/or wind correction for a rifle under given conditions. *Bad dope* is misinformation.

Dungarees: Marine Corps utility clothing (obsolete).

Eight-ball: Worthless, troublesome individual; one who deservedly remains "behind the eight-ball."

Emblem: U.S. Marine Corps Emblem, or Corps badge, adopted in 1868, frequently referred to as the Globe and Anchor or the Eagle, Globe, and Anchor.

EPD: Extra police duties.

Extend: To lengthen a current enlistment by contracting to remain in the service one or more years after the enlistment would ordinarily expire.

Fall out: To assemble outside barracks, immediately prior to a formation.

Field boots: Heavy half-boots designed and issued for field service; boondockers.

Field day: Day or portion of a day set aside for general cleanup or policing of an organization or area.

Field-grade officer: An officer of grade major through colonel.

First soldier: First sergeant (obsolete).

Flag allowance: Marines assigned to duty in an admiral's headquarters.

FMF: Fleet Marine Force.

Fore-and-aft cap: Garrison cap; also referred to as a "p-ss cutter."

Foul up: (1) A mistake, botch, bungle, or confused situation; (2) to confuse or bungle. *Fouled up*: badly confused.

Frock: To grant official permission for an officer who has been selected for promotion but has not yet made his or her number to assume the style, title, uniform, and authority of the next higher grade.

Frost-call: A procedure within a command whereby all officers and other key personnel may be alerted by sequential telephone calls or other notification.

Furlough: Period of authorized leave for enlisted personnel, not to be confused with a "48" (forty-eight-hour period of liberty) or a "72" (seventy-two-hour period of liberty).

Galley: (1) Kitchen of a mess hall; (2) mobile field kitchen; (3) ship's kitchen.

Gear: Equipment.

General mess: The enlisted mess.

Gizmo: Any miscellaneous, nondescript, unidentified thing or gadget.

Globe and Anchor: Marine Corps Emblem; sometimes Eagle, Globe, and Anchor.

Go ashore: Go on liberty, or leave the reservation.

Greens: Marine Corps service uniform.

Grinder: Drill field.

Ground pounder: See **grunt**.

Grunt: Aviation term for a rifleman.

Gung-ho: (1) Aggressive esprit de corps; (2) hard-charging.

Gunner: Short for "Marine Gunner," a title for line warrant officers.

Gunny: Diminutive of "gunnery sergeant."

Gunship: Armed helicopter.

Hack: (n) Arrest, officer's; *To be in* or *to be under hack*: to be under arrest, although the phrase sometimes refers to the less egregious situation of merely having one's liberty secured for a time after a prior unfortunate episode on liberty.

Hack it: To be competent or successful in a job or assignment: "Do you think Corporal Calkoff can *hack it* as a squad leader?"

Happy Hour: Late afternoon period during which the price of drinks at an officers' or NCOs' mess is sharply reduced.

Hard charger: Aggressive, dynamic, zealous, indefatigable officer or enlisted Marine; one who is professionally keen.

Hashmark: Service stripe worn on the uniform sleeve by enlisted personnel for completion of an honorable four-year enlistment in any of the U.S. armed services.

Head: Toilet facility; latrine.

Heel-and-toe watch: A condition during which watch standers alternate tours, one individual relieving the other and vice versa for an indefinite period.

Hill, to go over the: To desert.

Hill, to run over the: To force an individual to desert or apply for a transfer or retirement: "Captain Hardnose certainly *ran* that brig rat *over the hill*."

Holiday routine: Condition during which routine drills, instruction, training, and work are knocked off (q.v.) throughout a command; routine followed on authorized holidays and Sundays.

I&I: Inspector-instructor; a regular officer assigned to supervise the training and readiness of a reserve unit.

ID card: Identification card issued to every member of the U.S. armed forces.

IG: The inspector general.

IG inspection: An official inspection of a command or unit (usually biennially) by the inspector general or representatives.

IPAC: Installation Personnel Administration Center, a single, consolidated personnel center servicing the administrative needs of all Marines assigned to the base or station.

Iron Mike: Nickname bestowed on statue of World War I Marine in front of old Post Headquarters, Quantico (now the Marine Corps Association offices). This also has a much more general meaning as a can-do, get-things-done Marine or soldier; as a result, there are at least eight statues named Iron Mike on Marine Corps and Army installations around the world.

JO: Junior officer.

Joe: Coffee.

Joe-pot: Coffee pot.

JORG: Junior officer requiring guidance, the most junior O-1.

Junk on the bunk: Periodic inspection of equipment or, more loosely, of clothing and equipment, displayed on the bunk.

Khakis: Summer service uniform (obsolete in the Marine Corps, although Navy officers and chief petty officers still wear a version as a working uniform).

Knock off: To cease forthwith.

Ladder: (1) Stairs or stairway; (2) to adjust gunfire by a series of graduated spots in range.

Liberty: Authorized free time ashore or off station, not counted as leave.

Lifer: Marine who intends to make a complete career in the Marine Corps.

Line company: Narrowly, any of the lettered Marine rifle companies within an infantry battalion, as opposed to the Headquarters and Service Company and Weapons Company, which are not considered line companies; more generally, a company within a battalion or other unit that spearheads execution of that battalion's mission, rather than playing a supporting role.

Line duty: General duty in a ground organization of the Marine Corps.

Lock up: To confine in a brig (enlisted); to place under arrest in quarters (officer).

Locked up: Confined or under arrest.

Main gate: Main entrance to a post, station, reservation, camp, or compound, at which a guard post is maintained.

Mainside: Main or traditional center of a naval installation, usually close by the base or station headquarters.

Manual, the: *Marine Corps Manual.*

Marine Online: Online resource for individual Marines, providing secure access to electronic individual administrative and personnel records; abbreviated as MOL.

Mast: Navy equivalent of Office Hours (q.v.); upright spar supporting signal yard and antennas in a naval ship.

MCRD: Marine Corps Recruit Depot; either of the two boot camp facilities, located at Parris Island, South Carolina, or San Diego, California.

Mess sergeant: Noncommissioned officer in charge of an enlisted mess.

Messman: Nonrated enlisted personnel assigned to duty in the mess hall for a period of one month; on board ship, called "mess cook."

Mount out: To load and embark for expeditionary service in amphibious shipping or transport aircraft.

NCO: Noncommissioned officer.

Nervous in the service: Jittery, fearful, apprehensive, especially when in forward areas.

Nonrated: Not of noncommissioned or petty officer rank; servicemember in pay grade E-3 or below.

Number, to make: (1) To be promoted, when a vacancy occurs, to a higher grade for which previously selected; (2) (colloquial) to pay one's respects to a senior.

OD: Officer of the day; sometimes abbreviated as OOD.

Office Hours: Periodic, usually weekly, occasion when the commanding officer receives requests, investigates offenses, reenlists and discharges enlisted men, and awards commendations (the latter is less common now, as the commanding officer normally prefers to decorate Marines at all-hands formations).

Officers' country: (1) Officers' living spaces on board ship; (2) any portion of a base or station allocated for the exclusive use of officers.

Oh-Three: Vernacular for infantry, i.e., occupational field 03; applies equally to oh-two for intelligence; oh-four, logistics; oh-six, communications; oh-eight, field artillery; eighteen hundred, armor; and seventy-five hundred, pilot/naval flight officer, to highlight a few of the larger occupational fields.

Old man: The commanding officer.

Old salt: (1) Old-timer, experienced Marine; (2) sardonically, person who thinks he knows all the answers.

Out-of-bounds: An area or space restricted from use by normal traffic or prohibited to enlisted men, sometimes called "restricted area." Avoid "Off Limits," the equivalent Army/Air Force term.

Outside: Civilian life: "Sergeant Boatspace is now on the *outside*."

Overhead: Ceiling of a room (ashore) or compartment (on board ship).

Pack the gear: Measure up to Marine standards.

Pass over: To omit an officer or staff NCO from a promotion list by promoting someone junior in rank.

Passed over: In the status of having failed selection for next higher commissioned or staff NCO rank.

People: (1) Enlisted sailors or Marines; (2) one's subordinates, regardless of rank.

Pick up: (v) To promote an officer who has previously been passed over (q.v.).

Picked up: In the status of having been selected for next higher rank after having been passed over one or more times.

Piece: (1) A Marine's rifle; (2) artillery piece.

Pipe up: Speak up.

Platoon sergeant: Senior noncommissioned officer in a platoon, executive to the platoon leader.

Pogey-bait: Candy, snacks.

Pogey-rope: Fourragère.

Police: (1) To straighten or tidy up an individual, area, or structure; (2) condition of neatness or cleanliness.

Police gang: Permanent working force assigned to the police sergeant.

Police shed: Structure or space assigned to the police sergeant for stowage of tools, gear, and supplies; the police sergeant's workshop.

Prisoner chaser: See **chaser**.

Property room: Storeroom for unit property, sometimes called "property shed."

PX: Post exchange, a retail store operated for sale of articles necessary for the health, comfort, and morale of the command; inherited from Army lingo and still used today; also, MCX, for the Marine Corps Exchange on board Marine installations.

Qualify: To attain the minimum qualifying score in weapons proficiency, to attain the rating of marksman.

Quarters: (1) Government housing at a base or station, for officers and NCOs with authorized dependents; (2) periodic, usually daily, muster of a ship's company (Navy).

Rack: Bed, bunk; sometimes referred to as "sack."

Rated Marine: Noncommissioned or petty officer.

Read off: (1) To reprimand severely; (2) to publish the findings and sentence of a court-martial.

Reading, take a: To sound out.

Record day: The day on which a Marine fires an individual weapon for record of qualification; alternately, "qual day."

Recruiter: Marine assigned to recruiting duty.

Reefer: Refrigerator, as in a mess hall.

Regulation: (1) Strictly in accordance with regulations or adopted specifications; (2) issued from government sources. Avoid "GI," an equivalent Army term.

RHIP: Initialism for the service phrase "rank has its privileges."

Rock-happy: Eccentric or mildly deranged as the result of long overseas duty at a remote station, often on an island such as Okinawa, "The Rock."

Rocks and shoals: Punitive articles of the Uniform Code of Military Justice.

Runner: Messenger.

Running guard: Guard duty in which individuals have one tour on duty, one off, and then back on again with no intervening free period.

Rustbucket: Old, worn-out ship; Navy transport.

Sack: See **rack**.

Saddle up: To put on individual combat equipment and prepare to move out. Also called "gear up."

Salty: A seasoned Marine of any rank.

Scoop, the: Latest news, information.

Scope out: To ascertain or verify a piece of information: "I'm not sure whether that's good or bad dope—you'd better *scope it out.*"

Scuttlebutt: (1) Drinking fountain, or a container of drinking water; (2) unconfirmed rumor.

Sea soldier: Marine.

Seabag: Canvas duffel bag issued to each Marine for storage and transportation of uniforms and personal gear.

Seagoing: (1) Sea duty; (2) pertaining to or assigned to sea duty; (3) the uniform combination of blue trousers and khaki shirt.

Sea story: Yarn calculated to impress recruits or other gullible individuals.

Secure: (1) To anchor firmly in place; (2) to cease or terminate an activity or exercise; (3) an outdated movement in the manual of arms.

782 gear or **equipment**: Individual combat equipment once issued on memorandum receipt to Marine officers and enlisted personnel, so called because of the designation of the original receipt form employed.

Shanghai: To get rid of an individual by involuntary or surprise transfer.

Shift: To change uniforms, or from uniform into civilian clothing and vice versa.

Ship over: To reenlist.

Shook: Dazed, groggy.

Shoot the breeze: To chat or conduct casual conversation.

Shooter: Marine whose avocation is marksmanship with the rifle or pistol; loosely, a Marine who has displayed special prowess with rifle or pistol, or who has served with distinction on a Marine Corps rifle or pistol team.

Short-fused: (1) Having a deadline for completion very near in time; (2) very quick-tempered. Sometimes derivatively used in the nominative sense: "Gunnery Sergeant Piledriver sure has a *short fuse*."

Short-timer: One whose enlistment or current tour of duty is about to expire.

Shove off: To depart or leave, to get under way; an order to a boat to leave a landing or a ship's side.

Sick bay: Ship or unit aid station, dispensary, or infirmary.

Sick-bay commando: (1) Individual who spends undue time in hospital or at sick call; (2) malingerer.

Sick call: Daily period when routine ailments are treated at the sick bay.

Sight in: In general, to aim a weapon at a target; loosely used as synonym for "zero."

Skipper: Colloquial term for a commanding officer of a company, battery, or squadron.

Skivvies: Underwear.

Slop down: To drink in quantity and rapidly, beer especially.

Slop up: To eat in quantity and rapidly, without regard to table manners; to gourmandize.

Slopchute: Base or station exchange restaurant or beer garden (equivalent of "Geedunk" on board ship).

Small chow: Hors d'oeuvres.

Smoking lamp is lighted (or **out**): Smoking is (or is not) permitted (originally, a lamp on board old-time ships used by men to light their pipes).

Snap in: (1) To conduct sighting and aiming exercises with an unloaded weapon; (2) to try out for, or break in at, a new job.

Snow: To fool, bewilder, mislead, or exaggerate.

Snow job: Misleading or grossly exaggerated report or sales talk.

Spit and polish: (1) Extreme individual or collective military neatness; (2) extreme devotion to the minutiae of traditional military procedures and ceremonies.

Spit shine: (1) To shine leather, employing spittle or tap water to remove excess grease and produce a high polish; (2) an extremely high polish on a piece of leather.

Squadbay: Barracks room occupied by privates and junior NCOs.

Square away: To align, set in place, or correctly arrange an article, articles, or living space; when applied to individuals, to take in hand and direct.

Staff NCO. Noncommissioned officer above the grade of sergeant.

Striker: (1) Apprentice or aspirant, attempting to learn a military specialty; on board ship, the Marine entrusted with the ordnance maintenance of a single gun, sometimes designated "gun-striker."

Swabbie: Sailor.

Survey: (1) Medical discharge; examination by authorized competent personnel to determine whether a piece of gear, equipment, stores, or supplies should be discarded or retained; (2) to effect discharge or retirement of an individual for medical reasons; to dispose of an item of government property by reason of unserviceability; to obtain a second, third, or fourth helping of food.

Sympathy chit: Chit supposedly issued by those in authority, or by chaplains, authorizing an individual with many woes to obtain a prescribed amount of sympathy; expression used derisively to indicate lack of sympathy or concern over the plight of another.

Take off your pack: Relax.

Thirty-year Marine: Marine who intends to make the Corps a career; see also **lifer**.

Top: Master sergeant. Avoid the Army term, "top-kick."

Troop and stomp: Morning troop inspection, followed by close-order drill.

Two-block: (1) To hoist a flag or pennant to the peak, truck, or yardarm; (2) to tighten and center a regulation Marine Corps necktie.

Under way, to get: To depart, or to start out for an objective.

Utilities: Green or camouflaged field and work uniform, first issued in World War II; now officially termed the Combat Utility Uniform in both woodland and desert camouflage patterns.

Watch: Official tour of duty of prescribed length, such as guard or officer of the day.

Wet down: To serve drinks in honor of one's promotion.

Wetting-down: Party in honor of a promotion.

Whites: Marine Corps or Navy white dress uniforms; in the Marine Corps, worn only by officers until discarded in the year 2000, although the white trousers are retained for use by Marines in ceremonies (blue-whites).

Wing-wiper: Enlisted aviation Marine.

WM: Women Marine (obsolete); avoid using this term as it is considered pejorative.

Word, the: Latest news, usually well verified and reliable.

Work one's bolt: To resort to special measures, either by energy or guile, to attain a particular end.

Work over: (1) To reprimand severely; (2) to place heavy fire on a target or area.

Working over: (1) Severe reprimand; (2) heavy attack by fire.

Zapped: Killed in action. Occasionally used as a verb: "Corporal Buttplate sure *zapped* that sniper."

Zero: (1) To determine by trial and error the sightsetting required to obtain a hit with an individual weapon at a given range; synonymous with "zero in"; (2) the sightsetting required to obtain a hit with a rifle at a given range.

TERMS AND USAGES TO BE AVOIDED

In recent years, as a side effect of increased jointness among the services, certain undesirable terms or expressions from outside the naval services have been picked up by a few individuals and used to the detriment of the authentic Marine Corps way of talking. Avoid especially the following unfortunate usages:

Career (as in "career officer"): Say "regular."

E-4 (and other similar ways of speaking of enlisted rank): Under no circumstances, refer to an enlisted person as "an E-3" or "an E-6," etc., as these are *pay* grades. Refer to Marines and all other servicemembers using their correct grade and titles.

EM: Just say "enlisted Marine." Even better, say, "Marine."

GI: Use "squared-away" or "regulation." Never speak of an enlisted Marine as a "GI."

Hitch: Use "enlistment." "Hitch" is an Army term dating from the horse cavalry.

Insignia (when you mean Emblem): Even though unified clothing procedures have designated the Marine Corps Emblem as "insignia, branch of service," this terminology should be absolutely shunned. The only acceptable word is "Emblem." The term "insignia of rank" is okay.

Medic: Army/Air Force term for a hospital corpsman or "aid man or woman" (also an Army/Air Force term). Always say "corpsman" when referring to the Navy hospital corpsman.

TDY: Army/Air Force term that now appears on many joint forms. Always use the Navy/Marine "TAD."

Trooper: Of Army airborne origin. Refer to an individual Marine as a Marine, never a "trooper." "Troops" as a plural is acceptable, but not "troopers." "Marine" or "Marines" is best; "people," second best.

ZI: Use "CONUS," or just "the United States."

APPENDIX VIII
ACRONYMS AND INITIALISMS

The terms included in this appendix either were used in the text or refer to terms, phrases, or organizations referred to in the text but not critical to your understanding of it. This appendix can be used as a reference tool like Joint Publication 1-02, *Department of Defense Dictionary of Military and Associated Terms.*

AAW	anti-air warfare
ACC	Air Combat Command (Air Force)
ACE	aviation combat element
ACIP	aviation career incentive pay
ACMC	assistant commandant of the Marine Corps
AC/S	assistant chief of staff
ACTSMAN	*Marine Corps Assignment, Classification, and Travel System Manual*
ADP	Advanced Degree Program
AEDC	Arnold Air Force Base and Arnold Engineering Development Complex
AETC	Air Education and Training Command (Air Force)
AFAA	Air Force Audit Agency
AFAMS	Air Force Agency for Modeling and Simulation
AFCEC	Air Force Civil Engineer Center

AFCENT	U.S. Air Forces Central Command
AFDW	Air Force District of Washington
AFFSA	Air Force Flight Standards Agency
AFGSC	Air Force Global Strike Command
AFHRA	Air Force Historical Research Agency
AFIA	Air Force Inspection Agency
AFISRA	Air Force Intelligence, Surveillance, and Reconnaissance Agency
AFMC	Air Force Materiel Command
AFNIC	Air Force Network Integration Center
AFOSI	Air Force Office of Special Investigations
AFOTEC	Air Force Operational Test and Evaluation Center
AFPA	Air Force Petroleum Agency
AFPAA	Air Force Public Affairs Agency
AFPC	Air Force Personnel Center
AFRC	Air Force Reserve Command
AFSC	Air Force Safety Center
AFSFC	Air Force Security Forces Center
AFSMO	Air Force Spectrum Management Office
AFSOC	Air Force Special Operations Command
AFSPC	Air Force Space Command
AFWA	Air Force Weather Agency
AIS	automated information system
AMC	U.S. Army Materiel Command; Air Mobility Command (Air Force)
ANG	Air National Guard (Air Force)
ANGLICO	air naval gunfire liaison company
APO	Army Post Office
AQI	al Qaeda in Iraq
AR	Active Reserve
ARG	amphibious ready group
ARPC	Air Reserve Personnel Center (Air Force)
ASN(EI&E)	assistant Secretary of the Navy (energy, installations, and environment)
ASN(FM&C)	assistant Secretary of the Navy (financial management and comptroller)

ASN(M&RA)	assistant Secretary of the Navy (manpower and reserve affairs)
ASN(RD&A)	assistant Secretary of the Navy (research, development, and acquisition)
ATEC	U.S. Army Test and Evaluation Command
BAH	basic allowance for housing
BAS	basic allowance for subsistence
BCNR	Board of Correction for Naval Records
BICMD	Blount Island Command
BIR	basic individual record
BLT	battalion landing team
BOQ	bachelor officer quarters
BTR	basic training record
C2CEWID	Command and Control/Cyber and Electronic Warfare Integration Division
CAC	common access card
CACO	casualty assistance calls officer
CATC	Combined Arms Training Center
CBRND-E	chemical, biological, radiological, and nuclear defense equipment
CDD	Capabilities Development Directorate
CDE	College of Distance Education
CDET	College of Distance Education and Training
CE	command element
CEC	Civil Engineer Corps
CHINFO	chief of information
CIA	Central Intelligence Agency
CIO	chief information officer
CIS	communications and information systems
CJCS	chairman of the Joint Chiefs of Staff
CLB	combat logistic battalion
CLR	combat logistic regiment
CMC	commandant of the Marine Corps
CMR	consolidated memorandum receipt
CNIC	commander, Navy Installations Command

CNO	chief of naval operations
CNR	chief of naval research
CO	commanding officer
COCOM	combatant commander
COMMARFOR	Marine Corps Forces commander
CONUS	continental United States
COT	commander of troops
CSCDEP	Command and Staff College Distance Education Program
CSP	career sea pay; Consolidated Storage Program
DARPA	Defense Advanced Research Projects Agency
DC	deputy commandant
DC Aviation	deputy commandant for aviation
DC CD&I	deputy commandant for combat development and integration
DC I&L	deputy commandant for installations and logistics
DC M&RA	deputy commandant for manpower and reserve affairs
DC P&R	deputy commandant for programs and resources
DC PP&O	deputy commandant for plans, policies, and operations
DCAA	Defense Contract Audit Agency
DCMA	Defense Contract Management Agency
DCNO	deputy chief of naval operations
DECA	Defense Commissary Agency
DEERS	Defense Enrollment Eligibility Reporting Service
DEP	distance education program
DFAS	Defense Finance and Accounting Service
DHA	Defense Health Agency
DHRA	Defense Human Resources Activity
DHS	Department of Homeland Security
DIA	Defense Intelligence Agency
DIC	dependency and indemnity compensation
DIMHRS–Pers/Pay	Defense Integrated Military Human Resource System (Personnel and Pay)

DISA	Defense Information Systems Agency
DLA	Defense Logistics Agency; dislocation allowance
DLSA	Defense Legal Services Agency
DMA	Defense Media Activity
DMC	Distribution Management Center
DMCS	director of the Marine Corps staff
DMO	distribution management office
DNI	director of national intelligence
DNS	director of Navy staff
DOD	Department of Defense
DODD	Department of Defense Directive
DODEA	Department of Defense Education Activity
DOE	Department of Energy
DON	Department of the Navy
DOPMA	Defense Officer Personnel Management Act
DPAA	Defense POW/MIA Accounting Agency
DRU	direct reporting unit
DSCA	Defense Security Cooperation Agency
DSS	Defense Security Service
DTIC	Defense Technical Information Center
DTOD	*Defense Table of Official Distances*
DTRA	Defense Threat Reduction Agency
DTSA	Defense Technology Security Administration
DUSN(M)	deputy under Secretary of the Navy (management)
DUSN(P)	deputy under Secretary of the Navy (policy)
E2O	Expeditionary Energy Office
ECP	Enlisted Commissioning Program
EOTG	expeditionary operations training group
ETA	estimated time of arrival
EWSDEP	Expeditionary Warfare School Distance Education Program
EWTGLANT	Expeditionary Warfare Training Group Atlantic
FAST	fleet antiterrorism security team
FLPP	foreign language proficiency pay
FM	field manual

FMCR	Fleet Marine Corps Reserve
FMF	fleet marine force
FMID	Fires and Maneuver Integration Division
FOA	field operating agency
FORSCOM	U.S. Army Forces Command
FPID	Force Protection Integration Division
FPO	Fleet Post Office
FSA	family separation allowance
FTS	full-time support
GC	general counsel
GCE	ground combat element
GCIC	Global Cyberspace Integration Center (Air Force)
GTR	government travel request
HHG	household goods
HMH	Marine heavy helicopter squadron
HMLA	Marine light attack helicopter squadron
HMX-1	Marine Helicopter Squadron One
HQMC	Headquarters, U.S. Marine Corps
I&I	inspector-instructor
ICE	individual combat equipment
IG	inspector general
IID	Intelligence Integration Division
IMA	individual mobilization augmentee
IMCOM	U.S. Army Installation Management Command
INSCOM	U.S. Army Intelligence and Security Command
IRR	Individual Ready Reserve
ISIS	Islamic State of Iraq and Syria
JAG	judge advocate general
JAGMAN	*Manual of the Judge Advocate General*
JCID	Joint Capabilities Integration Division
JCS	Joint Chiefs of Staff
JGSDF	Japan Ground Self Defense Force
JRC	joint reception center
JTF	joint task force
JTR	*Joint Travel Regulations*

LCC	Logistics Capabilities Center
LCE	logistic combat element
LDO	limited duty officer
LES	leave and earnings statement
LID	Logistics Integration Division
LSMC	Logistics Services Management Center
MAGTF	Marine air-ground task force
MAJCOM	major command
MALS	Marine aviation logistics squadron
MARCENT	U.S. Marine Corps Forces Central Command
MARCORLOGCOM	Marine Corps Logistics Command
MARCORSYSCOM	Marine Corps Systems Command
MARDET	Marine detachment
MARDIV	Marine division
MARFOR	Marine Corps Forces
MARFORCOM	U.S. Marine Corps Forces Command
MARFORCYBER	U.S. Marine Corps Forces Cyberspace
MARFOREUR	U.S. Marine Corps Forces Europe and Africa
MARFORK	U.S. Marine Corps Forces Korea
MARFORPAC	U.S. Marine Corps Forces Pacific
MARFORRES	U.S. Marine Corps Forces Reserve
MARFORSOUTH	U.S. Marine Corps Forces South
MARFORSTRAT	U.S. Marine Corps Forces Strategic Command
MARSOC	U.S. Marine Corps Forces Special Operations Command
MARTD	Marine air reserve training detachment
MATCD	Marine air traffic control detachment
MAW	Marine aircraft wing
MB	Marine barracks
MCA	Marine Corps Association
MCA&F	Marine Corps Association and Foundation
MCAF	Marine Corps air facility
MCAGCC	Marine Corps Air-Ground Combat Center
MCAS	Marine Corps air station
MCB	Marine Corps base

MCBH	Marine Corps Base Hawaii
MCCDC	Marine Corps Combat Development Command
MCCS	Marine Corps Community Services
MCDEC	Marine Corps Development and Education Command
MCESG	Marine Corps Embassy Security Group
MCI	Marine Corps Institute
MCIA	Marine Corps Intelligence Activity
MCICOM	Marine Corps Installations Command
MCIEAST	Marine Corps Installations East
MCINCR	Marine Corps Installations National Capital Region
MCIPAC	Marine Corps Installations Pacific
MCIWEST	Marine Corps Installations West
MCLB	Marine Corps logistics base
MCM	*Manual for Courts-Martial, United States*
MCMWTC	Marine Corps Mountain Warfare Training Center
MCNOSC	Marine Corps Network Operations and Security Center
MCO	military claims office
MCRC	Marine Corps Recruiting Command
MCRD	Marine Corps recruit depot
MCSCG	Marine Corps Security Cooperation Group
MCSF	Marine Corps security forces; Marine Corps support facility
MCSFR	Marine Corps Security Force Regiment
MCTFS	Marine Corps total force system
MCU	Marine Corps University
MCWL/FD	Marine Corps Warfighting Lab/Futures Directorate
MCWP	Marine Corps Warfighting Publication
MCX	Marine Corps exchange
MDA	Missile Defense Agency
MDMC	Marine Depot Maintenance Command
MDW	U.S. Army Military District of Washington
MEB	Marine expeditionary brigade
MECEP	Marine Enlisted Commissioning Education Program

MEDCOM	U.S. Army Medical Command
MEF	Marine expeditionary force
MEU	Marine expeditionary unit
MGIB-AD	Montgomery GI Bill–Active Duty
MHG	MEF headquarters group
MIA	missing in action
MID	MAGTF Integration Division
MLG	Marine logistic group
MMC	Maintenance Management Center
MOQ	married officer quarters
MOS	military occupational specialty
MP	military police
MPF	maritime prepositioning force
MSC	major subordinate command; Military Sealift Command
MSG	Marine security guard
MSO	mandatory service obligation
MSOAG	Marine Special Operations Advisor Group
MSOB	Marine Special Operations Battalion
MSOSG	Marine Special Operations Support Group
MTU	mobilization training unit
MWR	morale, welfare, and recreation
MWSS	Marine wing support squadron
NASA	National Aeronautics and Space Administration
NATO	North Atlantic Treaty Organization
NCA	National Command Authorities
NCIS	Naval Criminal Investigative Service
NCO	noncommissioned officer
NECC	Navy Expeditionary Combat Command
NETCOM/9th SC(A)	U.S. Army Network Enterprise Technology Command/9th Signal Command (Army)
NFO	naval flight officer
NGA	National Geospatial-Intelligence Agency
NRO	National Reconnaissance Office
NROTC	Naval Reserve Officers' Training Corps

NSA/CSS	National Security Agency/Central Security Service
NSC	National Security Council
NUC	Navy Unit Commendation
NWC	Nuclear Weapons Council
NWDC	Navy Warfare Development Command
OAS	offensive air support
OCC	Officer Candidate Course
OCS	Officer Candidate School
OD	officer of the day
ODNI	Office of the Director of National Intelligence
OEA	Office of Economic Adjustment
OEF	Operation Enduring Freedom
OGC	Office of General Counsel
OHA	overseas housing allowance
OIF	Operation Iraqi Freedom
OMB	Office of Management and Budget
OMPF	official military personnel file
OOD	officer of the deck
OPCON	operational control
OPNAV	Office of the Chief of Naval Operations
OQR	officer qualification record
OSD	Office of the Secretary of Defense
PAC	personnel administration center
PACAF	Pacific Air Forces
PBP&E	professional books, papers, and equipment
PCS	permanent change of station
PEB	physical examination board
PEO LS	Program Executive Office, Land Systems
PERB	performance evaluation review board
PES	performance evaluation system
PFPA	Pentagon Force Protection Agency
PLC	Platoon Leaders Class
PME	professional military education
POV	privately owned vehicle
POW	prisoner of war

RCT	regimental combat team
RED	record of emergency data
RLT	regimental landing team
ROTC	Reserve Officers' Training Corps
SAPR	sexual assault prevention and response
SBP	Survivor Benefit Plan
SCM	summary court-martial
SCRA	Servicemembers' Civil Relief Act
SDDC	Military Surface Deployment and Distribution Command
SECNAV	Secretary of the Navy
SEP	special education program
SGLI	Servicemembers' Group Life Insurance
SJA	staff judge advocate
SMCR	Selected Marine Corps Reserve
SMMC	sergeant major of the Marine Corps
SOP	standard operating procedure
SORM	"Ship's Organization and Readiness Manual"
SP	shore patrol
SPMAGTF	special purpose Marine air-ground task force
SPMAGTF-CR-AF	Special Purpose Marine Air-Ground Task Force–Crisis Response–Africa
SPMAGTF-CR-CC	Special Purpose Marine Air-Ground Task Force–Crisis Response–Central Command
STAP	special training allowance pool
SWCIWID	Small Wars Center and Irregular Warfare Integration Division
SWS&CN	soft-walled shelters and camouflage netting
T/A	table of allowance
TACP	tactical air control party
TAD	temporary additional duty
TAPS	Tragedy Assistance Program for Survivors
TBS	The Basic School
TD	temporary duty
T/E	table of equipment

TF	task force
TG	task group
TMO	traffic management office
T/O	table of organization
TOQ	transient officer quarters
TRADOC	U.S. Army Training and Doctrine Command
TRAP	tactical recovery of aircraft and personnel
TRDP	TRICARE Retiree Dental Program
TRMC	Test Resource Management Center
TSC	theater security cooperation
TU	task unit
UCMJ	Uniform Code of Military Justice
UPB	unit punishment book
USAA	United Services Automobile Association
USAASC	U.S. Army Acquisition Support Center
USACE	U.S. Army Corps of Engineers
USACIDC	U.S. Army Criminal Investigation Command
USAFA	U.S. Air Force Academy
USAFE-AFRICA	U.S. Air Forces in Europe and Air Forces Africa
USAFRICOM	U.S. Africa Command
USARAF	U.S. Army Africa
USARC	U.S. Army Reserve Command
USARCENT	U.S. Army Central
USARCYBER	U.S. Army Cyber Command
USAREUR	U.S. Army Europe
USARNORTH	U.S. Army North
USARPAC	U.S. Army Pacific
USARSO	U.S. Army South
USASMDC/ARSTRAT	U.S. Army Space and Missile Defense Command/ Army Strategic Command
USASOC	U.S. Army Special Operations Command
USCENTCOM	U.S. Central Command
USEUCOM	U.S. European Command
USFK	U.S. Forces Korea
USMA	U.S. Military Academy

USNA	U.S. Naval Academy
USNORTHCOM	U.S. Northern Command
USO	United Service Organizations
USPACOM	U.S. Pacific Command
USSOCOM	U.S. Special Operations Command
USSOUTHCOM	U.S. Southern Command
USSTRATCOM	U.S. Strategic Command
USTRANSCOM	U.S. Transportation Command
VA	Department of Veterans Affairs
VCNO	vice chief of naval operations
VGLI	Veterans' Group Life Insurance
VMA	Marine attack squadron
VMM	Marine medium tiltrotor squadron
VMU	Marine unmanned aerial vehicle squadron
WAVES	Women Accepted for Volunteer Emergency Service
WHS	Washington Headquarters Services
WO	warrant officer
WSMC	Weapon System Management Center
XO	executive officer

INDEX

Note: Page references followed by an f, p, or t indicate information contained in figures, photographs, or tables, respectively.

ABOUT THE AUTHOR

Christian N. Haliday received his commission through the Naval Reserve Officers' Training Corps program after graduating from Duke University in 1984. During his twenty-eight-year active-duty career, he served in a variety of Marine Corps and joint assignments, including company, battalion, and installation command. Along the way, he earned a master's degree in security studies from the Marine Corps University and completed additional graduate work at the *Institut d'Etudes Politiques de Paris*, better known as *Sciences Po.*

The Naval Institute Press is the book-publishing arm of the U.S. Naval Institute, a private, nonprofit, membership society for sea service professionals and others who share an interest in naval and maritime affairs. Established in 1873 at the U.S. Naval Academy in Annapolis, Maryland, where its offices remain today, the Naval Institute has members worldwide.

Members of the Naval Institute support the education programs of the society and receive the influential monthly magazine *Proceedings* or the colorful bimonthly magazine *Naval History* and discounts on fine nautical prints and on ship and aircraft photos. They also have access to the transcripts of the Institute's Oral History Program and get discounted admission to any of the Institute-sponsored seminars offered around the country.

The Naval Institute's book-publishing program, begun in 1898 with basic guides to naval practices, has broadened its scope to include books of more general interest. Now the Naval Institute Press publishes about seventy titles each year, ranging from how-to books on boating and navigation to battle histories, biographies, ship and aircraft guides, and novels. Institute members receive significant discounts on the Press's more than eight hundred books in print.

Full-time students are eligible for special half-price membership rates. Life memberships are also available.

For a free catalog describing Naval Institute Press books currently available, and for further information about joining the U.S. Naval Institute, please write to:

Member Services
U.S. NAVAL INSTITUTE
291 Wood Road
Annapolis, MD 21402-5034
Telephone: (800) 233-8764
Fax: (410) 571-1703
Web address: www.usni.org